# The McGraw-Hill
# Multimedia Handbook

# The McGraw-Hill Multimedia Handbook

**Jessica Keyes**

*Editor*

**McGraw-Hill, Inc.**

New York   San Francisco   Washington, D.C.   Auckland   Bogotá
Caracas   Lisbon   London   Madrid   Mexico City   Milan
Montreal   New Delhi   San Juan   Singapore
Sydney   Tokyo   Toronto

**Library of Congress Cataloging-in-Publication Data**

The McGraw-Hill multimedia handbook / Jessica Keyes, editor.
      p.    cm.
  Includes index.
  ISBN 0-07-034475-2
   1. Multimedia systems.   I. Keyes, Jessica, date.
  QA76.575.M34    1994                94-10682
  006.6—dc20                       CIP

1 2 3 4 5 6 7 8 9 0  DOH/DOH  9 0 9 8 7 6 5 4

ISBN 0-07-034475-2

*The sponsoring editor for this book was Ron Powers, the editing supervisor was Stephen M. Smith, and the production supervisor was Donald F. Schmidt. It was set in Century Schoolbook by McGraw-Hill's Professional Book Group composition unit.*

*Printed and bound by R. R. Donnelley & Sons Company.*

*To order or receive additional information on these or any other McGraw-Hill titles, in the United States please call 1-800-822-8158. In other countries, contact your local McGraw-Hill representative.*    **BC14BCZ**

*This book is most appreciatively dedicated to my clients and friends, old and new, my family, and my editors.*

# Contents

## Part 2    Authoring

## Part 3    Animation, Video, and Sound

# Contributors

**Phil Abram**   *Eastman Kodak Company, Rochester, New York* (Chap. 50)

**Rex J. Allen**   *Allen Communication, Salt Lake City, Utah* (Chap. 13)

**Barbara Baker**   *Starlight Networks, Inc., Mountain View, California* (Chap. 48)

**Glenn Becker**   *NuMedia Corporation, Alexandria, Virginia* (Chap. 39)

**Bob Bennett**   *Autodesk Multimedia, Sausalito, California* (Chap. 26)

**Pam Berger**   *Byram Hills High School, Armonk, New York* (Chap. 14)

**Peter B. Blakeney**   *IBM, Atlanta, Georgia* (Chap. 44)

**Jesse Bornfreund**   *UNIX International, Parsippany, New Jersey* (Chap. 45)

**Tim Brock**   *St. Petersburg Junior College, St. Petersburg, Florida* (Chap. 25)

**John F. Buford**   *University of Massachusetts, Lowell, Massachusetts* (Chap. 45)

**Red Burns**   *New York University, New York, New York* (Chap. 2)

**Alton Christensen**   *CoSA, Providence, Rhode Island* (Chap. 30)

**John Colligan**   *Macromedia, San Francisco, California* (Chap. 43)

**Joan Davies**   *Mathematica, Inc., Lakeland, Florida* (Chap. 21)

**Mark Doran**   *UNIX International, Parsippany, New Jersey* (Chap. 45)

**Les Dunaway**   *Technology Helping People, Inc., Kennesaw, Georgia* (Chap. 40)

**Joseph Dunn**   *Macromedia, San Francisco, California* (Chap. 43)

**Mike Evans**   *National Semiconductor, Santa Clara, California* (Chap. 41)

**Joseph Fantuzzi**   *Macromedia, San Francisco, California* (Chap. 43)

**Ken Gerlach**   *Hewlett-Packard, Cupertino, California* (Chap. 4)

**Lewis Gruskin**   *IBM, Atlanta, Georgia* (Chap. 24)

**Satish Gupta**   *Media Vision, Fremont, California* (Chap. 9)

**Harry Hallman**   *Corporate Media Communications, Atlanta, Georgia* (Chap. 11)

**Guy Hancock**   *St. Petersburg Junior College, St. Petersburg, Florida* (Chap. 12)

**Ray Harris**   *Optibase, Dallas, Texas* (Chap. 31)

**David E. Hartman**   *St. Petersburg Junior College, St. Petersburg, Florida* (Chap. 25)

**Donna Hefner**   *Macromedia, San Francisco, California* (Chap. 43)

**Josh Hendrix**   *CoSA, Providence, Rhode Island* (Chap. 30)

**Jeff Hooks**   *St. Petersburg Junior College, St. Petersburg, Florida* (Chap. 8)

**Roger Karr**  *Digital Equipment Corporation, Marlboro, Massachusetts* (Chap. 19)

**Michael Kellner**  *Apple Computer, Santa Clara, California* (Chap. 20)

**Richard V. Kelly, Jr.**  *Digital Equipment Corporation, Marlboro, Massachusetts* (Chap. 46)

**Jessica Keyes**  *Techinsider, New York, New York* (Chaps. 1, 15)

**Susan Kinnell**  *UCSB, Santa Barbara, California* (Chap. 14)

**Cliff Kondratiuk**  *Sierra Semiconductor, British Columbia, Canada* (Chap. 27)

**Lucy Lediaev**  *Philips Interactive Media of America, Los Angeles, California* (Chap. 22)

**Claude Leglise**  *Intel Corporation, Santa Clara, California* (Chap. 33)

**James Long**  *Starlight Networks, Inc., Mountain View, California* (Chap. 48)

**Mike McGonagle**  *Computer Corporation of America, Cambridge, Massachusetts* (Chap. 35)

**Glenn K. Morrissey**  *Asymetrix Corporation, Bellevue, Washington* (Chap. 18)

**Ken Morse**  *Kaleida Labs, Inc., Mountain View, California* (Chaps. 32, 47)

**Kurt Mueller**  *Dataware Technologies, Cambridge, Massachusetts* (Chap. 23)

**Amy Pearl**  *SunSoft, Mountain View, California* (Chap. 34)

**Tim Picraux**  *Unisys Corp., Blue Bell, Pennsylvania* (Chap. 5)

**Marco Pinter**  *Digital Media International, Sunbury, Pennsylvania* (Chap. 37)

**Rudy Prokupets**  *Lenel Systems International, Fairport, New York* (Chap. 6)

**Steven L. Raber**  *IBM, Atlanta, Georgia* (Chap. 3)

**Bruce A. Rady**  *TouchVision Systems, Chicago, Illinois* (Chap. 38)

**Lex van Sonderen**  *Philips Interactive Media of America, Los Angeles, California* (Chap. 22)

**Serge Timacheff**  *Logitech, Fremont, California* (Chap. 28)

**Prem Uppaluru**  *Fluent, Natick, Massachusetts* (Chap. 42)

**Vince Walisko**  *The Walisko Group, Washington, D.C.* (Chap. 39)

**Rob Wallace**  *Wallace Music & Sound, Glendale, Arizona* (Chap. 36)

**Joseph Weintraub**  *Thinking Software, Woodside, New York* (Chap. 10)

**J. Alan Whiteside**  *Multimedia Learning, Inc., Irving, Texas* (Chaps. 7, 29)

**Mary F. Whiteside**  *Southwestern Medical Center, University of Texas, Dallas, Texas* (Chaps. 7, 29)

**Frederic M. Wilf**  *Elman, Wilf & Fried, Media, Pennsylvania* (Chap. 17)

**Les Wilson**  *National Semiconductor, Santa Clara, California* (Chap. 49)

**Andrew Young**  *Young Minds, Inc., Redlands, California* (Chap. 16)

# Foreword

Industry experts predict that by 1995, multimedia will have exploded into a $15 to $20 billion industry. These same pundits forecast that by the year 2000 every computer will be a multimedia machine. The question is, will you be prepared to ride the crest of this tidal wave of change?

And it *will* be massive. Even though information technologists have long been familiar with developing interactive systems, multimedia adds a startling new dimensionality. It adds real life.

Computer systems needn't be two-dimensional. The addition of sound, animation, and video does much more than just liven things up. It adds real content.

Picture a real estate organization whose computer system sports a "video tour" through various real estate holdings. Or an insurance claims system that captures the devastation of a hurricane in full color. Or a meeting that actually ends on time!

A 1992 study by Market Vision found that 43 percent of corporate executives surveyed found their business meetings boring (no surprise), and 40 percent admitted that they've fallen asleep. In a 1991 study by Inteco Corp., it was found that video presentations can cut a meeting's time by 40 percent and *boost audience retention of information by up to 38 percent.*

Retention of information is one-half of the promise of multimedia. The other half is *understanding* information. Multimedia provides the tactility (i.e., the "feel" of information through listening and viewing) that we so desperately need in today's information-intensive world.

McCaw Cellular understands this, and is using multimedia for the often difficult task of troubleshooting cellular phones. A McCaw serviceperson merely plays tones stored on his or her work station until the customer recognizes the errant sound, at which point the customer is provided with information about that particular problem.

Like McCaw, hardware and software vendors, large and small, mainframe, work station, and PC, are all joining the multimedia ranks. By the time you read this book, Oracle8 just might be gracing your desktop. It will be a major breakthrough. That's because Oracle is the first major RDBMS (Relational Database Management System) vendor to fully incorporate interactive multimedia into the fold.

The point is, multimedia is here to stay. The question is, will you be prepared? The answer will be yes if you follow the advice offered by the dozens of contributors to this book. For within the confines of this rather thick tome is the collected wisdom of the intelligentsia of the multimedia community. Included are 50 chapters and over 200 illustrations filled with techniques, checklists, standards, and guidelines that will help you to create systems that dazzle users with sound, animation, graphics, and video.

This book wouldn't have been possible without the help and encouragement of many people. I certainly want to thank my husband Robert, without whose unwavering support this book would never have been finished, and Stephen Smith of McGraw-Hill, who tackled this book with expertise, patience, and humor.

But I'd also like to thank the many contributors to this book who gave willingly of their time and expertise. These are the real heroes. I know they hope, as I do, that this book will serve as the wings that make multimedia fly.

*Jessica Keyes*

# Preface

Multimedia's a hot topic. But that's not the whole reason for this book. As a technologist with some 18 years of experience, I can't remember a time when a technology has so caught the minds and hearts of so many people. Myself included.

True, it started life on the consumer side of the house with Nintendo and Sega taking a huge chunk out of our kids' allowances. But then something funny happened. People began to realize the potential of "sight and sound" on business.

For more than two decades we've been at the mercy of the computer's flat representation of data. Precious little insight can be gleaned from a myriad of rows and columns of multidigit numbers. But even though a bit of multidimensionality was introduced to the process with the advent of the spreadsheet and various and sundry graphics programs, information visualization requires much more: a complete immersion of the senses.

The term *multimedia* is familiar to most. After all, we used it almost every day in grade school. That was back when "multimedia" meant nothing more than going to the audiovisual department to gather up the projector to view the requisite film on hygiene. But wait. This sounds eerily like what we're doing today. It couldn't be that Mrs. Applegate, our fourth grade teacher, was on the cutting edge of the multimedia revolution?

Well, maybe she was. For Mrs. Applegate knew full well the value of involving all of the senses in a learning experience. Information visualization isn't so very far afield from Mrs. Applegate's fourth grade classroom.

By using any combination of video, sound, graphics, and animation, we open up an unlimited vista and make the world understandable, not only to children but to adults working in business, academia, and the sciences.

The human body interprets input from the five senses almost simultaneously. A combination of sight, sound, smell, touch, and hearing enables us to react intelligently to the current situation. If multimedia is to be successful, then multimedia productions must follow this lead.

But doing so will require some pretty powerful hardware and software. For those readers who thought that multimedia was just a presentation with some sound or animation piped in—think again.

Multimedia calls for a fluidity between system resources that, to speak frankly, is rarely found today. Just ask your systems administrator about the vagaries of LAN systems response and you'll begin to understand just what I'm talking about. Today most system users suffer silently at the hands of what we optimistically refer to as "the client/server environment." Having too many users slows the system. Too much data routed between client and server slows it down even more.

Fortunately, our senses can easily accommodate variable speeds in populating a textual data screen. But just try that when populating a display with a video, and you'll wind up with what looks like a movie made by a three-year-old on a tricycle!

It's a good thing that technology is (as ever) moving rapidly to accommodate multimedia's intense requirements. But it would be erroneous to think that "computing" is leading the way. For multimedia is actually a convergence of many industries. Publishing, consumer electronics, computing, cable and broadcast television, telephone, communications, and film have been referred to as "seven octopuses," all with tentacles in each other's pockets.

As if to demonstrate the truth of this analogy, as I put pen to paper the ink is drying on the agreement between Microsoft, General Instrument, and Intel Corp. This prestigious trio has teamed up to build a Windows-based platform for interactive television or, as they call it, *infotainment*. The tool you'll use to channel-surf? The "air mouse"?

On the flip side, Bill Gates, Microsoft's perennially innovative chairman, has created a new company whose goal is to develop a technology that will merge moving images with text and art with history. Continuum Productions, Inc., is out to create a database that combines art, music, photographs, and historical information, giving new meaning to the term *performance art*.

Where as Gates's artistic vision might seem pure whimsy, the post office has embarked on the ultimate in practical applications of multimedia—especially for those of us who have to wait more than five minutes to get a roll of stamps. The U.S. Postal Service has introduced some high-tech multimedia kiosks that offer stamps, address-change services, and custom printing. And they're not even rude.

Perhaps the most intriguing of all multimedia applications are the ones that virtually breath. At Carnegie Mellon's Studio for Creative Inquiry, a virtual gallery is under wraps that, when completed, will permit people to take a stroll through ancient Egypt. Even more interestingly, Digital Equipment Corp. is one of the organizations whose Artificial Life & Virtual Reality Applications Group is working on something called a "virtual cadaver." Virtual cadavers provide a "body" to surgeons-in-training, allowing them to rush in where they would normally fear to tread. Dick Kelly, one of the contributors to this book, expounds on this subject in more depth later on.

But for those business users or technologists who don't have much of a taste for cadavers, or art for that matter, and who still have multibillions invested in enterprise systems—fear not. Multimedia is coming your way.

Oracle is one of the most-used of all database management systems. Thousands of payroll systems, personnel systems, and the like are run using Oracle's ralational database model. There was a time when relational was considered "old hat"—it just stored data. But times change. Today's Oracle incorporates interactive multimedia services such as electronic libraries and multimedia messaging, as well as audio and video. So even enterprise users can perform such esoteric multimedia functions as videoconferencing, video on demand, and even home shopping.

So, how do you get on the road to information visualization through multimedia? Easy. Just read on. In the coming pages you'll find the answers to the perennial questions, "where, what, when, how, and why."

The *Handbook* is not meant to be read cover to cover. You'll get more mileage out of it if you turn to the part or chapter of particular interest to you at a particular moment. However, the book is configured in a logical manner, of sorts.

In the beginning, there was a beginning. All books have one. And the *Handbook* is no different. So in Part 1, you'll find your basic introduction to the salient issues of multimedia: what it is, and how it's used (or should be used). Some real heavy hitters have contributed to this part, so even the multimedia aficionado would do well to peruse it.

In Part 2 you'll find chapters on creating and authoring a multimedia system. Producing an effective multimedia system takes a lot more than sound and video dumping. Dumping aside, those interested in attaching sound, speech, or music, or video or animation, would do well to flip to Part 3, where you'll be able to benefit from widely diverse expertise. We've even got a composer for you.

Part 4 is where we tackle the heady issues of networking, virtual reality, and standards. Even if you're an expert in multimedia, you'll find many a worthy nugget of information here.

Finally we come to Part 5. While there are several compendiums of multimedia products out there, I find them overwhelming. So in this part I've provided an "annotated" version. In other words, I've sifted through tons of literature from scads of vendors, and the ones listed are the ones I found to be of interest to me. You'll find a wealth of resources that I find intriguing, including those in the areas of authoring software, soundboards, CD-ROMs, consultants, publications, associations, clip art, clip sound, and clip videos.

So read on, and multimediate!

*Jessica Keyes*

# Multimedia Issues

# Getting Started in Multimedia

**Jessica Keyes**

## How Is Multimedia Different from Traditional Data Processing?

When computers first made their entrance into the corporate arena some three decades ago, they were thought of merely as numerical processors (i.e., number crunchers). In fact, the very first commercial application (albeit governmental) was to count the census. But monumental change was in the offing. Largely due to staggering advances in chip technology, no longer are computers relegated to the basements of large organizations. Today, (personal) computers can be found in millions of organizations on an equal number of desktops.

When the computer migrated from the basement to the desktop, precepts about programming migrated as well. As any professional programmer will attest to, no longer are monolithic systems developed. Instead, systems are composed of a series of distributed modules, some running on the PC and some running on the mainframe (or server), which taken together are collectively referred to as *client/server*.

Dispersion of system components to the PC, or client, required a change in the way programmers think about user interfaces. Where mainframe-based systems were largely character-based, these newer PC-based systems were much more icon-, or image-, based.

Even though image-oriented processing is a step in the right direction, multimedia, for the most part, has not yet caught on to any great degree in the corporate arena. There are several possible reasons for this.

The primary reason is that multimedia is so "different" from traditional systems development. Even though so much of today's PC-based development sports enhanced imagery as a user interface, there the similarity ends. For traditional systems simply do not (usually) handle audio, video, or animation. And these are the three key components of multimedia.

The majority of corporate systems, in spite of their colorful GUIs (graphical user interfaces) are numerical or text-oriented. Even though the advent of client/server has added an additional layer of complexity to the process, development of traditional systems is largely a straightforward process. One requests a record. One transfers this record to the client. The client processes the record and then transfers it back to the source from whence it originated. The "source" is usually a database, often relational in nature, that stores simply numbers or characters.

But even here things seem to be changing. Developing these GUIs saw the increase in new software development tools that enable programmers to quickly build user interfaces from a set of building blocks. Programmers had just discovered a mode of programming that had long been popular in the rarefied environments of artificial intelligence labs and in the domain of the vendors themselves. Object-oriented programming made its entrance in a big way and continues, to this very day, to have a radical effect on how systems are built.

Perhaps the biggest change is in the way we *think* about systems. Instead of a kluge of code which serves the purpose of building a system from top to bottom, we now tend to think in terms of *objects*. Objects are discrete, for lack of a better term, *things* that are self-contained and independent. They contain all the data and logic they need to carry out their designated functions. In essence, then, systems are built simply by connecting one or more objects.

Objects, of course, can be anything. No longer are we confined to the world of numbers or characters. An object can just as easily be a picture of a house as the number 23. Or a video clip as well as the text string, "123 Main Street." And because objects can be a number, a character, an image, a video clip, or sound, the world of multimedia is, for the first time, readily available to anyone who cares to dabble.

In essence, the technical skillsets needed to build a multimedia system are not dissimilar to those required to build any object-oriented system. One just uses a different set of tools. But in this era of a cacophony of different toolsets, systems developers have grown used to this diversity.

The biggest difference is in handling the three-dimensionality of multimedia. Where traditional systems present one view of the information, multimedia systems are "alive" with many views of the system—its sight as well as its sound. No longer are we confined to a rather one-sighted and very flat view of information. With multimedia we can look at information from all sides, sort of take a walk around it surveying it from all sides. And with virtual reality, we can even talk a walk inside of it.

In essence, one could describe traditional systems as "static" and multimedia systems as very much "dynamic" in nature. The big question then becomes, especially for those just getting involved in multimedia development, "*Just when and where do you add those elements of multimedia (i.e., animation, sound, video, imagery) to make the largest impact?*"

## A Question of Content

Aside from the technical aspects of developing a multimedia application, perhaps the biggest bugaboo for system developers, when presented with their first multimedia project, is content. But how to best integrate sound, video, animation, graphics, and text is largely in the domain of the content specialist. It is usual in the case of development of traditional systems to actively solicit the involvement of an expert from the area being automated. Why should the development of multimedia systems be any different?

User experts are natural content specialists. It is their understanding of the "business" that will enable them to direct (which is an appropriate verb here) the multimedia production. Essentially, their expertise should be able to accurately dictate the most logical placement of text, graphics, sound, and video.

Indeed, many of the consumer CD titles on the market today have been directed by just these content experts. *The Family Doctor,* authored and edited by Dr. Allan Bruckheim, is one of many examples. But even the good doctor needed a goodly dosage of technical expertise to put his production together.

Unless the title being produced is about computer topics, where the content and technical expert may be one and the same, the minimal human resource requirement for a multimedia production should always be at least one technical expert and one content expert.

Similar to other data processing applications, a multimedia application has a systems life cycle. And it should be followed. Some get the impression, because multimedia is infinitely interactive, that this type of system can be thrown together in one great kluge. Actually, there is nothing to prevent this sort of "development by chaos." But as in any software system, the end result really does reflect the hard work and organization of the software development process.

For those just getting started in multimedia, the difficulty is compounded by the unfamiliarity of the terrain. As already mentioned, the tools (both hardware and software) are quite different from traditional data processing tools. But this should not really faze the hardy stock of techno-gurus that have cut their teeth of late on such esoteric technologies as client/server, object-orientation, and even artificial intelligence. Ultimately, multimedia is just one more tool for the system developer's toolbox.

## A Quick Jump Start into Multimedia

Getting started in multimedia will be one of the more eye-opening experiences of your career. I know it was for me. Even though I already had 15 years of experience and had built a multiplicity of systems, multimedia was (and is), well…different.

Right off the bat, I had to make a slew of decisions about what software and hardware I would use. Because my experience is largely in the IBM PC–compatible arena, this last decision was already premade for me. A mere five years ago, the platform of choice was the Apple or the Amiga. And these are still wonderful platforms. However, the surge toward multimedia in the IBM PC (and clones) arena is nothing short of staggering. There are probably few hardware vendors who don't sell multimedia PCs. And even if you bought yours years ago, there's a plethora of upgrade kits to choose from. Just perusing the annotated appendix at the end of this book will make your head spin with the number of choices available.

The remainder of this chapter will take you through a typical multimedia "getting started" process. Although not everyone will make the same choices given their individual environments, this chapter will give you an excellent overview of what you need to get quickly started in building your very first multimedia title.

## Choosing your hardware

As was true in my case, part of your decision may already have been made for you. If your organization is predominantly IBM PC compatible–based, then this should be your delivery platform. Alternatively, if you're Apple-based, then a Mac it is. Or Amiga. In other words, you first need to find out who you're delivering the system to. And it's insufficient to presume that, since the data-processing group is IBM PC–based, the entire organization is IBM PC–based.

There are many organizations who offload development to the PC, but ultimately deploy on a mainframe, midrange, or workstation. The delivery platform of the ultimate end user, then, is of prime importance in making any hardware decision.

In some cases, especially where the multimedia system is marketing-oriented, the ultimate hardware platform is not known. In other words some users may have Macs, some PCs, and some only mainframes.

First let's address the mainframe issue. Developing multimedia applications on a mainframe is, as of this writing, nearly an impossible feat. Mainframe resources are highly leveraged and, as a result, operational folks would frown mightily at the mere mention of such a resource-intensive operation. With often hundreds (and sometimes thousands) of users sharing slices of time, resource allocation becomes an art form in these environments. Given that even 1 minute of compressed video gobbles up somewhere around 9 Mbytes, you can envision a rather nice traffic jam (although chapters in Part 4, Advanced Topics, will show you how to get around this—at least from a workstation or PC perspective).

Another nail in the mainframe coffin is the lack of available authoring software. Although it's not impossible to "grow your own" multimedia application using any number of traditional programming languages, authoring software has those "hooks" that make the development of multimedia software...if not a breeze, then at least a lot easier.

Finally, mainframes that use purely dumb terminals, as opposed to PCs, are for the most part precluded from the element of sound altogether.

That multimedia appears to be excluded from the mainframe domain is really an anomaly, as far as I'm concerned. In spite of the reasons stated above, the mainframe is really a natural platform for multimedia. With its nearly unlimited storage capacity, the storage of even 60 minutes of video (or sound) is only a drop in the bucket.

It really wouldn't take much to make the mainframe a multimedia server. It certainly has the capacity, and the network is already in place. In fact, a variant of multimedia has been practiced for years in just this fashion. *Imaging* is the convergence of two very different forms of media: text and graphics. Literally thousands of organizations are already using their mainframe to view documents along with their associated images. So adding video and sound is just two giant steps forward in the game of multimedia.

There's no reason why multimedia-enabled PCs can't be tethered to mainframes that act as the repository of the database, which stores not only text but sound, imagery, and video. While object-oriented databases are a natural for this task, some relational database vendors (such as Oracle) are moving quickly to provide these very capabilities.

For those organizations that rely on "dumb" terminals as clients of their mainframes, I can only hope that these terminals become not so dumb in the near feature. There's just no reason why these terminals can't be sound-equipped.

But even if your organization decides not to deploy on the mainframe, there's still the sticky wicket of the possibility of a diversity of hardware platforms. Fortunately, there are some software vendors who see this as an opportunity. One of them, Lenel Systems, markets MultiMedia Works, which is a universal player that supports 40 file formats including AVI, Quicktime, DVI, FLC, FLI, CD-Audio, Wave, and Midi. What this means is that you can write one smart system that determines the runtime environment and acts accordingly.

### Upgrading your hardware

The majority of PCs out in the field are IBM PC–compatible. But not all of them are multimedia-enabled. What this means is that few of them have enough hard-disk capacity, the ability to reproduce sound, a CD-ROM drive, a super VGA graphics card, or enough memory or speed to put it all together. Of course, it is entirely possible to successfully create and run a multimedia application without any of the above features—but the result may be less satisfactory. However, I've created and run very small applications without benefit of a sound card (I used a Windows driver to enable the speaker that comes with the PC—tinny, but usable) or CD-ROM. One caveat here is that if the application fits on a high-density diskette, then that should be the deployment media, since not many organizational PCs with a few years on them have a CD-ROM drive.

One thing you'll discover sooner rather than later is that there's a plethora of standards to consider (see Chap. 15 for much more on this). But why should multimedia be any different from any other technology? After all, proprietary standards are what sells hardware.

Whereas IBM calls their entry Ultimedia, the rest of the world has labeled it *multimedia*. The Multimedia Marketing Council (MMC) has developed a specification for a PC that ensures quality playback of multimedia productions. While it relies heavily on Microsoft's Windows as an operating system (whereas IBM bases its standard on its very own OS/2 or DOS), Ultimedia and the Multimedia Marketing Council's MPC (multimedia PC) are so similar as to be nearly indistinguishable.

The MPC Level 2 Specification is as follows:

25-MHz 486SX microprocessor

4 Mbytes of memory

3.5-inch floppy drive

160-Mbyte hard disk

16-bit sound

Two-button mouse

Windows 3.0, plus Multimedia Extensions or Windows 3.1

Color monitor with 640 × 480 resolution with 65,536 colors

Serial port, parallel port, MIDI I/O port, joystick port

But this is a specification for new PCs. If you need to upgrade the one already on your desk, then the MMC has graciously accommodated you with the following:

CD-ROM drive with a 300 kbyte-per-second transfer rate
   CD-ROM XA–ready (Photo CD)
   Multisession-capable
   Average seek time of 400 milliseconds

16-bit sound

MIDI I/O port and joystick port

You'll notice that nowhere do you see a reference to a video card (I don't mean a VGA card here, but one that processes digital video feeds). That's because part of the standard is the use of Microsoft's very own AVI (audio/video interleaved) video file format. AVI files require no special adapter card to play back video. This is its strength. Its weakness is that to get a superior video image, you really do need a digital video adapter.

The MPC standard actually provides the minimum requirements you need to "do good multimedia" at the lowest cost. Scratching the need for a video adapter greatly reduces the cost and enables multimedia applications to be more widely disseminated.

The first thing that people usually purchase when they decide to go multi-media is a CD-ROM drive. These greatly vary in price (see the appendix). You can buy very inexpensive CD-ROM drives ($199) at most computer stores—or even through catalogs. Of course, the cheaper the drive, the slower it'll be. And a slow speed is something you may regret later on.

From an organizational perspective, there are several alternatives to be considered when planning a department- or company-wide implementation. Purchasing a CD-ROM drive for each and every corporate PC (even at the low price of $199) can be very costly. You might want to consider networking those PCs (if they aren't already) and then networking a series of CD-ROM drives at the server.

If we remember that one rather small CD disc can hold somewhere around 250,000 pages of information, just think how much information a series of 3 or 4 or even 10 CD-ROM drives can handle. Just be sure to buy the very fastest CD-ROM drives if you're thinking of stacking them together.

While networking CD-ROM drives will require the expertise of a specialist (again, see the appendix), installing a single CD-ROM drive just requires perseverance. It's really no different from installing any other adapter card, except that in this case you must also install a drive. For those who are fainthearted at the prospect of installing another drive, or haven't the room for another, consider installing an external CD-ROM drive. It takes up some space on the desk, but it's a fairly easy installation process.

Multimedia loses much of its pizzazz without sound. And even though it's possible to get sound from the PC's built-in speaker if you install the right drivers (in the Windows control panel), there's nothing quite as exciting as good quality sound coming out of your PC through either attached headphones or speakers. For this you need a sound card.

There are many on the market. If you're planning on using pure voice annotation (no music), an 8-bit sound board will be sufficient and the least expensive solution. There are also several external devices available, such as Logitech's Audioman, which simply connect up to the PC's parallel port and voilà, sound!

If you're considering sound clips and/or music along with pure voice annotation, then a 16-bit card will provide about the same quality as the CD audio in your stereo system. But as you'll soon find out, there are great variations. A rule of thumb: the more expensive the sound card, the better the quality. And don't expect your local PC dealer to even stock some of the high-end cards.

Most sound cards come complete with a microphone and software that lets you "edit" the sound file. In a Windows-compatible environment, sounds are generally captured as .WAV files. Non-Windows systems store sounds in completely different formats. Although both store sound, they are incompatible without translating one to the other.

There's really no nice neat way to sum up what you'll need. Perhaps the following list from the June 1993 *Windows Sources* (p. 392) does the best job of explaining the requirements—and expenditures—of multimedia:

*If you want to run authored multimedia titles,* then use a 20-MHz 386SX-based PC with 2–4 Mbytes of RAM, a 256-color VGA display, an 80-Mbyte hard disk, a sound board, and earphones or speakers. It will cost between $1000 and $2000.

*If you want a system for authoring applications,* then upgrade to a 25-MHz 486DX-based PC with 8 Mbytes of RAM, 200-Mbyte hard disk, and a CD-ROM drive that transfers 300K or 600K of data per second. It will cost between $2500 and $3500.

*If you want to author full-motion video applications,* then upgrade to either a 33-MHz 486DX-based PC or a 66-MHz 486DX/2-based PC with a 300- to 500-Mbyte hard disk. It will cost between $4000 and $5500.

*If you want to master applications for CD-ROMs,* then upgrade your 66-MHz 486DX/2 to include a 1-GB hard disk, 16 Mbytes of RAM, and a 24-bit color board. Cost is between $3000 and $8000.

*If you want to play commercial CD titles,* then add a CD-ROM player with audio output that's controlled by a sound card. It will cost between $350 and $700.

*If you want to record sound,* then add a studio-quality microphone and high-end sound board. It will cost $150 for a good microphone, $300 to $600 for a sound board.

*If you want to compose music,* then add a MIDI keyboard. It will cost between $350 and $800.

*If you want to digitize photos,* then add a color scanner. It will cost between $1200 and $1500.

*If you want to add video,* then add a camcorder, VCR, and a video capture card. The video capture card will cost between $550 and $1200.

Yet another caveat is called for here. Windows-based systems are nowhere near as robust as either the Mac or (especially) workstations, in spite of the PC's popularity. The more you put inside of your computer, the higher the risk of incompatibility. For example adding sound, video, and a scanner requires three additional adapter boards. Each adapter board uses a system interrupt (IRQ) and a memory location. Conflicts, which arise when more than one device is configured for the same interrupt or memory location, are ticklish at best to sort out and fix.

If you intend to do heavy-duty multimedia development on your PC, then the minimum MPC requirement that I've listed above actually is insufficient. My advice is to double the memory and hard-disk storage requirements at a minimum, and to make sure your PC is as fast as they come. Also, be sure to spend a good deal of time with your Windows manual, figuring out ways to optimize the way Windows runs.

Perhaps the best advice I can give, and it's advice that I've taken myself, is to split development across more than one PC. I wouldn't be exaggerating if I told you that digital video work can hog all of the horsepower of a fairly high-end PC—and then some. By offloading your digital video work to a separate PC, you'll leave yourself plenty of room on your main PC for authoring, graphics, and sound. *And* you won't experience the memory conflicts that seem to be standard multimedia fare in the PC arena.

### A question of peripherals

Of course, all of this software and hardware means little if you have no way of "inputting" your multimedia element of choice into your application. While most sound cards come with a microphone, no digital video cards come with camcorders or VCRs (it's a pity). And while the microphone in question is quite functional, it is not of high quality.

**Sound.**   On the sound side you'll need a high-quality microphone as well as some extension cabling if you want to plug your stereo system into the back of the sound card. This last item lets you feed the music from your CDs, LPs, cassettes, and even radio directly into your computer through the "line in" port of your sound card, without the ambient noise a microphone picks up. So if you have some great background music for your multimedia production, this is the way to go. Use the microphone only when you want to add the "human" element to your production—that is, a voice-over.

Figure 1.1 shows the real bargain you're getting by buying a sound card. The one I'm using for the purposes of this chapter is Creative Labs' Sound

**Figure 1.1**  Sound board connectors.

Blaster 16ASP. As its name implies, it's a 16-bit sound card that enables me to get some pretty good audio fidelity in spite of the card's fairly low cost. Actually I'm quite pleased with it, and I don't see any reason why you should spend a cent more on a higher-quality sound board (unless, of course, you're a musician).

Probably the connection that is the biggest mystery to first-time multimedia developers is the one for MIDI. Because it's explained in infinite detail in other chapters of this book, I'll just provide you with a quick peek into this musician's dream.

In general there are two types of sound files, Wave and Midi. Wave files capture the entire sound, which is why they take up so much space. Just 7 seconds of sound, recorded in stereo at 16 bits and sampled at 44 kHz, takes well over one million bytes of disk storage. As shown in Fig. 1.2, you can minimize disk storage by changing some of the recording parameters.

Soundo'LE, bundled with the Creative Labs sound cards, gives you just this capability. For example, recording in mono, in 8 bits, and at a sampling rate of 11 kHz will take less than 75K—a big difference. And if you apply one of the compression algorithms, even less space is required. Using Creative's ADPCM (Adaptive Differential Pulse Code Modulation) algorithm will reduce the disk requirement to a mere 36K.

Whereas Wave files store the actual (digital version) sound, MIDI files store instructions for MIDI devices. Actually MIDI is an acronym for Musical Instrument Digital Interface, which is an industry-standard connection for computer control of electronic musical instruments and devices. Perhaps the most popular is the synthesizer.

If you don't have a MIDI instrument then, depending on the software you have installed you can still take advantage of the power of MIDI. Figure 1.3 shows the full range of capabilities of this type of software. Turtle Beach Systems' Turtle Tools comes with several applications. One of them, KeyPlayer, lets you use your own computer keyboard to "create" anything from a new symphony to rock music. Even rap. Starting with a base of MIDI files supplied with the product, you can become an instant Madonna.

Since Windows-based systems play either MIDI or Wave files, the inexpensive software and hardware that I've just described can really enhance your multimedia production, making it look and "sound" a lot more professional than it really is.

**Images.**  Although you can buy ready-made "clip art" and even photographs from any number of multimedia (and desktop publishing) vendors, there are times when you want to do your own. Sure, you can use a high-end paint package to draw your own, but not everyone is artistically gifted. That's where a good scanner comes in.

There are probably as many scanners on the market as there are printers. Even facsimile machines have gotten into the act by "claiming" that you can use a faxed image as input to a design or paint program. Actually they're quite right. Before I bought my scanner that's exactly what I did (and was

**Figure 1.2** Recording options for WAVE files.

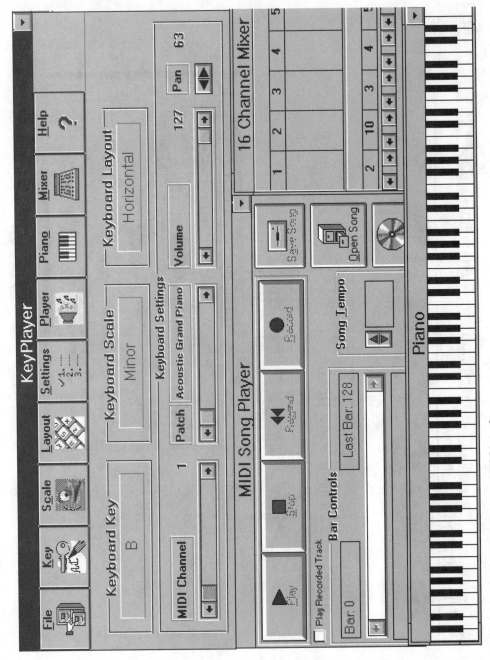

**Figure 1.3** Turtle Beach Systems MIDI interface.

quite smug about it). Faxed images are of extremely low quality, so the best advice I can give you is to search out a better alternative.

And as mentioned, there are plenty of options. For the most part, even though handheld scanners are quite reasonable in price, unless your eye-hand coordination is perfect, opt for a flatbed. Since there are variations even here, you'll want to look at the competitors carefully.

If you're like me, you'll want the best ratio between price and functionality. I wanted a flatbed, color, the highest possible DPI (dot per inch) when scanning, and a bunch of bundled-in software.

That's just what I got with the Microtek Scanmaker IIXE. It scans in full color, lets me set the resolution (it can scan to a virtual 1200 dpi), and came bundled with Aldus's PhotoStyler. About a month after I purchased the scanner I saw an ad that indicated they were now bundling it with Adobe's PhotoShop. After I wrote them a letter indicating that I had just purchased mine, they sent me a copy of PhotoShop. What a deal! I got both PhotoStyler and PhotoShop.

PhotoShop has much more functionality than PhotoStyler. But PhotoStyler is easier to use and takes a lot less memory. The rule of thumb here is don't overindulge on the software. Buy the capability that you actually need. Although PhotoShop has some great features, I really don't need them. Of course, *you* may!

Having a scanner means being able to take your own pictures (Ansel Adams, beware) and input them directly into your multimedia project. This is why having a *color* scanner is so important, since vivid color is the base of all multimedia. Figure 1.4 shows that just by putting a photograph inside the scanner and setting a few variables you can easily scan a picture.

Once the picture has been scanned, the software (in this case PhotoStyler) provides plenty of options that you can use to alter your image, as shown in Fig. 1.5. You can even crop out parts of the image and just use a section of it. This, in fact, is the method I used to build the graphics for the sampler multimedia applications that we'll be building in just a few minutes.

There are alternatives to scanning, such as the new digital video cameras, but from my perspective owning a scanner is one smart move. Not only will it permit you to scan images but you can also use it to scan text, along with some robust OCR (optical character recognition) software.

For this purpose, I use Caere's OmniPage. I simply put my sheet of text facedown on the scanner, open my word processor, and scan, as shown in Fig. 1.6. What comes out the other end is an editable file.

Of course, this is imaging from a PC perspective. Imaging has had a long life of its own, even before multimedia became a household buzzword.

There are literally thousands of organizations that have incorporated imaging as a major component of their "paperless" office plans. Even the government is doing it. The U.S. Customs Service uses imaging to transmit information about would-be drug smugglers.

**Video.**    Perhaps the multimedia element that gives developers the biggest "twinkle in the eye" is video. It's fun. It's as simple as that.

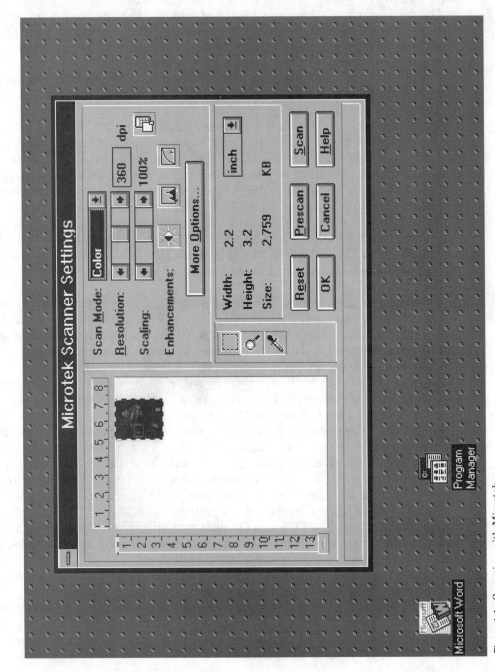

**Figure 1.4** Scanning with Microtek.

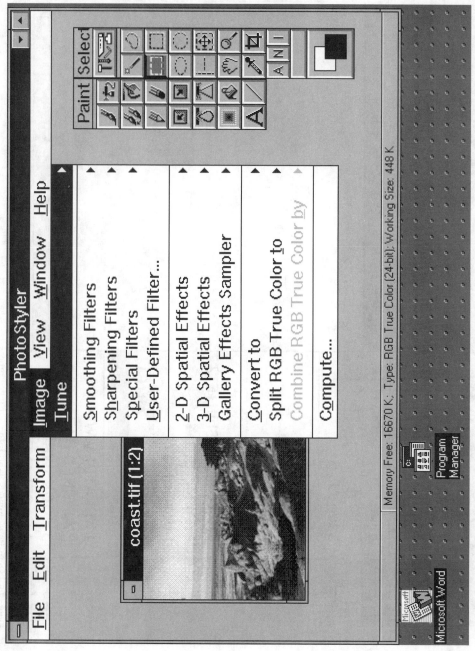

**Figure 1.5** PhotoStyler lets you alter images.

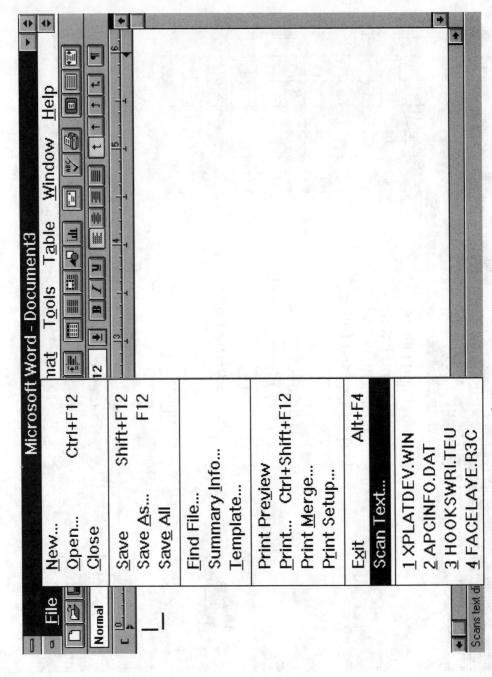

**Figure 1.6** OmmiPage embeds itself into your word processor—scan text.

It's quite possible to add video to a multimedia production without ever having a digital video card. If you're creating in a Windows environment, video is stored as AVI (Audio Video Interleave) files. Although the quality is far less than other digital delivery mechanisms, AVI does have a distinct advantage. That is, it permits the playback of video segments without a digital video adapter. In other words, AVI is a software-only solution. And because you can purchase literally thousands of minutes of video clips from dozens of multimedia vendors, you can add video to your production without getting your hands dirty.

Of course, if you want to tailor video to your own specifications you will need some additional software to do this. And if you want to shoot your own videos, not only do you need a camcorder or VCR as an input source, but a video capture card as well.

The card I used for the purposes of this chapter is the VideoSpigot. Originally developed by SuperMac Technology, the Windows version has since been sold to Creative Labs, leaving SuperMac free to concentrate on the market they like best: Macintosh.

The VideoSpigot itself is no more than a board and some compression software. The software that actually enables you to capture, import into your computer, and then edit the video image is Microsoft's very own Video for Windows, as seen in Fig. 1.7.

VFW is easy to use, but it's not nearly as robust as some of the higher-end digital video packages listed in the appendix. Additionally, it's not as popular as Microsoft had hoped it would be. As I write these words, Microsoft has sold only 50,000 copies of VFW. Perhaps this is because the original standard for video, Quicktime, now runs on the PC as well as on its original Mac platform.

If video is a central part of your multimedia project and you need to do some fancy footwork, then VFW is not the package for you. However, if all you require is the ability to capture a stream of video and then clip out only the frames you really need, then VFW is a most cost-effective choice.

Video is perhaps the most storage-intensive of all the multimedia elements. One minute, uncompressed, takes about 50 megs of hard disk. It doesn't take a mathematician to figure out that you'll quickly run out of storage space at this rate. Fortunately, VFW enables you to store the video clip you've created in a compressed format—and it enables you to select the best compression method for your needs.

VideoSpigot loads VFW with several compression methods (called *codecs*). One of the most popular is Intel's Indeo, which will trim that 50 megs down to an almost manageable 9 megs.

**Animation.**  Simply put, animation is the process of creating, usually graphically, a series of frames, and then having them display rapidly to get a sense of movement. Sort of like Bugs Bunny. In the world of multimedia, especially on a PC platform, multimedia and video overlap somewhat. It is quite possible to run an AVI (video) file that was created via animated means rather than through a camera.

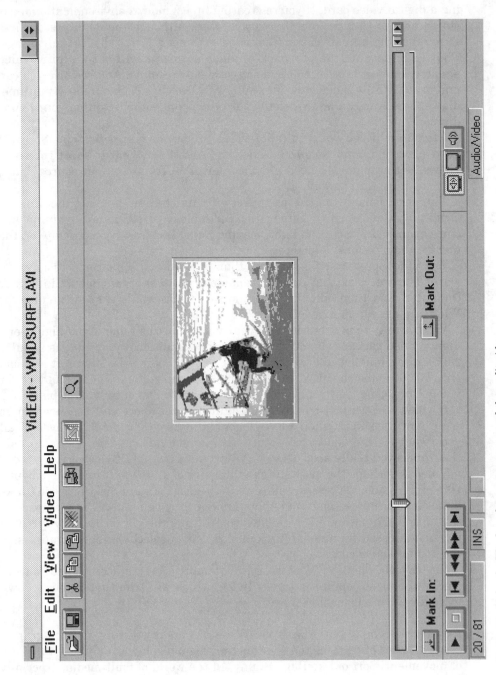

**Figure 1.7** Video for Windows lets you capture and then edit video.

There is a plethora of software packages that provide wonderful abilities to draw and then animate objects. Sometimes even the authoring tool provides the ability to animate objects created within the context of the authoring package. Asymetrix's Toolbook lets you create an object and then "drag" it around the screen. Toolbook monitors the direction in which you are moving and then creates an animation from it.

Other packages, such as IBM's Storybook Live, give you a series of animated sprites to use inside your multimedia titles.

### Video display adapters

Most developers, especially those who have never worked with interactive systems, fail to consider the ramifications of the video card that they're using either in development or production. When you're working with text there is little difference between adapter boards, but it's an entirely different matter when you're dealing with graphics.

The following table clearly illustrates the differences between the four categories of video cards. Note that the higher the resolution, the more colors you can display. However, you'll also notice that the higher the resolution, the more memory you'll need.

| Board | Pixel resolution | No. of colors | Memory for 1 image |
|---|---|---|---|
| CGA | 320 × 200 | 4 | 16,000 |
| EGA | 640 × 350 | 16 | 112,000 |
| VGA | 640 × 480 | 256 | 224,000 |
| SuperVGA | 512 × 480 | 16,777,216 | 983,000 |

Even though the majority of multimedia developers will work on a SVGA-enabled platform, where graphics are riveting in all their full-blown colorful glory, developers should be cognizant of the fact that not all delivery platforms are so well endowed. Believe me when I say that graphics that look wonderful under SVGA will look somewhat paltry in an EGA mode. Therefore, developers must "plan" their systems accordingly.

If the ultimate implementation platform is known beforehand, then all development work should be done (or at least well tested) on that particular platform. Unfortunately, there are many occasions when the developer knows only that the ultimate implementation platform will be a generic PC. Since the video adapter may well be SVGA or VGA—or even EGA—the development team has some hard decisions to make.

One method for solving this problem is to choose only those graphic images and digital video clips that display equally well on all platforms. Alternatively, different imagery can be used on the different platforms. The system can be programmed to "detect" the graphic adapter and then display those images targeted for that device.

Unfortunately, this last piece of advice is seldom followed, even by many of the makers of multimedia products. The result? When first-time users load up that demo disk, they invariably are disappointed. In the end, sloppy miscasting of target hardware can only do damage to the professional image of the industry.

## Building a Multimedia System

Now that the stage has been set, it's time to get down to the nitty-gritty of building your multimedia application. Although it's entirely possible to simply add a little video here and a sound clip there, you'll soon find out that the very best multimedia productions are those that have been carefully planned and executed.

The very first step of the planning process, however, is budgeting, and here Steve Bainbridge of the Wilson Learning Corporation, located in Eden Prairies, Minnesota, has thoughtfully provided a good rule of thumb for this process. By his estimate, a 2-to-4-hour interactive multimedia system will cost about $150,000, with the following distribution of resources:

| | |
|---|---|
| Document design | 2% |
| Research and writing | 10% |
| Video and audio production | 56% |
| Graphics and text | 6% |
| Programming | 9% |
| Project management | 8% |
| Mastering/check disc | 6% |
| 25 copies of videodisc | 5% |

Andersen Consulting's Ed Smith, who is based in San Diego, uses a consulting model approach to budgeting. The following example was calculated for development of a half-day of multimedia instruction.

| | |
|---|---|
| Design and development (300 days × $500/day) | $150,000 |
| Administration and management (60 days × $600/day) | 36,000 |
| Video subcontract (40 finished minutes) | 80,000 |
| Direct reimbursable (travel, mastering, etc.) | 11,500 |
| Total | $277,500 |

Smith uses two yardsticks when developing multimedia budgets:

1. The ratio of development hours to user contact hours:

| | |
|---|---|
| Low | 400:1 |
| Medium | 800:1 |
| High | 1200:1 |

2. Cost per finished minute:

| Low | $1000 to 1500 |
| Medium | $1500 to 2200 |
| High | Over $2200 |

## Start with a plan

All professional system developers use the system requirement and specification as their starting point. These documents are the blueprint of the deliverable system. Nothing less should be done for a multimedia application.

In the case of multimedia, though, a requirements specification contains much more than programming instructions. It also contains the overall graphic layout of the system, including the placement of any and all video, sound, imagery, and hypertext.

For the remainder of this chapter, we are going to use the example of the development of a first aid system. The system will contain text and graphics, as well as some sound and video. Even though this example is rather simplistic, it will serve a useful purpose as a demonstration of the steps one takes to design and develop a working multimedia system.

The purpose of the *First Aid Manual* (we'll call it FAM for short) is to provide end users with specific information about how to handle emergency first aid situations. The user should be able to do the following:

1. Choose a topic from a Table of Contents

2. Use the capability of hypertext to get a clarification of relevant topics and terms

3. Perform a word search to "find" any words or phrases of interest

4. See relevant graphics and videos, as well as hear relevant sound clips

The makeup of the developmental team is reflective of the problem at hand. A team can consist of from 1 to $n$ members, with the lower number indicating a simple problem with the source information readily available and the higher number indicating a complex system—both hardware- and information-wise. For example, a multimedia system for stock market trading that incorporates live digital video feeds, sound, and graphics and is distributed to a thousand locations worldwide will call for a fairly large developmental team. This team will be composed of content specialists (i.e., experts in trading) as well as a multitude of system development experts (i.e., a specialist in digital video, a specialist in distributed systems, programmers, etc).

FAM, on the other hand, is a rather simple system (for the purposes of this chapter). Our purpose is to take a manual that has already been written and translate it for a multimedia platform. Because the information is already available we won't need a content specialist, unless we want to verify the currency of the information.

Many multimedia titles on the market today have been developed in just this manner. This seems to be the modus operandi for organizations that are already publishers of huge amounts of information. Quite a large number of the technical trade magazines and newspapers have dusted off their back issues and republished them on CD-ROM. Packaged with robust retrieval software, the final product lets the user search for any title or author name, or virtually any key word or phrase, for up to 10 years of back issues.

When developing a multimedia title in this manner, you must make absolutely sure that the project is legally within bounds. That is, you can't just pick a title and decide to multimediate it (see Chap. 17 on legal issues in multimedia). You must either already own the copyright or secure it from the person or organization that does. In our case, the text of the first aid manual comes from the *First Aid Book,* published by the U.S. Department of Labor. And most of what is published by the government is copyright-free—that is, you can use it free and clear without worrying about infringing on anyone's copyright. In fact, I recently saw an advertisement for a CD-ROM that contains the full text of all the pamphlets published by the government's Consumer Information bureau.

Because the government did not thoughtfully provide me with their first aid manual on disk, I had to take the preliminary step of converting the printed page to something a computer can work with. Although there is always the option of rekeying the manual into a word processor, a far simpler method is to use your scanner.

As I already mentioned, I find a scanner indispensable. But a scanner is only as good as the software that you use with it. For the purposes of OCR (optical character recognition), I have been using Caere's OmniPage. In spite of some peculiar installation problems (which I will discuss in my next book, *The Productivity Paradox*), the software works like a charm. I merely place a page of text facedown on the scanner (much the same as with a copier), click on the "scan text" item in my word processor's file menu, and lo and behold: editable text.

### Picking an authoring tool

As you browse through the appendix at the back of this book you will notice that there is no dearth of choices in the area of authoring tools. Not all of these tools have the same functionality, so you'll want to spend some time assessing a selection of tools before you make your final decision.

Most organizations seem to "centralize" on one tool for each software category. For example, they prefer to use one CASE tool, one programming language, and so on. Unfortunately, not all business problems fit so neatly into such a unitary approach. This is especially true in the multimedia arena. There are tools for DOS, tools for the Mac, tools for Unix, scripting tools, hypertext tools, and on and on.

To narrow the field, you'll first have to decide what platform your final product will run on. In our case, FAM will run under Windows on the PC. Therefore I can ignore all authoring and other types of products that run on the DOS-only Mac or Unix platforms.

The characteristics of the product you want to develop should dictate the type of authoring tool you will use. FAM is extremely text-oriented; will require the ability to easily navigate around the text; requires the ability to use "hot words" to enable the user to get more detailed information about a particular area of interest; will not require a high level of interactivity in the use of selectable buttons; and will require the ability to integrate sound, video, and graphics.

As you review this attribute list, you may come to the conclusion that a hypertext-type product would be the best fit for your system. Those of you who are regular Windows users have no doubt had occasion to use the Windows Help function. Windows Help is a hypertext module that rather nicely enables the user to easily navigate through a lot of textual information. Microsoft's Multimedia Viewer (which is purchased separately from Windows itself) gives developers the very same functionality.

Since FAM's target end users are already Windows-literate, I've decided that the best authoring tool for the project is Multimedia Viewer.

## A Quick Tour of Multimedia Viewer

Microsoft's Multimedia Viewer is really a set of eight different tools. There is a ninth tool, Microsoft Word for Windows, that doesn't come with the toolkit, although many of us already have it. In fact, this is one of the reasons I decided to use Viewer. Given the confusion factor that this product presents to first-time users, I'm not sure I would have selected Viewer over some of the other hypertext tools on the market. In other words, Viewer is less than intuitive. But it does let you create robust multimedia systems, as shown in Fig. 1.8.

Viewer's eight tools can be described as follows:

| | |
|---|---|
| Viewer Project Editor | This is used to create the user interface, to configure the search features, identify the external files you'll be using, run the program that builds (compiles) your title, and also give you test capabilities. |
| Viewer Topic Editor | This module, which is activated through Word for Windows, is used to add features such as sound, graphics, digital video (in the form of Microsoft's AVI), hypertext links, etc. |
| Hotspot Editor | This is used to add "hot spot" regions to pictures so that the user can click on a picture, for example, and jump to another topic. |
| Viewer Compiler | Used to build your titles. |
| WaveEdit | Used to record, play, edit, and add special effects to sound files. |
| BitEdit | Used to edit bitmapped graphics. |
| PalEdit | Used with BitEdit to change the colors in an image or apply a particular palette. If you're going to use a large number of graphics for your title, you'll be using this a |

**Figure 1.8** Sample of viewer's capabilities.

great deal, since you'll want to have a certain consistency in the colors you use in your title. Also, the more colors you use, the more memory it takes.

Convert        This is used to convert audio and graphics file formats into formats that can run under Viewer.

The Multimedia Viewer development kit also comes with a royalty-free run-time viewer also called, quite confusingly, Multimedia Viewer.

The nice thing about Viewer (and most other multimedia authoring tools) is that you can develop simple systems or incredibly complicated systems by using basically the same steps. Figure 1.8 shows the startup screen of one of the titles that Microsoft ships with their product. The intent of "Viewer Gallery" is to walk developers through the many capabilities of the Viewer development tool. Although the picture is reproduced here in black-and-white, the actual screen is in full, vivid color—chockful of graphics.

The FAM system will be much simpler. We merely want to build a hyper-text version of the paper manual and throw in a few multimedia elements for good measure. But the steps we take to build FAM are also the steps that we would take to build a system as complex and graphical as the Viewer Gallery. So we're getting off to an excellent start.

### The first step

The very first step in creating a Viewer title is to create a project file using the Project Editor. In essence, a project file is a collection of pointers that point the way to the text file, sound file(s), graphic file(s), and video file(s), with the text being stored in the RTF section of the project and everything else being stored in the colloquially named "Baggage" section as shown in Fig 1.9.

The RTF section is actually a Word for Windows file, stored in Rich Text Format (RTF). Although many word processors have the ability to store text as RTF files, there actually is (believe it or not) no set RTF standard. So if you think you can get around the requirement to install a copy of Word for Windows, think again. Microsoft is smarter than that.

When setting up Viewer, you have an opportunity to indicate the drive/directory location of Microsoft Word, so getting to the appropriate file is as simple as entering the appropriate file name if the title is new, or "point-and-clicking" to the file name from a list. Since we've already scanned a file into the system and saved it in the RTF format, all we need to do is click on the file name. In all cases, we need to make sure that we maintain this file in RTF format. This adds an additional query from Word every time we want to open our file, as shown in Fig. 1.10.

Developing a title in Viewer is largely an exercise in word processing. Viewer relies on hidden text and footnotes to embed the commands that the run-time system interprets. Unfortunately, this plethora of footnotes is less than intuitive.

**Figure 1.9** Viewer project editor.

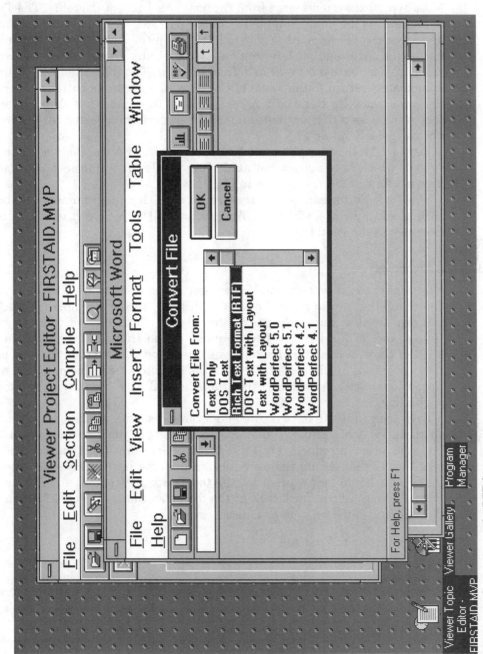

**Figure 1.10** Converting to the RTF format.

**The table of contents**

Most hypertext systems start from the base of a Table of Contents. The Table of Contents is the jumping-off point for the user to select and "jump to" any of a wide variety of topics. As you'll see later on, one of Viewer's nicer features is its starter menu and push-button bar. Without any programming whatsoever, your users have a built-in help function as well as the automatic ability to immediately return to the Table of Contents (the Contents button), return to the prior topic (Go Back button), see a list of all topics viewed in the order they were chosen (History button), as well as perform a search for a word or phrase (Search button).

Figure 1.11 shows a Microsoft Word screen with FAM's Table of Contents screen, which is heavily annotated. To get this far required much use of Viewer's Topic Editor, as shown in Fig. 1.12.

The Topic Editor enables me to select in English a programming attribute, such as add a picture, which the Topic Editor will then convert to one or more footnotes as shown in Fig. 1.13.

**Dividing text into topics**

Essentially, the developer (and/or content expert) has to review the text to determine the beginning and end of each topic. In our example (Fig. 1.11), you can see that there are quite a few topics: "Introduction to First Aid," "Importance of First Aid," "The Anatomy of the Human Body," and so on. Each of these is considered a topic and starts on a new page. Since a hard carriage return (CTRL + Enter key) is the dividing line between topics, multipage topics are easily done using the standard page break (i.e., automatic paginating).

Each topic needs to have a title and a context string, which is essentially a shorthand way of getting to the topic. For example you'll notice that in Fig. 1.11, the topic "Introduction to First Aid" has the word "Intro" next to it. This tells Viewer that should the user click on this line in the Table of Contents, the action should be to "jump to" the topic with the context string value of "Intro." If you take a quick look at the footnotes shown in Fig. 1.13, you see that the first two lines read as follows:

$Introduction to First Aid

#Intro

Translating the $ (Fig. 1.12), we discover that this first line indicates that it is a title. And the # sign indicates a context string (see, I told you it was a bit convoluted!).

Because Viewer is a true Windows product, I have the ability to designate things such as the color of the screen (or even use a graphic background, as Microsoft did in Fig. 1.8), the font and size of the text, as well as the color of the text. I can even give my system a title. Figure 1.14 shows (although in black-and-white) the Table of Contents in the finished product.

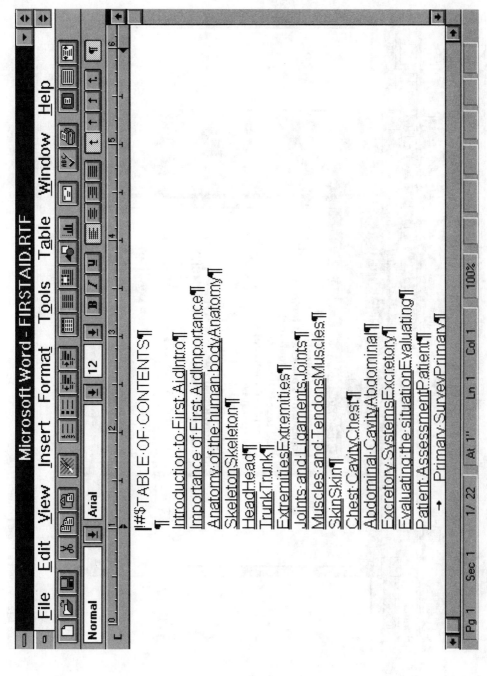

**Figure 1.11**  RTF version of the table of contents.

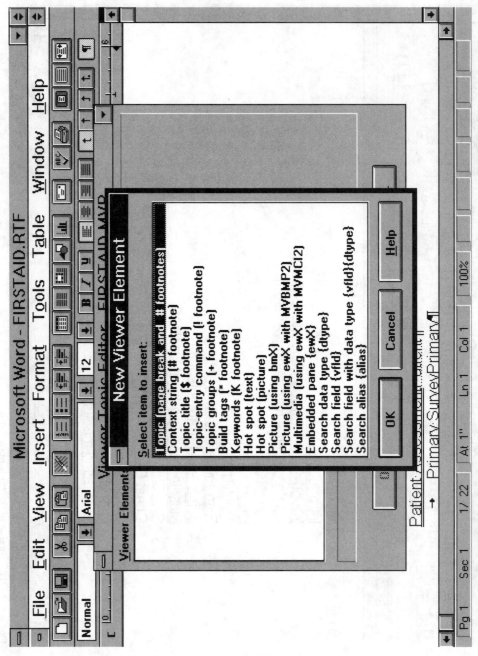

**Figure 1.12** Viewer's Topic Editor.

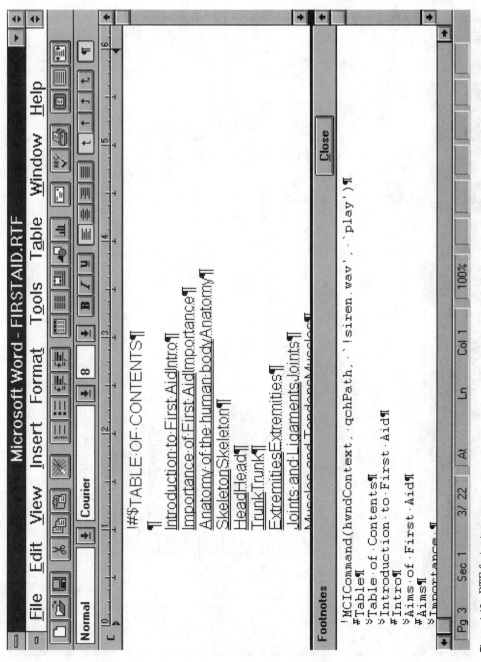

**Figure 1.13** RTF footnotes.

First Aid Manual

File   Edit   Bookmark   Help

Contents   Go Back   History   Search   <<   >>

TABLE OF CONTENTS

Introduction to First Aid
Importance of First Aid
Anatomy of the human body
Skeleton
Head
Trunk
Extremities
Joints and Ligaments
Muscles and Tendons
Skin
Chest Cavity
Abdominal Cavity
Excretory Systems
Evaluating the situation
Patient Assessment
Primary Survey
Secondary Survey
General Principles

**Figure 1.14**   Finished table of contents.

Because Viewer is hypertext-oriented, I have the ability to display text in one or more windows or panes—or I can display text in pop-up windows.

In the topic "Introduction to First Aid," I want to add a sort of disclaimer. I want the user to know the philosophy of first aid. To do this I can create a hot key out of either a picture or some text. I'll choose the later. In Fig. 1.15, you'll see the text of the topic "Introduction to First Aid." The third paragraph down starts with the phrase, "First aid does not replace the physician...." Note that this is underlined. That's because I designed it as a hot key. In this way the user knows that there's more information to be found if he or she scrolls over to this sentence. Clicking the hot key displays a pop-up screen that discusses the aims of first aid.

### Adding multimedia

Up to now we've worked only with the hypertext capabilities of Viewer. Now it's time to add some multimedia.

The government's publication on first aid had graphics as well as text. I scanned these separately, storing the graphics in several TIF files. In order to use graphics, though, I must first convert these files into a graphical format that Viewer can use. Figure 1.16 demonstrates the Convert capability that comes bundled with Viewer.

I must associate each of the graphic images, once converted, with its proper location in the RTF file. To do this I merely scroll to the correct location in the RTF file and press the hot key to get into Viewer's Topic Editor. From Topic Editor I choose "Picture (using ewX With MVBMP2)". Figure 1.17 displays the interactive screen the developer is presented with. Here you get to indicate the file name of the graphic, store it in Baggage (in the Project File), and dictate the placement of the image.

Figure 1.18 shows how FAM looks when it's all put together. While all "commands" are actually a series of footnotes, and therefore it is possible to bypass Topic Editor altogether and just code it yourself, unless you're really experienced and do this sort of thing frequently, I wouldn't hazard it.

Adding digital video and digital sound is done in much the same way as with pictures. I happened to have a digital sound file in Wave format of an ambulance siren, so I added it to the Table of Contents. Unfortunately I can't show you sound, but I *can* show you what the embedded command (located in the footnotes) for sound looks like:

    !MCICommand(hwndContext, qchPath, '!siren.wav', 'play')

Sound and video require use of the Media Control Interface (MCI). MCI is a platform-independent multimedia specification that was published in 1990 by Microsoft and other vendors to provide a consistent way to control devices such as CD-ROM and video playback units. In the example, I simply loaded the file "siren.wav" into Baggage and used the Topic Editor to "place" the sound in my text file.

# First Aid Manual

File    Edit    Bookmark    Help

Contents | Go Back | History | Search | << | >>

## Introduction to First Aid

First aid is the immediate care given to a person who is injured or ill. Sudden illness or injury can often cause irreversible damage or death to the patient unless proper care is initiated as soon as possible. First aid includes recognizing life threatening conditions and taking action to prevent death or further injury, to relieve pain, and to counteract shock until medical treatment can be obtained.

The urgent need for treating life_threatening situations makes it the responsibility of everyone to be able to give proper emergency care until the victim is transported to a medical facility.

First aid does not replace the physician, but it protects the victim until medical assistance can be obtained.

One of the first prin... [Aims of First Aid]

### Aims of First Aid

The principal aims of first aid are as follows:

. Care for life_threatening conditions
. Protect from further injury and complications
. Arrange transportation for the victim to a medical
  facility in such a manner as not to complicate
  the injury or subject the victim to unnecessary
  discomfort
. Make the victim as comfortable as possible to conserve strength

... ous injury. Even minor

...control bleeding, reduce
...onserve the victim's
...s of recovery are greatly

...and reducing accidents,
...lm while working under
...well_selected words of
...ing possible to reassure

When first aid is pr...
the severity of shoc...
strength. If these st...
improved.

Experience has sho...
as well as saving liv...
pressure, and organ...
encouragement, firs...
the apprehensive victim.

**Figure 1.15**  Pop-up screen.

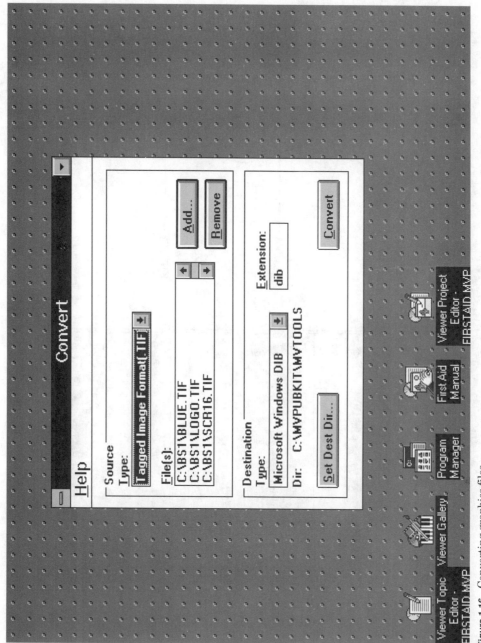

**Figure 1.16** Converting graphics files.

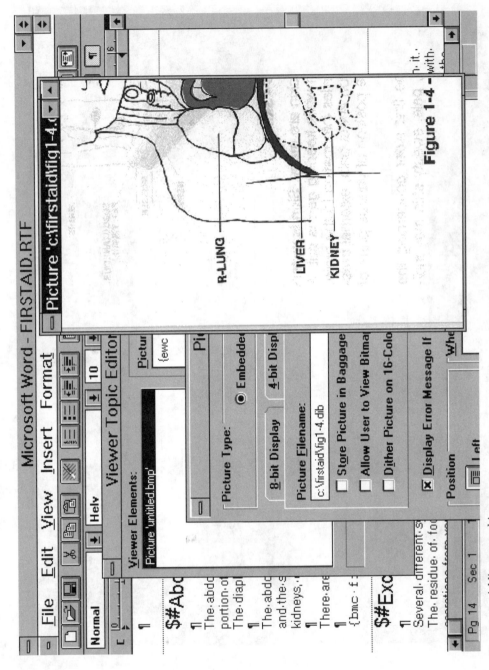

**Figure 1.17** Adding a graphic.

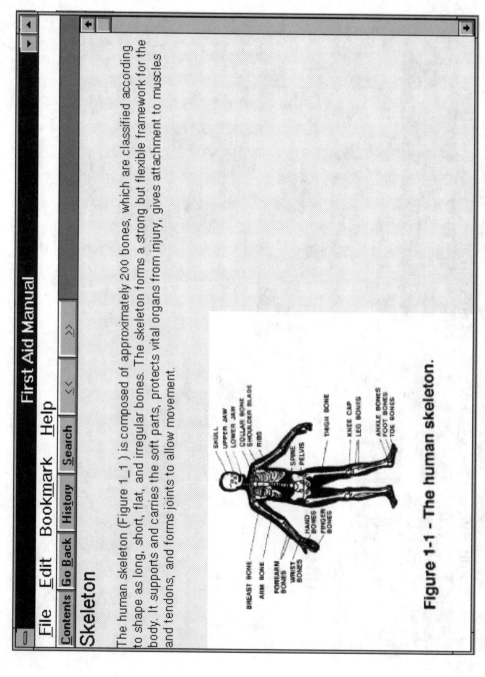

**First Aid Manual**

File  Edit  Bookmark  Help

Contents | Go Back | History | Search | << | >>

## Skeleton

The human skeleton (Figure 1_1) is composed of approximately 200 bones, which are classified according to shape as long, short, flat, and irregular bones. The skeleton forms a strong but flexible framework for the body. It supports and carries the soft parts, protects vital organs from injury, gives attachment to muscles and tendons, and forms joints to allow movement.

SKULL
UPPER JAW
LOWER JAW
COLLAR BONE
SHOULDER BLADE
RIBS
SPINE
PELVIS
THIGH BONE
KNEE CAP
LEG BONES
ANKLE BONES
FOOT BONES
TOE BONES
BREAST BONE
ARM BONE
FOREARM BONES
WRIST BONES
HAND BONES
FINGER BONES

## Figure 1-1 - The human skeleton.

**Figure 1.18**  Viewer title with graphic added.

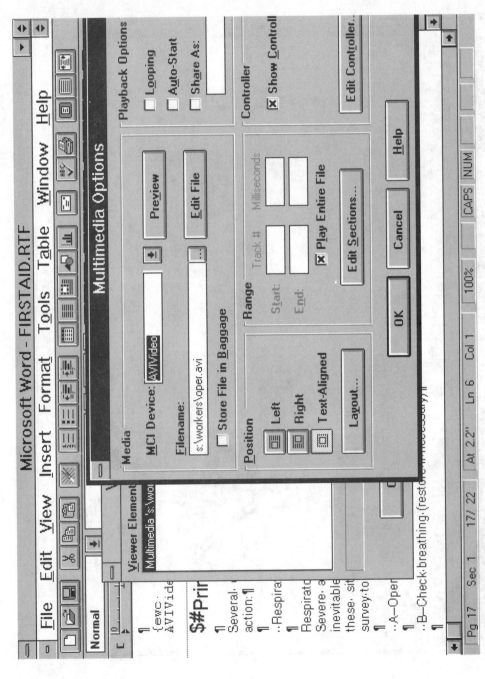

**Figure 1.19** Adding video to a viewer title.

Video is done in a like manner. Figure 1.19 shows the development environment at the point in time the developer has told the Topic Editor that he or she would like to add video to the text file. In the upper-left-hand corner, you'll see the image itself. It's a color image of doctors in an operating room. Viewer utilizes the AVI file format that was developed by Microsoft to allow playback of video files without any video hardware. Also note how small the video clip actually is. The quality of video is dependent upon a lot of things. For most systems, the limited amount of memory and hard-disk space precludes the use of full-screen video—hence tiny video clips like "oper.avi."

You'll also notice the multitude of options the video MCI driver gives the developer. And of course, you can take a gander at the convoluted command structure of the MCI command.

### Putting it all together

Although so far I haven't mentioned compiling the title at all, I really wouldn't wait until you've added everything before you compile for the first time. It's best to test the system continually. Both Build (compile) and Test are available as items on the Project Editor menu.

Although FAM is a small and simple system, it clearly demonstrates how to combine hypertext, graphics, and audio as well as video to produce a fairly interactive system.

Once you've tested your system thoroughly, you should be ready to package and distribute it. The distribution medium, however, is largely dependent upon how big your system is. FAM has a limited amount of text, only five graphics, one video clip, and one sound clip. But even such a limited system may be too big to deliver on one floppy diskette. Because even 1 minute of compressed video can take up 9 Mbytes of storage, the delivery medium of choice for most multimedia systems is CD-ROM. And here I'll direct you once again to the appendix, from which you can get a list of vendors who will gladly transfer your system to CD-ROM, or where you can find one or more vendors who will be more than happy to sell you your very own CD-R drive that will enable you to create your own CD-ROMs.

No matter which route you take, remember to test, test, and test again. You should especially make sure that your system runs on a PC other than the one on which it was created. For instance if you created it on an ALR machine, then test it on a Compaq, a Dell, or an IBM.

### Conclusion

The multimedia developer should be prepared to master a number of tools. And as the market is changing rapidly, it's a good idea to keep abreast of these changes. For example, over lunch the other day I heard that there is a company in Norway that has just about perfected a compression algorithm that will permit the storage of up to 90 minutes of video on just a floppy. Steven Spielberg, move over!

# Cultural Identity
# and Integration
# in the New Media World

**Red Burns**

In the last 50 years there has been an overwhelming change in communications. This change has not yet been fully understood by any of us who are in the middle of it. It is of the order of change occasioned by the introduction of writing and the printing press. Knowledge, power, and material relationships are changing radically as a result of the new forms of communications.

The electronics revolution in communications is multifaceted. On the surface there are the startling convergences of computing, audio, video, graphics, and text. To these convergences we can add the expanding temporal and spatial reach of the new distribution networks.

As each new form of communications develops, it promises new opportunities and resulting benefits to society. Yet there is enormous potential for abuse. And one of these abuses is an antiseptic technological world that cannot easily handle human paradox.

## The New Media

These new communications technologies have an almost irresistible allure, and their promise surrounds us. Extravagant claims are everywhere. And in fact there is much to be excited about. Yet we need to avoid becoming blindly seduced if we are to create desirable and equitable applications that justify our efforts and investment.

For individual users, it won't be long before a single wire comes into the home providing access to local as well as international information. This wire will serve as the link for voice, data, and video transmission.

This mode of communication and expression can be used by one voice or by many. Determining whose voice gets heard, determining an equitable use of this new power, is an important issue to consider.

The technology itself is as straightforward as a mathematical equation. The applications, however, are myriad. In the end it is people, not machines, who design applications.

My own engagement with communications technologies began a long time ago in documentary film at the National Film Board of Canada. At that time a filmmaker went into a community, took notes, wrote a script, shot a film, edited it, and sent it off to be distributed. A most worthy occupation—telling other people's stories. We, the filmmakers, felt quite comfortable with our interpretation of others—their values, their lives, their aspirations. We were the professionals. We created a world about others. We selected material we thought was important to represent them, rather than letting them represent themselves. In some cultures, it might be said that we were robbing others of their identity. At the time, I believed we were performing a valuable communications service: telling people's stories. The professional framed the message; this was an accepted practice.

A current example of this kind of representation can be seen on Cable News Network. CNN is broadcast to almost every major city in the world. During the Gulf War, CNN reached Israel, Saudi Arabia, and Iraq, as well as my home in New York City. Each viewer regardless of her/his culture received the same information at the same time. CNN is representing the world to us not only in America, but internationally. After the Army censors, the editors at CNN were essentially editing the war for all of us. That is very powerful!

As electronic media become the main mode of communications between peoples, the danger is that we may recreate the kind of colonialism found in classical literature where only one voice was represented. Interactive networks can provide a means for different voices, and certainly for more than one.

An example of a global interactive network was seen during the August 1991 activities in Russia. Computer conferencing provided an electronic link between Russia and the outside world. While it is estimated that there are only 1.5 million personal computers in the Soviet Union—and probably only 2 percent have modems—the personal and public communications they make possible didn't exist a few years ago. It has been reported that many Muscovites received scanned images of *The Washington Post* and *The New York Times* during the attempted coup, describing the reaction of the West to the events unfolding in Russia.

In one instance, NATO officials wanted to send a message of support to Boris Yeltsin and could not communicate directly from Brussels to Moscow. They sent their message through the Sovam teleport in San Francisco to Nikolai Kapranov, a top adviser to Yeltsin. Kapranov had an account on the computer mailbox. He sent a message back saying he had translated the NATO message and distributed it in the form of leaflets. He reported that the people inside the parliament building were grateful to know that they had a connection with democratic countries.

In the field of video, one of the first technologies I found that offered the possibility of this kind of self-representation was a Sony Portapak reel-to-reel ½-inch video, which I witnessed a demonstration of in 1970. I was astounded! The skills required to operate the camera were not out of reach for nonprofessionals. The cost was not prohibitive, and for the first time it was possible for ordinary people to make their own video documents. Interpreters became unnecessary. An option was available that had not existed before. The feeling of empowerment was thrilling to those who chose to use this new means of communications. By thinking about how they presented themselves, people learned about themselves and their community. Often that learning process was as important as the documentary ultimately produced. This modest-looking advancement was quite revolutionary in its potential to allow people to tell their own stories and control their information. Combined with a cable distribution system, people were able to present their own point of view in the dominant medium of American society: television.

This was an important time in the history of television in the United States. Broadcast television had always been a medium of scarcity, using a great deal of bandwidth and expensive equipment. Television production clearly was not available to ordinary people. The development of cable television changed all that. Not only were over-the-air television signals transmitted, but new origination opportunities arose.

The convergence of the low-cost, portable video equipment and an equally low-cost distribution network—cable television—created an unusual opportunity in the United States in the 1970s. At the time, cable television reached about 20 percent of American homes (now it reaches an estimated 60 percent). While the initial purpose of cable was to bring television reception to areas blocked by physical obstructions, the cable carried with it much more bandwidth than was then available to broadcast stations. With very little investment, small communities and cable systems could originate programming. No spectrum space scarcity here! You could originate channels as well as retransmit over-the-air television.

## Empowerment through Media

My research group, The Alternate Media Center at New York University, was set up in 1971 to examine possible relationships between communities, video, and cable. We set out to train people to develop and distribute their original documents locally on new cable channels. We set up models of Public Access Centers in partnership with cable systems in several U.S. cities from New York to California. We provided equipment and training for community members to shoot and edit videotapes of local concern.

People who were not media professionals, but who had community interests, were offered training and time on the cable systems on a first-come, first-served basis. City council meetings and protests were videotaped, interviews were conducted, conditions in schools and neighborhoods were recorded. Discussions of community problems were raised. It was an extraordinary political opportunity. Ultimately these access centers were absorbed by the cable systems and mandated by the Federal Communications Commission. Public Access in the United States is now established in communities across the country.

While this is an enticing story of empowerment through technology, there are important lessons to be learned from it. Many of the programs, on these channels, were ignored by the communities. Producers anxious to imitate the broadcast style of commercial television but with none of its resources or professional know-how lost their audiences quickly.

When communities stopped trying to mimic broadcast television and found their own voice, their own appropriate use for the video technology and the distribution channel, their audiences returned. Authenticity—a real and original voice—made community cable appealing. When people were themselves, not what they thought they should be, they were far more interesting than they had realized. There was now an alternative. It clearly pointed out the difference between access to a communications channel and access to an audience.

The flip side of the access issue is CNN. In the late seventies CNN exploited cable and combined it with satellite technology to distribute news worldwide from Atlanta, Georgia.

While this service is available worldwide, it is not distributed to many individual homes in many countries because the requisite satellite dishes are still very expensive. So outside of the United States, CNN usually is found in hotels and government offices and newsrooms. Its influence is even more powerful under these circumstances, since many of those who have access to it are members of government or the local press—in other words, the most influential people.

## Interactivity

Marshall McLuhan's global village may be too simple a model for today's complex interactions of culture, politics, technology, and media.

One way to better navigate the course of the future global technologies might be to examine these complex issues and international situations in terms of smaller, local ones.

With technological change comes the widening opportunity for interactivity. One of the attributes of interactivity is two-way communication. Television broadcasting is an example of one-way communication.

One-way media as we know them originate from one source and go to many. Interactive media create very different opportunities. They allow exchange and origination from many different sources.

Two-way communications and one-way communications are as different as a conversation and a lecture.

Interactivity has the potential to provide a new perspective on the issues of access to an audience, access to technology, and access to information. It can give a voice where one was not heard before. How we use it is a question of some significance.

Earlier I spoke of projects developed by the Alternate Media Center, which demonstrated to me the importance of allowing users to design their own systems, of allowing the content to create the application. In the mid-seventies, we responded to a National Science Foundation question about whether two-way television could deliver social services in a cost-effective manner. We chose to work with old people, because we knew they are large consumers of social services. We believed that the key was to design a communications system that would be used by senior citizens and programmed by them for their own use. The technology had to be transparent and unthreatening. The real job was to find a way to have the users make the system their own. There are many ways to communicate information. One way is to push the information out and the other is to pull the information out. We chose to organize a system that would have people pull the information out.

We began in 1975. One of our first efforts was to set up a governing board of community members to help us design and implement a two-way interactive television system for senior citizens in Reading, Pennsylvania. Using a return band of the local cable system, we originated from three neighborhood communication centers in existing senior citizen facilities. These were our permanent origination points. We also set up several mobile origination points from different city agencies such as City Hall, the social security office, schools, and the county commissioner's offices. These locations were introduced once a week.

Four separate origination sources were sent to the head end of the cable system. Only one channel was transmitted to cable subscribers. This was done by combining two locations on one split screen with a simple switcher. Switching was determined by who was talking. Because the cameras were placed directly beside the receiving signal, people were able to look at each other while talking from different locations. Those at home could participate by way of a telephone patched in at the head end and heard by everyone on the cable system.

While I have briefly described the technical grid, this project was not about technology. Communications technology does not exist apart from the people who create and use it. This was not broadcast television, although initially everyone wanted to emulate what they saw on television. Our analogy was the telephone. We said, "You don't make a program when you call someone on the telephone—you begin with the reason for the call, and the content is the dialogue that follows."

The important aspect of the programming was exchange and interaction.

A few examples. We found a woman in her eighties who had been active in local politics. She was a natural to "host" the weekly "live" exchange between the mayor and city council members. Other people hosted discussion programs that took place in four different locations at the same time. Those who hosted were in fact producers, but we avoided the jargon of television and instead used the metaphor of a telephone to suggest conversation rather than one-way television. Presenters determined the topic of the day, invited the participants, and stimulated discussion in four different locations.

Another woman who was interested in nursing homes took a camera person to various homes in the area and brought back a "taped" report for others to share. Her questions to the nursing home staff were far more relevant to the needs of older people than any questions we might have come up with. The videotape and the organizer's accompanying live commentary provided a lively exchange of questions and answers about the nursing home from people who didn't have the opportunity to visit.

Research and planning of programs was required, and many of the old folks became completely engaged in the process. I suspect the benefit of the activity kept many a mind agile. Voluntary committees that were responsible for the programming developed original ideas. The programming these folks created could never have been developed by a program director who didn't share their interests and problems. As a result of the broadcasts, people who hadn't seen each other in years discovered each other on television. When they waved to each other on camera, some thought it would trivialize the system; it turned out to be an unexpected benefit because our intent all along had been to encourage communication.

As familiarity and comfort were the order of the day, we needed to have open microphones at each of the centers. People had to be able to jump up and get involved in the discussion easily. The engineers advised that we could not have open audio with 14 microphones, because of feedback, but we knew that if the system was not spontaneous and easy to use people would reject it. So we found an engineer who listened to our concerns. He designed a feedback suppressor to solve the problem. The difficulties we encountered strengthened our conviction that users ought to drive the technology—not the other way around. It is a point I feel very strongly about. Too often technology drives an application because users are intimidated by the technology and do not have a hand in its design.

This project demonstrated that if people are given the tools, the environment, and the encouragement, they can create something that reflects them.

I remember vividly the day I was driving in Reading, Pennsylvania, and on my car radio a local news announcer referred to a comment that someone had made on one of the programs. I knew then that the channel had been accepted and become a permanent fixture in the community. The board of elders that we left in place in 1977 still operates to this day. They found the funds to sustain the system and manage the governance of what is now a model program in the United States. They don't remember that we were ever there, and we consider that our greatest success.

## What global networks can learn from this model

The global reach of television has made *globalization* a current buzzword in media. And multinational companies are rushing to serve new markets, with the promise of profit not far behind.

There are many options. Nowhere will issues of design and transparency be more important than in the interactive global networks now being formed. They are facing multinational issues of control, ownership, intellectual property, and transborder dataflow. But if, as these networks develop, these issues overshadow user issues such as accessibility and ease of use, we will lose an extraordinary opportunity to create interesting and exciting new forms.

The same factors that proved to be crucial at Reading apply to global networks. Transparency and clear and simple design are essential to demystifying technology and making it accessible to its users.

The telephone is a wonderful example of interactive applications designed by users. The telephone company provides an empty pipe and a universal interface, and the telephone is easy to use. Adults discuss business, teenagers discuss whatever teenagers discuss; some use it to combat loneliness, others to order groceries; some to make appointments, still others to make love. It is truly a user-generated medium.

The June 27, 1991 issue of *The Washington Post* featured a story about the telephone. A sociologist with Bellcore, the research arm of the Baby Bells, was quoted:

> When the Eskimos in remote northern Canada first got direct-satellite telephone communications about 20 years ago, the Canadian government figured they would just use it to talk to each other. Instead, the Eskimos started calling Seattle to check the market for seal meat and started cutting their own deals. That kind of thing has happened all over the Third World.

The historic landscape is littered with technologies that were developed for one purpose but used for vastly different ones. If flexibility is included in the design, users are able to adapt technology to their own needs.

Initially, when Bell developed the telephone, Western Union refused to invest in the new company. Western Union was convinced that people would not conduct business on the telephone because they needed information in writing. But the convenience of use, the transparency of the technology (we don't know whether a phone call is carried on terrestrial lines or through a satellite), ease of use (you don't need a manual), and most important, the opportunity to use it for a variety of communications, has made it an indispensable part of our lives.

Tomorrow's high-speed networks will have the capacity to carry multimedia in real time. The same need for transparency and ease of use applies to these networks. If a doctor is about to operate on a critically ill patient and needs to consult with doctors elsewhere, whether the distance is small or great a CAT scan can be sent down the network quickly. Museums and libraries can use these same networks to increase their distribution and availability to many more people in distant locations. Physical distances can be cut dramatically. As with the early days of the telephone, we can now only imagine applications. But once the empty pipe has been laid and is accessible, imagination and need will drive new uses.

## The People, Not the Technology

It is startling how quickly virtually any discussion of the future of computing, entertainment, publishing, broadcasting, office technology, and education evolves into speculation about the technology. But the technology is as straightforward as a mathematical equation. What *isn't* clear is how we can benefit from these new and powerful developments.

Now that users and artists can use these new tools because of lower costs and less obtuse interfaces, something new has been added to the mix. I use the term *artists* in a general sense. Art traditionally has shown us new ways to look at the world. The sensitivity and sensibility of the artist can temper a singular technological approach.

There is no question that we will have the ability to move large amounts of digital information across space and time. Fiber optics, digital switching, compressed video, direct satellite transmission, will take us to this electronic nirvana. Broadband digital switched networks will be accessible almost anywhere in the industrialized world, television receivers will be computers, imaging technology will get cheaper and smaller, and improved displays will incorporate graphics chips capable of decompressing full-motion video. High-resolution video will merge with computer displays. This new digital technology translates images, graphics, text, video, and sound into a common language.

But it is still *people* who lead the development of applications, *people* who bring humanity to the machines, *people* who will speak this common language. How we train people, how we encourage people to recognize a moral as well as an aesthetic responsibility, are serious considerations.

### Training the new technology designers

In 1979, the Alternate Media Center developed a graduate program in the Tisch School of the Arts at New York University: the Interactive Telecommunications Program. Its focus is telecommunications and the production of multimedia applications. The fact that the program is in the School of the Arts is significant. We are not housed in schools such as those of Computer Science, Social Science, Education, Business, or Journalism. We are in the School of the Arts because our primary interest is in creative communication.

The focus on interactivity requires that we look to the new technologies as the engine; that we look at technology as the verb, not the noun; that our commitment is to people, not technology. There is a new community of disciplines. Today fields that were once worlds apart are converging.

Our students and faculty come from a wide range of backgrounds. Computer scientists work with students from the fine arts, sound engineers, video makers, musicians, writers, journalists, architects—all are in the mix. What can they teach other? A great deal, and perhaps most importantly, that there is no one way to create, rather many different ways. Skills and approaches are exchanged. This is an environment with no fixed circumference, fluid enough to move with the acceleration of technological change.

The field has yet to be defined. The ability to communicate must be combined with creative vision. This is not an inherent attribute of the technology, however; it comes about when the technology is accessible to talented and imaginative people.

We believe that a new kind of communications professional is needed, one who can adapt to changes, who is aware of issues of power, control, representation, interface, and aesthetics, one who is able to demystify technology and yet has enough knowledge of its attributes to put it in perspective.

This new kind of professional is comfortable with both creative and analytical modes of learning. Our curriculum is set up for the student who wants to *learn* rather than for the student who merely wants to acquire a skill. This student is a new breed of person. One who understands the value of pictures, words, critical thinking, judgment, understanding, technology, and aesthetics. One who has the ability to manipulate tools, and the critical capacity to sort out information. In short, a student who reflects the knowledge shift from static knowledge to a dynamic, searching paradigm.

We believe that technology is not value-free. It takes on the values of the designers. How do you provide an environment where diverse talented people can harness these technologies so that they add to the human spirit?

We encourage collaboration rather than competition. The emphasis on collaboration creates a kind of collegiality that is exciting in any learning environment. Group projects allow students to add their particular skills to a project even as they learn about other disciplines. Students are encouraged to fail, to try out ideas and concepts that may or may not work and to learn from their mistakes. We prefer to ask questions rather than look for solutions.

Along with classes, students work on projects—experimenting with pushing the technology to the edge of the possible, combining tools and ideas in new ways. The tools are personal computers, video, graphics, sound, animation, and text—the medium is transmission. These new convergences of technologies are providing capabilities to individual users that once were reserved for highly skilled technicians operating very expensive equipment.

Labs are the heart of our graduate program, a crucible in which a mix of ideas and talents creates new forms and applications. Students in the Interactive Telecommunications Program developed and produce a program called *Window* which is cablecast each evening over Manhattan Cable, the local cable television company. The topics ranges from homelessness, racism, and sexism to other community issues.

Interactive videodiscs and telephone call-ins allow viewers to choose portions of a videodisc produced by students. The telephone interface was designed by one of our students—he is not an engineer, but was interested in experimenting with interactivity in a mass medium. The opportunity to control a television program is appealing to people who watch *Window*. We know that the audience is involved, because the call-in lines are constantly in use during the cablecasts.

The tools to mix and edit audio and video and electronic text are now accessible to a broad range of creative professionals—producers and artists—who want to take direct control of the process. Computer technology was once the domain of the computer scientist. Now, because of miniaturization and less obtuse interfaces, artists are working with computers. This may prove to be one of the most exciting developments, because artists will bring a new dimension and creative investigation of the possibilities of communications technology.

The computer can be a creative partner, but it can't do anything by itself. Only a talented and imaginative creator can make it *sing*.

We are now able to move beyond traditional linear exposition to explore interactivity, a nonlinear presentation of information. Parallel, even concurrent story lines are possible in this new medium.

This is an entirely new art form. We are freeing the music, film, video broadcast, and publishing industries from the limitations and practices imposed by previous generations of technology.

Our students are joining the ranks of the experimenters and the "imaginers." We expect them to raise the ethical questions, the aesthetic requirements, and the empowerment issues, and to address the design needs we emphasize when they go out and create the technology applications of our future.

Many of our graduates have set up their own companies, while others work in many different areas for both profit and nonprofit corporations such as the Nynex Media Lab, Apple Computer's Advanced Technology Group, the American Museum of Natural History, Chase Manhattan Bank, Educational Testing Service, the Telecommunications Office of the City of New York, Philip Morris, IBM, Optical Data, HBO, and ABC News Interactive, to name only a few.

In our graduate program, we try to maintain a balance between the excitement and allure of potential new and enhanced forms of communication and the responsibilities and pitfalls inherent in technological advances. We walk a tightrope, learning as we go.

Sometimes a technology's use is not obvious, and it needs to be introduced into a community of users who can design one themselves. Sometimes a technology can be adapted by a creative team or an event. Often a need creates an application.

However a communications technology comes to life, it is sure to take on the values of its creators and the users. It is important to remember that there is no one way but rather many different ways. In a time when big popular, centralized media can control how a person, a political point of view, or a cultural group is represented, it is crucially important that we come up with ways to provide alternate means for people to create their own media and, as a result, their own ways of representing themselves.

A Zen monk once asked a Zen teacher, "What is the way?" The teacher answered, "Ordinary mind is the way." The monk asked, "Then should we direct ourselves toward it, or not?" The teacher replied, "If you direct yourself toward it, you go away from it." The monk said, "If I don't direct myself toward it, how can I know the way?"

The teacher said, "The way is beyond knowing or not knowing."

---

This chapter was originally presented at the Cultural Identity and Integration in the New Media World conference at the University of Industrial Arts, Helsinki, Finland, November 1991.

# Tapping the Power of Multimedia

**Steven L. Raber**

## Introduction

A Michigan power company replaces a grueling, 12-hour standup training class with a self-paced multimedia training program that is more consistent, accurate, and detailed. A museum uses multimedia to teach the rigors of seventeenth-century maritime life to youngsters raised on microwave dinners and MTV. An NBA team immediately translates floor action into crowd-inspiring music with a multimedia system that responds to a touch on a screen.

These are just a few of the thousands of multimedia applications currently in use in homes, schools, and businesses, with thousands more under development. These applications are being used to teach, entertain, persuade, document, sell, and communicate in more powerful and exciting ways than anything that's ever existed before. And the power of multimedia is spreading rapidly. Less than three years ago, a multimedia system cost more than $10,000. Now the price has fallen to less than a fifth of that, and before long every PC will come equipped with multimedia capabilities. In fact, a McGraw-Hill poll of Fall 1992 Comdex attendees discovered that 41 percent believe that multimedia will have the greatest practical impact on computing during the next five years. Portability, wireless communications, and other technologies ranked far behind.

Multimedia represents a technological crossroads at which increasing PC power, digital technology, and video access have converged, personalizing, for the first time, the information revolution. Multimedia takes yesterday's training film, PC graphics presentation, audio tape, and other common media and merges them into impactful presentations that are much, much greater than the sum of their parts. It incorporates such information-handling technology as hyperlinking, which allows nonlinear navigation through data, and object orientation, which simplifies complex operations with point-and-click utility.

As a result, multimedia heralds a new way of learning and communicating as it moves from being a programmer's playground to a technology as familiar as the VCR and as necessary as the fax. In other words, if the eighties spawned PCs and networking belongs to the nineties, then multimedia will be the technological breakthrough of the millennium.

But exactly what is this revolution called "multimedia," and how can you put it to work for you? Is it another one of those technological fantasies that never seem to make the transition into everyday life, like videophones or intra-city "people-movers"? Is it one of those technologies where it pays to be cautious until the market has matured, like the early days of the VCR? Or is it more like today's telephone, a once-revolutionary technology that no one can now live without?

The answer is that if multimedia is not already having an impact on your life, it soon will be (see Fig. 3.1). That's why it's important to know not only what multimedia is, but how you can make it work for you. Don't be put off by unfamiliar buzzwords like DVI and MPEG, or fears of making irremediable mistakes. Instead, think of using multimedia as being similar to driving one of today's cars: a lot of advanced technology is hidden under the hood, but driving is still easy enough for everyone to learn.

## Using Multimedia at Home

Look at many of today's top-selling multimedia titles—*Sherlock Holmes, National Geographic Society's Mammals,* and *Where in the World Is Carmen*

Figure 3.1  Applications for multimedia.

*Sandiego?*—and you'll see how multimedia impacts the home. If your kids think Nintendo is awesome, then wait till they learn how multimedia immerses them in intergalactic space battles, rock 'n' roll theme parks of the future, and danger-packed voyages to the bottom of the sea. As one observer put it: MTV to the max.

*Mad Dog McCree,* for example, brings home the old action movies we watched at theaters as kids. Shoot the bad guy, and he keels over. Miss him, and you risk being plugged by the outlaw.

But, fortunately, home applications of multimedia are not limited to shoot-'em-ups. National Geographic's *Presidents* lets children explore timelines of history and experience famous presidential speeches at a click of the mouse. *The New Grolier MultiMedia Encyclopedia* combines the depth of traditional encyclopedias with exciting visualization of the moonwalk and other events. And *The 1991 Time Magazine Compact Almanac* captures the twentieth century, with over 10,000 articles and video footage ranging from Henry Ford's Model T to Boris Yeltsin and the Soviet coup.

Undoubtedly slowing the spread of multimedia into the home is the cost of commercial multimedia applications, which can range from less than $30 to several hundred dollars. Few consumers are willing to make that kind of entertainment investment, sight unseen. To help consumers overcome this hurdle, a major multimedia publisher and distributor has introduced a multimedia "test-drive" program. The publisher is entering into agreements with video rental stores to let consumers rent a new title for $3 per day, then buy it if they like it. Other major publishers are rumored to be looking at similar programs, which means that, before long, multimedia franchises may fill every shopping mall.

## Multimedia Goes to School

In the classroom, multimedia also can bridge the chasm between theory and practice by giving students the opportunity to practice what they have learned in a safe and controlled environment. And by making the theory real, multimedia engages students, turning them into active rather than passive learners.

Multimedia in the schools can be used to enhance learning and aid simulations. Seventh- and eighth-graders in a Rhode Island high school created a multimedia presentation that explored the historical significance of the *Titanic,* its tragic fate, the long search for the wreckage, and the technology used to find it. The students used IBM's LinkWay and Storyboard Live!, two programs that can combine text, graphics, animation, still photographs, and motion video into one document on the computer. In the process the students not only learned about geography, history, and math, but also developed higher-order thinking skills and problem-solving abilities.

Simulation also unlocks the power of multimedia. For example, a major midwestern university uses multimedia to teach introductory chemistry to more than 2000 students per semester. Students perform such experiments as the ionization of salt in water or determining the acidity of unknown solutions. The lessons allow students to perform procedures and make decisions about experiments that would be much more difficult with traditional instruction. The benefits include allowing students to study reactions that are too hazardous, expensive, or time-consuming to be completed in the standard chemical laboratory. Less hazardous waste is generated, and teachers can spend more time one-on-one. Instructors report that students seem to be better prepared for actual lab work and more motivated to study chemistry, perhaps because multimedia gives them the opportunity to learn from mistakes in a hazard-free setting.

High schools nationwide are using a class of multimedia that IBM calls "knowledge systems." These systems include *The Illuminated Books and Manuscripts* and *Columbus: Encounter, Discovery, and Beyond,* each incorporating 180 hours of interactive learning. *Illuminated Books* studies five classic works of literature, including Shakespeare's *Hamlet* and Alfred Tennyson's "Ulysses," while *Columbus* is a cross-disciplinary study of the Renaissance and the Age of Discovery.

## Getting Down to Business

The power of multimedia has been recognized by business and government as well. Already multimedia is having a significant impact in training/education, retail sales, business presentations, communications enhancement, and even public information access.

### Training

It's every manager's nightmare: overhearing an employee tell a customer, "I don't know. It's not my area."

Training employees so as to eliminate this problem is expensive. But the cost pales next to the price of untrained or poorly trained employees on customer relations, safety, or internal efficiencies. As a result businesses, always looking for ways to cut costs and improve productivity, have embraced multimedia as enthusiastically as an investment tax credit.

It's easy to understand why. Multimedia has the power to teach and train according to an individual's ability, without the intrinsic handicaps of classroom training, videos, and instructional manuals. An oft-quoted study says that people remember about 25 percent of what they see, 40 percent of what they see and hear, and almost 75 percent of what they see, hear, and do. While other forms of instruction are often merely variations on one-time show-and-tell, multimedia is see-and-do, with multiple opportunities to repeat if the information is not understood. The learning process is greatly accelerated when the user is in control.

Therefore, multimedia represents the best tool for business to bring what is commonly acknowledged to be an underskilled work force up to the demands of the twenty-first century.

Just open a copy of *BusinessWeek* or *The Wall Street Journal* to learn about multimedia in action. Before, the best one of the nation's largest telecommunications companies could offer trainees were flip charts and prerecorded videotapes and audiotapes. Now it's taking multimedia to its 43,000 employees, providing everything from technical training to simulated customer encounters to creative problem solving and decision making. The payoffs: employees learn more in less time with longer retention, while the company ensures consistent training nationwide and keeps employees on the job and out of the classroom longer.

Companies nationwide report similar benefits. A major steel company reported a 20 to 40 percent reduction in training time and a 20 to 40 percent increase in retention. A retail sporting goods chain cut average training time per employee from 8 to 4 hours. An overnight express company slashed instructor-led classroom time from 7.5 to 2.6 hours without cutting content. Multimedia courses save a Big Six consulting firm $10 million annually.

Currently, this business training occurs at stand-alone stations, each equipped with the necessary add-ons. But if companies put multimedia training programs on a network, the costs of current decentralized approaches will decline dramatically even as the benefits expand exponentially. The power of multimedia to teach and train will increase even more as courseware increasingly incorporates pattern-recognition features that automatically adjust information according to individual responses.

## Retail

Businesses also are using multimedia to extend their sales reach through multimedia "kiosk catalogs" and "kiosk sales representatives." These kiosks—stand-alone multimedia devices that look like ATMs and feature touchscreens, color images, video, and audio—are being placed in high-traffic areas, delivering accessible information to targeted prospects when they are in a buying mood. Information can be accessed through a touchscreen and viewed on the monitor, or even printed out. With the right communications links, kiosks can even be programmed and updated from a central facility.

Kiosks not only represent low-cost (less than $15,000), high-return sales tools but also can distinguish a business from its competition. Companies can collect information about their customers, either by recording the options chosen or by asking questions directly. Consumers benefit from reduced costs, since a manufacturer or retailer has no human, inventory, or operating costs.

With multimedia kiosks, customers can browse through colorful presentations of products before placing orders. Multilingual audio can serve a heterogeneous population, or even support a beachhead in international markets. A telephone link could allow the prospect to speak to a sales representatives while a credit card reader takes the order. A major Ohio bank is even testing videoconferencing on its kiosks, which will allow customers to see the customer service representative "live."

At the current rate, multimedia kiosks soon will be as ubiquitous as ATMs. Major league baseball teams are using kiosks that permit ticket buyers not only to buy game seats with a credit card, but also to see a view of the playing field from that particular seat! A major computer company plans to sell software for its palmtop computers via kiosks. Another company has used kiosks to provide sheet music to customers in whatever score, key, or arrangement they desire.

The benefits of multimedia just begin with consumer sales. Architects and engineers can use multimedia to transform blueprints and drawings into simulations of buildings and products, complete with interior visualizations including furnishings and decorations. Other companies can use multimedia to demonstrate those hard-to-inventory items such as handmade furniture, industrial equipment, or earthwork. Real estate agents can show prospects the interiors and exteriors of homes that meet their pricing, location, and other criteria, eliminating wasted trips to unsatisfactory sites. In fact, one Denmark agency used such a system to increase prospect traffic by 400 percent while reducing the number of house visits per purchase by almost 50 percent.

Waves gently kissing palm-shrouded shores...the ethereal chimes of medieval cathedrals...mountain panoramas ringing pristine ski trails—nothing can sell a vacation or trip like multimedia. Plus, multimedia can provide all of the extra details as to lodging, tours, special attractions, and all that really makes a trip. And when the entire family needs persuading, travel agencies can even "print" a custom videotape for the client to take home.

## Business presentations

But multimedia is not limited to special business needs such as sales or training. It can also deliver benefits every day in your office. You can improve every PC application with business audio, taking advantage of voice recording, annotation, and even supplementing other input devices. For example, you can eliminate all of the yellow "stickies" that grow on every business document by embedding audio comments, suggestions, or explanations in the spreadsheet, letter, or other document. This technology is easily networkable, which means that voice files can be moved around and shared on the network like any other type of computer data. The productivity benefits are obvious. You can speak faster than you can write, plus you can more easily convey nuance or feeling.

Other applications of business audio include checking the clarity of your grammar or thought process by having the computer "read" back documents. Or you can even train your PC to be a faithful servant, teaching it to "save file" or "print" with a spoken command.

## Documentation

Multimedia has proven to be a highly effective form of documentation for three reasons. First, it provides a visual means to show complex events, such as the routing of a phone call; second, it can rapidly access information required for installation or repairs; and third, it can show events chronologically in real time. For example, a major telephone firm now uses 90 seconds of visual animation to convey information that once took 20 pages to explain.

Multimedia documentation offers other benefits as well. It can provide examples of warning bells and lights, a capability no written documentation can provide. It can be much more current that old-fashioned manuals, since information stored on a server can be updated daily, if necessary.

## Public information access

Government touches our lives in so many ways—through our schools, taxes, and services—yet the most common citizen complaint is that you can't get information out of governmental agencies, as anyone who has every tried to call the Division of Motor Vehicles can testify. But multimedia kiosks offer governments a new avenue to communicate with citizens and help build a sense of community—24 hours a day. They can easily be placed in lobbies, shopping malls, public parks and facilities, convention centers, airports, museums, art galleries, and anywhere else people congregate and need information.

For example, the "L.A. Project" used multimedia to help citizens recover from the devastating 1992 Los Angeles riots. The multimedia kiosks, located in central community sites, offered citizens information on "Where Can I Get Help?" or "What Can I Do To Help?" The information connected victims with resources concerning financial aid, legal rights, food and clothing, shelter, small business assistance, and other categories. The information, displayed in English, Spanish, or Korean and reinforced with an audio recording, made the system accessible to persons with limited literacy. A similar system was used in Florida to help citizens recover from the devastation of Hurricane Andrew.

Other locales presently linking government to multimedia include Hawaii, which offers residents health, human services, and employment information; California, which is planning to provide vehicle registration renewals via touch-screen transaction kiosks; Oregon, which uses multimedia kiosks to give drivers' tests; and the Long Beach, California, Municipal Court, which allows violators to pay for traffic citations at an "Auto Clerk" kiosk.

## Collaborative multimedia computing

Multimedia can help to provide a new solution for work-group productivity that is best termed *collaborative multimedia*. Using advanced videoconferencing technology, collaborative multimedia allows real-time interaction between people who need to work together but who can't be in the same place at the same time. This permits "multimedia meetings" to occur as spontaneously as a phone call. As a result organizations can reduce travel costs and the nonproductive time spent traveling, allow work groups to span wider geographies, and improve productivity through work-group interaction.

The IBM Person to Person/2 is a videoconferencing system that incorporates a camera placed beside a computer so that participants can see each other as if they were in a face-to-face meeting. All desktop applications—spreadsheets, graphics, text—become de facto groupware because they are shared simultaneously among all participants. Once these applications have been moved into an open window called a "chalkboard," participants can use a set of drawing tools to highlight some points or delete others as if they were all standing together at a blackboard.

## How to Get Started with Multimedia

The benefits of multimedia are clear. But how can you turn the promise into reality? It's easier than you think. In fact if you can program a VCR, you can probably build a cutting-edge multimedia application.

Essentially, there are three avenues you can go down to get into multimedia on PCs (see Fig. 3.2):

1. Buy a complete, ready-to-go system based on standardized platform.

2. Upgrade your current system.

3. Use a "best-of-breed" approach, assembling a customized system with individual components optimized for specific needs.

Which avenue you will take depends on several factors: your budget (of course), potential applications, technical and/or programming skills, and your choice of operating systems.

In many ways the choice of an operating system for PCs is the most fundamental, since it will shape your choice of applications, upgrade paths, and total functionality. The three choices are DOS, Windows, and OS/2.

DOS was once the powerful engine that propelled the PC revolution, but now it's showing its age. Other operating systems long ago surpassed DOS in terms of power and functionality. However, although one day it may be as hard to find a DOS-based PC as it is now to find a car running on leaded

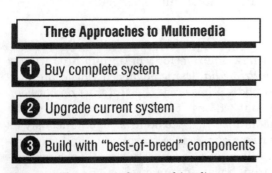

**Figure 3.2**  Three approaches to multimedia.

gasoline, there are still millions of users worldwide whose PCs provide all the functionality they need. These users can take advantage of some multimedia training applications that offer interactive response, some animation, and links to a VCR, videodisc player, or other analog device. Additionally, DOS-based PCs can be linked in a network that contains more powerful multimedia capabilities in a central repository.

Microsoft's Windows opened the door to graphical user interfaces in the PC world, and has consequently been incorporated into many multimedia applications. Windows permits a computer's additional memory to be tapped, thus giving multimedia applications the extra "room" to strut their stuff. Windows 3.1 incorporates multimedia extensions, which essentially means that it provides the necessary "hooks" to synchronize and orchestrate the sound, video, and other capabilities of most multimedia applications. As a result, Windows is heavily used for education and "edutainment" applications.

IBM's OS/2 is a 32-bit operating system, which is nothing more than a fancy way of saying that it provides a much wider "data highway" than the 8- or 16-bit capabilities of DOS and Windows. OS/2 can incorporate all the capabilities and functionality of DOS and Windows, plus provide the capacity for preemptive multitasking, which manages multiple streams of data (or applications) simultaneously. OS/2 with Multimedia Presentation Manager/2 (MMPM/2) provides a consistent platform for applications to incorporate sound, graphics, video, and images through the use of any easy-to-program, high-level interface. MMPM/2 is device-independent, which means that applications and tools can be written independently of the wide variety of multimedia devices and formats. MMPM/2 also allows multimedia hardware to be more fully exploited through device-sharing. Eventually, all advanced operating systems will be able to exploit the power of today's 32-bit microprocessors.

### The stand-alone path

The easiest way to get into PC multimedia is to buy a complete system from IBM, AST, Advanced Logic Research, or other manufacturers. For maximum functionality, make sure the system includes MPC Level 2 certification. This MPC specification is the electronic equivalent of the Good Housekeeping seal of approval, which means that the computer has been tested to ensure compliance with an industrywide minimum standard for enhanced multimedia computing.

To receive Level 2 certification (see Fig. 3.3), computers must have: 486 25-MHz or compatible processor; 4-Mbyte RAM; 160-Mbyte hard drive; double-speed (which means it has a data-transfer rate of both 150 and 300 bytes-per-second), XA (extended architecture)-ready, multisession-capable CD-ROM drive; 16-bit sound; and a monitor that offers a display resolution of 640 × 480 with 64K colors. (If some terms are unfamiliar, don't worry; they will be explained later in the chapter.) Buying an MPC Level 2 certified computer ensures compatibility with a wide range of powerful off-the-shelf multimedia software.

**MPC II Standard**

25-MHz 486SX microprocessor

4-MB RAM (8 MB recommended)

Display resolution of 640 x 480
with 65,536 colors

CD-ROM
• Doublespeed
• XA ready
• Multisession capable

160-MB or larger hard drive

**Figure 3.3**   MPC II standard.

### Upgrading a PC

If you're not ready to turn your current system out to pasture, then a multimedia upgrade kit may be best for you. In fact, upgrade products currently constitute the majority of multimedia hardware sales.

Before you take this path, first be sure that your existing system has sufficient horsepower. Pass those outdated IBM PC/XTs and ATs down to the kids; effective multimedia requires at least a 386SX with 4 Mbytes of memory. A 486 with 8 Mbytes of memory is even better. Add Windows to the mix, since it (or its equivalent) not only provides a graphical user interface (GUI) but also serves as the umbrella that lets such disparate elements as CD-ROM drives and video capture boards work together. The larger the hard-disk capacity, the better.

Multimedia upgrade kits usually contain a compatible CD-ROM drive and sound board, along with some bundled multimedia applications. For example, one popular upgrade kit that includes the sound board and drive comes with Compton's Multimedia Encyclopedia, Lotus 1-2-3 Multimedia for Windows, Nautilus Multimedia magazine, MacroMedia Action!, the Deluxe CD-ROM version of Carmen Sandiego, and Sierra's King's Quest V. As a result, these kits can represent a tremendous bargain, since buying these titles separately could cost thousands of dollars or more. Some even buy upgrade kits based not on the technology but solely on the type of titles they will receive.

### "Roll your own"

Or you might want to "roll your own" multimedia system, adding one kind of CD-ROM drive and a top-of-the-line sound card. But remember that you may pay a price for such freedom of choice. Compatibility becomes a problem, and it may be troublesome getting the individual components to work with one another. But if you do decide to go this route, it's time to get down to multimedia basics.

## Getting Down to Basics

A CD-ROM drive, either internal or external, is often the heart of a multimedia system. CD-ROM drives access the information contained on CD-ROM disks, which are just like audio CD disks except for special error-correction coding to ensure accuracy. CD-ROM disks hold about 650 Mbytes of data (the equivalent of 300,000 pages of information) or about 70 minutes of audio.

The two most critical specifications for choosing a CD-ROM drive are data-transfer rate and access time. Look for a continuous data-transfer rate of at least 150K per second. Slower rates will turn video and animation into herky-jerky screen stutters and may cause compatibility problems with the rest of your system. The newest—and most expensive—drives can wear two hats, spinning the disc at 300K per second for text or graphics, and slowing to 150K per second so that music and speech sound normal.

Access time is determined by how fast a drive scans a CD-ROM disk for information. Older drives take a half-second (500 milliseconds) or more to find data, while newer ones have access times as fast as 150 milliseconds. (Still slow compared to hard drives, which have access times of about 10 to 20 milliseconds.) The faster the better, but don't get one with an access time of less than 400 milliseconds, especially if you are going to depend on your PC for search-and-retrieval applications.

Look for a drive that meets the ISO 9660 standard data format, and avoid those with the older High Sierra (named after the Nevada hotel where the standards committee met in 1983) format. To avoid potential obsolescence down the road, get a CD-ROM player that can accommodate the emerging extended architecture (XA) format. The XA technology allows interleaved audio, video, and data streams on a CD-ROM disc. The standard is also compatible with Kodak's Photo CD technology, which lets you store photo images on CD.

Internal or external? Like modems, both offer the same functionality, so the choice essentially depends on your pocketbook and how handy you are with a screwdriver. Internal CD-ROM drives cost about $100 less than external drives, but require installation of drive rails and power-supply cabling inside a $5\frac{1}{4}$-inch half-height drivebay. (Check the documentation to make sure it explains installation clearly enough.) If you typically set your computer on its side to save space, then make sure the CD-ROM can operate in this position.

For external drives, just install an interface card (also called an *adapter* or *controller* card) in an empty slot and connect a cable to the drive. Remember that some external drives plug into proprietary interface cards while others use industry-standard SCSI connections. The interface makes no difference in performance, but SCSI-compatible CD-ROM drives will let other SCSI devices such as hard drives or tape drives "daisy-chain," or share the same adapter. On the other hand, using proprietary interface cards usually is cheaper, and it eliminates potential configuration headaches. If you do choose a proprietary card, make sure a controller is included. Buying one separately could add several hundred dollars to the cost.

Portable drives are small, lightweight external drives that plug into the parallel port through an adapter. They are usually used with portable computers. Remember, however, that all CD-ROM drives will run more slowly when connected to the parallel port.

Some drives permit disks to be directly loaded into the machine; others require CD-ROM caddies. There's no difference in performance, but caddies will help keep fingerprints and foreign matter from affecting the integrity of your disk. Handle with care! If dust does get inside the drive, it can interfere with the optical mechanism's ability to "read" information on the disk. Ideally, the CD-ROM drive also will have front-access controls for head-phones and volume control.

All CD-ROM drives should come with an installation disk that will add Microsoft's CD-ROM extension drivers (MSCDEX Version 2.2 or later) and a device driver to your system's CONFIG.SYS file, ensuring that the computer recognizes that a read-only drive is attached. Changes to your AUTOEXEC.BAT file may also have to be made so that your computer knows how to handle the new drive.

The type of application will determine whether you need a buffer or not. For text search and retrieval, a buffer isn't necessary, although it can speed up searches. However, smoothly displaying graphics, video, and animation requires a consistent transfer rate of 150 kbytes per second. To ensure this type of performance, look for a drive with a 32K to 54K buffer.

Of course, other important criteria that apply to all the components of a multimedia system include reliability, ease of setup, pricing, and technical support.

## Sound boards

Yes, all PCs do come with audio capabilities, but most can do no more than deliver one-note hoots and toots. Sound boards (Fig. 3.4) give your PC the ability to talk, sing, and entertain. Better sound boards can take sounds from a microphone, stereo, CD disk, or even a hard drive and mix them all together before outputting the result through speakers and headphones. This comes in handy, for example, if you want soft background music behind a travelogue narration.

The heart of a sound board is an analog-to-digital (ADC) chip that digitizes audio so it can be handled by your computer, and a digital-to-analog converter (DAC) chip that can turn computer output into sound. Almost every sound board will advertise compatibility with Creative Labs' Sound Blaster.

Minimally, a sound board should support CD Audio (so you can play the same CDs used in your stereo), MIDI files, and "waveform audio," better

| Determining the Quality of Sound Boards | | |
| --- | --- | --- |
| **Sound Quality** | **Sample Size** | **Sample Rate** |
| Low | 8-bit | 11 kHz |
| Medium | 16-bit | 22 kHz |
| High | 16-bit | 44 kHz |

**Figure 3.4**   Determining the quality of sound boards.

known as the WAV file format supported by Windows 3.1. WAV files are just a way to capture, store, and play back audio with a computer.

The quality of digitized audio is directly dependent on the "sample size," or how much data the ADC and DAC chips can process at once, and the "sample rate," or how fast the ADC and DAC chips can process the data. The sample size and sample rate seem like obscure terminologies until you know your specific application. Buy a sound card with an 8-bit sample size and a 22.05-kHz sample rate, and the audio output is going to sound like AM radio in an older car. In truth, this probably is adequate for games, but it may handicap more sophisticated business presentations or many newer multimedia titles.

For typical CD player output, look for higher-level cards with 16-bit sample sizes and a higher, FM-quality, 44.1-kHz sample rate. However, there's a price to be paid for higher fidelity: greater storage requirements. Sound sampled at 16 bits and 44.1 kHz takes 16 times as much disk space as the same sound sampled in 8-bit mono at 11 kHz. Of course compression can relieve the burden on your hard disk, but remember that the more you compress, the worse it sounds. There also currently aren't any standards for compression, which means that files compressed with one board and its software may not be readable by another board. Again, determine your entertainment, business audio, CD-ROM, and input requirements before you buy. 8-bit mono is fine for spreadsheet annotation, but probably inadequate for wooing prospects or making presentations.

Also consider cards with a MIDI interface, which means you can connect a computer to such electronic instruments as keyboards and drum machines. The MPC specifications call for MIDI support, although you can probably get along without it for most multimedia applications.

Almost all sound boards come with bundled software that let you record, edit, play MIDI and digital audio, or even author a multimedia presentation. For sound editing, check to see if the software supports Windows' OLE links. Most also include text-to-speech programs that read what you type.

Remember, however, that bundled software often has minimal capabilities, and serious applications may require software with additional capabilities.

If you already have a CD-ROM drive, check for compatibility. Several popular sound boards come with a CD-ROM connection, but some of these have a proprietary interface. For the widest—and safest—selection, look for a sound board that includes a SCSI connector. Better boards also will come with a microphone input jack and RCA output jacks for headphones or stereo speakers as well. When installing the sound board inside your computer, place it as far as possible from the power supply and hard drive so as to minimize potential interference.

### Video (still images)

Mention multimedia, and inevitably it will be defined in terms of "video." However, multimedia experts often stretch the word *video* to cover two meanings (see Fig. 3.5). The first is a series of static images, much like those seen in a slide show, and the other is "full-motion" video, which is comparable to watching TV or a movie.

Getting static images into a computer requires a video capture board, sometimes called an *NTSC/VGA board.* This expansion board digitizes an analog video signal from a VCR, camcorder, TV, or other NTSC source so that it can be stored and manipulated by a computer. With the proper software you can then shrink, edit, or crop the image, and augment it with text and graphics. Often this software is bundled with the board, but separate applications will offer greater functionality. More sophisticated boards provide the additional capability of controlling hue, contrast, and brightness and letting you crop, pan, and zoom in on a single image before saving it to disk in a popular graphics file format.

Unfortunately, getting the right video board is more complicated than buying a sound board. Video boards use a variety of signals and connections and follow different standards, and even the digital output can differ. And that doesn't include the differences in color-handling, resolutions, and file format

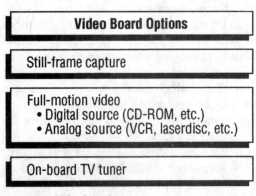

**Figure 3.5**  Video board options.

support. This means that you often have to adjust DIP switches or jumpers on both the expansion board and the motherboard to match signal type and monitor usage. For example, if your video capture board has VGA capabilities, you must switch off the system-board video to avoid interference from the add-in VGA.

### Video (full-motion)

Full-motion video can come from two sources: a CD-ROM disk or other digital storage device, or from such familiar items as VCRs or laserdiscs. Full-motion video—defined as 30 frames per second—from a digital source has a great deal more potential. You can, for example, add new images or clips to existing video as easily as inserting a sentence in a word processing document, eliminating the endless back-and-forth tape winds required for analog editing.

But at the same time, digital video is much more difficult to accomplish, mainly because full-motion video requires an extremely large data-transfer rate (up to 30 Mbytes per second) to display on the typical monitor. This means the average hard disk with dozens of applications and hundreds of files can support about 3 seconds of full-motion video. There are two approaches to reducing the vast burden digital video places on PCs: reducing the image (often to one-quarter of the monitor's size) or number of colors displayed, and compression.

JPEG, MPEG, P*64, DVI, and C-Cube are the best-known compression methodologies that permit digital video. All have their strengths and weaknesses, and each is best suited to particular applications. But the technology used most often in today's multimedia presentations is DVI (Digital Video Interactive), a proprietary, programmable compression/decompression technology based on the Intel i750 chip set. DVI can compress full-motion (30 frames per second) video at ratios between 80:1 and 160:1 and play it back in full-frame size and color. The IBM PS/2 ActionMedia II, an adapter card available for Micro Channel PS/2s, PS/ValuePoint, and other ISA-compatible computers, incorporates DVI technology and can support two modes of real-time compression and write to any digital medium.

Systems with DVI technology allow up to 72 minutes of full-screen, full-motion video playback from a CD-ROM disc, which can be produced for significantly less cost than laserdiscs. Images can also be easily edited or combined on-screen with computer-generated text and graphics. DVI technology, incorporated on IBM's PS/2 ActionMedia II adapter card, also permits you to capture, digitize, and compress multiple images and store them on disk or tape. While typical analog multimedia technology cannot produce laserdiscs in real time, DVI-based ActionMedia II applications can be created "on the fly" and stored on hard discs and other media.

Playback also is available from software-only compression, although there are some tradeoffs involved. Intel Indeo software can let any 486 computer with OS/2 or Windows play back video, although you'll only see 24 frames per second on one-quarter of the screen. Other software-only compression applications include IBM's PhotoMotion. This software, used in National Geographic's *Mammals, The New Grolier's MultiMedia Encyclopedia,* and many of the leading consumer/education titles on the market today, provides full-motion video playback with synchronized audio from a hard drive, and permits more than two hours of quarter-screen motion video, complete with audio.

Because of digital's storage and compression requirements, many people use a graphics board that allows full-motion video to be displayed from a VCR or laserdisc player. Laserdiscs look like large CD-ROM disks but incorporate analog—not digital—recording. As a result they provide high-quality video, exceeding the resolution of broadcast TV by about 40 percent.

VCRs and laserdisc players require an adapter board to be installed in the computer, which allows graphics to be mixed with video "windows." These boards, exemplified by the IBM M-Motion Video Adapter/A adapter card or VideoLogic's DVA4000 board, essentially let a PC serve as the brains of a VCR or other player. Some boards have two-way capabilities, allowing you to record computer-altered images on videotape.

### Other components

Of course the better the speaker, the better the audio. Make sure they are magnetically shielded to prevent interference with your PC. Some sound boards have enough power to drive loudspeakers directly. However, you'll get better sound by using speakers with built-in amplifiers or by linking the speakers to your stereo system. Most stereos and sound boards use pin plugs—also called *RCA* or *phono* plugs—although adapters may be required for different kinds of speakers and sound boards.

Many retail applications require touchscreen technology. It is a direct and intuitive way to control a computer, and extends the power of multimedia to those who may be uncomfortable with using a mouse or a keyboard. Some monitors, such as the 8516 Touch Display, offer integrated touchscreen capabilities, or use add-on touch panels to bring touchscreen technology to existing monitors.

### Getting into Multimedia—Software

Once the system has been set up, you need the necessary software to create and run multimedia presentations. This software will fall into one of five categories:

1. Authoring tools, which bind text, sound, graphics, and video into a coherent whole while adding interactive capabilities

2. Graphics tools, which are used to create still graphics, images, and special effects

3. Animation tools, which add motion to graphics and text

4. Audio tools, to capture and edit sound

5. Video tools, which capture and/or edit digital motion video.

Unfortunately, no one piece of software can do it all, which has its advantages and disadvantages. On the plus side, you can get software optimized for each particular application, but you risk incompatibility and the constant need to "shop around" for suitable applications (see Fig. 3.6).

To solve this problem, IBM, working with independent software vendors, developed the Ultimedia Tools Series, which represents the best-of-breed in multimedia software tools, all designed to work together. Currently, there are more than 80 applications that are part of the Ultimedia Tools Series, including MacroMedia's Authorware Professional (authoring software); Fractal Design's Painter (graphics); Turtle Beach Systems' Wave for Windows (audio); Autodesk's Animator Pro (animation); and other applications.

All the UTS-certified applications share a common architecture, which means that compliant applications running under DOS, Windows, or OS/2 will look and act as similarly as possible and be able to exchange data. Depending on the programs, you can manipulate multimedia objects across programs, use a clipboard to copy and paste items from one application to another, and use DDE (Dynamic Data Exchange) techniques across Windows applications. The eventual goal of the Ultimedia Tools Series architecture is to offer seamless interoperability among all multimedia applications.

### Clip media

If you, like many others, believe it's video that gives multimedia its punch, then you had better start assembling all the useful video images you can. Start taping those customer demonstrations or training sessions. Record your company president when he sets goals. Ask employees what they like about your company, and record the results.

And it doesn't have to be just video. Start taking digital photos with the Canon Xapshot, or have pictures digitized with the Kodak Photo CD system.

Figure 3.6  Tools for multimedia presentations.

Another alternative is to use a scanner, which looks like a desktop copy machine. The scanner digitizes your photo or artwork, allowing it to be imported into a computer application and manipulated like any other piece of art.

But be careful of what you copy. You don't want to run afoul of copyright law by illegally copying and using video, audio images, or text that belongs to someone else. That's why it's safest to generate your own multimedia material, or rely on the large library of material that producers permit to be used at will.

For example, Jasmine Stock Video offers a collection of video and production music for multimedia producers using Video for Windows. The Jasmine Stock Video Library can be used in the same way that "clip art" collections are used in desktop publishing. Using Indeo video software and these clip art CD-ROMs, PCs can show everything from Neil Armstrong's walk on the moon to the Great Wall of China, even to parachuting dogs and human cannonballs.

## Conclusion

Soon after Alexander Graham Bell invented the telephone in the late 1800s, companies rushed to connect homes to this wonderful new technology. Unfortunately, these companies weren't linked together, and often a homeowner couldn't call his neighbor across the street because they were on different systems. The situation was resolved only after all the phone companies had been unified into a single company.

In some ways, that situation is mirrored in the multimedia world of today. Multimedia is still in its infancy, which means there is a variety of competing standards. This is a minor problem if you have standardized on a multimedia platform within your firm, but it does inhibit your ability to write a best-selling application for the mass market. Ultimately, many of the problems will be resolved when full-blown multimedia standards and capabilities are integrated into operating systems.

But that shouldn't stop you from getting into multimedia, any more than the lack of automatic guidance systems for your car keeps you from driving to work each day. Multimedia can produce significant paybacks for you at home, in school, and in your business, for a relatively small investment of time and money. Now, for the first time, you have the power to capture the promise of the information revolution and make it work for you.

# The Virtual Classroom—
# A Business Necessity

**Ken Gerlach**

## The Training Challenge

### The training gap

Corporate educational and training programs face serious obstacles and are not keeping pace with the reality and needs of a changing work force. As John Naisbitt writes, "We have essentially the same education system we had for the industrial society and we are trying to use it to equip us for the information age."[1]

In the past decade we have seen constant, revolutionary change in products, technology, and customer requirements, and in the skills and knowledge needed by companies' employees. As a consequence, corporate America must confront the huge challenge of retraining its work force to compete in a new and changing world economy. The American Society for Training and Development estimates that 55 million Americans, about 45 percent of the work force currently employed, will need to be retrained in the next decade in technical, executive management, supervisory, customer service, and basic skills training. Moreover, "it is estimated that corporations will have spent in excess of $30 billion in 1992 to train employees,"[2] but that has not been sufficient to solve the problem.

Training can be accomplished through traditional courses (over half of America's corporate training takes place in a traditional classroom), tutorials, or informal, "grapevine" learning. Structured, formalized training is more productive than informal training, and much more effective when done in house. The average U.S. company invests less than 2 percent of its payroll in formal training, reaching only one-tenth of the work force. The average amount of time corporations spend on training their employees each year varies by industry, ranging from 5 days per year for industries with established technologies to 10 days per year for industries with rapidly changing technologies. At Hewlett-Packard Company, the average for technical people is between 22 to 27 days per year. The surplus trained labor force of a few years ago has been considerably reduced, so each employee's current skills are especially crucial if a company is to remain competitive.

The typical corporate training environment is comprised of a face-to-face class, either in a central facility or in field offices to which a trainer is sent in each location. But traditional training cannot keep pace in an era when technical obsolescence of an employee's skills can occur within 5 years of graduation from training. Increased competition, driven by accelerated product obsolescence (decreasing product life due to shorter development and marketing cycles) also impacts the necessity for constant and ongoing training. For instance, the average shelf life of a personal computer is less than 9 months. At HP, 50 percent of revenues are generated with products introduced within the last 2 years—a very rapid turnover of products. With limited product life and rapid product development, the pressure to accomplish training goals within a limited time frame is enormous.

HP's field engineers became vulnerable during the 1980s, when the accelerated development of new products was coming faster than technology updates could be transmitted. The interval between new product release and the accomplishment of marketing/training functions had to be cut dramatically. Training was struggling to keep up with the technology—field engineers were required to learn more in less time, but there wasn't enough time.

Traveling trainers, sent from corporate headquarters to the company divisions and field offices, can take months to deliver training to all sites. The optimal solution is to bring the training to all the employees at the same time—have the subject expert or panel of experts deliver the same information to all company sites simultaneously via some reliable and proven technological delivery system such as satellite. Tom Wilkins, an R & D manager for Distance Learning products at HP, says, "Between completion of course materials and delivery, a critical gap develops, sometimes as long as six months. The longer it lasts, the more likely it is that the training will be outdated before it can be delivered to the students."

Traditional classroom training will become increasingly less viable in terms of delivery time, cost, and user downtime, since rapid changes in technology and product obsolescence are becoming the norm across industries. A company needs to train its people on new products or communicate new strategies in a way that collapses time and distance. The challenge will be to retrain employees while maintaining competitiveness, reducing soaring costs, and managing limited time.

### Training to compete

If companies are to remain competitive, it is necessary that they plan for and quickly identify opportunities in a world that is truly becoming a global village. Local, parochial markets are disappearing, forcing organizations to either be responsive to changing market conditions or perish.

It is impossible for most corporations to be successful today without a worldwide strategy. In the 1960s, only 6 percent of U.S. business was exposed to international competition—today it's more than 70 percent, and increasing. At HP, more than half of its revenues come from overseas markets.

Frequent training and effective communication are fundamental if a company is to be responsive to changing markets and products and achieve a competitive advantage. Owing to evolving technology, collaborative management, and market-responsive production, a premium is now placed on employees who are multiskilled, multitrained, and who can be easily reassigned as needed.

"America's competitors in other countries commit significant resources to building a well-trained work force," but the United States has the "lowest percentage of spending on training compared to all the nations we…compete with" in Europe and in Japan.[3] In the United States the amount spent on upgrading employees' skills is only about 3 percent of what is spent on capital improvements to plant and equipment. Yet "the gains in productivity from workplace learning exceed the gains from capital investment by more than two to one."[3]

In today's global economy, the United States can no longer compete on the basis of mass production alone. We must respond faster to market needs and dramatically shorten product life cycles, bringing products to market in record time. Time-to-market will be crucial, with companies dependent on a smaller work force that must continually revise skills and use more technology in order to compete.

## The Training Solution

In spite of the traditional classroom's inability to keep pace with growing training requirements, there has been a serious underutilization of available technology that could be used to solve the training/education dilemma.

For a company that needs to update and quickly train geographically dispersed employees, delivering a consistent message worldwide, there is one technology that will enable them to quickly and efficiently respond to the training challenge: distance learning. Distance learning (DL) is an electronically assisted teaching/learning environment in which teacher and student are geographically separated, rely on electronic devices, and interact within a format that closely resembles the traditional classroom.

In the past, technology has focused on improving discrete instructional tools and access to outside information. The new generation of technology is aimed at creating a "virtual classroom" where artificial or physical boundaries are removed. Students in different locations across the country not only observe and listen but participate and become involved in subject matter that is delivered by the most knowledgeable and effective learning facilitators available and flavored by applicable, real-world case studies.

An effective DL environment creates a virtual classroom by using a telecommunications channel (i.e., satellite telecast) to link people at a number of locations. Interactive, two-way communication and real-time feedback is provided, which encourages the users' active participation. Given this technology, class size is unlimited, time and distance boundaries are removed, and the student has direct access to experts. Corporate training can be conducted quickly and cost-effectively.

Training via HP's Interactive Network grew out of a strategic need to provide a cost-effective and rapid delivery system for continuous information transfer from the factory to worldwide field sales and support groups. Sixty percent of HP's technical field people now participate in DL (see Fig. 4.1).

In adopting a new training technology, a valid criterion to consider is whether it lowers cost and decreases time while maintaining or exceeding quality. HP has found that DL can deliver more training simultaneously to all locations, for lower cost with consistent quality. Instead of sending instructors to the field, one expert presents the same message to everyone, at the same time, across multiple sites. It certainly is more efficient than physically moving people across the country to training classes. The ability to share resources through technology is also a viable alternative to building more buildings and individual classrooms. DL can maximize resources and combine assets with other groups to produce programming.

DL is a strategic solution for corporations—an effective means to train employees quickly, cost-effectively, and with enhanced quality, for the training is delivered undiluted by an expert. DL can be a crucial part of an enterprise's strategy to better manage and continually improve its competitive position.

## A Distance Learning System

### Description

In the virtual classroom that a DL system creates, specially designed hardware and software enable real-time interaction between an instructor at a host site and students who may be located at multiple global remote sites. It employs two-way interactive telecommunications and electronic devices to teach from a distance.

There are various delivery technologies for DL to choose from: satellite, fiber optics, cable, codecs over telephone lines, and microwave. Computer-response units, scanners, facsimile machines, CD-ROM, videodisc, and radio also are utilized. For the purposes of focusing on larger numbers of students and widely dispersed receiving sites, satellite delivery best meets the objective.

Transmission via traditional analog satellite signals broadcasts audio and video to multiple receiving sites, with return audio and two-way data communication supported over conventional land phone lines. High-quality audio is paramount in learning environments; important considerations are speech delivered without excessive reverberation, noise, feedback, distortion, or the returning echo characteristic of a satellite transmission delay.

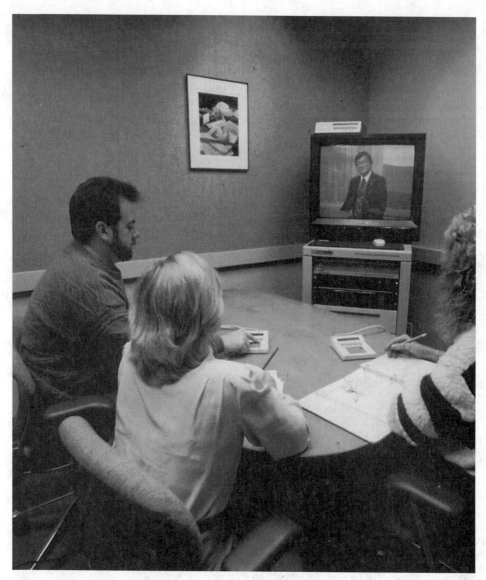

**Figure 4.1**   Participating in distance learning.

Video compression eliminates the redundant part of the analog signal, taking the analog video transmission and converting it to digital. With digital, there is no degradation of signal as it is retransmitted; and an additional benefit is that it requires significantly less bandwidth. Advances in digital compression will lower transmission costs, but more importantly will double or triple channel capacity (the number of channels that can be sent over any transmission medium).

A total distance learning solution (production, video, audio, and control system) is pulled together from various suppliers. A full integration of components requires expertise in audio, video, data, and control. This integration has been a barrier to market acceptance, because users do not have all the necessary expertise. Outside services usually are required for hardware/software installation and for test, design, production, training, and prototyping of the specific training/educational programming.

Let's consider the various configurations of communication technology presently available, and how they are applied.

#### Synchronous mode

One-way audio: radio program
Two-way audio: telephone conferences, radio talk show
One-way audio/one-way video: television program and videotape distribution

#### Asynchronous or virtual classroom

Two-way audio/two-way video: videoconferencing with compressed digital over telephone lines

The most economic and effective configuration for training environments is

Two-way audio/one-way video: DL transmitted over a high-quality analog satellite to multiple sites over a vast area

The virtual classroom simulates the feeling of a large number of students sitting in one classroom together, even though they are physically dispersed. Technology is applied seamlessly, and it is the most transparent to learners and instructors when the TV-quality image is maintained and the two-way questioning/answering process is unimpeded. Interaction is supported through computer-assisted response devices and communication technologies that enhance further feedback.

### System configuration

For simplicity, DL configurations include a host site, mode of signal transmission, and receiving sites, as shown in Fig. 4.2.

**Host site.**  The program originates from the host site, a studio classroom from which the session is broadcast. This teleclassroom includes a lectern/console where an instructor has the ability to either take complete control of the console features or have the production crew handle them. The lectern is equipped with a computer-based console that facilitates interaction between the instructor and students at remote sites through voice or electronic question-and-answer, as shown in Fig. 4.3.

The broadcasting facility, or uplink, is equipped with a control room where a technician has duplicate controls to assist the instructor if needed. It may

**Figure 4.2**  Distance learning configuration.

also include a director's console, various special-effects generators including VideoShow, stillstore, animation, chromakey (for displaying and annotating one image in combination with another), and camera and sound system controls. Video editing and duplicating equipment might also be included in this facility.

**Transmission chain.**  The first mile of communication link between the studio and satellite uplink usually consists of cable, fiber optics, microwave, laser, or telephone land line. The program signal is delivered to an uplink antenna or dish, then transmitted to a geosynchronous satellite in a fixed position 22,300 miles above the equator. Satellites have transponders (video channels) that receive and retransmit the video signal. If a broadcast is encrypted, the encoder or scrambler is colocated with the uplink and each receiver location needs a decoder to unscramble a broadcast.

**Receive sites.**  A satellite downlink receives and decodes the satellite signal into channels. Equipment configurations may include satellite dish; low-noise block converter; satellite video receiver; decoder for encrypted, scrambled code to maintain confidentiality and security; connectors; power supply; and video display.

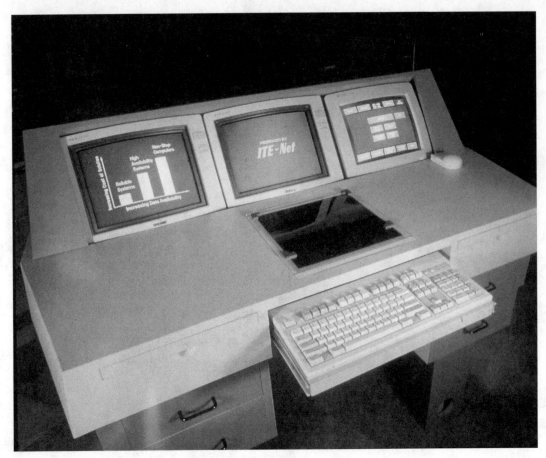

**Figure 4.3**    Electronic Q & A. (*Source: Hewlett-Packard Company.*)

**Interactivity.**   This distinguishes DL from one-way, passive, instructional television. Interactivity allows each student to join in with the instructor and
with the other students, giving a sense of being connected with the remote
class members and facilitating their active involvement. Interaction is accomplished via telephone, two-way audio, video, and two-way electronic text
and/or graphics interactivity. Interactive response units (IRUs) or keypad
devices allow remote and local students to interact electronically with the
instructor and among themselves during live classes. With IRUs, students
can receive quick and meaningful feedback and actively participate when
directly linked with the instructor. Instructors also receive immediate feedback from compiled student responses to numerical or multiple-choice questions via the interactive keypad system, and are able to immediately assess
the students' comprehension of the material and thereby modify the content,
rate, or presentation style in real time. A database can be used to gather all
the transactions for later evaluation and analysis.

## Instructor Preparation

When instructors are under pressure to improve efficiency in training, their choices typically are either to change the technology, change the way they teach, or some combination of the two. The task at hand involves putting the technological pieces together via system integration—bringing proven hardware and software into the mainstream of training.

The first obstacle for instructors to overcome is the paradigm shift from traditional, central training to DL, and one determining factor for acceptance is whether the technology is transparent to the learning. If the technology overwhelms the instructional process instead of serving as an effective teaching tool, then this approach will be resisted. Technology must be practical and easy for students and instructors to use. The goal is to take the face-to-face training environment and make the technology "invisible" so both the instructor and students can be actively involved in the learning process.

### Production staff

There are production staff who can aid the instructor and ensure that the technology does not inhibit the process. The instructor is then free to concentrate on content and leave the production to the experts, who might include

*Administrator.*   Schedules the facilities and satellite time, organizes timely distribution of materials to all remote sites.

*Remote site (field) coordinator.*   Communicates directly with each receiving site coordinator. Reserves room and equipment, sets up a room for satellite signal receiving, troubleshoots technical problems, arranges participants' question procedure, and follows up with student evaluations.

*Producer.*   Oversees the entire production. Conducts initial meeting to define what is needed and to advise the instructor on techniques, resources, media, and production methods. The producer facilitates the process and makes sure the instructor's teaching aides (e.g., live product demonstrations, videotapes) are properly integrated into the class.

*Director.*   Works with instructor and directs the crew during rehearsal and broadcast to plan and select the best way to "shoot" the program, timing and pacing, camera angles, placement of graphics.

*Additional crew (when necessary).*   Videotape recorder operator, additional camera operator, character generator/graphics operator, production assistant.

### Instructor skills

Televised teaching requires skills different from traditional teaching. Instructors need to familiarize themselves with the studio environment, the control room, and computer console, and learn new teaching skills for telecourses. An array of electronic educational tools including stored graphics, animation, videotape (roll-ins), drawing tablets, and remote cameras will need to be mastered so that they can be effortlessly incorporated in the program, as shown in Fig. 4.4.

Since timing is critical, there must be detailed organization of the class and explicit preplanning of the presentation. You should

- Develop a script to ensure that broadcast time constraints are adhered to.

- Establish procedures for course administration (e.g., fielding student questions and distribution/retrieval of materials).

- Foster new presentation skills suited to the medium, such as responding to camera movement, cueing, and speaking directly to the camera in an unhurried fashion while occasionally varying the tone of voice.

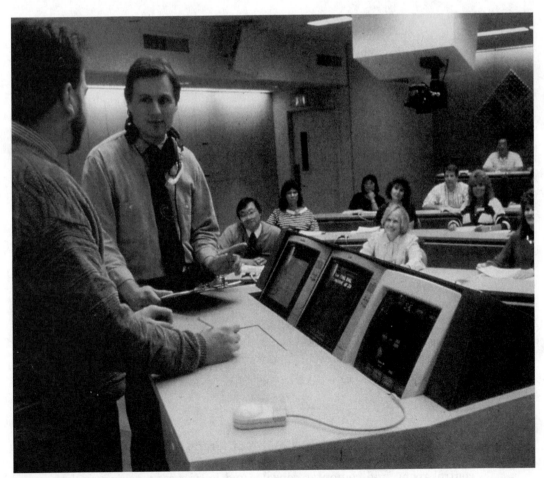

**Figure 4.4**   Learning console. (*Source: Hewlett-Packard Company.*)

- Select clothing with bright and bold colors but avoid plaids, stripes, and patterns that cause video interference.

- Orchestrate frequent interaction with students through predefined questioning strategies that stimulate discussion.

- Practice and rehearse in order to perfect timing and transitions, and to become comfortable with the technological tools. This is an extremely important objective; the instructor should be comfortable enough to easily focus on the student and use the technology to modify the course pacing or content to meet students' needs.

## Benefits of Distance Learning

Using technology for technology's sake can often prove less than optimal. However, a new training methodology or technology should be adopted if it meets two objectives:

1. Reduces costs associated with conventional training by reaching more students in less time

2. Provides effective learning as well as, or better than, conventional face-to-face training

Distance learning fulfills these needs by offering the following benefits:

1. *Time savings.* Content presented by a single source is received in many locations simultaneously and instantly. Information is disseminated to all employees at once, not just to a few at a time. Travel is reduced, there is less "down" time, and productivity is maintained without travel disruption or the need for "catch-up" time. DL can greatly reduce the time required to retrain a large, geographically diverse population and deliver time-critical messages immediately.

2. *Larger audiences.* More people can attend. The larger the audience, the lower the cost per person. Delivery to the workplace at low cost provides the access to training that has been denied lower-level employees. A company can increase the number of students trained without increasing training resources and can eliminate or minimize trickle-down training, road shows, and information "gate-keepers."

3. *Lower costs.* Travel, meals, and lodging costs are reduced by keeping employees in the office. In addition, lost opportunities for revenue generation are diminished, since field sales personnel get the necessary training with minimal disruption to their time spent with customers. HP continually has experienced significant cost reductions in delivering DL (compared to centralized training), with an average return on investment of $20 million per year over the last 5 years. The initial cost to install the entire studio and control room was paid for with the first two-week teleclass delivered to 750 students worldwide.

4. *Improved learning.*   HP surveys students to evaluate DL teleclasses, and results show that consistently more than 70 to 80 percent select interactive teleclasses as the optimal method for instructional delivery—students felt they learned more than in a conventional classroom. This is further supported by institutional and business studies which demonstrate that training at a distance is as effective as face-to-face training.

5. *Limited expertise leveraged across locations.*   The expertise of the best instructors can be delivered to thousands of people without sending trainers to conduct numerous training sessions at various locations. Topical experts spend more time in the office doing research and productive work rather than traveling. Each student, no matter how large the class, has direct access to the experts rather than to another representative instructor "trained by the trainer."

6. *Accessibility and flexibility.*   With a remote transmit or receive truck, a transmit or receive site can be located anywhere in the world; a benefit of the pervasive nature of satellite delivery.

7. *Usability.*   Useful for business, associations, hospitals or universities to present, inform, train or educate. Company updates, training, meetings, and other events can be broadcast live to multiple locations.

8. *Security.*   Encryption keeps out unauthorized outside viewers and protects confidential data.

9. *Interactivity.*   This defeats the boredom and passivity of one-way television classes. DL requires greater emphasis on involvement strategies and methods than traditional, teacher-centered strategies. A condition of effective learning is an environment where ideas can be freely communicated. Students receive not only visual and audio stimuli, but through interactivity (i.e., quizzes, telephone dialogue, and surveys) they participate in active, experiential ways. With distance learning the students can interact with the instructor when they need more discussion, enabling the instructor to respond to questions in real time, which is critical to students' learning and retention. Interactive keypads provide for immediate response and feedback, a crucial element since a student who does not receive feedback in a timely fashion quickly becomes demotivated. The dynamic exchange of ideas and questions keeps students alert, makes them feel they are involved and participating, and increases information retention and comprehension.[4]

## Future Directions

The next decade promises greater access to and expansion of national and international education and training networks utilizing interactive telecommunications. The traditional classroom at a central location, or alternatively "train-the-trainer" strategies, are being displaced by real-time interactive virtual classrooms at regional locations where instructor and students no longer need to be in the same place at the same time.

**Figure 4.5** Distance learning network. (*Source: Hewlett-Packard Company.*)

The next major step will be toward workstation-to-workstation training and education that will replace DL studio-to-receiving-sites classroom training. Multimedia, interactively manipulating text, images, animation, graphics, sounds, digitized voice, and video, will enhance the desktop as the premier delivery vehicle.

Eventually, encapsulated training packages will be delivered on demand—individualized training that is self-paced and delivered when and where a student needs it. Students will have the ability to acquire new skills and knowledge when they need them, where they need them, and in as much depth as they need them, as shown in Fig. 4.5. Responsive training, delivered to the workstation, will enable employees to meet the demands of an increasingly competitive global marketplace.

Given rapid product development and changing worker skills requirements, it is critical that a training system be (a) distributed and (b) just-in-time. Training will be responsive to the individual's needs, taking place when and where needed. Multimedia will provide the necessary visual and auditory stimuli and facilitate interactivity. The components will be modular, so that the student need select only those training elements that are demanded for the immediate task.

The virtual classroom returns full circle, focusing once again on the individual student's needs. The future promises to be a time of individual freedom and control, in which the important skills required to efficiently compete in an ever-changing world economy can be easily revised and enhanced as needed.

## References

1. Naisbitt, John and Aburdene, Patricia, *Reinventing the Corporation,* Warner Books, New York, 1985.
2. Roelandts, Willem P., "Distance Learning Solution," keynote address to Telecon XII, San Jose, CA, October 1992.
3. Portway, Patrick S. and Lane, Carla, "Corporate Training," in *Technical Guide to Teleconferencing and Distance Learning,* Applied Business Telecommunications, pp. 279–315, 1992.
4. Lane, Carla, "What is Teleconferencing?", in *Business Television and Distance Education: Partnerships in the 90s,* An ITVA Industry and Education National Videoconference Resource Manual, pp. 10–12, Feb. 12, 1992.

# Imaging as a Corporate Multimedia Tool

**Tim Picraux**

## Paper versus Images

Most organizations use some form of micrographics (i.e., microfilm or micro-fiche) as their archival storage medium of choice. Popular for well over a decade as an efficient and cost-economical storage medium for seldom-used but still important company documents, micrographics was seen as the per-fect solution for historical or "passive" paper. But passive paper accounts for only a small percentage of an organization's paper flow. For there to be a dis-cernible increase in productivity and quality, organizations must somehow be able to manage their "active" paper as well.

Managing active paper flow is perhaps the key component of the work-flow analysis process. Although a technique that has been practiced for years, the current emphasis on business reengineering has brought work-flow analysis to the fore.

Work-flow analysis examines the organization and the processes within it to find ways to significantly improve productivity and/or quality. In short the analyst, or a team of analysts, studies the various interdepartment and intradepartment business processes to pinpoint areas of improvement. Interestingly, the precursor to this technique was born of micrographics' younger cousin: imaging.

## Imaging as a Work-Flow Paradigm

Whereas micrographics is limited both by its storage medium (i.e., fiche or film) and its relatively unsophisticated software and hardware environment, imaging suffers from neither limitation. Whereas micrographics was limited solely to the passive archiving of paper, imaging can be an active participant in the day-to-day interactivity of the typical work process.

This robustness alone accounts for the dramatic growth in the imaging market. According to BIS Strategic Decisions in Norwell, Massachusetts, the imaging market doubled in 1992 to $2.35 billion. And in a recent member survey by the Association for Information and Image Management, 56 percent of those responding said they were using imaging today, while another 29 percent said they were investigating it.

The benefits of imaging are manifold: work reduction and elimination; reduced costs; improved customer service; improved utilization of resources; better use of information; faster and more informed decision making; reduced time to market; expanded revenue opportunities; enhanced corporate image; increased flexibility; higher quality; and, ultimately, increased control by management and staff alike.

When imaging vendors first entered the organizational fray, what they found was a web of interconnected business processes that were largely unstructured, sometimes irrational, and always less than efficient. To sell their wares, vendors were forced to "prove" the worthiness of their products by implementing not only imaging systems but more efficient work flows as well. And although the concept of work-flow analysis was by no means invented by imaging vendors, these same vendors are largely responsible for fine-tuning the technique and perhaps even making it a part of the popular vocabulary.

Today, work-flow analysis is a subset of reengineering and is performed by a wide variety of professionals, from systems integrators to work-flow consultants to the imaging vendors themselves. The dramatic growth in the numbers of this breed of professional is at least partially attributable to the newer, faster, and more robust imaging environments now available.

## The Imaging Environment

Imaging shares some of the basic features of the older micrographics systems. Systems consist of at least four components: a scanner (facsimile machines are often used as well), a printing device, an end-user workstation, and a storage medium. But there the similarity ends.

Whereas micrographics systems merely captured the "still" image of a document, imaging systems are powered by robust environments that permit a wide range of "interactivity" with the document. This feature set includes

- Rapid retrieval of document
- Retrieval and simultaneous viewing of a document by multiple viewers
- Ability to "zoom in and out" on any level of magnification
- Ability to "pan" the document in any direction
- Ability to rotate the displayed image
- Ability to display one or more overlays, or electronic transparencies, for a single document
- Ability to mark up imaged documents with text and graphical annotations

- Extensive editing capabilities, including the capability to copy, cut, paste, merge, and erase documents or portions of them, as well as manipulate document graphics

- Permanent storage of revised documents

- Ability to print on a wide variety of devices, including plotters, located throughout the organization

But today's very highly automated organizations require even more. They require that today's imaging systems be well integrated with the organization's existing applications, systems, and networks. This means that integration goes well beyond providing accessibility to the imaged document base across a wide range of heterogeneous hardware platforms. Integration also extends to enabling the end user to merge an image document to the very application that he or she is working with. For example, if an end user is working with Microsoft's Excel spreadsheet, there should be no barrier to being able to store the spreadsheet along with one or more complementary documents.

## The Folder Metaphor

Vendors, for the most part, have tailored their generic systems to specific vertical industries (e.g., insurance, engineering), such that end users are provided an electronic desktop with familiar tools using the vocabulary of their particular industries. However, the concept of the "folder" can serve as an apt metaphor to explain how imaging works in general. But we must explain the concept of the automated folder in the context of the entire imaging process.

### Scanning the document

In this first step of the process, scanners or fax machines can be used to convert hard copy into what is referred to as *raster data*. In selecting an input device, organizations should be aware that there is some variability in the quality of the output, which is largely dependent on the scanner used as input. Documents imaged with simple facsimile devices have a lower-overall-quality image than those imaged with a high-resolution scanner device. Measured in dots per inch (dpi), a rule of thumb is that the higher the dpi the better the resolution. In general, high-quality scanners scan at a resolution level of between 200 and 400 dpi. Additionally, different models of scanners vary in their speed anywhere from 8 pages a minute up to 50 pages a minute. Since scanners can be networked, several staff members working in tandem can scan quite literally thousands of documents a day.

### Converting it to text

Although not all organizations require this functionality, today's robust imaging environments have the ability to convert imaged text into usable text through optical character recognition (OCR). What this means is that an end user can import text from a scanned document directly into his/her word processor.

### Storing the document

Whereas micrographics systems stored documents on off-line microfilm and microfiche, imaging systems store documents directly on-line; therefore, these are always immediately available to the end user. Although magnetic disk (sometimes referred to as *hard-disk*) technology has been available for quite some time, newer advances in optical technologies have provided greater storage capacity at vastly reduced prices (i.e., an optical disk contains approximately 5.6 Gbytes of data, which translates roughly to 120,000 to 150,000 pages and costs just a few hundred dollars). Optical disks, which physically resemble CDs but can be as large as an LP record, use the light of a laser to etch information bits onto the surface of the platter. Although there are other, more expensive, technologies that permit both multiple-reads and multiple-writes, the preponderance of imaging systems use what is referred to as *WORM* (write once, read many).

### Indexing the document

Whereas storage of the document relies on the attributes of the hardware, success in indexing the document very much relies on the sophistication of the software. Indexing itself can be viewed as a means to an end. The ultimate goal of indexing is to provide the organization with the ability to quickly retrieve the document by its important attributes. For example, a loan application might be indexed by loan identification number, name of applicant, geographic location, and so on. Although most imaging systems do offer the ability to browse, the availability of indices quickens the search process dramatically. Since indices are crucial to the ultimate success of the imaging system, it follows that determining what they are is an important process. This is truly the domain of the work-flow analysts. Performed by in-house staff, consultants, or systems integrators who know the business the organization is in, the critical task is to analyze the document in the context of the entire organization, not just look at it in its own right. For example, in our loan example above, a work-flow analysis could conceivably determine that loan documents should also be indexed by the loan officer, providing management with oversight capabilities.

### Retrieving the document

While the document itself is stored on optical media, the indices can be stored on a database located in the organization's computer. If the imaging environment adheres to either de facto or de jure standards, organizations will have a variety of means to access their information. Whereas a standards-oriented imaging environment adheres to the CCITT (Consultative Committee for

International Telegraph and Telephone) Group 3 and Group 4 standard for facsimile transmissions, the same imaging environment should follow set standards that enable organizations to access documents outside of their imaging software. For example, indices stored in a proprietary database preclude organizations from using the index database in any of their applications. But an index database using the SQL (Standard Query Language) standard is immediately accessible to all. In nonopen, or proprietary systems, the imaged document often cannot be accessed by other systems or applications. An open system stores documents in an easily readable format such as TIFF (Tag Image File Format), which is a de facto standard file format designed to promote the interchange of digital image data and which easily provides access to the images from other systems and applications.

But if the imaging environment is truly robust, organizations need never go outside of it to access their document data. Using a folder metaphor, these systems contain advanced functionality for document management fully integrated within the automated environment with which the user is fully familiar. The end user need never leave his or her desk to walk over to an "imaging workstation." Instead, he or she could access the document(s) in question right at the PC on the desktop. The features of a robust imaging-integrated desktop environment include

- Compliance with the predominant windowing standards of a workstation, including Windows and Unix.

- Direct access at the user's desktop to information on existing mainframe computers.

- Storage of applicable documents and corresponding word processing documents and spreadsheet documents in an automated folder similar to the paper folders of yore. For example, a loan image would be stored in an automated folder alongside a spreadsheet that contained the loan worksheet and any letters that were sent to the customer.

- Ability to perform index searches and nonindex browsing, as well as boolean logic. Boolean search logic provides the organization with sophisticated exception reporting. Using our loan example, we could use boolean search logic to find those documents "where loans were over $70,000, customers were located in New York, and the loan was for a secondary residence."

- Ability to attach annotational notes to documents.

## Controlling the Work Flow

Most imaging systems provide the organization with the technology to ably process the work flow within the organization. Some more robust imaging environments, however, provide management and control capabilities as well. Over and above basic routing of paperwork, advanced imaging systems provide event management. This ultrasophisticated software provides the bonus of being able to create site-specific work flows; represent the work flow graphically; test the work flow with a simulation capability; route work loads; set priorities; query the status of work-in-progress; as well as provide supervisor control to manage and reallocate work loads.

Imaging solutions are applicable to any type of industry, although banking, insurance, government, and manufacturing tend to be the technology leaders. But the attributes of these four industries are really generic to industry-at-large. Most organizations suffer from too-large paper flows, interdependent business processes, and a requirement for real-time access to their information resource. Ultimately, organizations that implement an imaging solution will increase productivity and quality—and also gain entry into the very heady world of multimedia.

## A Short Imaging Glossary

*Archival.*   Readable (and sometimes writable) for a long time; "long" can mean from 5 to more than 100 years.

*Boolean capabilities.*   A feature of document-indexing software that permits the logical coordination of two or more index search specifications.

*Browsing.*   A system's ability to find an undefined feature or set of features in a database.

*CCIT Group 3 and Group 4.*   International compression/decompression standards for black-and-white images specified by the Consultative Committee for International Telegraph and Telephone (CCITT); the international standard for facsimile communications.

*COLD (Computer Output to Laser Disk).*   A system used to control the transfer of computer-generated output to optical disk for on-line or off-line storage.

*Compression.*   Conversion of a digital image to a lower number of bits for storage.

*Compression algorithms.*   Procedures according to which digital data sets representing images are compressed. Some of the most successful of these are contained in the CCITT Group 3 standards for digital facsimile.

*Decompression.*   Reconstruction of a compressed image for display or printing.

*DPI (dots per inch).*   A measurement of resolution referring to the number of pixels per inch on a workstation display monitor.

*Folder management system.*   A computer-based system that provides for the electronic capture, storage, distribution, annotation, display, and printing of images previously available only on paper or other hard-copy media. The emphasis of a folder management system is on the file folder, which contains multiple documents of varying numbers of pages and for which the tracking of work flow is important.

*Jukebox.*    An automatic selection-and-retrieval device that provides rapid, on-line access to multiple optical disks.

*Optical disk.*    A platter-shaped medium coated with an optical recording material.

*ODSR (Optical Disk Storage and Retrieval).*    A mechanical device that manages multiple WORM (Write Once, Read Many times) optical disks.

*Optical storage.*    Technologies, equipment, and media that use light—specifically, light generated by lasers—to record and/or retrieve information.

*Platter.*    A large, round disk for storing information.

*Scanner.*    A device that resolves a two-dimensional object, such as a business document, into a stream of bits by raster scanning and quantization.

*TIFF (Tag Image File Format).*    A de facto standard file format designed to promote the interchange of digital image data.

*WORM (Write Once, Read Many times).*    An attribute of certain optical disks. Once information has been "burned" into a sector of the disk it cannot be deleted or overwritten, but can be read any number of times.

# Multimedia at Your Fingertips

## Issues and Practical
## Implementations for
## Managing Multimedia Information

**Rudy Prokupets**

Multimedia is fundamentally changing the way we use information on our desktops. Personal computers traditionally presented information as text and graphics. Only very recently have certain breakthrough technologies evolved to become affordable and usable by personal computers. Audio technology has matured such that, with current hardware and software, users can record, play, and edit high-quality music, sound effects, and voice. The ability to play full-motion video in a scalable window on a desktop computer brought an array of video overlay boards to replace the very expensive still frame capture boards of yesterday. Newer boards added the ability to record compressed full-motion video onto a computer's hard disk, and new software integrates compression to minimize file size requirements. The capability now exists to take an analog video signal and convert it to a digital file, in real time and on a desktop. It will soon be possible to create high-quality digital movies on computer. In short, the era of inexpensive video on a desktop PC is now arriving.

## At Your Fingertips

With the explosive growth of the new market for multimedia, many end users, application developers, and content providers face the problem of how to effectively organize, manage, and instantly access the vast amount of multimedia information they accumulate. One major stumbling block is the tremendous diversity of incompatible file and media formats for audio, digital and analog video, animation, graphics, and text. Another problem is the growing number of incompatible multimedia peripherals and "computer-ready" consumer devices, such as full-motion video boards, camcorders, VCRs, and laserdisc players.

Software developers wishing to create new multimedia applications, or to incorporate multimedia into existing applications, usually must work in authoring environments. Typically these development environments are closed, requiring the developer to learn a proprietary scripting language. Even then, authoring environments sometimes offer only limited capabilities. Many developers would prefer to create applications using more familiar software tools. End users, too, would like to be able to add vitality to documents, spreadsheets, or presentations, and multimedia offers that extra dimension.

What's needed is software that can satisfy the requirements of users at all levels: casual users with home computers, software designers, business professionals. All of these people need software that can not only simplify working with multimedia information but also enable them to use that information in new and productive ways. If these fundamental user requirements are to be met, such software must allow the user to

- Organize, manage, and find when needed all sorts of multimedia information

- Retrieve and access all of his/her multimedia data, without having to move among several software packages

- Simplify working with a diversity of formats and peripheral devices

- Add multimedia to other software applications without having to become a multimedia expert

## Multimedia Object Manager

The phrase "object-oriented" has become a buzzword in the computer industry; as such, it is often misused by many multimedia companies. Essentially, a multimedia object is any discrete piece of information that can be represented—displayed or played—by a computer. In a truly object-oriented environment, all information—regardless of its format, type, or location—is accessed by the user in the same manner. It doesn't matter if the object is a graphic element, an animation, or an audio file, a digital video clip or a video clip from an analog device.

This generic approach has distinct advantages for both software designers and end users. Developers can use object-oriented programming to create a library of reusable objects. Once tested, these objects do not need to be retested for use in other applications, and they provide a consistent object-oriented interface from application to application. End users benefit from the developers' ability to quickly and efficiently respond to customer needs with upgrades and new products.

Because multimedia deals with real-world objects, it lends itself well to object orientation. Many users who work with multimedia quickly encounter the problem of managing the great quantity of data that they accumulate. Whether you have a CD-ROM with tens of thousands of art clips, or just a hard disk full of audio segments, locating files pertaining to a particular subject or stored in a specific format can be a nightmare. If you are a Windows user, you can use File Manager to search by file extension, file name, or directory; or you can rely on your own recollection. Each of these approaches can be extremely time-consuming.

Fortunately, multimedia content- and object-management software has emerged to address this need. By simplifying the processes of organizing, retrieving, displaying, and using important information, these products maximize user productivity. An example of a *content manager* is Aldus's Fetch, designed for the Macintosh computers. By contrast, MpcOrganizer and MediaOrganizer from Lenel Systems are *object managers* for the Windows platform. Lenel's approach has been to develop products that integrate user-critical functions, are truly object-oriented by design, and provide a consistent, user-friendly interface.

The ideal multimedia object manager is a highly integrated, object-oriented software package with three important functional components (see Fig. 6.1). The Multimedia Cataloging Database organizes all information as objects, enabling the user to quickly locate and retrieve them when needed. Once objects have been retrieved, they can easily be displayed by the Universal Multimedia Player. Finally, the Universal Multimedia-Enabling Server simplifies the process of incorporating the objects into other applications. These capabilities will be described individually in the following sections.

### Multimedia cataloging database

There are a number of features that make multimedia cataloging database software powerful, flexible, and simple to use. Most importantly, it should be able to organize and manage all media types and all popular formats. It should, for instance, be capable of cataloging

- Analog and digital video, including full-motion segments and still frames

**Figure 6.1**  Integrated multimedia object manager.

- Scanned photographs, artwork, slides, and negatives
- Animation files
- Bitmap and vector graphics
- ASCII text and a variety of word processing documents
- Digital audio data from both audio CDs and audio files
- Data stored on hard-disk drives, diskettes, CD-ROMs, videotapes, and laserdiscs

It should even provide a method for cataloging nonelectronic reference materials: three-dimensional objects such as printed documents and magazine articles; folders containing hard-copy information; and artifacts.

The software should combine the power of a full-functioned relational database engine with a superimposed object-oriented layer. This will enable the user to create object records, collections of records, and databases with user-definable fields and free-text descriptions. It should support pointing device shortcuts such as drag-and-drop and double-click, to simplify record creation.

It should provide the ability to browse through records using visual representations such as object thumbnails. A *thumbnail* is a miniature view of an object. When organized into collections called *galleries,* multiple thumbnails can be quickly retrieved and simultaneously displayed. For optimal flexibility, galleries should not be limited in size.

Some software applications create thumbnails that each require 10 to 20 kbytes of disk storage. When such large thumbnails are embedded in a collection of object records, the results are very large records, excessive memory requirements, and a virtually unmanageable database. Keeping this in mind, we see that a cataloging database's object thumbnails should need no more than 5 kbytes to be useful in large database applications.

A user should be able to supply information to narrow the search for desired objects. The user should be able to locate objects using a single search criterion or multiple search criteria. Comparative searches specifying an *either / or* or an *and* condition should also be supported.

The software should support the use of thesauruses—collections of keyword synonyms enabling the user to search for and retrieve desired objects. With this feature, the user can create a thesaurus containing, for example, the synonyms *blue, lake, sea, river, liquid,* and *well* for the keyword *water.* Even a disorganized user would then be able to search the database for the keyword *water* and retrieve objects that were cataloged in association with *blue, lake, liquid,* etc. The user should also be able to generate reports of keyword and thesaurus search results.

Once an object has been located, the cataloging database software should provide automatic object playback. This implies that, as long as the computer has the capabilities to provide it, the user will be able to see a graphic or document, hear an audio clip, or see and hear full-motion video or animations. On-screen device controls should enable the user to adjust video attributes, sound volume, and size and position, if applicable.

Finally, well-designed cataloging database software should be flexible enough to allow access by multiple users on a network. If you work in a corporate environment, it's very important for you to be able to organize your data for use by your project team, department, or entire organization. This implies the ability to create, access, and update shared records, thesauruses, and databases, and the ability for multiple users to simultaneously play the same object on a file server.

## Universal Multimedia Player

Whether you're a casual user with a computer that contains a little bit of everything, or a professional artist dealing with volumes of graphics and animations, if you work with multimedia, one of the first difficulties you encounter is how to display all of your files on your computer. For many of us, that means acquiring all of the necessary software and moving from package to package to view each type of file. This approach can be both costly and very time-consuming. Programs called *viewers* can display multiple formats of a single media type, but they don't address the great need for application software that can handle all formats—animations, audio, graphics, video, and documents—in a single environment.

This problem is compounded by the fact that virtually every industry-leading program has its own proprietary file format or formats. There are, for example, more than 20 widely used formats for graphics. Paint programs create files in formats such as BMP and PCX. Drawing packages work with formats such as CDR, DRW, AI, and WMF. Scanners often create files in TIFF format. Some on-line services and bulletin boards provide graphics in GIF format. None of these formats has become the industry standard, but many have become very popular. Even now, new formats, such as the Kodak Photo CD format for images, are being introduced. As a result, users frequently find themselves accumulating a large variety of files.

As new computer-based technologies have reached the commodity level, a growing number of incompatible multimedia peripherals and "computer-ready" consumer devices such as full-motion video boards, camcorders, VCRs, and laserdisc players have become available. Although some vendors provide device drivers with their equipment, such software often is designed with the technical end user in mind, making it difficult for others to use.

Some companies have understood these problems and have brought Multimedia Player software to the marketplace. Microsoft Windows includes Media Player. It's a good player but, unfortunately, it supports a very limited number of formats.

Lenel introduced the concept of a Universal Multimedia Player. With support for over 40 file formats, it can play graphics, documents, video from analog and digital sources, animations, and audio clips in all of the industry-leading formats.

A well-designed multimedia player should be intuitive enough to allow the user to play media objects using simple drag-and-drop or double-click methods.

In addition to all popular industry formats, it should fully support the Windows Media Control Interface (MCI) specification for controlling time-based objects and peripheral devices, such as analog and digital video, audio and VCR/laserdisc, and animation. This will enable the user to, if pertinent, adjust video attributes and sound volume on-screen as the object plays. The user should also be able to adjust the size and on-screen positioning of the object display window. The user should be able to make these adjustments quickly and easily, using features such as scroll boxes, radio buttons, and drop-down lists.

The user should be able to create a new object from an existing one—a portion of a video clip or audio segment—without having to make a copy of the original. Instead, the new object should include a reference to the original, thereby minimizing the new object's size. Furthermore, if the original object is an analog file, the new object could be digital and could be manipulated as such.

As an integral component of content management software, the universal multimedia player should provide auto playback of an object once the object has been located and retrieved by the cataloging database function.

Once a user has the capability to catalog, locate, retrieve, and play multimedia data, as well as the ability to control peripheral devices on-screen, it should be straightforward to string together a series of object plays to create dynamic multimedia presentations. A multimedia show combining text, graphics, analog and digital video, animations, and audio achieves greater message impact. The final component of an integrated multimedia content management package, a multimedia-enabling server, makes it easy for you to embed multimedia objects and shows into other applications.

## Universal Multimedia-Enabling Server

The use of multimedia-enabling technology implies the ability to incorporate multimedia elements into other horizontal application software, such as documents, spreadsheets, and databases. You can bring an animation file into a word processing document, embed full-motion digital video in a graphic file, or add CD-quality audio to a spreadsheet. Multimedia can add vitality to an otherwise static file, increasing the effectiveness of your message.

There are a number of methods by which applications can be multimedia-enabled. These include object linking and embedding (OLE), cut-and-paste using the Windows clipboard, application macros, dynamic data exchange (DDE), a command line interface, and an application programming interface (API).

The two most powerful and flexible of these are OLE and an API (Fig. 6.2). An API has open architecture and is a set of functions. The functions can be accessed using traditional C function calls, or via the more innovative object-class libraries and visual controls. API functions provide high- and low-level device and data controls, resulting in much tighter integration than OLE. However, working with an API is strictly a programmer's task.

**Figure 6.2** Multimedia-enabling technologies.

By contrast, object linking and embedding is interactive and doesn't require programming. A computer-literate end user can use OLE to add multimedia elements to other applications. When you *link* an object, you create a reference (link) to the source document in the destination document. When you *embed* an object, you make a copy of the object in the destination document. Embedding an object calls for a simple cut-and-paste operation.

OLE release 2.0 provides advanced features such as In-Place Editing and Automation, which enable users and developers to seamlessly integrate different object components—even entire applications—into new applications in very little time.

Applications that support OLE fall into two categories. *Servers* are applications whose objects can be embedded or linked into other applications. *Clients* are applications that can accept embedded or linked objects. An application can be both client and server. Most applications are being developed as OLE clients; very few are OLE servers.

Microsoft's Video for Windows and Gold Disk's Add Impact are multimedia-enabling servers. MultiMedia Works, from Lenel Systems, brought to the marketplace the first Universal Multimedia-Enabling Server, which allows you to integrate *any* multimedia objects into OLE-client applications and also includes API, Macro, and DDE interfaces.

A well-designed multimedia-enabling server should be flexible enough to allow users to integrate multimedia objects into other Windows applications using a variety of methods. This universality enables users to incorporate multimedia data into other commercial or custom applications using their method of choice. Novice users may prefer the cut-and-paste simplicity of the Windows clipboard and OLE. A software developer may prefer the flexibility and control of API functions.

A multimedia-enabling server should support all industry-leading formats for animation, audio, analog video, digital video, graphics, and text. It is especially important for the server to have a consistent user interface for all media types. Millions of individuals and corporations have video information stored on videotape devices, such as VCRs and camcorders. These devices essentially become information storage devices. The server should be able to control these analog devices, embed information from them into other applications, and treat that information the same way that it does digital information. Users should be able to incorporate analog objects into other software quickly and easily, without having to worry about the intricacies of device control and file manipulation.

### Integrated solution

A recent poll by a leading personal computing publication found that a majority of users intend to use the forthcoming generation of computers for the following purposes (in order of preference):

1. Multimedia or video production
2. Database management
3. Application development
4. Personal productivity

If this is a reflection of typical needs, what then should a user look for to put multimedia at his or her fingertips?

The ideal multimedia management solution is an object-oriented, tightly integrated package that provides all of the capabilities just listed (Fig. 6.3):

- Content management with thumbnails
- Universal multimedia playback
- Universal multimedia server
- External device control

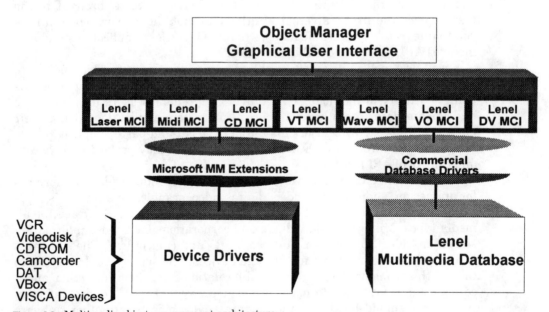

**Figure 6.3**  Multimedia object-management architecture.

Multimedia object-management software should be an integrated solution—the single solution to multimedia productivity. For this to be so, it must have a low cost/performance ratio. It must be capable of working with all industry-leading formats and media types. Furthermore, it must be positioned to proactively employ the emerging technologies and de facto standards of tomorrow. In short, it must be able to maximize the user's investment in hardware and software, even to the extent of adding multimedia elements to otherwise static software such as spreadsheets and documents.

It must be based on standards, avoiding proprietary interfaces. For the Windows user, this means supporting leading-edge technologies such as object linking and embedding (OLE) and media control interface (MCI). It must be powerful enough to give the user control over peripheral devices right from within the object management software.

Such a product should have a simple, intuitive, graphical user interface, employing flexible features such as a toolbar, context-sensitive help, "hotkeys," scroll bars, and buttons. The software should be simple enough such that users at all levels can immediately start to use the product's capabilities. It should be powerful enough to provide full relational database functions, yet intelligent enough to enable the user to execute these capabilities by simple mouse clicks or drag-and-drop actions.

A wise investment translates into long-term benefits for the user. For the casual user, high-quality object-management software takes the mystery out of working with multimedia, and provides a tool to organize and use information in new ways. For the professional, choosing well-designed multimedia object-management software can maximize hardware and software investment, provide a dramatic increase in productivity, create more effective business applications, and enhance message impact.

# The Successful Multimedia Development Team

## Expertise and Interaction

**Mary F. Whiteside**

**J. Alan Whiteside**

### Expertise and Interaction: Components of a Successful Interactive Multimedia Project Team

Gone are the days when one or two individuals—usually a programmer and a designer or content expert—could create an interactive training program, especially if it involved multimedia. Creating an instructionally sound, sophisticated multimedia application requires individuals with a wide variety of talents and competencies to collaborate as a team. In other words, the way to meet clients' demands for technical and content sophistication in a multimedia program within today's amazingly short development time frames is by facilitating interaction among the members of a team who possess the required types of expertise for the project.

The skills required to execute a high-quality interactive multimedia project in today's business climate span a number of disciplines and departments or organizations. The development organization must be able to make smooth transitions from initial marketing contacts and project definition to analysis and design, through prototyping and actual development, to implementation and evaluation. The successful team should include one or more members of the client organization or department. Demonstrated expertise in a number of critical areas is essential if a project is to meet its objectives and stay within budget and time frame.

The field of multimedia is simply too broad and deep for one person to sufficiently comprehend it. Also the playing field changes almost daily, as new development approaches and technical functionalities leap onto the scene.

Generalists (those who have a working knowledge of several areas) are a mainstay of a team, because they can help to identify issues, synthesize information, ask insightful questions, and keep a team headed in the right direction. In fact, successful teams are composed of individuals who are continually gaining experience and knowledge in related areas.

A superior multimedia project team, however, will draw upon the collective knowledge and experience of "experts" in various fields related to the development of interactive applications. Expertise is here defined as *proficiency in or mastery of a given skill,* often combined with experience in using that skill in various circumstances. For an even relatively sophisticated project to be successful, the team should either include as members, or have access to, experts in a number of areas. The second half of this chapter lists many of the types of "experts" that a successful project team should include, along with their specific responsibilities.

Assembling a group of experts is not enough. If they are to succeed, the individuals must be unified as a team. Decisions made by one individual invariably affect many other team members. The very fact that there are more than one or two people developing the multimedia application means that more conscious communication among the individuals is required. Schedules must be agreed upon and set, with appropriate assignments made. The failure of one individual to meet the schedule can mean that a milestone is missed. Whenever more than one person is creating interactive sequences, consistency of style and approach is a concern. Another issue is whether some portion of content has been duplicated in another part of the program or whether sections of content have "fallen through the cracks" and haven't been included at all. From a positive perspective, when a group of individuals acts collaboratively as a team, productivity can be increased markedly, the voice of the customer can be more accurately discerned, and creativity can be enhanced.

This chapter cannot address the principles and practice of team building, interpersonal communication, or empowerment of employees. These topics are vital to an understanding of the "team of experts" approach to multimedia development, but they are the subjects of many enlightening articles and books. Instead, this chapter will focus on the need or rationale for both expertise and interaction on a successful project team.

### The need for expertise

The need to have individuals with expertise in various areas either on or accessible to a multimedia development team can be substantiated from many perspectives. The situation is similar to that of an individual who needs medical attention. Generalists (in this case, primary-care physicians) play an integral part in the treatment of the individual, but specialists (experts in specific fields, such as orthopedists, surgeons, allergists, cardiologists, and radiologists) are called upon to consult with the principal physician in their specialty areas when necessary. In this way, needed expertise is brought to bear upon a problem. A similar relationship exists between experts in various disciplines and members of a successful multimedia development team.

The expertise required to develop multimedia applications can be broken down into three broad categories: (1) business/administrative, (2) instructional and artistic, and (3) technical. The business/administrative skills include, e.g., client relations; contract interpretation and negotiation; project scheduling; and team leadership. This type of expertise is provided mainly by the account representative, the project lead, and the program manager. (Specific responsibilities of all team members are detailed in the second half of this chapter.)

The instructional and artistic skills include, e.g., assessing end user/learner characteristics; specifying appropriate instructional strategies; defining and describing the subject matter or technical content for multimedia developers; evaluating courseware; importing, creating, and manipulating images of all types; and developing courseware with specified authoring tools. Instructional designers, multimedia developers, subject matter experts, and graphic artists typically provide these skills.

A multimedia development team also relies upon technical expertise, such as is required to: produce audio, photographic, and video elements for inclusion in the application; create software tools to facilitate the development of multimedia applications. Audio-video specialists and programmers or software engineers bring their skills to bear in this category.

Reasons are now given for including on a multimedia development team experts from each of these categories.

**Client sophistication varies greatly.** Clients and potential clients span the spectrum of literacy about multimedia. Many have become well informed about the design, development, and delivery of multimedia, including issues in both the technical and instructional design domains. Other client contacts with little or no experience in this area have assumed, perhaps owing to the effects of downsizing, the responsibilities for implementing instructional or training programs.

An education effort on the part of the development team is therefore necessary to ensure that (1) the client understands the benefits and limitations of the technology solution being proposed; (2) the client's expectations match the services and products to be developed; and (3) the provisions of the contract are clear, especially with regard to ownership of the materials produced, client changes, and missed milestones. This education process typically is begun by the account representative. However, the program manager and project lead are, to the greatest extent, responsible for the business/administrative task of dealing with client expectations and ensuring that all come out of the project feeling successful.

**Clients' expectation levels are rising.** Clients are expecting increased levels of sophistication and entertainment value in their final products. The artistic and technical members of the team are constantly challenged to be more creative and create added value in the multimedia products. For instance, we all have become accustomed to seeing intricate and engaging computer graphics on television and in films. Once clients have been tantalized by what they see and intrigued by reports of the latest breakthroughs in computer-delivered presentations, their expectations for a multimedia program are set. While some clients are coveting compact-disc-quality audio and full-motion video for their applications, this is not the full extent of their wish lists.

Individuals with expertise are required to implement other features, such as elaborate user or learner performance-measuring and -tracking systems that link to existing client databases. Creation of such tracking or monitoring systems requires programming or authoring system expertise, or both. Some multimedia applications (such as electronic performance support systems) require real-time links between the main program and external tools, such as the spreadsheets or databases that end users access as part of their jobs. Again, a programmer or authoring system specialist must be involved with the team. The development of specialized animation sequences, the creation of photorealistic graphics, and the incorporation of certain instructional strategies (such as giving a learner the ability to record and play back verbal responses to the program) also require distinctive expertise.

**Multimedia demands new instructional approaches.**   The instructional designer is responsible for designing effective informational or instructional programs. With the advancements being made in the hardware and software that support multimedia (e.g., increased desktop computing speed and power; wider bandwidths for increased transmission over networks; decreasing costs for storage space), new instructional approaches and solutions must be developed that will make use of the new opportunities while still ensuring that the program's objectives are met. The limitations of a few years ago have disappeared (remember CGA graphics, a maximum of 16 colors, and the single computer "beep"?). Technology has advanced to the point where we can now produce the kinds of informational and instructional applications that designers and developers knew should be created but that were unattainable, given the state of technology.

Also, the audiences who interact with a multimedia program have become more diverse, and multimedia solutions must speak to that diversity. Multimedia programs must be carefully designed to accommodate users who speak different languages, have different learning styles, reading levels, and years of experience with computers. Instructional designers also must keep in mind individuals with disabilities and cultural perceptions that may be different from the designers' perceptions (Schneiderman, 1992, pp. 26–31).

Given the new technological capabilities and the increasing instructional requirements, instructional designers and courseware developers must leverage the resources available and find new ways of ensuring that learners develop the required competencies. This will require using new types of interaction, such as having learners click and drag objects on the screen or record, play back, and critique their oral responses to questions. Leveraging the technology also means increasing the use of realistic simulations, scenario-based learning, and performance tracking, as well as a move toward techniques such as adaptive instruction/testing and intelligent tutoring.

**Multimedia is a technically complex field.**  More technical disciplines than ever before are represented within a successful multimedia development effort, and those disciplines are becoming increasingly complex. For instance audio, video, and sophisticated animation are relatively new to interactive programs, especially instructional applications. While instructional designers, content specialists, and programmers know something about each of these areas, expertise in them is rarely a part of their repertoire.

Similarly, graphics software has become both more functional and more complex, calling for additional skills from the graphic artist. The skills required of an artist to previsualize and then sculpt a three-dimensional object are different from those required for two-dimensional drawings. While new tools facilitate the construction of photorealistic three-dimensional graphic objects, artists must bring to bear on a project advanced visualization skills, as well as learn to use the new tools.

**New authoring tools abound.**  The range of multimedia authoring tools has expanded on every hardware platform, with each touting certain benefits. Sometimes a client specifies that multimedia development must be done with a certain tool (so that the client's own personnel can maintain the courseware). Not all projects will be completed on the same platform, and even on a given platform, some tools are more appropriate for certain projects than others. For instance, some multimedia tools are designed specifically for creating hypertext applications or linear presentations, while others are more appropriate for developing simulations or tutorials. Some tools create applications that will run under DOS, while others require the client to have Microsoft Windows installed on the delivery computer.

To be prepared for projects that fall into such different categories, the development group must be comprised of individuals who have technical expertise with different authoring tools. These individuals must not only be able to move efficiently from one tool to another depending upon the project, but often they must be able to understand the features, benefits, and limitations of each tool well enough to coherently explain them to clients and potential clients.

**An integrated multimedia system is necessary.**  The hardware and software components of sophisticated multimedia solutions are becoming so numerous and complex that it requires real dedication to read and assimilate all that is written, even about a relatively narrow topic. Only the systems analyst or integrator with a high level of expertise can recommend a complete and integrated system of hardware and software components that matches a client's needs.

Individuals with this type of expertise are also called upon to recommend or create special-purpose hardware or software tools for a multimedia application. For instance, new types of interaction devices (beyond the typical keyboard) have made dramatic appearances in the last few years. Pointing devices, once limited to function keys and alphanumeric keys, now include light pens, mice, touchscreens, trackballs, joysticks, and even voice input.

Occasionally, a unique interaction or pointing device is required to bring a higher level of fidelity to the program. The task of integrating such a device would most certainly fall to a systems analyst and/or software engineer.

### The need for interaction

A successful team is much more than a group of individuals. Coordination and interaction are required to arrive at a successful solution within today's typical development time frames. Interaction among the various types of experts (including members of the client organization) is necessary because of the interrelatedness of the disciplines required for effective interactive program development. Several examples of the overlap will illustrate this requirement.

Changes in the workplace have meant that workers often need more than the one-shot training of a few years ago. Given the advent of electronic performance support systems (EPSSs), the need for a melding of technical and instructional design expertise has never been greater. Determining the types of supportive resources a user might need (such as database access, reference materials, glossaries, and coaching systems, as well as minitutorials on very specific topics) requires interaction between client representatives (most likely subject matter experts and master performers), instructional designers, and system analysts. Only with input from these sectors can the development of an effective multimedia program be ensured.

Other examples abound of tasks requiring the expertise of systems analysts and instructional designers. Consider how delivery platform choices have expanded since the term *multimedia* first gained prominence. A multimedia system can be configured with an internal or external hard drive. It may or may not be accompanied by a laserdisc player or a CD-ROM drive. The solution may not involve a computer at all, as in the case of CD-I or 3DO. Printers and audio speakers increasingly are becoming typical elements of a multimedia solution. Integrating all these components to reach a certain level of functionality often requires a skilled systems analyst or integrator.

The disciplines of graphic art and instructional design also must be correlated. For instance, a multimedia developer cannot request that a certain graphic be produced for a lesson without entering into the domain of the graphic artist. If the artist who receives the request is isolated from the project team, the resulting graphic may either be inappropriate for the program or not at all what the developer had in mind. The likelihood of this problem occurring is lessened if the artist is assigned to the project team, included as an integral member of the design meetings, and even physically colocated with the team.

Similarly, if the subject matter expert(s) from the client organization is (are) not made a functioning part of the development team, the content may not be represented accurately in the final program. The client's representatives also are less likely to "buy into" design decisions made by the team without substantive input and consideration of their perspectives. The subject matter expert is a prime protagonist for "the voice of the customer," and the administrative skills of the team must be used skillfully to bring to bear on the project the SME's technical skills.

The options for implementing multimedia programs are expanding with each new technology advance. For example, users may access multimedia programs via LANs (local-area networks), WANs (wide-area networks), or in a stand-alone mode. Decisions about implementation and maintenance of the application involve at least the business/administrative and the technical skills represented on the team.

Similarly, the methods of providing updated courseware or applications to the users have changed. No longer is it feasible for a single individual to have the responsibility of ensuring that all users have the latest version of the software. This process may be done via modem, over a company network, by sending users a new CD-ROM, or by various other means. The decision about which of these methods is best in a given situation must incorporate input from individuals who thoroughly understand the technical benefits, limitations, and constraints of each method, as well as from persons who understand the business implications of each option and can explain them to the client.

It is important to note that integrating a group of experts not only is essential to successful multimedia development, it also provides several important benefits for the development organization. These include: (1) enhanced productivity; (2) greater ease in discerning the "voice of the customer"; (3) formulation of more creative solutions; (4) the positioning of team members for professional growth.

Working smarter rather than harder is essential to a department's or company's profitability and viability. While it may seem at first that the "collaborative approach" requires more time to complete an interactive program than the "assembly line approach," interaction among members of a project team can result in significant productivity gains. When team members take joint responsibility for every major decision, there is less chance for confusion or for individuals to recklessly "do their own thing" at the team's expense. Also, barriers between functional areas can be reduced or eliminated when everyone has been identified as part of the project team. The process then becomes more important than departmental affiliations. As issues are discussed, various areas of expertise can be tapped to find creative approaches to problems and to keep individuals, and the team as a whole, from pursuing inappropriate or unproductive approaches.

For instance, while the graphic artist and the instructional designer may agree that the use of motion video would be beneficial at a given point in the program, if the team has been wise enough to include the systems analyst in the discussion he or she may object that the delivery platform specified by the client is not adequate to accommodate this type of solution. Similarly, an authoring system specialist who has been made part of the team may be able to construct a template that will automate the development of a certain type of interaction that the instructional designer wants to implement. This will save course developers a significant amount of time, since they will not have to recreate a particular sequence of code or icons in the authoring system every time that type of interaction is called for.

Hearing and understanding the voice of the customer throughout the project is crucial in multimedia development, just as it is in other business ventures. When a whole team (including members of the client organization) is involved in a give-and-take process, a clearer understanding of the desired outcome is achieved, and, very importantly, shared by all who contribute to the project. The inclusion of the client representatives goes a long way toward ensuring that the final outcome of the development process is a product that matches the expectations and needs of the customer. All members of the development team should first listen to their counterparts on the client's side or to the client representatives in general. Then they should provide input, based on their areas of expertise, about how best to use technology and sound instructional-message design principles to produce a product that is well received and effective in meeting the client's goals.

Taking the project team approach to interactive program development fosters creativity among the team members, and this is an important issue in multimedia development. Creativity by itself is not sufficient, but without it even the best instructional design may result in a dull, dry program. The informational goals or instructional objectives may even be compromised without an appropriately creative approach. An infusion of creativity among the developers can often make the difference between an adequate or mediocre program and an exceptional one.

Existing theoretical literature maintains that a person's level of creativity is directly related to his or her own interest in the work (intrinsic motivation). One organizational development consultant set up a research project in an effort to prove that "settings that encourage and promote individualized, unforced, even autonomous production boost intrinsic motivation and, accordingly, promote creativity" (Plunkett, 1988, pp. 68–71). In the experimental group (which received a participative management intervention), the participants showed an increase in feelings of input and participation. As determined by objective, independent judges, only the experimental group showed a definite and dramatic increase in creativity. Neither the placebo nor the control group showed a significant increase in creativity.

This study suggests that having a team of people shoulder the responsibility for a project is beneficial, in that more creative ideas are generated. Many organizations employing a project team approach could likely provide anecdotal support for this conclusion. Where participation and commitment to a project are increased, the creativity of the team members is likely to increase also.

One final benefit of having a collaborative, integrated multimedia development team is that each member is naturally positioned for professional growth as the group takes on issues, works through alternatives, and makes decisions that must be implemented. Each individual has a chance both to hear and to be heard in an open exchange of ideas, which can lead to a deepening and an extension of competencies as diverse perspectives are brought to the table. As multimedia screen design considerations are being discussed, for instance, graphic artists, instructional designers, subject matter experts, and others will have input. As differing opinions and views are expressed, team members should be evaluating their assumptions and biases about the new ideas, as well as the ideas themselves.

## Summary of the case for experts and interaction

Without deliberate interaction among a team of experts charged with producing a multimedia product, several negative outcomes are likely. First, inappropriate multimedia solutions may be created that will not match the client's specifications, needs, or desires. These "solutions" may not be solutions at all; they may fail miserably to meet the program's stated goals and objectives. Second, productivity may suffer from lack of communication. If an expert doesn't know that an issue needs resolution, no solution is likely to be forthcoming, and the project schedule, budget, or both may suffer. Third, even if the application nominally meets the intended goals (e.g., the audience is adequately informed about a topic, or passes a posttest after a training intervention), the application may lack the cohesiveness, unity, and sparkle that a dedicated project team can provide.

On the positive side, designating a project team helps to ensure that all members are responsible for setting and meeting the schedule. Such an arrangement helps to bring focus to each individual's work efforts; he or she is part of a team whose goal is to complete a project they can be proud of on time and within budget. From a practical standpoint, project teams can contribute to higher-quality interactive solutions, individual growth of team members, and organizational productivity. From the perspective of client satisfaction, the creativity generated by interactions among a talented group of individuals is invaluable.

This approach to multimedia development may require a fundamental reorganization of a development organization's resources (physical and personnel). Internal shops that do not have in house all the expertise needed to complete a sophisticated multimedia project may have to rethink their approach to working with outside vendors and consultants. The project team is definitely the most efficient way to produce effective informational and instructional software that meets the client's needs, because it focuses everyone's attention and efforts on the "whole" rather than on isolated portions of the whole. Side benefits of the project team approach are that team members expand their horizons and learn new skills (thus becoming more productive and valuable to the company), and tend to bring more creative solutions to the design table. Furthermore, they can be genuinely proud that their input helped to shape a successful product.

## Typical Team Roles and Responsibilities

Depending upon the scope and nature of the interactive multimedia project being considered, different types of expertise should be represented on the project team. The titles or designations described next are likely to differ from organization to organization, and responsibilities may be distributed differently. To a certain extent, the size of the development department or organization determines how the responsibilities are divided. Some individuals may "wear more than one hat." However, the key is to have all the functions covered by individuals who possess expertise in these areas.

While this is not an exhaustive list, each job discussed next is potentially important to the successful outcome of a multimedia project. The roles and responsibilities listed for each are recommendations. Since each multimedia development entity is different, modifications to the roles and responsibilities descriptions are likely.

### Project lead/manager

The project lead is responsible for overseeing each phase of the project, from kickoff to completion and delivery. Planning, scheduling, and allocating resources are in the project lead's domain. This individual must be skilled in dealing with the administrative and business aspects of a project as well as the personnel and team-related issues. The project lead must also manage communication well, both among team members and between the team and the client representatives. Specific responsibilities of the project lead include

- Facilitating meetings between the client and the multimedia development organization
- Creating and monitoring

  Project schedule and budget
  Approval and sign-off process
  Roles and responsibilities
  Hardware and travel requirements
  Project team roles and responsibilities

- Managing the client review process and approval of each deliverable
- Acting as primary contact between client and multimedia development organization for project-management-related issues
- Communicating project status to multimedia development organization's management
- Setting project milestones and managing project to that schedule
- Coordinating approval/sign-off of materials with clients
- Selecting vendors for outsourced efforts

### Program manager

The program manager brings business and administrative expertise to the team. While usually not a part of the everyday development activities, the program manager serves an integral function nonetheless by attending to contract-related issues, budgets, schedules, and resource requirements. In some organizations, especially those in which only a small number of projects are under way at one time, this function may be handled by the project lead or manager. Specific responsibilities of the program manager include

- Coordinating with all the development team project leads on

  Personnel assignments
  Milestone status vs. billing schedule
  Project personnel, and equipment resources and requirements

- Maintaining communication with client, especially on topics such as

  Overall project status
  Billing status
  Contract modifications

- Managing development-team budgets

### Account representative/marketing representative

This individual's role in the multimedia development process also relates to the business/administrative aspects. The account representative initiates contact with a prospective client and provides the contact person(s) with the first glimpse of the development organization.

For outside vendors, it is important to communicate the salient features about one's company and why it should be the vendor of choice for a given project. While this process is begun by the marketing representatives, it often requires reinforcement from team members with expertise in the various technical disciplines.

Once an initial contract with a client has been secured, each member of the team becomes a selling agent, reinforcing the client's choice of vendors and assisting in the education process so that additional contracts will come with less intensive marketing efforts.

The account representative usually is responsible, throughout the life of the contract, for ensuring that effective communication is maintained with the client and that the "voice of the client" is heard and understood by the development team. When wearing this hat, it is important that the account representative not "oversell" the organization's capabilities or underestimate the time and budget required to produce what the client has in mind. Typical responsibilities of the account representative in this area include

- Ensuring that funding for the project being considered exists in the client organization

- Providing to the client sufficient background information about the development organization

- Describing for the client the types of services available to it through the development organization

- Gaining an initial determination of the type of need and/or project in which the client is interested
- Communicating to the development organization's management the scope of the project under consideration and the degree of probability that it will be funded

### Instructional designer

The instructional designer (sometimes there is more than one) is the cornerstone of a multimedia development team. This individual's educational and experiential background is crucial in bringing together into a unified whole from the seemingly disparate fields represented on a development team, the team's principles, approaches, and ideas. The fields of graphic art and instructional design, and the various technical domains, should be given equal consideration in the multimedia application to be developed, and the instructional designer is key to this effort.

In general, this person is responsible for the processes used to develop the multimedia program and, if it is to be an instructional piece, for the effectiveness of that program. More specifically, the tasks of the instructional designer include

- Directing the technical activities of course developers, graphic artists, and other team members assigned to the project
- In technical meetings, leading the discussion related to content and instructional approaches
- Keeping in close touch with individuals from the client organization
- Having final responsibility for

  Definition of training issues
  Assessment of learner characteristics
  Definition of instructional strategies and approaches
  Analysis of end-user tasks
  Review of existing training materials and/or relevant documentation

- Having final responsibility for the development of

  Performance objectives
  Learning strategies
  Courseware styles and standards document
  Evaluation criteria
  Quality-control processes (jointly with project lead)
  Multimedia authoring procedures (jointly with project lead)
  Implementation plan

- Creating and securing agreement on the instructional approaches applied to the project
- Reviewing products of the instructional design process to ensure instructional integrity and consistency in style, organization, and level of detail

- Planning and conducting formative evaluation of the program, including data analysis

## Multimedia developers/courseware developers/courseware authors/instructional specialists/technical writers

The multimedia developers are charged with implementing the design for the application agreed to by the team. Reporting to the lead instructional designer, these individuals must produce a sound informational or instructional program, following the styles and standards delineated for the project.

Staffs are becoming leaner, individuals are acquiring new skills, and authoring tools are becoming easier to use. Thus, multimedia or courseware developers are becoming responsible for actually creating the on-line materials that end users interact with. This trend is a departure from the approach that divided the development process into writing/storyboarding on the one side and, on the other, "packaging" or manipulating the authoring system to put materials on line. Specific responsibilities of multimedia developers include

- Conducting instructional analysis with subject matter experts (SMEs), software developers, and other resources as required
- Researching the content related to the project in order to determine how to structure the multimedia
- Detailing any procedural steps for the completion of tasks that audience members will need to perform
- Participating in review meetings
- Developing instructional materials that are consistent with the styles and standards agreed to by the team
- Specifying for the artist the graphics to be included in the multimedia program
- Authoring assigned multimedia modules, using the authoring tool(s) selected for the project
- Providing first-level quality control for assigned on-line modules and print materials (if applicable)

## Graphic artists

Visuals provide one of the most effective and efficient means of communicating. The graphic artist, whose sphere of interest and expertise often extends beyond visuals per se, brings invaluable benefit to the multimedia development team. He or she does so not only by creating graphic materials to complement other media, but also by introducing an insightful dose of creativity to discussions about the project.

It is important to ensure that at least one graphic artist is included in the design process from the beginning of a project. Not only will the team benefit from the artist's input, but the artist needs to be informed about factors affecting final artwork, such as purpose and tone of the program, the intended audience characteristics, and the technical constraints within which the visuals are to be created.

The graphic artist or artists may work strictly within the realm of original graphics, or they may also have responsibility for manipulating existing images (such as digitized photographs and so-called "clip art"). In addition, graphic artists are not limited to creating visual materials with computer-based tools. In some instances it may be appropriate to create a graphic manually and scan it into the computer for manipulation. The graphic artist's specific responsibilities include

- Working closely with other team members to formulate graphical approaches and strategies for the program
- Creating visuals that concisely and effectively convey information
- Producing visuals that provide a consistent look and feel throughout the application

### Art director

When a multimedia development organization is large enough to warrant having an art director, his or her primary role is to ensure that the graphic artist(s) assigned to a multimedia project produce visual materials that are consistent with the purpose, style, and tone of the application. The art director may also serve as a graphic artist on the project, and should be involved at least in the initial team meetings. As the project matures and changes, the art director must be kept abreast of changes that could affect the number, type, or level of sophistication of the visuals being produced. Informal interaction between the project lead and the art director may be sufficient, or the art director may want to join the artist(s) assigned to the team at the regularly scheduled team meetings.

On a project that involves more than one graphic artist, the art director usually will be called upon to make assignments and track the progress of visuals as they move from the "request" stage to the "completed" stage. Specific responsibilities of the art director include

- Ensuring that project standards are maintained (from a visual perspective)
- Ensuring that graphic requests are appropriately assigned to the team's artists
- Tracking the flow of visual material production from graphic request through completion

### Subject matter experts/content specialists/reviewers

Subject matter experts (SMEs) play a vital role in the instructional design process. These individuals not only supply knowledge of the content to the development team, they also often provide them with valuable insights concerning the target audience, pertinent examples to include in the program, and guidance about effective presentational strategies.

In short, SMEs help to ensure that the multimedia application reaches the desired goals. Most often they are employees of the client organization, but they also may be full-time employees of the multimedia development organization, or consultants hired for the duration of the project because of their special expertise. The subject matter experts for a project should be selected as soon after the start of the project as possible, in order to involve them in the audience and content analysis as well as the initial design process. Since SMEs for a project may have little or no experience with multimedia applications, each member of the team should consider spending a little extra time with the SMEs explaining how his or her part of the work effort is accomplished. The better the SMEs and developers understand each other's contributions to the process, the more smoothly the project will move forward and the more valuable will be the information the SMEs are likely to provide.

On some projects, other individuals besides the primary SMEs will serve as reviewers. These individuals may represent the actual target audience, or they may represent various technical disciplines within the client organization that have a stake in the content and/or the success of the multimedia program. Thus, specific responsibilities of subject matter experts/reviewers include

- Helping the development team understand and structure the content of the multimedia program
- Helping the development team understand the target audience characteristics and how they will relate to the multimedia program
- Supplying to the development team specific, relevant examples and anticipated common errors and misinterpretations likely to be made by the target audience
- Reviewing the multimedia program at interim stages and submitting written corrections and/or suggestions related to content accuracy, completeness, and relevance to the target audience

## Systems analyst/integrator

When informational and instructional programs were first delivered by computer, they consisted mostly of text on the screen, with an occasional low-resolution graphic. Today's requirements for successful multimedia programs demand hardware and software that can present sophisticated animations, video-like effects, motion video, and audio. If users need to be able to access different types of peripherals (such as printers, CD-ROM drives, and modems), the ante is raised again. Even more complex multimedia challenges are becoming common, such as electronic performance support systems

(EPSSs) that are coupled with a client's existing software application, and training programs that will be accessed by users with different types of computers over local-area and wide-area networks. In these situations, planning and implementing solutions calls for a level of expertise beyond an ability to attach the right cables to the right equipment.

The systems analyst or integrator is responsible for planning and constructing a cost-effective system for the client. It goes without saying that the system recommended for the client must actually reach the objectives of the multimedia program. All the components must work together without manipulations by the client. Further, the systems analyst must adequately communicate to the team any constraints or limitations within which the multimedia program must be developed. Specific responsibilities of the systems analyst include

- Ensuring that a cost-effective system can be constructed that meets program objectives
- Ensuring that the features and benefits of the system are described (in understandable terminology) in such a way that the client can make an educated decision as to possible implementation of the specified configuration of hardware and software
- Communicating to the multimedia development team any constraints or limitations (as well as features and benefits) of the hardware/software platform
- Ensuring that all multimedia materials developed for the project will work with the proposed system
- Loading the multimedia program and any other required software onto the client's hardware, and installing the equipment at designated locations
- Troubleshooting any problems that seem to be hardware- and/or software-related
- Maintaining the hardware and software (this includes handling equipment failures and software upgrades) if this service has been contracted for

### Authoring systems specialist

Depending upon a number of factors, an authoring systems specialist may be part of the multimedia development team and may play different roles. If the authoring tool being used is not very complex and the multimedia developers are experienced in the use of it, then the authoring systems specialist may be of more use to another development team. If, as is often the case with sophisticated multimedia programs, the authoring tool is a powerful one and some of the instructional or informational interactions have a number of branching options, the authoring systems specialist will serve as a primary resource for team members.

This individual should have mastered the system used by team members in order to troubleshoot very quickly any difficulties they might have. The authoring systems specialist also should perform a quality-control check on each segment of the program to ensure complete technical functionality. More specifically, the authoring systems specialist is responsible for

- Ensuring that the same version of the authoring system is installed on the computer of each team member who will be developing lessons on-line

- Creating and modifying as necessary any authoring system models or templates that increase productivity and facilitate consistency among the developers

- Troubleshooting any problems that arise related to the authoring system or when implementing the types of interactions the developers want to use

- Coordinating with the systems analyst on such issues as how the authoring system should be configured to meet the program objectives, and how the runtime versions of the multimedia program should be installed on the client's equipment

- Instructing users as to the procedures associated with putting multimedia materials on-line with the specified authoring system

- "Programming" any special or difficult sequences (such as a complicated animation or a branching structure)

- Ensuring that each segment of the multimedia application has full technical functionality

## Quality assurance specialists

No products should leave the multimedia development organization without significant input from these guardians of quality. The quality assurance specialists should be involved early in the project so as to enable the sharing of design issues and potential areas of concern. It is sound business practice to proactively include individuals who can look for potential inconsistencies among developers and questionable instructional approaches, as well as pounce on the "typo" that no one else has found.

While the quality assurance specialists may not review all the materials themselves, their oversight of the review process is vitally important. More specifically, quality assurance specialists' responsibilities include

- Coordinating with the project lead to ensure that an adequate plan of reviews and sign-offs is in place when the project begins

- Ensuring that each part of the multimedia application undergoes appropriate review and testing (e.g., congruence of on-line materials with supporting paper-based materials; consistency of content across the application; soundness of instructional approach; technical functionality)

- Coordinating with the project lead as to the process for making changes to multimedia materials and documenting that appropriate changes have been made

- Checking the consistency, instructional approach, and technical functionality of at least a subset of the materials

- Checking to ensure that the established review process is being followed and that it is effective
- Managing the pilot test procedures

### Audio/video specialist

The functions of the audio/video specialist may be performed by one or more individuals. These persons may be employees of the multimedia development organization or they may be consultants, called upon when their services are required. In reality, if complex audio or video requirements are part of a given project, the necessary staff is usually contracted for through a vendor who specializes in audio and/or video. For less demanding applications, an in-house expert can be called upon to perform one or both of these functions.

For a moderately sophisticated project, the audio/video specialist may be required to acquire and insert audio and video segments into the application. In other projects, an expanded team is required that might include, among others, a professional narrator, a sound engineer, a video producer, and one or more videographers. For a moderately sophisticated multimedia application, the responsibilities of the audio/video specialist include

- Providing the multimedia development team with input as to the types of audio and video that will best capture the "look and feel" the team is after
- Acquiring and/or shooting video clips that will be incorporated into the program
- Acquiring and/or recording audio clips that will be incorporated into the program
- Troubleshooting any technical problems related to the use of audio and video in the application
- Coordinating with the project lead about production schedules, so that the appropriate media are ready when they are needed during development
- Negotiating with vendors for the rights to media that are to be used in the program
- Serving as liaison between the multimedia development organization and those vendors selected to provide services such as narration, sound recording, and video production/editing
- Ensuring that the audio and video selected for the project blend with the established style and tone of the program, and that the media help the team to reach the program's objectives
- Helping to inform the team about issues related to copyright infringement and fair use laws

### Software engineer/programmer

Not every project calls for the expertise of a software engineer or programmer. However, on certain projects, this individual is indispensable. Broadly speaking, the software engineer's domain is the planning and implementing of software tools that facilitate the development of multimedia programs. The scope of such tools ranges from the development of an entire authoring system to a few lines of code to add new functionality to an existing authoring system.

In the case of a multimedia-based electronic performance support system (EPSS), the software engineer may be called upon to program an interface between the client's software system and the EPSS itself. This interface enables data to be passed between the two systems so that the end user can access context-specific help, advice, coaching, reference, and instruction without leaving the main software system. Some typical responsibilities of the software engineer include

- Collaborating with the multimedia team to determine what software tools are necessary for success

- Collaborating with the client's technical staff (usually programmers) to determine how best to couple the multimedia application and the client's software system (applies to the development of an EPSS)

- Programming specialized pieces of code to accomplish certain functions that are required for the future by the development team

- Ensuring that extensions to an existing authoring system function correctly and do not adversely affect any other function

## Client's project lead

The client's project lead represents the multimedia project to the client's management and serves as liaison to the development organization, whether internal or external to the client organization. This individual is often the development organization's main contact with the client, although the individual may or may not have the authority to officially accept the program as complete. In many cases a member of the client's management team is ultimately responsible for signing off on a completed project.

The role of the client's project lead is quite similar to that of the development team's project lead, but in this case as seen from the perspective of the client. It is a role that is crucial to the success of any multimedia project, because this person is usually charged with ensuring a successful product. It pays to take pains to ensure that the client's project lead is an integral part of the multimedia development team, since this person can be either the team's advocate or its adversary.

Since this person represents the client, and the team's approach should always be to please the client, the team certainly needs to listen to and act upon the input provided by this person. Note the crucial responsibilities of the client's project lead, and consider how they can impact the multimedia project, either positively or negatively:

- Securing corporate approval to begin each phase of the program

- Providing the needed logistical and economic support when the involvement of SMEs and other reviewers necessary for project success is being solicited

- Providing the development team with access to the most current resource materials and information about the target audience
- Providing the development team with equipment and space if some of the development effort will take place at the client's site
- Securing a commitment from the client's team members (such as SMEs and other reviewers) concerning time frames and schedules
- Monitoring project activities from the client's perspective
- Serving as the client's point of contact for the multimedia development team members
- Providing feedback to the multimedia development team as to the progress and quality of project activities and deliverables
- Consolidating and communicating the inputs from SMEs and other reviewers about the multimedia program
- Providing consultation to the project team about the client's technical, schedule, and budgetary constraints
- Providing information to the development team about such issues as corporate culture and previous training efforts, issues that may affect the development team's recommendations about this project
- Making final decisions for the client in review meetings
- Supervising/managing the pilot testing and roll-out of the multimedia application from the client's perspective
- Making arrangements for the facilities and with the test participants for pilot testing of the new application
- Approving and signing off on each deliverable through final completion date (optional)

**Other potential team members**

As seen from the broadest perspective, many other individuals could be considered part of a multimedia development team. For instance, if the multimedia application is to be used as part of an instructor-based training program, those instructors need to become part of the team, much like SMEs, not only to provide input about the audience and the content but also to understand how the multimedia program will be used in their classrooms.

Before an application is delivered in its "final deliverable" form, it needs to be thoroughly tested. While much testing is done by the development team members (including quality assurance specialists), members of the target audience usually are asked to pilot-test the new application. Input from these individuals can be invaluable in ensuring that the program meets the expectations of the eventual audience and has adequately considered the audience's entry-level skills and knowledge.

Other client representatives or consultants also may be called upon for their unique expertise. Corporate culture really does differ from entity to entity, and it is important to know how the culture of an organization should be reflected in a multimedia program, lest the program run counter to that prevailing culture. Many companies have an almost hallowed set of technical terminology and/or stylistic conventions that must be accommodated or adhered to. Others have policies and procedures that may affect the development and delivery of the application. Having an "insider" provide this type of information can greatly increase the likelihood of success for the final product.

If the client's project lead cannot provide sufficient information about the culture in which the multimedia application will be fielded, then perhaps someone else within the organization can share that information with the team. Taking pains to integrate that person into the development team, and then to share ideas about the tone and style of the multimedia program, can prevent those culture clashes that make a project less than successful or cause portions of it to have to be redone.

Equally important when it comes to understanding the corporate culture is understanding the specific *international* culture in which the multimedia application will be fielded. Within most organizations that do business overseas, there are knowledgeable individuals who can advise the team both on technical matters (e.g., what form of electrical power is typical) and on content-related issues (e.g., whether a golf analogy is appropriate). It is prudent for the project lead to explore with the client's project lead what types of resources on international issues are available to be consulted before moving ahead too quickly with the design of the application.

Last, perhaps, but not least, are those individuals who provide the team with administrative services. The people who perform these services or keep equipment operational often do not get the credit they deserve. On any given project there is a wealth of tasks, such as photocopying and securing couriers for materials, that must be accomplished. Computers, printers, and copiers seem to require service at just the wrong moments. But the individuals who gain visibility only when things go awry also must be considered part of the multimedia development team.

## References

Schneiderman, B., *Designing the User Interface: Strategies for Effective Human-Computer Interaction,* 2d ed., Addison-Wesley Publishing Company, Reading, MA, 1992.

Plunkett, D., "Intervention for Creativity: An OD Approach," *Training and Development Journal,* 42(8), 68–71, 1988.

# 8

# Virtual Reality as Multimedia: A Teacher's Pet

**Jeff Hooks**

### Anecdotally...

An old joke about testing the nature of reality tells of some empiricists walking down a railroad track and finding an object. Each uses a different sense to examine it: the first looks, the second touches, the third smells, and the last tastes. After they have determined the nature of the object, the last empiricist declares, "I'm sure glad I didn't step in it."

### Defining Virtual Reality

*Virtual reality* (*VR*) is a technology that provides one with sensations and the control of perspective so that one experiences the illusion of being in the presence of an object, within a situation, or surrounded by a place. The illusion seems more real if different kinds of sensations are provided by media.

### Combined with audio/video

Today, VR relies on audio and video technology augmented by a computer interface that reads the movements of a participant's body. These act as triggers that change the direction of sounds and the perspective of sights so that one sees and hears an artificial world that appears to respond in relation to one's body movement, just as the real world does. In the future, researchers can be expected to refine olfactory and tactile media to the point where they give users of VR the opportunity to rejoice over not having stepped in it, even though "it" is not really there.

## VR as an Industry

Howard Rheingold's *Virtual Reality,* an encyclopedic account of the origins of VR, introduces the technology that, since the book's publication in 1991, has more than doubled in size and become a significant industry.

### In the military

During the Persian Gulf War, the U.S. military used VR applications to allow pilots and tank commanders to experience a computer model of the Kuwaiti landscape.

In the premiere issue of the slick periodical *Wired,* cyberpunk author Bruce Sterling reported on his visit to the U.S. Army's Combined Arms and Tactical Training Center at Fort Knox, Kentucky: "The Pentagon has a virtual Kuwait on a hard disk—SAKI, the Saudi Arabia-Kuwait-Iraq database. It has the country mapped out meter by meter, pixel by pixel, in 3-D, with weather optional" (p. 95).

American soldiers used SAKI to give them a virtual experience of driving tanks and flying planes. It gave them skills in maneuvering over the terrain—skills as good as, and sometimes (especially during sandstorms) better than, the skills of the country's residents.

Today, the VR technology developed during that war has created a new standard for digital terrains, a standard for all American armed forces, called "Project 2851." Sterling: "Project 2851 is about the virtual reproduction and archiving of the entire planet. Simulator technology has reached a point today in which satellite photographs can be transformed into 3-D virtual landscapes" (p. 98).

### In the marketplace

VR also has entered the marketplace in the form of video games, performance art, and telepresence. (Telepresence is similar to VR, but different in that it creates experiences by using actual sounds and pictures transmitted from distant locations rather than a computer-generated model.) Thanks to VR, arcade and home video games now can give players the sensations of climbing over 3-D cartoon landscapes, launching bombs from handheld guns, and avoiding capture by flying dinosaurs.

### Bringing people together

Earlier this year, performance artists Billy Idol and Thomas Dolby were preparing tours of concert performances around the United States in which audiences would be transported into virtual worlds, i.e., live 3-D music videos (Thomas, p. 18). With telepresence, musicians and audiences, lecturers and students, conference participants, even lovers soon will meet together from distant locations without the difficulties of travel because sophisticated cameras and microphones will bring people together virtually.

## VR in Education

Most revolutionary, however, is the transforming power this technology will have in education.

### Known uses

Multimedia combined with interactive computer technology already has enabled students and teachers to bring the world into their classrooms. Soon students will don headsets with stereo video screens and stereo speakers that will enable them and their teachers to explore virtual volcanoes or medieval cathedrals. Medical students will practice on virtual patients, permitting them to perfect their techniques without endangering lives. Students of language will virtually join in on native-tongue conversations in foreign countries.

### Uses unknown

So many possibilities exist that creative teachers will discover ways of using VR that are inconceivable today.

### Adaptations and ramifications

VR can be implemented on computers that already are in many classrooms—especially when combined with videodisc players, CD-ROM players, and digitized recordings. Multimedia packages can be adapted so that, as students move mice or click keys, they look, listen, and control their perspectives while viewing a video screen that has become a window on a world—a window that looks into a remote location or a remote possibility.

Whatever the equipment, the result of VR in the classroom—the result of multimedia combined with interactive computer technology—will be an unprecedented enhancement of the educational experience in terms of creativity and efficiency.

## An Early Experience

My first project using virtual reality as a classroom tool was the Virtual Library (Fig. 8.1), a HyperCard stack that I used in a classroom of networked Macintoshes, a CD-ROM player, and a modem. I had little computer experience outside of word processing when I developed the Virtual Library as part of St. Petersburg Junior College's Project Flamingo (the plan by which all seven campus sites are being computer-networked). SPJC provided training, equipment, and release time for teachers to develop Macintosh applications for classroom use.

### A persistent problem

Most of my previous education had been in literature, and I had taught college classes, primarily in writing, for about 15 years. One task that had

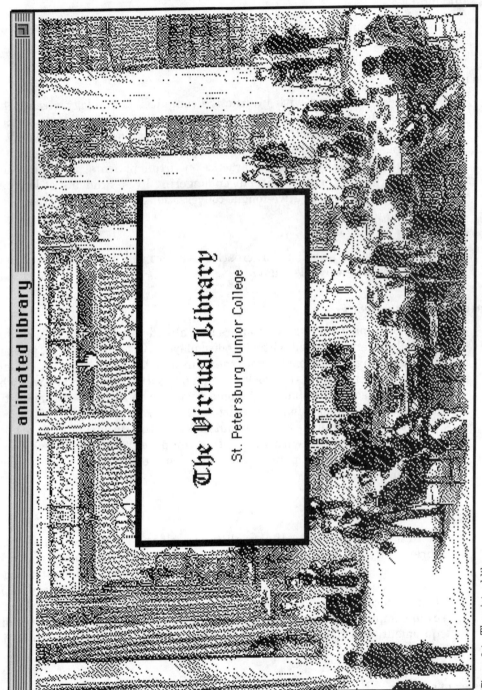

**Figure 8.1** The virtual library.

always presented me with problems was introducing students to library research. Because each student confronted different challenges in the library, I found the best method for teaching research was to physically visit the library with the students individually, offering suggestions and asking questions as they sought information.

Although this worked very well, the time it took was an impossible obstacle. Teaching an average of five classes of 25 to 35 students made this method unworkable, simply because there were not enough hours in a week.

### A HyperCard solution

Solution: I created a model of the library as a HyperCard stack. The students would access the class model, which automatically dialed and connected with LUIS, the databank of Florida's university library system. Using this computer catalog, I could stay in the classroom and help students to sort through the lists of library materials displayed on their Macintosh screens. Then they could access some CD-ROM disks that contained a variety of bibliographical materials.

Lastly, the students were presented with the Virtual Library. I had scanned graphic representations of the interior architecture of the library as seen from a variety of angles and distances. I pasted these onto a series of coded HyperCard cards so that as the students moved the mouse, an appropriate view of the library's architecture was displayed on the screen. Thus, the students saw an animated representation of the library as if they were looking through a window and controlling a vehicle while they traveled in it inside the building.

When the students clicked the mouse following display of a book on a shelf, the book floated off the shelf and opened before them. With another click, the pages turned. Bibliographical data about the book was placed automatically in the students' virtual notebooks, where they also could take notes. A virtual photocopy machine could copy text and graphics from displayed books and then store them in the students' notebooks.

Upon leaving the Virtual Library, the students would be prompted to decide whether they wanted to print their notebooks. If they did, the classroom laser printer provided hard copies of the material they had gathered.

The material in the Virtual Library was extremely limited, of course. Only a few books could be opened, and only a few pictures in the books contained words and pictures. Other library resources, such as audio recordings, videotapes, and computer software, were included and could be viewed and listened to by the students, but for only the briefest duration.

### Some advantages

One difference that made the Virtual Library a better teaching tool than an actual library, however, was that HyperCard enabled the texts, images, and sounds in the library sources to be electronically cross-referenced. They were *hypertexts* (Figs. 8.2, 8.3, and 8.4).

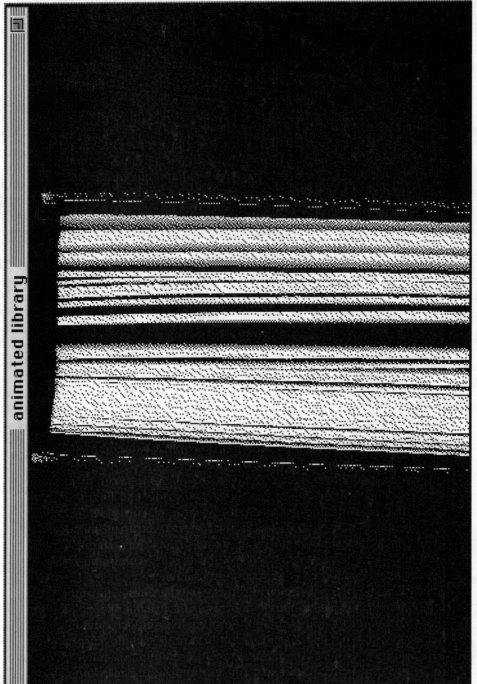

**Figure 8.2** Frame 1 of book opening.

**Figure 8.3**  Frame 2 of book opening.

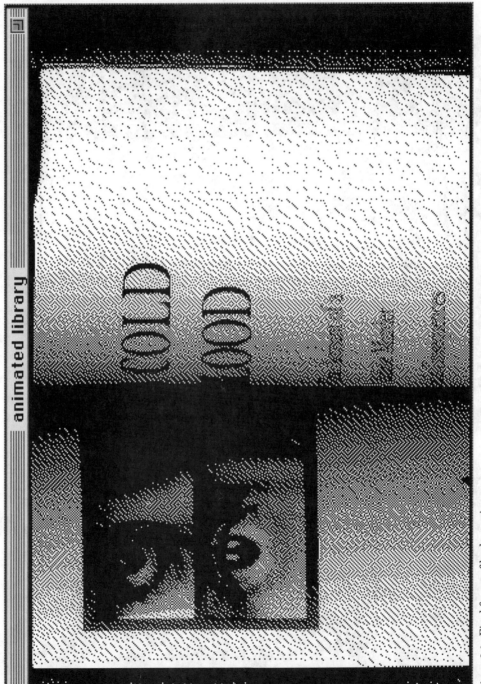

**Figure 8.4** Final frame of book opening.

For example, a passage from Truman Capote's *In Cold Blood* contained words and phrases that acted as hot spots. When students clicked on the appropriate spots in the text, their view would be shifted automatically to a *National Geographic* map of Kansas, an entry in the *Oxford English Dictionary,* a photo of a grain elevator in an encyclopedia, or a sequence of dialogue from director Ken Russell's film version of the novel.

**Positive fallout**

The advantages of the Virtual Library actually amounted to more than time, efficiency, and ease. Students using the tool acted as if they were playing an exciting video game. Instead of exhibiting the yawning and foot-dragging behavior that I am sure most teachers recognize when announcing "the library tour," my students were eager to learn. They came to class early, and it was difficult to get them to leave so the next class could begin.

**A Final Word**

This experience made me a convert. Now, no matter what I am teaching, I try to find a method to use multimedia packages and interactive technology. In the future, I hope that all my teaching will be an exploration within a virtual world instead of a lecture in a conventional classroom.

**References**

Rheingold, Howard, *Virtual Reality,* Summit Books, New York, 1991.
Sterling, Bruce, "War Is Virtual Hell," *Wired,* 1.1 (Premiere Issue), pp. 46–51, 94–99, 1993.
Thomas, Wes, "VR Update," *Mondo 2000,* pp. 18–19, February 1993.

# The Multimedia Odyssey

## Satish Gupta

## Introduction

Nations and companies are being called upon to speed up the development of products so as to remain competitive in a global, fast-paced economy. They need more rapid dissemination of the latest research information, and faster training and retraining of design, production, and service (human) resources. But today's communications methods already are being pushed to extremes. In short, if we are to succeed, we need more effective communications capabilities than those we've relied on until now.

We need not start from scratch, however. Print, audio, and video have a panoply of benefits upon which we can draw. The challenge is to combine them in such a way as to obtain the greatest advantages of each in a cohesive and coordinated way. That is the essence of multimedia.

Multimedia, like other new technologies, is progressing through a variety of developmental stages, each of which has implications for *applications, cost and justification, infrastructure,* and *standards.* We can chart multimedia's present location and course quite precisely. This information is essential for planning at which stage of its development one is prepared to adopt this technology. We can also identify some of the rocky shoals around which multimedia may have to navigate. Be assured, however, that multimedia has been established, is progressing, and will become pervasive.

## Starting the Journey

In making our way from traditional communications methods to multimedia, we need to address the differences among those methods and the obstacles keeping us from combining them effectively.

**Print and graphics**

Different media have widely different information-transfer properties. Print, for example, requires the reader to scan coded sequences and decode them into cognitive constructs—words, sentences, paragraphs. Vision is our highest bandwidth sense, but it is hamstrung by the decoding speed required of reading. By their natures, writing and reading are sequential access methods. Indices may offer a reader some degree of random access, but always at the risk of loss of context or perspective.

Graphics (pictures, diagrams, charts, tables, etc.) can often replace many words and make it easier to describe a concept or idea. Like a snapshot, however, a graphic is static. It offers no inherent clues about the temporal relationships of its elements. Also, most graphics require captions to assist readers in understanding the ideas they are meant to convey.

On its positive side, print (with or without graphics) is a mature technology and requires no special systems on the part of the reader. It is portable, requires no batteries, and is very durable.

**Animation**

No one is sure who first drew simple sequences of pictures on the pages of a pad, then flipped through them rapidly to create an animated effect. We do know that nickelodeons had hand-cranked animators before the turn of the nineteenth century.

Animation offers the temporal juxtapositions that graphics lack. Unlike print or graphics, animation is a dynamic medium. We get a sense of relative timing, position, direction, and speed of action. We need no captions, because the message is conveyed by the motion and the scene.

**Audio**

We can assume that early man's first forms of communication were gestures and sounds. Oration was a revered art form among some of the earliest civilizations. Spoken words have power not only to convey meaning but to add subtleties, as well. For example, a person's "tone" may be more important than his or her actual words in understanding the importance of something. One need only watch film footage of Roosevelt, Mussolini, or Hitler to feel the emotional effect that voice can wield.

Like animation, audio is a dynamic medium. It depicts sounds and their sequences and give us a sense of their chronology. Also like animation, voice or music can be synthesized artificially.

The telephone and radio permit us to "carry" (electrical) voice signals over great distances. Of course, audio is more than spoken words. It provides the alternative to attending a live concert if one wishes to hear music. It also permits us to use music as a communication vehicle in conjunction with words and images. Hollywood has long recognized the value of background music for manipulating an audience's emotions. Consider the shrieking violins in

Hitchcock's *Psycho,* the ominous-sounding bassoons in *Jaws,* the tubular bells in *The Exorcist.*

## Images

The term *image,* here, refers to reproductions of real objects that reflect light through lenses onto film or photoelectric transducers. A photographic snapshot of a statue, for instance, would fit this definition; a drawing of the statue would not. A picture is a high-speed information-transfer medium. The eyes can take in great amounts of information in an instant. Even the pattern-recognition processing that serves to identify the objects is much faster, say, than the processing rate of reading written words and phrases. ·

An image is reproduced in a static medium. It is a moment in time, captured, with no ability to convey what preceded that moment or what followed it.

## Video

Video (e.g., motion images) both provides high-speed information transfer and shows temporal relationships. Video is produced by successive capture and storage of images as they change with time. In addition to the high-speed information-transfer properties of images, video adds more information by incorporating the element of time along with the images.

Like animation and audio, video is dynamic. For example, an entire service operation can be viewed from beginning to end, showing each step in sequence. The viewer sees exactly where each part is located, exactly how to make the adjustments, and exactly how long it should take. This is information that it is impossible to convey fully with any type of written material.

## Artificial-world media

Words, graphics, animated graphics, and synthesized sounds allow us to create within an imaginary or artificial world. Using words, we can describe things that are not real, or real yet. We can draw pictures of atoms with electrons orbiting the nuclei—scenes we will never see of real atoms. With animation, we can make those electrons move. These media provide us with important tools for communicating about abstractions and conceptualizations.

## Real-world media

Since audio, images, and video all involve reproduction of real sounds or physical objects, they are categorized as *real-world media.* In conjunction with *artificial-world media,* real-world media offer ways of reinforcing conceptual ideas with actual examples that are similar. Together, the two categories of media (artificial- and real-world) offer a powerful combination of communications capabilities (see Fig. 9.1).

**Figure 9.1**   Temporal relationships.

### Obstacles to combining the various media

The processing speeds, storage capacities, and input/output data-transfer rates needed to support text and static graphics are far different from those needed to support animation, digitized audio, and digitized video.

A system that meets the minimum requirements for digital audio and video could support text and graphics; however, one that meets the minimum requirements for text and graphics would be unable to support digital audio and video. Also, systems that can handle digital audio and video have proved much more costly than those that handle only text and graphics.

Also complicating things are the differences in the technologies used to support text, graphics, audio, and video. In computer systems, artificial-world variables (e.g., alphabetic characters, primitive graphic features) are all represented and processed using digital encoding and decoding of electrical signals. Digital electrical signals representing a page of text look much like those representing a page of graphics. What's more, the same circuits and components can be used to process either signal.

Audio and video have traditionally been represented and processed using analog technologies. The electrical signal's properties (voltages and frequencies) were made to vary in direct accordance with the physical variable's properties (e.g., loudness and pitch of sound; brightness and color of light). Mixing digital and analog signals has been a bit like mixing oil and water. Digitizing the audio and video is necessary before they can be fully integrated with text and graphics.

Fortunately, two factors are helping us to overcome these obstacles. Affordable personal computers and their related technologies are now being built that can handle the requirements of digitized audio and video. And all communications technologies are rapidly moving toward digital representation and processing.

## Moving All Information toward Digital Encoding

Although analog systems appear simpler, digital systems generally provide better quality and more functions, and at a lower cost. For example a phonograph, which is an analog system, converts the movement of a stylus in a record's groove directly into an analog electrical signal. This is amplified and converted directly into a physical vibration by a loudspeaker.

A compact disc (CD) player, on the other hand, is a digital system. Instead of a groove, the surface of the CD is patterned with tiny "pits" or laser-burned holes, each representing a digital bit. As the CD turns, an infrared light source and detector detects and encodes these surface-reflection variations as digital 1's and 0's. The 1's and 0's are combinations of bits representing the magnitude of a sound's original analog signal at some sampling interval. A CD, for example, contains digital data sampled at a rate of 44,000 samples per second.

A microcomputer in a CD player processes the digital samples and controls their conversion into analog voltage levels. Each sample produces a voltage level, and the varying levels are sequenced at the sampling rate. Using signal processing techniques, the CD player connects the sequential analog levels together into a smooth representation of the original analog signal. This processed signal is then amplified and reproduced by a loudspeaker.

Comparing the phonograph to the CD player, it is obvious that the latter is a more complicated system. Yet sophisticated CD players can now be purchased for about $100, or less than the cost of an inexpensive phonograph. And the CD player provides nearly perfect resolution, without surface noise, wow and flutter, and other characteristics of phonograph reproduction. Logic says the CD system should cost much more than the phonograph, but digital microcircuit technology has literally turned this logic upside down.

### The move to digital is unstoppable

When signals representing text, sound, and images are all digital signals, they can all be carried on a single network, stored using digital mass-storage techniques, and processed using digital microprocessor technology. This capability is essential for communication when people are separated in time and space.

Every communication approach is rapidly shifting to digital. Music in digital form on CDs has already been described. The telephone industry is using its Integrated Services Digital Network (ISDN) to transport voice and data. Photographs are becoming digitized, too. Kodak now makes it possible to get a Photo CD containing digitized versions of one's photographic images for display on a television. And television, too, is moving toward an all-digital, high-definition format.

### The shift to digital makes multimedia practical

If text, graphics, animation, audio, and video were all done digitally, then combining them into a multimedia communications technology would immediately go from feasible to practical. The architectures of present-day personal computers are inherently capable of handling digital versions of text, graphics, animation, audio, and video. By plugging in innovative accessory circuit boards, a present-day PC can be suitably equipped to support multimedia for an additional $500 to $1000.

### From Information to Communication Processing

We are witnessing a transition of computing from information processing to communication processing. Communications, once only an option for early PCs, has become a standard feature of contemporary PCs.

Since the first IBM PC was introduced in 1981, personal computers have rapidly shifted from being stand-alone personal productivity tools to being networked systems sharing peripherals, storage, and messages.

Current Macintosh computers, from the lowest (even the notebook models) to the highest end, come equipped with networking capability built in. Other PCs are easily configured for networking. Built-in and add-on modems permit PCs to participate in wide-area networks supporting public e-mail services (e.g., MCI and EasyLink) and more sophisticated networks, such as Apple's AppleLink.

Just as information processing evolved from a text-only orientation to text and graphics, so communications processing is now passing through a text-only stage to one of compound "documents" containing text, graphics, audio, and video. The proof that these multiple media are serious components of today's and tomorrow's personal computers is to be found in the changes taking place in computer operating systems. The Macintosh operating system includes QuickDraw and QuickTime, modules that support images and motion images. Microsoft's Windows and Windows NT include Video for Windows, its QuickTime counterpart (see Fig. 9.2).

## Telecom-, Television-, and Computer-Centered Multimedia

Multimedia is not solely the province of computers. It is a technology that will be present in telecom, television, and computer systems. However, there

**Figure 9.2**   Multimedia changes the PC to a personal communication system.

are several distinctions that set these multimedia implementations apart, and there will be distinctions in how each is applied.

## Telecom and television

Looking first at telecom and television, these two communications technologies are based on established infrastructure standards. There are very specific formats for signals meant to travel over telecom circuits, and for those that travel to television receivers via RF transmissions and via cable. These infrastructure standards are templates within which the multimedia technologies for telecom and television must conform.

The signals presently carried by telecom circuits are analog signals. However, switching and many other supporting functions have been done digitally for more than two decades. The Integrated Services Digital Network (or ISDN) is the telecom industry's current, fully digital network. ISDN provides end-to-end connectivity to support a wide range of both voice and nonvoice (e.g., data) services.

A Broadband Integrated Services Digital Network (BISDN) standard was proposed and accepted in 1992 that will operate at bandwidths of 1.5 Mbits per second and higher. Unlike ISDN, which is designed to make use of the existing copper-wire telecom infrastructure, BISDN will require fiber-optic transmission media.

The point, however, is not the type of media nor the data-transfer rates. The point is that the telecom industry does not first create an innovative technology, then permit a standard to emerge; it first creates a standard, then builds technologies that comply with that standard. We will see the same approach taken with telecom-centered multimedia. The limits of multimedia capability will be determined not by innovative design but by constraints imposed by preestablished standards.

Television, like telecom, also tightly conforms to standards. In the United States, television signals conform to the National Television Standards Committee (NTSC) standard. This calls for 525 lines of resolution transmitted at 60 half-frames (odd and even lines, interlaced) per second. The composite signal transmitted from a broadcast television facility includes the RF carrier plus video signals containing color and luminosity information, audio signals containing sound information, and a Modular Television System (MTS) signal for deriving stereophonic audio separation. The composite signal minus the carrier is used for direct connection (i.e., wired connection) of video and audio signals. As with telecom, today's television signals are analog signals. The proposed standard for high-definition television (HDTV), however, is likely to be a fully digital one.

## Personal computers

In complete contrast with telecom and television, computer systems and technologies have evolved by first building innovative systems, then letting the market drive standards.

We've seen this scenario with peripheral interface standards, such as the Small Computer System Interface (SCSI), Shugart Associates System Interface (SASI), Centronics' parallel port for printers, and the like. We've also seen it with software standards, such as MS-DOS, and network standards, such as IEEE 802.3 (Ethernet) and IEEE 802.5 (Token Ring). Hayes Microsystems' AT Command set is the de facto standard for computer control of modems. What all of these have in common is that they were deployed long before they became standards. That is the way in the computer industry.

As a result, computer-centered multimedia can proceed apace without the constraint of standards such as those of telecom and television. One would therefore expect that the pace and degree of innovation would be highest in computer-centered multimedia. And it is.

### Different strokes

Aside from the differences in infrastructure standards, telecom-, television-, and computer-centered multimedia will be applied in different ways. This is a function not only of technology but of a precedent, as well.

### Teleconferencing

To some degree, telecom is already applying multimedia in an application called *teleconferencing*. Here we have essentially a closed-circuit connection linking two or more specially equipped conference rooms, permitting those in each room to see and hear those in the other room(s). Today's videoconferencing is generally a preplanned, orchestrated, televised meeting of people held in locations equipped for that purpose. Teleconferencing, on the other hand, can combine audio, video, text, and graphics, as well as people. Microphones capture the voices; television cameras capture images; and scanners are used to capture and transmit text and images that were initially on paper.

Despite the cameras and scanners, the primary focus of teleconferencing is verbal communication. Image motion is usually confined to the proverbial "talking heads." Rapid motion cannot be supported, because it causes differential data bursts that exceed the typical telecom channel capacity. Hence, waving hands disappear from the screen and reappear in jerky rather than smooth motion.

Further developments in multimedia are likely to make teleconferencing simpler and less costly, but they are not likely to change the nature—that is, formal organized meeting with a verbal-communication focus—of that application. By contrast, teleconferencing in a computer-centered context would likely result in more informal "meetings" pulled together in a much more spontaneous fashion.

### Interactive television

So far, all attempts to establish an interactive television presence that is appealing to viewers and profitable to providers have been failures in the

United States. This is not to say that interactive television will never succeed, just not in the ways it has been implemented thus far.

Advances in multimedia technology will make it less costly to support interactive television—of sorts—but do not count on using your television for buying tickets to the theater or making reservations on airlines. Like telecom and teleconferencing, television and television-centered multimedia will have a focus closely related to its current success factor. For telecom, that factor is verbal communication; for television, the success factor is entertainment.

This is the lure attracting such notables as Time Warner and its alliance partner, U.S. West; Tele-Communications, Inc., the United States' largest cable operator; News Corporation, owner of the Fox Cable Network; and Sony, owner of Columbia's huge studio library. Each has different visions of interactive television, but entertainment is solidly at the core of them all.

### Computer-centered multimedia—no limits

Computer-centered multimedia will be as multifaceted as computers themselves. What has shaped and continues to shape the implementations, applications, and costs of computer-centered multimedia is technology itself. More specifically, the four technology areas that are key to continued progress in computer-centered multimedia are *audio, high-capacity mass storage, video,* and *networking.*

As mentioned earlier, computer-centered multimedia can be viewed as an ongoing voyage whose present position and future course are both clearly discernible. This ship's sails are filled not with wind but with technology innovation. With each fresh breeze of innovation, the ship moves faster and covers a wider area.

We can look at where computer-centered multimedia was, where it is, and where it is going. We can see what effect the levels of technology have had, and will have, upon applications, costs, and justifications, infrastructure and standards. This will be very helpful in deciding at what point, and to what extent, one wishes to embrace multimedia.

### The Voyage

Virtually every new technology, in becoming a success, passes through evolutionary phases. These correspond roughly to a market's adaptation sequence. The *enable* phase occurs early in the evolution and is utilized by the market's early adopters. During the *enhance* phase, many of the early technology's rough edges have been smoothed and a more mainstream group of users begins to adopt it. In the final stage, *pervade,* the technology becomes so well integrated and affordable that it has mass appeal and brings in the late adopters.

It took over four decades for mainframe computers to make this journey, but less than one for personal computers to do it. In the process, personal computers have revolutionized the way we live and work, and multimedia is creating a revolution of its own within that personal computer revolution.

## Global problems provide the push and pull

Multimedia is being pushed and pulled into the business market by a combination of global problems. The developed nations of the world are in a state of information overload. The average U.S. citizen is exposed to thousands of items of information every day. This leads more to confusion than to increased understanding.

In today's globally competitive economy, knowledge has become one of the most valuable assets, but unlike most other assets, knowledge has a very short shelf life.

Technology markets have been a lifeblood for most of today's developed nations, but current markets are rapidly saturating, causing worldwide recessions and their related problems.

Another global problem is the changing-societal-work-ethic model. There are now many more things to enjoy when one is not working, and employees covet their leisure now as never before. Thus, if companies are to raise employees' collective productivity while giving them the leisure time they demand, they must find more effective ways of training them and having them do their jobs.

While they do not constitute a panacea, multimedia technologies, suitably applied, do promise to make a significant dent in these seemingly intractable problems.

## The Enable Phase

The enable phase occurred during multimedia's infancy. This was the period during which analog and digital media were combined in rather inelegant ways, with rather cumbersome implementations. Nevertheless, to those early adopters who began using enable-phase multimedia, it made their applications cheaper, faster, and better. This was the case despite the high cost of employing dynamic media and the lack of tools to be used by those who were expert in the subject matter to be presented.

During the enable phase, a number of application areas depended upon the interactive use of multimedia. Computer-based training, for one, used this technology, when the objective was to train an employee in the repair of a specific piece of equipment. It permitted the student to view the repair process as often as desired and in the sequence preferred by the trainee.

In such a case, a trainer would have used a videotape that showed an expert making the repair. Student and trainer could then review the tape as often as necessary to achieve the required level of comprehension. In the absence of videotape or laserdisc, the repair would have had to be a live demonstration. Indexing signals on the videotape in conjunction with computer-based control functions would have made the viewing and reviewing process more precise and efficient.

Seeing and hearing information leads to greater retention than when simply reading it. Being able to interact with the information adds even greater retention. People generally retain about 20 percent of what they hear, 40 percent of what they see and hear, and up to 75 percent of what they see, hear, and do. Therefore, the interactivity afforded by a multimedia computer can significantly increase the effectiveness of training.

The value of this solution during the enable phase was so great for some applications that it was easy to justify the use of new and expensive technology. Even spending $100,000 to develop an hour's worth of interactive video training was acceptable, because it allowed more students to be trained in less time, reduced travel expenses, and kept students off the job for shorter amounts of time. Trainers were able to handle more students and with greater scheduling flexibility. The training pace was also very flexible, resulting in even more effective retention and learning.

### Cost and justification

Multimedia during the enable phase was targeted at a few well-defined vertical applications and user groups. Justification was fairly straightforward, involving cost reductions, productivity improvements, and/or revenue increases as a consequence of adopting this technology.

### Infrastructure

During the enable phase, multimedia equipment was relatively expensive, software tools were not mature, and the number of skilled users was limited. Those who were experts in training subject matter could not wield the tools themselves. Instead, they had to work in conjunction with those who were multimedia experts.

### Standards

During the enable phase, each application was for all intents and purposes a custom implementation. Very little of what was used for one application could be adapted for use in another. What standards existed were related to individual media (e.g., VHS or Beta). Integrating the media into a multimedia application, however, proceeded with virtually no standards to speak of.

### Results

Current multimedia applications developed during the enable phase are almost exclusively in the areas of training, education, and merchandising, and all are mostly interactive presentations.

## The Enhance Phase

Multimedia is currently in the enhance phase. Here, the technology has become significantly less expensive, faster, and easier to use. Enable-phase applications have prompted development of new products and tools, creating an infrastructure capable of sustaining more growth.

The lower cost of multimedia makes it more appealing to those developing a broader spectrum of applications. While not critical to these applications, multimedia enhances their functionality and distinctiveness. Such applications include spreadsheets, word processors, electronic mail systems, groupware, document imaging systems, and database management systems.

Spreadsheets and word processors, for example, can be enhanced using voice annotation. Help functions in any application can be more effective when they make use of voice and/or video sequences. As hardware support for multimedia proliferates, software vendors will enhance their products with multimedia features. This will allow them to differentiate their products and gain competitive advantage.

The rate of growth and acceptance during the enhance phase rests on two factors: the number of systems capable of supporting multimedia, and the number of applications that employ multimedia. These factors are also mutually dependent. Obviously, multimedia hardware solutions that require an installed base of new systems will slow down the process. On the other hand, solutions that can take advantage of affordable upgrades for existing systems can catalyze the multimedia adoption process.

## Cost and justification

Justification for using multimedia is harder to come by in the enhance phase than it was in the enable phase. Multimedia's contribution to horizontal applications such as spreadsheets, word processors, and the like is not critically important. In this case, "demand" means something like "want to have" rather than "need to have."

As it becomes easy to voice-annotate individual cells in a spreadsheet or a particular paragraph in a document, communication between coworkers will improve and information interchange will happen much faster. As the new technology continues to have a positive impact, its evolutionary growth becomes even more irreversible.

## Infrastructure

In this phase of development, new tools are emerging that enable large numbers of people, unskilled in multimedia technologies, to perform simple, necessary functions (such as voice annotation or video-clip insertion) that are supported by many different horizontal applications.

As compared with earlier tools, these new tools will be lower-cost and therefore more appealing to a broader and larger group of users.

## Standards

With the shift from vertical to horizontal applications, standards become much more important. A Pulse Code Modulation (PCM) standard for digitized voice is already part of the Multimedia Personal Computer (MPC) standard. Adaptive Delta PCM is the emerging standard for audio compression in the Compact Disc Read-Only Memory Extended Architecture (CD-ROM XA) definition.

For images and video, the Joint Photographic Experts Group (JPEG) and Motion Pictures Expert Group (MPEG) are in the process of meeting on compression standards. Intel, with its Digital Video Interactive (DVI), is seeking, as of this writing, to have it become a de facto standard.

These standards, however, have a different focus than the requirements of personal-computer-centered multimedia. As such, they do not appear to be compatible with the large number of existing 80386-based PCs.

Another candidate standard is currently called "Captain Crunch" and was developed in 1993 by Media Vision Inc. This video compression standard is significantly different from MPEG and DVI, making it much simpler to implement. As a result, Captain Crunch could provide the necessary full-motion-video multimedia support to tens of millions of existing PC systems. Media Vision foresees upgrade costs of only a few hundred dollars.

Candidate standards like Captain Crunch that can extend multimedia backward into the large installed base of current systems should help to propel multimedia much more quickly to the next development phase.

## The Pervade Phase

By 1995 or 1996, virtually all personal computers will have multimedia capabilities. By then the cost of designing in multimedia, and the popularity of the technology, will have made it a standard feature. Concomitantly, personal computers will have become personal communications systems. On these systems, text, graphics, sound, voice, images, and motion images will be as easy to produce and manipulate as text and graphics are now. Application developers will include multimedia features as routinely as they now include *Help* and graphical-user-interface features.

Multimedia will be seen as the most effective way to communicate information in any business environment. It will be part of operating systems, networks, and database management tools. Product developers will have the benefit of a fundamental multimedia standard set.

We see evidence of these changes already in Microsoft's Multimedia Extensions (MME) to Windows, and in IBM's OS/2 Multimedia Presentation Manager and Apple's QuickTime.

Networks and networking software will also undergo changes that make them capable of supporting computer-centered multimedia applications and files. Local-area networks will be enhanced to support the transport of dynamic media. Wide-area networks will have the benefit of ISDN and BISDN running on the Synchronous Optical Network (SONET), or Asynchronous Transfer Mode (ATM). ATM is an international standard developed by CCITT for transporting voice, data, image, and video independent of rate, media, or services.

## Cost and justification

At this phase of development, cost justification for multimedia will be irrelevant. All new computers will come equipped with basic multimedia capabilities, and software products will use those capabilities to create new applications and raise the value of the computers themselves.

Multimedia technology, like the graphical user interface, will become part of the user interface. Applications will use audio and video wherever they are best suited to the delivery of particular information.

## Infrastructure

Multimedia capabilities will be built into system software, and improved user interfaces will make using multimedia both easy and intuitive. The skill issue will evaporate as users become more accustomed to working with audio and video, just as they now are to working with text and graphics.

## Standards

Today, when one hits a key on a keyboard and a character appears on a computer display screen, no one cares that between the keystroke event and that of the displayed character, all kinds of encoding and decoding may have taken place.

Similarly, in the pervade phase of multimedia, users will not need to know or care about what happens to the voice spoken into the microphone, or the images captured from the camera or other video source. Multimedia files created on one platform will be readily movable to another platform, just as ASCII text files now move easily over WANs from platform to platform (see Table 9.1).

**TABLE 9.1  Phases of Multimedia Evolution**

|  | Enable | Enhance | Pervade |
|---|---|---|---|
| Applications | Vertical, training-oriented | Horizontal, included in popular personal productivity tools | Multimedia used virtually everywhere |
| Costs | High but justifiable | Much lower cost due to emerging standards and higher volumes | Irrelevant, because multimedia is standard part of all systems |
| Infrastructure | Hybrid analog and digital systems | Moving toward all-digital implementations | As easy to use as today's mouse and keyboard |
| Standards | None, except for individual subsystem standards | Standards for audio and video emerging | Comprehensive and transparent |

## Moving One "Byte" at a Time

The move from the personal computer of today to the personal communications system of tomorrow will be a giant step accomplished by making a sequence of smaller steps. These smaller steps relate to the four technologies at the core of computer-centered multimedia: *audio, high-capacity mass storage, video,* and *networking.*

## Audio

Adding audio to personal computers meant handling a dynamic medium for the first time in an environment geared to static media. The requirements for handling audio, however, are easier to meet than those for video. Thus, audio was the first small step.

Computer games and applications such as Microsoft's Flight Simulator take advantage of a computer's audio-processing capabilities. Computer games have been the most prolific users of computer sound, and their popularity helped to drive the cost of add-in sound boards down well below $100.

The availability of sound for little or no extra cost is enticing software developers of business products to add sound to their wares. Lotus Development Corp., for example, was among the first to offer a software product—Lotus Sound—that enabled users of office applications (e.g., word processors, spreadsheets, and e-mail) to add voice annotations.

Microsoft has enhanced its Windows system to support sound, and both OS/2 and the Macintosh operating system have also been modified to support sound capabilities.

## High-capacity mass storage

Digital sound and video consume huge quantities of data storage. For example, audio CD–quality stereo sound is sampled at 44.1 kHz with 16 bits per sample. This translates into a data-transfer rate of 705,600 bits per second per channel. At that rate, a 1.44-Mbyte flexible diskette can store 8 seconds of CD-quality sound.

Lower-quality sound can be sampled at 22 kHz with 8 bits per sample requiring a 176,000-bits-per-second-per-channel transfer rate. The flexible diskette could then store up to 32 seconds of stereo sound or 64 seconds of monaural sound. An hour's worth of monaural sound (sampled at 22 kHz with 8 bits per sample) would practically fill up an 80-Mbyte hard disk. Obviously, magnetic storage technologies, such as flexible and hard-disk drives, were a poor match for audio storage.

CD-ROM technology, on the other hand, offers inexpensive, removable, high-capacity (e.g., 650 Mbytes) storage. Audio CDs have largely displaced vinyl phonograph records as the medium of choice for music distribution and reproduction. CD-ROMs are becoming the primary medium for storing huge volumes of text, static images, and sound. As shown next, with suitable compression, CD-ROM technology is also the right medium for video.

## Full-motion video

Real-color, full-motion video is incredibly memory-intensive. For example, a display screen with a picture element (pixel) array of 640 × 480 pixels, each pixel requiring 24 bits of data, represents over 7 million bits of data! If the screen were redrawn 30 times per second, the data rate would be greater than 200 million bits per second. One second's worth of video (e.g., 30 frames) would require more than 27 Mbytes of storage. Thus, an 80-Mbyte disk drive would be more than filled by 3 seconds' worth of video data, and a CD-ROM would hold about 24 seconds' worth!

Both the data-transfer rate and storage capacity requirements can be mitigated by choosing a smaller display area, using a 256-color scheme (e.g., 8 bits per pixel), or lowering the frame rate from 30 to 15. Each compromise, however, downgrades the quality of the video image.

The standards proposed by MPEG and Captain Crunch would compress the raw video data output into a much reduced amount of data, while preserving much of the video information. The end result of such compression is the ability to store more than an hour of video on a CD-ROM.

With MPEG, the raw video data must first be stored temporarily, then compressed, then stored in compressed form. Thus even though the final stored result is compressed, a large-capacity storage system is required for the interim data. Captain Crunch, however, performs real-time compression on incoming video data. Thus there is no need for a large-capacity buffer storage system. This real-time compression makes it feasible to process video on an affordable desktop.

Both video compression methods (MPEG and Captain Crunch) provide on-the-fly video decompression and display.

## Multimedia networking

The fourth and final step in multimedia evolution involves networking. Today's networked personal computers are usually connected to local-area networks, or LANs. These networks allow users to share information, access data from on-line services, and handle transactions on corporate databases.

Today's LANs are designed for static media (e.g., text and graphics) and are optimized for use where data traffic is bursty rather than lengthy or continuous. This is not a good match for dynamic media, which need to preserve the time relationships very precisely.

Tomorrow's LANs, however, will be modified so as to efficiently manage audio and video data streams, thus forging multimedia into a pervasive business resource.

Wide-area networks are well along the path toward handling multimedia data. BISDN running on SONET or ATM is capable of supporting text, graphics, animation, audio, and compressed full-motion video.

## The Pieces Fall into Place

With audio and video joining text and graphics as all-digital technologies, the way is now open to combine these multiple media within a common system and over a common network.

Personal computer technology keeps advancing, and with each advance another step is taken along the path of multimedia evolution that leads from feasibility to practicality. Once, audio on an 8-bit machine with 16-bit data paths and flexible diskette drives was feasible; today, audio on a 32-bit machine with 32-bit data paths and a CD-ROM drive is practical.

Video, because of its data intensity, called for the most in the way of computing resources, and a practical solution to the data-compression requirement. The computing resources are here, and so is the practical data-compression solution.

We will now begin to see an increase in the development of multimedia authoring tools, and a particular surge in those applications that employ multimedia. This will be due in part to the increasing number of systems capable of supporting multimedia, and in part to the communications value provided by this technology.

With systems capable of quickly and easily mixing text, graphics, sounds, and moving images, we can begin to meet the needs of twenty-first-century communications by using the right choices of communications media to their best advantages.

# 10

# Multimedia on a Budget

**Joseph Weintraub**

## Getting Started

True multimedia, with full-motion video, can be fantastically expensive today. The high-end JPEG video accelerator boards alone are currently $2000, about the price of a new 486DX33 PC with 200-meg hard drive. In addition, just 60 seconds of this high-definition video can consume more than 52 Mbytes of hard-disk space. A ten-minute MPC video production would require 10 × 52, or an astounding 520 Mbytes. How big is your hard drive right now? As a user you can get somewhat over 520 Mbytes on a single CD-ROM, but as an MPC Developer you would need several gigabytes of hard disk to work with and to store this video before it is converted to CD-ROM. Gbyte hard drives are available, and in fact a 2.1-Gbyte SCSI hard drive and controller would add just about $3000 to the cost of this hypothetical 486, now hovering around $8000 or $9000.

Our first multimedia disk was produced on a very tight budget, on a 386 PC with just a 120-meg hard drive, yet it is still a visually exciting and powerful half-hour presentation. It can be viewed on almost any DOS Machine with a color monitor, giving a potential audience of over 200,000 users, compared with the current installed MPC Base of under 12,000.

In this article I will show you, step-by-step, how we produced this sophisticated and professional automated VGA Slide Show on a 3.5-inch high-density diskette for the IBM/PC for under $2500 and how we can sell it profitably for just $29.95.

## Step 1.   Prepare your slides and photographs

The easiest way, by far, to create your first multimedia presentation is to adapt a slide show or video for playback on the VGA or Super VGA Monitor of your PC. That way you don't have to worry too much about "creating" the presentation, and can concentrate on the technical details associated with getting it onto your PC's hard drive.

If you are creating a new presentation from scratch, you might consider shooting a few hundred Kodachrome slides with your Nikon, then selecting and arranging them in sequence in a slide projector tray till they do a good job of presenting your ideas visually. Later you will bring that slide presentation into your computer room and digitize it! Of course if you can afford a Fotoman Digital Camera from Logitech, you will save a good deal of time, not to mention film. (It uses magnetic disks.)

### Step 2.    Write your narration

Present your slide show to a roomful of people, or even just one other person. As the slide show proceeds, narrate in a loud, clear voice so as to emphasize and explain your ideas fully. Capture the narration on a quality tape recorder!

Later, you can have this tape typed onto the computer, or perhaps even digitized directly into a MPC soundtrack on your hard drive. (Note that digitized voice also takes up a lot of hard-disk space. Do not plan to digitize more than 20 minutes of voice and music. If your narration is longer than 20 minutes, plan on presenting the text as bright-white on a blue background, or some other eye-pleasing combination.)

### Step 3.    Install software and study the manuals cover-to-cover

At a minimum, you will need some sort of digitizer board installed in your computer, some sort of video camera to capture your slides, and the software that comes with your digitizer board that "takes the digital picture" and stores it on your hard drive. In addition you will probably want PC Paint or Aldus's PhotoStyler to touch up and perhaps add text to your digitized images.

If your slides, photos, video camera, or digitizer are black-and-white, you can "colorize" the images effectively once they are on your hard drive, and often come up with a more creative presentation than if you had started with perfect high-resolution color.

You will also need a multimedia run-time program or "slide show" software package so as to present your finished images with sophisticated wipes and dissolves between screens. We used Show Partner from Brightbill-Roberts with extremely good results. You will actually learn to use your software by working with it, but you can save yourself a lot of trouble by *reading the manual from cover to cover!*

### Step 4.    Get your hardware installed and ready to use

We purchased a very simple but effective b & w Digitizer board with a b & w video camera. The total outlay for hardware and software was under $500. While the board we used is no longer available, you can still get a low-resolution board from Video Eyes for under $300.

Instructions for installing your hardware will vary with the board, but in general you just turn off your 386 or 486 computer, slip the board into an open slot, and secure it in place with just one screw. If no jumper switches have to be set, this should take you all of 10 minutes.

### Step 5. Prepare your work environment and try the tutorial

Someone once said to me, "When you work, *ONLY* work!" and I consider this very good advice. Get the family out of the house or office. Put out the dog and feed the cat. Turn off that darn TV and put on your "creativity music," which should not be so loud that you can't hear yourself think! Forget about your diet, your doctor, your spouse, your kids, your income, your taxes, your health, and any other worries that might be sabotaging your creative impulses!

Why is creative thought like meditation? Because they both require a certain mental discipline, solitude, and quiet time and space. What is the sound of one hand clapping? How many angels can dance on the head of a pin? How many pixels are there on a Super VGA Screen? What is the secret of a successful PC slide show or multimedia presentation? For me, the secret is in keeping my use of unusual special effects to a minimum. For you, it may be something else. Working with your specific hardware and software in a "loose" experimental way, without worrying too much about perfect results, may allow you to create moods and styles that are effective and very new!

### Step 6. Go through a minipresentation with just three slides

Don't mechanically record every slide in your tray just to get it done, only to find out after days of work that you have repeated the same mistake 300 times. Instead, take just your first three slides all the way to a finished presentation. Save your results on a floppy disk. Turn off your PC and leave the room. Go have a beer and a few pretzels...maybe a pastrami sandwich...or some brussels sprouts with garlic and butter...whatever...then come back, turn on the PC, make believe you are the audience, and start your three-slide presentation. Does it work? If not, fix it. If it does work, you are on the right track. Go on to slide number four.

My work consisted of a lot of mental leaps and bounds, but basically came in two flavors:

1. Grunt work
2. Creative play

The grunt work involved turning on the slide projector, focusing the next slide, focusing the b & w video camera on the projected image, endlessly adjusting the size of the image, observing the image on the PC screen, and pressing some keys to save it to the hard disk.

The creative play involved colorizing the image in PC Paint and trying out the seemingly endless variety of wipes, drips, weaves, and dissolves available in Show Partner! That's the most fun I've ever had.

### Step 7.    Prepare your full visual presentation. Add text where appropriate.

Now that you know what works and doesn't, continue until you have completed your full presentation. Don't be afraid to continue to experiment with timing, color, text, dissolves and wipes, and other special effects. The longer your presentation, the more you must do to hold the viewers' interest through the entire show. You may be adding text to the bottom of screens or you may be alternating screenfuls of text and VGA images.

Be sure your screens don't zip by so fast that your audience can't finish reading the text. Since machines vary so much in speed, it is safest to ask the user to "press any key" to continue to the next screen. A show that drags along on an old 286 may zip by about 10 times too fast on a new 486.

Of course if you're using a soundtrack with digitized speech, you will want to keep text to a minimum—perhaps just titles and credits.

### Step 8.    Check your spelling and continuity

Nothing destroys your professional image like a misspelled word. If you know you can't spell, use a spellchecker (or a literate friend) to check the spelling of your text. Don't get too fancy with fonts. Two or three font styles in bright-white against blue is just perfect! Blue on white or yellow is also quite readable. Avoid tiny type that older folks won't be able to read. Old English is tempting for some applications, but can be difficult to read on a PC screen.

### Step 9.    Add voice or music as a planned part of your presentation

Add any special effects, but in moderation, please—this is not a psychedelic light show for a rock concert!

A good presentation does not require digitized voice, music, or special-effect sounds, but if you have the time and equipment, a soundtrack can add a lot. However, not all of your customers will have a SoundBlaster Pro with stereo speakers, so be sure your show stands on its own, even if no sound system is available to the viewer. Don't count on the PC speaker to deliver intelligible speech. It varies too much in quality from one PC to another, and some laptops have no speaker at all.

It is best to create your soundtrack on a high-quality multitrack tape recorder, for later translation to a variety of digital formats.

### Step 10.    Make backup copies of all your work

How would you feel if you had worked for 48 straight hours, completed the first multimedia presentation of your life, and then had a fatal hard disk *CRASH* that Wiped out all of your work with no hope of recovery of even one single screen?! You'd feel pretty sick, right? So backup, backup, backup, backup! We now have a Jumbo Colorado Tape Backup that backs up the entire 212-meg hard drive in under 20 minutes, just by pressing F1.

But even if you can't afford a tape backup, you can afford a stack of floppy disks! It only takes five minutes to copy your presentation to a floppy, but it can save you *days of work*.

**Step 11.  Prepare your "Silver Master"**

You are getting down to the short strokes now. Your presentation is almost complete. Arrange all your PIC Files neatly in a single directory with your runtime software. View it from start to finish. Does it look good? Yes? Then *copy it to a floppy* and stash it securely in your bottom drawer! That is your *extra insurance backup*. Now copy to *another* floppy. That is your "Silver Master."

**Step 12.  Alpha-test your Silver Master by yourself**

Modify it if required. If you can sleep on it, this is a good time to do so. When you wake up the next day, view your Silver Master. Any required changes will stick out like a sore thumb. Make those required changes. Update your backups and Silver Master with the changes.

**Step 13.  Show your Silver Master to a friend**

Your first exposure to the world should be to a friendly part of the world: a friend or a loved one.

**Step 14.  Ask for honest criticism, then revise as required.**

You don't want false praise, you want honest, constructive criticism. You must learn to accept criticism from others, and develop the knack of seeing your work through their eyes. What sings to you may not sing to everyone.

Ask yourself: How general is my intended audience? Am I aiming my work at a special group? If so, show it to a representative member of that special group. If you feel that anyone could enjoy and learn from your multimedia presentation, then grab anyone off the street and show it to anyone! Communication involves you, your medium, your creation, and your audience! Check it out before you try to sell it.

**Step 15.  Prepare your "Golden Master"**

Your Golden Master is the master from which all sale copies will be reproduced. It should be perfect. I like to use Norton Utilities VL (volume label) to give my Golden Master a special unique volume name, and then use Norton FD (file date) to revise the file date and time so that they are the same on every file. These two steps add that small professional finishing touch you will find on many professional disks. You will notice that every file is dated 01/01/94, and every file was created at 12:00 am. This is of course impossible, yet it has become the mark of a professional multimedia disk.

**Step 16.   Beta-test your Golden Master with a coworker or other person whose opinion you respect**

> I know you think you have tested more than enough, and everything is perfect, but there is always one more bug. Now is the time to enlist the help of a coworker and find that last misspelled word or other tiny error that will be so irritating after it has been copied onto your first 100 labeled diskettes!

**Step 17.   Ask for honest, constructive feedback; make final revisions.**

> If you still have to make a few creative changes or clarifications, now is the time to bite the bullet and do so. There will not be another chance like this to get it right. Once it is right, if you are unfortunate enough to have a boss, this is when you show it to your boss.

**Step 18.   Make a small production run of about 100 disks and manuals.**

> Wow! You have "published" your first multimedia presentation. If it is unusual and wonderful, perhaps your next run will be 5000 or 10,000 copies! Or maybe a few hundred thousand! Or maybe you will have a million-seller on your hands, and get rich and famous!

**Step 19.   Run ads in *PC* magazine, *BYTE, PC Computing,* and *Computer Shopper.* Damn the expense!**

> Also send review copies to every reviewer in the world. Install an 800 number for orders. Get credit card vendor status. Your phone is ringing off the hook! Wealth, freedom, more creative time, and a visit from the bluebird of happiness!

# 11

# The Competitive Edge

## Harry Hallman

## Introduction

Athletes train for it! Students learn for it! Governments go to war for it! But perhaps the most fiercely fought battles for obtaining a competitive edge are waged on the international playing fields of business and industry. The complexity and fast-changing business environment of today's world has wreaked havoc with organizations that were considered to be, just 10 years ago, the most formidable marketing forces on the face of the earth.

Now they, along with thousands of new startups, are scrambling to gain what little advantage they can. Cost-cutting, redesign of products, "right-sizing," and a host of other modern business techniques are being employed in order to allow these companies not so much to prosper as simply to survive.

An organization's ability to accurately and effectively communicate has never been more important. And any tool that allows companies to communicate better with their customers, employees, and stakeholders is or at least should be valued. Multimedia is one such technology.

## What *Is* Multimedia, Anyway?

It's interesting that the most promising communications tool ever to be invented has started its life with such a confusing name. The term *multimedia* has different meanings to different groups of people.

To the advertising community, multimedia means the use of various media, such as print ads, broadcast television and radio, to conduct an advertising campaign. To schoolteachers in the 1950s and 1960s, multimedia was the use of audio, film strips, and books to help in the teaching effort.

In 1970, the term *multimedia* was invented to describe the use of multiple slide projectors synchronized with audio and shown on the same screen. That was changed, in the United States, to the term *multi-image*.

Then came the late eighties and early nineties. Multimedia now means the use of computers to communicate, inform, and educate through an interactive mix of graphics, video, text, and audio. The term has become so confusing that IBM created its own brand by renaming it Ultimedia. Others have decided that an appropriate name for this media should be *new media*.

Whatever you want to call it, multimedia is audiovisual communication with one important distinction—interactivity. And it is the interactive part of these media that offers to provide companies with a competitive marketing edge.

The advantages interactive audiovisuals offer in the field of training are fairly self-evident, but it is in marketing that we may see these media truly excel. Virtually all current marketing communication tools are linear in nature. That is, they make a specific statement and cannot deviate from that statement. They move in a straight line.

Unfortunately, prospects' minds very rarely move in straight lines. As they view a video or listen to a live presentation they get thoughts, have questions, develop concerns. Most salespeople correctly view these interactions as opportunities to move the sale closer to a close. Yet how many times have you heard a presenter tell a prospect that he or she will answer all questions at the end of the presentation, simply because he or she didn't want to deviate from the order of the slides in the tray? By then most of the good questions—and the sale—may have been forgotten.

Clearly, the more interactivity you create, the better. And the only tool better at this important task than interactive audio-visuals is prone to miscues, affected by the physical and mental atmosphere of the meeting place, and requires thousands of dollars in shipping costs just to get it in front of the prospect. That tool, of course, is the salesperson.

This is not to say that the salesperson will ever be replaced. That simply won't happen, but we can make them more productive, more articulate, more professional, and more knowledgeable. And that can be accomplished by using this new audiovisual tool we are now calling "multimedia."

## Two Multimedia Success Stories

Thousands of people are using multimedia to help them in their marketing efforts and to create marketing successes. But two stories stand out as testimonies to the real power of multimedia. One involves the selling of a city, and the other netted a $110 million contract.

### Atlanta's bid for the 1996 Olympics

How do you convince an international committee to consider your city for the Olympics? First you assemble a great team of city leaders, then you devise a method for that team to portray the city as a modern metropolis capable of handling millions of visitors. That's exactly what some citizens of Atlanta did.

Once the team of leaders had been put together, its members went to Fred Dyer of Georgia Tech University to help them develop some marketing tools that could show what the city would look like in 1996 when the Olympics came to town. Dyer and his group came up with a plan to create two different multimedia presentations. The first was a kiosk using full-motion video and sophisticated animation, all controlled by a roller ball.

Using the roller ball, the viewer visually flies in any selected direction across the metro Atlanta area. The rate of speed is controlled by how fast the viewer moves the ball. As he or she comes upon a part of the city that will house a specific building, the computer switches to 3-D animation of that facility. Again using the roller ball, the viewer tours the facility, receiving information on the go.

The second presentation the Georgia Tech group put together was a three-screen projected-video, computer-controlled extravaganza, all located in a minitheater. The theater houses a small grouping of chairs and a control panel that is a model of the city covered in Plexiglas. The panel is a sort of multimedia presentation of its own. Cars, trucks, and other vehicles move through the city streets as the viewer is asked to start the show and select one of two languages available.

The show was an interactive sight-and-sound extravaganza that provided the viewer with a realistic glimpse of what the 1996 Olympics would be like if held in Atlanta.

Of course the city of Atlanta *was* selected as the site for the 1996 Summer Olympic Games. While the effort to attract the Olympic Games and the millions of dollars that go with it was a major team effort, the leaders of that effort are quick to tout the power that their multimedia tools provided.

### ETS expected excellence, and got it

In 1992, Educational Testing Services, the world's largest testing organization, was asked to bid (along with two competitors) to help a prestigious medical council computerize their current paper-and-pencil certification test. ETS was given three months to create a plan and present it at the council's national meeting.

Each competitor would make a two-hour presentation to the entire council of over 125 people. They also would be given the opportunity to operate a week-long technical center, where council members and their staff could see firsthand the type of work ETS was doing in the field.

While the ETS staff worked on the actual proposal, it turned to Lynn Tumulty of ETS's communications department to help it create the necessary materials needed to convince the council to select ETS for the project.

Tumulty devised a plan that included a mixed-media presentation of slides, video, audio, and live speaker for the two-hour presentation to the council. She then designed a strategy for the technical center that included the use of multimedia.

To help her in the creation of both the presentation and the multimedia, Tumulty asked Michael Olenski, Vice President of Corporate Media Communications of Philadelphia, PA, to create all the audiovisual materials, including the multimedia, and set them up on-site at the hotel where the event was to take place.

Olenski's staff created several free-running multimedia animated kiosks for the event. But perhaps the most powerful use of multimedia was in the creation of a simulated management software package. ETS wanted to show the council how the computer software that would manage the testing process would work. There simply were not enough time or resources to create a real working copy of this custom package.

Olenski's staff used Autodesk's Animator Pro animation software to create the computer software simulation. The program used standard graphic effects and interactivity to give the Council a realistic view of how the software would work. Both ETS and CMC staff helped to make over 150 one-on-one presentations of this simulation during the week-long event.

On Friday, as the council meeting came to a close, council members voted on their vendor of choice. ETS was selected to implement the five-year, $110 million effort. Both ETS and the council management acknowledged the impact that both the more traditional presentation materials and the multimedia software simulation had had on the selection process.

## Other Practical Applications

Not all marketing opportunities are million-dollar babies. In fact, most are simple day-to-day events that lead in time to millions of dollars. Let's explore some possible uses of multimedia in helping to increase the effectiveness of communications in several important marketing efforts, including

1. Lead generation
2. Sales presentations
3. Proposals
4. Point of sale
5. Customer education
6. Customer satisfaction
7. Marketing/advertising research

These ideas are meant only to stimulate your own thought processes. It is the marketer's own imagination that will, of course, create unlimited uses for interactive audiovisuals.

### Lead or sales generation

Multimedia kiosks placed in high-traffic areas, such as malls and trade shows, can collect names and addresses of interested prospects. They can issue coupons to be redeemed later at a business location. Through the proper collection of data, these devices can even help you to qualify the prospects.

While in the past this task has been taken care of with relative ease by standard computers, it is the advent of the colorful and exciting combination of graphics, sounds, and motion, all provided at reasonable prices, that makes multimedia so attractive for lead generation.

## Sales presentations

Salespeople complain that the more traditional presentations, using slides and overheads, distract from the selling process. Those types of media are bulky and cumbersome, and because they are linear, the salesperson cannot always take advantage of the power of total interaction with the customer.

Perhaps one of the most powerful forms of multimedia for use in presentation is *compact-disc interactive* (CD-I). Imagine being able to store thousands of images, numerous full-motion, full-screen videos, all linked to high-quality sound, on one 5-inch compact disc. Now imagine opening your briefcase, plopping a small presentation unit onto the customer's desk, inserting the disc, and making a presentation you had programmed just hours before. No cumbersome trays and projection units. No changing from the slide projector to the videotape player and back again. And most importantly, when the customer asks a question that may deviate from the formal presentation, you will be able to immediately interact with your presentation media to answer that question.

Using standard computers and multimedia can provide the same benefits for conference-room or large-audience presentations.

## Proposals

One of the most difficult aspects of the proposal presentation is making the ideas you are presenting come alive for the prospect. In the case of ETS, mentioned above, it was necessary to show how a specific software would function. Multimedia made that possible. If you were selling a new construction project, you might want to show what the building would look like when it was completed. And if you were an ad agency seeking a multimillion-dollar contract, you would certainly need to show and let the prospect hear your ideas. Multimedia makes all of these concepts come to life, and it can do this for virtually any product or service.

## Point of sale

Audiovisuals have been used as point-of-sale tools for years, and have proven to be very effective. With multimedia you can add the dimension of interactivity (at a reasonable cost), and allow customers to see and hear exactly what they desire. They won't have to sit through a five-minute videotape to learn what they want to know. Instead they will go directly to the subject and get the answer quickly. That in turn will get them to the checkout counter faster.

## Customer education

One of the most powerful tools a marketer has at its fingertips is customer/prospect education. The concept is simple. You, as a supplier, provide critical information that educates the customer or prospect so that they can make a logical buying decision. In doing this, you show your trust and your willingness to provide service, and this predisposes the customer to buy from you. One large telecommunications company has traced over $250 million in sales to a two-year customer education program they conducted.

Creating customer education materials in the form of CD-ROM or CD-I discs, and making them available to prospects and clients, will help to cut the cost of the more traditional approaches to conducting seminars. While seminars are extremely valuable for one-on-one interaction, and do facilitate sales, it is not always practical to have seminars in every city or to fly every prospect to your location. In such cases, an interactive multimedia customer education program could be sent to the prospect.

In the case of CD-I, a company could send the playback unit and disc to the prospect and it would be less expensive than the average air fare to fly a prospect to a location. And in those cases where seminars are practical, the multimedia can be distributed to the attendees so that they can share the important information with colleagues back home.

### Customer satisfaction

Imagine getting a multimedia instruction disc every time you purchased one of those "impossible-to-put-together" toys for your child. Surely it would increase your satisfaction to be able to put the toy together faster and more easily. While packaging a multimedia instruction disc with every hard-to-put-together toy may not be practical, the $2 or so it would cost is certainly practical for automobiles, lawnmowers, manufacturing equipment, and thousands of other products that require assembly or special knowledge to operate.

Not only will you help to create satisfied customers, you may even attract new customers who see the multimedia as added value.

### New products

Most companies have intellectual assets they have gathered over their years of being in business. Often this knowledge can be turned into new information-based products. The product could be a training program useful in other industries, or a database of facts that have value to others. In either case this information could be turned into multimedia programs offered for sale within the industry or even to the consumer market.

This is, of course, not a new idea, in that many companies already have done this successfully. But with the advent of multimedia and especially the new compact-disc technology, the creation of CD-I titles for now paper-intensive information may be more practical for many smaller organizations.

### Is Computer Technology the Competitive Edge?

There are those who do believe that computer technology provides a competitive advantage for companies that are able to buy it. But study after study has proven that simply "buying" this type of technology has little effect on those factors that make a company a better competitor. In fact, in some cases productivity, customer service, and profitability have suffered, thus making the company *less* competitive.

It is the manner in which the technology is implemented that is the most important factor. Applications, applications, applications! A word that should be thrice emblazoned on every multimedia product. Every user, every provider, and every manufacturer of multimedia products and services should be thinking in terms of the applications, not just the features of a product.

"Build it and they will come" only works in the movies. In the real world of business you must first find out what the customer wants and needs, then build it better than your hundreds of competitors, and finally get up on the highest mountaintop you can find and shout to the world that you have an application that will fill their wants and needs. And you need to do it *often*. Multimedia can help companies do just this.

# 12

# Virtual Anesthesia

**Guy Hancock**

## Understanding Virtual Reality

Virtual reality can be understood as a substitution of man-made input for natural input to one or more of the senses, usually sight and sound. At the extremes of imagination are virtual environments that also provide coordinated stimulation of the five senses.

### Using multimedia

Multimedia can be used to approximate a virtual environment by including recognizable visual, audio, and other cues that help the viewer/user to suspend disbelief and become engrossed in the virtual experience. Multimedia simulations can include many aspects of virtual reality to enhance believability for the user. In education, the simulations are designed to prepare the student for real-life situations. Although they are not primarily entertainment, they must be entertaining in order to keep students interested and to be used more than a few times.

### Elements of interactive multimedia

Some interactive multimedia include instruments or controls that are connected to the computer. The most common example is the joystick for flight simulators. A more exotic example is found in advanced flight trainers, which tilt and bump to give realistic proprioception sensations; that is, within the apparatus itself, sensations are produced much like those a person would experience in an actual-reality situation. Some elements available to an author wishing to create a computer simulation include graphics, still video, video, sound, interactivity, and sequencing. Certain techniques and principles guiding the application of each of these elements contribute to making the multimedia simulation more like a virtual reality.

## One Project, at SPJC

Under development at Florida's oldest two-year institution of higher learning, St. Petersburg Junior College, is an anesthesia tutorial and simulation for veterinary technology students. While designing *More Anesthesia, Please!,* we repeatedly examined and revised the use of graphic images, sound, video, timing, and interactivity.

*More Anesthesia, Please!* is authored in SuperCard and runs on any Macintosh with a color monitor. SuperCard has many similarities to HyperCard but allows full use of color. The computer is connected to a laserdisc player with a separate monitor. It is fairly easy to write script in the software, which directs the player to play particular frames, sounds, or video segments from the laserdisc.

The scripts are activated by various events such as mouse clicks or cards opening or closing. The student goes through all the steps, from picking a case to making choices about the equipment to inducing and maintaining anesthesia. Examples from this project will be used to illustrate the application of these elements so as to enhance the realism and engage the user.

## Available Elements for Computer Simulation

### Graphic images

Graphic images can enhance a simulation if they realistically convey some aspect of the environment modeled by the simulation. The arrangement, size, colors, position, textures, and shading can all contribute to increasing the realism. Graphic images can complement video images when a separate monitor is being used to display video in a two-monitor system. Graphic images also can trigger recognition and familiarity if they closely resemble real objects the student has seen or will see.

We created graphic images for a floor plan of the hospital, for the monitors, and for the patient's chart, which indicates floating palette windows, button icons, and an anatomical diagram. We used a cartoon in the opening sequence that was scanned in from the artist's drawing (Fig. 12.1).

### Still video images

Still video images most enhance the realism of a simulation when the pictures are taken from real-life situations. Further enhancement occurs if the pictures are taken from the perspective of the participant in the real-life experience. For example, the picture that most closely simulates driving a car is taken from the driver's seat looking through the windshield. It is more realistic if the location of the picture approximates the simulation, and if the car is actually moving so that objects at the edges are blurred slightly.

For *More Anesthesia, Please!,* still video images were taken from the video disk itself and with a still video camera. Bottles of drugs, pictures of patients, and pictures of the anesthesia machine were used (Fig. 12.2).

**Figure 12.1**  Opening sequence for virtual anesthesia. (*Source: Michon Pratt.*)

### Video

Video offers much potential to draw the viewer into a virtual world. We are accustomed to watching television to such a degree that it may have become a reality of its own. A lot of TV is live video of real events, so we may be more willing to imagine that simulated events are real. Video usually includes sound, and combining the two media gives a more powerful representation of reality.

People are very attuned to the sounds that accompany actions, activities, and events. Seeing motion, shadows, and colors while hearing the expected sounds helps us to enter the virtual world. The disbelief caused by the smaller-than-life-size screen, lack of depth perception, two-dimensional image, and colors that are not quite true is more easily overcome by the combination of sound and motion video.

For *More Anesthesia, Please!,* the video disk was repurposed. This means the video choices were limited to what the original author had filmed. The particular disk was well thought out, of good quality, and very complete. Nevertheless, there are video scenes we wanted to use that are not on the disk.

Our challenge was to use as much of the video as possible, as long as it enhanced our project. Another option was to include QuickTime video of our

**Figure 12.2** Still video imagery.

own if there were scenes missing that we felt were essential—the tradeoff being that the storage size for the project would increase dramatically as more QuickTime was added. However, video is so compelling in creating the virtual environment and engaging the user that it may well overcome this disadvantage.

## Sound

By itself, sound can contribute to a more realistic simulation of reality. It has been found that the combination of wire-frame visuals and sound is very effective in helping people to suspend disbelief. With the use of sound, it is not necessary to have realistic visual images in order to achieve immersion of the user in the virtual environment.

We are not highly conscious of the many sounds that accompany daily activities and actions, but we expect to hear them. The real-life absence of concurrent sounds would be noticed immediately. Conversely, the presence of these sounds, coordinated with graphics or video images in a simulation, adds a lot to the perception of reality.

Some of the sounds used in our project include a cow's moo, the click of knobs being turned on the anesthetic vaporizer, the click of switches on monitors, the sound of gas filling the rebreathing bag, and the beep of ECG monitors in surgery.

## Interactivity

Interactivity means that the user receives appropriate and expected feedback in response to actions taken. In a simulation of doing a blood-cell count under the microscope, the student might wish to change magnification from $10 \times$ to $40 \times$. In real life, she would move an objective mounted on a turret. In a computer simulation she might click on a button with the mouse, or click on a picture of a microscope objective. As the view changes to the larger magnification, the sound of the new objective clicking into place is heard.

The sound reinforces the realism of the simulation because it is familiar, but also because it occurs in response to a user's action. The more interactivity has been built into a multimedia program, the more it can achieve in creating a virtual reality.

## Sequencing and timing

The sequencing and timing of a multimedia program or simulation are important in creating a virtual reality. People are accustomed to events occurring in predictable sequences, to actions causing events or reactions. The multimedia program faithfully represents reality by not violating the beliefs and expectations of the users.

The designer of a multimedia program has to make many decisions about which events in a sequence A–Z are important, and which ones can be modeled or represented effectively. Not every step will be included, but if enough of the important steps are represented effectively, the program will come closer to creating a virtual reality.

Another aspect of sequencing is allowing the user to control the sequence of events. This mimics real life, and the feedback given to the user can further enhance the sense of realism.

## More Examples of the Use of Multimedia

The interactive canine anesthesia tutorial and simulation provide more examples of the various aspects of multimedia used to enhance the reality of the program.

### The chart

Veterinary technicians must examine each patient's chart for information that affects the administration of anesthetics. In developing the simulation, we attempted to make the on-screen chart look as much like a real patient chart as possible. Lots of information is there, just as in a real chart, forcing the technician to review the entire record and pick out the relevant items.

The student is required to recall information from the chart—or go back to the chart and look it up again—when calculating drug doses. Sometimes the units must be converted from pounds to kilograms before the calculations can be done, another real-life complication.

### The vaporizer

In another section of the program, the student will change the setting of the anesthetic vaporizer. The video disk being repurposed has a segment showing a close-up of a hand turning the vaporizer knob to the new setting. The parallel sound track includes the sounds of the vaporizer clicking into the new setting. When the anesthesia machine flush valve is pushed, a sound track segment from the video disk plays the sound of oxygen filling the rebreathing bag (Fig. 12.3).

### Surgery

In surgery, the video is shot from the perspective of the anesthetist at the head of the table. Whenever something needs adjustment, the head technician turns and looks straight at the viewer, waiting for a response. This is an effective technique for getting the student involved in the tensions and emotions of doing anesthesia.

## Hardware and Software

The development of *More Anesthesia, Please!* proceeded on a Macintosh IIcx and a Quadra 950. It is very helpful to have 8 to 12 (or more) Mbytes of RAM memory, so that multiple applications can be opened simultaneously. Both

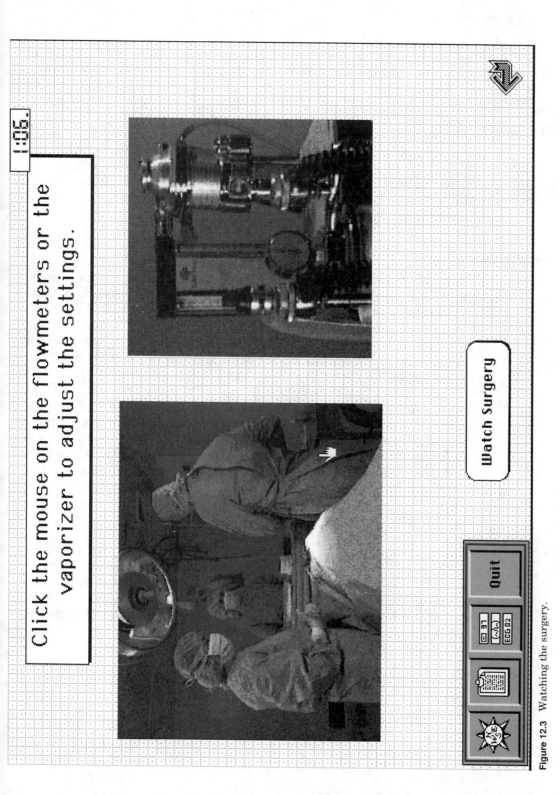

Click the mouse on the flowmeters or the vaporizer to adjust the settings.

1:05.

Watch Surgery

Quit

91
ECG 02

**Figure 12.3** Watching the surgery.

VideoSpigot and QuickImage video digitizer boards were used. Video sources used were the laser player, video camera, Canon XapShot!, still video camera, and videotape.

### The Soundtrack

Sound was incorporated by using MacRecorder and SoundEdit to record and edit sounds, and by directing the laser player to play one or the other of the audio tracks. The laser player audio can be played either through the speaker in the monitor or through amplified speakers. It is helpful to have paint and draw programs to create graphics and edit pictures.

### Repurposing

In repurposing a video disk, a major task is to index all the video and audio segments. We used a HyperCard stack designed for this purpose. It includes player controls to start and stop the disk as well as to find specific frames.

It took approximately 6 hours to create the index for one side of the laserdisc for *More Anesthesia, Please!* This work paid off when searching for each audio or video segment to include in the project. The lower the hardware requirements are for your project, the more units on which it will be able to play.

This was one reason for our choice to plan for a separate monitor with the laser player. There are video digitizer boards capable of playing external video in a window on the Macintosh screen. However, these boards are not found in most machines, and they are more costly than a video monitor. We decided color was an essential aspect of this project. By that choice we gave up the potential to run the project on monochrome Macintoshes.

### In Summary

By involving more senses and by more closely reflecting the real world, we can stimulate a virtual reality in the mind of the viewer. Learning via multimedia-virtual-reality can be nearly as memorable and influential as real life-experiences. The advantages are that it can be much less costly to provide, can be repeated, and can allow the student to gain experience that cannot always be provided by real life.

# Who Had Better Be on First

## Getting Optimal Results
## from Multimedia Training

**Rex J. Allen**

## The Great Irony

There is great irony in a book about multimedia—but it's not what you think.

You might think the irony lies in hefty chapters of printed matter that speak dryly of magnificent media in living color. But the chief irony is not in the contrast of digital video animations and dull chapter headings. A very good book, combined with a fertile imagination, can still grow mental media that not even Hollywood can afford to produce.

Or you may be thinking of the ironic contrast between a *passive* book and the exciting *interactive* technologies of multimedia of which we write. Actually, I found Hugo's *Les Misérables* to be profoundly interactive, and anything but passive.

So wherein lies the great irony? I have spent every working day of the past 14 years "in" multimedia—hardware, software, courseware. For me, the irony of this chapter in this book is that I don't know *you*. I don't know why you bought this book, or why you are reading this chapter. I don't know what you plan to do with multimedia technologies, or what motivates you, or what you knew before you began reading, or what TV shows you watch, or your background in instruction. Aye, there's the rub! You see, we at Allen Communication have enjoyed some remarkable successes with multimedia instruction *because* we worry incessantly about these very questions. We've learned that *who* must be on first.

Get to the point, you say. Okay, look at it this way. You are walking down the hallway in a high school and you meet someone who looks like a teacher—older, less colorful, unarmed. You ask, "What do you teach?" Or perhaps you are taking a break in the company lunch room and you overhear a group talking about their training classes. "Oh," you ask, "what do you teach?" The answers are predictable. In the school he or she will say, "I teach biology," or math, or English. In the training department they will say, "I teach software applications," or management skills, or forklift operation. And you will be terribly disappointed. You want them to say, "I teach kids!" or "I teach coworkers!"

This is the point. In education and training we go about, for the most part, teaching physics and OSHA compliance. *What* is on first, not *who*. Content experts become teachers and trainers, and then they teach content. Quite incidentally, in that process, *some people* learn *something*. They may even "meet the objectives," if there are any. But the learning is very, very far from optimized. If you think back on the handful of truly great teachers you have known, you may recall that they *cared,* or they *knew you,* or they made *it* (content) make sense to *you* (person).

## Haven't We Met Somewhere?

So, I have to write this chapter based on some very general assumptions. If I knew you, I would write it differently and it would help you much, much more. For example, if I knew you as a college student in an instructional technology course, I'd interview lots of people like you. I would study your language, your values, your motivations. I would use pictures and diagrams and examples and questions that made sense to you. I would try to use a tone and pace that worked for you. I would try to acknowledge your fears or cynicism about learning, and even make you face these concerns. I might let you explore the content and come to your own conclusions, then dare you to make this content come alive in a personal project or simulation. *And* if I had multimedia technologies to help, I'd have a heyday with pictures and sounds and experiences that made sense to you.

Now, if I knew you to be a tired trainer in a hospital, I would write still differently. Maybe you want some very general ideas about "audience-centered" training design—a theoretical treatise about the why. Maybe you have inherited a ton of "traditional" instruction (i.e. boring, content-centered overhead transparencies) that you want to bring to life. You want a checklist or recipe that will help you to increase the value and interest of your training. Maybe you know all this stuff I'm talking about and just need a way to justify optimal learning to your boss. Or maybe, if you're lucky, your management has decided that training and education ought to become an integral part of organization strategy. You've been told to help increase profits and decrease costs, to make training accountable for real change in performance—to make it pay! *Good for you.* Now you have the motivation to optimize your impact. You will *want* to put who on first.

Here at Allen Communications, we have had our most important successes with multimedia instruction when we have taught people, not just content. Specifically, we and our clients have achieved real results (profits, savings, strategic positioning, quality, empowerment, etc.) when we hit the right audience with the right combination of methods and multimedia muscle. And we had to know the people before we could optimize their learning. It's very hard to do this, because everyone and their dogs will want you to focus on the content—especially the dogs. They will want you to cut the fluff and get to the meat of the subject. They will agonize over each step in a procedure, each word describing the system, each question about the schematic. But in their content-world they have forgotten that all dogs are hungry and *all learners are not.* So, *you* must put who on first.

## So What's New About That?

But that's just good training, you complain. What's *new* here, and how does this apply to multimedia, anyway?

What's new is actually *doing* "good training," because we don't do it very often, and *how it applies* is the subject of the following paragraphs.

First, we will talk about the instructional development process, and where in that process the audience must be evaluated, acknowledged, loved, and taught. We'll even attempt to offer a checklist of sorts, including when and how to bring the learners back into learning. Then we'll offer three case studies that used this focus and process to achieve some remarkable results. My strong desire is that you, whoever you are, will be touched and taught. Then we will have bridged the "great irony" together.

## An Instructional Design Process

So where can we reinsert the learner in learning? Let's look first at a rather standard and effective instructional development process. Now, don't get worried. This is not a soapbox sermon on any one particular instructional systems design (ISD) model. Nor will we argue the theoretical underpinnings of the various models. We will not debate the cognitive or social learning or behavioral doctrines, nor the "new" constructivist versus "old" structured approaches, nor the relative value of values and attitudes in learning.

Quite frankly, I would love to have these discussions with you some time. *Our* motivations and values as designers make a *big* difference in *their* learning as students! But we will not get into that now. Instead, take a look at Fig. 13.1, which shows the basic "systems" development model to which most of us subscribe.

But where do we focus on the learner? The picture of the process seen in Fig. 13.1 is too general, too far removed from actual development steps to help. We know that we must capture and understand the audience during the Analysis phase. But when and where? And how do we translate audience awareness into the remainder of the phases? Figure 13.2 represents a more specific model that works for interactive multimedia courseware development. It was adapted from my teachers, Walt Dick and Robert Gagné, with a touch of Mager and Merrill, and a lot of Allen thrown in. (See Dick and

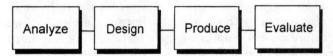

**Figure 13.1**   The systems development model.

Carey, 1990; Gagné, 1970; Mager, 1988; Merrill, et al., 1989.) Hopefully it is much like your approach. Note that not all critical steps, such as approvals, are included.

Is Fig. 13.2 similar to your process? Are you overwhelmed at the complexity, or underwhelmed by the simplicity? Or are you basically cynical about the whole "boxes and arrows" thing? We have found that this sort of instructional

**Figure 13.2**   The instructional design process.

model works only when we work it, of course. It is important to note, however, that it is not a whimsical arrangement of steps. It is based on many decades of research and the results from many "real" applications. Specific checklists and tools are applied to each activity, and it works. If you are not following such a model, you can make great strides toward optimal learning simply by studying and adopting some such approach.

That said, the chief questions of this discussion now return: Where in all these activities can we focus to bring the audience to life? Which of these steps matters most, when it comes to final results?

## Where and How Do We Put Who on First?

It has been our experience that *all* of the steps in our process make a difference to our instructional success. However, three of the major steps within the model seem to most influence our ability to create optimal learning, in conjunction with ongoing formative evaluation throughout the process. These include (1) the audience analysis itself, (2) the definition of strategies, and (3) the specification of a course treatment, including a style guide for "look and feel." (In order to make your reading interactive, look back at Fig. 3.12 and imagine that those three boxes are now colored differently and that they are flashing on and off. Cool, huh?!)

Of all the steps required to create great courseware, these three matter most. We have also found that these steps are least emphasized by most developers and trainers. For the most part, we have observed that a trainer will receive a mandate from the boss (the mission), collect and assess the content from subject matter experts (SMEs), organize it into "chunks" or modules, and then start writing a script, making transparencies, scheduling rooms, etc. After all, is there time for anything else—the dogs are after us, aren't they? So the trainer teaches content, and hopes the learning is caught, if not taught. No! There *is* time to do it right!

### Analyze and profile the audience

During audience analysis, we try to find answers to the following kinds of questions. In our questionnaires and interviews, these are offered in a more random order, and "second questions" are often asked about a given area once someone is talking freely. Notice that we often combine additional content analysis with the audience analysis. Again, these are just sample items.

- In your opinion, what skills are most critical to success at your job?
- What is the most important attitude for someone in your job to have?
- What is most satisfying about the work you do?
- What do you find to be the most difficult aspect of your responsibilities?
- Why do some people "wash out" in your job area?
- What makes a real "star performer" in your area?

- In your mind, what is the most difficult part about working with _____ (specific skill, system, procedure to be taught)?
- In what area of _____ do you feel most certain about your skill and ability? Least certain?
- How did you learn _____? What was most helpful about this training? Least helpful?
- If you were to teach _____ to a friend, how would you do it?
- What motivates you to do a good job with _____?
- If you were "the boss," and could change anything about the way _____ is trained, what would you do?
- When you get stuck with _____, where do you go for help?
- Please *rank* the following activities in order of importance ("A" is most important, "B" next most important, etc.) on the left. Then *rate* their difficulty on the right ("5" is most difficult, "1" is least difficult).

| Rank activity/task/issue | Difficulty | Comments |
|---|---|---|
| _____ Perform start-up procedure | 5  4  3  2  1 | |
| _____ Ask for the purchase order | 5  4  3  2  1 | |
| _____ Prepare the agenda | 5  4  3  2  1 | |

Etc.

- What is your favorite sport or activity after work?
- What subject did you enjoy most in school?
- What is your favorite magazine and TV show?
- What music do you enjoy most?
- What do you do in your spare time (hobbies, interests, study, etc.)?
- How often do you think or read about something new to you (astronomy, geography, science, art)? What was the last thing that caught your attention?
- What else should we be asking about, so that we can make the new _____ training most effective?

As we gather audience data, we tend to follow this process:

1. Discuss the audience with our direct clients, management, and assigned SMEs.

2. Create questionnaires, and distribute to as many in the audience as is practical, or at least representative samples from known audience segments. Ensure anonymity, unless they choose to provide their names.

3. Gather and tabulate the data, then build follow-up interview questionnaires.

4. Conduct one-on-one interviews and focus groups, if possible.

5. Analyze the data and develop a short, concise Audience Profile, then gain client approval and acceptance of this description.

6. Encourage *everyone* on the design team to put this profile in front of them and to salute the audience daily. Focus on the profile in meetings. Challenge all subsequent decisions based on this profile.

As a result of all this effort, we become much more acquainted with our "whos," and if this understanding seeps into every crack of our courses, optimal results can begin to accrue. So, in addition to the omnipresence of the audience profile, how do you get that sort of transfer from analysis to courseware?

## Define the instructional strategies

Walt Dick's book, *The Systematic Design of Instruction,* includes a fine chapter on the need to carefully, thoughtfully, creatively define instructional strategies in a course or course module (Dick and Carey, 1990). He starts with a basic outline of possible instructional events or strategies that have been shown to be most effective in most situations. They are modeled after Gagné's events of instruction (Gagné, 1970). He suggests that the designer consider the following options for each "chunk" of instruction. I am paraphrasing and adjusting Walt's list based on our experience.

### Preinstructional activities

Gain learners' attention and build relevance/motivation.

Orient them as to what they should learn (objectives).

Verify that they know enough to start (prerequisites).

Get them comfortable with flow, options, grading.

### Instructional activities

Present the key concepts and ideas.

Offer examples and nonexamples.

Provide practice with the concepts, and helpful feedback.

Guide students through integration of learning.

Focus on transfer of learning to the learner's job.

### Postinstructional activities

Provide review as necessary/desired.

Require some sort of testing with feedback/scoring.

Provide remediation if necessary, and/or enrichment as desired.

All these events of learning are important. They may not all apply to every module or course, and they may not all be best used in this order every time. But the fact is that as you use these general strategies, your courseware will get better. How much better? That depends.

You see, even with the use of this tested outline, critical questions still arise. How will you gain the learners' attention? How will you present the key concepts? How will you help them to transfer learning to their job? *The answers are in the audience analysis.* Let's use an example.

### Tulips, juvenile delinquents, and you

Suppose you offer your instructional design expertise to your community leaders on a voluntary basis. You want to contribute. You want to get involved. (I'm impressed!) They come back and tell you that they need a short course on planting tulips. The Beautification Committee has decided that tulips are the key to community success. Okay. You can do this!

You ask about the audience, of course, and they explain that there is quite a large group of "volunteers" from a local counseling clinic who know nothing about tulips, but who need to learn. They want every volunteer to be able to plant hundreds of bulbs quickly and correctly, so that none is wasted. (That's your "mission.") Volunteers are available at various odd hours for training, and they will need individualized instruction. The committee members strongly suggest computer-based training, and offer a solid rationale and the needed delivery systems. Good luck, they say, and you're off.

Here is the result of your discussions with your neighbor, a tulip expert. The lessons or modules break out rather nicely. You've got the content.

- Soil preparation (consistency, acidity, proximity to water, etc.)
- Bulb preparation (age, health signs, color combinations, etc.)
- Planting the bulb (depth, orientation, soil packing, etc.)
- Tools to use (spade, rake, trowel, ruler, etc.)

Then you go to the clinic to learn about the audience. You talk to management, conduct interviews, even use a questionnaire. You find *two* very *interesting* audiences.

Audience One

Juvenile delinquents on parole, ages 13–18
Hate-the-establishment adults in general
Love hard-rock music, *The Simpsons*
Court-ordered to do community service
Never gardened, but some love flowers
Live in jail at night

Audience Two

Older men (55–65), recently widowed

Getting counseling to overcome grief
Like classical music, *MacNeil-Lehrer*
Counseled to do service as therapy
Never gardened, but willing to learn
Live alone at home

You begin to write objectives based on the content outline and to build your evaluation plan. It becomes clear that both audiences need the same basic content. They will need to meet ᵗhe same "performance objectives." That will make it easier, right? Wrong.

As you begin to select instructional strategies, you begin to see how the audience must drive your selections. Think about this for your "Planting the Bulb" module:

| How would you... | For Audience One... | For Audience Two... |
|---|---|---|
| Motivate, build relevance? | _____ | _____ |
| Present the key concepts? | _____ | _____ |
| Provide practice, exercises? | _____ | _____ |
| Guide integration? | _____ | _____ |
| Test and remediate? | _____ | _____ |

Do you see how the audience must drive the specific strategies? Can you imagine someone trying to simply "teach tulips" to these two audiences? Can you picture the results? What would happen if you had not discovered the two different audience segments?

We have found that a table like the one above, with columns for each identifiable audience segment, is very helpful. As we select specific strategies, we force ourselves to design for the learner. Audience One may best relate to games and competition as the primary mode for presenting a key concept, and to testing and testimonials from credible peers for motivation. Audience Two may best relate to a self-help course where they discover what they need to know and then practice with simple, on-screen simulations.

When you really understand your audience and then drive your strategy definition based on that audience or set of audience segments, you take a long step toward optimal learning. Don't just teach tulips. Help troubled kids and mourning grandpas!

## Specify the treatment and style guide

The third step in the design process that seems to be most critical to optimal learning, especially when the course will be delivered via computer, is what we call the *treatment*. That is, how will the course look and feel? Here are six examples of the issues most critical at this juncture that should be considered for each audience:

1. What is an appropriate general motif or overall look and feel (borders, icons, creative theme, cartoon character, tough guy)?

2. What will be the tone and pace of the instruction?

3. What colors and music are most appropriate for the customer?

4. What will the basic screen layout look like, and why?

5. What about reading level?

6. What about navigation conventions?

Did your treatment recommendations change, based on the audience? With these questions answered, we strongly recommend that someone on the project team (or from Quality Assurance) take the time to document all treatment decisions made and compile a binding style guide for all who work on the project. We like to make this an "on-line" style guide or a working prototype, so that everyone understands how the course will look and feel as early as possible. This approach also ensures consistency and eventually reduces costs, sometimes significantly.

And remember, remember: the treatment is taken from the audience analysis. In the case-study screen examples we'll be looking at next, you may be able to pick up on the way our designers adapted "look and feel" to each audience, even without the ability to discern color, animations, video, audio, etc.

Well, we have reviewed the three areas of the instructional design process that make the most difference to overall courseware results. I have tried to provide some checklists, some samples, and some examples that could help. In the next paragraphs, I'd like to share some real-world experiences in which audience-centered learning has made all the difference.

## Three Case Studies

### Union Pacific Railroad (see Fig. 13.3)

**The problem.**   Deregulation and competition led to massive layoffs, restructuring and relocations, high-tech solutions in a low-tech environment, and overall poor performance. The reliability of their service was dangerously low. People inside the company were very unhappy, as were customers. Significant, traditional training efforts had failed to induce change.

**Analysis.**   The content analysis suggested that the information and skills to be learned were not very complex. Why hadn't training worked? The audience analysis revealed that labor-management relations were poor, that relations

**Figure 13.3**   Union Pacific course.

among people in different job functions were weak or hostile, that few employees saw any big picture or much hope in the face of discouraging news. They had not changed because they did not want any more change. They were afraid and suspicious. We learned that they still valued the Union Pacific tradition (many third- and fourth-generation workers) and shield (logo), railroading in general, and country music. Deep down they wanted the railroad to make it, and they knew how to work.

**Strategies.**   Create a short course that *all* employees would have to experience. It would openly address their real problems, attack issues honestly, acknowledge the company's cultural issues, challenge their thinking, persuade them to give learning and change a chance, and do it all in a surprising way. Here are just a few of the selected strategies:

**Catch attention and motivate.**   Create a country-and-western music video that expresses anger, fear, and concern, but also hope and vision for the future.

**Present key concepts.**   Create an interactive "argument" on-screen among employees and with management. Let learners participate so as to understand and to vent frustrations.

**Provide practice and feedback.**  Show learners an employee error and have them discover how this mistake impacts all other employees in the organization. Show the "shield" breaking up, and have learners decide how to put it back together.

**Provide enrichment.**  Allow learners to see an alternative ending of the music video, then take it home to share with families, change attitudes at home.

**Treatment.**  Use Union Pacific colors, trains, and textures on the screen. Use extensive testimonials of real people to enhance credibility. Use simple navigation options to overcome fears of technology. Maintain simpler reading level, direct "voice," down-to-earth language. Create video and audio with very high production values to add credibility. Use UP shield throughout to capture tradition.

**Outcomes.**  Over 120 hours of courseware have now been developed—all rolling out of the first "culture change" course. Over 10,000 people have been trained, and all have achieved 90 percent or better on posttests. UP has saved over 10,000 training days with the multimedia approach, plus related travel, per diem, time off the job, etc. They have enjoyed very high transfer of training to job performance, as evidenced by an increase in on-time deliveries of over 30 percent in areas where training has occurred. That represents a positive impact of millions in savings, and new opportunities. They believe training has given UP a significant strategic advantage over its competitors. The employees like the training and want more. It hit home. This series of courses was awarded the prestigious 1993 "Nebby" award for best interactive multimedia training in industry, as well as other awards.

## U.S. Air Force maintenance continuation training program
(see Fig. 13.4)

**The problem.**  F-16 and F-15 fighter planes are very complex and expensive, and extremely critical to our national defense. Those who maintain them are not highly educated, although a few are extremely expert in troubleshooting and fixing aircraft. Overall, of every three parts pulled off the aircraft, one was fully functional. This created a huge waste of costs in labor, parts, distribution, etc. (Please note that we have since found that most organizations have a similar "miss rate" in their maintenance areas.) The idea of the training was to improve troubleshooting skills and devise better cognitive strategies in order to reduce the number of parts pulled in error by 5 percent. The result would be a savings of $110 million over 5 years.

**Analysis.**  Content analysis was performed through a relatively new technique we call "cognitive task analysis." We were able to capture the "mental maps" of the rare experts, their view of the various aircraft systems, as well as their "cognitive paths" through those systems, the thinking process they

**Figure 13.4** U.S. Air Force maintenance training course.

use to troubleshoot. The audience analysis showed that the maintenance technicians were young, had little if any formal education beyond high school, enjoyed rock music, had limited knowledge of aircraft system intricacies, and had gained the habit of "swaptronics" in maintenance—i.e., continually replacing parts until the problem goes away. Unhappily, the "swaptronics" approach was reinforced by the technicians' immediate supervisors, who emphasized number of flights rather than quality maintenance. Finally, these technicians were patriotic and cared about their mission, and the experts were motivated primarily by pride.

### Strategies

**Establish relevance and motivate.**  Create a rock-music video introduction and theme that emphasizes pride in country and job, demonstrates results of great performance, and uses credible peer experts to provide testimonials.

**Present key concepts.**  Use a Socratic "dialogue" approach to let learners show what they already know and to focus them on their gaps in knowledge. Build all instruction around problems to be solved. Use "tips from the experts" to present key ideas and skills.

**Provide exercises and feedback.**  Use powerful, free-play simulations that allow technicians to think through many different problems. Demonstrate the impact of their decisions on time, cost, and mission readiness. Then show them how their thinking process compares to an expert's approach.

**Provide remediation.**  Encourage technicians to experience the simulations over and over, until their thinking process has captured the power of the expert's approach.

**Treatment.**  Use red-white-and-blue borders and icons based on aviation themes. Use a rock-music theme at all transition points and "under" key attitude messages. Use "expert" mentors to provide continuity and credibility. Design and use a limited number of screen layouts across all courses to enhance consistency and learner "comfort" with the instruction.

**Outcomes.**  Over 220 hours of interactive instruction, delivered on-time and within budget. Hundreds of learners have been exposed to the instruction in pilot implementations. Attitude rankings by learners are very high. System knowledge improved by an average of about 35 percent among both experts and novices taking the courses. Ability to accurately troubleshoot aircraft breakdowns increased by nearly 80 percent across all courses, all audiences. Transfer of training to the flight line, and changes in overall performance, are currently being tracked. Initial indications are very positive. This series of courses was awarded the prestigious 1993 "Nebby" award for best interactive multimedia training in military/government, as well as other awards.

## Alyeska berth operations center emergency training
(see Fig. 13.5)

**The problem.**  While the chance of an emergency along the Alaskan Pipeline and at the docks (berth) in Valdez is remote, the potential impact of such an emergency is great—as shown by the *Exxon Valdez* oil spill in recent years. Yet the ability to train personnel in emergency preparedness is limited, since they cannot afford to shut down the pipeline for even a few minutes a year. The problem was how to create realistic, powerful simulations that would test technicians' abilities to quickly and properly respond to emergencies.

**Analysis.**  Content analysis was performed through the same techniques previously described for the Air Force project, including "cognitive task analysis." We were able to capture the "mental maps" of system experts and the "best practices" procedures for dealing with emergencies. The audience analysis showed that these Alaskan technicians were rugged individualists who disliked "hype and fluff" and wanted to get their hands on their systems to test their abilities. They did not want lots of tutorials or "commercials" for management, or any other "frills." They simply wanted to have the knowl-

**Figure 13.5**  Alyeska Pipeline operations training course.

edge, confidence, and skill to deal with emergencies well. They were of all ages and backgrounds, with one common love: Alaska.

### Strategies

**Establish relevance and motivate.**  Put learners in a simulated emergency situation immediately and test their ability to respond, providing helpful feedback along the way. Use graphics, animations, sounds to recreate the tension of the environment.

**Allow for practice.**  Use powerful, free-play simulations that allow technicians to think through many different problems. Demonstrate the impact of their decisions on time and cost. Then show them how their thinking process compares to an expert's approach.

**Provide enrichment.**  Allow technicians to record their scores for the simulations and compare them to others'.

**Treatment.**  Use cool Alaskan colors and images for borders, menus, and icons, including the "midnight sun," float planes, etc. Use lifelike graphics and animations to provide as realistic an environment as possible. Make the user interface as lifelike as possible by allowing learners to touch "real" buttons, read gauges, move in any direction, etc.

**Outcomes.**   One emergency training course is now installed along the pipeline and is in active use by the operators. This Berth Operations course is now in pilot-test and the design, based on simulations with remedial instruction based on simulation performance, has been well received by all technicians. They become very excited during the simulations and enjoy competing for time/cost productivity. Learner confidence in ability to handle emergencies is now higher.

## In Closing, I'd Like to Thank You...

So, who are you, and what's in this for you? If you are still reading, you must be both disciplined and patient (or an insomniac?). In any case, thank you. I want this chapter to make a difference for you, and more importantly, for the learners in your care and keeping. To make optimal learning happen, we all have to grasp the broader vision. We have to care about real results in terms of people who change and perform better, faster, cheaper. Once again, that is very difficult, and all the tempest about us would have us focus elsewhere, it seems. In *Open Boat,* Stephen Crane wrote one of the best first lines ever to open a short story:

None of them knew the color of the sky.

He went on to immerse the reader in the message:

None of them knew the color of the sky.
Their eyes glanced level, and were fastened upon the waves that
swept toward them. These waves were of the hue of slate, save
for the tops, which were of foaming white,
and all of the men knew the colors of the sea.
The horizon narrowed and widened, and dipped and rose,
and at all times its edge was jagged with waves...
most wrongfully and barbarously abrupt and tall,
and each froth-top was a problem in small boat navigation.

Indeed, it is very hard for us to notice the sky when the storm rages around us. Navigation on the "sea" of training, especially multimedia training, is becoming increasingly difficult. Many would have you focus on bits and bytes, graphic resolutions and bandwidths, CD-I and DVI and MMCD and WHONOSWHAT. Others would lead you into the desert of content-contentedness. Amidst this tempest, the temptation—indeed, the *requirement*—is to focus at least some attention on the waves. However, real success—real *results*—demand that you pay *additional* attention to the sky. The color of the sky, the big picture, the *audience* will guide the boat and instill the needed courage into the sailors. The audience will help us to focus on what really counts, if we give them the chance. The rewards are real, and ultimately essential to our success both as individuals and as an "industry."

Thank you for listening, whoever you are. At least you now know *who* is on first!

## Bibliography

Crane, Stephen, "The Open Boat," in *The "Secret Sharer" and Other Great Stories,* Abraham H. Lass and Norma L. Tasman, eds., New American Library, New York, pp. 217–218.

Dick, Walter and Lou Carey, *The Systematic Design of Instruction,* 3d ed, Harper Collins, New York, 1990.

Gagné, Robert M., *The Conditions of Learning,* 2d ed, Holt, Rinehart and Winston, New York, 1970.

Mager, Robert F., *Making Instruction Work,* David S. Lake Publishers, Belmont, CA, 1988.

Merrill, M. David, Zhongmin Li, and Mark K. Jones, "Second Generation Instructional Design," *Educational Technology,* September 1989.

# 14

# CD-ROM and Its Impact on Education

**Susan Kinnell**

**Pam Berger**

## Introduction

CD-ROM, which stands for compact disc–read only memory, is an optical technology used for the storage of and the gaining access to large amounts of information on a plastic 12-centimeter disc. This information can be read and subsequently used in a number of ways, but not altered on the disc in any way. (Although newer technological developments are under way for discs that can be erased and/or rewritten.)

The capacity for storage on a CD-ROM is impressive—over 650 Mbytes of data. That's the equivalent of 300,000 printed pages, one million library catalog cards, one hour of sound, or 15,000 graphic images. Because the discs are small and relatively indestructible, they have become very practical for use in schools.

This technology was first announced in 1983, a development of Philips and Sony. The first commercially available disc was BiblioFile, which was issued in 1985. Later in 1985, a group of industry leaders met at the High Sierra Casino and Hotel in Lake Tahoe, California, for the purpose of setting standards for the structural organization of files and data on a CD-ROM. This became known as the High Sierra standard, and subsequently it was amended slightly and formalized by the International Standards Organization as ISO 9660. Virtually every disc since that time has met those standards and is thus playable and usable on a variety of CD-ROM drives.

The first CD-ROM product for the school market was Grolier's Electronic Encyclopedia, which was announced in 1986 and became available along with Microsoft's Bookshelf in 1987.

In 1987, there were approximately 120 titles available for use on any type of CD-ROM drive. Fifty percent of these were indexing and abstract databases, priced in the $1000 to $3000 range. By 1989 there were more than 500 commercially available titles, and prices were beginning to come down to from $500 to $2000. Forty-five percent of the discs were source databases containing full-text, numeric data, or computer programs.

As of 1993 the number of available titles has grown to almost 4000, and the price range is from $20 to $3000. No longer are the majority of titles print-based; no longer are the choices limited to just a few resources specifically for schools. As the number of CD-ROM titles produced multiplies dramatically each year, the number of these available for schools increases proportionally. According to a recent survey by University Microfilm Inc., within the next two years 85 percent of school libraries are likely to be using CD-ROM, as compared with just 25 percent in 1987.

## How CD-ROM Works

### The disc

A standard CD-ROM is physically composed of three layers: a clear polycarbonate substrate layer, a metal layer, and an acrylic layer. Polycarbonate is used for strength and rigidity (it is the same material that's used for bulletproofing). Aluminum is used for the metal layer, and a clear acrylic material is used for the top layer where the label and company information are printed.

The data on a disc are encoded and stored on a disc in the form of "pits" and "lands." Pits are depressions or hollows in the metal, and lands are perfectly flat areas. A laser beam reflects off the flat areas and is detected by the sensors in the drive. The light shining on the pits is deflected sideways, or defused so that it cannot be detected by the sensors. This pattern of nonreflective and reflective areas on the disc is interpreted by the drive circuitry as a pattern of 0's and 1's, and is thus translatable into machine language as binary code.

The focal plane of the laser is directly on the metal layer of the disc, so any scratches or marks on the polycarbonate should not interfere with the readings from the sensors. The pits and lands on a disc are on a single spiral track that is less than one one-hundredth the width of a human hair. If unwound, this track would be almost 4 miles long.

The disc, unlike a magnetic disk in a hard drive, spins at a varying rate of speed, called *constant linear velocity*. A magnetic disk, spinning at the same rate of speed (*constant angular velocity*), has tracks near the edge of the disk that are moving faster than tracks near the center. The sectors on these tracks must then be of bigger size to hold the same amount of data as the slower-moving sectors on the tracks at the center of the disk. The critical point is that the data must all pass the read head at the same speed. The sectors on an optical disc are all of equal size, which allows for many more sectors on any given disc. The tradeoff is less storage and more speed (of access and transfer) on a magnetic disk, and more storage and less speed on an optical disc.

**The drive**

Within the CD-ROM drive are various components and circuits:

- A small motor that spins the disc
- A laser that projects a beam of light onto the disc
- A detector that reads the reflected light from the disc
- A prism that deflects the reflected light onto a light-sensing diode
- A circuit that reads the voltages generated by the diode

When the disc is spinning in the drive, a detector is positioned to receive the reflected light from the laser beam. This detector moves to that part of the disc being read. The motor spins the disc at a varying rate of speed called constant linear velocity (as just noted), so that no matter which part of the disc is being read, it is spinning at exactly the same rate over the detector.

The reflected light from the lands (and the absence of reflected light from the pits) is deflected onto a light-sensing diode. Each pulse of reflected light generates a tiny electrical current in the diode, which is then passed on to the computer as a stream of 1's. These 1's are interspersed with 0's, which represent the places where no light was reflected.

Speed of access is one of the important criteria for a CD-ROM drive. When a CD-ROM disc is in the drive, the user searches for a piece of information on that disc by putting in a search query, by clicking on a button, or by typing in a word. There is a delay while the light on the drive goes on and the motor hums, and then finally the response to the query appears on the computer screen. How fast the drive finds the requested information and gets to its exact location on the disc is its *access time. Transfer time* is the amount of time it takes for that information to be transferred to the computer screen. The access time for today's new drives ranges between 200 and 380 milliseconds. Note that for this measure, the smaller number is better; that is, the fewer number of milliseconds it takes to access the data, the better. (Remember, CD-ROM drives are not fast by other standards in the computer world. A hard-disk drive accesses information in 15 to 50 milliseconds.)

Transfer time is measured differently on a CD-ROM drive than access time. Transfer time is measured by how many kilobytes of information are passed from the disc to the computer per second. This is called "kilobytes per second," or kbps. For many years the industry norm was 150 kbps, but in late 1992 and early 1993 there were many new drives introduced in the market that were rated at more than 300 kbps. Rumor has it that by mid-1994 there will be 600-kbps drives readily available, at similar prices to today's 300-kbps drives.

Remember that for transfer speed, the bigger number is better—more data gets passed from the disc to the computer faster. This is slow by other computer standards: the transfer rate of a hard drive is 600 to 2000 kbps.

The newer type of disc drives, called *double-speed, double-spin,* or "MultiSpin" (a NEC trademark), have the ability to transfer data from the disc to the computer at two different speeds. Audio data is sent at 150 kbytes per second (kbps), while video and graphics are transferred at 300 + kbps. This is a different measure of speed than the varying rate at which the disc is spinning in the drive, and should not be confused with that speed or the speed of access.

During the latter part of 1992, Eastman Kodak unveiled its new PhotoCD system. With this system, slide film is developed and the images placed on a compact disc called PhotoCD, using Kodak's proprietary process. A revolutionary aspect of this new process is its ability to store subsequent groups of images on the same disc. These discs, with multiple groups of images stored at various times, are called *multisession* discs. The images on the disc can then be viewed on a television monitor using a CD player, either Kodak's own player or any of the newer players or drives that are designated "PhotoCD-compatible." These drives are called *CD-ROM XA*—the XA stands for "eXtended Architecture." While all such CD-ROM drives will read a PhotoCD, some of them are rated for single-session compatibility and others for multisession compatibility. The difference is that multisession CD-ROM drives can read those PhotoCDs to which more than one group of images has been added.

The single-session drives can only read a PhotoCD's first group of images. This has a lot of ramifications for long-term school use—school pictures, yearbooks, and the like.

### The computer

Essentially CD-ROM provides the capability to access very large storage files, with the added benefit of being able to change the information in those large files by simply changing the disc in the drive. The kind of computer attached to the drive will determine to some extent the kind of CD-ROM usable in the drive, and how fast its information can be accessed. If the computer is a vintage 8088 machine (the old PC XT model), the fastest CD-ROM drive on the market will not function at its best levels. If the computer monitor is not a high-resolution monitor, preferably in color, a great deal of the visual excitement of CD-ROM will be lost. If there is no added sound board in the IBM-compatible type of machine, then the audio files on the CD-ROM will be silent. If there is a small amount of RAM (working, temporary storage in the computer), then the computer may not even be able to handle the CD-ROM at all.

There are some minimum requirements for running certain kinds of discs. Clearly if it is a text-based disc, an older and slower machine without sound and color will be able to handle it. However, if there are graphics, video sequences, audio files, or animation as well as text, then the computer behind the CD-ROM drive also has to have certain capabilities.

The Multimedia PC Marketing Council in Washington, D.C., established a level of minimum hardware requirements in an effort to standardize what people would need to be able to run a certain kind of multimedia disc. In May of 1993, they announced a second level of minimum requirements that extends the original list and also provides recommendations for maximum performance. Any CD-ROM that carries the label *MPC,* or now carries the label *MPC Level 2,* will run only on machines that meet those minimum requirements. The new MPC Level 2 minimum requirements are:

- A computer with 4-Mbyte RAM, 25 MHz, 486SX, and a 160-Mbyte hard drive

- A CD-ROM drive with 300-kbps sustained transfer rate, maximum average seek time 400 milliseconds, CD-ROM XA-ready, multisession-capable

- A sound board with 16-bit digital sound, 8-note synthesizer, and MIDI playback

- A video display with 640 × 480 resolution and 65,536 colors

- Ports for MIDI input/output, and a joystick.

### The software

**On the computer.** The next element to consider in connecting a CD-ROM drive to a computer is the software that enables that connection. If the drive were simply plugged into the computer's SCSI port (or, in some cases, to a serial port), the computer would have no internal instructions that would help it recognize the device or understand how to communicate with it. Those instructions come in the form of software, usually a single floppy disk, that is loaded in with the other operating system software.

If the machine attached to the drive is a Macintosh, then the process is simply one of copying four or five basic files onto the System folder. If the machine is IBM or IBM-compatible, then the enabling software is called *MSCDEX,* which stands for Microsoft Compact Disc Extensions. These are extension files for DOS, the internal disk-operating system. DOS can only recognize a file up to a certain size; most CD-ROM files are considerably larger than that. A statement is added to both the AUTOEXEC.BAT and the CONFIG.SYS files so that the computer will look for and recognize the presence of the CD-ROM drive when it is started up. There is also an application start-up file, which is simply a file that tells the computer how to start the CD-ROM application.

**To search the disc.** The second kind of software is supplied with the disc to enable the user to search the disc or access the programs, files, or information on the disc. Sometimes this search software is accessed straight from the disc, and sometimes it is recommended that the software be copied from the disc to the hard drive. This approach lets the speed and power of the computer run the search software, so the CD-ROM drive only has to deal with accessing and transferring the information from the disc.

**On the disc itself (dataware).**   The information that is encoded on the actual disc has been called "dataware." Since this data takes many forms—text, illustrations and pictures, audio, video, and animation, for example—how it is physically placed on the disc can have some impact on the efficiency of the search software in finding the information on the disc. The capability to search the disc also takes many forms: single words may be searched; lists of topics or subject headings may be browsed; menus can be utilized; words can be located in relationship to other words or in their context; parts of words may be searched, with a whole variety of possibilities as a search result.

This whole process takes place when the disc is first created, or mastered. Databases of information, files of pictures or sounds, sequences of video or animation—whatever forms the data take are loaded into an authoring system. This system organizes the information according to the ISO standards, creates indexes of all the words, their relationships and contexts, filters out problems and misleading data, and arranges the final files, folders, directories, lists, pointers, flags and tags, and everything the authors can think of that will make the job of locating information on the disc easier for the user. In addition, error detection and correction routines are added to the file so that no mistakes will arise out of the disc's information.

Once the final version of the material has been settled and the master disc has been made, it is then replicated as many times as needed. Each disc is a perfect copy of the original file and contains the exact material as authored and indexed.

## The network

One of the most exciting developments in the CD-ROM world is the enhanced ability to include CD-ROM on any given network. Although it is not yet feasible to network a fully multimedia disc (full-motion video is not yet networkable), networking of most CD-ROMs is both possible and desirable.

One of the main problems with a CD-ROM collection is the limited access to a particular product. For example, if the school library holds a 21-volume encyclopedia, it is possible for 21 different students to access that encyclopedia at the same time. (Not at all likely, since they would be looking for similar information a majority of times, but possible.) The same encyclopedia on a single CD-ROM would not provide as much access, therefore, as the print version. But by making that encyclopedia available on a network, with multiple workstations in various areas, many more students could access the same information. Since it is also likely that the research process will be speeded up on the CD-ROM, the number of students who can use the disc will be close to, if not equal to, the number of students using the print version.

Along with the computer, CD-ROM drive, and shared access software (such as MSCDEX provides), the requirements for networking CD-ROM fall into two categories, hardware and software. The hardware is a network interface card (NIC) that goes into every computer on the network. The kind of interface card will determine the kind of network, such as star, ring, tree, line, etc. These physical arrangements of computers linked to each other with cabling are called the *topology* or *architecture* of a network. The architecture also determines the speed of the data being transmitted between workstations.

The software required is a *network operating system (NOS)*. This works in conjunction with the computer's individual operating system to enable it to recognize the network and the individual protocols for sending and receiving data along the network. Also required is the *host* or *server* software, which enables it to store and regulate the sharing of files or programs by members of the network.

Each networking situation is different and depends on the number and location of the computers, as well as the age and capacity of those machines.

## Management of CD-ROM in Schools and Libraries

CD-ROM is having a major impact on school and academic libraries. The depth and breath of its influence will come as a surprise to some people, especially those who are accustomed to the idea of research and information resources as being primarily print-based.

This relatively new technology is changing how business is carried out in school libraries and dramatically impacting library management and collection development, in addition to the instruction program and the curriculum of each school. Journal articles, conference presentations, and discussions with library media specialists all reveal not only ardent acceptance of CD-ROM, but a dawning awareness of some underlying problems and issues pertaining to CD-ROM's use and integration in schools.

Some of the issues that must be addressed by school library media centers fall into the following major categories:

1. Needs assessment and technology planning

2. Equipment decision making

3. Staff development and training issues

4. Collection development

5. Budgeting

Issues such as these are being explored at national conferences, such as the Databases in Schools Conference, professional literature such as *School Library Media Quarterly* and the *Information Searcher,* and even on the Internet in School Library Media and Network Communications listserve, "LM_NET." As these issues are addressed and resolved, the full impact of CD-ROM technology on student learning will be better realized.

## Impact of CD-ROM on Students

The impact of CD-ROM technology on students is different from that on the administration, faculty, and staff. Students will be approaching CD-ROM as a source of information, as a tool for learning, as a reference or guide to other sources, and as a source of entertainment. Where they use the discs will depend on the school's facilities and arrangements. How they use the discs, and the results (both short- and long-term) they get, will depend on a number of other factors.

First of all, the success a student has in using a CD-ROM will depend in large measure on his or her familiarity with computers. Keyboarding, the use of function keys, understanding screen appearance, file management, and manual/visual dexterity are all part of the preliminary skills a student must have to succeed with CD-ROM.

Second, a student needs to understand the concepts of searching or using an electronic database, such as that found on a particular CD-ROM. Although students usually don't like to be instructed in the use of CD-ROM, preferring instead to explore by trial and error, it has been found that the very scope and size of the database causes it to elude the explorer. The depth of the sub-ject material on the disc is not visually obvious to students, and they are therefore not aware of what they may or may not have missed in their research. In this case, practice does not make perfect. In fact, practice itself often is precluded because of the limited number of machines, sometimes the large number of students, and the limited time per student that is available for searching.

Therefore instruction of some kind is almost always necessary, and that brings up a whole variety of further issues: what kind of training (individual or group)? where and when? on individual CD-ROMs, or by sort/type of CD-ROM? and so on. Further, it has been shown that students at the secondary level who have received no skills training in searching electronic databases—training that will certainly be of great use to them in their college years—do not understand the complexities of such searches.

With regard to Bloom's Taxonomy, a scale of learning that ranges from simple identification through comparison and up to evaluation and synthesis, the CD-ROM search process ranks quite high. For students, there is no longer a feeling that simple identification and reiteration is enough; the chal-lenge to find different sources, more material, and then evaluate those sources leads to a higher order of thinking skills and more active learning processes. There is an increase in student achievement with a corresponding decrease in student frustration, both of which will find favor with teachers, librarians, and parents.

The final issue is one that has wider scope than just using or not using CD-ROM. Today's generation of students is visually oriented, from lifelong expo-sure to television, movies, videos, video games, and the like. Attempting to teach low-motivated students with traditional print sources may prove diffi-cult, and will meet with increasing resistance and frustration.

## A Look at the Future

The future is bright for CD-ROM in schools. The incredible expansion in the number of available titles, the developments in hardware and networking, and the reliability of the medium itself mean that more and more schools will be turning to CD-ROM. The market really picked up speed when some kind of a breakeven point was reached—there were enough discs being published to make further hardware development feasible, and there were enough drives around to make publishing discs a profitable enterprise. Once that point had been reached, an enormous spurt of growth took place, with internal CD-ROM drives being included with new computers and with new discs being published every day and week. Developments in miniaturization along with increases in speed will bring machines that are easier to use and portable; chip and processor developments will continue to drive prices lower and make the technology more and more affordable. As this happens, more machines will be found in homes, and that will greatly encourage the use of CD-ROM in education.

With the accompanying proliferation of titles, teachers, librarians, and parents will be able to evaluate a wide number of discs, selecting only those that best meet their criteria. No longer will they be forced to buy the *only* disc on the market, but rather be enabled to buy the *best* disc.

As more and more schools turn to electronic resources—computers, disk-based materials, optical materials, and on-line resources—the result will be more and more students fluent in the use of computers to assist them in their studying, research, and schoolwork.

# 15

# A Discussion of Standards

## Jessica Keyes

## Introduction

As a whole, standards are technical documents, most quite lengthy, that make for dry reading. This chapter will serve as an introduction to the current standards-based terminology that the multimedia developer should have a passing knowledge of. It is presented in an alphabetical glossary format.

## The Standards

**AVI** (audio video interleave). This particular technology was developed by Microsoft for its Video for Windows products. Although hardware is required for video capture, AVI requires no special hardware for playback.

**CD** (as explained by Andrew Davidson of Philips Interactive Media of America to a Compuserve forum). In the beginning, there was CD-DA (compact disc–digital audio), or standard music CDs. CD-DA begat CD-ROM when people realized that you could store a whole bunch of computer data on a 12-centimer optical disc (650 Mbytes). CD-ROM drives are simply another kind of digital storage media for computers, albeit read-only. They are peripherals, just like hard disks and floppy drives. (Incidentally, the convention is that when referring to *magnetic* media, it is spelled "dis*k*." Optical media such as CDs, laserdiscs, and all the other formats I'm about to explain are spelled "dis*c*.")

*CD-I (compact disc–interactive)* came next. This is a consumer electronics format that uses the optical disc in combination with a computer to provide a home entertainment system that delivers music, graphics, text, animation, and video in the living room. Unlike a CD-ROM drive, a CD-I player is a stand-alone system that requires no external computer. It plugs directly into a TV and stereo system and comes with a remote control to allow the user to interact with software programs sold on discs. It looks and feels much like a CD player, except that you get images as well as music out of it and you can actively control what you see and hear. In fact it is a CD-DA player, and all of your standard music CDs will play on a CD-I player; there is just no video in that case.

Next came *CD-ROM-XA (eXtended Architecture)*. Now we go back to computer peripherals—a CD-ROM drive, but with some of the compressed audio capabilities found in a CD-I player (called *ADPCM*). This allows interleaving of audio and other data so that an XA drive can simultaneously play audio and display pictures (or other things). There is special hardware in an XA drive controller to handle the audio playback. This format arose from the industry's desire to inject some of the features of CD-I back into the professional market.

Now along comes the idea from Kodak for *Photo CD*—digital pictures on compact disc. They teamed up with Philips to develop the standard for Photo CD discs. At this point a new problem enters the picture, if you'll pardon the expression. All of the disc formats mentioned so far are read-only; there is no way for anyone but the producer of one of these discs to store his/her own content on the disc—that is, to write to it. But there already existed a technology called *WORM (Write Once, Read Many times)*. This is an optical disc that can be written to, but exactly *once*. You can "burn" data on it, but once burned the data cannot be erased, although it can then be used like a CD-ROM disc and read forever. (Depending on your definition of *forever*, of course.)

CD-ROM, CD-ROM-XA, and CD-I discs are normally "mastered" as opposed to burned. That means that one master copy is made and then hundreds, or thousands, or millions (if you're lucky enough to need that many) of replicates (or replicants, if you're a *Blade Runner* fan) are pressed from the master. For quantities above a few dozen or so, this process is much cheaper than burning. Generally, disc-pressing plants can handle all of these formats, as the underlying technology is the same; the only differences are in the data and in the disc format.

The reason that WORM technology was critical to the formulation of Photo CD is obvious: the content of these discs is not determined by the manufacturer or publisher. For Photo CD, each disc will be different—a roll or a few rolls of film per disc from a customer.

Kodak and Philips wanted Photo CD discs to be playable on both computer peripherals for desktop publishing uses *and* on a consumer device for home viewing. For the former, CD-ROM-XA was chosen as a carrier, and for the latter both CD-I, which had already been designed as a consumer electronics device, and dedicated Photo CD players. This desire for a hybrid disc, or one with multiplatform compatibility, led to the development of the "CD-I Bridge" disc format. A Bridge disc is one that is readable on both a CD-I player and a CD-ROM-XA drive.

This Bridge format is the reason there is so much confusion about CD-

ROM drives for Photo CD. A drive that supports Photo CD must be a CD-ROM-XA drive that is also Bridge-compatible. (The technical description of Bridge discs calls for supporting certain kinds of sectors identified by "form" and "mode" bits, which is what you usually hear instead of the "Bridge" disc label.) That almost completes the picture, except for the concept of *sessions*.

Although a WORM disc can be written to only once, it is not necessary to write, or burn, the entire disc all at once. You can burn the disc initially with, say, a few hundred megabytes of data, then go back later and burn some more data onto it. Of course, each burn must be to a virgin part of the disc; once a spot on the disc has been burned, it cannot be reburned. Each burn operation is referred to as a *session,* and a drive or disc that supports this multiple burning operation is referred to as being *multisession-capable.*

Originally, all WORMs were single-session only. That is, you could not go back and add data to a WORM disc once it had been burned, even if it was not full. For Photo CD, they wanted the consumer to be able to add more pictures to an existing disc as additional rolls of film were processed. So the extension of WORM technology to multisession use was developed and adopted for the Bridge disc format. This required hardware changes to CD-ROM-XA drives, and that is why there are a fair number of single-session XA drives on the market and more and more multisession ones appearing.

A single-session drive can read a multisession disc, but it can only read the contents of the first session that was burned. Incidentally, all Philips CD-I players are multisession, although all current CD-I discs have only a single session on them. (Generally, being mastered means a single session, although it is possible to master a multisession disc. I don't know of any software that currently supports this, however.)

**CD-audio.**  See Redbook audio.

**CD-Bridge.**  Digital data may be written in any one of a number of logical formats such as CD-Audio, ISO 9660, XA, CD-I. The CD-Bridge format conforms to both the CD-I and CD-ROM-XA specifications. This format assigns two separate disc label locations, allowing a CD-ROM-XA track to be played on a CD-I player. Kodak Photo CD discs are CD-Bridge discs, and thus can be played on CD-ROM-XA drives or on CD-I players.

**CD-I** (the Green Book, as described by Lucy Lediaev, Manager of Developer Services for Philips Interactive Media of America).  The "CD-I Full Functional Specification" (commonly known as "the Green Book") is a comprehensive and detailed description of the standards for compact disc–interactive hardware, operating systems, and software. CD-I technology is licensed by Philips and Sony Corporation, and the Green Book is published by the two companies to assure worldwide adherence to a single standard for this licensed technology. The Green Book describes a "base-case" player that is the target for CD-I software developed all over the world. A base-case player contains the minimum set of functions that assures adherence to the CD-I standard. The Green Book also describes extensions to the base case, such as full-screen, full-motion video (FMV).

In the United States, the Green Book is available to prospective CD-I developers from the CD-I Association of North America (301-444-6613). CD-I licensees receive the Green Book as part of the licensing process. For information on licensing CD-I technology, or for more information regarding policies governing distribution and use of the Green Book, contact:

Bert Gall
Coordination Office for Optical and
  Magnetic Media Systems
Philips CEC
PO Box 80002, Building SWA1
5600 JB Eindhoven
The Netherlands
Telephone  + 31 40 726409
Fax:  + 31 40 732113

**CD-ROM.**  The Yellow Book—ISO 10149:1989. See also CD-ROM-XA.

**CD-ROM-XA.**  The major problem with first-generation CD-ROM technology is its inefficiency in dealing with multiple data types. With CD-ROM, different data types such as video, graphics, text, and video need to reside in different files on the CD-ROM. The result is increased access time, as the drive must seek data in multiple disk locations.

Standard CD-ROM is a two-step process, First, graphics, video, and text files are loaded into RAM. Second, the information in RAM is sent to the display adapter while the drive accesses and plays back the audio file. Not only does this slow down the access time, but this process relies on large RAM buffers.

CD-ROM-XA (XA stands for eXtended Architecture) is considered the next generation of CD-ROM technology, since it solves the problems discussed above. XA uses a technology known as *interleaving* that allows audio, video, graphics, and text to be combined together in a single file. CD-ROM-XA was developed by Sony, Philips, and Microsoft in 1989. Many others such as Kodak, IBM, Toshiba, are following suit.

Each of the separate multimedia elements is divided into a number of smaller packets, which are then intermixed into a single interleaved file as shown in Fig. 15.1. Although data packets can be arranged in any way, the packets themselves are organized in repeating synchronized patterns. Each data packet is approximately 2.3K and comprises $\frac{1}{75}$ of a second of playback time.

Reading information from the CD-ROM is a process known as *streaming*. Here the packets are reassembled and output to the display adapter or speakers. Because all the data on an CD-ROM-XA is synchronized, it appears as if all video and audio data is being played simultaneously.

To achieve this degree of precision, CD-ROM-XA uses ADPCM (Adaptive Differential Pulse Code Modulation) compression. ADPCM enables a compression ratio of up to 16 to 1 depending on the sampling rate and audio level. The following listing shows what is possible.

**Figure 15.1**   Streaming: synchronized audio and video.

|            | Sampling rate | Compression | Hours |
|------------|---------------|-------------|-------|
| B-Stereo   | 37.8 kHz      | 4:1         | 4+    |
| B-Mono     | 37.8 kHz      | 8:1         | 9+    |
| C-Stereo   | 18.9 kHz      | 8:1         | 9+    |
| C-Mono     | 18.9 kHz      | 16:1        | 18+   |

*Note:* B audio is equivalent to FM sound; C is equivalent to AM.

CD-ROM-XA can contain any data type, including:

8- and 16-bit bitmaps, and motion video

Compression video such as JPEG, MPEG, and INDEO

Text

Binary executable code

Data

PCM and ADPCM audio

A single interleaved CD-ROM-XA file that is pressed onto a disc as a continuous track is called a *stream*. While the length of a stream can vary, the
maximum length is the length of the CD-ROM itself: 74 minutes. When playing back the CD-ROM from an XA drive, the data packets from the disc are
split apart in real time, with the audio components being routed to a digital-
to-audio converter and all the image data (video, graphics, and text) routed to
the display adapter. In essence, streaming ensures that each audio and video
packet reaches its destination in a synchronized manner, affording the user
of the CD-ROM a seamless viewing and listening experience.

There are two other advantages as well. Since there is no waiting for files
to preload, playback is immediate. And since it requires neither a large RAM
buffer nor a disk cache, use of CD-ROM-XA requires less system resources.

**CDTV.** This is Commodore's entry into the home-based CD-ROM market. Its competitors are both CD-I and VIS.

**COSE** (common open software environment). A loosely affiliated grouping of Unix product vendors, including IM, HP, Sun, SCO, Novell, and USL, whose goal is to develop a common desktop environment (CDE). Once CDE is in place, portable Unix-based multimedia will be possible.

The elements of this emerging standard are as follows:

Based on motif

A front panel, based on Hewlett Packard's VUE, for storage of commonly used tools and icons

Windows management, object and folder management, and tools for basic administrative tasks such as interapplication communications and message passing

Personal productivity tools such as clock, note pad, text editor, and mail front end

**DVI** (digital video–interactive). Hardware and software vendors (including IBM and Intel) got together and standardized on a hardware/software combination that yields very high compression ratios (up to 150:1) and smoother playback, since it plays back full-color motion video at 30 frames per second. When it ties in with a mainframe computer, DVI playback approaches the quality of broadcast video.

DVI is a proprietary, programmable, compression/decompression technology based on the Intel i750 chip set. This hardware consists of two VLSI (very-large-scale integrated) components to separate the image-processing and display functions.

Two levels of compression/decompression are provided. Production-level video (PLV) is a proprietary asymmetrical compression technique for encoding full-motion color video. It requires that compression be performed either by Intel at its facilities or at licensed encoding facilities set up by Intel. Real-time video (RTV) provides image quality comparable to frame-rate (motion) JPEG and uses a symmetrical, variable-rate compression. PLV and RTV both use variable compression rates.

**Gold Sound Standard Council.** Founded in 1992 by a group of sound-card vendors (Ad-Lib Multimedia Inc., Cardinal Technologies, Inc., CPS, Focus Information Systems, Inc., and Yamaha Corp. of America), this group's goal is to promote an open audio standard so that sound-card developers will need to write only one set of drivers for DOS and one for Windows. Even if the group is successful, the standard it creates will be competing against the popular de facto standards created by Creative Labs' Sound Blaster and Microsoft's Windows Sound System. The council can be reached via Yamaha in San Jose, CA, at 800-543-7457.

**Green Book.** See CD-I.

**High Sierra Standard.**  Developed by a group of systems manufacturers and CD-ROM publishers at a 1984 meeting at the High Sierra Hotel in Lake Tahoe, this standard has been absorbed by the ISO 9660 standard.

**JPEG** (Joint Photographic Experts Group).  A compression standard for still images. JPEG compresses at about 20:1 before the image is visibly degraded. JPEG also compresses rather slowly: about 1 to 3 seconds for a 1-Mbyte image, depending on the computer.

JPEG uses a technique known as *lossy compression*. As its name implies, data is lost during the compression process, which is accomplished algorithmically. JPEG breaks the image down into smaller, more manageable blocks, compresses the block, and then moves on to the next. What this enables is compression-on-the-fly and much higher compression rates (up to 20:1), compared to typical text compression ratios, which hover in the area of 3:1.

**MPEG** (Motion Picture Experts Group).  A compression standard for video (motion) images. MPEG can deliver decompressed data at 1.2 to 1.5 Mbytes per second. This allows CD players to play full-motion color movies at 30 frames per second. MPEG compresses at about a 150:1 ratio before degradation, although rates as high as 200:1 are attainable.

The Moving Picture Experts Group achieved its milestone of defining the MPEG-2 Video Main Profile. In its work toward developing a multichannel audio-coding standard, MPEG made important progress by merging several previous proposals into a single unified proposal. In its work on the MPEG-2 Systems Standard, MPEG created an initial specification for multiplexing multiple audio, video, and data streams into a single stream so as to meet the transmission, storage, and access requirements of many applications.

These achievements signal the convergence of such diverse industries as broadcast (including cable, satellite, and terrestrial), telecommunications, entertainment, and computing to a single worldwide, digital, video-coding standard for a wide range of resolutions, including TV and HDTV.

**MPEG-2 Video.**  A developing international standard that will specify the coded bit-stream for high-quality digital video. MPEG-2 Video builds on the success of the completed MPEG-1 Video Standard (ISO/IEC IS 11172-2) by additionally supporting interlaced video formats, increased image quality, and a number of other advanced features, including features to support HDTV. MPEG-2 Main Profile is a compatible extension of MPEG-1, meaning that an MPEG-2 Video decoder can decode MPEG-1 bit-streams. Also like MPEG-1, MPEG-2 can support interoperability with the CCITT H.261 video telephony standard.

As a generic international standard, MPEG-2 Video is being defined in terms of extensible profiles, each of which will support the features needed by an important class of applications. Among the applications supported by the Main Profile will be digital video transmission in the range of about 2 to 15 Mbits per second over cable, satellite, and other broadcast channels, enabling exciting new consumer video services. Because the MPEG-2 Video Main

Profile can be implemented at reasonable cost using today's technology, it will be possible to introduce these services by early 1994. With the Main Profile now defined, manufacturers can complete their initial MPEG-2 Video encoder and decoder designs. Some manufacturers expect prototypes to be operational by mid-1993. Another feature of the Main Profile is support for several picture-aspect ratios, including 4:3, 16:9, and others.

The development of further profiles is already well under way. The collaboration between MPEG and the CCIR is bearing fruit with the definition of an hierarchical profile, which extends the features of the Main Profile. This profile is well suited to applications such as terrestrial broadcasting, which may require multilevel coding. For example, this system could give the consumer the option of using either a small portable receiver to decode standard-definition TV, or a larger fixed receiver to decode HDTV from the same broadcast signal.

**MPEG-2 Audio.**  MPEG is developing the MPEG-2 Audio Standard for multichannel audio coding, which will be compatible with the existing MPEG-1 Audio Standard (ISO/IEC IS 11172-3). MPEG-2 audio-coding will supply up to five full bandwidth channels (left, right, center, and two surround channels), plus an additional low-frequency-enhancement channel, and/or up to seven commentary/multilingual channels. This week in Sydney, MPEG merged several proposals from the November 1992 London MPEG meeting into a unified specification. In its audio work, MPEG is collaborating with the CCIR to conduct subjective tests of the proposed multichannel system.

The MPEG-2 Audio Standard also will provide improved quality coding of mono and conventional stereo signals for bit-rates at or below 64 kbits per second per channel.

**MPEG-2 Systems.**  The MPEG-2 Systems Standard will specify how to combine multiple audio, video, and private-data streams into a single multiplexed stream, allowing for the transmission, storage, access, and retrieval of the original streams, while maintaining accurate synchronization. MPEG-2 Systems will be targeted at a wider range of applications than the MPEG-1 Systems Standard (ISO/IEC IS 11172-1). As a generic standard, MPEG-2 Systems will support a wide range of broadcast, telecommunications, computing, and storage applications.

To provide support for these features, the MPEG-2 Systems Standard will define two kinds of streams. The Program Stream provides for the creation of an audiovisual program, which could have multiple views and multichannel audio. It is similar to the Systems Stream of MPEG-1, with extensions for encoding program-specific information such as multiple-language audio channels. The Transport Stream is new to MPEG-2. It multiplexes a number of programs, comprised of video, audio, and private data, for transmission and storage using a wide variety of media. The Transport Stream supports multiprogram broadcast, storage of single programs on digital videotape, robust performance against channel errors, conditional access to programs, and the maintenance of synchronization over complex networks and through editing operations.

**Multimedia PC** (MPC). An MPC is a regular PC that has been upgraded with hardware and software add-ons to take advantage of multimedia. The following specification is the minimum required to ensure multimedia compatibility:

80386SX or higher processor

2M of RAM

30M or greater hard disk

VGA or SVGA display

Two-button mouse

101-key keyboard

CD-ROM with a transfer rate of at least 150K per second; a maximum seek time of 1 second; drive cannot use more than 40 percent of the computer's CPU processing power

Audio board with the following capabilities: music synthesizer; on-board analog mixing capabilities; digitized sound in 8-bit samples at an 11-kHz input sampling rate; 8-bit samples at both 11-kHz and 22-kHz output sampling rate

Serial and parallel ports

MIDI I/O Port

Joystick port

Headphones or speakers

Microsoft Windows 3.1

MS-DOS CD-ROM Extensions (MSCDEX), Version 2.2 or later

Windows 3.1 is a big part of the MPC standard, in that it provides the Media Control Interface (MCI). MCI is a unified, command-driven method for software to talk to related multimedia peripheral devices including: AVI; Red Book audio; dat (digital audio tape player); digital video in a window; video overlay; image scanner; MIDI sequencer; videotape recorder or player; videodisc; waveform audio device.

As more and more multimedia products began to flood the market, the Multimedia Marketing Council found that the Level 1 specification (described previously) was not robust enough. What follows are the newly revised MPC Level 2 specifications.

For systems:

25-MHz 486SX microprocessor

4 Mbytes of memory

3.5-inch floppy drive

160-Mbyte hard disk

16-bit sound

Two-button mouse

Windows 3.0, plus Multimedia Extensions or Windows 3.1

Color monitor with 640 × 480 resolution with 65,536 colors

Serial port, parallel port, MIDI I/O port, joystick port

For upgrade kits:

CD-ROM drive with a 300-kbyte-per-second transfer rate

CD-ROM-XA–ready (Photo CD)

Multisession-capable

Average seek time of 400 milliseconds

16-bit sound

MIDI I/O port and joystick port

**NISO** (National Information Standards Organization).  NISO is a national standards developing organization that develops and promotes voluntary standards for information science, libraries, and publishing practices. Of the many NISO standards, the one of greatest interest for those in the multimedia community is NISO 9660, which is also known as ISO 9660 or ANSI 9660. 9660 is the operative international standard for the placement of data on compact read-only optical disks (CD-ROM). It sets forth the volume and file structure for CD-ROM and specifies placement of files to ensure interoperability of CCD-ROM products. This is a 64-page standard and is priced at $48. It can be purchased through Transaction Publishers, Dept NIS092, Rutgers University, New Brunswick, NJ 08903. From a practical perspective, you need to purchase this volume only if you are the makers of a CD-ROM drive. For the rest of us, just make sure that the CD-ROM drive that you purchase is 9660-compatible. If you absolutely must take a look at this standard, but don't want to spend the money, try an association library such as that of the IEEE, located in New York City.

New (draft) NISO standards in development include

ANSI/NISO Z39.72-199x. CD-ROM standard format for the submission of data for multimedia CD-ROM mastering. $30.

ANSI/NISO Z39-199x. CD-ROM standard interface retrieval protocol.

Both may be obtained from

National Information Standards Organization.
P.O. Box 1056
Bethesda, MD 20827
(301) 975-2814

**NTSC** (National Television Standards Committee).  This is the video standard for North America. All signals, whether they be from a TV, VCR, laserdisc, or camcorder, conform to this standard.

This standard, which has been in existence since 1952, decreed that a single frame of video consists of up to 525 horizontal scan lines, each taking $\frac{1}{60}$ of a second to draw, drawn every $\frac{1}{30}$ of a second on the inside face of a phosphor-coated picture tube by a fast-moving electron beam.

**Orange Book.** This standard specifies the format for write-once and magneto-optical CD technologies (MO CD).

**P*64.** This is a video telephone conferencing standard from the International Telegraph and Telephone Consultative Committee (CCITT) for compression audio and motion-video images. The standard incorporates multiplexing, demultiplexing, framing of data, transmission protocol, bandwidth congruence, and call setup and teardown. P*64 encodes real-time motion video and audio for transmission over copper or fiber-optic telephone lines at 30 frames per second, at a bandwidth between 40 kbits and 4 Mbits per second.

**PAL.** This is the European version of the NTSC standard. Unfortunately, NTSC and PAL are incompatible. However, much of the video software on the market enables you to output to either NTSC or PAL. PAL paints 625 lines at a frame rate of 25 per second, each field taking $\frac{1}{50}$ of a second to draw.

**QuickTime.** This is the video codec written for the Macintosh. QuickTime video players are available to play QuickTime video on MPC platforms.

**Redbook audio** (CD-Audio—The Red Book—CEI IEC 908). This is the standard that controls the creation of audio CDs. It is an international standard, ISO 10149. It's also known as "the Red Book Standard" simply due to the color of the standard's book jacket. Many CD-ROMS (and all MPC standard drives) allow the playing of audio CDs through the PC's CD-ROM drive.

The entire specification can be found in the International Electrotechnical Commission's "Compact Disk Digital Audio System 908; 1987." It covers such specifics as dimensions; optical parameters of the plastic; recording and playback environment; signal measurement and fidelity; and the structure of the digital files that contain the music waveforms.

Digitally, Redbook audio is recorded as 16-bit words using a sampling frequency of 44.1 kHz and recorded in a 2-channel, linear format.

**SECAM** (The Sequential Color and Memory video system). This system is used in France, among other places. Although like PAL it is a 625-line, 50-Hz system, its base technology and broadcast method is different from PAL.

**SGML** (Standard Generalized Markup Language). Adopted as an ISO standard in 1986, it allows organizations to structure and manage information in a cross-platform, application-independent manner. It tags documents as a series of data objects rather than storing them as huge files.

**SFBA** (Shared Frame Buffer Architecture). Intel Corp. and ATI Technologies have joined forces to develop a new hardware architecture that combines graphics and video technology, reducing the cost of putting multimedia in a PC. SFBA is an open specification that enables makers of graphics chips and board makers to build a single card that combines graphics acceleration, video compression and decompression, and video-capture capabilities. SFBA supports system buses, including EISA (Extended Industry Standard Architecture), ISA, VESA-local bus, Micro Channel, and Peripheral Component Interconnect.

**Standard for Electronic Manuscript Preparation and Markup.**  Version 2.0, introduced in August 1987, describes standard methods for authors and publishers to keyboard and mark up books, articles, and serials on a computer. The document contains explanatory information about the Association of American Publishers' (AAP) application of SGML, defines the application's formal syntax, and is, along with its appendices, the formal Electronic Manuscript Standard approved by the American National Standards Institute.

The standard is the result of the three-year Electronic Manuscript Project, sponsored by the Association of American Publishers and the Council on Library Resources, which drew on the expertise of over 60 publishing, bibliographic, and office industry groups around the world. The Electronic Manuscript Standard offers the first industrywide application of SGML for the publishing industry.

A series of guidebooks is available for those interested: The *Author's Guide to Electronic Manuscript Preparation and Markup* explains how to prepare a manuscript with Electronic Manuscript Standard markup. The *Reference Manual on Electronic Manuscript Preparation and Markup* condenses major concepts of the Standard into an easily consulted guide with examples. For more information contact EPSIG (Electronic Manuscript Preparation Special Interest Group), c/o OCLC (Online Computer Library Center), 6565 Frantz Road, Dublin, Ohio 43017. Or call 614-764-6195.

**VIS** (Video Information System).  This is Tandy's competitive offering to CD-I. The device is physically similar to Photo-CD or CD-I but is based on Microsoft Windows.

**Yellow Book.**  See CD-ROM.

**XA.**  See CD-ROM-XA.

# CD-ROM Standards for Unix

**Andrew Young**

## Introduction

The Unix market, also known as the "open-systems" market, is driven by standards. Essentially and by definition, proprietary products are not "open," thus every major component of the Unix operating environment has in one form or another undergone a standardization process. Early adopters of the Unix operating system generally were universities and technical organizations whose primary interest was in pushing the envelope of whatever technology they could acquire. These users were price/performance buyers and did not exhibit a high level of brand loyalty. This was one of their primary reasons for selecting Unix systems; using Unix did not lock them into a permanent commitment to a vendor's proprietary products.

From very early on, many different computers ran very similar, though usually not identical, versions of Unix. While there has always been competition among vendors to deliver the most advanced Unix implementations, the market demanded reasonable interoperability among different Unix products. This led to a variety of efforts to bring workable standards to the industry. In the two decades since Unix was originally released, many components of the Unix environment have been standardized. The command structure and system interface both became standards through the POSIX committees of the IEEE, and subsequently were adopted by the International Standards Organization (ISO). Most of the programming on Unix systems has been done in the "C" language, which is commonly provided with the operating system since most of the operating system itself was written in "C." This language essentially became a de facto Unix industry standard at its inception, but it has also been formally standardized by the American National Standards Institute (ANSI).

## Unix and Standards

The combination of these standards has offered Unix users an unprecedented level of code portability. Even in the early days, users wanted to, and in many cases actually could, port their software relatively easily to whatever were the newest and hottest platforms available in each new generation of Unix systems. Since these users generally did not discard their old machines, it quickly became important to connect these systems in extensive heterogeneous networks. Thus the next areas to undergo broad standardization were the physical and logical aspects of networking.

There are two primary types of standards in the computer industry: formal standards, developed and adopted by official standards bodies, and de facto standards, usually developed by one or more industry participants to solve a specific problem but made widely available to avoid the emergence of multiple conflicting solutions. Though there is a natural bias toward formal standards, in many ways it doesn't matter whether a standard is formal or de facto, as long as the industry as a whole supports the standard. The Unix market tends to adopt standards with its feet. In other words, one can usually identify the viable standards by looking at the various alternatives and identifying the one the crowd is flocking toward. In some cases this may mean that a formal standard will win out over another "technically superior" solution, but in such situations adequate, functional interoperability, enabling widespread support, is generally of primary importance.

## CD-ROM Standards

One of the reasons CD-ROM (Compact Disc Read Only Memory) has become such a universal success is that the entire foundation of CD-ROM technology, from the physical structure of the disc to the logical organization of the information recorded thereon, has been standardized. Here the process began as proprietary, licensed, consumer audio technology, but the licensing terms were reasonable and the technology was so compelling that CD-DA (Compact Disc–Digital Audio) products became the biggest success in the history of consumer electronics. In the decade since the CD was invented, several variations on the basic technology have been released, of which CD-ROM is probably the best known. The fundamental specifications defining the successful variants generally have been codified as published international standards.

At the most fundamental level, the physical parameters and encoding of data on a compact disc are specified in a document known as "the IEC 908." This contains much of the information presented in the so-called Red Book, which specifies the physical size and structure of manufactured CD-DA discs, how digital audio data is to be physically recorded on the disc, how the individual data blocks are to be identified, the implementation of error-detection and -correction codes, and a variety of other details.

Layered on top of this specification is the ISO 10149, which encompasses the content of "the Yellow Book." This is the basis for CD-ROM technology. It details the extensions to the IEC 908 that support recording computer-readable digital data from a compact disc. This involves mechanisms for determining which of the recorded information is audio data and which computer data, and which of the available forms for recording this information are to be used. Further it specifies the use of an additional layer of error-detection and -correction encoding that increases the reliability of the medium from the relatively limited needs of digital audio to the high reliability required of computer storage.

Once raw computer data is able to be recorded on a high-capacity, random-access medium such as CD-ROM, one or more file systems usually will be designed to take advantage of this. Early work on CD-ROM file systems followed one of two main paths: adapting or porting file systems designed for other media to CD-ROM, or development of proprietary, CD-ROM-specific file systems.

Neither of these added significant flexibility to this new medium. File systems designed for other media were generally ill suited to the performance characteristics of CD-ROM drives. Proprietary file systems were not widely available and tended to be tuned to the applications, and sometimes hardware, provided by the developing vendor. The market floundered in the sea of incompatible solutions in which it was awash.

Soon a group of vendors decided they would all benefit from the adoption of a common file system standard specifically designed to perform well with the wide class of applications for which CD-ROM technology was expected to be used. Out of this effort the High Sierra format was born in 1986. Two years later a slightly modified version was adopted as the ISO 9660 standard. The ISO 9660 has become one of the major successes of the standardization process. More computers of different types from different manufacturers can read ISO 9660–format discs than any other disk or tape format, including floppy and hard-disk formats.

## Standard Limitations

Yet the ISO 9660 has limitations which have raised concerns that vendors may choose to bend, break, or ignore the standard altogether in certain situations. Much of the concern is rooted in the "lowest-common-denominator" nature of the file system. In order to reach the widest possible range of target platforms, the file system places substantial restrictions on the character set acceptable for file and directory names, the depth of directory structures, and the range of file system features supported. While the ISO 9660 is well suited to DOS and VAX VMS systems, it leaves much to be desired when applied in the Unix and Macintosh environments.

Under the Unix operating system specifically, much early application of CD-ROM technology has been in the area of application and operating system software distribution. It is here that robust support for Unix file system features is most important. Many vendors found it difficult or impossible to create an acceptable model for distribution of their materials within a strict ISO

9660 structure, so a variety of non- or nearly ISO 9660 CD-ROM discs appeared, usually simply dumps of Unix file system (UFS) hard disk images onto CDs.

This trend caused concern for many in the traditionally standards-oriented Unix market. UFS, more a general set of file system design principles than an actual standard, does not provide any real interchange capability. UFS discs created on one system usually cannot be read on a system of a different type, sometimes even if they are from the same vendor. Further, UFS images dumped onto CD-ROMs generally were hit with substantial performance penalties compared to similar ISO 9660 discs, since UFS was designed to work well on fast hard disks.

## The Rock Ridge Group

In 1990 a group of Unix and CD-ROM industry vendors formed the Rock Ridge Group to address this issue. Their goal was to develop a CD-ROM file system that would provide complete support for Unix/POSIX file systems and that could form the basis for a formal international standard. After considering a variety of possible routes to go down, the group settled on a draft proposal, submitted by this author, as the basis for their subsequent work. This proposal embedded the additional Unix file system information transparently within an ISO 9660 directory structure. This allowed a single disc, with a single physical directory structure, to have two logical appearances. In a compatible Unix environment, the disc would appear to be a complete Unix file system. To a system that understands only the basic ISO 9660, the disc would appear to be a normal ISO 9660 disc.

This approach supports the primary goal of the ISO 9660: universal information interchange. Since there is only one actual directory structure through which the data can be accessed, all the files are accessible from either view. The file names and even the directory structure may be different, but all the file contents are available. Further, to allay the concern of other, non-Unix vendors that use of the Rock Ridge Protocols may preclude simultaneous recording of other file system extensions, the proposal was split into two parts. The System Use Sharing Protocol (SUSP) defines a shareable, extensible, non-Unix-specific mechanism for recording additional information within the ISO 9660 directory record's System Use Area. The Rock Ridge Interchange Protocol (RRIP) uses the SUSP specifically to record the information required for a complete Unix/POSIX file system. Both of these proposals were released in the spring of 1991 with the support of more than a dozen major Unix and CD-ROM vendors.

When the SUSP was being constructed, features were added to allow coexistence with as many of the current uses of the System Use Area as we could find. When the fields that would be required for the RRIP were being defined, extra effort was made to make the encoding as flexible and non-system-specific as possible, to encourage the use of these fields in other non-Unix environments that also could benefit from extensions to the ISO 9660 such as

OS/2, Windows NT, the Macintosh, or the Amiga. This strategy has substantially reduced the number of possible conflicts with other industry interests and has nearly eliminated all resistance to support for the protocols.

The Rock Ridge Protocols currently have the status of a de facto industry standard. They constitute the only proposal that addresses the needs of the Unix market while remaining completely ISO 9660–compliant. Every major Unix industry vendor that is seriously concerned with CD-ROM support has implemented the Rock Ridge Protocols. Most of these vendors were themselves actively involved in the development of the protocols. Some are still involved as members of the IEEE Computer Society standards working group, chaired by this author, which is formalizing the proposals in preparation for their adoption as an official IEEE standard.

### The Official UNIX Standard—XCDR

The only existing, official, Unix-specific CD-ROM standard is the XCDR, adopted by X/open, a Unix industry organization formed to promote open, standards-based computing. An ISO 9660 volume and directory structure provides fields for storing a wide variety of information about the disc that it describes, such as who published the disc, who prepared the data, multiple time stamps (creation, modification, effective and expiration dates), and whether the disc was designed to operate on a specific system or with a particular application. Much of this information is not directly accessible through a normal directory listing, which is all that most computer systems know how to provide.

The XCDR defines an application programming interface (API) for accessing all of the ISO 9660 volume and directory information. Support of this API would allow application or system programmers to conveniently utilize this information where this is awkward now, since each programmer must have sufficient knowledge of the ISO 9660 (and patience) to find and decode the data. The RRIP also proposes to extend this API to support the specific features it provides. Though the XCDR has been around for over two years, it has only recently begun to generate any significant interest from the Unix vendors. This interest is expected to grow as more diverse applications of CD-ROM technology are developed.

### Standards on the Way

A variety of other CD-ROM-related standards efforts of interest to the Unix community are under way. Perhaps the most visible is the Frankfurt Format/ECMA 168/DIS 13490. This format provides an incrementally updatable file system to support the new generation of "Orange Book," CD-recordable (CD-R) drives. While the ISO 9660 and the Rock Ridge Protocols are widely being used with CD-R drives, they can be used only in a batch-write (disc-at-once) mode, in which the entire disc is written in one pass. This encompasses a large segment of the CD-R market, including the entire CD-

ROM publishing market, most batch backup situations, and virtually all custom data distribution applications, primarily because the vast majority of installed CD-ROM drives are not capable of reading incrementally written discs. Still, there are many applications for which incremental writing of information to CD-R would be useful. Owing to fundamental design decisions, the ISO 9660 cannot support this function, so another format is required and the Frankfurt/ECMA 168 serves this need well.

Whereas the High Sierra Group was composed almost exclusively of MS-DOS PC-oriented vendors, the developers of the Frankfurt proposal represented a much wider cross-section of the computer industry. Specifically, the Unix vendors were well represented, resulting in strong Unix/POSIX support within the Frankfurt proposal. Thankfully, this precludes the need to develop a Rock-Ridge-style extension to this proposal and assures that all vendors that implement Frankfurt/ECMA 168 drivers for Unix systems will provide full POSIX-style file system support immediately. Such products are expected to begin appearing in 1994, after the expected adoption of the Frankfurt/ECMA 168 as an ISO standard early that year.

There are other areas that beg for standardization. Several data-exchange (client-server search-and-retrieval) protocols are being promoted for standardization, but as of yet none has caught the attention of the market. Which, if any, of these will become either de facto or formal industry standards has yet to be determined.

There is a crying need for a baseline, full-text indexing standard. Currently few CD-ROM titles can be accessed under Unix without using DOS-emulation. An indexing standard would allow information vendors to sell their information on CD-ROM to anyone, and retrieval software, perhaps using enhanced proprietary index structures, only to those markets that the vendors believe justify their investment. On platforms not supported directly by the vendors, third-party software houses could develop retrieval software that could access many vendors' discs, or the users could develop their own retrieval software.

CD-ROM is the medium of choice for the distribution of multimedia applications, in part because of the level of standardization. This allows vendors to deliver multimedia products on a single disc to multiple platforms. Many of the standard formats used in the PC environment (TIFF, PCX, WAV) are becoming de facto standards under Unix as well, but the biggest barrier to Unix multimedia is actually having adequate support for multimedia delivery on a wide range of Unix platforms. Ironically, it is much more likely that one could establish a motion-video standard than an audio standard under Unix today, because a wider variety of Unix boxes support powerful color graphics processing than support even adequate audio output. Only recently have we seen a trend toward providing audio support on Unix workstations, yet no major vendor provides audio support standardly on its entire product line. Only when audio can essentially be assumed to be available on all desktop workstations from the major manufacturers will multimedia be able to show substantial growth in the Unix workstation market.

Clearly, support for CD-ROM under Unix has come a long way in the last few years, and this growth strongly parallels the development of appropriate standards. Before the ISO 9660 was introduced in 1988, there was no Unix CD-ROM market. While some progress was made in the interim, use of CD-ROM under Unix really started to grow only after the introduction of the Rock Ridge Protocols in 1991. Today CD-ROM is an accepted, often even required, component of the Unix workstation environment. If multimedia is ever to flourish in the Unix environment, it will be because adequate standards have been developed to support this function. To paraphrase Vince Lombardi, the legendary Green Bay Packers coach, under Unix "standards aren't everything, they're the only thing."

# 17

# Legal Aspects of Multimedia Productions

**Frederic M. Wilf**

## Why Multimedia Is Different, from a Legal Perspective

The law responds to each new technological challenge by first studying it and then, if appropriate, doing something about it. For example, the Copyright Office started accepting copyright registrations of computer programs as early as 1964, but it was not until 1980 that Congress amended the U.S. Copyright Act to explicitly protect computer programs.

Until the advent of multimedia, the Copyright Office and the users and owners of copyright-protected works had placed each type of work in its own pigeonhole. Photographs were registered in one way, and licensed by photographers and stock houses. Musical compositions were registered in another way, and licensed through ASCAP, BMI, and other organizations. The movie and television studios handled their own copyright registrations and licensing, with the help of the Harry Fox Agency and the distribution houses. However, multimedia blurs these distinctions.

A single multimedia work can contain

- Text from an encyclopedia
- Photographs from a magazine
- Music composed by one person and performed by another
- Sound recordings from a record album
- Video from an old movie

all of which have been altered and arranged to form a single integrated work. Indeed, the initials of the term *multimedia* are shared with an older, Yiddish word for a similar blending of many things into one: *mishmash*.

This sort of mishmash makes for some interesting legal issues. So far, the law has dealt with multimedia legal issues by reversing the process that created the mishmash. The law looks at and analyzes each element that goes into a multimedia work as if that element were by itself. Eventually the law will deal with the final result (the mishmash), but until that happens it is best to analyze each element separately.

An element-by-element analysis may take a little more time to complete, but as you will see, you do not need a lawyer to conduct this analysis. Much of it you can do yourself.

### What this chapter covers

This chapter discusses legal issues that multimedia artists should be aware of under U.S. law. For example, if an artist would like to digitize and incorporate a photograph from a recent magazine, and there is no copyright notice, can the artist do this?

Suppose an artist has completed a multimedia work on CD-ROM that consists of hypertext, video, and sound, as well as searching software. How can the artist protect the work, or at least have the right to sue anyone who pirates it?

There are fairly simple techniques to protect what the artist has created, as well as methods to enforce that protection. The other side of the coin is that the artist does not want to unwittingly infringe on the rights of others, so a basic understanding of common legal problems can be helpful.

This chapter briefly discusses copyright, privacy, and contract law as they apply to multimedia works.

### What this chapter does *not* cover

This chapter discusses a number of legal issues that multimedia artists face, but it does not cover every legal issue. Nor does it say everything that needs to be said about each issue that it does cover.

This chapter discusses the law in the United States. It does not discuss the law in any other country. More importantly, many issues (such as contract law) are subjects of state law, which means that the law will be different from one state to the next.

This chapter does not provide the "final word" on the state of the law. The law is a moving target, because it continues to change. One example is the U.S. Copyright Act, which was completely rewritten in 1976. However, Congress has seen fit to amend the Copyright Act about a dozen times since then. All the other areas of law discussed in this chapter are also subject to constant change.

Finally, this chapter does not provide legal, accounting, or other professional advice. If legal advice or other expert assistance is required, the services of a competent professional should be sought.

## Copyright Law

Copyright law is the primary means to protect multimedia works. It is designed to protect "expressions" of ideas, while making available to others the underlying ideas, facts, and information. Copyright law defines what is and is not protected, as well the methods by which protection is enforced.

This section will discuss the legal rights that make up a copyright.

### Owning a copyright, as opposed to owning an object

When a person buys a book or a record, that person then owns the physical object—the book or record. Owning the book or record does not give the purchaser the right to copy the book or record, or make new versions of the book or record.

So if you purchase a videotape of a ten-year-old movie, you can watch that movie and show it to your friends. However, you cannot copy scenes from the movie into your CD-ROM-based guide to cinema without the permission of the person or company that owns the copyright to the movie.

As for the videotape, you can sell it to another person, so long as you don't keep any copies for yourself. In copyright law, this is called the *first sale doctrine*. Once the physical copy embodying the copyrighted work has been sold, the purchaser can use or dispose of that copy in any way she likes, so long as she does not make copies of all or part of the work.

### Source of law

The United States Copyright Act is the sole copyright statute in the United States. This has been so since Congress preempted the field with the Copyright Act of 1976, which became effective on January 1, 1978.

No state is allowed to legislate in the area of copyright law, so there is no state copyright law. Nor is there a "common law" (judge-made) copyright law, meaning that judges do not make up new rights or responsibilities as they do in other areas of the law. Judges are only allowed to interpret the U.S. Copyright Act, which means that the most they can do is come up with explanations and structures for resolving disputes whenever the Copyright Act seems ambiguous, unclear, or incomplete.

For those who have access to federal statutes, the Copyright Act may be found in Title 17 of the United States Code. When this chapter refers to a section number, it will be to a section number of Title 17. For example, the definitions of copyright terms are found in Section 101 of the Copyright Act.

### Definitions of key copyright terms

Copyright law is whatever Congress says it is. Key to an understanding of copyright law are the terms that Congress uses in the Copyright Act. The definitions are important, because a particular term will have one meaning in copyright law and a different meaning in a different area of the law. For example, in copyright law the term *publication* means "dissemination to the general public"; in libel law, however, *publication* means "*any* dissemination of libelous matter to any other person, in public or private."

The following are the key terms defined in Section 101 of the Copyright Act.

**Work.**  A *work* in the copyright lingo is any embodiment that contains expression that may be protected under the copyright law. Works include building designs, drawings, books or any kind of text, two-dimensional and three-dimensional art, computer programs, movies, etc.

**Audiovisual work.**  An audiovisual work is a series of related images and any accompanying sounds that are intended to be shown by the use of machines such as projectors or electronic equipment, including computers and televisions. It does not matter whether the audiovisual work is embodied in tape, on film, or on disk. Most multimedia works are considered audiovisual works for copyright purposes.

**Derivative work.**  A derivative work is a work that is based upon one or more preexisting works, regardless of the type of preexisting work. The derivative work can be in any form in which a work may be recast, transformed, or adapted. Digitizing a photograph creates a derivative work (the digital version) of a preexisting work (the photograph). A derivative work can constitute an original work of authorship that is separate and distinct from the preexisting work. As noted above, however, it is the copyright owner who decides whether a person is allowed to make derivative works of the copyright owner's work.

One key issue involving derivative works is the point at which a derivative work is no longer considered derivative. For example, if you digitize a photograph, that creates a derivative work that can be recognized as a copy of the original. If however you then alter the digitized version to a point where it is no longer recognizable in any way as a derivative of the original, then you have created a new work.

Think of it as melting down a bronze statue. If you melt it down partially, and part of the original is still recognizable (even a small part), then you have a derivative work. However if the bronze is melted completely into a liquid and then poured into a new mold, an original work is created that no longer owes anything to the prior work, except for the raw material.

**Fixed in a tangible medium of expression.**  The Copyright Act automatically protects all works—including multimedia works—as soon as they are written on paper, stored on a disk, or saved in some other medium. As an example, if one person talks to another person, no copyrighted work is created. However, if one person records the conversation on audio- or video-tape, then a copyrighted work has been created on tape.

**Copyright exclusive rights.**  The Copyright Act grants five exclusive rights to a copyright owner, who may (1) copy or reproduce the work, (2) prepare derivative works, (3) distribute copies, (4) perform the work, and (5) display the work. Thus the owner of the copyright can control who copies the work, who can make new versions of the work, who can distribute copies of the work, who can perform the work on stage or screen, and who can display the work on the walls or monitors of an art gallery.

**Author and owner.**  The *author* is the person who creates a work. The creator of the work is called an *author* even though he or she may be creating a photograph, a videotape, or a sound recording.

The *owner* is the owner of the copyright at any given time. Initially the author and the owner are the same person, because the author is the initial owner of the copyright. But the author may transfer the copyright to another person, who then becomes the owner. Often, the terms *copyright owner* and *copyright holder* are used interchangeably.

**License.**  A *license* is a contract by which the copyright owner allows another person to exercise any one or more of the five exclusive rights. An *exclusive license* means that only the licensee can exercise the licensed rights. A *nonexclusive license* means that the owner is free to allow people other than the licensee to exercise the licensed rights.

**Assignment.**  An *assignment* is a document by which the copyright owner transfers all of the exclusive rights to another person, who then becomes the copyright owner.

**Publication.**  *Publication* refers to the distribution of a work by sale, rent, or lending copies of the work. Generally speaking, any distribution of a copyrighted work to the general public is deemed a publication of the work, regardless of whether copies of the work are sold by mail order, door-to-door, or while standing on a street corner.

## When copyright attaches

Copyright law automatically protects any copyrightable work that is "fixed in a tangible medium of expression" (see earlier entry). Another way to think of it is that copyright law protects any work that has some physical embodiment, even if it is only a series of magnetic blips on a tape or disk.

You do not have to register your copyright, although registration is recommended for most works that can be copied and that are worth more than the few dollars it costs to register the copyright with the Copyright Office. (See Copyright Registration, p. 17.8.)

## What copyright protects

At its most basic, a copyright is a right to copy. The owner of the copyright controls who can have a copy and what can be done with it.

The copyright owner can allow one person to have five copies and another person three, and refuse to allow a third person to have any.

The copyright owner of a photograph can allow one person to make a copy of the photograph and incorporate it into a multimedia work.

### The idea/expression dichotomy

Copyright law does not protect ideas, only the *expressions* of ideas. If there are many ways to express an idea, then copyright law will protect one expression from being copied or incorporated into another expression without the permission of the copyright owner. In copyright lingo, this separation of ideas and expressions is called "the idea/expression dichotomy."

If there is only one way, or just a handful of ways to express an idea, then the Copyright Act may not be used to protect that idea, and other people may use any expression of that idea.

The problem with drawing a line between ideas and the expressions of them is that the line is drawn at a different place for each work. Thus the line may be drawn in one place for one computer program, in another for another program. Moreover, since most copyrightable works contain many elements and pieces, each element is separately evaluated for the purpose of drawing the line between idea and expression.

So if a brochure contains photographs, text, and drawings, then each photograph, each paragraph of text, and each drawing constitutes a separate element that must be evaluated to determine where the line should be drawn between idea and expression. Is one photograph an unadorned picture of a man in a business suit? If so, then while anyone can use the idea of photographing a man in a business suit, this particular photograph cannot be copied or reproduced without the permission of the copyright owner.

## Who Is the Copyright Owner?

Under Section 201 of the Copyright Act, ownership of the copyright goes to the person or persons who created the work (the "authors" of the work). Thereafter the copyright owner may transfer ownership to another person, partnership, corporation, or other entity that can own property.

The exception to this general rule is "work for hire," which has two distinct and different definitions.

### Work for hire in employment relationships

Under the first definition of *work made for hire,* an employer is deemed to be the "author" of all works created by an employee within the scope of his or her employment.

It does not matter whether the work was created at the office or at the employee's home, and it does not matter whether it was created when the employee was being paid or was on a lunch break. As long as the type of work created falls within the types of work that the employee is paid to do, then the employer shall automatically own the copyright. No written documents are necessary.

For example, if a person who works as an accountant in a large accounting firm creates rock videos at night, then that accountant would personally own the copyright to the rock videos. Creating videos is not within the *scope of employment* of the accountant.

By contrast, if by day a person is as an employee of a production firm to create rock videos, then her employer would own the copyright to any rock videos she creates at night.

### Work for hire in independent contractor relationships

The first definition of work for hire is limited to employment relationships. The second definition applies to independent contractors who create certain types of copyrightable works, and it requires that each contributor sign a written document.

This second definition of *work made for hire* states that the copyright in specially ordered or commissioned works will be owned by one party, when all the parties expressly agree in a written document or documents signed by all of them that the work to be created is a work for hire.

This definition is limited to (1) contributions to collective works, (2) parts of a motion picture or audiovisual work, (3) translations, (4) supplementary works, (5) compilations, (6) instructional texts, (7) tests, (8) answers to tests, and (9) atlases. These nine classes of works may be thought of as *commissioned work for hire*. This definition of work for hire does not apply to any other type of work.

### When work for hire does not attach

Work for hire does not apply to self-employed individuals who are creating copyrightable works by themselves. A person working alone (and not as an employee of anybody else or of any partnership or corporation) will own the copyright and will be called the "author" of the work.

Work for hire does not apply to independent contractors creating works that are not commissioned works for hire (see section above). Thus, a photographer who takes photographs of a product for an advertising campaign does not come under either definition of work for hire, and he or she will own the copyright for each photograph. Photographs are not one of the nine types of commissioned work for hire discussed in the Copyright Act, even though the photographer was commissioned by someone else.

Work for hire does not apply to independent contractors creating commissioned work for hire where there is no written agreement. If 10 people agree to contribute to the making of a film but there is no written document signed by them, then the film is not a work for hire. Instead, all 10 people who contribute will be joint owners of the copyright in the film.

### How to ensure that only one person or company owns the copyright

The Copyright Act defines who will own the copyright by default. However, the default may be changed at any time by use of a written document signed by the parties.

Regardless of whether either definition of "work for hire" applies to a type of work, you can always write and sign an agreement stating that, among those who contribute to a work, one person or company owns the copyright. Thus the freelance photographer who takes photographs for an advertising campaign can assign her copyright to her client in writing. An employee and an employer can agree in writing that the employee will own the copyright to everything she creates, regardless of whether it is within the scope of her employment.

## Copyright Notice

Copyright notices consist of three parts: (1) "Copyright," "Copr." or "©"; (2) if the work is "published" (see previous discussion), the year of first publication; and (3) the name of the copyright owner. Copyright notices are still strongly recommended but are no longer required for any work first created or first published after March 1, 1989.

For works published for the first time prior to March 1, 1989, a copyright notice should be placed on the work. Otherwise the artist will likely lose the copyright to the work.

If the artist places a copyright notice on a work, then later sues an infringer, the infringer cannot claim in court that she did not know the work was protected by the artist's copyright.

## Copyright Registration

The first thing you should know about copyright registration is that it is optional, but recommended for many works. The second thing you should know is that you do not need a lawyer to do it for you. Registering a copyright is a fairly simple and painless process.

Copyright registration is optional to protect works created or first published after March 1, 1989. Registration is now required only as a first step prior to filing a copyright infringement lawsuit. Thus a copyright registration serves, so to speak, as the keys to the courthouse.

### Why you should register your copyright early and often

Copyright registration is recommended for any work worth more than the filing fee (presently, $20) and for any work that may be stolen or otherwise infringed. If the work is worth less than the filing fee, why bother? If the work cannot be stolen or infringed (which is not the case for most works), then there is no need to bother.

There are several reasons why early registration of copyright is recommended. First, you need to have a certificate that shows that the copyright is registered before you can sue anyone for infringement (although Congress has been debating removing this requirement). Since it normally takes several months to receive the certificate of registration, you could be forced to wait several months before suing an infringer, unless you paid an additional fee so as to get the certificate of registration back within a week. By filing early, you already have the certificate of registration in hand in case you have to sue someone.

Second, in a copyright infringement suit, the copyright owner may get attorney's fees and additional types of damages if the copyright application was filed prior to the start of the infringement, or shortly after publication (i.e., within three months of the date of first publication). If the copyright was registered after the infringement began, then the copyright owner cannot ask for attorney's fees or additional types of damages.

### How to get and file an application for copyright registration

You should not need a lawyer to file a copyright registration. Unlike federal trademark and patent applications, the process is simple.

To get applications for copyright registration, call the U.S. Copyright Office. If you call 202-707-3000, you will reach a live human being, who is very likely to be helpful. The people at the Copyright Office will tell you how to file your applications, but they will not give you a "legal opinion." If you call 202-707-9100, you will reach an answering machine that will take your order for forms and other information. It usually takes 4 to 6 weeks to get the forms. Once you have them, you can always make more forms for yourself by photocopying them onto a good-quality white bond paper. This will make the Copyright Office happy, because it doesn't want to mail out any more forms than it has to. See examples of copyright application forms at the end of this chapter.

To register a copyright, you need to send the completed application (two sides of one piece of paper), a check for the filing fee (presently, $20), and a copy or other specimen of the work. Different forms are used for different types of works, and the specimen also will be different from one type of work to the next. The specimen could be one video or audio tape, or some other piece of the work that will help the Copyright Office to identify it.

Once you have filed the application, it often takes 2 or 3 months to receive the certificate of copyright registration. Neatness counts on the application, because the Copyright Office will make a few marks on it and then photocopy it onto a nicer piece of paper to create the certificate of copyright registration. If you can't easily read the application, no one else will be able to either, least of all a judge who is trying to enforce the registration as shown on the certificate. If you later lose or misplace the certificate that you receive, you can always get another from the Copyright Office for a small fee.

## Transfer of Copyright

A copyright owner may transfer all or part of a copyright by a written document, or by bequeathing the copyright in a will like any other family heirloom. A copyright may not be transferred by an oral agreement, although the parties can make an oral agreement effective by following it up with a written document.

If the copyright is transferred by a written document, the person transferring the copyright needs to sign the document. The person receiving the copyright may sign the document, but it is not effective unless the person transferring the copyright signs the document.

A copyright is *divisible,* which means that the owner of all five exclusive rights can transfer one of the five rights to one person, another to a second person, the rest to a third person. This often makes it difficult to track down who owns which rights, when the copyright has been parceled out among several owners.

## Copyright Term

Understanding copyright term is useful, since it allows you to know how long you will have the rights to your own work and also helps you to determine whether another person's copyright has expired.

### Works created since 1978

For all works created by individuals since 1978, the copyright is good for the life of the author, plus 50 years. If two or more individuals are the creators of a work, then the copyright expires 50 years after the death of the last author.

Thus, if a particular work is created by an artist in 1994 and the artist dies in 2030, the copyright will be good until the year 2080 (assuming that the copyright is not changed again in the interim).

For all anonymous works, pseudonymous works, and works made for hire, the copyright is good for 75 years from the date of first publication or 100 years from the creation of the work, whichever occurs first.

Thus, for an audiovisual work where all the contributors signed "work-for-hire" agreements, the copyright will last for 100 years from the date that the work was created, or 75 years from the date that it was first made available to the public, whichever term is shorter. Another example: If an employee creates a multimedia work for her employer in 1995 but the work is not seen outside the employer's company and is not publicly distributed, then the copyright will be good until the year 2095.

### Works created before 1978

During the period from 1909 through 1977, a copyright was good for 28 years and then had to be renewed (by filing a paper with the Copyright Office) for another 28 years. Just to complicate things, Congress decided that the copyright in any work created prior to 1978, but still protected as of 1978, would be protected for up to 75 years. As you might expect, this led to confusion that made a lot of work for copyright attorneys.

As a rule of thumb, you should assume that any work created before about 1922 is in the public domain (which means that anyone can use it), and that any work created in or after 1922 is protected by the Copyright Act (until proven otherwise).

## The Real Meaning of "Public Domain"

In the copyright context, the term *public domain* means that nobody owns or has a claim to a particular copyrightable work. Thus anyone can use, copy, or make derivative works of a public domain work. Some people confuse the specific term *"public domain"* with general references to a "published work" or "publication." A work that is publicly available or published is not necessarily in the public domain.

When a copyrightable work enters the public domain, it never leaves the public domain. However, anyone can take a public domain work, add new expression to it, and claim a copyright for the new work. However, the copyright in that circumstance covers only the new expression (the aspects that were added), so the original work will continue to be in the public domain for anyone else to use.

For example, the stories of the Brothers Grimm are now in the public domain because they were written well before 1922. Anyone can copy the original stories, translate them into English, edit them, add new artwork, and publish the result in a book. Copyright law will protect the new artwork, the new translation (translations of human languages are considered derivative works), as well the editing if the editing is more than trivial. If anyone copies that particular book or protected elements of it, that person can be sued for copyright infringement. However, copyright law does not prevent anyone else from going back to the original stories, making their own translation, and publishing them with other artwork.

## Infringement of Copyright

Once you have a copyright, you may need to sue a pirate. On the other hand you may need to know what you are facing if someone accuses *you* of being a copyright pirate.

### Filing a copyright infringement action

As noted above, U.S. citizens cannot file a copyright infringement action unless they have received a certificate of copyright registration from the Copyright Office. Although Congress has debated removing this requirement, it was still in effect when this book went to press in early 1994.

You should always have an experienced attorney represent you in court. To paraphrase those warnings one sometimes hears on television commercials that show professional race car drivers on race tracks, this is a job for a professional—you should not try to litigate a copyright infringement case by yourself.

Your attorney will investigate the facts and make sure that your case can go forward. As part of this investigation, the attorney will likely need to speak with other people who know the facts and circumstances, especially if the infringer is someone known to you.

Once your attorney has investigated the case, he or she will file several documents with the court, including a "complaint" that documents your claims to the courts. Once the papers have been filed, they must be served on the opposing party, who will then have the right to file motions to dismiss the case or file an "answer" that responds to each of the allegations and claims in the complaint.

### Seeking a temporary restraining order "ex parte"

If someone is infringing your copyright, then that person may destroy any evidence of infringement as soon as she or he is sued. In that case, your attorney will file an additional set of motion papers and ask to see the judge. Since your attorney will be seeing the judge without anyone representing the other side, this procedure is referred to as being *ex parte,* a legal term meaning "on or from one side only."

The judge will order a seizure of the evidence prior to trial if she or he is convinced that you have a very strong case and that seizure is the only way to preserve evidence prior to trial. If the judge does order seizure, then you will have to post a rather large bond to cover any damages that you may cause during the seizure, especially if it turns out that you were wrong and the defendant is not a pirate.

### Pretrial and trial

After the initial round of pleadings, and assuming that the case has not been dismissed by the court, the parties then begin a phase known as *discovery.* In discovery, each party has the opportunity to ask questions of the other party in writing or in person (while a court reporter takes down the person's answers to the questions). Each party can also demand access to all of the original materials that went into the copyrighted work, as well as all other documents and materials that may lead to information that is relevant to the case. Often the parties will use the information gleaned during discovery to file a round of motions with the court asking it to make a decision about the case prior to trial. Many times enough information is collected during discovery that a motion is filed to decide the case without a trial, or to limit the issues to be decided at trial.

If the case makes it to trial, then the defendant will have the right to a jury. Whether or not the defendant requests a jury trial, the parties will often take several days in court to present witnesses and enter exhibits. The judge will always decide the strictly legal issues, such as whether a particular document will be allowed in as evidence. The jury (or the judge, in the case of a nonjury trial) will apply the evidence and reach a decision.

### Damages and remedies that a court may award

Under the United States Copyright Act, the copyright owner asks the judge to award either *actual damages* or *statutory damages.*

Actual damages are measured by taking the amount of money lost by the copyright owner and adding to that the amount made by the infringer as a result of the infringement.

When statutory damages are awarded, this means that the judge picks a number in a range (presently, $500 to $20,000) and awards that amount, per work infringed, as damages. Moreover, if the judge finds that the infringement was committed "willfully," then he or she picks a number from a larger range (presently, $500 to $100,000) and awards that amount per work infringed. Statutory damages usually are chosen when the copyright owner has not lost much money as a result of the infringement, yet needs to teach the infringer a lesson by making the damage award much higher. Unfortunately, statutory damages are available to the copyright owner only when the copyright was registered prior to the beginning of the infringement or shortly after the work was first published.

The judge can always assess court costs and order destruction of all infringing copies. If the copyright was registered prior to the infringement, the judge can make the infringer pay the attorney's fees and expenses of the copyright owner, which can total tens or hundreds of thousands of dollars.

## Fair Use of Copyrighted Works

Certain uses of a copyrighted work may not be prosecuted. One set of uses is called *fair use* and is defined in Section 107 of the Copyright Act. Fair use is not a magic formula that instantly turns copying into a permitted use. Rather, it is a set of guidelines that balances the rights of the copyright owner with other rights and needs, including First Amendment concerns and the need to give students and teachers a certain leeway for educational purposes. However, that leeway has its limits.

In one case, several publishers sued a nationwide chain of copy shops located on college campuses. College professors were assembling a sort of textbook out of magazine and journal articles and having this new "textbook" copied at a copy shop. The professors then told their students to go to the copy shop and pay for one copy of the handmade textbook. When the publishers sued the copy shop, the copy shop claimed that it was allowed to make copies as a fair use because the professors wanted the copies for teaching purposes. The courts sided with the publishers, because the professors had not bothered to ask permission from the copyright owners before copying the articles, and because the handmade textbooks competed with textbooks sold by the publishers.

Thus we see that the making of copies without permission is excused as a fair use only when the purpose of the use is criticism, comment, news reporting, teaching (including, in some cases, multiple copies for classroom use), scholarship, or research.

These purposes are fairly narrowly constrained. Thus teachers can invoke fair use when they make copies for their classroom, but publishers of classroom books cannot do so because they are not directly teaching students.

## Types of Uses Recognized as Fair Uses

Fair use is limited to a handful of certain types of uses, mostly related to teaching and criticism. Four factors are weighed to determine whether a particular circumstance is a fair use or an infringement.

### First factor: purpose and character of the use

The first factor weighed is the purpose and character of the use, including whether such use is of a commercial nature or is for nonprofit educational purposes. Thus if the person making the copies is doing so for a profit, that weighs against fair use. However, if the person is making copies for teaching at church, that factor will weigh in favor of fair use.

### Second factor: nature of the copyrighted work

If the copyrighted work is one that generates large amounts of money such as popular books, records, or movies, then any copying will be closely scrutinized. If the copyrighted work is not a money-maker, then fair use is easier to prove.

### Third factor: amount used

It is an axiom of copyright law that an infringement occurs when even a small part of a work is copied, especially if the portion copied is of high quality or is important to the rest of the work.

The third fair-use factor honors that axiom by weighing the amount and substantiality of the portion copied in relation to the copyrighted work as a whole. If one paragraph is copied from an 800-page book, then the portion is not substantial. However, if 20 seconds are sampled from a 2-minute song, that is substantial, especially if the 20 seconds contain the chorus of the song.

### Fourth factor: effect on the market

One of the primary purposes of the Copyright Act is to ensure that authors of copyrighted works are compensated. So it is not surprising that the fourth factor of fair use is the effect of the copying on the potential market for, or value of, the original copyrighted work. If each copy made without permission replaces a copy that would have been sold, then that weighs against fair use. If the copies made do not affect the sales of the original, then this factor weighs in favor of fair use.

## Application of Fair Use

Before one can apply the principle of fair use, one first must determine into which of the categories (criticism, comment, etc.) the use of the copy fits. Then all four of the factors are weighed together, some perhaps being more important than others. There is no mechanical application along the lines of "three out of four factors wins."

For example, what happens when a publisher prepares and sells laserdiscs containing the copyrighted works of a recent playwright without the playwright's permission? The laserdisc contains all of the text of all of the plays, plus full-motion video of one play that the publisher captured off a television rebroadcasting of an old movie version of one of the plays. The laserdiscs are intended for classroom use at a price of $100 each. Is this a fair use?

First, you must consider the type of work. Teaching, scholarship, and research are all included as fair-use purposes, so the laserdisc should be weighed under the four factors. In this case, the first factor cuts against fair use. The publisher is making money from this venture, even though the purchasers may be nonprofit educational users. Second, the copyrighted work consists of highly profitable works (plays and movies, which are subject to video rental income and broadcast royalties), even though the sales of texts of the plays probably do not generate large amounts of income for the playwright or other copyright owners (since the producer of the movie may own the copyright to that production).

The third factor also cuts against fair use, because the laserdisc contains the entire movie and the entire text of each play. Finally, the fourth factor also cuts against fair use, since each laserdisc sold replaces one copy of each play text that could have been sold, as well as one copy of the movie that could have been sold. So this is not a fair use, and the publisher should first seek licenses from the playwright and the owner of the copyright to the movie.

## Copyright Collectives, Stock Houses, and Agencies

It is quite easy to get from others a license to use copyrighted works, by using stock houses, copyright collectives, and other agencies. Each agency has the right to license the use of copyrighted works to others on the basis of a set scale of fees; they also have the power to negotiate fees with you on behalf of the copyright owner.

The agencies provide a large selection of works to choose from, which makes it easier for you to conduct one-stop shopping for licenses to the copyrighted works you hope to use in your multimedia presentations.

There are hundreds of agencies from which to choose, a number of them having offices around the country. The names and principal addresses of several of the better-known agencies follow, under the appropriate headings.

## Music

The licensing of music is broken down into several categories based on the type of music-related work and the type of license sought.

Multimedia works may need (1) an original composition license, if the final product includes covers of original compositions not previously recorded; (2) a mechanical license to cover a previously recorded song; and (3) a synchronization license, when music is combined with video.

### Licensing of Original Compositions

The term *original composition* refers to the sheet music and lyrics written by composers and lyricists. Anyone who wants to record or perform an original composition should contact the appropriate rights organization for that purpose. Two of the best known are

American Society of Composers,
  Authors and Publishers (ASCAP)
One Lincoln Plaza
New York, NY 10023
212-621-6000

Broadcast Music, Inc. (BMI)
320 West 57th Street
New York, NY 10019
800-366-4264
212-586-2000

## Mechanical and synchronization rights

Once a music record or CD has been made available to the public for private
home use, any song (original composition) on that record or CD may be recorded by another artist or group. The composer grants a license. This is required
pursuant to Section 115 of the United States Copyright Act. The type of license
is called a *mechanical license* (because records used to be considered "mechanical" reproductions) or a *compulsory license* (because the Copyright Act makes it
difficult for the copyright owner to refuse permission). Mechanical licenses do
not apply to music used for movies, television, or other visual images.

*Synchronization licenses* are licenses to use music in combination with visual
images in movies, television, or home video. Synchronization licenses are nego-
tiated on a case-by-case basis, and are not subject to compulsory license rates.

The agency best known for mechanical, synchronization, and related
licenses is

The Harry Fox Agency, Inc.
National Music Publishers' Association, Inc.
205 East 42nd Street
New York, NY 10017
212-370-5330

## Photography

Photographs often are licensed through stock photography agencies, one of
which can be found in virtually every city and many large towns (check the
phone book).

Almost all of the stock agencies are aware of digital uses, and many offer
images in digital form in popular binary formats.

License rates depend on the type of use and on how many people are likely
to see the photo or other image.

One agency on the cutting edge of the digital uses of images is

Media Photographers Copyright Agency
American Society of Media Photographers, Inc.
Washington Park, Suite 502
14 Washington Road
Princeton Junction, NJ 08550-1033
609-799-8300

## Movies and Video

Several stock houses that handle still photography also license video stock. Movies and television video can be licensed directly from the copyright owners (usually the production firms) or from their distributors.

You have to be careful about using movies and television because, like other audiovisual works, they incorporate the copyrighted works of others, including music and still photographs. The copyright owners of the movies may not have the right to license to you the background music or other preexisting works incorporated into those movies. In those cases, you should ask the copyright owners for their licensing information so that you can get all of the permissions that you need in writing.

## Privacy and Publicity Law

This is a growing area of law. California and New York have passed statutes that protect privacy, and other states are likely to follow.

The rights of privacy and of publicity are the two sides of the same coin. The rights of privacy and of publicity apply even if you photograph or record (video, audio, or both) a person out-of-doors in a public location, whether sitting in a park or town square or walking down the street. The law deems that a person has the right to control how his or her image is used.

If the person is a private person, then she may prohibit the use of her image for your profit or gain. She has the right to remain private. Don't make private people "public" without their permission.

If the person is a public person or celebrity, she may be able to prohibit your use of her image without proper compensation, primarily because she is deemed to have a property interest in her image. In other words, she can make money from her status as a celebrity, so you cannot use her status to help sell your product without her permission. Celebrities have the right to control their publicity.

One good example of the right of publicity is the Bette Midler case. A car manufacturer wanted to run a series of commercials that featured Ms. Midler's singing. Ms. Midler decided not to participate, so the car manufacturer hired someone else who sang just like Bette Midler. Ms. Midler sued and won about $400,000, because people who listened to the commercials thought that she was singing in the commercial. Even though no image of Ms. Midler was used, her vocal style is sufficiently distinctive to serve as her trademark. Since everyone agreed that Ms. Midler's vocal style had helped to sell cars, Ms. Midler was held by the court to have the right to control when and if her voice and vocal style can be used to help sell cars.

## Releases

There is no better way to ensure that you have all the rights you need to use a person's image or other distinctive features than to get a release.

Professional photographers use releases all the time. An example of one such release, prepared by the American Society of Media Photographers, may be seen on p. 17.25 at the end of this chapter. However, you may need to consult an attorney to ensure that the release is enforceable under the law of those states in which you will use it, and to make sure that it covers every type of use that you are contemplating.

## When You Can Use the Works of Another Person

There are several ways in which you can legally incorporate the works of others into your own works. Ask yourself a few questions.

First, is the work in the public domain? As explained earlier, the term public domain means that no one owns the copyright or other rights to a work. If you have access to a Leonardo da Vinci painting or the manuscript of a Mozart concerto, then go ahead and make your own copies without fear of copyright violation.

Second, if the work is *not* in the public domain, can you get a license to use or copy the work? The saying has it that "it is easier to beg forgiveness afterwards than to ask for permission beforehand." When it comes to copyrighted works, however, permission is often easy to get and costs very little, while the price of forgiveness can be very high indeed. At the very least, forgiveness (including legal fees, court costs, and damages) costs a great deal more than permission.

Third, will any original work that you copy be recognizable as a derivative work? As noted previously, a derivative work remains a derivative work only so long as any part of it is still recognizable as originating with its predecessor.

Fourth, does the work affect anyone else's privacy or publicity rights? If a person can be recognized by his or her looks, voice, or other distinctive attribute, he or she can request compensation. So long as you or the person to whom you have licensed the work has the appropriate releases from each individual, then this will not be an issue.

## Forms

This section contains the following sample forms: form PA (pages 1 and 2), for a work in the performing arts (Fig. 17.1); form TX (pages 1 and 2), for a literary work (Fig. 17.2); form VA (pages 1 and 2), copyright registration (Fig. 17.3); and a photographic release (Fig. 17.4).

PA        PAU

EFFECTIVE DATE OF REGISTRATION

Month          Day          Year

DO NOT WRITE ABOVE THIS LINE. IF YOU NEED MORE SPACE, USE A SEPARATE CONTINUATION SHEET.

**1**

**TITLE OF THIS WORK ▼**

**PREVIOUS OR ALTERNATIVE TITLES ▼**

**NATURE OF THIS WORK ▼** See instructions

**2**

a

**NAME OF AUTHOR ▼**

**DATES OF BIRTH AND DEATH**
Year Born ▼          Year Died ▼

Was this contribution to the work a "work made for hire"?
☐ Yes
☐ No

**AUTHOR'S NATIONALITY OR DOMICILE**
Name of Country
OR { Citizen of ▶
{ Domiciled in ▶

**WAS THIS AUTHOR'S CONTRIBUTION TO THE WORK**
Anonymous?      ☐ Yes ☐ No
Pseudonymous?   ☐ Yes ☐ No

If the answer to either of these questions is "Yes," see detailed instructions.

**NATURE OF AUTHORSHIP** Briefly describe nature of the material created by this author in which copyright is claimed. ▼

**NOTE**
Under the law, the "author" of a "work made for hire" is generally the employer, not the employee (see instructions). For any part of this work that was "made for hire" check "Yes" in the space provided, give the employer (or other person for whom the work was prepared) as "Author" of that part, and leave the space for dates of birth and death blank.

b

**NAME OF AUTHOR ▼**

**DATES OF BIRTH AND DEATH**
Year Born ▼          Year Died ▼

Was this contribution to the work a "work made for hire"?
☐ Yes
☐ No

**AUTHOR'S NATIONALITY OR DOMICILE**
Name of country
OR { Citizen of ▶
{ Domiciled in ▶

**WAS THIS AUTHOR'S CONTRIBUTION TO THE WORK**
Anonymous?      ☐ Yes ☐ No
Pseudonymous?   ☐ Yes ☐ No

If the answer to either of these questions is "Yes," see detailed instructions.

**NATURE OF AUTHORSHIP** Briefly describe nature of the material created by this author in which copyright is claimed. ▼

c

**NAME OF AUTHOR ▼**

**DATES OF BIRTH AND DEATH**
Year Born ▼          Year Died ▼

Was this contribution to the work a "work made for hire"?
☐ Yes
☐ No

**AUTHOR'S NATIONALITY OR DOMICILE**
Name of Country
OR { Citizen of ▶
{ Domiciled in ▶

**WAS THIS AUTHOR'S CONTRIBUTION TO THE WORK**
Anonymous?      ☐ Yes ☐ No
Pseudonymous?   ☐ Yes ☐ No

If the answer to either of these questions is "Yes," see detailed instructions.

**NATURE OF AUTHORSHIP** Briefly describe nature of the material created by this author in which copyright is claimed. ▼

**3**

a

**YEAR IN WHICH CREATION OF THIS WORK WAS COMPLETED** This information must be given in all cases.
◀ Year

b

**DATE AND NATION OF FIRST PUBLICATION OF THIS PARTICULAR WORK**
Complete this information ONLY if this work has been published.
Month ▶          Day ▶          Year ▶
◀ Nation

**4**

See instructions before completing this space.

**COPYRIGHT CLAIMANT(S)** Name and address must be given even if the claimant is the same as the author given in space 2.▼

APPLICATION RECEIVED

ONE DEPOSIT RECEIVED

TWO DEPOSITS RECEIVED

REMITTANCE NUMBER AND DATE

DO NOT WRITE HERE OFFICE USE ONLY

**TRANSFER** If the claimant(s) named here in space 4 are different from the author(s) named in space 2, give a brief statement of how the claimant(s) obtained ownership of the copyright.▼

**MORE ON BACK ▶**
• Complete all applicable spaces (numbers 5-9) on the reverse side of this page.
• See detailed instructions.
• Sign the form at line 8.

**DO NOT WRITE HERE**

Page 1 of _____ pages

**Figure 17.1a** Form PA (front).

| EXAMINED BY | | FORM PA |
| CHECKED BY | | |

☐ CORRESPONDENCE
Yes

FOR
COPYRIGHT
OFFICE
USE
ONLY

**DO NOT WRITE ABOVE THIS LINE. IF YOU NEED MORE SPACE, USE A SEPARATE CONTINUATION SHEET.**

**PREVIOUS REGISTRATION** Has registration for this work, or for an earlier version of this work, already been made in the Copyright Office?

☐ Yes  ☐ No  If your answer is "Yes," why is another registration being sought? (Check appropriate box) ▼

a. ☐ This is the first published edition of a work previously registered in unpublished form.

b. ☐ This is the first application submitted by this author as copyright claimant.

c. ☐ This is a changed version of the work, as shown by space 6 on this application.

If your answer is "Yes," give: **Previous Registration Number ▼**          **Year of Registration ▼**

**5**

**DERIVATIVE WORK OR COMPILATION**  Complete both space 6a & 6b for a derivative work; complete only 6b for a compilation.

a. **Preexisting Material**  Identify any preexisting work or works that this work is based on or incorporates. ▼

**6**

See instructions
before completing
this space.

b. **Material Added to This Work**  Give a brief, general statement of the material that has been added to this work and in which copyright is claimed.▼

**DEPOSIT ACCOUNT** If the registration fee is to be charged to a Deposit Account established in the Copyright Office, give name and number of Account.

Name ▼                                              **Account Number ▼**

**7**

**CORRESPONDENCE**  Give name and address to which correspondence about this application should be sent.   Name/Address/Apt/City/State/Zip ▼

Area Code & Telephone Number ▶

Be sure to
give your
daytime phone
◀ number

**CERTIFICATION\***    I, the undersigned, hereby certify that I am the

Check only one ▼

☐ author

☐ other copyright claimant

☐ owner of exclusive right(s)

☐ authorized agent of _____
                        Name of author or other copyright claimant, or owner of exclusive right(s) ▲

**8**

of the work identified in this application and that the statements made
by me in this application are correct to the best of my knowledge.

**Typed or printed name and date ▼** If this application gives a date of publication in space 3, do not sign and submit it before that date.

_____     date ▶  _____

Handwritten signature (X) ▼

| MAIL<br>CERTIFI-<br>CATE TO | Name ▼ | YOU MUST:<br>• Complete all necessary spaces<br>• Sign your application in space 8 | **9** |
| Certificate<br>will be<br>mailed in<br>window<br>envelope | Number Street Apartment Number ▼<br><br>City State ZIP ▼ | SEND ALL 3 ELEMENTS<br>IN THE SAME PACKAGE:<br>1. Application form<br>2. Nonrefundable $20 filing fee<br>   in check or money order<br>   payable to *Register of Copyrights*<br>3. Deposit material<br>MAIL TO:<br>Register of Copyrights<br>Library of Congress<br>Washington, D.C. 20559 | Copyright fees are ad-<br>justed at 5-year inter-<br>vals, based on in-<br>creases or decreases in<br>the Consumer Price In-<br>dex. The next adjust-<br>ment is due in 1995.<br>Contact the Copyright<br>Office in January 1995<br>for the new fee sched-<br>ule. |

\* 17 U.S.C. § 506(e). Any person who knowingly makes a false representation of a material fact in the application for copyright registration provided for by section 409, or in any written statement filed in connection with the application, shall be fined not more than $2,500.

▲ July 1992—100,000                                        ☆ U.S. GOVERNMENT PRINTING OFFICE: 1992—312-432/60,005

**Figure 17.1***b*   Form PA (back).

# FORM TX

**For a Literary Work**
UNITED STATES COPYRIGHT OFFICE

REGISTRATION NUMBER

|  |  |
|---|---|
| TX | TXU |

EFFECTIVE DATE OF REGISTRATION

| Month | Day | Year |

**DO NOT WRITE ABOVE THIS LINE. IF YOU NEED MORE SPACE, USE A SEPARATE CONTINUATION SHEET.**

**1** **TITLE OF THIS WORK ▼**

**PREVIOUS OR ALTERNATIVE TITLES ▼**

**PUBLICATION AS A CONTRIBUTION** If this work was published as a contribution to a periodical, serial, or collection, give information about the collective work in which the contribution appeared.   **Title of Collective Work ▼**

If published in a periodical or serial give: **Volume ▼**      **Number ▼**      **Issue Date ▼**      **On Pages ▼**

**2** **NAME OF AUTHOR ▼**

a

**DATES OF BIRTH AND DEATH**
Year Born ▼      Year Died ▼

Was this contribution to the work a "work made for hire"?
☐ Yes  ☐ No

**AUTHOR'S NATIONALITY OR DOMICILE**
Name of Country
OR { Citizen of ▶
{ Domiciled in ▶

**WAS THIS AUTHOR'S CONTRIBUTION TO THE WORK**
Anonymous?  ☐ Yes ☐ No
Pseudonymous?  ☐ Yes ☐ No
If the answer to either of these questions is "Yes," see detailed instructions.

**NATURE OF AUTHORSHIP** Briefly describe nature of the material created by this author in which copyright is claimed. ▼

**NOTE**
Under the law, the "author" of a "work made for hire" is generally the employer, not the employee (see instructions). For any part of this work that was "made for hire" check "Yes" in the space provided, give the employer (or other person for whom the work was prepared) as "Author" of that part, and leave the space for dates of birth and death blank.

b

**NAME OF AUTHOR ▼**

**DATES OF BIRTH AND DEATH**
Year Born ▼      Year Died ▼

Was this contribution to the work a "work made for hire"?
☐ Yes  ☐ No

**AUTHOR'S NATIONALITY OR DOMICILE**
Name of country
OR { Citizen of ▶
{ Domiciled in ▶

**WAS THIS AUTHOR'S CONTRIBUTION TO THE WORK**
Anonymous?  ☐ Yes ☐ No
Pseudonymous?  ☐ Yes ☐ No
If the answer to either of these questions is "Yes," see detailed instructions.

**NATURE OF AUTHORSHIP** Briefly describe nature of the material created by this author in which copyright is claimed. ▼

c

**NAME OF AUTHOR ▼**

**DATES OF BIRTH AND DEATH**
Year Born ▼      Year Died ▼

Was this contribution to the work a "work made for hire"?
☐ Yes  ☐ No

**AUTHOR'S NATIONALITY OR DOMICILE**
Name of Country
OR { Citizen of ▶
{ Domiciled in ▶

**WAS THIS AUTHOR'S CONTRIBUTION TO THE WORK**
Anonymous?  ☐ Yes ☐ No
Pseudonymous?  ☐ Yes ☐ No
If the answer to either of these questions is "Yes," see detailed instructions.

**NATURE OF AUTHORSHIP** Briefly describe nature of the material created by this author in which copyright is claimed. ▼

**3** a **YEAR IN WHICH CREATION OF THIS WORK WAS COMPLETED** This information must be given in all cases. ◀ Year

b **DATE AND NATION OF FIRST PUBLICATION OF THIS PARTICULAR WORK** Complete this information Month ▶ _____ Day ▶ _____ Year ▶ _____ ONLY If this work has been published. ◀ Nation

**4** **COPYRIGHT CLAIMANT(S)** Name and address must be given even if the claimant is the same as the author given in space 2.▼

See instructions before completing this space.

**TRANSFER** If the claimant(s) named here in space 4 are different from the author(s) named in space 2, give a brief statement of how the claimant(s) obtained ownership of the copyright.▼

DO NOT WRITE HERE OFFICE USE ONLY
APPLICATION RECEIVED
ONE DEPOSIT RECEIVED
TWO DEPOSITS RECEIVED
REMITTANCE NUMBER AND DATE

**MORE ON BACK ▶** • Complete all applicable spaces (numbers 5-11) on the reverse side of this page.
• See detailed instructions.  • Sign the form at line 10.

**DO NOT WRITE HERE**
Page 1 of _____ pages

**Figure 17.2a**  Form TX (front).

| EXAMINED BY | **FORM TX** |
| --- | --- |
| CHECKED BY | |

☐ CORRESPONDENCE
Yes

FOR
COPYRIGHT
OFFICE
USE
ONLY

**DO NOT WRITE ABOVE THIS LINE. IF YOU NEED MORE SPACE, USE A SEPARATE CONTINUATION SHEET.**

**PREVIOUS REGISTRATION** Has registration for this work, or for an earlier version of this work, already been made in the Copyright Office?

☐ **Yes** ☐ **No** If your answer is "Yes," why is another registration being sought? (Check appropriate box) ▼

**a.** ☐ This is the first published edition of a work previously registered in unpublished form.

**b.** ☐ This is the first application submitted by this author as copyright claimant.

**c.** ☐ This is a changed version of the work, as shown by space 6 on this application.

If your answer is "Yes," give: **Previous Registration Number ▼**       **Year of Registration ▼**

**5**

**DERIVATIVE WORK OR COMPILATION** Complete both space 6a & 6b for a derivative work; complete only 6b for a compilation.

**a. Preexisting Material** Identify any preexisting work or works that this work is based on or incorporates. ▼

**b. Material Added to This Work** Give a brief, general statement of the material that has been added to this work and in which copyright is claimed. ▼

See instructions
before completing
this space.

**6**

—space deleted—

**7**

**REPRODUCTION FOR USE OF BLIND OR PHYSICALLY HANDICAPPED INDIVIDUALS**      A signature on this form at space 10, and a check in one of the boxes here in space 8, constitutes a non-exclusive grant of permission to the Library of Congress to reproduce and distribute solely for the blind and physically handicapped and under the conditions and limitations prescribed by the regulations of the Copyright Office: (1) copies of the work identified in space 1 of this application in Braille (or similar tactile symbols); or (2) phonorecords embodying a fixation of a reading of that work; or (3) both.

a ☐ Copies and Phonorecords       b ☐ Copies Only       c ☐ Phonorecords Only

See instructions

**8**

**DEPOSIT ACCOUNT** If the registration fee is to be charged to a Deposit Account established in the Copyright Office, give name and number of Account.
**Name ▼**       **Account Number ▼**

**9**

**CORRESPONDENCE** Give name and address to which correspondence about this application should be sent. Name/Address/Apt/City/State/Zip ▼

Area Code & Telephone Number ▶

Be sure to
give your
daytime phone
◀ number

**CERTIFICATION\*** I, the undersigned, hereby certify that I am the

Check one ▶

☐ author
☐ other copyright claimant
☐ owner of exclusive right(s)
☐ authorized agent of _____

of the work identified in this application and that the statements made
by me in this application are correct to the best of my knowledge.

Name of author or other copyright claimant, or owner of exclusive right(s) ▲

**10**

**Typed or printed name and date ▼** If this application gives a date of publication in space 3, do not sign and submit it before that date.

date ▶

Handwritten signature (X) ▼

| MAIL CERTIFI-CATE TO | Name ▼ | YOU MUST: · Complete all necessary spaces · Sign your application in space 10 |
| --- | --- | --- |
| **Certificate will be mailed in window envelope** | Number·Street·Apartment Number ▼ | **SEND ALL 3 ELEMENTS IN THE SAME PACKAGE:** 1. Application form 2. Nonrefundable $20 filing fee in check or money order payable to *Register of Copyrights* 3. Deposit material |
| | City·State·ZIP ▼ | **MAIL TO:** Register of Copyrights Library of Congress Washington, D.C. 20559 |

Copyright fees are adjusted at 5-year intervals, based on increases or decreases in the Consumer Price Index. The next adjustment is due in 1995. Contact the Copyright Office in January 1995 for the new fee schedule.

**11**

\* 17 U.S.C. § 506(e) Any person who knowingly makes a false representation of a material fact in the application for copyright registration provided for by section 409, or in any written statement filed in connection with the application, shall be fined not more than $2,500

July 1992—100,000

☆ U.S. GOVERNMENT PRINTING OFFICE: 1992—312-432/60,006

**Figure 17.2b** Form TX (back).

# FORM VA

UNITED STATES COPYRIGHT OFFICE

REGISTRATION NUMBER

VA                    VAU

EFFECTIVE DATE OF REGISTRATION

Month          Day          Year

---

**DO NOT WRITE ABOVE THIS LINE. IF YOU NEED MORE SPACE, USE A SEPARATE CONTINUATION SHEET.**

**1**

**TITLE OF THIS WORK ▼**                    **NATURE OF THIS WORK ▼** See instructions

**PREVIOUS OR ALTERNATIVE TITLES ▼**

**PUBLICATION AS A CONTRIBUTION**   If this work was published as a contribution to a periodical, serial, or collection, give information about the collective work in which the contribution appeared.   **Title of Collective Work ▼**

If published in a periodical or serial give: **Volume ▼**          **Number ▼**          **Issue Date ▼**          **On Pages ▼**

**2**

**a**

**NAME OF AUTHOR ▼**                    **DATES OF BIRTH AND DEATH**
Year Born ▼          Year Died ▼

Was this contribution to the work a "work made for hire"?
☐ Yes
☐ No

**AUTHOR'S NATIONALITY OR DOMICILE**
Name of Country
OR { Citizen of ▶
Domiciled in ▶

**WAS THIS AUTHOR'S CONTRIBUTION TO THE WORK**
Anonymous?   ☐ Yes ☐ No
Pseudonymous?   ☐ Yes ☐ No
If the answer to either of these questions is "Yes," see detailed instructions.

**NATURE OF AUTHORSHIP**   Briefly describe nature of the material created by this author in which copyright is claimed. ▼

**NOTE**

Under the law, the "author" of a "work made for hire" is generally the employer, not the employee (see instructions). For any part of this work that was "made for hire" check "Yes" in the space provided, give the employer (or other person for whom the work was prepared) as "Author" of that part, and leave the space for dates of birth and death blank.

**b**

**NAME OF AUTHOR ▼**                    **DATES OF BIRTH AND DEATH**
Year Born ▼          Year Died ▼

Was this contribution to the work a "work made for hire"?
☐ Yes
☐ No

**AUTHOR'S NATIONALITY OR DOMICILE**
Name of country
OR { Citizen of ▶
Domiciled in ▶

**WAS THIS AUTHOR'S CONTRIBUTION TO THE WORK**
Anonymous?   ☐ Yes ☐ No
Pseudonymous?   ☐ Yes ☐ No
If the answer to either of these questions is "Yes," see detailed instructions.

**NATURE OF AUTHORSHIP**   Briefly describe nature of the material created by this author in which copyright is claimed. ▼

**c**

**NAME OF AUTHOR ▼**                    **DATES OF BIRTH AND DEATH**
Year Born ▼          Year Died ▼

Was this contribution to the work a "work made for hire"?
☐ Yes
☐ No

**AUTHOR'S NATIONALITY OR DOMICILE**
Name of Country
OR { Citizen of ▶
Domiciled in ▶

**WAS THIS AUTHOR'S CONTRIBUTION TO THE WORK**
Anonymous?   ☐ Yes ☐ No
Pseudonymous?   ☐ Yes ☐ No
If the answer to either of these questions is "Yes," see detailed instructions.

**NATURE OF AUTHORSHIP**   Briefly describe nature of the material created by this author in which copyright is claimed. ▼

**3**

**YEAR IN WHICH CREATION OF THIS WORK WAS COMPLETED** This information must be given in all cases.
◀ Year

**DATE AND NATION OF FIRST PUBLICATION OF THIS PARTICULAR WORK**
Complete this information ONLY if this work has been published.   Month ▶          Day ▶          Year ▶          ◀ Nation

**4**

See instructions before completing this space.

**COPYRIGHT CLAIMANT(S)** Name and address must be given even if the claimant is the same as the author given in space 2.▼

**TRANSFER** If the claimant(s) named here in space 4 are different from the author(s) named in space 2, give a brief statement of how the claimant(s) obtained ownership of the copyright.▼

APPLICATION RECEIVED

ONE DEPOSIT RECEIVED

TWO DEPOSITS RECEIVED

REMITTANCE NUMBER AND DATE

DO NOT WRITE HERE   OFFICE USE ONLY

**MORE ON BACK ▶**   • Complete all applicable spaces (numbers 5-9) on the reverse side of this page.
• See detailed instructions.          • Sign the form at line 8.

**DO NOT WRITE HERE**
Page 1 of ____ pages

**Figure 17.3a**   Form VA (front).

| | |
|---|---|
| EXAMINED BY | **FORM VA** |
| CHECKED BY | |
| ☐ CORRESPONDENCE Yes | FOR COPYRIGHT OFFICE USE ONLY |
| ☐ DEPOSIT ACCOUNT FUNDS USED | |

**DO NOT WRITE ABOVE THIS LINE. IF YOU NEED MORE SPACE, USE A SEPARATE CONTINUATION SHEET.**

**PREVIOUS REGISTRATION**   Has registration for this work, or for an earlier version of this work, already been made in the Copyright Office?
☐ Yes  ☐ No   If your answer is "Yes," why is another registration being sought? (Check appropriate box) ▼
☐ This is the first published edition of a work previously registered in unpublished form.
☐ This is the first application submitted by this author as copyright claimant.
☐ This is a changed version of the work, as shown by space 6 on this application.
If your answer is "Yes," give: **Previous Registration Number ▼**          **Year of Registration ▼**

**5**

**DERIVATIVE WORK OR COMPILATION**   Complete both space 6a & 6b for a derivative work; complete only 6b for a compilation.
a.   **Preexisting Material**   Identify any preexisting work or works that this work is based on or incorporates. ▼

b.   **Material Added to This Work**   Give a brief, general statement of the material that has been added to this work and in which copyright is claimed.▼

**6**

See instructions
before completing
this space.

**DEPOSIT ACCOUNT**   If the registration fee is to be charged to a Deposit Account established in the Copyright Office, give name and number of Account.
**Name ▼**                                    **Account Number ▼**

**7**

**CORRESPONDENCE**   Give name and address to which correspondence about this application should be sent.   Name/Address/Apt/City/State/Zip ▼

Area Code & Telephone Number ▶

Be sure to
give your
daytime phone
◀ number.

**CERTIFICATION***   I, the undersigned, hereby certify that I am the
Check only one ▼
☐ author
☐ other copyright claimant
☐ owner of exclusive right(s)
☐ authorized agent of_____
                      Name of author or other copyright claimant, or owner of exclusive right(s) ▲

**8**

of the work identified in this application and that the statements made
by me in this application are correct to the best of my knowledge.

**Typed or printed name and date ▼** If this is a published work, this date must be the same as or later than the date of publication given in space 3.

_____ date ▶ _____

**Handwritten signature (X) ▼**

| | Have you: | |
|---|---|---|
| **MAIL CERTIFI-CATE TO** | Name ▼ | • Completed all necessary spaces? • Signed your application in space 8? |
| **Certificate will be mailed in window envelope** | Number/Street/Apartment Number ▼ | • Enclosed check or money order for $10 payable to *Register of Copyrights?* • Enclosed your deposit material with the application and fee? |
| | City/State/ZIP ▼ | **MAIL TO:** Register of Copyrights, Library of Congress, Washington, D.C. 20559. |

**9**

* 17 U.S.C. § 506(e): Any person who knowingly makes a false representation of a material fact in the application for copyright registration provided for by section 409, or in any written statement filed in connection with the application, shall be fined not more than $2,500.
☆U.S. GOVERNMENT PRINTING OFFICE: 1987—181—531/60,010

August 1987—100.000

**Figure 17.3*b***   Form VA (back).

## SIMPLIFIED ADULT RELEASE

For valuable consideration received, I hereby grant to [PHOTOGRAPHER] the absolute and irrevocable right and permission, in respect of the photographs that he/she had taken of me or in which I may be included with others, to copyright the same, in his/her own name or otherwise; to use, re-use, publish, and re-publish the same in whole or in part, individually or in conjunction with other photographs, and in conjunction with any printed matter, in any and all media now or hereafter known, and for any purpose whatsoever, for illustration, promotion, art, advertising and trade, or any other purpose whatsoever; and to use my name in connection therewith if he/she so chooses.

I hereby release and discharge [PHOTOGRAPHER] from any and all claims and demands arising out of or in connection with the use of the photographs, including without limitation any and all claims for libel or invasion of privacy.

This authorization and release shall also inure to the benefit of the heirs, legal representatives, licensees, and assigns of [PHOTOGRAPHER], as well as the person(s) for whom he/she took the photographs.

I am of full age and have the right to contract in my own name. I have read the foregoing and fully understand the contents thereof. This release shall be binding upon me and my heirs, legal representatives, and assigns.


DATE: _____     _____
                                                         (NAME)


_____       _____
        (WITNESS)                               (ADDRESS)

**Figure 17.4**  Photographic release. (*Source: The American Society of Media Photographers, Inc. Copyright © 1986. All rights reserved. Reprinted with permission.*)

# Authoring

# 18

# Using Object-Oriented Tools for Faster, Easier Software Development

**Glenn K. Morrissey**

## Why the Multimedia Market is Expanding

The use of multimedia technology is exploding for a myriad of reasons:

- *It's effective.* Multimedia lets users communicate faster and still produces better retention of communicated information.

- *It's cost-effective.* Multimedia-enabled hardware is rushing to market, with prices for components from CD-ROM drives to audio and video boards lower than ever before.

- *It's a safe bet.* In 1992, Microsoft Corp. brought multimedia into the PC mainstream by including multimedia in its Windows operating system software. With a clear standard, buyers and sellers can now participate in the multimedia market without worrying about betting on the wrong technology or specification.

- *It's compelling.* Users can't use multimedia without multimedia application software. And they won't use it if those applications aren't compelling. Happily, a new generation of affordable, easy-to-use software tools is spurring the rapid development of those vital applications.

The affordability and ease of use of these new-generation software-development tools is producing two profound changes in the multimedia marketplace:

1. *An expansion in the base of software developers.* Until recently, applications were written by programming experts—those who understood the

requisite programming languages. Today, applications can be written by "content" or subject-area experts with little or no training in programming. This means that the communication between expert and user is more direct, producing more useful software. It also means that more content experts can author titles, thus expanding the base of multimedia titles.

2. *A reduction in time- and cost-to-market.*   For developers, new tools replace a considerable amount of time-consuming code-writing with a fast, easy graphical interface (much as Windows has replaced the text-based interface of MS-DOS for users). Much of the multimedia functionality that developers might otherwise have had to create for themselves is already built in—and reusable. Applications under development can be tested without time-consuming recompiling. All of this cuts the time required for title development from years to months or less. And shorter time-to-market both expands the universe of available titles and reduces the prices that need to be charged for them.

## Introducing Object-Oriented Tools

Several development tools now on the market provide varying levels of this new functionality. A key example is Multimedia ToolBook, a popular multimedia development tool made for Microsoft Windows by Asymetrix Corp.

Multimedia ToolBook, introduced in 1991, has been used to create more than 25 percent of the multimedia MPC titles now available, including Microsoft's Beethoven; Macmillan's Macmillan Dictionary for Children—Multimedia Edition; and Dr. T's Music Software's Composer Quest. Companies including Lotus and Turtle Beach use Multimedia ToolBook for their own MPC demos. And thousands of corporate developers such as Andersen Consulting, Lockheed, and Intel use it for in-house title development.

The tool is a software construction set that lets users build customized Windows multimedia applications. Exemplifying the features of new-generation tools, Multimedia ToolBook uses an intuitive graphical user interface; an object-oriented programming language called OpenScript; hypernavigation and linking among video, audio, animation, images, and text; and tools for editing and debugging applications.

### How Multimedia ToolBook differs from traditional environments

Multimedia ToolBook differs from conventional development environments in at least three ways:

1. *ToolBook handles screen imaging automatically.*   Instead of writing code to display text and graphics, you create objects with Multimedia ToolBook's drawing tools. Objects persist between executions of your application, and Multimedia ToolBook handles all imaging for you.

2. *Multimedia ToolBook objects are "smart."* Because these objects come with built-in behaviors, you don't have to program every action for your application, only those behaviors that are unique. A Multimedia ToolBook field knows how to display and scroll text. A Multimedia ToolBook player knows how to run a video clip, etc.

3. *Multimedia ToolBook handles memory management.* You no longer need to worry about writing to specific memory segments. Multimedia ToolBook, working with Windows, handles memory management for you.

### How Multimedia ToolBook leverages multimedia functionality

Multimedia expands your development options. The challenge for tool-providers is to offer new flexibility without adding complexity for developers. In Multimedia ToolBook, that has been accomplished by building multimedia functionality into prescripted objects, called *widgets,* that make multimedia use a simple matter of cutting and pasting widgets, or their scripts, into the target application.

For example a prebuilt, VCR-like control panel can be pasted directly into an application to provide features such as play, pause, stop, fast-forward, and rewind, all without writing any programming. Users can link to and control any standard Windows multimedia device, including CD-ROM, laserdisc player, animation software, waveform audio card, overlay video boards, and MIDI sequencer.

Meanwhile, experienced developers can integrate customized multimedia functionality from whatever level they wish, using the C compiler language, Windows SDK, or other tools. And for developers who feel comfortable with a modest level of direct script-writing, Multimedia ToolBook permits this approach too, using clear, English-based commands. Whereas widgets offer greatest ease-of-use, and C and similar tools offer the greatest power and customization, simple scripting brings together the benefits of both approaches.

The following sections will show you the advantages of multimedia development using an object-oriented development tool, and how to leverage those advantages so as to develop specific applications.

### Using an Event-Driven System

Unlike earlier tools, Multimedia ToolBook is an event-driven system. Understanding how that system works will enable you to leverage its advantages.

An *event* is any action the user takes in a window, such as pressing a key, clicking or dragging the mouse, or choosing a menu option. These events occur in random order—"at the whim of the mouse"—and the application must respond to them. An event-driven system can do this; traditional programming, with its linear code, can't.

Every event generates a message, which Multimedia ToolBook responds to. Programming a Multimedia ToolBook application, therefore, is essentially a matter of reacting to messages. Multimedia ToolBook generates idle messages at Reader level when there is no other input. Even when the user is doing nothing, the application still receives messages. Reader-level changes, unlike those created by the developer at Author level, do not change the content of the title.

Input to a Multimedia ToolBook application comes in the form of keyboard events, mouse events, and menu events. Keywords in the OpenScript programming language correspond to the messages sent as a result of those events. Multimedia ToolBook has built-in responses to event-driven messages. For example if a user clicks a menu command, Multimedia ToolBook's built-in response is to display the appropriate dialogue box or carry out the action indicated by the command. Additional events come from system notification. For example, Multimedia ToolBook gives you an enterPage event every time a new page is displayed, and a leaveBook message is sent as the application closes down.

### Sending messages

Although events occur "at the whim of the mouse," the messages triggered by events travel in a predictable direction. Messages are sent to objects in "books"—the metaphor for the Multimedia ToolBook application. Which object receives a given message depends on the message. For instance,

- Mouse event messages are sent to the object with the mouse pointer.
- Menu command messages are sent to the currently displayed page in the application.
- Keyboard event messages are sent to the object with the "focus," that is, the button, field, or record field where the keystrokes will be typed.

Because Multimedia ToolBook is designed to be flexible, you aren't limited to its built-in messages. You can define your own, as needed for specific applications.

### Handling messages

A message is sent; how will the Multimedia ToolBook application handle it? You program the response to an event-driven message in a *handler*. Handlers live in *scripts*. Any object can have a script. The handler receiving the message directs the response to the event. A handler does not have to live in the script of the object it handles. Messages are forwarded from object to object until a corresponding handler for the message is found. The direction in which a message is forwarded is based upon the object hierarchy. Messages travel up the hierarchy in search of a handler, as shown in Fig. 18.1.

The place in the object hierarchy where a message enters is called the *target*. For example, a buttonUp message is sent upon releasing the left mouse button during a mouse click. The target of a buttonUp message is the object clicked. If no handler for the message resides in the object's script, the mes-

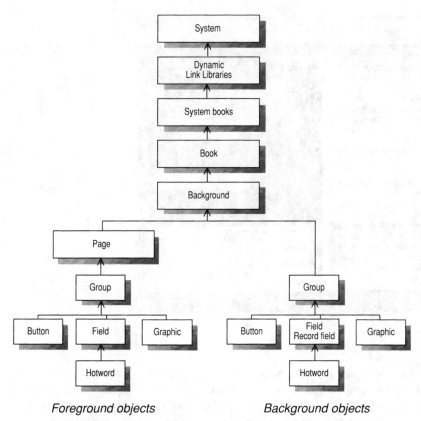

**Figure 18.1** Toolbook object hierarchy.

sage is forwarded to the group script if the object belongs to a group; then it is forwarded to the page. If none of the objects' scripts in the hierarchy contains a handler for a message, the message is forwarded to the Multimedia ToolBook system. At the system level, Multimedia ToolBook responds to a message with the default, or built-in, behavior. Because a Multimedia ToolBook application can rely on Multimedia ToolBook's built-in responses for much of its behavior, you can concentrate on writing handlers to add new or different behavior (Fig. 18.2).

## Writing handlers

Often, you will place a handler in the script of the target object. However, placing handlers at different levels in the hierarchy gives you greater flexibility in defining object behaviors such as

- *General behavior for multiple objects.* Placing a handler higher in the hierarchy defines general behavior for the objects below. The higher the handler, the greater its scope.

**Figure 18.2**   Toolbook handlers.

- *Exceptional behavior for an object.*   Placing a handler lower in the hierarchy intercepts a message to block general behavior, whether defined by a handler in the application or by the Multimedia ToolBook system. For example, Multimedia ToolBook has built-in responses to menu command messages; a handler could be placed specifically to substitute a different response behavior.

- *"Staged" behavior for an object.*   Including a forward statement in a handler forwards a message for more processing. A message can be forwarded up the hierarchy, directly to another object, or directly to the Multimedia ToolBook system. For example, a handler can use staged behavior by prompting a user to provide additional input and then forwarding a message conditionally based on the user's response.

## Developing Applications Using Object-Oriented Tools

You can use object-oriented development tools to create a range of multimedia applications, including

- *On-line kiosks.*   Stand-alone installations that provide user-directed information and more, such as accepting names and addresses to which to send additional information or products, and printing out maps or other data at the user's request.

- *Interactive training.*   On-line tutorials and interactive education programs.

- *Hypermedia documents.*   Encyclopedias and help systems, with links so that readers can explore topics dynamically.
- *Databases.*   Complete flat-file databases in Multimedia ToolBook, or front-ends to data from external sources.

Now let's take a closer look at using object-oriented tools to develop these applications.

## Presentations and kiosks

In the era of music videos and video games, people are used to flashy visual input. On-line presentations and kiosks appeal to this visually sophisticated audience, far more than traditional media do (Fig. 18.3). The presenter controls the presentation with the mouse or keyboard, so it's easy to branch out to corollary topics, include animation, or modify a screen during the presentation. In general, on-line presentations require even less programming than do other types of object-oriented applications. Kiosks provide even greater functionality. First, they operate without the need for a presenter; the user navigates through the information directly. Second, the kiosk can accept user information such as names, addresses, and credit card data, so as to send additional information or products. Users also can receive hard copies of requested information—such as ordering lists or maps—to take with them.

As shown in Fig. 18.3, developers can create bullet lists that reveal themselves one bullet at a time. They can size the screen to hide the menu bar. And they can insert buttons with built-in functionality (e.g., "go to the next screen when clicked") that don't require any additional programming for use.

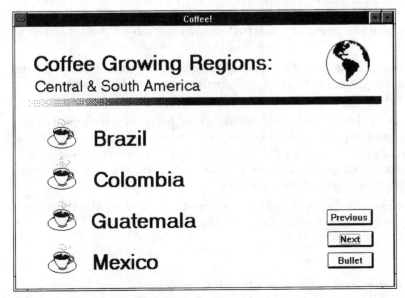

**Figure 18.3**  A multimedia kiosk.

**Scripts in kiosks.**  A self-running kiosk needs few controls beyond automated page-turning. A scripted control structure flips through the pages at regular intervals. Using Multimedia ToolBook, you can provide this control via an idle handler. For example:

```
to handle idle
    send next
    pause 5 seconds
end
```

While idle messages are being received—i.e., while no user action is taking place—the application displays the next page. When the user presses a key, the keyDown message is sent and intercepted by a handler like this:

```
to handle keyDown
    request "Quit?" with "Yes" or "No"
    if it is "Yes"
        send exit
    end
end
```

If the user answers "yes" to the Request Dialog Box, the application quits.

**Tips for developing effective kiosks.**  Here's a set of guidelines you can use to develop effective kiosks:

1. You may wish to customize the interface for your kiosk. That's easy to do using a tool such as Multimedia ToolBook. Hiding menu bars is as simple as inserting the instruction "hide menuBar at reader" in an enterBook handler. You can hide the title bar by positioning the window to a negative $y$ coordinate, using the instruction "set bounds of mainWindow to coordinates."

2. Keep screens simple for better comprehension. In the case of bulleted lists, a good rule of thumb is to keep to a maximum of five lines, with three to four words per line.

3. If your kiosk is being made to accommodate a group, be sure to use colors, typefaces, and type sizes that can be seen by everyone. Sans serif type (e.g., Helvetica) is easier to read than serif type (e.g., Times). Subtle background colors (e.g., gray) are easier to view than bold colors. Avoid dithered colors; they provide insufficient contrast.

4. Use a simple, consistent technique for smooth page navigation. Create a summary page that serves as a map for the user.

## Interactive training

An object-oriented tool such as Multimedia ToolBook is ideal for authoring interactive training applications, because you can easily create screens with rich color graphics, place customized text where you want it, and use animation to illustrate or to capture a student's attention. You can create quizzes and store student responses, display hints, acknowledge correct answers, and track a student's progress from lesson to lesson.

**Designing a workbook.**   Your interactive training application can be in the form of a "workbook," with different types of pages serving different functions. For instance,

- A table of contents page lists topics to be covered in the workbook. The background for these pages can include a script that places a checkmark beside topics that have been viewed by the student.

- Explanation pages present the concepts associated with a topic and introduce the exercises to follow.

- Exercise pages contain specific instructions and objects that the student can use to complete the exercise.

**Tips for effective interactive training.**   In designing an interactive training application, you should

- Keep the design simple, so students can spend time learning your content—not your format. Hide the menu bar or menu elements that are not needed for training. And use a few, varied backgrounds that can be keyed to—and provide an intuitive clue to—the type of information being displayed.

- Establish user-defined properties to hold information about a student such as the student's name, completed lessons, or quiz scores.

- Use "request" and "ask" commands to display hints or prompt the student for information.

- Organize information in manageable portions. One concept per lesson is a good rule of thumb.

- Provide clear, consistent navigation controls so that students will know where they are in an application and how to move around in it.

- Keep your design general and flexible, so that it can be readily updated with additional lessons, as needed over time.

## Hypermedia documents

Hypermedia documents use hotwords, buttons, and other linking devices to allow end users to navigate through your information at their own direction and pace. Electronic textbooks, encyclopedias, kiosks, and point-of-purchase displays can all benefit from the linking tools in development products such as Multimedia ToolBook. Those tools include navigational links and context-sensitive information.

**Navigation links.** Readers can browse topics by clicking buttons or hotwords linked to other pages in the book. When using these links, you should organize your document in a branching structure. Each main topic starts a new page in a linear progression; subtopics branch off the main path on their own pages.

The flexibility of open navigation through a book can also be a drawback, if the reader becomes—or just feels—lost. Control buttons on subtopic pages can let the reader decide whether to return to the main topic or go to a new one. Other icons and tools can restore even more user control. For example, a compass icon on each page can display an index to all book topics, showing their relationships and allowing readers to move to new topics of their choosing.

Another way to illustrate a book's structure is to use a contents page. Clicking a topic (a button with a buttonUp handler) can reveal subtopics (hidden grouped objects) under it. Readers can use the contents page to move directly to the desired part of the application.

The contents page from the "Multimedia Tour" title in Multimedia ToolBook (Fig. 18.4) is a hypermedia document. It uses navigational links to let readers move directly to subjects of particular interest. Navigational buttons on this page appear in the same location throughout the book, making it easier for readers to navigate.

**Context-sensitive links.** Context-sensitive links provide additional help to readers where and when they need it. The tasks they perform are based on where the reader is working. Using context-sensitive hotwords and buttons keeps pages uncluttered yet provides quick access to additional information.

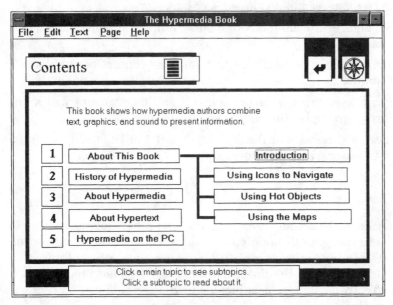

**Figure 18.4** A table of contents structure.

In Multimedia ToolBook's "Multimedia Tour," for example, a glossary page is made up entirely of context-sensitive hot buttons. Each button's script is a user-defined message that gets forwarded to a handler in the book's script. The handler displays a specific line of text in a request dialogue box. Hotwords throughout the book bring up similar context-sensitive definitions by sending user-defined messages to the book. Both the glossary buttons and the hotwords use the request command to present the definitions.

By the user's handling the buttonUp message in the book's script, consistent behavior is guaranteed for any hotword or button in the book. For example in an on-line personnel manual, every mention of the word *overtime* could be a hotword that brings up a description of the overtime policy when clicked. To make script-writing simple, you would set the name of the page to overtime. Now, the following handler in the book's script takes care of navigation for all overtime hotwords in the book:

```
to handle buttonUp
    if target contains "hotword"
        go to page (text of target)
    end
end buttonUp
```

The target is the overtime hotword, whose script is empty. When a reader clicks this hotword, the buttonUp message floats up the object hierarchy to the book in search of a handler. When the handler in the book script runs, Multimedia ToolBook goes to the page whose name is the same as the target's text.

**Tips for designing hypermedia documents.**   Because information is so accessible in hypermedia documents, you will need to take special care to organize that information effectively. You should

- Divide your information into discrete units of single concepts or ideas. Devote a new page to each. When you build links among the pages, the interrelation of ideas will appear more natural.

- Design your book around a relevant metaphor. For example, Macmillan New Media's *Macmillan Dictionary for Children–Multimedia Edition* uses a book metaphor. Asymetrix's *MediaBlitz!* uses a time-line metaphor. A metaphor helps the end user to place your information in an immediately recognizable context.

- Use animation instead of text to explain actions that are better shown than described, such as how objects appear or act under different conditions or from different perspectives.

## Database applications

A multimedia database can easily include video, photographic images, even audio, along with traditional text and graphics. Realtors, insurance adjusters, and museum curators are just three types of end users who would benefit from maintaining multimedia databases.

**Flat-file databases.**   Multimedia ToolBook can be used to create flat-file databases or front-ends to external data sources. A flat-file database has a structure represented by a single nonhierarchical set of fields, unlike a relational database, which can include multiple sets of fields with relationships established among them. Front-ends give users an easy interface to large, complex, centralized databases.

A flat-file database written in Multimedia ToolBook can use graphics, buttons, and record fields to construct a simple screen useful for both data entry and browsing. Buttons and graphic controls on the background can contain scripts for creating, copying, and deleting pages and searching the database for character strings.

You can create a database quickly by importing an ASCII-delimited or ASCII fixed-field file into Multimedia ToolBook. Importing an ASCII file automatically creates a background with record fields to hold the data you import.

A flat-file database in Multimedia ToolBook can include buttons and graphics that serve as controls for modifying records, searching, and navigation (Fig. 18.5).

**Database front-ends.**   When you need to maintain data in its original form, rather than import it into the Multimedia ToolBook application, you'll want to use Multimedia ToolBook to create a front-end. This is useful, for example, for data that needs to be accessed by other software. To access the data from Multimedia ToolBook, you can use Object Linking and Embedding (OLE), a Dynamic Link Library (DLL), or Dynamic Data Exchange (DDE).

A DLL is an external file, usually written in C, that defines the functions a Multimedia ToolBook application can use. To use a DLL, you write statements in a script that link to the DLL and declare the functions you want. Then you can use those functions in any handler in the book. Database access is just one example of what a DLL might do. DLLs can extend Multimedia ToolBook in other ways, such as driving multimedia devices or interacting with other programs.

DDE is a Windows communication protocol that makes it possible for two programs that support DDE to exchange data and issue commands to each other. DDE allows you to integrate applications to take advantage of the strengths of each. For example, Microsoft Excel is better than Multimedia ToolBook at number-crunching, but Multimedia ToolBook provides more flexible, exciting graphics for a better GUI. You might maintain data in Excel and access it from your Multimedia ToolBook application.

DDE in Multimedia ToolBook is built into a set of OpenScript® commands you can use in scripts. To use DDE, you need a copy of the program with which you are exchanging data, and you need to know what DDE syntax that program expects.

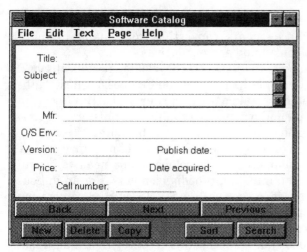

**Figure 18.5**  A flat-file database.

Here's an example of using DDE in Multimedia ToolBook. It calls for the Multimedia ToolBook application to obtain updated information from an Excel database and display it in the Multimedia ToolBook front-end:

—Update a summary field in the Multimedia ToolBook instance by
—requesting data from Excel
to handle buttonUp
   getRemote "Regional __ Totals" application excel topic "region.xls"
   put It into text of field "summary"
end buttonUp

**Tips for designing databases.**  Here are some additional ideas for database design:

- When you use record fields in a book, whether for a database, presentation, or other purpose, don't place objects over the record fields on the background. Overlapping background objects can have a significant impact on the speed of page flipping and scrolling.

- When you create a database front-end with Multimedia ToolBook, you don't need to use record fields. The work of accessing and displaying data is done by the scripts that communicate with the external database, so you can use regular fields on the foreground of a page.

## New Budgetary Considerations

Software development used to require a tremendous budget for programming work. With event-driven, object-oriented application development, that's no longer the case. Meanwhile, other parts of the multimedia development process—researching audio and video clips, negotiating and obtaining rights, producing original multimedia elements, converting from analog to digital, etc.—have become both time-consuming and expensive.

For example, using Multimedia ToolBook, the development staff at Dr. T's Music Software needed just two months to assemble Composer Quest, rather than the two years it might have taken with earlier tools. But recording musical selections, researching and writing biographies and history/art cross-references, scanning photographs, etc. took many months more.

Developers need to be aware of these new time-line and budgetary realities when they plan the development process. Developers also need to be fully aware of all their options for obtaining multimedia elements. For an in-house application, a nonprofessional video shot with a S-VHS or Hi-8 camera may be sufficient; certainly, it will be inexpensive. But for commercial applications or high-end corporate applications for use with clients, etc., developers may need professional-quality video that can cost up to several thousand dollars per minute of finished production. It is a good idea to construct a flowchart, identifying all needed multimedia elements and detailing explicit plans for their inclusion in the application.

## Bibliography

*DLL Reference: A Guide to Using Dynamic Link Libraries,* Asymetrix Corporation, Bellevue, WA, 1989–1991.

*Toolbook Ideas: An Author's Introduction to Programming in ToolBook,* Asymetrix Corporation, Bellevue, WA, 1989–1991.

*Using Multimedia ToolBook,* Asymetrix Corporation, Bellevue, WA, 1989–1991.

# 19

# Design Considerations for Multimedia-Based Executive Information Systems

**Roger Karr**

## Executive Multimedia

Multimedia has been submerged in a wide range of definitions, ranging from "a PC that can play back an audio file" to "a sophisticated, high-powered workstation that can digitize, and with additional 'hooks,' analyze data in the form of video, audio, graphics, images, and text." When GUIs (graphical-user interfaces) were introduced in the early 1980s, few predicted how critical these interfaces would be to our ability to work more effectively, use tools more efficiently, and provide richer information in an easier-to-use and more understandable way. Today, there is not much future for software packages or application tools that are built *without* such interfaces.

Multimedia for executive-level applications is the "new" interface. It is no longer a considered a "toy box" technology that technocrats play in. The next step in the revolution of transforming raw data into information and information into knowledge is now considered to be the form in which this knowledge can be represented. It has been said that new forms of knowledge-representation will continue to revolutionize the way people use and deal with information.

With the click of a button, you can now receive a desktop video of your marketing vice president presenting a corporatewide strategy for introducing your new widget to the market. This revolutionizes the way information, and in its purest sense knowledge, is acquired, transformed, and communicated. Having knowledge of new product information, revenue projections, new management-team goals and deliverables, has translated into better-informed decision making and significantly improved corporate performance. And after all, improving the bottom line *is* the bottom line.

Focused work that improves the quality of interactions between top managers and at the same time upgrades the quality of the information and knowledge to be shared can do remarkable things for a corporation's level of global performance. The integration of multimedia technology into existing corporate legacy systems, databases, document management systems, and corporate communication systems has been shown to dramatically enhance the quality of both executive and line-management interaction. It does this by improving the quality of information—an absolute requirement in today's global marketplace.

Without getting much of a brain cramp, most people in the computer industry can define, in their own terms, what multimedia is. In the context of executive information applications, multimedia is *the ability to select any or all forms of data, manipulate them into meaningful information, and effectively integrate that information into a solution that solves a business problem and results in more efficient decision making.* Understanding the importance of integration is just as important as understanding how to choose the right medium or combination of media that will maximize technological advantage while transforming information into knowledge.

## Multimedia applications for the executive

Perhaps the most obvious application of multimedia for the executive is in the area of corporate communications. Most executives, from senior managers right up to the CEO, have a need to communicate to all employees at all levels. As a general rule, a corporate communications session is developed and delivered once every quarter. Usually this is a big production (literally) and requires significant resources so as to coordinate a general assembly (or broadcast) and then reproduce and distribute it. More often than not, those who need to hear or see the session don't do so for a multitude of reasons:

- Companies typically are required to broadcast to multiple locations, but it may be that not all work sites have the satellite capability to receive the broadcast. Additionally, the costs for private broadcasts may be prohibitive.

- Videotape reproduction can be quite costly. Then too, the distributed videocassette often seems to get lost or to sit on a shelf in some person's office, collecting dust.

- The person receiving the videotape has the problem of trying to find the right time to play it, not to mention finding the answer to the age-old question, "Where do I get the TV and VCR?"

With a multimedia information kiosk positioned in a cafeteria, lobby, work bullpen, shop floor, or anywhere that "people take a break," people have immediate or "on-demand" access to the latest presidential address to employees, results and ramifications of the recent merger, shift in corporate strategies, incentive plans, etc. This communication vehicle, because of the richness of its multimedia interface, can also be entertaining even as it delivers vital information to the employees.

The results can be dramatic at all levels of the organization. One should never underestimate the value and importance of having a work force whose access to information is free and easy. The richness of information, when transformed into employee knowledge, can have a resounding effect on general work-force morale and on the whole concept of effective leadership. Take that transformation and apply it to your sales force, customer service division, Information Systems groups, and any other departments within the business and watch its effect on the bottom line. An effective organization is a well-informed organization.

## Multimedia-enabled succession planning

Multimedia at the executive's desktop takes the shape of many specific applications. One such application would be succession planning for medium to large corporations. Succession planning has often been done the "good ole boy" way; what matters is who you know, what you know, and how well connected you are. The development of a multimedia-rich application that integrates corporate databases, corporate planning, and strategic planning processes can provide executives with the information they need when they need it. Avoiding the "good ole boy" approach enables more objective decision making.

Executive Information applications can use multimedia to break through the barriers that have long prevented management teams from getting the information they need to make well-informed decisions. Multimedia is the delivery mechanism to communicate messages in easy, efficient, and effective ways. In fact it is the new integration tool for giving a second life to existing corporate legacy systems, document management systems, and corporate personnel databases in which millions of dollars have been invested. Multimedia provides the ability to represent this wealth of information in one seamless, easy-to-use application.

A number of considerations are critical to the successful development and deployment of multivendor, multimedia applications for the executive's desktop. They vary in importance depending on the type of business opportunity/problem you are trying to achieve or solve. It is important to note that the operative word in this statement is *multivendor*. Until the market has been defined, most if not all successful multimedia applications will be multivendor solutions.

## Configuring Worldwide Executive Multimedia Systems

The PC market is moving at such a rapid pace, it is hard to imagine any standard platform that can be used. Often the configuration of the desktop is driven by whether the application will reside in a distributed computing environment or as part of a single-user, stand-alone application. In the case of most multimedia applications designed for the executive desktop, many people have access to some of the same information, limited access to other levels of information. In these environments, distributed computing is the most efficient way to get information sorted and made available to whoever needs to use it.

In the context of succession planning, for example, information in all forms needs to be available: detailed performance data that allows effective analysis by the hiring executive; business segment performance; views on goals for both the individual and the corporation where he/she is employed; spreadsheet data to review budgeted versus actual spending; ROI calculations and overall budget performance. Using multimedia as the integration point, this data can be delivered in the form of text, graphs or bar charts, static images, audio, and audio combined with video. In most cases, during the succession planning process, the ability to collaborate with colleagues about the same information is crucial; therefore, allowing information and knowledge to be shared in a timely fashion is critical.

### Broadcast-quality video

In this environment, networking is the key. Delivering near-broadcast-quality video over a 10-Mbyte network is a challenge. It also limits the number of clients or users that can be served at any given time. Distributing this information requires network servers that allow for the storage of large, data-driven files, files that have been stored digitally on a magnetic disk residing on a file server. In terms of configuration, the file server must have a sizable amount of storage. Specific size depends on how much video and audio will be used by the application, along with database and image type information. In general terms, a 1-minute video file that was digitized at 2 kbits per second will consume an average of 20 Mbytes of hard-disk storage. At this record rate, the video can be delivered to the desktop at 30 frames per second with excellent resolution.

The amount of storage required can vary significantly depending on the hardware and software used for digitization. Different compression algorithms—JPEG, MPEG, MPEG+, and now Fractal (none of which can be considered standard)—can drastically change the storage requirements. Careful consideration must be given to the hardware and software selected to handle the task in terms of audio and video digitization. For a network distributed solution, the "gotchas" would be in the form of network protocols being used, throughput of the network, and the configuration requirements of the file server.

### Networking considerations

The type of network installed will determine the number of clients that can access the same file server. A 10-Mbyte network can safely handle an average of 6 clients at a data record rate of 1.5 kbits per second. Usable bandwidth on a 10-Mbyte network hovers around 7 or 8 Mbytes before significant through-put degradation is experienced. However, through the use of network repeaters the number of clients can be increased significantly at a relatively low cost.

A 100-Mbyte fiber-optic network can handle up to 80 clients from a single file server without experiencing any degradation in network performance. Splitting the network into several segments allows one to increase the num-ber of clients per server almost twofold. These figures serve as examples of what different networks can support in the way of multimedia applications. It should also be noted that if video is not part of the equation, the storage requirements are significantly reduced.

Many considerations must be taken into account when identifying the number of clients on the network that can be served from one network server. When you are ready to head down the road of "state-of-the-art" multimedia solutions, be sure to have a dedicated network engineer develop your network topology. This person plays a critical role in the overall functional specifica-tion and design of the multimedia solution.

Depending on the size of the application and the types of data that need to be integrated into the solution, the configuration may include several file servers. For integration into a document management system, for example, a file server may be required to store the document images. This server may employ the use of optical storage devices that have the ability to store many terabytes of information on the file server. Another file server may be required as an audio and video server only.

The message here is that, in addition to acquiring the services of a network expert, it is also critical to the success and implementation of your solution that you have on-board an experienced application architect who understands the business opportunity or problem. With these two resources in place, the process of developing a high-level design can get under way.

The development of a high-level design is an iterative process, and it requires tight communication among the customer (in this case the execu-tive), engineering, and delivery resources. With these components you now have a team that can design, develop, and deliver a high-powered multimedia solution for the executive(s). If you think that an army of engineers, archi-tects, and project managers must be required to complete such work, note that Digital Equipment Corporation developed such an application with just a "few good [people]."

### The PC configuration

In terms of desktop PC configurations, there are basically three areas that will significantly impact the performance of such applications. Again, it depends on whether they are distributed applications or stand-alone applications.

The first is the memory requirement for the desktop PC. In order to achieve the proper throughput on the desktop, a minimum of 12 Mbytes of memory should be configured. If the desktop is configured in a distributed environment, you may be able to get away with 8 Mbytes depending on other desktop applications you run locally. If the desktop is stand-alone, ideally 16 Mbytes should be configured into the desktop. As if to point up the fact that the personal computer industry is rapidly changing, Windows NT™ could transform the approach these applications take in a distributed computing environment.

The second consideration is disk storage. Again, in a distributed environment where you may require access to large amounts of storage on the server, disk storage does not play a critical role at the client level. Depending on whether you like to run your applications locally, aside from the multimedia application, a 160-Mbyte disk is more than sufficient. If the multimedia application resides locally on the desktop, local disk capacity is critical. This, however, depends on the types of data that have been integrated into the solution.

With video and audio files local and digitized at a 1.5-kbit record rate, 1 minute will consume roughly 20 Mbytes. Often this intense storage requirement scares people. However, if you consider the amount of information that can be communicated in a 1-minute video clip, the storage requirement suddenly becomes very reasonable. It also can be reduced significantly, depending on the required quality of the video. For example, if the record rate is 1.0 kbits and the video display requirement is 15 frames per second, that 1-minute segment now requires somewhere in the area of 5 to 7 Mbytes.

Executive-level multimedia applications have a tendency to need high-end video quality, especially if it is a corporate communications type of application. For these applications, disk storage requirements can range from 0.5 to 1 Gbyte. With this in mind, one of the major advantages to distributed computing is clear: investing in a well-configured file server can actually save in the area of client PC costs. In addition to the disk storage requirements for high-quality video, a good noninterlaced, multisync monitor should be part of the PC configuration.

The third desktop configuration consideration is the CODEC device used for compression/decompression. There are a number of these devices on the market. Many are hardware assisted and others are software playback only. Investing the time to learn about these many different devices is important.

## Steps for Integrating Multimedia into the Executive Suite

### Application content

Application content is perhaps the one area most critical to any executive information application, or multimedia application for that matter. In the case of executive multimedia applications, the content must be what the executive needs, not what you think the executive needs. In terms of a succession planning application or corporate communications application, the content must be current, professionally produced, and easily updated at a moment's notice.

When integrating a multimedia solution into existing corporate information systems, it is important to integrate only that data that enhances or enables the management team to make valued use of the application and, even more importantly, more effective decisions. For example, if the need is to integrate personnel profile records, pay attention only to the specific types (records) of information needed from the profile, not the entire profile. This will help you to manage the huge amount of data that needs to be changed or modified on a regular basis. Rather than use data just because it is there, use only that data that the application requires. This concept may spin off other work that needs to be done outside the application itself.

An example of this would be to execute database extractions outside of the multimedia application. When the extraction is complete, the manipulation of data may be done within or outside the application, depending on application dependencies. In layperson's terms, you should, when integrating large databases, do as much data manipulation/extraction as possible outside the application before importing to the executive information application. The "wins" here are (1) performance and (2) the advantage of distributed computing in another form.

## Audio and video

In terms of video and audio content, make no mistake, this must be done professionally, particularly when the application is to be used by senior executive staff members. When you are using these data types in an executive succession application, it is absolutely critical that each person being viewed in video form has their best foot forward. Keep in mind that seeing a person presenting themselves on your desktop should be the same, in terms of quality, as seeing a person speak on television. There is an unspoken expectation that the video and audio segments seen on the desktop will be of equal or greater quality as those we all see daily on broadcast television.

To meet this expectation, most medium to large corporations and government agencies have a communications division that consists of a fully equipped production studio. Engage these folks early, for they have a wealth of knowledge and insight most application developers and architects do not have when designing a multimedia application that draws on the full array of data types including video and audio. This also leads to the advantage of having a human-interface engineer review the look and feel and flow of the application. (This is often a part-time job for experts in the field.)

Other content such as images, text, and graphics all need to be integrated, keeping one question in mind: Is the information useful and easy to understand, and does it flow well? From the end user's point of view, the ability to navigate easily from one data type to another is just as important as the actual content itself. "Popping" from an interactive spreadsheet session (say, a budget projection), to a business plan, to the divisional executive presenting the new fiscal-year strategy, is where a multimedia application really shows its stuff.

## Business process considerations

Multimedia executive applications touch on a wide variety of traditional business processes, particularly in the succession planning procedure, where usually there are many processes that an executive board of directors goes through to select the next chief financial officer.

One must look at how these traditional processes are impacted. You may find that some are impacted very positively and others not so positively. An example of how a process was impacted by the development and deployment of an executive profiling application is one company's review of worldwide corporate performance. In this case, the board of directors wanted to get closer to the business. The first problem was the unfamiliarity of board members with the individuals responsible for particular business divisions, units, or segments. The challenge was to provide a tool that would not only introduce these individuals to senior management, but also deliver an electronic file folder for each individual containing information such as biographies, resumés, financial performance information, fiscal-year goals, personal performance data, personal development plans, etc.

In order to solve this seemingly intractable problem, processes were put in place to acquire this information in all forms. Standard formats were developed in terms of written reports, spreadsheet data, resumés, etc. Perhaps the most influential module of this application was the 10-minute video interview, in which the interviewees were asked specific questions about current corporate performance and what the corporation's strategy should be as it entered the twenty-first century. These very pointed and difficult questions were provided to the interviewer by the board of directors. The bottom line is that the board members now had the ability to learn, in a single day, about many divisions within the corporation, as opposed to the more traditional approach that could take up to 18 months.

This process required significant coordination by the individuals who set up the interview time with 30 senior executives worldwide. For those executives who were not in the corporate headquarters area, filming was done locally, while the actual interview was conducted via telephone. Significant savings were realized in terms of travel costs, and at the same time this process did not take the busy executive away from the business issues requiring his or her attention.

The other forms of data made it necessary to modify other processes. Most of the modifications were in the area of format and standards for reporting. Again, these were processes that were closely looked at prior to the actual commencement of work.

An example of the positive results accrued during this information-acquisition process: when an existing process for reporting was looked at to accommodate requirements for a multimedia succession planning application, it was determined that there were much better, more efficient ways to get this work done. Therefore the adoption of these practices became permanent. In addition the cost associated with putting together this application was far less than the cost (including executives' time) of getting 30 senior executives into the boardroom as candidates for not just one but many different positions.

Again, the processes that an executive information application uses are those that require significant attention. In today's business environment, companies are spending significant time and investing significant resources on process reengineering. Multimedia applications for executives can assist and become the "standard" way to deliver the results of this reengineering effort. Note as well that these types of applications can be of significant help in training executives in the results of such reengineering efforts.

## Support

Finally, there is always the need for support. The term *support,* in the context of this chapter, refers to the need for a person, group, or division to maintain the application. This maintenance comes in many forms. A few to touch upon would be network maintenance, application maintenance and enhancements, application content, and updates. Unlike many point-of-information multimedia kiosk applications, where much of the content is static for a period of time, executive information applications require that the data be absolutely up-to-date on a moment's notice. Often an executive needs to update information or annotate certain documents and pass them on to a colleague. This can all be done with significant attention being paid to the design, maintenance, and support of the application.

It is critical that the system have the ability to update this information easily. The data may change monthly, weekly, and oftentimes daily. The ability to rid the application of old information and replace it with current information is critical to the success of the application. This task is often designed into the application in such a way that a nontechnical support person can update its content dynamically. Often executives want to have the option to update or purge information on their own. In such cases, having a knowledgeable support person in place when the executive gets himself/herself in trouble (lets face it, it happens) is vital. This support person must be fully trained in the use of the application, and he or she should also have immediate access to the development or engineering team. In many instances, support is provided by the same team that designed and developed the application.

Support also falls into the realm of those business processes we discussed earlier. These should be designed in a way that supports the use of the application and makes possible the automated update of information in a standard format. Make no mistake, these applications *are* highly sophisticated, but sometimes they require no more support than what the executive needs today, simply a better way to pull it all together. Often this provides a refocus and training opportunity for those who are the support staff for the executive office and the executives themselves.

## Conclusion

We have only scratched the surface and looked at a very small sampling of how multimedia can be a significant competitive advantage for the management team of a company. We have discussed several ways in which such applications can produce significant cost savings in terms of succession planning and reengineered processes.

We have also discussed configuration considerations, the most important being those that impact network design, integration, and platform configuration.

Given the rate at which this technology is changing, perhaps the best advice I can give to you is to keep abreast of what tools (hardware and software) are hitting the marketplace and to learn how to turn them into a solution that will give executives a clear competitive advantage. But let's not forget that the application can also be a lot of fun to build and use!

# Macintosh Multimedia Tools

## Michael Kellner

## The Elusive Paperless Office

With the advent of desktop computing and communication, the idea of a paperless office arose. Electronic documents, conveyed by wire to one's colleagues...a very compelling thought. Alas, the computer revolution has produced the biggest paper explosion ever.

Nonetheless, with new technologies, it is becoming increasingly difficult to portray certain types of information on paper. We are seeing an increased push toward the paperless office as it becomes necessary to keep the electronic document "on line" to fully receive much of this information.

How much of the information you see around you would you like to have at your fingertips, indexed and easily accessed? With current technology you can bring text, images, sound, and motion video into your desktop working environment.

This chapter will describe a variety of different hardware and software tools that you can use with your Macintosh to capture both dynamic and static information for use in your multimedia documents.

### Types of information

There are two major types of information: *dynamic* and *static*. Dynamic information is composed of elements that change over time. For instance, video is composed of a sequence of pictures that change in time. Sound, stock quotes, and telemetry output also change over time.

Static information is data that does not convey its information based on time. For instance, one day's edition of a newspaper does not change over time. The information from that edition can be archived and obtained at any time. How the information is *interpreted* over time may change, but the data itself remains static. Other examples here include artwork, a company's quarterly results, and a photograph.

Computers traditionally have been good at handling static information. Recently desktop computers have been endowed with the ability to handle time-based information. Since there are so many types of dynamic information, it is necessary for a computer to have a solid architecture upon which to build the facilities that can manipulate dynamic data.

### The Macintosh is designed for multimedia

Since its inception, the Macintosh has been able to handle various forms of static information easily and consistently. Graphics and text were manipulated in the same way throughout the entire environment. There were no graphics modes. Pictures could be copied and pasted in the same way as text.

The Macintosh was built around a solid architecture for static data processing. Being a well-designed architecture, it was easy for Apple to extend it seamlessly with new technologies such as true-color image manipulation. Extensions were made to the system without adversely affecting the current applications. In fact, extensions could be made to the system that added functionality to existing programs without changing or upgrading the applications.

In 1991, Apple released QuickTime—a set of technologies packaged as a Macintosh system extension. QuickTime was designed as an architecture for handling time-based data. Being an architecture, it defines in general terms how time-based data is to be handled. QuickTime is expandable, and as of this writing has been extended twice beyond the initial implementation to include new data types and digital image-compression schemes.

With the installation of QuickTime, all programs that used pictures, a standard Macintosh data-type, could now use compressed pictures automatically. New applications were written to take advantage of QuickTime's motion video capabilities, and upgrades to applications were released that allowed QuickTime movies to be inserted into electronic documents. A movie embedded within a document provides an opportunity to better explain a concept described within the document.

The benefits of multimedia documents are fewer if you are limited to one computer platform. If the electronic document you create cannot be shared with the audience you are trying to reach, you will either have to bring the computer and the audience together or convert the document to a paper representation of the data, losing much of the information contained therein.

QuickTime and the QuickTime movie files are becoming a de facto industry standard. There are currently versions of QuickTime that operate on the Macintosh, Microsoft Windows, and A/UX (Apple's UNIX) platforms that can use the same data files. QuickTime movie file support is even more widespread. Hundreds of Macintosh and Windows applications support creation and/or playback of movie files. Apple has also licensed some key compression technologies to Silicon Graphics Inc., so their machines can support the creation and playback of QuickTime movie files.

With the proliferation of media produced using QuickTime, and the increasing popularity of the QuickTime movie file format, it is only a matter of time before QuickTime tools are available on other platforms. The incorporation of the Kaleida joint venture between IBM and Apple, and the collaboration of Apple with key consumer products manufacturers, ensure that QuickTime will continue to be the premiere dynamic data technology.

## Macintosh Multimedia Hardware Tools

Out of the box, the Macintosh comes with considerable multimedia capabilities built in. There are many additional multimedia tools available to you, to add to or extend those capabilities. But remember: *always* turn off your computer and all devices before connecting or disconnecting any device.

### Scanners

A *scanner* is a device that converts an image on a piece of paper to a picture that the computer can manipulate. It is used to bring a picture or text into the computer so that you don't have to draw or type it in yourself. Used with OCR (optical character recognition) software, your computer can transcribe a text document into a file that you can save, modify, transmit, or otherwise manipulate.

**Hardware.** There are many types of scanners, with various capabilities. *Flatbed scanners* are common, and operate somewhat like a photocopy machine. There is a glass surface upon which the document or book is placed. The scanner then passes a light and lens under the glass to make an image of what is on the glass. Some full-color scanners require three passes under the image.

*Hand-held scanners* require you to pass a small scanning device over the top of what you want to scan into the computer. They have a limit to the width that they can scan. If you can't cover the whole picture in one pass, you will have to connect the pieces together yourself, using a software tool such as PhotoShop. It can be difficult to align the scanned pieces so that the image looks coherent.

*Slide scanners* are used to scan 35-mm photographic slides. They produce high-quality, high-resolution images. However, slide scanners are of limited use. Not all the text or images you scan will be developed on 35-mm slides.

**Software.** Most scanners come with DAs (desk accessories) or with applications that allow you to scan documents and save them as graphics files. Some come with software that allows you to scan from within your favorite drawing package (such as Photoshop). This makes scanning and manipulating images one step easier.

**Connecting.** Most scanners that connect to the Macintosh do so through the SCSI port. Connect a SCSI cable and a SCSI terminator to the scanner. If there are no other SCSI devices such as external hard disks connected to your computer, connect the SCSI cable to your computer. If you have other devices, remove the terminator from the last device in the chain and connect the SCSI cable to the last device. Set the SCSI ID on the scanner to a number different than those of the other devices. Turn on all devices, then your computer. Install the scanner software provided with the scanner. For more information on SCSI, see the subsection SCSI Notes on p. 20.17 at the end of this chapter.

### Video input

A computer with video input capabilities can be quite useful. Much as a scanner is used to bring pictures on paper into the computer, so video input and a video camera can be used to bring pictures of objects into the computer. For instance, using a scanner to get a picture of a building would require that you take a picture of the building, have it developed and printed, then scan it using a scanner. With a video camera, you can videotape the building from many angles, connect the camera to your computer, then use a frame-grabbing program to capture the picture (or pictures) that you want.

Instant pictures can be made by connecting the video camera to the computer and running it "live." This can be useful for making pictures of small, movable objects, people, or even, with proper lighting and setup, photographs. However, the quality of a video image is not nearly as good as an image obtained by using a scanner.

Used in conjunction with QuickTime, video digitizers can be used to "grab" sequences of video for storage and playback. These are known as *QuickTime movies.*

**Hardware.**  If your Macintosh is not equipped for video input, you can get a video digitizing card. There is a plethora of these cards currently available. Many are combination display/video digitizing cards that can be used to add another monitor to your Macintosh, increasing your on-screen work area. Most digitizing cards have the capability to use S-Video as well as composite video input. S-Video is useful only if your video source (camera or videotape recorder) has it as well. Some cards offer hardware compression built in or as an upgrade option. Some cards combine audio and video input to offer a one-card solution to making digital movies.

Whichever digitizer you choose, make sure it is compatible with the model of your computer and offers the capabilities you need.

**Software.**  Video digitizers come with system software that allow you to use their capabilities. These system extensions are known as *VDIGs (video DIGitizing components)* that allow QuickTime to use the card. With the VDIG, any program that uses QuickTime to grab movies will work with the digitizer. As well, many companies package software to grab pictures, make movies, and otherwise manipulate video images.

**Connecting.**  With everything turned off, take the lid off your computer, find an empty slot, and push the card into it. Put the lid back onto your computer. If the board has display capabilities, connect the monitor cable to the card. This will result in faster video digitizing if you digitize to this display. Connect the appropriate cables to the card–S-Video cable, composite video cable, and/or audio cables. Turn on the computer and install the supplied software.

### Hardware-assisted video compression

Hardware-assisted compression for video input takes the burden of compression off of your computer by processing the video with components designed specifically for this purpose. This allows you to make larger movies at a faster frame rate.

The frame rate is the number of different pictures per second that the movie displays. Standard television in the United States uses a standard known as NTSC, which runs at 29.97 frames per second. Movies run at 24 frames per second.

**Hardware.**   Compression boards are designed either as a "daughter board" card, which plugs into an existing video input card, or as a separate card. Some video input cards, such as SuperMac's Digital Film, come with hardware-assisted compression built in. The MoviePak is an example of a daughter-board from RasterOps that plugs into a range of their existing video cards.

**Software.**   Hardware compression cards come with system software that you put into your System Folder. QuickTime will notice that the card is installed and add it to the list of compression options available. When you create a movie using a movie recorder or an editing package, select the compressor that came with the hardware. Note, however, that if you create a movie with a hardware compressor, it is likely you will need the hardware to play back the movie. If the hardware compressor is a JPEG compressor (a standard type), you can play back the movie without the hardware but at a much lower speed than it was recorded at.

### Video output

Video encoders give you the capability to record to videotape or display on a large screen everything that is displayed on your computer screen. This allows you to display presentations live to a large audience, or record to a videotape for archiving or viewing at a future time.

**Hardware.**   Certain video input boards such as the Radius Video Vision have composite and S-Video output sockets that connect directly to a VCR or large-screen display. The Video Vision has a feature called *image convolution* that reduces the flicker of narrow horizontal lines at the expense of some image clarity.

Other video output solutions consist of external boxes that connect between your computer and your display. The box converts the computer's video signal to S-Video, composite video, or component video, all of which can be connected to videotape recorders, large projection monitors, and television sets.

**Software.**   Combination cards such as VideoVision come with software that controls all features of the card, including video output. The external boxes require no software at all.

**Connecting.**   For the combination cards, connecting is as easy as plugging a cable into the output of the card and the input of the VCR or other video device. Other solutions have unique connection requirements. For example, the RasterOp's Video Expander II is an external box that connects to the video card in your computer. The box has output connectors for S-Video, composite video, and component RGB.

Consult the instructions included with your video converters to see exactly how they are to be connected.

(*Note:* You can try to videotape your computer screen with your video camera, but usually the results are less than satisfying. When you view the tape, a horizontal band appears on the computer display and slowly scrolls upward, only to reappear at the bottom. You may have noticed this on the local news or in poorly produced movies. Professional video cameras sometimes have a scan-rate adjustment that allows you to synchronize the camera and the display to alleviate the problem. Other solutions include using a time-based converter to convert the scan rate of the computer to a rate suitable for the video recorder.)

### Audio input

Audio digitizers are used to record sounds into your computer. If your Macintosh is equipped with an audio digitizer, you can send voice mail, annotate documents, or record sound effects for multimedia presentations. With QuickTime, an audio digitizer is used to record the audio portion of a movie.

**Hardware.**   Some Macintoshes have an audio digitizer built in. If yours doesn't, use an external box such as MacroMedia's MacRecorder to connect through the serial port to your machine. Some video-digitizing cards have an audio digitizer built in. There are also dedicated audio-digitizing cards, which provide professional-quality sound digitizing and manipulation.

**Software.**   System software included with audio digitizers allow them to be used in a standard way. With the software installed, all programs that use sound input operate similarly. For example, you can record a sound from within the "Sound" control panel no matter which audio digitizer you have. Just press the Add button and the recording controls will come up in a dialogue.

The audio digitizer you buy will come with software that allows you to record and manipulate sounds. QuickTime uses all digitizers in a common way and allows you to adjust the capabilities of the digitizer, such as the sampling rate and whether or not to use sound compression. For general multimedia presentations, a sampling rate of 22 kHz is fine.

[*Note:* The sampling rate can be defined as the number of times per second the computer records a segment of sound. Sound is vibrating air that moves your eardrum. The faster the vibrations, the higher the pitch of the sound. To record high-pitched sounds, the computer must check the digitizer many times per second. The sampling rate must be twice the frequency of the sound you are trying to record. Telephone voice quality requires a sampling rate of about 8 kHz (8000 times per second), whereas compact disc quality requires 44 kHz.]

**Connecting.**   For built-in sound digitizers, there is a port on the back of the computer indicated by a microphone icon. This port takes a $\frac{1}{8}$-inch mono minijack (see the Cables subsection on p. 20.11). Some external sound digitizers such as the MacRecorder use the same type of plug. Other digitizers use RCA plugs, which are common to most audio devices such as amplifiers and VCRs.

Adapters are available that convert RCA plugs to the $\frac{1}{8}$-inch minijack. This allows you to connect your VCR or other audio source to your Macintosh's internal sound input port.

## Audio output

All Macintoshes come with a built-in speaker that is adequate for nondemanding multimedia applications. To go beyond adequate, you can use the sound output port indicated by a speaker icon. Similar to the sound input port, this is a $\frac{1}{8}$-inch minijack that may be capable of stereo output depending on the model of your Macintosh. An adapter can be used to connect this port to a videotape recorder or to external amplifier and speakers for playback to an audience.

**Hardware.**   High-quality audio-digitizing cards and some combination video/audio-digitizing cards have output capabilities. These are either RCA-type jacks, which can be connected directly to VCRs or amplifiers, or $\frac{1}{8}$-inch minijacks.

**Software.**   Software included with some digitizing boards allow control of the sound output. For example, the VideoVision card has a control panel that allows you to adjust volume and mixing of its sound sources. The Macintosh "Sound" control panel allows you to choose between built-in audio output (which includes the sound output port) and external audio.

**Connecting.**   Sound output connectors are either RCA-type stereo, or $\frac{1}{8}$-inch stereo minijack. A minijack-to-stereo RCA adapter can be used for conversion of the two. From the RCA cables, you can connect to audio components such as amplifiers, mixers, equalizers, and recorders.

### Graphics tablets

Graphics tablets are used instead of or in conjunction with a mouse, to draw and manipulate the cursor. For drawing pictures or painting, a graphics tablet is an easier and more accurate device to use than a mouse.

**Hardware.** A graphics tablet uses a pen or a puck to move the cursor on the screen. A *puck* is a hand-held device like a mouse with buttons and cross-hairs that can be used to accurately trace images placed on the tablet. Some tablets can detect pressure sensitivity that is used, for instance, to draw a line thicker when the pen is pressed harder. Programmable buttons on the pen or puck can be set up to perform common tasks such as a double-click. Pens or pucks can be wireless or connected by a flexible cable to the tablet. The wireless pens are easier to manipulate but there is an increased risk of misplacement or loss.

**Software.** Graphics tablets come with system software that allow them to be used as a replacement for the mouse. A control panel is used to configure the tablet along the lines of pressure sensitivity, pen button function, and tablet orientation.

**Connecting.** Some graphics tablets such as the Wacom ArtZ use the Apple Desktop Bus (ADB) to connect to your Macintosh. This is the same port where the keyboard and mouse are connected. Connecting these tablets is as easy as finding a free ADB port on your computer or keyboard and plugging in the tablet's connector.

Other graphics tablets require an external interface box that connects between the tablet and the computer's serial port.

(*Note:* Since you can connect a number of devices to the ADB chain, connecting a digitizing tablet using ADB will leave a serial port free for something else, such as a MIDI interface or a modem.)

### Light pens

Light pens are used to directly manipulate the cursor on the screen. A pen connected by a cable is used to move the cursor or to draw directly to the screen. The cursor is moved by putting the tip of the pen on the computer's screen. Mouse clicks are accomplished by either pressing a button on the side of the pen or pushing the pen to the screen.

While light pens give you a more direct manipulation of the cursor on the screen, it can sometimes be unwieldy to hold the pen to the screen. Also there are times when the pen obscures the item you are trying to manipulate.

**Hardware.** Light pens use the signals that the computer sends to the monitor to determine where the pen is located. An external box is connected between your computer and monitor, and another cable connects to your serial port to tell your computer where the pen is located.

**Software.** Like graphics tablets, system software is included that allows the Macintosh to use the pen as a cursor, instead of or in addition to the mouse. A control panel is used to calibrate the pen as well as to configure attributes such as which serial port shall be used.

**Connecting.** Using FTG Data System's PXL-780 light pen as an example: Connect the monitor cable from your computer to the pen interface box. Connect the box's monitor-out cable to your monitor. Plug the serial connector into an unused serial port. Plug the pen into the box and connect the power connector to the box. Install the supplied software. Use the software to configure the pen and to calibrate it with your computer and display.

## Touch screens

Touch screens are used in stand-alone multimedia displays, interactive kiosks, and in schools. They come either as a complete monitor or as an overlay for an existing monitor. Similar to but not as accurate as light pens, they provide direct manipulation of the cursor on the screen. A person needs only a single finger to manipulate the cursor.

For kiosks, a touch screen is very useful. The user can manipulate the program directly from the screen, and all fragile hardware can be protected in an enclosure. Touch screens are good for specific applications that require the user to select an item from a group of items. They are not very good for use as an everyday alternative to a mouse. It can be difficult to perform double-clicks or to accurately press a small screen item such as a window's Close box.

**Hardware.** Touch screens come as a complete monitor, or as an overlay that attaches to an existing monitor. The control hardware typically is contained within an external interface box that connects between the screen and a serial port or an ADB port.

**Software.** Like light pens and graphics tablets, system software is included to allow the touch screen to be used as a replacement for or in addition to the mouse. A control panel is used to configure and calibrate the screen.

**Connecting.** Using the Elographics Acutouch monitor as an example: Connect the monitor as usual to your computer's display card. Connect the appropriate cable from the interface box to the interface connector at the back of the monitor. Attach the serial cable from the interface box to an unused serial port on your computer. Connect the power connector to the external box. Turn on the monitor, and apply power to the external box. Install the supplied software. Configure and calibrate the monitor.

## MIDI

MIDI (musical instrument digital interface) is used to connect musical synthesizers and equipment to each other and to a computer. MIDI transmits control information, not sound, to the devices connected to it. By doing this, MIDI allows you to record the performance of a musician. The instruments, the key, or the tempo of the piece can be adjusted at any time. In order to use MIDI with your computer, you must have either a MIDI interface box or a MIDI sound module card.

To process digital audio, your computer must do much more work than MIDI. Liken MIDI to a conductor (the computer itself) directing an orchestra (MIDI devices). The conductor does not have to put forth the entire effort to produce the music.

MIDI songs require much less storage space than digitally recorded music. They typically require 25 Kbytes per minute to produce high-quality music, whereas comparable digital music requires over 10,000 kbytes per minute. However, talent is required to generate the compositions to be played. There are software packages of precomposed music to include in your presentation if you don't have the time or talent to produce it yourself.

**Hardware.**  A MIDI interface is a small box that connects to your computer through a serial port and has MIDI input and output ports. A MIDI sound module card is a whole synthesizer contained on a card that you plug into your computer. Audio-output cables connect the MIDI module to an external amplifier.

**Software.**  The preferred method of using MIDI with the Macintosh is with Apple's MIDI Manager software, which is bundled with most MIDI software packages. This software allows easy connection of different sources of MIDI information (e.g., music software) to destinations (e.g., MIDI keyboards or sound modules). Some MIDI software packages also have their own means of communicating with MIDI interfaces.

**Connecting.**  Using Apple's MIDI interface and a MIDI keyboard as an example: Connect the serial cable from the MIDI interface to your computer. Connect a MIDI cable from the output port of the interface box to the input port of your MIDI keyboard. Connect another MIDI cable from the input of the interface box to the output of the MIDI keyboard. Connect the power to the MIDI interface. Install the software and configure the MIDI Manager, specifying the appropriate serial port.

## Storage

**Hardware.**  Multimedia can require massive amounts of data storage space, and digital video requires high data-access speeds. If you intend to work with digital video, you need as much disk space as possible. RAID (redundant arrays of inexpensive disks) are excellent for video acquisition, as they are faster than single drives and offer large capacities.

Removable media can be useful for long-term storage as well as data transfer. Since short (30-second) movies can occupy many megabytes of storage, floppy disks just won't do the trick. Syquest, Bernoullis, or magneto-optical drives are a good solution. Important factors to take into account are media cost and compatibility issues. If you do get a removable-media storage device to transfer presentations, make sure your destination computer also has the same type of removable-media device, or else you will have to tote your drive around (which defeats the purpose of removable media).

## Cables

Behind most multimedia workstations is a rat's nest of cables. There are many different types of connectors and cables (see Fig. 20.1). In some cases the same type of plug and cable is used to make completely different connections.

(*Note:* Make sure that the two ends of a cable connect compatible components, otherwise you may damage your equipment.)

The following describes Fig. 20.1 in detail.

**(A) Phono plug.** Also known as *patch cords,* these are used for audio connections and are the same as those used for stereo components. These cables are

**Figure 20.1**  Connectors.

usually found as a pair (red plug—right channel; black or white plug—left channel). Some have a third plug for composite video (yellow). Some have only one cable (mono sound), while others have a mono sound channel and a composite video channel (yellow—video; white—audio).

**(A) Composite video.**   These are used to connect video sources to video inputs. They have the same phono plug as audio cables, but the cable itself is slightly different. They also are called *75-ohm video cables*.

**(B) Component video/BNC connector.**   Component video is used in high-end equipment and with some RGB monitors. The cable end is comprised of one or three BNC-type connectors. The quality of component video is higher than that of S-Video but is not as common. Some component video cables have a monitor plug (DB-13) at one end and three BNC-type connectors at the other. This cable is used to connect a video-display card to a component video monitor. This connector also is used to connect ethernet networks.

**(C) ⅛-inch stereo minijack.**   This connector comes in stereo and mono versions. Typically it is used to connect microphones and earphones. With an adaptor, it can be connected to phono-plugs as well.

**(D) ⅛-inch mono minijack/Control-L.**   This connector is found on microphones and monophonic earphones. It is also used in Control-L applications that control certain VCRs and video cameras for synchronization and automated control.

**(E) S-Video/ADB connector.**   S-Video is a video standard that provides better quality than composite video. The cable is the same as that used by the Macintosh's ADB (Apple Desktop Bus) devices such as the keyboard. In a pinch, an extra keyboard cable can be used in place of an S-Video cable. Make sure that the S-Video cable is connected only to S-Video sockets, and *never* connect an S-Video source to your keyboard socket.

**(F) MIDI/5-pin DIN.**   A MIDI connector is larger in size than the mini-DIN plug and S-Video plug. A MIDI cable is used for MIDI-in, MIDI-out, and MIDI-thru connections. This same connector occasionally is used for power connectors. Be careful not to connect a power connector to your MIDI ports.

**(G) Serial RS-422/VISCA/8-pin mini-DIN.**   The Macintosh serial port uses an 8-pin plug to connect to serial devices. Cables can have the mini-DIN plug on each end or a DB-25 on one end to connect to serial devices such as modems. A VISCA cable (mini-DIN 8 on each end of the cable) is the same as a serial cable and can be used interchangeably.

**(H) Monitor cable/DB-13.**   This cable is used to connect a video-display card to an RGB monitor. It has a DB-13 connector at the computer end and another DB-13, BNC connectors, or a custom connector at the monitor end. Some display systems use a connector that fits between the monitor connector and the monitor itself to allow the presenter or operator to see the display while projecting it to a large audience.

**(I) Serial RS-232/DB-25/System SCSI connector.** A DB-25 connector commonly is used as a port on modems and other serial devices. It also is used as the System SCSI connector on the Macintosh.

**(J) SCSI (Small Computers Standard Interface).** This cable can connect a variety of devices including scanners, hard disks, tape storage units, printers, and some high-end audio digitizers. There are three types of plugs for SCSI connections. The 50-pin connector is used to daisy-chain SCSI devices together. A DB-25 plug is used to connect the Macintosh to the SCSI chain and, sometimes, to connect SCSI devices together. The HDI-30 connector is used with the Macintosh PowerBooks to connect them to the SCSI chain.

## Macintosh Multimedia Software Tools

### Recorders/editors

In order to use the hardware tools to bring information into your computer, you need to have software that knows how to access the hardware.

### Scanning software

Most scanners are supplied with the software used to access them. Many of these software packages are limited in their capabilities, and you will want to supplement their usage with additional, more specialized software. LightSource's Ofoto is a comprehensive image-acquisition tool. It provides image-manipulation tools such as color correction, rotation, and cropping. Ofoto is unique in that you can place a picture on the scanner's surface and press a single button. Ofoto will then scan the picture, rotate it so that it is straight, crop it, and adjust brightness and contrast to produce a usable picture without a lot of adjustments.

Adobe's Photoshop is a well-known image-processing package that has the capability to access a scanner directly. All that is required is a "plug-in module" that specifically works with Photoshop and your scanner. Other packages such as optical character recognition (OCR) software will also have a way to work directly with your scanner. ExperVisions's TypeReader OCR package has drivers for many popular scanners.

### Movie recorders

With QuickTime and a video input card, you can use your Macintosh to capture movies for viewing and editing. Movie-recording software is used to control the video card so as to capture sequences of video and/or audio and save it to disk. Movie-recording software also allows you to set the compression methods to allow you to make the space-versus-quality compromise. Typically, better-quality images require greater storage space. Certain compressors do a better job of compressing than others but may produce lower-quality images. There are also compressors, such as SuperMac's Compact Video compressor, that produce a good-quality, highly compressed image at the expense of compression speed. With Compact Video, it is necessary to record the video with another compressor (or none at all) and compress after you're done recording.

With a QuickTime-compatible video card, any movie-recording software will work with your video card. Apple's Movie Recorder program is a basic video-capture program. It allows you to capture audio and video and set compression parameters. It also allows basic cut-and-paste of video segments.

Adobe's Premiere is a comprehensive video-capture and -editing package. Premiere not only works with QuickTime, it can produce an edit decision list (EDL) for use with professional video-editing equipment. You can use your Macintosh with Premiere to edit your video and use the EDL to produce the final cut. Premiere also allows you to add transitions to your video segments, such as fade-in/fade-out, zoom-in, and page-turn.

### Tips on making good movies

1. *Experiment.*   Try the suggestions listed here, and try different things. The only way to find out how to make good movies is to try it under a variety of conditions. Some of the tips given here are surefire winners, while others depend on your particular computer setup and the subject of your video.

2. *Always use the best-quality equipment available.*   For example, if you have a VHS and a Hi-8 video camera, use the Hi-8, because the quality of Hi-8 is better than VHS. Likewise, if you have composite and S-Video output available on your playback video deck, use S-Video.

3. *Use hardware-assisted compression.*   Using hardware compression frees the Macintosh to perform other tasks such as digitizing audio and saving the video to disk. With hardware assistance, full-screen movies can be recorded at 30 frames per second.

4. *If you have more than one monitor connected, make sure the recording window is completely on the screen that is connected to your video digitizer.*   Most video digitizer cards that offer display capabilities will display digitized video to their own screen much faster than to another one.

5. *Don't pan the film—use a still background instead.*   Compression doesn't work well with moving backgrounds.

6. *Get lots of memory.*   With an abundance of memory you can record movies to RAM, which is faster than recording to disk. Note, however, that without huge amounts of memory (20 + megabytes), you will only be able to record small (size and length) movies before space runs out.

7. *Don't use virtual memory.*   Virtual memory uses your hard disk as extra memory. Since the hard disk is much slower than RAM, using VM to increase your memory space will not give you the speed increase that extra RAM will. VM will just slow the computer down and prevent it from making good movies.

8. *Don't use unnecessary system extensions.*   Many extensions force your computer to give them processing time at periodic intervals. The time that your computer gives to these extensions is that much less time it has to work on your movies.

9. *Use an appropriate compressor for the image contents.*   Compressors usually are developed for a particular image type. The compact video and video compressors are good for recorded video, whereas the animation and graphics compressors are good for computer-generated graphics. JPEG produces small, good-quality photo images but is too slow for motion video (unless it is sped up with hardware).

10. *Turn off automatic file compression software.*   QuickTime does the compression itself. Programs such as DiskDoubler or Stuffit SpaceSaver will try to compress files that have already been compressed.

11. *Turn off file sharing.*   File sharing takes a lot of effort on your computer's part. Turn it off when you are recording movies, and let the computer concentrate on making good movies.

## Audio recorders

Most movie-recording software can be used for audio recording as well, by setting the option to not record video. This is a direct way of recording audio, but typically the output file is a movie file. Specialized audio-recording software such as MacroMedia's SoundEdit Pro has many effects that can be applied to recorded sounds. Reverberation effects, noise filtering, bending, and compression are a few of the effects available. SoundEdit Pro also can save the sound in formats other than the "Movie" format.

## MIDI recorders

MIDI recorders (sequencers) are used to capture a musical performance from a MIDI-capable instrument, typically a MIDI keyboard. These recorders allow you to manipulate the notes that were recorded as well as the tempo and arrangement of the composition. They let you record one instrument, then record another while the first is being played back. In this way you can record a musical arrangement with multiple instruments entirely by yourself.

## Titling software

Your Macintosh can be used to produce impressive titles both for digital video on your computer and for your videotape productions. Generic graphics packages such as MacDraw Pro will suffice for simple titles. Specific tools for manipulating text as graphics objects, such as Strata's Strata Type 3D, can produce intricate title screens using any font on your computer. They can also use graphics created by most paint or drawing programs. Strata Type creates three-dimensional objects and allows you to designate what the surface is made out of, such as gold or chrome. You can specify colored light sources and special effects, such as light coming through a window pane. Using tools such as Strata Type, you can produce results similar to the titles seen on broadcast television.

## Media integration

Many multimedia packages are geared primarily to a specific type of media. For example, Adobe Premiere is an excellent digital video editing package, but it cannot manipulate MIDI data. To bring all of your multimedia information together, you will need a media integration package. Passport's Producer is a program that brings together slides (from presentation packages such as Persuasion), movies, pictures, sounds (such as speech), animations, MIDI, and music directly from compact discs. Producer allows you to arrange a presentation using time to specify when an item is supposed to display or play. For example you can produce a 30-second commercial with a montage of pictures and some music from a compact disc, then put spoken dialog in at the appropriate time.

With a video output device, you can use the Print-to-video feature to save the presentation onto a videotape.

## Format conversion

A frustrating aspect of working with different computers and software packages is data incompatibility. Getting information from one program to another is much easier than getting it from one kind of computer to another. The Macintosh has many utilities to assist in format conversion.

To use data from an IBM PC–compatible computer, you can use Apple's PC Exchange software. With it, IBM PC–compatible disks look and act like Macintosh disks. Files on the disk can be viewed as icons and copied to and from Macintosh disks.

For conversion of data from IBM-compatible computers to the Macintosh, you can use Apple's Easy Open software in conjunction with translators from companies such as DataVis. These translators convert your data among the common formats found on each computer.

DeBabelizer from Equilibrium Technologies is a graphics-processing utility that has tremendous conversion capabilities. It can convert between 55 different graphics formats found on Macintosh, DOS/Windows, Amiga, Sun, X Windows, SGI, and other computers. DeBabelizer is scriptable, which means that you can tell the computer how to perform a graphics conversion once, then have it do the same thing for a number of files automatically. This is very useful when you have to use a large number of graphics files between different computers.

## Cataloging

It is very easy to lose track of all of the information you have on your computer. With a media-cataloging program such as Imspace Systems' Kudo Image Browser, or Aldus's Fetch, you can keep track of all of your media files. Image

Browser has an interesting "riffle" feature that allows you to scan a large catalog of images quickly. With compatible software such as Quark Express, you also can drag and drop pictures from the database directly into your documents.

### SCSI notes

1. Make sure your computer and all of the SCSI devices are turned off before you add or remove devices from the chain.

2. Devices on the SCSI chain are identified by the computer with SCSI IDs. Each ID must be unique and in the range of 0 to 6. If conflicting IDs are assigned to devices (e.g., if both a hard disk and a CD-ROM have an ID of 0), the computer will not operate properly or may not start at all. Turn off all devices, reset the IDs, and the computer will work properly.

3. If there is one internal hard disk, it usually will be set to ID 0. If there is more than one internal SCSI device, you can check their IDs by selecting their icons from the Finder and selecting "Get Info" from the Finder's file menu. If you reconfigure your devices often, it may be a good idea to label the device's front with the ID to save some confusion later. Alternatively, there are shareware tools available that allow you to scan and identify devices on the SCSI bus.

4. The terminator used for the Macintosh IIfx is different than the terminators used for all of the other Macintosh models. It is black, while the more common terminator is gray. Make sure you use a black terminator with the IIfx. You may not immediately notice a problem, but incorrect usage can result in data corruption.

5. Be aware that some SCSI devices are internally terminated. Check the documentation that accompanies the device to determine if this is the case. The internally terminated device needs to be at the end of the SCSI chain, and no external termination should be used. If you have any internally terminated devices in the middle of the SCSI chain, you must remove the internal termination before using.

6. Some advanced devices have self-determining termination; i.e., the device decides if it needs termination or not. See the documentation supplied with the device to determine if it has this feature.

7. If you've just been adding or removing SCSI devices or other cables behind your computer, make sure all the cables are securely connected. A partially connected SCSI cable or an unterminated SCSI chain is capable of causing data loss. If your computer starts to act strangely (spurious disk-read errors, incorrect icons, etc.), it's possible that your SCSI chain is incorrectly configured.

# 21

# Stop the Presses!
# Creating an Electronic Brochure

**Joan Davies**

## Introduction

Marketing and advertising professionals continually brainstorm in their search for new ways to attract attention, sell a product or service, or heighten awareness of a particular company or person. The effort to motivate mass markets by means of dynamic or inspirational messages has resulted in an evolution of marketing ploys from junk mail and fax fliers to sales videotapes. But in this high-tech age, when an influx of paper advertising breeds greater contempt than interest, and when it's commonplace to transmit information to thousands of people simultaneously through such services as electronic mailboxes, these techniques have lost their edge.

From ever-developing computer technology there is now emerging, however, a new marketing strategy that seems destined to a longer life than the fax flier (a marketing fad still used, but less frequently and more cautiously, since it lost popularity almost from the beginning when recipients realized it was their paper, and therefore their dollars, that advertisers were using). Corporate advertisers now are turning to multimedia as a viable marketing alternative, recognizing the powerful impact of novel delivery vehicles such as interactive kiosks and electronic brochures and catalogs.

Electronic brochures offer a high-volume, quick-production resource that is not only economically beneficial (especially since the price of 3.5-inch floppy disks has gone down about 50 percent in the course of 1993) but also environmentally correct. Paper waste is a primary drawback of traditional mass-market mailings, one that the use of electronic brochures eliminates. Electronic brochures minimize the panic that sets in when advertisers suddenly notice an inaccurate phone number or date, or a misspelled name. Glaring, perhaps harmful, mistakes can be corrected in a snap, and disks reduplicated at a fraction of the cost of reprinting an entire run of four-color brochures. Marketers can get extended mileage from an ad campaign that uses electronic brochures by simply updating and duplicating more diskettes as products or services change or in order to target different audiences. Additionally, electronic brochures encourage recycling, since the recipient can reformat and reuse brochure disks.

Until they lose their appeal (and that is not likely to happen for a long time), electronic brochures will elicit a curiosity factor that almost guarantees the recipient will pop the disk into a computer and watch and/or interact with it. Because electronic brochures are more personal and flexible than paper or videos, customers feel more in control of the information they're receiving—a sales tactic that translates into more sales revenues.

## Electronic Brochures, the New Marketing Tool

### Setting the norms

Computers are quickly becoming a household and business staple, in much the same way as television sets became less of a novelty and more of a standard item in the mid-1950s. Soon basic statistics will measure families and corporations by the number of computers they own and operate, and the two-computer family will be as normal as the two-car family. Since many computer users communicate through electronic mail, electronic brochures are an obvious vehicle. Even those who don't log on to CompuServe or Prodigy can witness a new dimension in marketing literature.

Electronic (or digital) brochures are distinguished from interactive kiosks, or from catalogs distributed on CD-ROM, because they are more representative of the traditional paper flier or brochure. Whereas kiosks and catalogs are fully developed and in-depth (often interactive) sales or information tools, electronic brochures generally are smaller-scaled, self-contained sales tools distributable on one or two floppy disks. They are not considered product demos because they sell features and benefits by making use of much the same tactics as paper brochures, perhaps blending animation and sound with color graphics. These are techniques that no piece of paper, however creatively designed, could ever hope to produce. (But note that the two terms are often used interchangeably by many end users, who aren't concerned with such fine distinctions.)

### Reaching the mass market

Despite the imminent and long-term benefits, electronic brochures do present a new problem that paper marketing materials don't. The very nature of electronic brochures potentially limits the marketer's audience. Before deciding that electronic brochures will work for them, marketers must determine who their audience is. This decision, of course, must be made in any direct-marketing campaign; however, it becomes even more vital with computer marketing. In addition to asking the obvious question, "Does my target have a computer?", marketers must determine exactly what kind of computer he or she has. The most wonderful digital brochure will have absolutely no impact if it cannot be viewed on someone's computer.

Electronic brochures distributed by direct mail for the PC industry face more pitfalls than those created for Macintosh computers. The only standard for personal computers is that there is no standard! So even when developers create the most generic brochure—for instance, a 320 × 200, 16-color VGA board—there is no guarantee that all—or even half—of the target market will be able to play it. Although most hard-core, sophisticated graphic artists and designers are dedicated to the 24-bit power of 16.7-million-color images, even low-end 256-color brochures developed for a generic market can have surprisingly effective results. While most designers opt for 320 × 200 resolution as the lowest common denominator when it comes to reaching mass audiences, the minimum high-quality standard is likely to become 640 × 480 as more super-VGA boards hit the market, especially with the price dropping from $6000 to about $1000 and under. That standard is evolving even now, with as many as 750,000 Tseng Labs chips shipping every month, giving Tseng Labs a 25 percent market share, according to Ron McCabe, Tseng Labs product manager.

Marketers who do their homework, like those noted in *NewMedia* magazine by Gillian Newson, will be able to generate a greater response rate:

> According to the Direct Marketing Association in New York City, a paper brochure direct-mail campaign that gets a response rate of 1 to 2 percent is successful. The lowest response rate mentioned by the producers of interactive brochures interviewed for that article was 12 percent, and some claimed responses of over 50 percent.*

An alternative distribution mode for electronic brochures is electronic mail. Such popular communication networks as CompuServe, Prodigy, and America On-line often prohibit advertisers from clogging the lines with electronic "junk mail," but others—like the Internet—encourage the international transmission of digital advertisements. In the latter case, the potential for marketing through networks becomes enormous, as Michael Schrage reports in *Adweek:*

> Once advertisers come onto the network, Internet usage (already growing 20 percent a month compounded) will skyrocket even faster, because more consumers will come on board. Of course, advertising will subsidize network growth for computers just as it did for radio and television.†

Regardless of the distribution method, the easier the brochure is to install and view, the higher the response rate is likely to be. Marketers should

---

*"Interactive Marketing Is Driven to Succeed," June 1993, p. 73.

†"The Ultimate Network," May 17, 1993, p. 26.

assume that audiences don't know what kind of hardware their systems contain, and relay instructions in the simplest language possible.

## Application Studies

### Tools of the trade

Electronic brochures, while a fairly new concept, are already far beyond the conceptual stage. Many marketers, from large ad firms and computer companies to independent multimedia producers, have been testing the waters—with very good results.

All of the application designers described in the next sections created electronic brochures using Mathematica's TEMPRA as the primary authoring tool. The whole authoring process may have included any of the TEMPRA products at some point: TEMPRA PRO for scanning, video capture, image editing, painting, and printing; TEMPRA Turbo Animator for creating or editing 8-bit or 16-bit animations; and either TEMPRA SHOW or TEMPRA Media Author for the actual scripting of the brochure. Each brochure fits on one 3.5-inch floppy disk and runs either $320 \times 200$ or $640 \times 480$ at 256 colors.

### The medium is the message

For Raymond Elman, director of creative services at Coopers & Lybrand, electronic brochures have become a differentiating means of marketing. Coopers & Lybrand is an international professional services firm that specializes in five core businesses: business assurance/audit, tax consulting, performance improvement, human resource advisory, and process management/outsourcing.

Elman has been creating multimedia presentations at the Coopers & Lybrand Boston office for the past four years, but it is only recently that he has realized the potential for marketing his company's services digitally. Electronic brochures are "living documents," Elman says, appropriate for his particular company because they make available, over his firmwide network, up-to-date marketing resources that employees can access instantly and present to clients. "They can simply say, 'Hey, I've got something interesting here on my computer. Can you take a few minutes to let me walk you through it?' At the moment, I don't think a lot of people in our business are doing this kind of thing."

Early in the fall of 1992, Elman produced a digital brochure inviting Harvard Business School students to attend a recruiting seminar for Coopers & Lybrand. Because Elman had heard that students at Harvard receive so much recruiting literature they don't read half of it, he wanted to develop a message that would make Coopers & Lybrand stand out from the rest of the crowd.

Using TEMPRA, Elman created a simple "flier," complete with photos and testimonials, which he sent on a 3.5-inch floppy to 900 Harvard students. Development of the brochure itself took Elman only about two days, although members of the recruiting staff had spent a month reaching agreement on the text to be included.

To reach more students, Elman built the brochure in two resolutions (to be viewed at 320 × 200 and 640 × 480). By showing a graphic of the Harvard Business School crest at the start of the brochure and asking the simple question, "Did you see all or part of the crest?", Elman could branch viewers to the appropriate display resolution for their computers. Aside from this interactive introduction, the recruiting brochure is self-running. The entire brochure was compressed to fit on one 3.5-inch floppy disk, which an outsourcing company duplicated (it also, Elman points out, sanitized the disks and ensured that they contained no viruses). Coopers & Lybrand then mailed the floppies and cover letters to 900 Harvard students.

"We tripled our attendance at the briefing," Elman said. "What we heard was that people were carrying their disks around, saying, 'Have you seen this?' The Harvard campus was sort of abuzz with having received it." In addition to successfully marketing the recruiting seminar, Elman's brochure sparked interest in multimedia as a messenger. "I received one letter from somebody at Harvard that said, 'I have been looking at recruiting literature for two years and this is certainly the most innovative and exciting document I have ever received. I have renewed interest in your firm because clearly you are on the cutting edge of technology.'"

Elman is now creating a brochure about Coopers & Lybrand that is in much the same format as the Harvard Business School digital brochure, including the opening graphic that lets viewers choose the display mode for their systems (see Fig. 21.1).

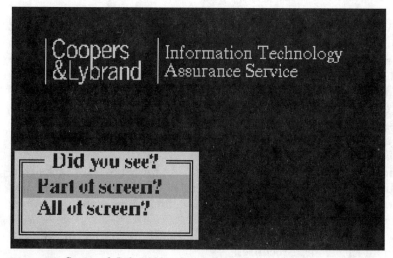

**Figure 21.1**  Coopers & Lybrand brochure.

**Selling the sizzle**

When Rich Bevis, director of photography at the Cincinnati-based Encore Productions, was contacted by an ad agency and a defense contractor to develop a sales video for a new product, his first instinct was "this is the perfect thing for multimedia." And when the reps from Martiney and Associates and KDI agreed that a multimedia brochure would be an appropriate way to market TV Link, a computer-to-video converter, the planning began.

Encore Productions created two electronic brochures and a videotape for TV Link. The electronic brochures serve double duty: one includes audio and plays in various computer stores like CompUSA and at computer trade shows, while the other is a nonaudio version that is distributed through mass mailing with an accompanying four-color spec sheet. Mailing recipients interested in getting more information are then sent the videotape. The brochures, each of which fits on one 3.5-inch floppy disk, were originally designed for KDI salesmen to display on notebook computers, but then, according to Bevis, "after they saw what we were doing, they said, 'Hey, we need to send this out to everybody.'" Bevis adds that the change in focus made the brochure more powerful, although they maintained the original 320 × 200 resolution to make the brochure look bigger.

As of this writing (late 1993), KDI has had about 20,000 disks duplicated over several runs. Bevis says that response to the brochures has been "terrific. People were really interested, and they [KDI] moved a lot of TV Links. It was more than they had expected and eventually more than a normal direct mail." With big, bold, flashing text and fast-moving graphics, Encore sold TV Link's sizzle: *success*.

During the development stage, Bevis said the designers discussed the pros and cons of interactive marketing versus self-running. They decided that a self-running brochure seemed more in keeping with the direct sales approach. Encore's primary business is video and film production, a high-motion industry that reveals its influence in the fast-paced action of their brochure.

Although TV Link is computer-related hardware, computer products aren't the only products that Encore Productions designs multimedia applications for. Bevis says they are in the process of developing a demo for an insurance company, and another for a shoe company, each of which may include kiosks positioned in various malls across the country. And Encore Productions is active in the toy industry as well, having developed an application for Kenner Toys that was displayed during the 1993 International Toy Fair in New York. They created another for the line of toys based on Steven Spielberg's megahit movie, *Jurassic Park*.

Bevis definitely believes in keeping pace with the industry—as quicksilver-like as it is. "If you sit back and just kind of relax and say, 'Oh, we use this and use it forever and ever,' somebody else is going to be doing something better than you," he says.

(To see how Bevis created the TV Link brochure, flip to p. 21.8 and the section Authoring an Electronic Brochure.)

## A case for interactive marketing

In Brooklyn Heights, New York, Jeff Beckerman, president of Beckerman Productions, is making the transition from film and video postproduction to multimedia. With a background in editing nationally televised commercials for such prominent companies as Budweiser and McDonald's, Beckerman is poised to take advantage of the creative opportunities of multimedia. And electronic brochures are just a step away from television commercials: same rhetoric, just a different vehicle.

"About two years ago I became enthralled in multimedia," he said. "I feel that digital brochures are going to be such a strong multimedia market that I'm concentrating all my spare time on them." Beckerman's focus is sales- and marketing-oriented interactive disk-based multimedia. To demonstrate his production ability, let's go back to a time when he first began to market his services.

Beckerman developed a demo of an interactive brochure that features imaginary scanners (Fig. 21.2). It also teaches the user the concept of scanning and the competitive advantages of an imaginary scanner brand. The brochure's interactivity includes having viewers type in their names, point to topic selections, and advance to the next screen. Beckerman believes that audiences want interactivity in electronic brochures: audiences who are involved personally in an activity tend to retain information longer than passive audiences.

To that end, the digital brochure's main menu includes four buttons for the viewer to select from: Scan, Speed, OCR, and Other. Each button branches

**Figure 21.2**  Interactive brochure.

into a segment of the brochure that uses graphics, animation, and text to describe some aspect of scanning. Like most brochures, Beckerman's is 8-bit (256 colors), although he started in 16-bit and compressed the images to the same palette to ensure consistency in colors. The brochure took Beckerman two weeks to complete, using TEMPRA to prepare the graphics and author the sequence.

Beckerman did not distribute this demonstration brochure by mail; however, he says that the people he has shown it to responded positively. Because of this response, he's developing a broader-based brochure to use in a pitch to businesses interested in digital marketing. Like many other marketers, Beckerman sees direct mail as being the most effective and efficient means of distribution.

"When you get something [in the mail] from a company with their logo on it, that's more friendly than just downloading a product demo from a bulletin board. It also seems more professional," he explains. But companies should consider a dual marketing approach, with both brochures and floppy disks. "When a customer calls an 800 number, the company's representative can ask, 'Do you want us to send you a brochure, a floppy disk that will run our demo, or both?' If the demo's interface is engaging, the favorable response will prove its worth."

## Authoring an Electronic Brochure

All the applications in this chapter used TEMPRA as the primary authoring tool for creating the electronic brochures. In authoring with TEMPRA SHOW

**Figure 21.3**  Authoring user interface.

or TEMPRA Media Author, designers create "sequences" composed of "events," which include graphics, animation, text, audio, timeouts, buttons, and other special effects. Each event appears on a single "line" and all the events interact for smooth playback, so that audio plays simultaneously as graphics and animations appear on the screen.

TEMPRA SHOW and TEMPRA Media Author both have two interfaces: a graphical user interface (Fig. 21.3) and a text-based interface. With the GUI, designers can review the brochure line-by-line as it is created. The benefit of the text interface is that is shows 20 lines of sequence at once, making it more efficient for complex authoring. At any time in either interface, designers can try the entire sequence as it's being created.

This section explains the details involved in creating Encore Productions' TV Link electronic brochure. As you look at Rick Bevis's script, you can see that it's distinguished by columns and lines. Each column contains a "field," with the information relevant to each particular event in each line. The fields are defined next.

*Label.*    Used for branching from one point in the sequence to another. A word that appears in the Label field has a matching word in the Next field to connect the two event lines together, depending on the action taken by the viewer. Not every line requires or will have a label, only those that branch.

*Type.*    This designates the actual event, whether graphic, audio, text, animation, and so on.

*File.*    Some events require a file. For instance, graphics use TIF and PCX files, text uses TXT files, and animations use FLI, FLC, and FLX files. Other events that are not connected to a file skip over this field.

*Method.*    This field varies depending on the event, but it determines how the event will appear on the computer screen. The Method for a graphic would be the wipe transition used to display the graphics, while the Method field for a text event would be the font style and size.

*Speed / Display.*    The Speed setting tells how fast a transition occurs or how fast a sprite travels across the screen, and the Display determines if a visual event is permanent or temporary.

*Parameters.*    The field contains information such as the color of backgrounds and text, position of buttons and scaled graphics, and the starting and stopping positions of sprites. This field can also be used for writing comments related to the sequence.

*Wait.*    The Wait determines if there's a delay between events, which can be either a timed pause or a key press.

*Next.*    Like the Label, the Next field is for branching. A word that appears in the Next field on one line is linked to another line that has a matching word in the Label field. With this capability, designers can create brochures that branch from anywhere to anywhere in the sequence.

| # | Label type | File | Method | Speed parameters | Wait | Next |
|---|---|---|---|---|---|---|
| 1 | Video | SetMode | VGA_13 | 320x200 | 256 | |
| 2 | Global | DropShad | 2x 2y 0c | | | |
| 3 | Global | PIC_PCX | | | | |
| 4 | Global | SPR_PCC | | | | |
| 5 | STARTBColor | Quick | 99 Solid 0c | 3 | | |
| 6 | Screen | LINK01 | Bot_Tp | | | |
| 7 | Sprite | BUSI | | 10P 302bx 151by 60ex 151ey | | |
| 8 | Sprite | VIDEOS | | 10 P -119bx -12by 77ex -12ey | | |
| 9 | Sprite | SALES | | 15 P -6bx -123by -6ex 57ey | | |
| 10 | Sprite | MARKET | | 15 P 304bx 86by 54ex 86ey | | |
| 11 | Sprite | TRAIN | | 15 P -143bx 32by 127ex 32ey | | |
| 12 | Screen | LINK01 | Hrz_Out | 1 | | |
| 13 | Text | QUALITY | HELV31 | P 001 116x 198y 15c 4w 3h nnl | 2 0/18 | |
| 14 | Text | VERSA | HELV31 | P 001 64x 117y 15c 5w 3h nnl | 2 0/18 | |
| 15 | Text | AFORD | HELV31 | P 001 14x 41y 15c 6w 3h nnl | 2 0/18 | |
| 16 | Screen | SUCCESS | Dissolve | 20 | 2 0/18 | |
| 17 | Video | KDILOGO | AaPlay | 99 P 0x 0y 1R | 3 0/18 | |
| 18 | BColor | | Vrt_Out | 99 Solid 0c | | |
| 19 | Screen | LINK04 | Hrz_Out | 50 | 2 0/18 | |
| 20 | Text | QUALITY | HELV40 | E 001 48x 90y 15c 5w 3h nnl | 3 0/18 | |
| 21 | Screen | LINK06 | Hrz_Out | 99 | 3 0/18 | |
| 22 | Screen | LINK04 | Hrz_In | 99 | | |
| 23 | Text | 7 | HELV20 | E 001 2x 120y 15c 14w 7h nnl | 3 0/18 | |
| 24 | Text | VERSA | HELV30 | E 001 65x 90y 15c 6w 3h nnl | 3 0/18 | |
| 25 8C | Screen | LINK08B | Hrz_In | 90 | | |
| 26 | Text | 8C | HELV30 | P 001 73x 88y 15c 6w 3h nnl | | |
| 27 | Sprite | KDI-ARRW | 33% | 5 E -31bx 100by 36ex 100ey | | |
| 28 | Sprite | KDI-ARRW | 33% | 5 E 36bx 100by 36ex 100ey | | |
| 29 | Sprite | KDI-ARRW | 33% | 5 E 36bx 100by 36ex 100ey | | |
| 30 | Sprite | KDI-ARRW | 33% | 5 E 36bx 100by 36ex 100ey | | |
| 31 | Sprite | KDI-ARRW | 33% | 5 E 36bx 100by 36ex 100ey | | |

| # | Type | Name | Format | Coordinates | |
|---|---|---|---|---|---|
| 32 | Sprite | KDI-ARRW | 33% | 5 E 36bx 100by 36ex 100ey | |
| 33 | Sprite | KDI-ARRW | 33% | 5 E 36bx 100by 36ex 100ey | 2 0/18 |
| 34 8G | Screen | LINK08B | Lft_Rt | 99 | |
| 35 | Text | 8G | HELV25 | P 001 19x 109y 15c 12w 5h nnl | |
| 36 | Sprite | KDI-ARRW | 33% | 5 E -31bx 100by 146ex 100ey | |
| 37 | Sprite | KDI-ARRW | 33% | 5 E 146bx 100by 146ex 100ey | |
| 38 | Sprite | KDI-ARRW | 33% | 5 E 146bx 100by 146ex 100ey | |
| 39 | Sprite | KDI-ARRW | 33% | 5 E 146bx 100by 146ex 100ey | |
| 40 | Sprite | KDI-ARRW | 33% | 5 E 146bx 100by 146ex 100ey | |
| 41 | Sprite | KDI-ARRW | 33% | 5 E 146bx 100by 146ex 100ey | |
| 42 | Sprite | KDI-ARRW | 33% | 5 E 146bx 100by 146ex 100ey | 2 0/18 |
| 43 8F | Screen | LINK08B | Lft_Rt | 99 | |
| 44 | Text | 8F | HELV25 | P 001 18x 109y 15c 13w 5h nnl | |
| 45 | Sprite | KDI-ARRW | 33% | 5 E -31bx 100by 119ex 100ey | |
| 46 | Sprite | KDI-ARRW | 33% | 5 E 119bx 100by 119ex 100ey | |
| 47 | Sprite | KDI-ARRW | 33% | 5 E 119bx 100by 119ex 100ey | |
| 48 | Sprite | KDI-ARRW | 33% | 5 E 119bx 100by 119ex 100ey | |
| 49 | Sprite | KDI-ARRW | 33% | 5 E 119bx 100by 119ex 100ey | |
| 50 | Sprite | KDI-ARRW | 33% | 5 E 119bx 100by 119ex 100ey | |
| 51 | Sprite | KDI-ARRW | 33% | 5 E 119bx 100by 119ex 100ey | 2 0/18 |
| 52 8H | Screen | LINK08B | Lft_Rt | 99 | |
| 53 | Text | 8H | HELV21 | P 001 25x 107y 15c 12w 5h nnl | |
| 54 | Sprite | KDI-ARRW | 33% | 5 E -31bx 100by 170ex 100ey | |
| 55 | Sprite | KDI-ARRW | 33% | 5 E 170bx 100by 170ex 100ey | |
| 56 | Sprite | KDI-ARRW | 33% | 5 E 170bx 100by 170ex 100ey | |
| 57 | Sprite | KDI-ARRW | 33% | 5 E 170bx 100by 170ex 100ey | |
| 58 | Sprite | KDI-ARRW | 33% | 5 E 170bx 100by 170ex 100ey | |
| 59 | Sprite | KDI-ARRW | 33% | 5 E 170bx 100by 170ex 100ey | |
| 60 | Sprite | KDI-ARRW | 33% | 5 E 170bx 100by 170ex 100ey | 2 0/18 |
| 61 8K | Screen | LINK08B | Lft_Rt | 99 | |
| 62 | Text | 8K | HELV21 | P 001 9x 105y 15c 13w 5h nnl | |
| 63 | Sprite | KDI-ARRW | 33% | 5 E -31bx 100by 246ex 100ey | |

**Figure 21.4** Script listing.

21.11

| # | Label type | File | Method | Speed parameters | Wait | Next |
|---|---|---|---|---|---|---|
| 64 | Sprite | KDI-ARRW | 33% | 5 E 246bx 100by 246ex 100ey | | |
| 65 | Sprite | KDI-ARRW | 33% | 5 E 246bx 100by 246ex 100ey | | |
| 66 | Sprite | KDI-ARRW | 33% | 5 E 246bx 100by 246ex 100ey | | |
| 67 | Sprite | KDI-ARRW | 33% | 5 E 246bx 100by 246ex 100ey | | |
| 68 | Sprite | KDI-ARRW | 33% | 5 E 246bx 100by 246ex 100ey | | |
| 69 | Sprite | KDI-ARRW | 33% | 5 E 246bx 100by 246ex 100ey | 2 0/18 | |
| 70 8l | Screen | LINK08B | Lft_Rt | 99 | | |
| 71 | Text | 8l | HELV25 | P 001 7x 107y 15c 13w 5h nnl | | |
| 72 | Sprite | KDI-ARRW | 33% | 5 E -31bx 100by 198ex 100ey | | |
| 73 | Sprite | KDI-ARRW | 33% | 5 E 198bx 100by 198ex 100ey | | |
| 74 | Sprite | KDI-ARRW | 33% | 5 E 198bx 100by 198ex 100ey | | |
| 75 | Sprite | KDI-ARRW | 33% | 5 E 198bx 100by 198ex 100ey | | |
| 76 | Sprite | KDI-ARRW | 33% | 5 E 198bx 100by 198ex 100ey | | |
| 77 | Sprite | KDI-ARRW | 33% | 5 E 198bx 100by 198ex 100ey | | |
| 78 | Sprite | KDI-ARRW | 33% | 5 E 198bx 100by 198ex 100ey | 2 0/18 | |
| 79 9A | Video | JITTER | AaPlay | 99 P 0x 0y 7R | | |
| 80 | Screen | LINK09A | Quick | 99 | | |
| 81 | Text | 9A | HELV25 | P 001 35x 113y 15c 11w 5h nnl | | |
| 82 | Sprite | KDI-ARRW | 33% | 5 E -31bx 114by 94ex 114ey | | |
| 83 | Sprite | KDI-ARRW | 33% | 5 E 94bx 114by 94ex 114ey | | |
| 84 | Sprite | KDI-ARRW | 33% | 5 E 94bx 114by 94ex 114ey | | |
| 85 | Sprite | KDI-ARRW | 33% | 5 E 94bx 114by 94ex 114ey | | |
| 86 | Sprite | KDI-ARRW | 33% | 5 E 94bx 114by 94ex 114ey | | |
| 87 | Sprite | KDI-ARRW | 33% | 5 E 94bx 114by 94ex 114ey | | |
| 88 | Sprite | KDI-ARRW | 33% | 5 E 94bx 114by 94ex 114ey | 2 0/18 | |
| 89 9B | Screen | LINK09A | Hrz_Out | 99 | | |
| 90 | Text | 9B | HELV25 | P 001 5x 112y 15c 13w 5h nnl | | |
| 91 | Sprite | KDI-ARRW | 33% | 5 E -31bx 114by 129ex 114ey | | |
| 92 | Sprite | KDI-ARRW | 33% | 5 E 129bx 114by 129ex 114ey | | |
| 93 | Sprite | KDI-ARRW | 33% | 5 E 129bx 114by 129ex 114ey | | |
| 94 | Sprite | KDI-ARRW | 33% | 5 E 129bx 114by 129ex 114ey | | |

| # | Type | Name | | Coordinates | |
|---|---|---|---|---|---|
| 95 | Sprite | KDI-ARRW | 33% | 5 E 129bx 114by 129ex 114ey | |
| 96 | Sprite | KDI-ARRW | 33% | 5 E 129bx 114by 129ex 114ey | |
| 97 | Sprite | KDI-ARRW | 33% | 5 E 129bx 114by 129ex 114ey | 2 0/18 |
| 98 9C | Screen | LINK09A | Hrz_Out | P 001 20x 112y 15c 11w 5h nnl | |
| 99 | Text | 9C | HELV25 | 5 E -31bx 114by 157ex 114ey . | |
| 100 | Sprite | KDI-ARRW | 33% | 5 E 157bx 114by 157ex 114ey | |
| 101 | Sprite | KDI-ARRW | 33% | 5 E 157bx 114by 157ex 114ey | |
| 102 | Sprite | KDI-ARRW | 33% | 5 E 157bx 114by 157ex 114ey | |
| 103 | Sprite | KDI-ARRW | 33% | 5 E 157bx 114by 157ex 114ey | |
| 104 | Sprite | KDI-ARRW | 33% | 5 E 157bx 114by 157ex 114ey | |
| 105 | Sprite | KDI-ARRW | 33% | 5 E 157bx 114by 157ex 114ey | |
| 106 | Sprite | KDI-ARRW | 33% | 5 E 157bx 114by 157ex 114ey | 2 0/18 |
| 107 9D | Screen | LINK09A | Hrz_Out | 99 | |
| 108 | Text | 9D | HELV21 | P 001 12x 107y 15c 13w 5h nnl | |
| 109 | Sprite | KDI-ARRW | 33% | 5 E -31bx 114by 189ex 114ey | |
| 110 | Sprite | KDI-ARRW | 33% | 5 E 189bx 114by 189ex 114ey | |
| 111 | Sprite | KDI-ARRW | 33% | 5 E 189bx 114by 189ex 114ey | |
| 112 | Sprite | KDI-ARRW | 33% | 5 E 189bx 114by 189ex 114ey | |
| 113 | Sprite | KDI-ARRW | 33% | 5 E 189bx 114by 189ex 114ey | |
| 114 | Sprite | KDI-ARRW | 33% | 5 E 189bx 114by 189ex 114ey | |
| 115 | Sprite | KDI-ARRW | 33% | 5 E 189bx 114by 189ex 114ey | 2 0/18 |
| 116 9E | Screen | LINK09A | Hrz_Out | 99 | |
| 117 | Text | 9E | HELV25 | P 001 14x 109y 15c 12w 5h nnl | |
| 118 | Sprite | KDI-ARRW | 33% | 5 E -31bx 113by 218ex 113ey | |
| 119 | Sprite | KDI-ARRW | 33% | 5 E 218bx 113by 218ex 113ey | |
| 120 | Sprite | KDI-ARRW | 33% | 5 E 218bx 113by 218ex 113ey | |
| 121 | Sprite | KDI-ARRW | 33% | 5 E 218bx 113by 218ex 113ey | |
| 122 | Sprite | KDI-ARRW | 33% | 5 E 218bx 113by 218ex 113ey | |
| 123 | Sprite | KDI-ARRW | 33% | 5 E 218bx 113by 218ex 113ey | |
| 124 | Sprite | KDI-ARRW | 33% | 5 E 218bx 113by 218ex 113ey | 2 0/18 |
| 125 10 | Screen | LINK10 | Hrz_Out | 99 | 2 0/18 |
| 126 | BColor | Tp_Bot | 99 | Solid 0c | |

**Figure 21.4** (*Continued*)

| # | Label type | File | Method | Speed parameters | Wait | Next |
|---|---|---|---|---|---|---|
| 127 | Screen | LINK10A | Dissolve | 50 | 3 0/18 | |
| 128 | Screen | LINK10BS | Sand_UP | 20 154bx 93by | 3 0/18 | |
| 129 | Screen | LINK10CS | Sand_UP | 20 65bx 138by | 4 0/18 | |
| 130 | BColor | Tp_Bot | 99 | Solid 0c | | |
| 131 11 | Screen | LINK11 | Slide_U | 99 | 5 0/18 | |
| 132 | BColor | Tp_Bot | 99 | Solid 0c | | |
| 133 11A | Screen | LINK01 | Drip_DN | 99 | 12 0/18 | |
| 134 | BColor | Tp_Bot | 99 | Solid 0c | | |
| 135 12 | Screen | LINK12 | Slide_D | 50 | 4 0/18 | |
| 136 | BColor | Tp_Bot | 99 | Solid 0c | | |
| 137 13 | Screen | LINK13 | Slide_R | 99 | | |
| 138 | Draw | SetBrush | Square Set 1s 106c | | | |
| 139 | Text | 13 | HELV21 | P 001 25x 176y 14c 12w 3h nnl | | |
| 140 | Draw | | FBox | P 40bx 92by 279ex 125ey | | |
| 141 | Text | 13A | HELV25 | E 001 79x 126y 15c 7w 3h nnl | 3 0/18 | |
| 142 | Text | 13B | HELV25 | E 001 39x 126y 15c 10w 3h nnl | 3 0/18 | |
| 143 | Text | 13C | HELV25 | E 001 37x 125y 15c 10w 3h nnl | 3 0/18 | |
| 144 | Text | 13D | HELV25 | E 001 64x 125y 15c 8w 3h nnl | 3 0/18 | |
| 145 | Text | 13E | HELV25 | E 001 50x 125y 15c 10w 3h nnl | 3 0/18 | |
| 146 | Text | 13F | HELV25 | E 001 32x 126y 15c 11w 3h nnl | 3 0/18 | |
| 147 | Text | 13G | HELV25 | E 001 51x 126y 15c 9w 3h nnl | 3 0/18 | |
| 148 | Draw | | FBox | P 34bx 63by 284ex 148ey | | |
| 149 | Text | 13H | HELV25 | E 001 29x 148y 15c 11w 5h nnm | 3 0/18 | |
| 150 | Screen | LINK13 | Dissolve | 50 | | |
| 151 | Text | 13I | HELV25 | P 001 84x 174y 15c 6w 6h nnm | 3 0/18 | |
| 152 | BColor | Quick | 99 Solid 0c | | | |
| 153 18 | Screen | LINK04 | Tp_Bot | 99 | | |
| 154 | Text | QUALITY | HELV30 | P 001 91x 107y 15c 4w 3h nnl | 2 0/18 | |
| 155 | Text | VERSA | HELV30 | P 001 69x 64y 15c 6w 3h nnl | 2 0/18 | |
| 156 | Screen | LINK04 | Tp_Bot | 99 | | |
| 157 | Text | SUCCESS | HELV40 | P 001 17x 94y 15c 6w 3h nnl | 3 0/18 | |

| 158 | BColor |        | Quick   |    |                              | Solid 0c |    |
|-----|--------|--------|---------|----|------------------------------|----------|----|
| 159 | Screen | LINK20B| Sand_UP | 99 |                              |          | ST |
|     |        |        |         | 99 |                              |          |    |
| 160 | Text   | 20B    | HELV15  |    | E 001 89x 21y 15c 9w 3h nnl  | 0 6/18   |    |
| 161 | Text   | 20B    | HELV15  |    | E 001 89x 21y 15c 9w 3h nnl  | 0 6/18   |    |
| 162 | Text   | 20B    | HELV15  |    | E 001 89x 21y 15c 9w 3h nnl  | 0 6/18   |    |
| 163 | Text   | 20B    | HELV15  |    | E 001 89x 21y 15c 9w 3h nnl  | 0 6/18   |    |
| 164 | Text   | 20B    | HELV15  |    | E 001 89x 21y 15c 9w 3h nnl  | 0 6/18   |    |
| 165 | Text   | 20B    | HELV15  |    | E 001 89x 21y 15c 9w 3h nnl  | 5 0/18   |    |

**Figure 21.4** (*Continued*)

When creating an event line with TEMPRA, designers typically start with the Label or Type field. Once the event has been selected, the menu for the following field related to that event automatically appears. These self-prompting menus make it easy and quick to script a sequence. Yet each field can be modified on the fly to change any part of a line—for instance, the font or color of a text event, or the position of a sprite.

Bevis's brochure is an excellent example of constant motion, full use of a 256-color palette, big text, and—most important of all—a sales message. As we follow the script, notice the attention Bevis pays to organization and structure. A clean script early in the design process makes modification easier later on.

Figure 21.4 shows the complete 165-line script that represents the TV Link brochure. You may want to refer to it throughout this explanation.

**Line 1.**   The first step you must take in working on almost any electronic brochure created with TEMPRA is to determine the video resolution at which the graphics will be displayed. Bevis set video mode for the TV Link sequence at standard $320 \times 200$ 8-bit VGA. By setting at this resolution, Bevis reached a larger audience than he would have using other hardware. Brochures designed at 16-bit resolution may have a more impressive creative impact, but 8-bit brochures are likely to have a greater sales impact.

**Lines 2–4.**   These three lines determine the global settings for text drop shadows, picture-file format, and sprite-file format. Global events (which include fonts and colors) set defaults. These defaults can be changed only by another Global event. In Line 2, the drop shadow to appear behind text has been set at an $x$ and $y$ axis of 2 pixels. The 0 represents the color black, which was chosen from a 256-color palette. Lines 3 and 4 really are not necessary, since an 8-bit (256-color) video-set mode automatically defaults graphics as PCX files, and sprites as PCC. But it doesn't hurt to ensure the proper settings in the brochure.

**Line 5.**   This is the first line the viewer will actually see in the brochure. It's a solid black background color that wipes onto the screen quickly. Starting a brochure with a solid color clears the screen of previous graphics and sets the stage for the information to be presented. Notice that the Label field includes the word START. This matches the word START on Line 165 in the Next field. Lines 5 and 165 are linked together so as to play a continuous loop.

**Line 6.**   QA Screen event is actually a graphic. In Line 6, the graphic is an introductory picture called LINK01 that wipes onto the screen from the bottom of the computer screen to the top at a speed of 3 pixels at a time. Note to remember: Wipes can be very resourceful communicators in themselves. If the graphic to be shown is read from left to right, wiping the graphic onto the screen from left to right is more effective than wiping the graphic as a rollup. Be sure to use wipes as part of the creative design process rather than just choose the first one because it seems interesting.

**Lines 7–11.** These lines are all text pictures treated as sprites. A *sprite* is basically a small moving clip or animation. Any still picture can be turned into a sprite to create motion in a brochure. Sprites are created against a black background, which becomes transparent as the clip is moved around on the computer. The speed of the sprite is determined by the amount of black around it, and since sprites are fairly small they don't have much black around them. Therefore they generally move at a slower speed than most other events. In Lines 7 and 8 the sprite speed is 10, whereas the sprites in Lines 9–11 move 15 pixels at a time. All six sprites are permanent, which means they stay on the screen until they're wiped off by another event. The Parameters field displays the beginning and ending $x$ and $y$ axes for the sprites. The negative parameters ($-119bx$, $-12by$) represent sprites positioned off the visible screen. Turning text into sprites is an effective way to add movement to brochures.

**Line 12.** The LINK01 graphic file wipes onto the screen again, using a horizontal-out wipe at a 1-pixel speed. Using the same image several times throughout a brochure is a technique that is used frequently in the film and video industry (ever notice how people traveling in a car seem to pass the same scenery over and over again?). Looping full-screen graphics and modifying text, smaller graphics, or sprites over it helps to give a brochure more mileage and looks more interesting than a single-color background.

**Lines 13–15.** All three of these lines are ASCII text files, assigned a Helvetica 31-point font and positioned diagonally over the LINK01 graphic. They are all permanent events, meaning they stay on the screen until wiped off by another graphic. The numbers in the Parameters field represent the location, color, and justification of the text. Notice the delay set in the Wait column. The 2 0/18 and other such numbers indicate the time in seconds to pause before continuing on to the next line.

**Line 16.** The graphic SUCCESS dissolves onto the screen in 20-pixel blocks in this line, and pauses for 3 seconds before going on to Line 17.

**Line 17.** Here, Bevis plays an animation of the KDI logo. The AaPlay signifies the runtime Autodesk uses for its 8-bit FLI and FLC animation files. TEMPRA uses these animation formats also, in addition to 16-bit FLX files. The animation plays at the highest speed, 99, and is permanent. The 0x and 0y are the location of the animation on the $x$ and $y$ axes, while the 1R means that the animation plays one time and then stops.

**Lines 18–24.** This series of lines wipes on a black background color, loads graphic files, and displays ASCII text. Note the pauses in the Wait field. One rule of thumb to keep in mind when creating the electronic brochure: Know your target audience. Designers working on 486 computers with lots of memory need to be aware of the speed of the brochure. If the audience will most likely have 386/25 or 386/33—or even 286—computers, the speed of the wipes, animations, and pauses should be created for the lowest common denominator. The ideal is to create the brochure on a faster system, build the distributable version, then watch it from a target system to ensure that it flows smoothly and in a timely fashion.

**Lines 25–33 (and all lines through 124).**   Line 25 begins a segment that is repeated throughout the brochure. Note the 8B displayed in the Label field. This is not meant to be a branching event; it is a comment line that shows at a glance the represented segment of the brochure (the comment line notes are continued throughout the script). Although the script shows nine lines of events, the viewer really sees only three activities: a graphic, some text, and a blinking arrow. The blinking arrow is actually a sprite that travels across the screen and then pops up and disappears at the same location six times, so that it appears to be blinking. In the Sprite event for lines 27–33, the sprite has been reduced 33 percent to make it the appropriate size for the brochure.

The other lines through line 124 are similar in setup to lines 25–33. Working with a script made the design of this particular brochure easy: Bevis simply copied and pasted the first nine-line segment and then made changes as necessary.

**Lines 125–136.**   This group of lines alternates between a graphic and a background color event using various wipe effects and delays. Again, note the use of delays between the graphic and the background color. On a fast machine, these delays prevent graphics from appearing and disappearing so fast that no one can read them.

**Lines 137–165.**   These last lines of the brochure display graphics and various text files associated with those graphics. Lines 138, 140, and 148 are Draw events that display a filled box on the screen, containing some of the Text events. On Line 165 in the Next field is the word START, which is the branch to Line 5, which loops the brochure continuously until the viewer presses the Ctrl-C keys on the keyboard to boot out of the brochure.

## Acknowledgment

I would like to thank Jennifer Kleman, communications specialist at Mathematica, Inc., for helping me to gather data for this chapter.

## Bibliography

Fitzgerald, Kate. "Catalogs Evolve into High-Tech Kiosks," *Advertising Age,* May 10, 1993, p. 47.
Levin, Gary, "Interactive Makes a Splash," *Advertising Age,* April 5, 1993, p. S-1.
Newson, Gillian, "Interactive Marketing Is Driven to Succeed," *NewMedia,* June 1993, p. 73.
Schrage, Michael, "The Ultimate Network," *Adweek,* May 17, 1993, p. 26.
Winski, Joseph M., "Interactive Man: Prodigy Proficient, Our Hero Seeks Thrills Via PC, Ennui Wins," *Advertising Age,* April 5, 1993, p. 24.
_____. "In Interactive, Consumers Taking Control," *Advertising Age,* April 5, 1993, p. S-2.

## Copyrights

# CD-I Developers' Source Guide

Lex van Sonderen

Lucy Lediaev

## What Is Digital Video?

### General features

Digital video (formerly called *full-motion video*) is an extension to the CD-I specification that adds the capability for playing moving natural pictures on the full screen with associated audio of compact-disc quality. Image quality is equal to or better than VHS. To play digital video, CD-I players need to be equipped with a digital video cartridge. Most base-case CD-I players have an extension slot for this cartridge. There will also be CD-I players with built-in digital video.

### Technical features

Digital video uses the MPEG ISO 11172 standard for compression. Digital video is noninterlaced video and can have playback rates of 24, 25, or 30 pictures per second for film, PAL/SECAM, and NTSC source material, respectively. Regardless of the picture rate, digital video can be played back on NTSC and PAL/SECAM systems. Digital video performs temporal-frame-rate conversion without impact on picture size. Aspect-ratio distortion does occur, because PAL/SECAM and NTSC have different aspect ratios. A compatible aspect ratio is loosely defined as one that results in minimal distortion on both PAL/SECAM and NTSC systems.

The maximum picture size depends on the picture rate: $352 \times 288$ at 25 Hz or $352 \times 240$ at 30 Hz. Short and wide pictures (for example, $704 \times 120$) or high and narrow pictures can also be coded.

You can display only a subrectangle of the digital video image, and you can define the position of that rectangle on the CD-I display.

Digital video is displayed in the backdrop plane of CD-I. It is visible only where the two CD-I base-case planes are transparent.

Audio allows bit rates for mono speech of from 4 kbytes per second up to 56 kbytes per second, where 24 kbytes per second subjectively equals stereo CD-quality audio. Digital-video audio is mixed with CD-I base-case audio.

A typical full-screen video stream uses 146 kbytes per second. The size of a video stream is determined by the picture quality, the picture size, and the picture rate. One can have multiple video and audio streams, but only one of each can be active at a time. The maximum data stream is 170 kbytes per second.

Digital video allows for the following play modes: forward play; forward slow motion; freeze frame; forward and reverse scan/skip.

### How do I make a title using digital video?

To play digital video, you will need an application program. There are three alternative ways of creating that application, depending on the level of interactivity needed:

1. For simple linear roll-over titles, a production system will be available shortly.

2. OptImage MediaMogul can be extended with plug-ins for lightly interactive titles. Contact OptImage (address, etc., is on p. 22.5) for further information.

3. For more interactive titles, custom programming is necessary. To write custom programs, you will need a C-cross compiler and software libraries. The digital video specification is an extension to the Green Book (Chapter IX); the OptImage Balboa Run-Time System has been extended to take digital video into account.

Production of the needed MPEG data streams occurs in three steps: (1) audio encoding, (2) video encoding, and (3) multiplexing. Audio encoding can be done using software encoders that are sold by CD-I tool developers such as OptImage. Multiplexing is the process of combining the audio and video streams into one MPEG data stream.

Encoding MPEG video is a very computation-intensive task. As of yet there are no adequate desktop solutions that give adequate image quality within an acceptable conversion time. The following companies provide MPEG encoding services:

Leon Silverman
Laser Pacific Media Corporation
809 N. Cahuenga Blvd.
Hollywood, CA 90038
Phone: 1-213-462-6266
Fax: 1-213-960-2195

Bentley Nelson
Pacific Video Resources
2339 Third Street
San Francisco, CA 94107
Phone: 1-415-864-5679
Fax: 1-415-864-2059

Steven Blumenfeld
GTE ImagiTrek
2385 Camino Vida Roble, Ste 200A
Carlsbad, CA 92009
Phone: 1-619-431-8801
Fax: 1-619-431-8755

Klaus Beunk
Valkieser Multi Media
's-Gravelandseweg 80a
1217 EW Hilversum
The Netherlands
Phone: 31-35-23-48-58
Fax: 31-35-23-27-11

## Launching CD-I

With the successful launch of CD-I in the United States, Philips is receiving an increasing number of calls from people who are interested in developing CD-I titles. Our goal is to encourage anyone to exploit this exciting new medium, and in the rest of this chapter we attempt to answer basic questions as well as to direct those who are new to CD-I to the many sources of CD-I development hardware, software, and information.

### Where can I buy CD-I players and CD-I discs?

Consumers in the United States who want to know where they can buy CD-I discs and/or Philips CD-I players can call the toll-free number of the Philips Consumer Electronics Hotline: 1-800-845-7301.

### Where and how can I sell my CD-I consumer titles and ideas?

**Philips Interactive Media of America (PIMA).**  PIMA's primary focus is on the publication of high-quality CD-I titles for the home entertainment market. PIMA enters into a limited number of agreements with other organizations to coproduce home-entertainment and educational titles. Because of the large number of inquiries, we ask that prospective coproducers mail background information to Senior Vice President in charge of Product Development, Sarina Simon. She can be reached at 11111 Santa Monica Blvd., Suite 700, Los Angeles, CA 90025.

When sending your proposals to Ms. Simon, please describe the subject matter for the proposed title in two or three sentences. Because we cannot guarantee confidentiality in the handling of your proposal at this early stage of the proposal process, we advise you not to send a detailed outline or discussion of your ideas. But do provide detailed information on your company (brochures, company background, etc.), its personnel (resumés or biographies), and facilities. Because Ms. Simon receives a large number of proposals, it will be at least three weeks before you get a response. Upon approval of your proposal for further consideration, the next step is a business plan and a mutual confidentiality agreement.

If you are an independent producer seeking distribution of CD-I titles, contact Robert E. Schaulis, Vice President of International Product Management and Distribution, at 11111 Santa Monica Blvd., Suite 400, Los Angeles, CA 90025 (310-444-6627).

As part of PIMA's publishing activity, independent producers are encouraged to seek distribution agreements for their CD-I titles. PIMA establishes and maintains distribution channels in North America. PIMA can also arrange distribution through foreign channels. The procedure for obtaining a distribution agreement with PIMA is outlined in a document entitled *Guidelines for Distribution License Agreements,* which is available upon request from the International Product Management and Distribution office.

### How can I make corporate or educational CD-I titles?

CD-I is not a proprietary system; therefore companies or individuals may develop their own CD-I titles. Suppliers of development systems can give assistance in finding complete solutions for CD-I development, and they often can provide courses for authoring and programming, as well as offer support.

### Where can I buy CD-I development systems?

**Philips Consumer Electronics (PCEC).**   PCEC is the supplier of Philips hardware in the United States. This organization provides CD-I development players, and it is very active in the commercial and industrial markets. In addition, PCEC can assist developers in designing and putting together hardware systems. For further information, please contact your regional sales manager:

West coast: John Hill; phone 1-615-521-3101

Central: Jerry Huffman; phone 1-317-841-0224

East coast: John Elicker; phone 1-908-827-8648

Southern: Linda Olsen; phone 1-404-952-0064

**OptImage.**   OptImage, a Philips joint-venture company, is a major supplier of development systems for CD-I. It has a large catalog of hardware and software tools for CD-I designers and engineers. OptImage also organizes courses and workshops for CD-I authoring and programming. For further information, please contact

OptImage
Attn.: Pam Wilber
1501 50th Street
West Des Moines, IA 50625
Phone: 1-515-222-2073
Fax: 1-515-222-2080
Western region: Barry Horton (1-714-859-9162)

**ISG.** ISG is a supplier of development systems for CD-I. It has a catalog of hardware and software tools for CD-I developers. ISG specializes in Macintosh-based CD-I engineering systems. For further information please contact, in America,

Interactive Support Group
Attn.: Anne Badger
9420 Topanga Canyon Blvd., Suite 200
Chatsworth, CA 91311
Phone: 1-818-709-7387
Fax: 1-818-709-8160

In Europe:

Attn.: William Vablais
St John's Innovation Centre
Cambridge, United Kingdom, CB4 4WS
44-223-426114
44-223-420015

**Script Systems.** Script Systems is a supplier of development systems for CD-I. It has a catalog of hardware and software tools for CD-I developers. Script Systems specializes in MS-DOS-based CD-I authoring systems. For further information, please contact, on the East Coast,

Attn.: Jim Bertlesman
The Market Place, Building 5
Manlius, NY 13104
Phone: 1-315-682-8714
Fax: 1-315-682-4730

On the West Coast:

Attn.: Tom Bertlesman
214 Spring Grove Lane
San Rafael, CA 94901
Phone: 1-415-258-9768
Fax: 1-415-258-0673

In Europe:

Attn: Peter Theihzen
Phone: 31 5700 10655
Fax: 31 5700 10621

**Where can I get information on CD-I outside of the United States and Canada?**

You may contact, in Europe,

Philips Interactive Media Systems U.K.
Attn.: David Ward
Freeland House
Station Road
Dorking
Surrey RH4 1UL
United Kingdom
Phone: 44-306-875777
Fax: 44-306-875789

Philips IMS Authoring Systems
Attn.: Cees van Versendaal
P.O. Box 80002
5600 JB Eindhoven
The Netherlands
Phone: 31-40-736228
Fax: 31-40-734234

In Asia and Australia:

Philips East Asia
Attn.: Frank Pauli
35-1 Sagmiohno 7-chome
Sagamihara
Kanagawa 288
Japan
Phone: 81-427-410255
Fax: 81-427-495094

Philips East Asia
Attn.: Chris Hofland
28th Floor, Hopewell Centre
17 Kennedy Road, Wanchai
Hong Kong
Phone: 852-821-5340
Fax: 852-528-2259

Philips Australia
Attn.: G. Lee
Australia Centre
3 Figtree Drive
Homobush NSW 2140
Australia
Phone: 61-2-7428311
Fax: 61-2-7644060

**What tools do I need to produce CD-I titles?**

You can make CD-I titles by using an authoring system or by writing custom programming. Authoring is a method for creating an interactive presentation using user-friendly, high-level tools. An authoring system enables the producer to make interactive presentations by integrating thousands of images, hours of sound, partial-screen video clips, and on-screen buttons and controls.

An authoring system consists of a personal computer system (Macintosh or MS-DOS PC), a professional CD-I player, an emulator, and software packages. Usually the video or audio assets are created or captured on the personal computer and then combined on the professional CD-I player. At the present time, one cannot use popular personal-computing authoring packages (for example Macromind Director, ToolBook) to create CD-I presentations; thus, one of the several specific CD-I authoring packages that exist should be used.

For more complex presentations that require greater interactivity and faster execution, custom programming is necessary. Programming for CD-I can be done on a Macintosh, an MS-DOS PC, or a Sun, using a C-cross compiler and software libraries.

### What system do I need for CD-I authoring?

The following are guidelines to some of the systems commonly used for CD-I authoring. No specific recommendation or price information is given here, because such information is best provided by the suppliers of the development systems. Before you make any decision as to which system to use, *consult your CD-I development system supplier first.*

**Hardware.**   Recommended equipment includes

High-end personal computer system

Macintosh II or Quadra, with at least 3 Nubus slots *or*

486-based MS-DOS-compatible PC, running MS-Windows, SCSI interface, and at least 3 empty slots

*Lots* of storage space

Minimal 2-Gbyte hard-disk space per production

8-mm Exabyte tape drive

**Connections.**   Recommended equipment includes

Ethernet cards + NFS software

Serial cables

SCSI cables

**Professional CD-I player.**   Recommended equipment includes

Philips CD-I 605

NTSC/RGB color monitor

Optionally: a low-end monitor to reflect end-user quality on the TV in the living room

**Emulator, including software.**   Recommended are

Philips CD-I emulator *or*

ISG emulator board for the Macintosh *or*

Script Systems emulator for PC-type systems

**Capture and encoding hardware, including software.**   We recommend

High-end audio-capture board

High-end video-capture board or scanner

**Software.**   There is a variety of software applicable to the task of producing a CD-I title.

### Authoring

Media Mogul, for the Philips CD-I 605, *or*

Media Showcase, for the Philips CD-I 605, *or*

Designer Work Bench, for MS-DOS

### Image and audio conversion

Audio-conversion utilities (ACUs)

Image-conversion utilities (ICUs)

Animation- and movie-conversion utilities

### Image and audio conversion and asset management

Media Stockroom, runs on MS-DOS PC under MS-Windows

### Audio- and image-editing applications

For example, for Macintosh: Adobe Photoshop, Studio 32, Macromind Director, DigiDesign SoundTools II

### File transfer software

To transfer files from Mac or PC to CD-I: OptImage, ISG, or Script Systems

## What system do I need for CD-I programming?

The following are guidelines to some of the systems commonly used for CD-I programming in the C programming language. No specific recommendation or price information is given here, because such information is best provided by the suppliers of the development systems. Before making any decision about the systems to use, *consult your CD-I development system supplier first.*

**Hardware.**   Recommended equipment includes

### Computer

High-end personal computer system or workstation

Macintosh II or Quadra with at least 3 Nubus slots *or*

486-based MS-DOS-compatible PC running MS-Windows, SCSI interface, and at least 3 empty slots, *or*

Sun Sparc

### Emulator

Philips CD-I emulator *or*

ISG Cassiopee board for the Macintosh *or*

ISG emulator board for the Macintosh *or*

Script Systems emulator board for the PC-type systems

### Professional CD-I player

Philips CD-I 605 *or*

ISG Cassiopee board for the Macintosh

NTSC/RGB color monitor

Optionally: a low-end monitor to reflect end-user quality on TV in the living room

### Connections

Ethernet cards + NFS software

Serial cables

SCSI cables

### Capture and encoding hardware

High-end audio-capture board

High-end video-capture board or scanner

**Software.**   Recommended software includes

### Programming

MPW on Macintosh, SunView on Sun

OS-9 Cross Compiler for Sun, Mac, or PC

OS-9 source-level debugger

ISG X-Link

GNU Cross-compiler on Sun or Mac

OptImage Balboa C Library

ISG C++ Library

Script Systems CD Vista C Library

### Image and audio conversion

Audio-conversion utilities (ACUs)

Image-conversion utilities (ICUs)

### Audio- and image-editing applications

For instance, for Macintosh: Adobe Photoshop, Studio 32, Macromind Director, DigiDesign SoundTools II

### File transfer software

Software to transfer files from Mac or PC to CD-I: OptImage, ISG, or Script Systems

### Disc building

OptImage Master/Green *or*

ISG CDL and BD

## What is an emulator?

During the development stage of CD-I production, software is continuously tested and run. Because of the specific characteristics of the CD-I medium, the software cannot be run and tested with just a hard disk. In particular, the data delivery, the data rate, and the (slow) access time of the CD need to be taken into account. An emulator is an intelligent, computer-peripheral device with a high-capacity hard disk. During the development stage, a disc image is built onto the hard disk of the emulator. Then, when the emulator is switched to the emulation mode, it behaves in the same manner as a real CD player. The alternative would be to burn a CD-I disc for each test run, which is slower and more expensive.

## Do I need a CD-recorder?

Usually, a CD-recorder is not required for development of CD-I titles. Typically an emulator is used, and only when the disc image is completely finished is it sent to a mastering house to be reproduced in compact-disc form. If one regularly needs to make a very small series of CDs (1–10), a CD-recorder can be useful.

**What is "the Green Book"?**

The *"Compact Disc–Interactive Full Functional Specification"* is better known as "the Green Book." The Green Book is the official standard for CD-I-compliant hardware and software. It is coauthored by Philips and Sony and is available only to official licensees of the Compact Disc–Interactive standard. To become a licensee, contact Philips, Sony, or the CD-I Association.

**What are the technical specifications for a CD-I player?**

A CD-I player plays all CD-I titles, CD digital audio (CD-DA), CD+Graphics, Photo CD, and CD-ROM-XA bridge discs.

**Memory**

2 banks of 512 kbytes RAM

8 kbytes nonvolatile RAM

650 Mbytes CD-ROM-XA

**Audio**

CD-DA: max. 72 minutes

ADPCM level A: max. 144 minutes, two channels, hi-fi quality

ADPCM level B: max. 288 minutes, two channels, normal quality

ADPCM level C: max. 576 minutes, two channels, speech quality

ADPCM audio can be played directly from disk, with negligible computer interaction, or can be loaded into memory to be played with precise timing.

**Video**

Resolution: $384 \times 240$ when displayed on NTSC, $384 \times 280$ when displayed on PAL

2 8-bit video planes

Background plane in 1 of 8 colors

$16 \times 16$ hardware cursor in 1 of 8 colors

Video effects: transparency, mattes, color-keying, pixel-hold, mosaic

Programmable video processor to execute video commands on a field and line basis. Commands include: change CLUT; change coding method; change transparency factor; define video memory address, etc.

Each plane can have multiple image-coding methods (video modes) selectable on a per-line basis

### Image-coding methods

CLUT4: 16 colors out of 16 million, double horizontal resolution (768 pixels)

CLUT7: 128 colors out of 16 million

DYUV: 16 million colors, for continuous-tone images

RL3: 8 colors out of 16 million, hardware run-length compression, double horizontal resolution (768 pixels)

RL7: 128 colors out of 16 million, hardware run-length compression. Note: DYUV and RL video modes do not allow direct access to the value of an individual pixel.

Two more video modes exist that are rarely used:

CLUT8: 256 colors out of 16 million; only possible in one plane, the other plane can only be DYUV; restricting compared to CLUT7.

RGB555: 32,768 colors, uses both planes, and requires twice as much data per screen; restricting and slow compared to the other video modes.

### Processor

68K family, equivalent to 8-MHz 68000

### Operating system

CD-RTOS: OS-9 with CD-I extensions. Lightweight, real-time, multitasking operating system

### Notes

No responsibility will be taken by Philips or the authors for the information presented herein. For comments, additions, corrections, or if you have remaining questions, contact

Lex van Sonderen
Manager, Knowledge Transfer
Philips Interactive Media of America
11050 Santa Monica Blvd.
Los Angeles, CA 90025
Phone: 1-310-444-6689
Fax: 1-310-477-4953
Internet: lex@aimla.com
CompuServe: 71552,2204

# Corporate Guide to Optical Publishing

**Kurt Mueller**

## Introduction

In virtually every industry, leading corporations are looking at CD-ROM (Compact Disc, Read Only Memory) as a powerful business tool. For example:

- A leading computer manufacturer significantly improves the delivery of documentation, training materials, and maintenance releases by bundling a CD-ROM drive in its latest product line.

- A Baby Bell company publishes 300 telephone directories—covering every published listing in a six-state area on a single CD-ROM disc, with room to spare.

- A farm equipment supplier significantly improves its dealer communications by publishing its parts and price catalogs on CD-ROM.

- A major software company provides better technical support by distributing technical bulletins and help-desk information on CD-ROM, increasing the effectiveness of telephone support and distinguishing its products in the process.

- A U.S. government agency converts its 20,000-page loose-leaf Procedures manual to CD-ROM. Monthly distribution to field offices saves time and reduces staff requirements.

- A major oil company publishes product and competitive information on CD-ROM for use by sales representatives with portable CD-ROM readers.

Why have these organizations made major commitments to CD-ROM? Why has there been so much talk about CD-ROM lately, particularly when the technology has been available for over seven years? This chapter will attempt to answer these questions.

## CD-ROM and Competitive Advantage

There are two reasons for the surge in popularity of CD-ROM. First, technological developments have substantially lowered the barriers to cost-effective use of CD-ROM. In the eighties, CD-ROM technology was still too expensive and applications too difficult to develop for many corporations. These conditions have changed dramatically. A technology that once was only potentially beneficial is now affordable, easy to use, and widely employed.

Second, CD-ROM has demonstrated clear benefits for business. More than 5000 CD-ROM titles are now in print for a broad range of applications, including over 3000 commercial products. One CD-ROM can hold the equivalent of 1500 floppy disks, 250,000 pages of text, or 12,000 scanned images, at an incremental media cost of only $2 per disc. This tremendous data-storage capacity and low cost have led many people to focus on the media cost savings alone.

Yet even greater benefits of the technology lie in the cost reduction and revenue generation it provides by delivering products and services more efficiently. CD-ROM technology is a powerful tool that can

- Improve sales performance
- Lower cost of sales
- Improve product and service quality
- Differentiate products in the marketplace
- Strengthen third-party distribution channels
- Dramatically improve customer service

For companies looking for a competitive edge, these are compelling benefits. Three areas are emerging as key competitive advantages for business in the nineties: knowledge, time, and information. CD-ROM can enhance improvement activities in these areas, and often serves as the core of a competitive solution.

### The three areas of competitive advantage

**1. Knowledge.** With product lines expanding, boutique manufacturing operations, and increasing pressure to customize products, businesses today are faced with the challenge of having to provide a bewildering array of product possibilities and options. Retail, distributor, and support personnel are increasingly expected to attain more in-depth knowledge about a broader product line. Often, simply finding the correct information is difficult. CD-ROM can not only provide correct and current product information, it can assist in training personnel in the sale and use of products as well.

Newly emerging self-contained, portable CD-ROM and multimedia players are revolutionizing the sales process. Each salesperson can now carry an electronic reference that includes complete product catalogs, specifications, sample product applications, and sales and marketing promotions. Sales training time for complex products is reduced, a consistent and professionally prepared product presentation is delivered, and customer questions can be answered on the spot. The competitive advantage gained by organizations employing these technologies is substantial.

**2. Time.**   Decisions are being made in increasingly complex environments, where any delay can mean lost revenues and customers. Measured through the parameters of market presence or response, time is emerging as a key competitive advantage.

CD-ROM can assist in providing up-to-date information in a readily searchable format. Precious time isn't wasted searching for pertinent facts, and all appropriate details can be quickly assembled at once.

A major manufacturer of industrial heating and cooling systems identified a lower response time in the answering of product questions as a key competitive advantage. A target of one minute or less to respond to any customer question about any of the company's products established the overriding objective. Given that there were over 60 product catalogs dating back more than 50 years, a complete reengineering of the company's information systems was required. The reengineering included CD-ROM delivery of product information. Rather than using information technology simply as a productivity enhancement tool, it was identified as a way to reengineer the company's customer communications.

**3. Information.**   Corporate America today captures significantly more data than can be integrated for decision making. Distilling this data into a set of information useful for guiding the business requires both a business and technical perspective. The information challenge isn't about how much data can be captured, but about how to make the best decisions with the available data. CD-ROM is used to provide databases from which knowledge can be extracted by managers using sophisticated access software and "what-if" analysis.

## CD-ROM Technology Today

### A technology takes off

CD-ROM has been a fortuitous technological development. It emerged through the coincidental convergence of several developments: the appearance of CD audio in the mass-market entertainment industry; the proliferation and standardization of personal computers in business; the need for information providers of all types to find alternatives to distributing increasingly higher volumes of information on paper.

## Over 3,000 Commercial CD-ROM Titles

| **Structured Data** | **Text** |
|---|---|
| • Bibliographic Data | • Books |
| • Corporate Directories | • Government Regulations |
| • Credit Data | • Legal/Tax Information |
| • Financial Data | • Loose-leaf Publications |
| • Geographical Data | • Manuals |
| • Patent Information | • Medical Information |
| • People Directories | • Reference Collections |
| • Statistics | • Standards Information |

## Over 2,000 Corporate CD-ROM Applications

| **Structured Data** | **Text** |
|---|---|
| • COM Replacement | • Audit Procedures |
| • Customer Data | • Contracts |
| • Forms Catalogs | • Engineering Standards |
| • Inventory | • Maintenance Releases |
| • Monthly Statements | • Policy Manuals |
| • Parts Catalogs | • Research |
| • Purchasing Data | • Technical Documentation |
| • Service Orders/Reports | • Training Manuals |
| • Spec Sheets | |
| • Transaction Histories | |

**Figure 23.1**   CD-ROM titles today.

CD-ROM derives its low price and manufacturing availability from the consumer audio marketplace. CD audio is the most successful consumer electronics product in history, and it has created a stable worldwide standard and manufacturing base. The success of CD audio has fostered spinoff technologies such as CD-ROM.

CD-ROM is well on its way to becoming the medium of choice for electronic distribution. Today there are over 3000 commercial CD-ROM titles and in excess of 2000 corporate in-house titles.* Figure 23.1 illustrates representative subject areas.

Besides technological advantages, CD-ROM owes its success to three key advantages it provides to users: multimedia, multiplatform, and multiple language applications.

**Multimedia.**    The term *multimedia* refers to the delivering of text, data, graphics, audio, and video to end users. CD-ROM facilitates delivery of all of these information types in an integrated package. Information sets can be accompanied by audio and video clips describing significant areas. For example a service manual could contain, along with the written text and diagrams, a video or animation sequence showing a critical procedure. Multimedia will play an increasingly important role in the way information is distributed and

---

*Source: Infotech.

used in the nineties. Because multimedia presentations and interactive sessions require significant amounts of storage space for digitized images, sound, and video, CD-ROM is uniquely positioned to become the medium of choice for these new information formats.

**Multiplatform.**   The term *multiplatform* refers to the use of one disc in different computer platforms. A formal CD-ROM standard, developed by an ad hoc industry group known as High Sierra, was approved by the International Standards Organization (ISO) in 1987. By laying out the CD-ROM files in ISO 9660 format, a publisher ensures that the CD-ROM will play on any standard CD drive attached to a computer with appropriate software. The ISO 9660 standard was developed to be operating-system-independent. If access software that provides for multiplatform support is employed, a correctly formatted CD-ROM disc can be used in any of a number of computer environments: PC, Macintosh, UNIX, and others. This has allowed CD-ROM producers to publish discs not just for the PC but for whatever workstation is on the end user's desk. CD-ROM can now replace paper, because it's accessible on every desktop.

**Multiple languages.**   The term *multilingual* usually implies a user interface that contains operations, hints, and help-text in different user-selected languages. An initialization parameter determines the start-up language to be displayed, with an option for the user to change the operating language interactively. The content of the CD-ROM often is in only one language, although a number of emerging applications include multiple versions of the source content in different languages. Multilingual applications help to circumvent communication and training issues for international organizations.

## The Software Challenge

A CD-ROM disc often contains 100 times more information than a typical personal-computer database, but the rate at which the CD-ROM drive can get to various locations on the disc is at least 10 times slower than a magnetic disk. The challenge for CD-ROM retrieval software is to gather a much greater volume of information quickly, despite an inherently slower hardware technology.

To create applications for CD-ROM, two kinds of software are required: software that helps the developer to build and prepare an application to be put onto the disc (known as *authoring software*), and software that allows the user to retrieve the information from the disc through his/her desktop computer (commonly referred to as *retrieval software*).

Because of CD-ROM's large capacity for data and its slow access speed, software originally designed for magnetic media is ineffective when applied to optical media. CD-ROM software must be optimized to minimize disc access. There are now several vendors offering software that has been optimized for optical media, and the best of these can equal or exceed magnetic media performance even while searching several hundred megabytes of data.

CD-ROM drives are increasingly attached to computers other than DOS-based PCs, such as Windows, Macintosh, and UNIX machines. The newest generation of CD-ROM development systems allows the development of discs on one platform that can then be accessed from a variety of hardware platforms and network environments. This new breed of software is often referred to as *multiplatform retrieval software.*

These next-generation systems increasingly will be required to prepare and deliver multimedia presentations in addition to data and text applications. The software challenges of the nineties will include not simply the delivery of multimedia but the integration of multimedia objects with corporate information collections, and the delivery of those integrated databases at exceedingly high performance levels on a variety of computer platforms.

### CD-ROM advances—more for less

These software improvements are among the most important developments to change the immediate outlook for cost-effective use of CD-ROM. Five years ago, the creation of a single CD-ROM application through a service bureau cost from $50,000 to $100,000. For less money today, corporations can install a complete internal CD-ROM publishing capability, including both the software and the premastering hardware. Installations such as these are capable of turning out more than 50 applications per year.

Here are some other advances:

- The cost of mastering and replicating 100 discs has fallen from $5000 to $1500. Incremental discs can be purchased for less than $2 each.
- Capacity has increased from 550 Mbytes to 700 + Mbytes per disc.
- Stand-alone drive prices have fallen from $1500 to under $500. Half-height drives for IBM PCs are available for under $400. Volume purchases yield even lower prices.
- Recordable CD-ROM systems now available support complete in-house production of CD-ROMs for low-volume or security-sensitive applications. Blank media in low quantities start under $30, with cost savings for volume purchases.

### Real Problems, Real Solutions

CD-ROM is solving real business problems today. Let's look at a few examples.

**Problem.**  Supporting a rapidly expanding product line cost-effectively.

**Solution.**  Take a cue from several computer manufacturers and improve the effectiveness of sales and service personnel by publishing broad-based and/or constantly changing product information on CD-ROM. This enables customers to help themselves when they might otherwise have called for support. Not only is the need for direct staff involvement reduced, but customer satisfaction is improved.

**Problem.**   Supporting a product in the dealer channel.

**Solution.**   Leading companies, from farm-equipment suppliers to airlines, are taking advantage of this technology in the competitive dealer environment. Comprehensive catalogs for all products, including prices and specifications, are distributed on CD-ROM. This makes it easier for dealers to locate the right product.

**Problem.**   Selling products internationally without getting snarled in regulations and rising administrative costs.

**Solution.**   Follow the lead of an international consumer products manufacturer operating in more than 50 countries. It has converted import/export databases to CD-ROM. The system reduces costly mistakes made by personnel, who must search among 50,000 products for shipping codes and regulations, and saves over $2 million per year.

**Problem.**   Improving sales training and efficiency.

**Solution.**   Adopt the strategy of a leading oil company that puts product and competitive information on CD-ROM and equips field salespeople with portable CD-ROM systems. Salespeople use the systems to identify the correct product and point out competitive advantages.

**Problem.**   Increasing the productivity of professional staff.

**Solution.**   Learn from a major drug company that scanned chemical-analysis reports to create a database of more than 100 years of research. Previously the information had been accessible only in paper files, and was therefore seldom used. The company has recovered the cost of the effort by eliminating the cost of duplicating previously performed tests.

A summary of the potential benefits of CD-ROM information integration and distribution is shown in Fig. 23.2.

## CD-ROM and other distribution technologies

Many years ago, the computer revolution promised the elimination of paper. We now know that the computer is the most voracious consumer of paper since the printing press. Paper has distinct advantages as an information distribution medium: it is completely portable, requires no additional hardware for access, and updates are simple (although incorporation of update pages can often be complex and time-consuming). Paper also has disadvantages: it's cumbersome, hard to search, and environmentally unfriendly.

Virtually every large corporation and most small businesses are now producing, editing, and updating information electronically. The natural next

Reduce Costs and Improve Efficiency
- Lower information distribution costs
- Save on information retrieval time
- Avoid duplication of efforts
- Reduce errors and mistakes
- Improve learning rates
- Share knowledge

Increase Revenues
- Broaden product scope
- Improve sales and channel performance
- Present/differentiate products
- Sell information

Increase Productivity
- Deliver information when, where, and how it is needed
- Make better decisions due to timely information access
- Increase product support capability

Improve Corporate/Product Image
- Satisfy customers
- Gain a reputation for technological leadership
- Increase channel loyalty

**Figure 23.2**   The strategic benefits of CD-ROM.

step in this process is electronic distribution, and the benefits are not simply improved access and increased efficiency. For efficiency, cost, and environmental reasons, corporations and government agencies alike are embarking on significant efforts to reduce the amount of paper produced and distributed.

The general term *electronic distribution* embraces telecommunications and local-area networks; magnetic, floppy, and cartridge disks; computer output to microfiche; facsimile; and CD-ROM. Each is appropriate for different types of information and different distribution objectives. Telecommunications is best for smaller amounts of information that have a short life-span or must be updated frequently. The significant cost of creating and maintaining a telecommunications capability, and the inherent bandwidth limitations, reserve this alternative primarily for high-priority information.

Magnetic media is most appropriate for small databases requiring fairly frequent updates. Much of the information created by work groups on local-area networks will be stored magnetically. As this information accumulates, storage becomes increasingly unwieldy.

Computer-output microfiche and microfilm are used for high-frequency distribution to multiple locations, and for information archiving when search requirements are minimal. Although these are mature technologies, this technology isn't seeing wide use today due to dissatisfaction with both the media and the delivery system. Today there are fewer than one million microfilm readers, as compared to more than 100 million business and personal computers.

Facsimile is ideal for fast delivery of small amounts of paper-based information.

CD-ROM has broad areas of application, due to the following unique advantages:

- It features digital-based media capable of delivering text, data, graphics, sound, and/or video.

- It is compatible with personal computers and local-area networks.

- It can be shared over both local- and wide-area networks.

- Information can be exported to other computers and software programs.

- It offers very high capacity at a significantly lower cost than other distribution alternatives.

- It has a searching, sorting, and retrieval capability superior to paper, computer-output microfiche,* microfilm, and on-line.†

- The cost for volume distribution is low.

CD-ROM has certain limitations that make it inappropriate for some applications and not a viable substitute for traditional storage:

- It is read-only, with no ability to modify the data on disc. However there are some emerging technological approaches that will allow for the appending of data to an already existing data set on CD-ROM.

- A mastering step is required to create the master and replicas. Mastering costs $1500 and takes three days, with faster turnaround available for an extra charge. CD-recordable technology allows in-house mastering for low volumes of discs, but the blank disc is more expensive than mastered CD replicas.

- The slow speed and large capacity of optical discs require special software to provide application performance comparable to magnetic disk.

- The drive must be added to the typical desktop workstation at a cost of $400 to $800. Many of the latest generation of PCs now come with CD-ROM drive already installed.

CD-ROM's strengths make it most appropriate for applications with any of the following requirements (Fig. 23.3):

- Information distributed to multiple locations

- Mixed text, data, graphic, and/or audio/video information

- Large data volumes

- Fast access time

- Extensive searching, sorting, and retrieval

## A Value Multiplier for Information Systems

Four current information-management technologies are emerging as high priorities for most organizations over the next decade: electronic publishing,

---

*Com fiche generally is searchable only on a single field. CD-ROM software permits every field to be indexed and searched in multiple ways.

†CD-ROM information retrieval is 3 to 5 times faster than on-line retrieval for large-volume databases.

**Figure 23.3**   Cost per megabyte.

local-area networking, client-server architectures, and transaction processing. CD-ROM can broaden the application of these systems and enhance their value to the corporation.

### Electronic publishing

To remain competitive, businesses that produce large volumes of paper-based information are moving to electronic publishing. Various types of information such as text, data, and graphics, can be combined electronically, saving substantial time in revising, reformatting, and producing a document. These advantages are great as far as they go, but usually they stop just short of distribution. Converting electronic information to a nonelectronic format when there are more than 25 million potential electronic readers on the desks of corporate America does not make sense for many applications. This is a large area for cost savings and productivity improvement.

### Local-area networks and work-group computing

The CD-ROM standards were established with networks as an expected requirement. The ISO 9660 standard incorporates the basic hardware and media specifications required to make a CD-ROM network compatible. Once a network has been equipped with drives and appropriate software, virtually any CD-ROM disc—assuming it has the appropriate network license agreements and meets the ISO 9660 standard—can be shared on the local-area network. Each attached drive provides over 700 Mbytes of read-only information to the network nodes. By placing one or more CD-ROM drives on each local-area network or in each department, an organization provides ready

**Service**

- Documentation
- Maintenance Releases
- Service Call Reports
- Trouble Shooting Guides
- Maintenance Histories
- Parts Lists
- Inventory
- Warranty Listings

**Operations**

- Inventory
- Parts Lists
- Stock Number Cross Reference
- Bill of Materials
- Order Data
- Engineering Standards
- Parts Where Used
- Facility and Equipment Registers

**Marketing and Sales**

- Catalogs
- Specification Sheets
- Parts Lists
- Prices
- Inventory
- Purchase History

**Procurement**

- Inventory
- Bill of Materials
- Cumulative Order Data
- Vendor Cross Reference Data
- Index of Suppliers

**Research and Development**

- Research Reports
- Standards Information
- Bibliographic Databases

**Figure 23.4**   Work-group information requirements.

access to internal information and to externally purchased information relevant to that department or work group. Examples of typical work-group information requirements are shown in Fig. 23.4.

### Downsizing and client-server architectures

Corporations and government agencies are rapidly replacing centrally located, monolithic information systems with distributed architectures. Driving forces include high maintenance on centrally located mainframe systems, long lead times on new application developments, and the increasing need for organizations to provide flexible and responsive information systems. Client-server architectures make possible a decentralized information enterprise, allowing local control and maintenance of information pertinent to the work group.

CD-ROM is often a vital component of downsizing efforts. While a new decision-support application for a centrally located information system may require lengthy lead time, extracting a copy of the information, committing it to CD-ROM, and using fourth-generation access tools for decision support is proving successful. This newly emerging use of CD-ROM is helping to accelerate many corporation's downsizing efforts.

### Transaction-processing systems

Some of the best examples of information as a competitive tool are found in those industries that have been transformed by electronic transaction processing such as banking, brokerage, and travel. Other examples include the pharmaceutical and auto parts industries, and a variety of other retail businesses where transaction information is essential to the successful operation of the business.

The leaders in transaction processing are now taking the next step in strategic information delivery: CD-ROM. Purchasing activity in corporate and government organizations is converted to CD-ROM for trend analysis. Retailers in the auto, trucking, and appliance replacement-parts business are using CD-ROM to find the right part and make the sale.

Using CD-ROM systems to augment point-of-transaction information, improve customer service, and boost sales is widely applicable to other industries. The two technologies work in partnership: on-line transaction processing delivers accurate and time-sensitive information, while large volumes of related but less time-sensitive information are delivered on CD-ROM.

## How CD-ROM Can Benefit Your Organization

### Existing content

CD-ROM can have a significant impact on an organization's bottom line, but identifying where in an organization to start with CD-ROM applications can be difficult. Most organizations that see an immediate impact with CD-ROM base their initial applications on preexisting content. CD-ROM is used to improve and expand existing information sources. As these organizations integrate CD-ROM into their business systems, they introduce new content sources to further leverage the investment in CD-ROM development platforms and readers.

### Information used and produced

To determine if optical information distribution is appropriate for an organization, it's appropriate to analyze the sources and uses of information. One recommended approach divides the organization's major activities between serving the customer and supporting infrastructure. Figure 23.5 illustrates a typical manufacturing company's primary and infrastructure activities. For each major activity, the information produced and the information used in performing critical functions is identified.

### CD-ROM applications portfolio

After the information used and produced has been arranged according to priority, it can be organized into an applications portfolio for the organization. The applications portfolio identifies high-return activities by classifying information mission/activity-critical, management/support, and archival. CD-ROM will have the greatest impact on mission- and activity-critical information. Figure 23.6 illustrates the applications portfolio for an insurance firm.

| Primary Activities | Operations | Marketing & Sales | Service | Customer |
|---|---|---|---|---|
| Information Used | Orders<br>Engineering Standards<br>Purchasing Information | Inventory Orders<br>Parts Lists<br>Design Specifications<br>Market Information<br>Sales Information<br>Inventory | Training<br>Parts Lists<br>Customer<br>Information<br>Inventory | Documentation<br>Maintenance<br>Parts Catalogs |
| Information Produced | Parts Lists<br>Inventory<br>Ship to Lists<br>Bill of Materials<br>Parts Where Used<br>Facility &<br>Equipment Registers | Parts Catalogs<br>Customer Database<br>Prospect Database<br>Purchase Histories<br>Spec Sheets<br>Pricing<br>Contracts | Service Call<br>Reports<br>Trouble-<br>Shooting Guides<br>Maintenance<br>History<br>Training<br>Service Orders<br>Warranty<br>Listings | Warranty<br>Information<br>Product<br>Improvements<br>Service Requests<br>Customer<br>Information<br>Orders |
| **Infrastructure Activities** | **Research & Development** | **Purchasing** | **Human Resources** | **Financial & Admin.** |
| Information Used | External Research<br>Patent Information<br>Standards Information<br>Bibliographic Research | Inventory<br>Orders<br>Bill of Materials<br>Vendor Information<br>Price Lists<br>Product Information | Government<br>Regulations<br>Recruiting<br>Information | Accounting<br>Standards<br>Government<br>Regulations<br>Accounting<br>Input<br>Budget Input |
| Information Produced | Internal Research<br>Engineering Standards | On Order Reports<br>Vendor Information<br>Product Information<br>Price Lists | Training<br>Manuals<br>Personnel<br>Records | Policy &<br>Procedure<br>General Audit<br>& Record<br>Retention<br>Budget<br>Information<br>Accounting<br>Information |

**Figure 23.5** Information used and produced.

This applications planning process results in a list of high-priority applications in which CD-ROM distribution yields substantial benefits. This application portfolio becomes the focal point in the technology acquisition process. Those applications that will serve as prototypes to test the technology warrant additional planning, so as to create a complete profile of the user, the information, and the anticipated benefits.

| | Value Multiplier | Agency Info | Marketing & Sales | Operations |
|---|---|---|---|---|
| | Electronic Publishing | | Renewal & Policy Changes | |
| | Database Publishing | | Policy Holders File | Claim Payment History |
| | Product & Service Info | Rate Books | Rate Books | |
| | Policy & Standards Info | Policy Manuals | | Cumulative Policy Register |
| | Customer & Transaction Info | | Renewal & Policy Changes | Transaction Register |

Activity Critical

Management Support

Archival

**Figure 23.6**   CD-ROM applications portfolio—insurance

## Multimedia applications portfolio

The term *multimedia* typically implies adding new content through additional data types (such as audio and video) to existing applications. Adding multimedia is reasonable only when it provides significant productivity or communications improvement. Starting with existing content is recommended, as multimedia production costs can quickly accumulate. As with CD-ROM applications, those selected for development should be the high-value, activity-critical applications in an organization.

As with the CD-ROM applications portfolio, a portfolio of multimedia applications will pinpoint those areas in which applications development will have the greatest impact. Figure 23.7 illustrates a representative multimedia applications portfolio.

It's important to note that as of today multimedia delivery is in its infancy. Hardware, software, and data standards are just emerging. While traditional CD-ROM data types (data, text, and graphics) have arrived at platform-neutral standards, multimedia sources, such as audio and video, have not. Today a CD-ROM application with traditional content can be portable across

| | Operations | Marketing & Sales | Service |
|---|---|---|---|
| Multimedia Publishing | | Product Catalog with Sound or Video | Tech Doc. with Sound |
| Multimedia Database | Employee Databases | | Parts Catalog with Sound |
| Multimedia Presentations | Management Presentations | Sales Presentations | |
| Multimedia Training | Personnel Training | | Service Training |
| Multimedia Sales Systems | | Multimedia Kiosks | |

**Figure 23.7**   Multimedia applications portfolio.

numerous end-user computer platforms (assuming that appropriate multi-platform software has been employed). A multimedia application must be designed for a specific computer platform.

## Selecting the Right CD-ROM Approach

Once CD-ROM has been identified as a viable technology given existing requirements, the next step is to determine the best approach to developing applications. This entails both a technical and business evaluation. As with most computer applications, software is the key component. Before considering the business options, it's important to understand the match of data type to software support.

### Matching content with software

When evaluating CD-ROM application software, the type of information supported becomes critical. A brief explanation of the key information types—structured data, text, graphics, audio, and video—is provided next.

**Structured data.**  Structured data is the most prevalent data type on CD-ROM. Examples of structured data are information from computer databases, bibliographies, directories, catalogs, and numeric data (as illustrated in Fig. 23.1). Structured information may contain text fields, but unlike full text, structured data does not have to be exclusively in the form of sentences, paragraphs, and chapters. It can also be partially or entirely in phrases or fields. In a parts catalog, for example, the part name and description fields would use a classic keyword text retrieval. The part-number-, model-, year-, price-, and date-issued fields would utilize numeric- and date-range searching. Queries from all fields can be combined with boolean logic to find unique "and," "or," or "not" related sets of information. With structured data, an index file is created for each field, but developers may elect to index only fields of interest. Because the records are arranged in structured order, index searching with structured data is normally faster and returns less irrelevant information.

**Text.**  Text includes information derived from books, journals, reports, and documentation. Textual information often is structured by an outline for browsing purposes. Users can select chapters, sections, and headings as convenient access points, provided they know that the material of interest is located within that part of the text.

Keyword searches provide another way of accessing text. Users can find information when its location is not obvious, or when its occurrence is so frequent that looking through a book index becomes tedious or impractical. Key terms may be combined to find unique "and," "or," and "not" related documents. The leading text systems offer proximity searching (word $A$ within 10 words of word $B$); truncation (entering a root word retrieves all variations);

and numeric-range searching. Phonetic searching and index browsing also are offered on some systems.

Many text-retrieval systems are enhancing search capabilities through the addition of hypertext. Hypertext describes different ways of linking related items to each other. In its simplest form, known as *sideways browsing,* the user selects a displayed word or phrase and with a single keystroke finds all documents that contain that word. More sophisticated systems search for related terms as well, or provide for item-linking created by the publisher or user.

**Graphics.**  Graphics includes pictures, charts, illustrations, and page images. These can exist as bitmapped images or structured graphics (vector). Graphics normally are associated with either structured data (such as a part catalog with part diagrams) or text (such as a maintenance manual with illustrations).

Some of the most common types of graphics found in CD-ROM products today are bitmapped page images. A scanner is used to capture an entire document page as a grid of black-and-white pixels. Text as well as drawings, pictures, and tables are represented as part of the same image. Captured this way, the text is not machine-readable and therefore not searchable. Only the whole page can be indexed and accessed. This approach is useful when the arrangement of the text on the page is complex and meaningful, when graphics appear with regularity, and when the user can find the desired page by means of a keyword or hierarchical index that points to the page image. The ability to integrate bitmapped images provides a general-purpose mechanism for incorporating a wide range of image types into optical applications. It is preferable to choose software with at least this capability. Vector graphics, prevalent in some technical-documentation applications, are supported by only a limited number of CD-ROM software products. Most CD-ROM software currently handles black-and-white, but some systems handle color. Color graphics are a key ingredient of multimedia applications.

**Audio.**  Audio includes voice, music, and sound clips. While the CD disc was originally developed for audio, the use of audio on CD-ROM is relatively new. Hardware and format standards are just now emerging, and often are computer-platform-specific. Developers who choose to add audio content to CD-ROM applications today must select from several emerging standards.

**Video.**  Video can range from animation sequences to full-screen, 30-frame-per-second display. Animation sequences usually are generated with a computer graphics package, while video is typically sampled from videotape or videodisc. Using CD-ROM for video is also new and immature. Hardware and media standards for rudimentary animation, much less video, are just emerging, and several standards are competing.

Many CD-ROM applications use graphics, audio, and video, and are developed with authoring software optimized for video, graphics, and sound, as opposed to data and text. Multimedia applications that also require sophisticated data- and text-searching must be merged with these multimedia "front-ends."

Because standards have not emerged for multimedia delivery, adding multimedia content to a CD-ROM title today typically limits the title to a specific computer platform. Some publishers elect to replicate the multimedia information on the CD-ROM, producing multimedia content specific to each target platform. This option requires substantial space on the disc for the multimedia objects.

## Application development options

The business alternatives for developing CD-ROM applications range from complete in-house development to complete service-bureau contracting. Figure 23.8 illustrates some of the tradeoffs. However, the right approach for your organization also will depend on the software development path selected. A discussion of the four common development paths follows.

**1. In-house software development.**   Writing customized CD-ROM software is the least popular option, because of the high development and maintenance costs. Keeping custom products updated in a rapidly changing multiplatform industry is also difficult. Many of the commercial publishers who opted to write their own software in the mid-eighties are now abandoning this approach and licensing software from vendors focused on multiplatform CD-ROM software development.

In those cases where the software developed in-house has been successful, the product typically was written for a single application of limited scope and duration. Unfortunately, when additional applications emerge, the original software frequently cannot be readily adapted or modified. Consequently the development process must begin all over again.

As a result, writing custom software is almost never cheaper than licensing. The cost of writing a simple program for CD-ROM access with documentation is a minimum of two person-years of senior programmer time. The best

| | Services | In-House |
|---|---|---|
| **Short Term Issues:** | Prove Concept<br>Overcome Data Prep<br>Ensure Optimal Launch<br>Learn from First Project | Data Availability<br>Staff Availability<br>Systems Availability<br>Up Front $$ Availability |
| **Long Term Issues:** | Technology Infrastructure<br>Keep Expense Variable<br>Assignable Responsibility<br>Insure Technical Response<br>Avoid Up Front $$ | Internalize Learning Curve<br>Development Close to Users<br>Lower Per Application Costs<br>Increase Enhancement Control<br>Avoid Priority Problems |

**Figure 23.8**   Services or in-house development.

packages available today represent at least 10 times that much investment in programmer time, and their developers have greater resources to add features and enhancements.

**2. Commercial software.**   Over 20 commercial CD-ROM software products are available today for building databases and retrieving information from those databases. These packages range from simple and inexpensive text-only packages, to highly flexible "tool kits" for programmers, to multifunction authoring systems.

Organizations developing CD-ROM titles have several options. While the authoring software and retrieval engine must be acquired from the same vendor, there are various ways in which the user interface can be developed. Most (but not all) CD-ROM development systems provide a "standard" user interface. This interface is performance-tuned to the retrieval engine, and should permit substantial customizing without programming.

Some advanced systems allow development of custom user interfaces by writing software. Dividing the retrieval software into user-interface and retrieval-engine is a useful differentiation—it allows corporations that wish to develop highly customized user interfaces to capitalize on the advanced technology available in CD-ROM-based retrieval engines. This approach involves more time and personnel than a standard user interface, but results in a custom product tailored to the organization's needs. Figure 23.9 illustrates the tradeoffs involved in user-interface development.

User-interface development systems are emerging that attach to retrieval engines through linking mechanisms such as Dynamic Linked Libraries in Microsoft Windows. These allow CD-ROM developers to attach a third-party user interface to a CD-ROM retrieval engine, but generally require some programming. With the increasing popularity of client-server applications, development systems that support this architectural approach are expected to gain popularity in the future.

The PC software industry has produced several text-retrieval products not originally designed for CD-ROM. While many of these offer good-to-excellent

\* Applications Programming Interface to commercial retrieval engine

**Figure 23.9**   Application development approaches.

| Type of Search | CD-ROM Software | Typical Text Retrieval |
|---|---|---|
| Keyword | X | X |
| Wildcard - Trailing Truncation | X | X |
| Wildcard - Leading Truncation | X | |
| Wildcard - Within Word | X | |
| Multiple Wildcards Per Word | X | |
| Phonetic | X | |
| Line/Entry | X | |
| Numerical | X | X |
| Vector | X | |
| Date | X | |
| Binary | X | |
| Pop-Up Browse of Any Index | X | |
| Stopword Lists | Many | 1 |
| Cross Reference Search | X | |
| Adjacency - Word Level | X | Maybe* |
| Adjacency - Sentence Level | X | |
| Adjacency - Field Level | X | |
| Order Required | X | |
| Order Not Required | X | |
| Boolean and Wildcards | X | |
| Boolean and Adjacency | X | |
| Multiple Search Screens | X | |
| Encryption/Password Protection | X | |
| Graphics - Link to File | X | Maybe** |
| Graphics - Decompress & Display | X | |
| Graphics - Zoom, Size & Pan | X | |

\* If there is any adjacency it is probably slow and limited.  True adjacency requires complex indexing of the location of  every word in the file. To avoid this, low-end software simply searches for all occurrences and then checks each occurrence to locate occurrences together. This is very slow, especially on optical media.

\*\*Most PC software has no graphics display functions and simply allows a link to an external graphics file. Programs which display graphics often don't zoom and size images, making it difficult to read detail on most PC screens.

**Figure 23.10**   CD-ROM software vs. low-end text-management software.

support for small collections of text stored on magnetic disk, they may be inadequate for CD-ROM. Some of the most important differences between mission-critical retrieval software and these low-end packages lie in the range, flexibility, and sophistication of the searches that may be performed. Without more powerful searching it's difficult to capture the needed information without being overwhelmed by unneeded material as well. Figure 23.10 illustrates some of the differences in the types of searching that may be performed with software designed for CD-ROM.

Applications vary according to the demand they place on the retrieval engine, and the engine's performance is only as good as the authoring software used to create the data structures. Thus before you purchase commercial software, it may be prudent to develop a product, and then have a service bureau evaluate the technology.

**Service bureaus.**    The early CD-ROM service bureaus became successful by creating CD-ROM products that provided them with a built-in opportunity for repeat business. In the beginning very little was known about making a good CD-ROM product, so publishers were captive customers, willing to pay high fees in order to avoid costly mistakes.

The biggest disadvantage of working with a traditional service bureau is the loss of control over the product. There is little flexibility to prototype or enhance a product quickly or easily. More importantly, the investment in a service bureau does not allow expertise in the technology to be leveraged within the corporation.

**CD-ROM publishing platform.**    A new type of company has emerged that is effectively a "hybrid" service bureau/software development company. This new generation of companies provides a transition strategy for organizations that would like to use CD-ROM but have not yet developed expertise in the technology. These new hybrids will both develop applications as well as license their CD-ROM development software in the form of a "publishing platform."

The hybrid service bureau/development company creates the first application by working closely with a company's technical staff. The technical staff learns how to create an application and can then bring the software platform in house for subsequent titles. A publisher can acquire a license to both the authoring software and the retrieval software it will distribute with the discs to its users.

The advantage of this approach is that control of the product development is in the hands of those most knowledgeable about the customer. In addition, software specifically designed for CD-ROM lowers the internal product-development costs and shortens the time required. CD-ROM expertise is developed internally, and as expertise increases, costs are reduced further.

The major disadvantage of the in-house publishing platform is the investment required for software, hardware, and support staff. These can be kept to a minimum in the early stages by creating a pilot application using the preferred publishing platform vendor as a service bureau. The vendor's product can later be brought in house so that the investment is not made until the software has proven successful and the applicability of the technology to the entire applications portfolio has been evaluated. While it may be required as a way of educating the vendor as to the data types and information-usage profile of your industry, the pilot program often is the optimal means of determining if the software is suitable. Staff can be added as needed, and the system brought in house when ready. This provides a smooth transition without inconveniencing existing customers.

Generally speaking, the more products, enhancements, and updates are planned, the more an in-house publishing platform makes sense. A publishing platform that can be leveraged across a wide variety of applications is the most cost-effective way to introduce CD-ROM technology into an organization.

### Successful CD-ROM publishing in house

Assuming that potential applications justify in-house development, and that the publishing-platform approach is preferable, the next step is to select the appropriate hardware and software. First choose software that meets the applications portfolio requirements, then choose hardware that can support it.

The applications portfolio drives requirements for the software. It is from the combining of identified requirements for all applications that the ultimate needs for an authoring capability are derived. Figure 23.11 is an example. Most organizations will identify, at a minimum, a requirement to integrate text, data, and graphics. A vendor's retrieval software engine should be able to demonstrate its viability in commercial use. Concentrating on vendors that have published titles and have licensed software for in-house use will give you a short list of finalists to evaluate. A list of commercial CD-ROM products produced by using the vendors' retrieval engines is a good indicator of credibility. Seeing a demonstration of published CD-ROM applications is even better.

### Other software considerations

Once software that meets the application requirements has been identified, several other factors should be considered before a decision is made.

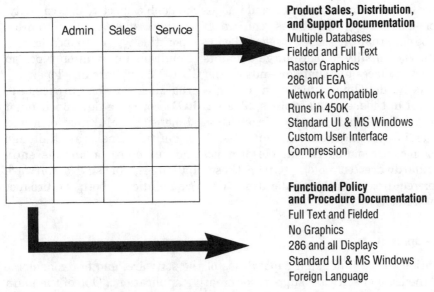

| | Admin | Sales | Service |
|---|---|---|---|
| | | | |
| | | | |
| | | | |
| | | | |

**Product Sales, Distribution, and Support Documentation**
Multiple Databases
Fielded and Full Text
Rastor Graphics
286 and EGA
Network Compatible
Runs in 450K
Standard UI & MS Windows
Custom User Interface
Compression

**Functional Policy and Procedure Documentation**
Full Text and Fielded
No Graphics
286 and all Displays
Standard UI & MS Windows
Foreign Language

**Figure 23.11** Applications portfolio defines requirements.

**Performance.**  Users familiar with applications on personal computers have developed certain performance expectations, with most actions requiring not more than a few seconds. Actions that take longer must give the user some feedback that the action is in progress and, optionally, tell him or her how much is complete.

CD-ROM applications generally involve searching hundreds of megabytes, with drives that are much slower than magnetic drives. To solve this problem, the software must be optimized for both CD-ROM and the type of data. Vendors should be able to demonstrate that their product can handle applications with the number of records and megabytes of information that you require. CD-ROM-optimized software should meet user expectations for magnetic-based searching, even when searching hundreds of megabytes.

**Multiplatform.**  With appropriate software, the same CD-ROM disc can be used in any computer platform such as DOS, Windows, Macintosh, and UNIX. However, the development software must support this multiplatform authoring and provide retrieval software for each desired environment. Many commercial products are available for developing Windows or Macintosh applications only. They preclude using the CD-ROM in any other environment.

Limiting the application to a single platform may limit the number of benefits to be gained. This is especially true when replacing paper, because printing must continue until everyone's workstation is supported.

**Information volume.**  Many databases exceed the 700-Mbyte capacity of a CD-ROM disc today. Some of these applications may fit on a single disc, if compression is available in the authoring software. While standard compression schemes for text, structured data, and images can double effective disc capacity, multiple-disc sets are sometimes required. If multidisc applications are anticipated, be sure that the software selected will support this type of application.

The unique ability to place large amounts of multiple information types on a single disc places unusual demands on the CD-ROM software developer.

Normally, developers focus on a single area such as word processing, numerical databases, or graphics. The CD-ROM software developed must push the technological envelope in all three dimensions. Multiplatform and multimedia add additional dimensions. This multidimensional challenge must be met without sacrificing performance and ease of use on an inherently slower hardware technology. Given these challenges, choosing a software partner requires careful consideration of the capabilities of both the product and the vendor.

## Application Development

In addition to the functional capabilities of the software, another consideration is the level of software support for creating applications. One of the main impediments to CD-ROM use has been the level of programming and the effort required to develop applications. For most organizations, only a few of the potential applications justify programming. The broad base of applications must be implemented by nonprogrammers. In evaluating CD-ROM authoring software, development capabilities that aid application-creation without coding should be considered.

Some advanced software authoring systems have front-end programs for reading and converting data from a variety of formats, including electronic publishing systems or on-line databases. These data-reading programs provide a broad funnel for capturing information. Photocomposition, database, and word processor formats can be supported by answering menu prompts, saving several person-weeks of conversion programming for each application. Publishers planning a CD-ROM product using a database that is already on line can usually format the database directly by using the authoring system.

Interface design and development determines how the end user will interact with the information. Query, display, print, export, and other capabilities are executed via the interface.

The most common model is a *fixed interface*. This option is popular with many text-only products, because the query options are limited. Products that integrate text, data, and graphics generally require a more sophisticated approach than is available in this model.

At the other end of the spectrum, the most flexible model is a "write-your-own" interface. The CD-ROM software consists of retrieval software and a set of calls to link the retrieval software to a custom-designed interface. This approach requires programming for every application. In addition, the programming investment is made prior to testing the match between the information and the retrieval software.

While clearly disadvantageous, many "tool-kit" products offer custom interface programming as the only option for publishers. While the capability to customize is essential to many applications, it should be viewed as an option, not a requirement, of the system.

The preferred approach borrows from the "application generator" techniques developed for DBMS access. The authoring software provides a model interface. Customizing is done by nonprogrammers through screen layout and painting, with the authoring software generating the code required in the background. Multiple user interfaces including search screens, data views, and print options are possible through switching and editing screens.

The more flexible this approach is, the less programming is required. Even when custom work is needed, the first complete application can be tested using the "standard" interface to ensure that the information and user requirements are met. The testing process also demonstrates the size of data and indexes, the amount of compression, the memory required, and performance if simulation capabilities are available. The test application can be used to obtain valuable feedback and to determine if the "standard" approach is in fact acceptable.

Testing and debugging of the application should be facilitated. System messages should be logged in a file for review. Indexes should be viewable, for instant access to all records containing an identified term. Reports on data size, index size, etc. should be available.

The software also should provide for application simulation prior to CD-ROM generation. Highly desirable are systems that simulate the slow CD-ROM access speed to give an indication of the actual performance of the finished product.

End-user application creation should include support for context-sensitive help screens, copyright notices, and an installation script generator to make end-user installation as foolproof as possible.

Foreign language version creation can be dramatically eased with proper support in the authoring system. Selection of the target language should provide automatic support for the appropriate keyboards, sorting sequences, character sets, and user-interface text files. Multiple language versions can be accessed by the user with a few keystrokes.

A robust authoring system contributes value in many ways. It increases the number of applications that can be produced, while improving the quality of each application. It increases learning throughout the organization and puts the technology in the hands of those people who best understand the user and the data. It saves time and money during development, and minimizes ongoing support and maintenance costs. Finally, it ensures that a majority of applications can be developed with a single system so that multiple systems need not be supported.

### Staffing requirements

A single application engineer can develop and update a significant number of applications using a properly designed development system. The steps in the first table in Fig. 23.12 indicate the level of staffing required to develop a typical CD-ROM application using commercial authoring software. The second table indicates the level of staffing required as the application is updated. (*Note:* Use of a programmer's tool kit requires higher skill levels and generally more time.)

Given the time involved in indexing and developing a full application, the ideal approach is to prototype a complete application using a small subset of data. This ensures up-front that the data and software will work together.

### Organizational requirements

For in-house CD-ROM publishing to be successful, there must be an organizational commitment to optical publishing. In some cases one division or group within an organization has taken the lead in successfully demonstrating the utility and cost-effectiveness of using CD-ROM for information delivery. In other organizations, a coordinated corporatewide effort has been launched simultaneously in many areas of the company.

Publishing corporate data on CD-ROM can be a high-profile activity. Getting discs into the hands of customers and distributors creates positive

## Steps and Staffing Requirements for Application Development

| Step | Skill Level | Time |
|------|-------------|------|
| Data Conversion and Filtering | Developer* | 1 day plus |
| Database Definitions | Developer | 1/2 day - 1 day |
| Screen Layout | Developer | 1 - 2 days ** |
| Indexing Specification | Developer | 1/2 - 2 days |
| Indexing and Binding | None | 10 Megabytes/hr. |
| Debugging and Texting | Developer | 1 - 2 days |
| Help Screens | Skilled User | 1/2 - 2 days |
| Install Program | Developer | 1/2 - 1 day |
| Creation of Premaster Tape | Developer | 1/2 - 1 day |

\*  PC DBMS Developer
\*\*Assumes screen painting interface design with no programming.

## Steps and Staffing Requirements for Updates to Applications

| Step | Skill Level | Time |
|------|-------------|------|
| Index and Bind | Skilled User | Set up, then machine time @ 10 Megabytes/Hr. |
| Quality Assurance | Skilled User | 1 hour - 1 Day |
| Creation of Premaster Tape | Developer | 1/2 - 1 day |

**Figure 23.12**  Steps and staffing requirements for development.

exposure for the company. Internal information takes on a high profile when it appears on the same media as Mozart or Madonna.

## Publishing partner

When you are making the commitment to optical publishing, make sure your technology partner is equally committed.

In a new and emerging industry, it is sometimes difficult to determine who the successful, long-term players will be. The credentials of the management team, the financial resources of the company, the reputation of the investors, and the company's track record become critical considerations. A history of software-development companies suggests that during the early stages of a new technology, having a focused product strategy is key to ultimate success. For example, most of the leading software products in the PC arena were originally developed by companies whose business was dedicated to one category, such as presentation graphics or word processing.

Finally, because of the high-profile nature of optical publishing, leading organizations have already taken the step and bet their reputation on the vendor they selected. The software developers most likely to be the long-term winners should already have a list of demanding yet satisfied customers.

## Summary

In an age suffering from "information overload," an age "drowning in paper," CD-ROM technology is positioned to deliver substantial benefits. CD-ROM provides a means for solving certain information problems when applied to critical activities and undertaken with a clear sense of how information is used by the knowledge worker. CD-ROM fits naturally into corporate computing strategies and leverages major trends, including electronic publishing, work-group computing, and transaction processing.

Successful CD-ROM applications integrate knowledge about the information user, information content, and software/hardware technology. The ideal CD-ROM publisher is the group that best understands the user and information content. The publisher resides within the organization, and must control the software and hardware technology to effectively serve the user.

Technology solutions are available from companies that have focused their business on creating CD-ROM technology for in-house use. This focus is critical because of the challenges inherent in CD-ROM development, ranging from performance to multiple information types to indexing gigabytes of data on multiple discs.

Those organizations that have acquired the technology and delivered the applications are the greatest proponents of CD-ROM. Their experience suggests that CD-ROM will become a major competitive tool in the hands of information managers. Organizations that put this technology to creative use will reap substantial benefits.

## Appendix A    Optical Publishing: An Industry Overview

*Optical publishing* is a term that describes the result as well as the process of distributing information on optical media. This is similar to the way in which the term *electronic publishing* refers to the distribution of information in digital form over telecommunication or broadcast systems, and *print publishing* refers to books, magazines, and reports on paper or microfiche. Estimates put print publishing at more than 90 percent of the publishing universe, with electronic at 10 percent. Optical publishing today represents about 5 percent of the electronic publishing share, or 0.5 percent overall.

The term *optical publishing* generally refers to information distributed on CD-ROM. Broadly speaking, it also can be used to refer to laser videodisc and interactive videodisc (used primarily for merchandising and training). The term *optical storage* (as opposed to optical *publishing*) refers to the use of write-once and erasable optical discs. The technologies are quite different, a critical distinction being that optical publishing embraces the idea of volume production and distribution.

The traditional publishing industry—book-publishing houses, magazine publishers, and educational textbook providers—increasingly is involved in optical publishing as the industry becomes more established. The publishers who took the initial risk to adopt the medium and get it established, however, are not household names with popular properties. They are publishers selling into library and technical markets with specialized information, new publishers with no prior publication history, and companies from the computer industry moving into publishing.

A majority of the first CD-ROM titles were transferred from the on-line publishing world, adapted from files already available by modem from remote host database services. Since then content has broadened to include numerous application areas, as indicated in Fig. 23.1. Most observers agree that this represents just the tip of the iceberg that is potential use of CD-ROM.

Libraries were among the first CD-ROM customers. The technology was a good fit for several reasons. A CD-ROM product has a known cost like a book or magazine subscription, and it can be budgeted and made accessible to all patrons without charging back variable on-line fees. Libraries are a known market that enable publishers to target those customers with particular needs and great purchasing power. Librarians also already had a great deal of experience with on-line searching. They were eager to learn about CD-ROM and to share their experiences with others in the field.

Corporations are the next major market for CD-ROM, and they have already significantly surpassed libraries in volume use. As was just pointed out about librarians, corporate users' broad familiarity with computers and on-line searching techniques puts them one step ahead of the game. Corporations are customers for reference products in resource centers; business, financial, and directory products at the departmental level; technical and scientific reference products at the research and engineering level; and desktop publishing and related products at the individual level. Corporations also are the leading producers of in-house titles for documentation, database distribution, corporate records, and other internal applications.

Computer software producers have become publishers and distributors. An increasing number are using CD-ROM to distribute software products, particularly when distribution on floppy disk is too unwieldy. In some products such as Lotus 1-2-3 and Apple Macintosh Hyper card, content becomes integrated with the application. Microsoft Corporation, the largest PC software producer, has made invaluable contributions to the optical publishing industry by means of numerous CD-ROM products, CD-ROM conferences, books about CD-ROM, and the MS-DOS extensions for CD-ROM.

Government is another major market. There are both commercial and in-house training applications in this market. Among the applications are documentation for military equipment, training programs, standards, and administrative information. Many government agencies are taking on a commercial publishing role with regard to government collections that are distributed to the Federal Depository Library network. They also have markets in the private sector such as patents, social, economic, agricultural and business data, and technical reports.

Other market sectors that today are primarily vertical and commercial include professions such as law, medicine, health, and education, as well as the emerging consumer market. CD-ROM has also been attractive to publishers and users in niche markets where very specialized information is used by a very specific group of customers.

Optical publishing is the subject of a major annual survey conducted by InfoTech,an international consulting and research firm specializing in optical-disc and information-technology markets. The most recent results (as of this writing) are published in the yearly *Optical Publishing Industry Assessment,* which is available from InfoTech, Woodstock, VT (802-257-1038). To create this report, InfoTech interviewed hundreds of publishers worldwide and applied a sophisticated methodology, drawing on over eight years of direct experience in the optical disc industry.

InfoTech established a tracking system in 1987, allowing it to measure the impressive growth in the industry from 1988 on. Titles in print have grown from fewer than 100 in 1986 to an estimated 5000 in 1992 (Fig. 23.13). The installed base of readers has grown from 9000 in 1986 to an estimated 4,000,000 in 1992 (Fig. 23.14). Total revenue, which includes titles and reader hardware for commercial and in-house applications, has increased from $31 million in 1986 to $3.9 billion worldwide in 1992 (Fig. 23.15).

InfoTech estimates that the commercial market shipped 3256 titles valued at nearly $2 billion in 1992, and it forecasts growth by 1995 to nearly 8000 titles valued at over $4 billion. Commercial revenue is calculated at retail prices and based on confidentially reported unit-sales data collected from over 80 percent of the publishers.

The in-house market is estimated to have released over 2000 titles in 1992, roughly 40 percent of all titles released. By 1995 the figure is forecast to be somewhere around 3500 titles. Titles published for in-house use are not directly counted, because of the great difficulty in identifying producers. They are

**Figure 23.13** Worldwide titles in print. 1992 figures are estimates. (*Source: Infotech.*)

**Figure 23.14** Worldwide installed base, in thousands of units. 1992 figures are estimates. (*Source: Infotech.*)

**Figure 23.15** Worldwide revenues, in thousands of dollars. 1992 figures are estimates. (*Source: Infotech.*)

estimated by the vendors serving that sector with software, media, and hardware. Although the in-house data is not statistically valid, it is still a strong indicator of what the in-house sector represents to the optical publishing industry and is widely regarded as the best available estimation of output.

## Appendix B   Estimating Costs

When you are considering CD-ROM, remember that costs must be viewed relative to alternative means of organizing, distributing, and retrieving information. Cost analysis is not complete without factoring in both performance and the competitive advantages that result from the availability of information on CD-ROM, such as ease of updating, accuracy of searching, ad hoc query capabilities, and inexpensive distribution.

### Application development costs

**Service bureau.**   The various steps of data preparation, indexing, interface creation, etc. require appropriate software and resources. This varies depending on the actual amount of data in the application, the complexity of the project, and the sophistication of the authoring software.

It is impossible to predict the cost of a CD-ROM application from a distance. For simple projects, a price of $10,000 to $40,000 would not be uncommon from a service bureau. This would include the use of its software, reading and "cleaning" the data, indexing, creating the user interface, pressing the discs, and licensing the retrieval software. Custom applications would cost more.

**Publishing platform—software.**  Software should be specifically designed for CD-ROM applications. It should be optimized to achieve maximum performance while minimizing the space requirements for the data and related indexes. Mature software specific to CD-ROM will offer substantial benefits, including sophisticated data-import capabilities, high-throughput indexing, and rich features and functionality in retrieving data from CD-ROM. Less sophisticated software sometimes costs more in the long run, because it requires more data conversion prior to indexing or more program development to add required features to the retrieval facilities. Worse still is the case where significant time is invested and the CD-ROM application is unacceptable because of slow performance.

Software specifically designed for the organization, indexing, and retrieval of information on CD-ROM can range from a few hundred dollars to $50,000. Cost differences lie in the type of information your application entails, the range of organization and indexing options available, the flexibility inherent in the software, and its performance.

Costs may also vary with the reliability and credibility of the vendor. Value is closely related to how complete the software is and how much custom development is required to create your CD-ROM application. A system that saves three person-months of programming per application is worth a significant premium over a programming tool kit.

Software for multimedia authoring also can range from a few hundred to thousands of dollars. The options and differences in costs here relate primarily to the types of information the authoring system supports.

**Publishing platform—hardware.**  Costs for the hardware for an in-house development capability vary. A minimum 486-based PC with extended memory is recommended if you are to achieve adequate index build performance. A price range of $2000 to $4000 is typical, not including disk drive, tape drive, or CD-recordable drive. Complete premastering systems range from $10,000 to $50,000 depending on features, memory, throughput, and vendor support. If you already have an installed 386 or 486 with sufficient magnetic-disk space, today a CD-recordable drive can be added for under $10,000.

A growing trend is indexing on high-performance UNIX-RISC-based machines. These machines offer substantial price/performance advantages if the throughput requirements warrant the higher processing speeds.

The major cost advantage of an in-house publishing platform is the ability to leverage the investment in software, hardware, and staffing across a number of applications. With as few as five applications, the fully loaded cost per CD-ROM disc falls below $20. In this report is a summary cost calculation for creating a complete application-development capability. Costs per PC, per disc, and per megabyte are included in this cost analysis.

If you are thinking about developing multimedia applications, the required components usually can be added to a publishing platform as needed. Depending on the type of multimedia (audio, video, etc.), various sound and video capture boards, videodisc players, cameras, and sound equipment may be necessary. Costs for these components vary greatly depending on quality, throughput, and features.

**Staffing.**  Personnel requirements for an individual project using an authoring system with no custom programming are summarized in Fig. 23.12. Projects that require custom interface development are more labor-intensive.

A single application engineer can develop and update a significant number of applications using a properly designed authoring system. Experience suggests that compared with a "tool kit," an authoring system increases application production 3 to 10 times.

### Retrieval software costs

Retrieval software licenses are offered in one or more of the following ways.

**CPU basis.**  Useful primarily for internal applications, this pricing method is similar to PC software that is licensed for use on a particular machine forever. Regardless of how many CD-ROMs your organization creates, the cost for the retrieval software for that PC doesn't change. Charges for this "pay-once" CPU license vary with vendor and quantity. Pricing tends to parallel mass-market PC software: $250 to $500 per CPU for low volumes, and roughly half that for quantity purchases.

**Per disc or per subscription.**  For applications in which the publisher doesn't know or control the end user (e.g., discs distributed outside the organization), retrieval software is charged on a per-disc or per-subscription basis. Per-disc pricing usually is tied to volume-based plateaus and will vary from vendor to vendor. For a 200-disc volume, a price range of $25 to $50 per disc is typical. For a volume of 5000, a range of $10 to $20 per disc should be expected. (*Note:* It's important to ascertain how "volume plateaus" are computed by the software vendor. Ideally, all licenses can be grouped together, so that an organization can quickly reach and remain at the highest discount level.)

Annual subscription pricing, while somewhat higher, offers the option of updating the users' products without limitation during the year. At a 200-subscription volume, prices in the range of $75 to $100 should be expected. At 5000 subscriptions, the price per year should be $25 to $50.

Pricing outside these ranges usually indicates an organization that is underfunded and/or a new entrant to the market, complete with the associated risks. Software companies that have survived the ups and downs of an emerging industry and are providing quality products and services generally offer their products in the price ranges identified above. To survive in the PC software business, companies typically need to reach and sustain sales in the $10 million range in their third or fourth year. This can be illustrated by reviewing the few survivors in word processing, spreadsheets, or graphics from the early eighties. A good "going-concern" viability test is to divide the vendor's price into $10 million. That will give you the number of new customers they must attract each year.

### Media costs—mastering the disc

If only a small number of replicas is required (less than 50, in today's economics), or if a prototype of the completed disc is desired, CD-recordable technology may be employed. Blank CD-recordable media today cost $30 in low quantities and less than $25 in high quantities, in addition to the costs for the CD-recordable drive.

Once a complete application exists, a premaster tape is created and sent to the pressing house. The first cost in this process is the setup charge (currently, $1000 to $2000). On the low end, five-day turnaround is typical. Higher prices can achieve one-day turnaround. The next cost is a disc charge, which is volume-related. Prices of $1.50 to $2.50 each are typical today. Because of the setup charge, companies normally produce the maximum number of discs likely to be required from each pressing.

### In-house cost summary

The cost of bringing a complete CD-ROM application development capability in house is summarized below. Costs are broken into logical groups and summarized in the final section. Organizational overheads have not been included, as these will vary from case to case.

**Initial investment.** These costs are one-time outlays for hardware and software that are assumed to have a useful life of 3 years (although actual life may be longer).

| | |
|---|---|
| Hardware | |
| Premastering system (1 Gbyte plus tape drive) | $11,000 |
| 486 personal computer | 4,000 |
| Subtotal | 15,000 |
| Software | |
| Authoring system | 30,000 |
| Total initial investment | $45,000 |

**Annual costs.** These are average annual outlays for personnel, office space, and supplies. Experience suggests that these costs and manpower levels are sufficient to produce up to five different applications, with an average bimonthly update frequency. More applications or more frequent updates may require more resources.

| | |
|---|---|
| Personnel | |
| Applications developer | $60,000 |
| Office space | 10,000 |
| Supplies | 5,000 |
| Total annual costs | $75,000 |

**Investment per workstation.** These costs assume that 500 PCs in the organization are outfitted with CD-ROM drives and retrieval software. Higher volumes result in somewhat lower per-workstation costs, due to volume discounting. These investments also are assumed to have a useful life of 3 years.

| | |
|---|---|
| CD-ROM drive with interface | $ 500 |
| Retrieval software (perpetual) | 200 |
| Total investment per workstation | $ 700 |
| | |
| Total workstation investment (500 PCs) | $350,000 |

**Costs per CD-ROM application update.** All steps in the application-development process, from acceptance of raw data on magnetic tape through generation of premaster tapes ready for the mastering/pressing facility, can be accomplished by the above personnel using the listed facilities. The premaster tapes are then forwarded to the mastering/pressing facility, where a setup charge is incurred for each master disc and a per-disc charge applied for the replication. Documentation can be prepared as a slip-insert to the CD-ROM jewel-case packaging.

| | |
|---|---|
| Mastering (per application/master disc) | $ 1500 |
| Replication (per CD-ROM disc) | 2 |
| Documentation (per CD-ROM disc) | 1 |

**Software maintenance cost.** Software maintenance is assumed to run at 15 percent annually, the industry norm.

**Cost summary.** This section assumes that the organization is producing three CD-ROM applications: one updated quarterly, one monthly, and one every six months. The volumes are 200, 500, and 300 units respectively.

|  | Annual total | Annual per PC | Per disc | Per megabyte* |
|---|---|---|---|---|
| Initial investment | | | | |
| (3-year life)† | $ 15,000 | $ 30.00 | $ 2.03 | $ 0.01 |
| Annual costs | 75,000 | 150.00 | 10.14 | 0.03 |
| Workstation costs | | | | |
| (3-year life)‡ | 116,667 | 233.34 | 15.77 | 0.05 |
| Application update costs§ | 49,200 | 98.40 | 6.65 | 0.02 |
| Software maintenance¶ | 9,500 | 39.00 | 2.64 | 0.01 |
| Totals | $275,367 | 550.74 | 37.23 | 0.12 |

*Assumes discs contain average 300 megabytes.

†45,000 / 3 = 15,000

‡350,000 / 3 = 116,667

§((4 + 12 + 2) * 1500) + ((200*4 + 500*12 + 300*2) * 3) = 49,200

¶(30,000 + 500*200) * 15% = 19,500

# 24

# Multimedia Consulting

## A New Frontier

**Lewis Gruskin**

## Introduction

Innovative applications of multimedia technology are now spotlighted in almost every business magazine. A major steel company is using multimedia to train employees, reducing training time by 20 to 40 percent. Large retail firms are implementing multimedia kiosks to extend their retail outlets. IBM, Apple, and other firms are announcing powerful multimedia software development tools, in addition to personal computers with multimedia capabilities at less cost. It's clear that multimedia will have a significant impact on business—and soon.

To achieve these benefits, companies must add multimedia to their business operations effectively while avoiding the mistakes many companies made during the early days of the PC revolution. Then PCs were introduced haphazardly, often without management direction. This approach resulted in a disparate collection of computing devices that often used different operating systems, ran incompatible software, and worse, could not communicate with the corporate computers or with each other. As a result, PCs did not deliver the much-promised boosts in productivity and job enhancement, and corporate management missed out on many of the competitive advantages they could have gained by using this new information tool more effectively.

When examining the potential of multimedia, corporate management must address several major questions. How can multimedia help to solve critical business problems? How are multimedia solutions created, implemented, and supported? What new issues in application design must be considered? Above all, what is the best way to get started in this new field?

### The Transformation of Business

The choices can be overwhelming, and the decisions crucial. Multimedia is much more than a recipe for jazzing up PCs with a mixture of speakers, video cards, and new software. It represents a new computing and business paradigm that affects the way people communicate, work, and learn. The multimedia synergy of incorporating voice, data, and video with computer power has the proven potential to become an integral part of corporate business processes and to radically change business operations—if it's introduced correctly.

Multimedia will transform a corporation's business activities in three areas. First, multimedia will provide interactive front-ends to existing applications to make them easier to use, a change that will affect every aspect of MIS operations. Second, multimedia will permit new MIS and business applications to be developed, such as sales automation, just-in-time training, and desktop conferencing, as companies learn to tap the power of interactive access to information in a variety of formats. Finally, the technology will serve as the cornerstone for new multimedia-based opportunities in much the same way that the potential of interactive TV is spawning new business ventures (see Fig. 24.1).

However, the full potential of multimedia to transform business can't be tapped just by using it to add impact to existing applications or to address individual or departmental problems. For maximum effectiveness, multimedia must be employed as a strategic information tool within a framework of long-term business requirements. Multimedia should be linked to other com-

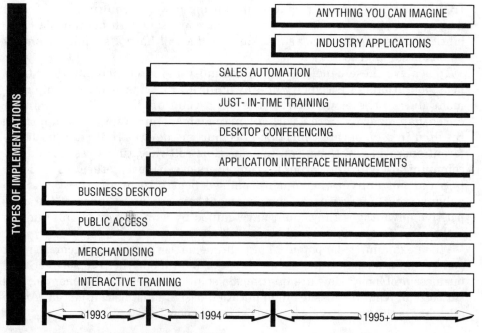

**Figure 24.1**   Range of multimedia opportunities.

puter resources and deployed with at least some understanding of how employees, customers, and vendors may react to the new technology.

The advantages of looking strategically at this new technology are clear. Think of the potential for individual and strategic advances if, from the very beginning, multimedia can be extended across a company's existing infra-structure of stand-alone and distributed computing. Imagine the strategic advantages of sharing information—whether in audio, video, image, or data format—throughout a distributed enterprise around the world. Consider the benefits of strengthening the links among employees, customers, and vendors through improved multimedia communication.

Yet achieving effective enterprisewide multimedia use is not easy, and the risks can be great. The technology involved in integrating data, text, and video is complex and confusing. Standards often differ. There are new categories of devel-opment tools to comprehend and presentation issues to be resolved, which can involve complex tradeoffs concerning storage, media file size, and bandwidth.

Multimedia also is a technological frontier whose landscape consists of numerous cutting-edge questions, ranging from, "Who owns the copyright for images used in multimedia presentations?" to "Which compression technolo-gies should be adopted?" Find the right answers, and the payoffs will be greater profitability and productivity. Guess wrong, and money, time, and opportunity will be wasted (see Fig. 24.2).

**Figure 24.2**  Customer needs.

## Looking for Help

Faced with those high stakes, many companies are turning to consultants to guide them through the jungle of competing technologies, unexplored applications, design issues, and user acceptance. A consultant traditionally provides many benefits, especially when new technologies are involved or deadlines are tight. A consultant can offer an objective view of a problem in order to help speed a solution. A consultant also provides specialized expertise often unavailable in house. This expertise allows a consultant to know what can be done, how technologies can be applied, and what fundamental challenges must be met. Sometimes a consultant is brought in as an additional resource to ensure timely completion of projects.

Companies should be cautious, however, about the type of consultant they use when it comes to a technology with the impact and implications of multimedia. Such a complex technology involves new tools and skills such as authoring, media production, and large-object handling. During application design, multimedia also affects the analysis of the problem, the type of information gathered, and the implementation requirements. To complicate matters even further, multimedia can impact not only information systems but every area of the company's business, by the way in which it creates complex interrelationships among business practices, technology, human/machine interfaces, and media-based communications. To be effective in this field, a consultant must do more than copy what has been done before with other technologies. Rather, the consultant must be able to help a company mold the unique functionality of multimedia to create new strategic solutions for business problems.

## Differences between Multimedia and Traditional Consulting

It's clear that if multimedia is to be introduced effectively, a new type of consulting must offer more than the traditional benefits provided by an MIS consultant. This new multimedia consulting works first to align the capabilities of the technology with the strategic goals and demands of the firm. Once this has been achieved, multimedia consulting can help the customer to define its requirements for specific situations.

Multimedia consulting for business applications requires more than just technical knowledge about multiple hardware platforms and operating systems, video compression, hardware and software compatibility, networking, and other complicated issues. It is a multidisciplined profession involving business analysis, goal-setting, benchmarking, programming, human factors, communications, and other skills, many of which require intensive and long-term training (see Fig. 24.3).

A qualified consultant should be trained—and experienced—in business and management systems. Industry knowledge is important too, such as familiarity with market trends and industry applications. A multimedia consultant should have project-management skills encompassing planning,

**Figure 24.3**  Strengths of the multimedia consultant.

tracking, risk management, and contracting. The consultant should understand how user expectations about interactive responses, nonlinear learning, video presentation skills, etc. are being transformed by today's communications industries, including television, movies, and advertising. Beyond business and media expertise, the consultant should possess strong personal skills, with the ability to lead, communicate, analyze, negotiate, and make decisions. The consultant should also have access to the multiple resources available from specialized consulting teams; the specialized teams can be part of the consultant's organization or associates of the firm.

Additionally, the international links of many businesses create a special need for cross-cultural sensitivities. As information in these businesses becomes distributed not only within the companies but across national borders, it becomes all the more imperative to use a consultant who understands the impact multimedia can have within different countries and cultures.

Extensive, diversified training and knowledge are only part of the arsenal of the multimedia consultant. Just as important is the consultant's perceptiveness about organizational and technological issues. The most knowledgeable and skilled consultant in the world will do little good unless he or she is sensitive to the client's concerns and focused on solving the client's business problems. After all, the central issue is not just introducing a new technology but rather solving business and operational problems, even if they don't necessarily involve multimedia.

When you review the capabilities of a multimedia consultant, it's also important that you distinguish between *consulting*—deciding what to do or how to do it—and *performing* or *executing* specific development tasks. The multimedia consultant concentrates on understanding the global business environment, the corporation's strategic goals, and the scope of the eventual implementation. After extensive client input, the consultant provides objectives, timetables, solution design, and performance standards. The consultant may lead prototype development so as to provide the "look and feel" of the multimedia solution and thereby gain client approval. However, once these parameters have been set, the project can be turned over to "perform teams" of people who are skilled in execution, such as graphic designers, script writers, video technicians, and interactive program authors. If appropriate, the multimedia consultant can play some of the "perform" roles, depending on the size and complexity of the project.

The benefit of using an experienced, qualified multimedia consultant will be new approaches and solutions to the age-old problems of increasing sales, improving productivity, and enhancing communications within and without your organization. Just as PCs should not be used merely to automate the old ways of doing business, so too the power of multimedia should not be frittered away by all those application "quick fixes" that often seem to be no further than an 800-number phone call away. Multimedia represents a historic opportunity to marry a high-potential technology with long-term business objectives. A multimedia consultant can help you to make the most of that opportunity.

## A Multimedia Consulting Methodology

The effective multimedia consultant is skilled in the use of an organized, transferable consulting methodology. This methodology provides a consistent, measurable structure for planning, organizing, tracking, and executing business applications linked to the unique demands of multimedia. These unique demands—such as ownership and performance rights, physical-environment considerations, and media production coordination—have not yet been incorporated into traditional applications and are not part of most companies' processes and methodologies.

To guide a project effectively and consistently from understanding the business problem through formulating a concept to completing a multimedia solution, a tested, flexible methodology is needed. The IBM Multimedia Consulting Practice, a unit of the IBM Consulting Group, has developed a unique, client-centered methodology for planning and executing multimedia projects. This methodology is flexible enough to work either for corporatewide distributed business process solutions or for stand-alone training solutions.

**Figure 24.4**  Consulting methodology.

When used by an experienced multimedia consultant, the methodology employs repeatable processes (essential, as multimedia projects evolve from single-purpose solutions to corporatewide applications), reduces project risks, and maintains constant client participation.

The methodology is structured around nine phases (see Fig. 24.4) beginning with analysis and ending with confirmation of the client's short- and long-term arrangements for evaluation, support, and maintenance:

1. Analysis

2. Design

3. Development

4. Media production

5. Authoring

6. Testing

7. Implementation

8. Support

9. Maintenance

The first phase, Analysis, collects data about the business context for the intended application, analyzes related requirements from other areas of the company, proposes alternative solutions, assesses the impact of each solution, and presents recommendations. Prototyping may be used to clarify the client's requirements or expectations.

The Analysis phase receives special emphasis in the Multimedia Solution Methodology, because later media decisions will depend on the information initially gathered about users and processes. For example, to plan the most effective interactive strategy (or strategies), the consultant must have information about all potential users. If users include the client's customers, market research may be the only way to determine the characteristics of those users. Similarly, the project team must identify all of the business processes that will be affected by the project, including existing processes that the project will automate, new processes that the project will create, and manual processes that may feed the multimedia-supported processes.

The Design and Development phases work out detailed specifications for the application, including exact content, presentation flow, user interaction patterns, screen and media element descriptions, and programming interface requirements. Media element specifications, from master storyboards through scripts, detailed storyboards, and authoring requirements, are also completed during these phases.

During the Media Production phase, media and programming "perform teams" create the media elements and programs that are pulled together during the Authoring phase into the interactive application. End-user documentation, training materials, and other supporting components must also be completed on schedule.

The Testing phase verifies that all elements of the application work as intended. This phase can include acceptance-testing by the client and legal reviews of the completed application. Testing is followed by the Implementation phase, which brings the application into general use in the client's organization and "tunes" the application and related processes so as to get the most efficient performance during daily business routines. Implementation includes migration and production pilot activities, if appropriate for the project.

The final phases, Support and Maintenance, confirm that the client has appropriate long-range evaluation, support, and maintenance procedures in place for the application. Full ownership of the application, along with all required supporting materials, are then turned over to the client.

## Special Features of the Multimedia Solution Methodology

The Multimedia Solution Methodology pays special attention to the unique requirements of multimedia work so that all major requirements are identified early in the project. For example, a client with seasonal business cycles may need to update the visual parts of an application every quarter. Traditional application development might consider this updating as a "maintenance" activity to be addressed late in the project. However, in a multimedia application, this updating can affect decisions about what kinds of visual elements should be used and how they should be stored. Consequently the multimedia methodology collects those requirements early, along with other business needs.

Similarly, the methodology organizes any specialized expertise that may be needed. For example, a distributed multimedia project may have need of someone knowledgeable about wide-area networking. In such a case, the IBM Multimedia Consulting Practice can recruit expertise from other IBM groups to design a solution. Other problems or activities may require the use of other skilled organizations. When a variety of skills is required on a project, the multimedia consultant can serve as "prime contractor." The structured topics, terminology, and tasks in the methodology help the multimedia consultant to coordinate the specialists and thereby meet the client's needs.

The methodology also distinguishes clearly between *consulting* and *perform* work. The consultant "consults" by helping the client to identify business requirements and potential solutions. The consultant can also help to work out (in the Design and Development phases) more detailed specifications for implementation. However, the closer the project gets to the "perform" work of creating storyboards, scripts, authoring structures, and media elements, the more the consultant functions as the client's representative, ensuring that designs and implementations meet the client's critical success factors and preestablished constraints, but not doing "hands-on" media work.

The Multimedia Solution Methodology emphasizes the crucial importance of keeping the client actively involved. More than in traditional application development, multimedia rework (such as reshooting a video segment or rerecording a voice-over) can be very expensive. To minimize these unnecessary costs, the consultant works to ensure that the client reviews and approves design, development, and media production activities at each stage to provide a solid foundation for the next round of project work. The methodology identifies major milestones and frequent checkpoints as a structure for involving the client.

Another special feature of the Multimedia Solution Methodology is that it provides a road map to define and transfer procedures and perspectives. The defined procedures establish a consistent baseline for measuring all outcomes. The processes also are transferable, so that the client's employees can leverage the consultant's knowledge and apply it to their own situation, using it to solve new problems. Transferability also allows a process to be used in multibranch or even multinational environments. Finally, if a process can be repeated, the risk from unexpected outcomes or even unexpected costs can be significantly reduced while encouraging a consistent implementation across the enterprise. This is much more than "not reinventing the wheel"; it is establishing a way to build wheel after wheel after wheel.

The benefits of these special features can be seen in several multimedia proposals in which the IBM Multimedia Consulting Practice became involved. A major telecommunications firm wanted to know whether multimedia was the best method for training and for improving retail sales. It also wanted to understand the best ways to ensure widespread acceptance of multimedia applications and to pinpoint the long-term costs and strategy of developing multimedia throughout the organization. IBM Multimedia Consulting suggested an approach that identified the company's business goals and objectives, multimedia's business value, the critical elements to be resolved with prototypes, and, finally, an approach for implementation. Then market research would determine potential market reaction to multimedia and would serve as the basis for a companywide implementation strategy.

In another instance, a major U.S. city expressed interest in placing service kiosks throughout the city. IBM Multimedia Consulting worked with a market research firm to plan how to determine both citizen acceptance of the kiosks and the most popular potential applications. The project also included a cost/benefit analysis to examine the costs of implementing different levels of kiosk networks and some potential revenue-generating options that could repay the city for its investment in the system. Finally, a conceptual model would be developed to define prototypes, outline steps to key milestones, and describe methods to validate success.

## Criteria for Successful Consulting

The result of using a tested, structured methodology is much more than producing an isolated multimedia application for a specific set of users. The company also has a solution that is integrated with strategic goals and business processes. The application is built upon an analysis of the unique requirements of the eventual target audience, whether that is employees, customers, or prospects. The multimedia solution links the latest technologies to a thorough understanding of how developmental issues must change to accommodate new data types and user interface issues, learning requirements and presentation effectiveness. The outcome is consistent with the client's business goals, satisfying all the requirements that were identified at the beginning of the project.

Successful consulting also provides a basis for identifying other uses of the technology. This reuse leverages the investment the firm makes in the multimedia consultant as well as reduces the risk inherent in single applications. In essence a good multimedia consultant is a teacher, guiding the firm to new levels of understanding about larger goals and strategies as well as upcoming technologies. This education provides a valuable foundation for the firm's growth even as it provides employees with those new capabilities that result from the enhanced use of multimedia.

None of this is possible, however, unless the consultant can bring to bear all of the expertise needed for the project. The consultant's own technical understanding is just the beginning. He or she should also be able to draw on the resources of an organization to deliver the unique expertise that may be necessary for a specific multimedia project. This expertise can include skills in networking, user interfaces, and market research.

The successful multimedia consultant can apply these skills to specific design, authoring, and implementation work, but only after the scope of the project has been outlined within the context of larger business and organizational issues. While sophisticated tools are available to almost anybody to develop multimedia applications, it makes little business sense to generate applications based solely on the skills of a programmer and the demands of the moment. To embark upon individual multimedia projects without this larger vision of corporate requirements is like setting off on a journey without a road map.

## Conclusion

Multimedia technology has advanced to the point where any company can easily buy or develop training, presentation, or retail applications. It's tempting for companies striving for every competitive advantage to jump into multimedia, especially when they read success stories about documented bottom-line savings.

But multimedia is so much more than the latest technology upgrades. If the power of multimedia is to provide maximum long-term benefits, multimedia must be closely integrated with larger business strategies as well as linked to immediate application needs. Those twin demands make it imperative that a multimedia consultant use a structured, consistent methodology to satisfy the client and to demonstrate a comprehensive approach to business application development. The payoffs will come in the form of tested solutions that make employees more productive and managers more effective, and that substantially improve communications in all parts of the enterprise.

# 25

# A Virtual Poem

## Extending Classroom Reality?

**David E. Hartman**

**Tim Brock**

## Taking the Plunge

When Jessica Keyes asked us to contribute a chapter on combining multimedia and virtual reality, we were faced with some unique challenges.

First, while we both had some experience with and understanding of virtual reality, neither of us considered ourselves "experts." Second, while our college had provided us with some pretty good equipment, we had no virtual-reality apparatus, such as gloves or head-mount displays. We were on the verge of saying "thanks, but no thanks," when the inspiration hit us: Why not accept our limitations and, better yet, turn them into parameters for a project that would demonstrate how useful virtual-reality work can be done without tens of thousands of dollars' worth of equipment?

It has been said that virtual reality is a solution in search of a problem. That certainly fit our dilemma. We needed to find a problem that could be solved using virtual reality. It goes without saying that the project would have to be effective and affordable. It would have to be limited in scope, too, because we had less than six weeks until our deadline! The result is "Petals," a virtual-reality exploration of a poem (see Fig. 25.1), and what follows is a week-by-week account of how the project came together.

## Week 1

In this short week we agreed to do the project, decided it should involve a poem, picked the poem, decided to focus on a single word in the poem, researched that word's etymology, began to search for an appropriate

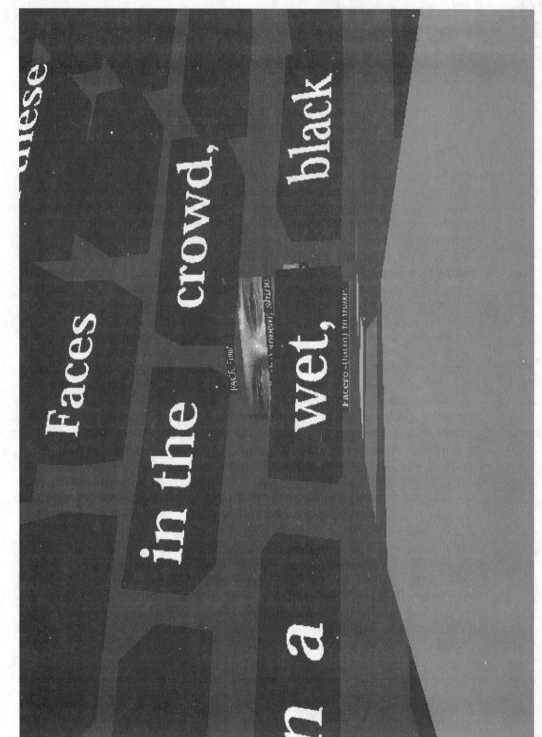

Figure 25.1 A virtual poem.

metaphor to serve as our virtual "world," and decided to use Virtus Walkthrough as our virtual-reality software.

### The poem

In searching for that suitable poem, we knew it would have to be short because our time was limited. It also would have to be rich in imagery to succeed in a multimedia/virtual-reality environment. We settled on Ezra Pound's "In a Station of the Metro":[1]

> The apparition of these faces in the crowd;
> Petals on a wet, black bough. (*Pound 109*)

The images were evocative and starkly contrasting. Better yet, nearly all of the words (see Fig. 25.2) were, themselves, "virtual environments"—teeming with images, emotions, sensations, and associations.

One of these rich words—*faces*—seemed to be the center around which the rest of the poem revolved. By exploring the word *faces* we would, of necessity, also be exploring much of the rest of the poem. An etymological exploration confirmed our choice of this as the focus for our virtual environment. We discovered that the words *appearance, facade,* and *shine* were tangled up in the translated Latin roots of *face.* It was decided: We would go "inside" the word *faces.*

### The software

We decided to use Virtus Corporation's Walkthrough because of its intuitive interface, affordable price (less than $250), and relatively modest equipment and memory needs. Walkthrough and its companion "playback-only" software, Voyager, were designed to allow the creation of virtual architectural spaces. An architect could, for example, create a home that prospective buyers could "enter," exploring rooms, checking for closet space, or even positioning furnishings. We would create a palace of poetry! And, because Walkthrough uses a "through-the-window" virtual-reality interface, we wouldn't need head-mount displays or any control devices more sophisticated than a mouse.

### Week 2

In this span, we discovered some things Walkthrough couldn't do, saw Virtus come to the rescue, explored the work of artists in our search for design ideas, and made some metaphoric decisions.

### Virtual dilemma

Our "poetic palace" very nearly became a tumbling house of cards when we discovered that Walkthrough 1.1 does not have QuickTime or texture-mapping capabilities. In order for our project to be a true marriage of virtual reality and multimedia, QuickTime and texture-mapping would be essential. A desperate

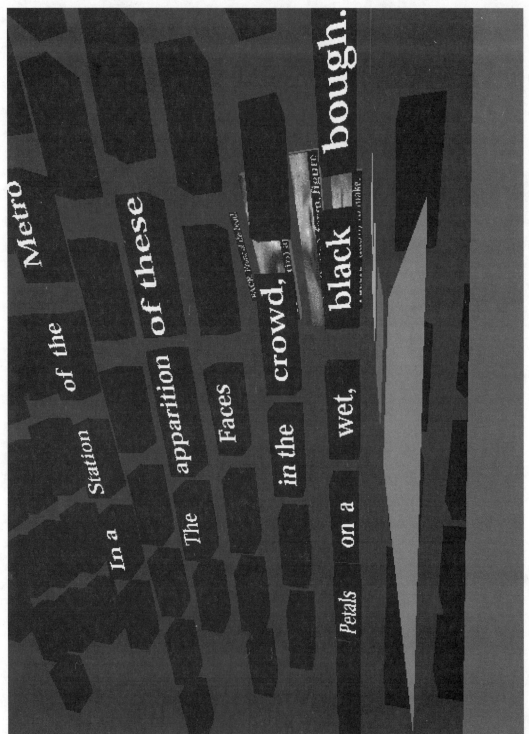

**Figure 25.2** Imaging an Ezra Pound poem.

phone call to Virtus Corp. proved to be providential. Virtus informed us that both QuickTime and texture-mapping were features of a "texture-enhanced version" of Walkthrough, which was at that time in beta testing. Virtus then graciously offered to send us a copy. It arrived during Week 3.

### Looking for some help

For inspiration we turned, like so many before us, to established visual artists—particularly Picasso, Escher, and Seurat. As we continued to gather material and ideas, we were drawn to Seurat's technique of pointillism, in which dots of primary colors are juxtaposed in such a way that, when viewed from a distance, they take on both form and hue. It is the distinctive feature of pointillism, however, that when viewed up close, only the individual bits of color are distinguishable.

Our approach to poetry would be similar. We would "walk" up to the poem until we were so close that only individual bits of data would be visible. The data of the poem—its "faceness," in this instance—could be explored fully before we "stepped back" to view the whole once again.

We also were intrigued by the recursive nature of much of Escher's work. One of the reasons the poetic experience fails for many students is that they read poems only once—and at a literal level, at that. If students are to read poetry successfully they must return to it repeatedly, from different angles and applying a variety of tools. We wanted the explorers of our project—like figures in one of Escher's "Möbius" paintings—to somehow find themselves ending at the beginning, and thus encouraged to begin the journey again.

Finally, Picasso's *Guernica* helped us to find expression. The elements of cubism and collage contained in *Guernica* gave us a sense of artistic direction while we were immersed in a world populated by rectangles and polygons.

### On the road to a metaphor

In the manner of the poem itself (which Pound reportedly cut down from 30 lines), we decided that representation would take precedence over realism. Rather than try to create a realistic human face, for example, we would represent one by using a set of vertically stacked bars arranged to approximate the shape of the human face. These bars would serve as three-dimensional billboards onto which we would place QuickTime movies and PICT files. And where there's a billboard, there must of course be a road—which we decided would be the most effective thread to tie our virtual layers together.

### Week 3

During this span we produced our first "sketches" of the virtual environment, explored types of faces, began to record QuickTime movies from TV and live sources, and practiced placing QuickTime movies onto surfaces in the newly arrived Walkthrough Beta software.

## Storyboarding

In our impatience to get started, we found ourselves using the fresh software as a virtual storyboard. If one of us got an idea, we would quickly draw it on Walkthrough (which renders instantly) and try it out. Storyboarding in this manner is more recursive than linear. If we decided we liked something we had storyboarded, it was already there in the virtual environment, ready to be incorporated.

## QuickTime

Using VideoSpigot hardware, we started to collect short movie clips of faces from television, focusing on various types. We knew we wanted to use facial parts for the first layer of "Petals"; however, we soon discovered that QuickTime movies cannot be cropped. Nothing on TV would give us that kind of close-up. We decided we would have to use live models.

We practiced placing in our virtual environment some of the QuickTime clips we had picked up from television. We learned—not unexpectedly—that as the number of simultaneously running QuickTime clips increased, speed decreased. Even using the RAM disk on our Quadra 950, we found that using any more than three QuickTime movies at one time slowed movement in Walkthrough unacceptably.

A silver lining appeared on this cloud, however, as we discovered that QuickTime movies exist only on the "front" of a layer. In other words, once we traveled through or around a layer, the QuickTime movies on the front of it ceased to exist for all practical purposes. By positioning our layers carefully, we realized we would be able to ensure that there would never be more than three QuickTime movies running at the same time.

## Week 4

We continued to pull QuickTime clips from television and edited some of them, videotaped models for facial close-ups, created text as texture, decided how text and QuickTime images would go together, applied textures to the first layer, and created a winding road for the virtual environment. We even managed to lose our Quadra (more later)!

## Facing our models

Using people from surrounding offices as our models, we videotaped a selection of eyes, noses, and mouths. We taped all three with the audio turned off, then taped the mouths saying the Latin roots of the word *face*. These clips were edited with Adobe Premiere.

## Text as texture

Because Walkthrough Beta does not have text-generation capability, any text we wanted to use had to be created elsewhere and applied to our layer as a texture. Using Adobe PhotoShop, we created the text of the poem as well as the Latin root words for *face*. We used 20 percent gray Palatino reversed on black for all of the text in "Petals."

### The first layer

We created five rectangular bars and stacked them—*floated* them might be better—with equal space separating each bar from the next. The middle bar was the longest, with bars getting successively shorter as they moved further—up or down—from the center. The road was made to pass between the bottom bar and the one above it.

It was time to add QuickTime. We found we could "stretch" our square QuickTime format to fit the horizontal bars we had created, but the distortion was unacceptable. We already knew we could not crop QuickTime in Premiere, so we had to come up with another solution. We learned we could "mask" QuickTime movies by covering unwanted portions with textures that were the same color as the background. While the method was somewhat crude, it served its purpose well without slowing things down appreciably.

A QuickTime clip of a pair of eyes was stripped across the second bar from the top. A clip of a nose was then stripped across the next bar, and a mouth was stripped across the next one. All three had to be created larger than needed and then masked. Because the facial parts were taken from three different models, the effect was startling, yet oddly cohesive. If examined long enough, they became working parts of a new, recognizable face (Fig. 25.3)!

A small strip of text containing a Latin root word and its English translation was textured at the bottom of each bar that contained a facial part. The words of the poem were textured onto a layer of widely spaced floating bricks, which were placed in front of the "face" layer. The effect was to make the QuickTime faces visible through the mesh of brickwork containing the poem.

The creation of the new layer and all of its bricks slowed things down considerably, adding a new problem: While QuickTime was active only in a 180° sweep, a complicated Walkthrough creation—such as our brick wall—was active as long as it appeared anywhere on the screen. It was time for some more creative engineering.

Our solution was to create a wall that was the same color as the background, which effectively made the wall invisible. This wall extended roughly parallel to the road, blocking the brick layer from view as travelers looped back around toward the starting point. The wall, which covered an area 10 times the size of the brick layer, slowed movement hardly at all! Evidently, having to recalculate large numbers of points really puts the brakes on Walkthrough—understandably enough. Our wall, massive as it was, still contained only 8 points—one for each corner. In comparison, each brick in the brick wall contained 8 points!

### Week 5

During this interval we replaced our crashed Quadra, experienced hard-drive failure, recovered our data and reinitialized the hard drive, grabbed and edit-

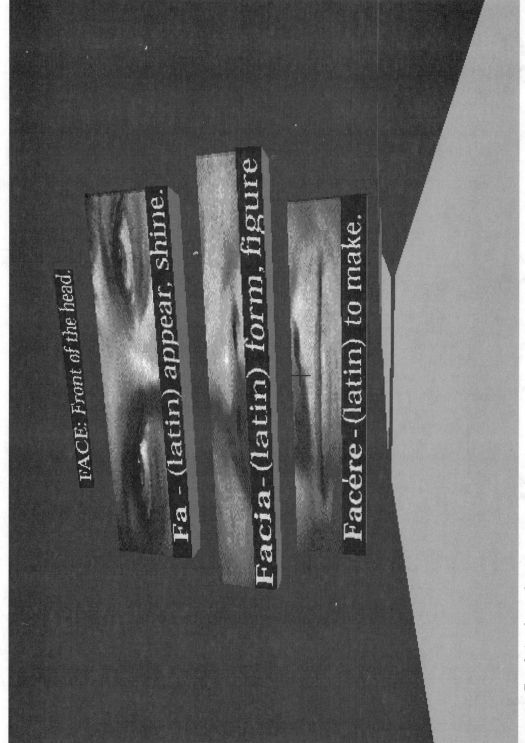

**Figure 25.3** Translating the words to imagery.

ed QuickTime clips of crowds from television for use in the second layer, roughed out the concepts for layers 2 and 3, videotaped models reciting the entire poem, scanned and edited slides of flowers for use in the third layer, created rooms to enclose layers 2 and 3, and edited sounds.

## System distress

No one likes to talk about equipment problems, but they do occur—especially in a project as complex as ours. And because equipment failure and system crashes were significant time thieves, particularly in weeks 5 and 6, they merit some attention here.

We never did determine the cause of our first system crash, which occurred at the end of Week 4. The machine refused to budge—even after the system was reinstalled. As is so often the case, the machine ran fine when the technicians booted it in the repair shop. The hard-drive crash was equally mysterious. We recovered the data and reinitialized the drive. It may have succumbed to excessive fragmentation.

It is worth noting that as our project's complexity increased, so did the number of reboots. We were working with a beta version of Walkthrough, so some crashes were to be expected. A more significant factor, though, is that we probably were asking Walkthrough to do things its designers hadn't envisioned or intended, stretching quite a few limits in the process. Despite several crashes during the final stages of development, however, very few were encountered during exploration of the virtual environment itself.

## Layer 2

We weren't sure yet how we wanted Layer 2 to look, but we knew we wanted to focus in on the first line of Pound's poem, "The apparition of these faces in the crowd." We began grabbing QuickTime clips of crowds from television, keeping the clips short to conserve memory. These were edited in Premiere. While we were in Premiere, we also created a composite movie of crowd clips and text (Fig. 25.4).

Two models were videotaped reciting the poem. Eventually one voice would be used for Layer 2, another for Layer 3. As in the previous videotapings, extreme close-ups were used.

## Layer 3

We had by now the vague notion that we wanted Layer 3 to actually be a room. In one of our earliest design sketches for "Petals" we had envisioned a room through which the viewer would move, viewing QuickTime movies, PICTs, and text on planes suspended at unusual angles. However, we discarded the idea as too confining and too reliant on an overworked paradigm. We returned to it now for Layer 3, but with a major difference: the room would be a black one. The effect on the traveler would be an impression of being suspended in the pure blackness of space.

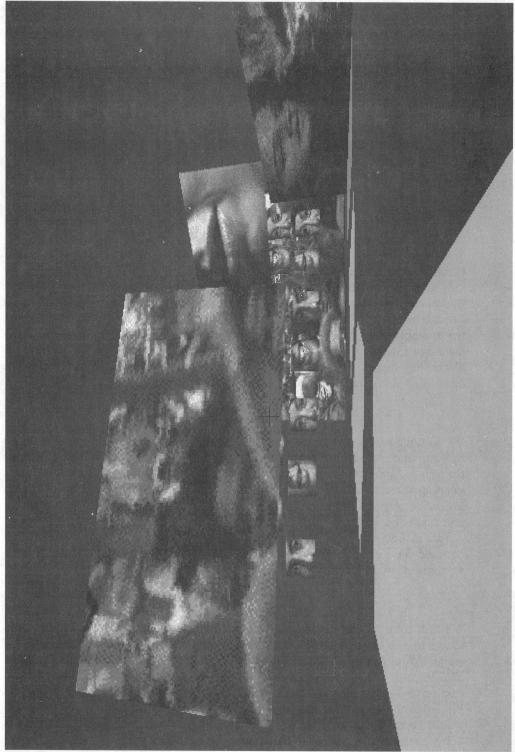

**Figure 25.4** Composite imagery.

While we were experimenting with Layer 3, we discovered that once we were inside a room, nothing outside of the room existed to slow us down. The room became a self-contained universe that existed in complete ignorance of anything that lay beyond its walls. The gain in speed was so significant that we decided to build a room around Layer 2 as well.

We scanned slides of flowers taken with a macro lens, using a Tamron Photovix Slide Scanner. The slides had either black or transparent backgrounds, which made them easy to edit out in PhotoShop. We wanted only the flowers themselves to appear, not their backgrounds.

## Week 6

During this final, short, hectic week, we produced the third layer, then the second—yes, the second—layer, and tweaked, tweaked, tweaked. Then we tested...and tweaked some more.

## Three comes before two

Because we had some idea of how we wanted Layer 3 to look, we produced it ahead of Layer 2. Black panels were created and arranged inside our black room, making the panels, in effect, invisible. Onto these panels were placed QuickTime movies and PICTs of the flowers. Once placed, the flowers and movies appeared to float in space. The road, of course, continued through the room to keep travelers oriented. At the far end of the "room" we placed a composite movie with a circular mask. The movie consisted of a time-lapse sequence of a flower opening, then fading into a pair of eyes.

The road took the traveler directly through the flower/eyes (Fig. 25.5).

Two sounds were edited and added to the final QuickTime sequence (that way they would be audible throughout the room). The first sound was of a model reciting the second line of the poem: "Petals on a wet, black bough." The second was of water running somewhere off in the distance. We used SoundEdit Pro to add reverb to the water sound.

Finally, we decided we wanted the journey into black space to be a surprise to the traveler. That posed a problem because a black room looks like a big black cube from the outside. Our solution? We created a room the same color as the background and just a tiny bit larger than the black room. We placed the black room inside the "invisible" room. A traveler standing outside the room would have no idea it existed, but in following the road, he or she suddenly would be thrust into black space.

## Last but not last

For the second layer, we decided on a more literal billboard approach. We wanted our QuickTime and PICTs to appear as signs along a short stretch of the road. This was fairly easy to accomplish. We created panels the same color as the background, then textured QuickTime and PICTs of crowds onto

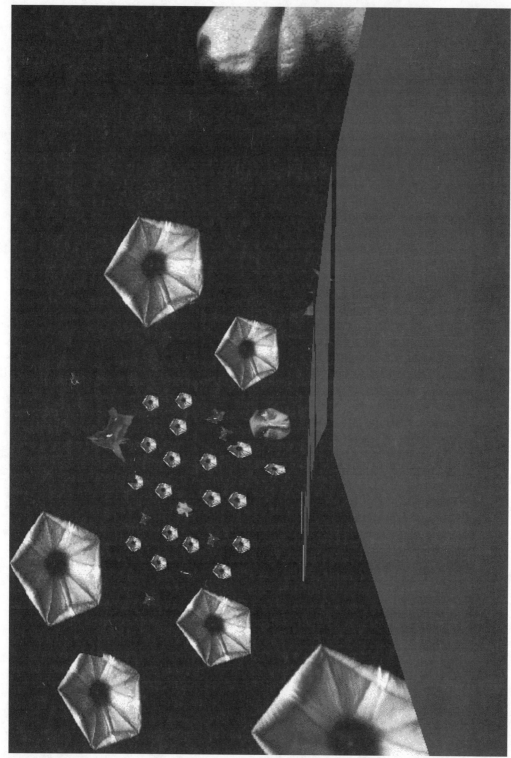

**Figure 25.5**  The road through the petals.

them. Much of the time spent on Layer 2 involved coming up with an effective arrangement of billboards.

At the very end of Layer 2, we placed a composite QuickTime clip of a road with faces along it. The movie was placed so that our road seemed to join the road in the QuickTime clip. The traveler was invited to literally go inside the movie. We then moved Layer 3 so that it was immediately on the other side of the QuickTime movie. In this way the traveler would go through the movie and suddenly be immersed in the blackness of Layer 3.

## Tweaking, tweaking, tweaking

Once the layers had been completed, there were numerous small adjustments to be made. We played with the final position of the billboards in Layer 2, added a few textures, reedited the water sound to push it further into the background, and reedited one of our composite movies in Layer 2. One large adjustment also was made: we moved Layer 1 so that it was closer to the end of Layer 3. This enabled travelers to see Layer 1 the moment they emerged from Layer 3.

## Done and done

Finally, we changed the viewer perspective slightly, moving the viewer/traveler closer to the level of the road. This made the road easier to follow and enhanced the three-dimensional effect of some of the layers.

The project was complete.

## Appendix    Production Notes by Tim Brock

### Using QuickTime in Virtus Walkthrough

For us, working with QuickTime in the beta, texture-enhanced version of Virtus Walkthrough was extremely straightforward and intuitive, provided enough memory was available.

In the Walkthrough Beta (WTB), QuickTime (QT) movies are applied as textures with the WTB surface editor. Once the specific plane of an object has been selected, the surface editor allows users to place numerous (we found no real limit except in terms of speed) textures or movies anywhere parallel to the selected plane. For example, textures or movies can be placed above or below the surface plane—without adhering to the actual dimensions of the surface. A movie or texture also can be assigned either transparent or opaque surface attributes.

Once the movie (including its audio) has been applied, it can be viewed and interacted with instantly in the WTB Walk View window. This immediate feedback is extremely helpful in testing the placement of the movies/textures in the virtual space. When viewed in the Walk View window, the movies continue to loop as long as the steering (mouse) is engaged, and remain active within a 180° radius. Because the movies, like PICT files, are textures, their images are bitmapped and pixelate when viewed up close (Fig. 25.6).

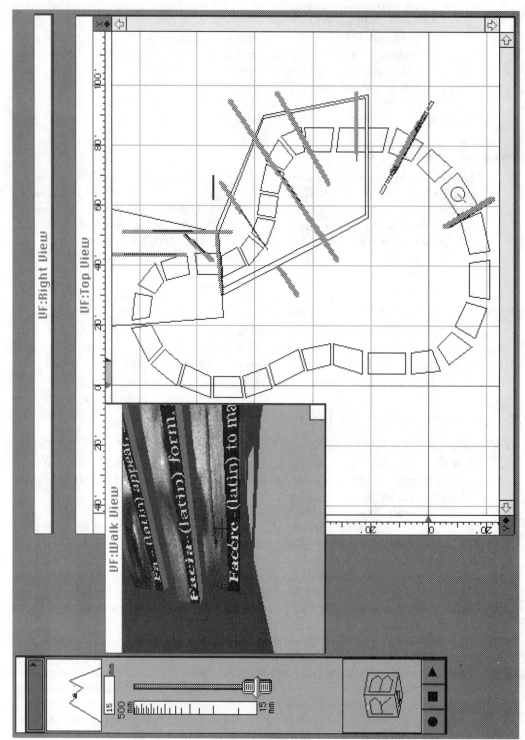

**Figure 25.6** Walkthrough window.

Overall, the extended capability of QuickTime in WTB adds an exciting and easy-to-use multimedia function within the virtual space.

### Hardware requirements

In order to effectively deal with numerous QT movies and textures in the WTB project, a Quadra 950 with 1 Mbyte of V-RAM and 64 Mbytes of D-RAM was used. The only other computer hardware needed besides the standard keyboard, mouse, and 17-inch monitor was a SuperMac VideoSpigot board for QT image/sound capture. Other noncomputer hardware included the following input devices: Super VHS recorder (with 12-inch NTSC monitor), cable TV, VHS video camcorder, and slide scanner. For production and presentation, external speakers were useful but not necessary.

### System/software requirements

In order to produce a virtual-reality product for the classroom, certain system requirements and various software programs were needed. System requirements included the QuickTime 1.5 or 1.6 extension and at least 40 Mbytes of RAM—including the ability to create a RAM disk. The software used was SuperMac ScreenPlay to grab QT movies, Adobe Premiere to edit QT, MacroMind SoundEdit Pro for editing audio, Virtus Walkthrough to create virtual environments, and Adobe PhotoShop for image-processing of PICT files for textures.

### TV Input and other sources for virtual reality

The input sources used included television, video clips, slides, and text editors. The hardware used was a cable TV/video hookup and Tamron slide scanner, both providing an NTSC signal (via RCA cable). These sources were plugged directly into the VideoSpigot board, which captured both digital video (QT) and video stills (PICTs). The stills were imported directly into WTB to be used as textures, while the QT movies almost always were edited and compressed in a QT editing program. Text was generated in a paint program as a PICT file and also used for texture-mapping in WTB.

### Creating QuickTime for virtual reality

To create QuickTime movies, several conditions were set to record both video and audio. First, a RAM disk was created (40 Mbytes). To record sound, RCA cables from a video source were plugged into the external inputs of the Quadra 950. In software (under Sounds on the control panel), external audio was selected. To record video, the video source was connected with one RCA cable to the VideoSpigot board in the Quadra. With all the groundwork done, ScreenPlay (VideoSpigot Software) was used to record QuickTime to the RAM disk at 320 × 240 pixels (10 frames per second) including audio at 22-kHz, 8-bit mono.

### Editing QuickTime for virtual reality

For this project, editing the QT movies for WTB required that the movies be reduced to half the original size: from 320 × 240 to 160 × 120 pixels, and from 10 to 8 frames per second. If sound wasn't necessary, audio channels were cleared. Movies were kept as short as possible and edited to loop continuously. Adobe Premiere was the QT editor used, providing easy editing and quality compression.

### QuickTime and sound design in virtual reality

When QuickTime was imported into WTB, if audio was included in the movie it became an integral part of the virtual space. In "Petals," the synchronized sound of the QT movies continued to loop with the video. This repetition was used as part of the design strategy. If the movies were too short, the audio would repeat often, which was not always desirable. To control this, portions of the audio would be edited out and the video channels extended. The portions of sound that were eliminated would then be placed in another movie that was looping at another rate. In various places, reverb was added to emphasize the content. This enhancing and overlapping of repeated sounds proved very effective in the total design.

### Editing QuickTime audio for virtual reality

In order to edit sounds in QuickTime, the audio track of the QT movie was exported from Premiere as an AIFF file to MacroMind's SoundEdit Pro, and processed. SoundEdit Pro was used to amplify, reverse, extend, and add reverb to sounds. The sounds then were saved again as an AIFF file and imported back to Premiere, to be either combined with another movie or recombined with the original.

### Through the windshield: navigation in the virtual classroom

In designing for classroom use, limitations were placed on navigation—not to hinder the student's ability to navigate, but to keep things simple and reduce confusion. In "Petals," the participant can move forward, backward, left, right, and the combinations thereof—but not up and down. In effect, participants are given a car, not an airplane.

### Maximizing QuickTime in Walkthrough

In "Petals," 9 QuickTime movies and 26 textures were used. Because of the large number of movies and textures, three techniques were applied in order to maximize memory and speed in WTB. First, all movies and textures were placed in RAM (a 40-Mbytes RAM disk was created, leaving 20 Mbytes of RAM free for the WTB application).

Second, in WTB, speed was increased considerably by selecting the "unshaded rendering" option. Unshaded rendering reduces program calculations by displaying objects without shading their various surfaces. For instance, a cube would have the same surface color on all six sides. This limitation, while providing speed for navigation, encouraged a creative use of textures, color, and scale to suggest form and depth in the virtual space.

Third, "invisible" rooms (rooms created with the same color as the background) were made to surround two of the areas that contained QT movies (we found that three movies per room was our maximum if we were to maintain navigation speed and adequate movie frame-rate). In WTB, movies are not calculated if viewed beyond a 180° radius, or if blocked by a room or partition. This allows for more discreet placement of movies, reducing calculation to movies seen only by the navigator. In "Petals," these invisible rooms were assigned transparent openings so that the navigator could "see in," initiating the QT movies to play at the appropriate time.

### VR applications for the classroom: maximum/minimum requirements

The total size of "Petals" is under 15 Mbytes—including the application. For classroom use and presentation, the ideal configuration is to have a 15-Mbytes RAM disk for the movies and textures, and enough additional RAM to set the application to 20 Mbytes.

However, with at least 12 Mbytes of RAM, "Petals" can run from the internal hard disk of any 040 machine (i.e., Quadra and Centris series computers). This configuration allows the WTB application to be set at 8 Mbytes of RAM, which is the absolute minimum to successfully run "Petals."

## Reference

1. Pound, Ezra, "In a Station of the Metro," *Personae: The Collected Shorter Poems of Ezra Pound,* New Directions, New York, 1971.

# Animation, Video, and Sound

# 26

# 3D Animation

## Bob Bennett

### 3D Then and Now

Few objects in the world are truly flat, and human beings are used to receiving their information in three dimensions. And yet much of human communication up to this point has been delivered on paper, the most familiar two-dimensional medium. Even the most complex three-dimensional structures are communicated in 2D drawings and blueprints that only professionals can decipher.

For centuries, designers have created 3D models out of wood, paper, or clay to help them communicate their concepts. But creating a 3D model in the real world is a tedious procedure that, once completed, can be modified only by means of even more work. As veteran builders of 3D models, architects, set designers, and design engineers were among the first to embrace the concept of computer-aided design. By generating their models on the computer they could enjoy many advantages.

For instance, they could attain viewpoints of the model unattainable with any physical model, regardless of size. They could travel "into" a computer-generated house to see it from the viewpoint of a prospective resident. They also could modify a computer-based model quickly and easily. Imagine being able to change the fabric or material of a chair from Naugahyde to canvas in a few moments using a computer. And even if you do go on to make changes in your original design, you can readily retain multiple versions of your model on the computer, without destroying the original.

The advantages of using the computer to generate models can be summed up in a single word: *control*. With the computer you have control over the shape and surface-appearance of objects without having to overcome the real-world constraints of physics. If you want to create a flower made out of concrete, your computer will happily oblige you. You can apply plaster, sculpt metal, or carve objects out of wood without having to learn each of these respective crafts.

**Figure 26.1**   Courtroom animation.

This level of control also extends to the environment around your model. With your desktop computer you can place your design on a glass pedestal or in a field of wheat. Lighting can be adjusted so that the perfect tint and the ideal shadow is cast upon your scene. With this degree of control, your 3D model can deliver the specific message intended, without superfluous details. It is precisely this capability that makes 3D computer imagery so powerful as a courtroom tool. Only those details of a court case that are truly known need be presented. Unknown persons in a scene can have blank faces, while known bullet trajectories can be exhibited with precise accuracy in the same scene. Figures 26.1 and 26.2 demonstrate this. Both of these images, created by Alec Jason, are wireframe models rendered and animated for a murder trial.

If the advantages of using computers to do 3D modeling have been so great, why is it such a recent phenomenon? The answer lies in the price/performance curve of desktop computers. 3D modeling requires substantial processing power. Only in the past 3 years have desktop computers been fast enough even to create complex 3D models. Now the Macintosh, AMIGA, and IBM PC are all fast enough for 3D work. As personal computers (PCs) have become more powerful, computer software developers have rushed to supply software for these potential new customers. While CAD software is a common means for building 3D models, its purpose is primarily to support the design and

**Figure 26.2**   Courtroom animation.

manufacturing processes. When communication is the main goal, specialized 3D modeling software such as Swivel 3D from Macromedia is generally opted for. With a 3D modeling package, one can create 3D objects that are ready for the next stages of rendering and animation.

## The Power of Animation

Often, people associate the word *animation* with "cartoons." Cartoons are great, but there is much more to animation than fun, animated characters. Animation has grown from being purely an entertainment medium to being one of the most powerful ways to get your point across. It has a universal appeal that transcends age and cultural boundaries. Delivered at 30 frames per second, it sends a concentrated message. Whether you are aiming to deliver complex visual information or simply to keep the viewer's attention, animation is truly a powerful medium.

Animation software on a desktop computer lets you exercise a tremendous amount of control over your final result. You can control form, color, lighting, and perspective using 3D animation software. You are not bound to physical laws of nature, and thus can create images that say exactly what you need to communicate.

Animation is, of course, a time-based, space-based medium. And as such it gives you control over the pace of your message. You can use animation to efficiently show in a few seconds a lengthy process (such as soil erosion) that takes months or years in the real world to occur. Conversely you can slow down an event that would normally be too fast to comprehend by making the animation take place over 5 to 10 seconds. You can show how things move over time—traffic, or a robot arm. You can vary the surface appearance of an object to show how a process such as rusting can alter an iron plate over time. Or, to really give your audience a feel for the space in which you have placed them, you can simply vary your viewpoint so as to travel through a 3D scene.

## The Process

There are five basic steps to creating 3D animation that are common to most software packages, regardless of the computer platform you are using. You should

1. Create a 3D model.

2. Apply realistic materials.

3. Add lights and cameras.

4. Make it move.

5. Render.

Let's look at these steps in more detail.

### Creating a 3D model

In a typical 3D modeler, there are numerous ways to construct a 3D model. First, objects can be generated from *primitives,* or simple 3D shapes such as cubes, spheres, cones, and cylinders. Many real-world items are in fact amalgamations of simple shapes such as these. For instance, a table often is comprised of four cylinders and a cube.

A second method involves creating 3D objects from 2D outlines. A profile of a wine glass can be "spun" 360° to form a solid 3D goblet. Similarly, a banana can be constructed by sending a circle along an arc, while its circumference is increased and decreased.

In addition, 3D models of common objects from cars to sharks are available in prebuilt form. Many of these models originally were created in CAD systems, and they are stored in standard Data Exchange Format (DXF) files. Some companies like Viewpoint Engineering now specialize in supplying 3D models to the multimedia developer. Often it is easier to purchase a model of the Statue of Liberty, for example, than to construct it anew yourself. Keep in mind that the suppliers of these models often use 3D digitizing equipment to speed the model-development process. In fact, many of these companies can

**Figure 26.3** Autocad model.

even digitize real-world 3D items on demand if you can provide them with the physical object to be digitized. If you are obtaining 3D objects from a vendor, make sure they are in a format you can accept, as there are numerous 3D data formats utilized, one of which is shown in Fig. 26.3.

In the computer, most computer models ultimately are comprised of small triangles, or polygons. A small model may have less than a dozen objects, with less than 10,000 polygons total in the scene. A large model may have hundreds of thousands of polygons. Other methods of representing models rely on mathematical surfaces and store data in a more efficient manner than do individual polygons.

The best computer models are constructed with easy-to-understand names assigned to their components, simplifying the subsequent tasks of applying materials and animating them. Even better, some models are sold with all of their material appearances preapplied.

### Applying realistic materials

Once geometry has been acquired or built, the next step in developing an animation is to apply material appearances to objects in the scene. Tabletops could be assigned a gray marble finish, chairs an oak-wood finish. Sometimes the goal is to make the scene look as believable as possible, a goal known as *photorealism*. Other times the goal is not so much to make the scene look real as to make it look fantastic or interesting. The ability to assign any material property to any object in the computer is one of the most powerful aspects of 3D animation. Often, computer software for 3D animation includes a built-in library of existing materials plus a "materials editor" for creating or modifying materials.

The most basic way to specify a material is to specify its color properties (e.g., how light will reflect off the object). Often these color properties are specified by using adjectives referring to three properties of light: diffuse, specular, and ambient. The *diffuse* component is the color of the object itself. For instance, you would want to assign a red color to the diffuse component to simulate a red plastic ball, as shown in Fig. 26.4.

The *specular* component is the shiny highlight on the surface of the object. If, for example, we wanted that same red ball to look as if it were made of glass, we might assign a small white specular highlight to the material (on a red surface, this will appear to be glass). By varying the size and color of the specular highlight we could also approximate the look of other common mate-

**Figure 26.4**  3D Studio's unique textures.

rials such as metal or rubber. The final color property, *ambience,* is the color of the surrounding light in the overall scene.

But color is only one basic way to create a realistic-looking material. Another way is through the use of texture maps. A simple use of a texture map is to apply a decal to an object, such as a red cross on the side of an ambulance. A texture map is simply a bitmap, that is, a raster file created in a paint program or perhaps scanned into the computer. If you wanted a certain carpet in your computer model, you could actually scan a sample of the carpet into the computer and apply it to the floor of an imaginary house. Any bitmap can be used as a texture map. Many computer artists believe that the skilled use of texture maps is one of the best ways of achieving believable results on a computer.

Texture mapping can be much more subtle than a pure decal such as the cross mentioned above. Textures can completely replace the base color of an object or be applied just as a percentage. For instance, if we were to add a marble texture to a yellow material and let it bleed through the yellow color, we could make the object look more complex—like a soup in need of stirring, perhaps. A texture map also can be applied to simulate a rough or pitted surface in a technique known as *bump-mapping.* Here the values in the texture map are used to simulate raised or depressed areas on a surface, so the resulting look is grainy, not smooth.

Texture maps also can be used to vary how transparent an object is, to make some portions shiny or dull, or to simulate the mirrored reflection of the surrounding scene in a surface, such as a wood tabletop. Textures need not be just still images, they can be a sequence of images. In this way you can simulate an event such as a burner on a stove getting bright red as it heats up, or make a television set in your scene appear to be tuned to a show.

One of the more advanced ways to create a material appearance is through a programmable procedure often called a *shader.* Let's say you want to have a brick appearance on a wall in your scene. You could either scan in a brick pattern and apply it as both a texture and bump map, or write a shader to simulate the look of real brick. Many common materials such as marble, wood, and brick can be approximated quite effectively through the use of computer algorithms. A "procedural" brick might have the additional advantage of appearing solid—that is, the brick material seems to pass all the way through the object. Procedural materials also generally lack the "seams" that classic texture-mapped materials sometimes exhibit. Finally, procedural materials tend to look good even when viewed from very close up, whereas a texture map can look highly pixelated (jagged) up close.

A wide variety of materials can be employed in a single scene. Objects in the background may not need very detailed materials to be assigned to them. An object that is the focus of attention may require a very detailed material that is applied with great care so as to avoid seams and other imperfections. A single scene may include hundreds of different materials. The materials used in a scene may actually occupy much more disk space than the geometry of the objects themselves!

### Adding cameras and lights

When it comes to this part of computer modeling, the terminology may be quite familiar to you, particularly if you have some background in photography.

Just as in the real world, we must have light in order to see anything that has been rendered. There are different kinds of lights in most computer software programs, just as there are around you everyday. *Ambient* light is the basic level and color of light in the whole scene. If red ambient light is used to simulate the look of a sunset, any blue objects will tend to look purple.

Spotlights often are used to send a cone of light in a particular direction. You decide on the size of the cone and where the light should point. The spotlight usually can have its own color—or even a bitmap—assigned to it, much like a slide projector. A spotlight generally will be able to cast shadows behind objects it encounters. The softness of the resulting shadow usually is another parameter associated with the spotlight.

Keep in mind that spotlights have no shape or mass themselves, so you can place them in a scene without having to worry whether they will be seen. You also can place them in locations where no real light could ever go. Figure 26.5 shows a "blotchy" shadow map projecting through a carefully placed spotlight. This gives the impression of watery shadows cast on an ocean floor.

Most computer software packages of this type also include an automated camera. You can place one or more cameras in a scene and then look through them, with the resulting perspective corresponding to the characteristics of the "lens" you have specified.

There are no lens defects in a computer camera, which means you can create a wide-angle lens that could never be manufactured in the real world! You can put a camera in places where no real camera could ever go due to heat, water, lack of physical space, or other constraint.

### The rendering process

Let's assume you have created a model and it has materials assigned to it. You can now easily move your camera to the desired position and "render" a single frame so as to get a nice picture. Rendering is the computationally intense part of the process, which means your computer may be tied up thinking for quite a while. It is sometimes said that rendering is "never fast enough."

There are several different levels of rendering, and these are sometimes referred to as *shading methods*. A common one is trading off rendering quality for rendering speed. The simplest and fastest shading method is *flat shading*. In fact, some computers can perform flat shading in hardware for instantaneous shading of small- to medium-sized models. But a flat-shaded rendering is not terribly impressive in appearance. Each polygon is assigned a single color, and the result is usually a faceted look that appears phony. Flat shading is useful during mode development and for producing motion tests prior to final rendering.

The next level of shading quality is *smooth* (often called *Gouraud*) *shading*. This type of rendering eliminates the faceted appearance of flat shading but

**Figure 26.5**  Automated camera.

takes a little longer to compute. Instead of each face getting a single color, a gradient of colors is assigned to each face to produce a smooth appearance. One level up from smooth shading is *Phong shading*. Phong shading looks even better than smooth shading, since it adds specular highlights to objects. While this takes longer to render, the presence of these highlights makes for a more convincing result. Imagine an excellent rendering of a billiard ball and you will have a good idea of what Phong rendering looks like. Figure 26.6 provides examples of various forms of rendering.

There are other kinds of shading methods, and rendering is still an area of very active research. *Radiosity* is a technique that makes it possible to simulate extremely realistic lighting of interior spaces. *Ray-tracing* is a very time-consuming technique that produces excellent results. With ray-tracing you get perfect reflections off shiny surfaces, and light is bent or refracted when it

**Figure 26.6** Various levels of rendering.

travels through an opaque or transparent object such as a wine glass. As mentioned earlier, you may not have the time to render using a technique such as ray-tracing, since it usually takes too long to be of practical value for creating on a desktop computer an animation of many frames.

### Making it move

By now you should have some idea of how you will create, model, develop material properties for, and render out a single frame or picture. But how will you actually animate?

In the case of classic 2D animation, you traditionally would draw each frame of an animation, with each moving object drawn in a slightly different

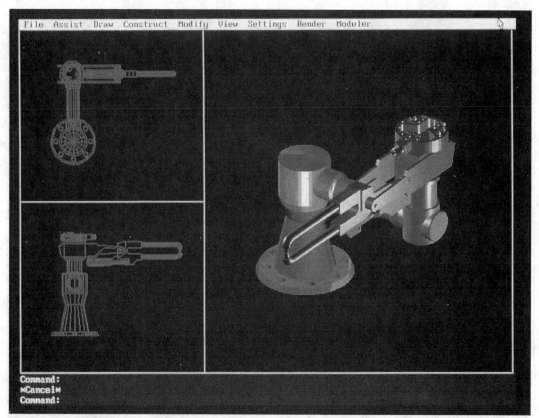

File  Assist  Draw  Construct  Modify  View  Settings  Render  Modeler

Command:
✳Cancel✳
Command:

**Figure 26.6**  (*Continued*)

position. Your point of view generally would be fixed, and objects would move in front of you. With 3D animation, the process is a bit different. You assign motion to objects on specific "keyframes" and move your camera on different frames to gain the best vantage point, and the software figures all of the "in-between" moves. This process is called *keyframe animation,* and it is the technique used to create most 3D animation today. Some 3D animation is produced in a slightly different manner, but before we get into that let's look at keyframing in more detail.

Keyframe animation can be defined as *the process of assigning motion to objects on specific numbered frames of an animation sequence and letting the computer interpolate the intervening motion.* If you position a ball up in the air on frame 30 and establish that as a keyframe, the computer will "move" the ball up smoothly from frame 0 to frame 30. Exactly how smoothly the ball begins and ends its journey is usually settable in the software. Sometimes you want an object at rest to move instantly (as in an explosion), while at other times you want it to move gradually (as when a boulder starts to roll down a slope). You have control over these "ease-in" and "ease-out" settings in

**Figure 26.6**   *(Continued)*

software products such as Autodesk 3D Studio. This is demonstrated in
Fig. 26.7, where a path is created for a helicopter to follow in an animation.

Often it is useful to establish a hierarchy of objects when performing
keyframe animation. In other words, you can establish links between objects
so that they are affected by the characteristics of other objects in the scene.
You may want to link a hand to an arm, so that if you move the arm, the
hand moves with it. A walking person may have a very detailed set of hierar-
chies, so that, as the head turns, the eyes and nose also move, but the eyes
can move independently of the head.

Just as you can keyframe objects to produce 3D animation, so too you can
keyframe lights and cameras. You may want a spotlight to pan across a
company logo for a Hollywood-type effect. Or you may want to assign a camera to follow a curving path as each frame is rendered. The possibilities are
limitless.

**Figure 26.6** (*Continued*)

Animation often boils down to a few basic types of movement. You can rotate an object around its local pivot point, or around some center point in the scene (such as a whirlpool). You can scale an object up or down, as when inflating or deflating a balloon. You can move an object from one location to another.

Some programs will allow you to "morph" objects from one shape into another. You could say by the keyframe on frame 120, "Morph the fish into a whale." This is a complex task for the software to accomplish, and restrictions may be placed on you such as requiring the number of points in the "begin" and "end" shapes to be identical. Often you can morph the material of the object, not just the shape. In this way you can make a leopard suddenly have the skin of a giraffe.

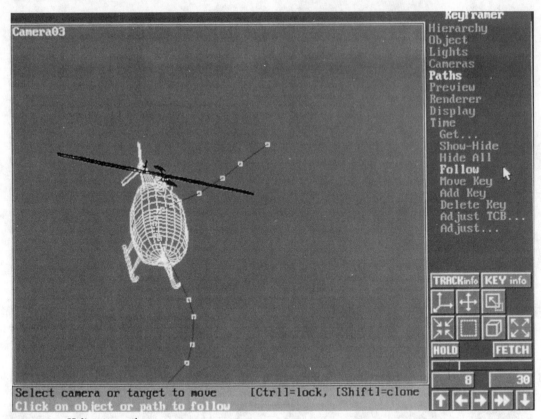

**Figure 26.7**   Helicopter path.

Generally, keyframing is done by using interactive graphics, where you visibly move objects in certain keyframes by means of a mouse or other pointing device. Sometimes a scripting language is used ("Move Ball 34,0,0 at Frame 30") to establish the animation sequence. Sometimes the process is even more automatic. Computer software is getting better and better at assisting the animator. In some cases the behavior of certain objects can be programmed. An explosion can be programmed to "shatter" an object in an animation—greatly simplifying the task of the animator. In professional animation software such as 3D Studio, airplanes can be automatically "banked" around turns, and balls can be set to bouncing without manually keyframing them up and down. Even effects such as waves and ripples can be automatically assigned using today's software. Expect tomorrow's software to increasingly take over the computation of common movements such as running and swimming.

In summary, the process of producing 3D animation can really be as simple or as complex as you choose to make it. One thing is certain: the personal computer technology necessary to produce 3D animation is now accessible, affordable, and understandable.

# 27

# Technical Aspects of Multimedia Audio

## Cliff Kondratiuk

### Digital Audio Systems

Fast growth in the PC sound card market is today fostering fierce competition among the hardware vendors in the field. As a result, the marketing machines are throwing around statistics and buzzwords that imply their products offer the same audio quality as that to be found in a good home-stereo system. In order to wade through this mountain of claims and advertisements, it is important to have a basic understanding of how the perception of human hearing relates to digital audio systems. The important factors that determine the quality of a digitized waveform are the sample rate, the number of bits used to encode the signal, and the proper design of the analog input and output sections.

While the audio signal is in the digital domain, the two determining factors of quality are the sample rate and the number of bits used to encode the waveform. Through Nyquist's theorem, the sample rate defines the reproducible bandwidth of the encoded signal. Nyquist's theorem states that a digitally encoded signal may be used to record and reproduce frequencies from DC to one-half of the sample rate without introducing aliased noise components. With the bandwidth of human hearing accepted as being from 20 Hz to 20 kHz, this theorem shows that a sample rate of greater than 40 kHz is required to reproduce the audible range of frequencies. To satisfy this requirement, Philips and Sony chose the 44.1-kHz sample rate when designing the compact disc (CD). This same sample rate is now also used as the highest rate supported by the multimedia audio extensions found in Windows 3.1™. The other sample rates supported under Windows are 11.025 kHz and

**Figure 27.1**  Bandwidths supported by Windows 3.1. A = 20 Hz to 20 kHz, bandwidth of human hearing; B = 20 Hz to 20 kHz, usable bandwidth of 44.1-kHz sample rate; C = 20 Hz to 10 kHz, usable bandwidth of 22.050-kHz sample rate; D = 20 Hz to 5 kHz, usable bandwidth of 11.025-kHz sample rate.

**TABLE 27.1   Frequency Range of Common Sounds**

| Instrument/sound | Frequency range fundamental | Frequency of fourth overtone/harmonic |
|---|---|---|
| Grand piano | $A_1$ to $C_8$ <br> 27.01 Hz to 4.186 kHz | 12.558 kHz |
| Flute | C3 to B6 <br> 261.63 Hz to 3.951 kHz | 11.853 kHz |
| Electric guitar | E1 to E5 <br> 82.41 Hz to 1.328 kHz | 3.984 kHz |
| Pipe organ | C2 to C10 <br> 32.7 Hz to 8.372 kHz | 25.116 kHz |
| Trumpet | E2 to B flat 4 <br> 164.81 Hz to 932.33 Hz | 2.797 kHz |
| Human speech | 50 Hz to 800 Hz | 2.4 kHz |

22.050 kHz. Figure 27.1 shows the bandwidths that may be reproduced by these three sample rates.

These usable bandwidths show the highest frequency to be less than the theoretical maximum stated by Nyquist's theorem. In practical applications, frequencies equal to and greater than the Nyquist frequency must be significantly attenuated to avoid the introduction of aliasing noise. This attenuation is assumed to occur between the highest usable frequency and the Nyquist frequency.

In an attempt to correlate these frequencies to the real world, Table 27.1 lists the frequency ranges of some common sounds.

From this table we can see that, with the exception of the pipe organ, the largest fundamental frequency of these sounds is less than 5 kHz, implying that they could all be recorded without any loss at the low rate of 11.025 kHz. This would be the case if all of these sounds were comprised of only the fundamental sine wave, with no overtones or harmonics. Fortunately these sounds also include the harmonic overtones, which help to define the timbre of the instrument. This tonal quality, together with the rates of amplitude change, is how we differentiate between various musical instruments and other everyday sounds. To maintain the unique quality of these sounds, the frequency range chosen for digital sampling must also include these harmonics. The value of the fourth harmonic of the highest note or fundamental shows that higher sample rates are required to capture the frequency content of the entire instrument.

Percussion instruments such as snare drums, crash cymbals, etc. do not exhibit a frequency range as shown above. These types of instruments generally contain fast-attack transients that are made up of frequencies from the fundamental of the instrument up to 20 kHz in some cases. Thus, to properly record many percussion instruments, the 44.1-kHz sample rate would be required.

The second factor of audio quality is the number of bits used to encode the signal. This determines the available dynamic range and the signal-to-error ratio of the digital sample. Available dynamic range is defined as *the difference between the quietest or lowest-level signal and the loudest or highest-level signal that may be encoded.* In order to provide a more straightforward description, the following discussion will relate to the use of a linear PCM encoding technique.

In a digital system, an analog signal is encoded by assigning finite levels to the analog waveform at discrete periodic intervals. This introduces two distinct limitations on the encoding. The first limitation will be defined as *available dynamic range* and is related to the amplitude of the signal and the number of bits used to encode the sample. If a 16-bit word length is used, the system is capable of assigning one of 65535 distinct levels to the ideal analog waveform. If the analog signal is limited to a maximum voltage level of 1 V peak-to-peak, then the loudest signal that may be encoded is equal to 1 V and the quietest equal to $\frac{1}{65535}$ V. This yields an available dynamic range of approximately 96 dB.

A digital system's dynamic range and the perception of loudness in human hearing are often difficult to compare. The threshold of human hearing is measured as being 0 dB sound pressure level (SPL), which is equal to $10^{-12}$ watts/$m^2$ in acoustic power. A 16-bit recording is able to reproduce signal differences from 0 dB to approximately 96 dB. If the output of this recording were connected to a loudspeaker system capable of producing an output power of .0063 watts/$m^2$, or 96 dB (typical home-stereo loudspeakers can reproduce an acoustic SPL from 85 to 92 dB), Figure 27.2 would directly relate the dynamic range of the digital system to the human perception of loudness.

**Figure 27.2**   Comparison of digital to human perception of loudness.

The second limitation is the signal-to-error ratio, or digital signal-to-noise ratio of the encoding technique. When a finite digital level is assigned to the ideal analog signal, a measurable difference exists between the assigned level and the ideal signal amplitude. This difference is a form of distortion introduced by the digital encoding and is generally referred to as *quantization error*. As in the measurement of dynamic range, the amount of distortion is directly related to the number of bits used in the encoding. The power of this distortion is determined by the size of the individual steps in amplitude available to the digital sampler. An example of this error is shown in Fig. 27.3.

Like dynamic range, the signal-to-error ratio also is measured in decibels. It is calculated by taking the ratio of the maximum RMS signal value to the energy in the error signal across one sample interval. The results of this measurement yield a signal-to-error ratio for linear PCM encoding of $6.02n + 1.76$ dB, where $n$ is the number of bits used.

For a 16-bit word length, this would yield a signal-to-error ratio of approximately 98 dB, which is about the same result obtained for the dynamic range. This holds true only for a linear PCM encoding technique. Other forms of digital encoding such as the μLaw/ALaw companding technique have signal-to-error ratios that are significantly lower than the reproducible dynamic range. μLaw/ALaw will be discussed later in the chapter.

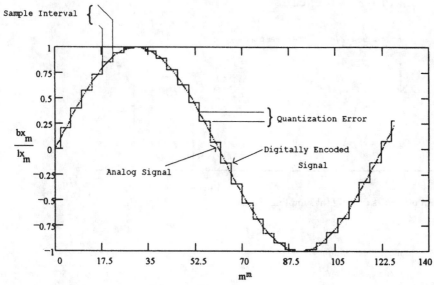

**Figure 27.3**  Distortion introduced by digital encoding.

The standard sample sizes offer the following ideal signal-to-error ratios:

| Sample size | Signal-to-error ratio | Equivalent |
|---|---|---|
| 8-bit | 49.88 dB | Telephone |
| 10-bit | 61.92 dB | AM radio |
| 12-bit | 73.96 dB | Metal tape |
| 16-bit | 98.04 dB | Compact disc |

These measurements show the ideal signal-to-quantization error for various encoding word sizes, and are the most often used to make dynamic-range or signal-to-noise ratio claims. There are additional noise components that may be present in a digital signal which are unrelated to the basic claim for dynamic range. The most unpleasant of these are a result of audible image frequencies and digital aliasing noise. Image frequencies are a component of digital systems that occur as a result of modeling a continuous time-analog signal with discrete time samples. Figure 27.4 shows the placement of these images in a digital sampling system.

When the sample rate, Fs, is 44.1 kHz, the Nyquist frequency, 0.5Fs, is set at 22.05 kHz. The images introduced from this sample rate will occur in between 22.05 kHz and 44.1 kHz, which is outside the accepted range of human hearing. Noise introduced from these image frequencies becomes a significant problem when the sample rate used for the signal is 22.05 or 11.025 kHz. These rates will create image frequencies well within the range of audible frequencies. To avoid a serious degradation in the output, these

**Figure 27.4**  Placement of images in a digital sampling system.

**Figure 27.5**  Oversampling image frequencies.

images must be removed by a steep rolloff-analog smoothing filter placed after the digital-to-analog converter. In order to accomplish this, a sound card would require an output filter with programmable cutoffs to match each of the supported sample rates.

Some digital systems have a set output sample rate matching the maximum supported rate of 44.1 kHz. To play samples designed for the lower rates, the system will interpolate, or oversample the data to the fixed output rate. This introduces more concerns with additional image frequencies created by the oversampling process. Figure 27.5 shows the additional images introduced when oversampling an 11.025-kHz signal to 44.1 kHz. Figure 27.6 shows the frequency spectrum of a 1-kHz tone sampled at 11.025 kHz and then oversampled to 44.1 kHz by merely repeating each sample four times.

The three additional peaks in Figure 27.6 are a result of failing to remove the images around the original 11.025-kHz sample rate after the signal was oversampled. In the digital domain, these frequencies must be removed through the execution of computation-intensive digital filter algorithms. Due to the processing power required, these algorithms must be performed on the sound card. Only digital signal processor (DSP)–based sound cards have the power available for this.

**Figure 27.6**   Frequency spectrum of noise.

Until now, our discussion of sound has been limited to the audio signal while it is still in the digital domain. Typically, the digital domain is where the lowest amount of noise is introduced into the signal. The high-speed digital signals found on the PC's ISA bus, and the lack of proper isolation between the analog and digital circuitry on the sound board, cause most of the signal degradation. Measurements of some popular sound cards show overall SNRs of less than 72 dB for 16-bit, 44.1-kHz sample recording and playback. The analog circuitry on some cards even picks up audible noise caused by data transfers from disk accesses and mouse movements. As a final determination of a given sound card's overall signal-to-noise ratio, the measurements taken from the output of the analog section should be used. To be of value, these measurements should be taken while there is a lot of activity on the ISA bus.

## General MIDI

MIDI (Musical Instrument Digital Interface) was introduced by the MIDI Manufacturers Association (MMA) in 1983 as a standardized serial-communications protocol for controlling electronic music devices. This protocol allowed electronic synthesizers to communicate with each other, regardless of the manufacturer. MIDI takes the form of byte-wide instructions that have been standardized for assigning track and patch IDs, triggering notes, controllers, channel volumes, etc. on any MIDI-compatible synthesizer. Although this marked a breakthrough in the music industry, one component was missing from the original specification. While keyboard manufacturers supported the MIDI protocols, they still maintained control over the patch IDs in which the individual instrument sounds are located. Although the devices could communicate with one another, a given MIDI sequence was useful only for the equipment for which it was written. To use the program with different hardware setups, the user had to edit the patch locations in order to trigger the correct instrument sounds. This problem recently has been addressed with the General MIDI System–Level 1 specification introduced by the MMA in 1991.

The General MIDI (GM) mode of operation was added to the MIDI specification as a means of standardizing where each instrument sound can be addressed on a given sound device. This mode specifies where 128 specific melodic-instrument and 46 percussive-instrument sounds can be addressed on a General MIDI–compatible device (see Fig. 27.7). The introduction of this standard instrument-mapping allows application developers and composers to generate one MIDI file that can be played through any compatible sound device. In addition to supporting the standard instrument locations, General MIDI–compatible devices must be able to respond to each of 16 MIDI channels simultaneously, with different timbres on each channel. Compatibility also requires that the device have a minimum of 24 voices that are dynamically allocated for either pitched timbres or fixed percussion, or 16 dynamically allocated voices for pitched timbres and 8 dedicated voices for percussion. Higher-quality sound cards will offer up to 32 dynamically allocated voices. A detailed overview of the General MIDI specification is offered next.

The MIDI Manufacturers Association introduced the General MIDI System–Level 1 specification to allow MIDI data sequences to play on any MIDI synthesizer that complies with the specification. This was accomplished by defining minimum performance requirements for compatible synthesizers, sound modules, cards, or keyboards. As taken from the General MIDI System–Level 1 specification (1991), a PC sound card or module must have

*Voices.*    A minimum of either 24 dynamically allocated voices, available simultaneously for both melodic and percussive sounds, or 16 dynamically allocated voices for melody plus 8 for percussion.

*Channels*

General MIDI support for all 16 MIDI channels
Variable number of voices on each channel (polyphony)
Different instrument sounds (timbres) on each channel
Key-based percussion on channel 10

*Instruments*

A minimum of 16 different timbres playing various instrument sounds
A minimum of 128 presets for instruments (MIDI program numbers)

*Note on / note off*

Middle C = midi key 60
All voices must respond to velocity
All voices dynamically allocated (note/drums reattack using free voices)

*Controller changes*

Controller 1—Modulation
Controller 7—Main Volume
Controller 10—Pan

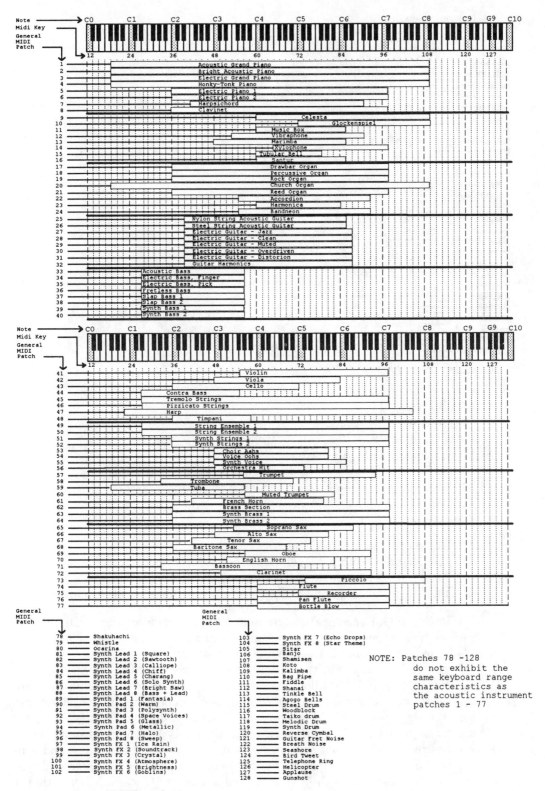

**Figure 27.7** General MIDI synthesizer ranges.

**Figure 27.8**  General MIDI percussion map.

Controller 11—Expression
Controller 64—Sustain
Controller 121—Reset all controllers
Controller 123—All notes off
Reg. Parameter 0—Pitch-bend sensitivity
Reg. Parameter 1—Fine-tuning
Reg. Parameter 2—Coarse-tuning

*Channel messages*

Channel Pressure (aftertouch)
Pitch bend—default ± 2 semitones
All channels respond to MIDI volume
Default powerup: pitch bend = 0; volume = 100; controllers normal

Within the GM specification, channel 10 is set aside as the MIDI channel used to trigger percussion timbres, as shown in Fig. 27.8. Channels 1–9 and 11–16 are used for any of the 128 melodic-instrument timbres.

It should be noted that this specification differs from the Microsoft implementation of MIDI. To allow for support of low-quality systems that are unable to meet the minimum voice and simultaneous-timbre requirements found in the General MIDI specification, Microsoft defined channels 1–10 for use by high-end music synthesizers and channels 11–16 for low-end music synthesizers. OPL2-based sound cards would be described as a low-end synthesizer and any GM-compatible device would be described as a high-end synthesizer. The concern with Microsoft's redefinition of General MIDI is that it essentially renders the upper MIDI channels useless to high-end synthesizers. A MIDI sequence authored to Microsoft's definition would use these channels for a simplified version of a song that could play on a low-end system. High-end synthesizers are not expected to respond to messages written to these upper channels, effectively reducing the usable number of MIDI channels from 16 to 10.

## Basic Sound Card Features

With a growing number of sound cards available on the market, it is important to know what features are available and what is required for their intended use. The features described next include the minimum requirements that should be found on any sound card for use in a multimedia application. These may be thought of as the necessary functions, and they do not include any of the application-specific features such as voice recognition, effects processing, etc.

### PCM playback and recording

The ability to play back and record PCM (pulse code modulation) files is considered a necessity for any useful audio device, given the large number of applications making use of digital audio. Among others these applications include voice annotation, speech recognition, speech synthesis, voice mail, sound clips for presentations/education, sound effects and speech for entertainment software. Although digital audio playback and recording is one of the base functions found on any sound card, the available formats, capabilities, and methods of implementation differ from card to card. These differences affect both the quality of the output and the number of applications able to make use of the card.

### Digital audio formats

Useful sample rates for digital audio in multimedia applications range from approximately 8 kHz for telephone-quality voice to 44.1 kHz for high-fidelity music. For use with the widest range of applications, the card should be capable of supporting each of the following playback and recording formats:

- 8-/16-bit mono/stereo at 11.025 kHz, 22.05 kHz, and 44.1 kHz
- Adaptive delta pulse code modulation (ADPCM) 4:1 compression/decompression
- μLaw/A-Law 2:1 companding

The first entry is made up of the base formats supported directly through the multimedia extensions found in Windows 3.1. These offer a wide enough range of quality versus storage space for the majority of applications. Any sound card being considered for purchase should, at a minimum, be able to record and play back samples in any of these base formats These formats offer quality ranges from a level as low as telephone speech to levels approaching CD audio.

ADPCM is a lossy digitizing technique that allows the application or user to record and store samples at a 4:1 compression ratio. The samples are then decompressed as they are played back. The obvious benefit of using this type of compression technique is the reduction of the amount of hard-disk space required for storing samples. Given that a thirty-second sound clip recorded in 16-bit stereo at 44.1 kHz requires over 5 Mbytes of storage, this type of compression can become extremely useful. The downside of this type of algorithm is the signal degradation resulting from the processing. The encoding/decoding of the 16-bit signal results in an overall dynamic range of approximately 60 dB, as compared to 96 dB in the original 16-bit signal. This equates to a drop in dynamic range from close to CD-quality to approximately AM-radio-quality. The reproducible bandwidth is also slightly reduced to approximately 8 kHz for a 22.05-kHz sample rate, or 16 kHz for a 44.1-kHz sample rate. At this time, 2:1 ADPCM algorithms are not in wide use on PC sound cards. Although the compression ratio is lower, the dynamic range is reduced from the ideal 96 dB to only 90 dB.

There is a formidable compatibility problem with the ADPCM algorithms in use. Each vendor offering this encoding technique has effectively implemented a proprietary compression algorithm whose files could be properly decompressed only by the inverse algorithm. This sometimes results in sample files compressed using one manufacturer's method being useless for playback on any other make of sound card. To alleviate this, Microsoft has recently released their ADPCM algorithm for use by any sound card manufacturer or ISV. This should give applications developers the confidence to incorporate a standard compression technique without risk of limited support by hardware.

The μ-Law/A-Law companding technique is commonly used in telecommunications for a fairly-good-quality 2:1 compression of speech signals. The companding algorithms defined by the Compaq Business Audio specification are the same as those used in the telecommunications industry. This method uses a piece-wise linear logarithmic compression characteristic that results in a quantization noise power that is proportional to the signal power over a wide dynamic range. Essentially, this system gives the ability to encode soft or lower-volume signals with the same signal-to-noise ratio as louder signals. The end result is a relatively constant signal-to-noise ratio of approximately 40 dB, with a dynamic range approaching that of 12-bit linear PCM encoding. This method of encoding will find its primary application in voice mail and voice annotation. The reduction in signal-to-error ratio makes it a poor choice for encoding music signals.

Table 27.2 offers a view of the formats supported for recording and playing back digital samples. Where applicable, listed bandwidths set the upper range at a reasonable point to allow for proper attenuation before reaching the Nyquist frequency. Listed signal-to-error ratios for the linear PCM formats are calculated as an ideal bandlimited value. Signal-to-error ratios for the ADPCM formats are approximated, as they will depend on the actual

**TABLE 27.2  Formats Supported for Recording/Playback of Digital Sample**

| Sample format | Linear PCM | | | | | | ADPCM CD-I algorithm | | μLaw/ALaw | | |
|---|---|---|---|---|---|---|---|---|---|---|---|
| Sample rate | 11.025 kHz | | 22.05 | | 44.1 kHz | | 22.05 kHz | 44.1 kHz | 11.025 kHz | 22.05 kHz | 44.1 kHz |
| Bandwidth | 20 Hz to 5 Hz | | 20 Hz to 10 kHz | | 20 Hz to 20 kHz | | 20 Hz to 8.5 kHz | 20 Hz to 17 kHz | 20 Hz to 5 kHz | 20 Hz to 8.5 kHz | 20 Hz to 17 kHz |
| Sample size | 16 | 8 | 16 | 8 | 16 | 8 | 16 to 4 | 16 to 4 | 14 to 8 | 14 to 8 | 14 to 8 |
| Ideal signal-to-error | 96 | 48 | 96 | 48 | 96 | 48 | 60 | 60 | 38 | 38 | 38 |
| Storage required(MEG) | 1.26 | 0.63 | 2.52 | 1.26 | 5.05 | 2.52 | 0.631 | 1.262 | 0.63 | 1.262 | 2.52 |

algorithm used. Signal-to-error ratios for the μ-Law/A-Law companding format are based on ideal bandlimited signals for each sample rate. The storage space required is based on a 30-second, stereo sample file.

## MIDI and Music Synthesis

Music synthesis and MIDI are closely related features on many sound cards. Different methods of designing the music synthesizer, General MIDI, and MPU-401 compatibility all lead to sound devices that have varying levels of performance and abilities. This section will first cover the basic methods of music synthesis being offered in today's market, and will then explain the different architectures and how they combine to become a General MIDI device.

### Music synthesis

The quality of music synthesis found on sound cards available today ranges from the poor tinny sounds of two-operator frequency modulation (FM) to almost professional-quality sample-based synthesis. The intended use of the sound card will go a long way toward determining what type of synthesis method is suitable for the task. A descriptive rating of each of the methods currently in use will now be given.

**Two-operator FM.**   Although two-operator FM offers relatively poor quality in terms of realistic musical instruments, this method enjoys the largest installed user base of any other form of music synthesis on the PC. At the time of introduction on the old Adlib and Soundblaster cards, the Yamaha YM3812 (OPL2) synthesis chip offered one of the only methods of generating musical-instrument sounds on a PC, and due to a lack of any real competition, soon became the standard still supported by most new applications. Even today many of the new "Soundblaster-Compatible" cards being introduced still make use of this outdated technology as their only method of synthesis. As newer technologies begin to take hold and their related price-points drop, it is hoped by many that two-operator FM synthesis will become a thing of the past.

The drawback of OPL2 is the inability of the simple two-operator FM algorithm to properly model the timbre of a real instrument. The results of the standard FM equation $x(t) = A\sin[(wct)+I\sin(wmt)]$ are generally waveforms made of a simple harmonic structure that lack any transients and inharmonic information. Synthesis of the unpitched sounds that define most percussion instruments is impossible to do realistically using this method, resulting in very poor sounds. Figure 27.9 shows the simplified waveform, amplitude envelope, and frequency spectrum that make up a piano sound as generated by the OPL2.

Figure 27.9*a* shows the relatively simple waveform created with the two-operator FM algorithm. The envelope for the sound is generated with a standard four-stage (attack/decay/sustain/release) ADSR, which results in a smooth shape that decays the fundamental at the same relative rate as the harmonics. This style of decay may be seen in the frequency spectrum of

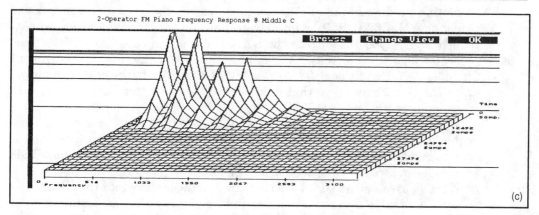

**Figure 27.9**  Waveform (*a*), amplitude (*b*), and frequency (*c*) of a piano sound.

Figure 27.9*c*. The frequency spectrum also shows that the resulting waveform does not contain any of the inharmonic data or transients that add to the coloring of a piano sound.

Apart from the poor quality of its music synthesis, the other problem with OPL2 is that it is able to generate only a very limited number of simultaneous voices. In what is referred to as the *melodic mode* of operation, this device is able to generate only nine simultaneous melodic instrument sounds. If a tenth note were to be struck while the other nine instruments were still decaying, one of those nine would be cut off to allow the new note to play.

The *percussive mode* of operation is somewhat more limiting. This mode sets the operators up for use as six melodic voices and five percussion voices. Within this, the percussion is limited to a kick drum, snare drum, tom-tom, hi-hat, and crash cymbal. Each of these percussion instruments also is assigned to a specific operator able to generate only that style of percussive sound, with any restriking of the instrument cutting off the previous sound.

The third mode of operation, referred to as the *additive mode,* is rarely used, as the instrument sounds generated by using the outputs of all 18 operators are usually of lower quality than those generated with the melodic mode. As all three modes of operation for the OPL2 fail to meet the minimum requirements laid out in the GM System–Level 1 specification, most General MIDI files would not be able to play properly. Many notes would cut out prematurely when new notes were triggered, resulting in a choppy-sounding sequence.

Sound cards that use the OPL2 can be viewed as a poor choice for anything but use as a game card for audio support in older games. MultiMedia presentations, newer entertainment software, and music composition require real-sounding instruments as well as compatibility with GM System–Level 1. The OPL2's shortfalls in these areas should take any sound card using two-operator FM out of the running as a serious multimedia product.

**Four-operator FM.**   The four-operator FM solution for music synthesis is considerably better than its two-operator predecessor. Although it was only recently introduced to the PC sound card market, the basic algorithms of the Yamaha YMF262 (OPL3) chipset have been in use for many years on consumer-level keyboards such as the DX100. The added complexity of the four-operator algorithm increases the quality of most of the melodic-instrument sounds. As an additional feature, the OPL3 is fully backwards-compatible with the OPL2 chipset, so that any older software written for the OPL2 will function properly on the OPL3.

When an instrument on the OPL3 is designed using the four-operator algorithm, the results usually are quite pleasing for many of the melodic-instrument sounds. Figures 27.10, 27.11, and 27.12 show the waveform, amplitude envelope, and frequency spectrum of a piano sound generated on the OPL3.

If the figures for the OPL3 are compared to those shown for the OPL2, it is readily noticeable that the waveform and frequency spectrum contain a great deal more harmonic information. This results in sound that is much closer to that of a real piano. There are however certain drawbacks with the OPL3. Sound cards using the OPL3 chipset generally claim to have a 20-voice synthesizer. What isn't widely known is that the number of available voices depends entirely on the mode of operation for which the chip is programmed. The first two modes of operation are for either 18 simultaneous melodic sounds or 15 melodic sounds with 5 percussive sounds.

When operating in one of these two modes, the chip is using two-operator

**Figure 27.10**   Wave of a piano sound—OPL3.

**Figure 27.11**   Amplitude of a piano sound—OPL3.

**Figure 27.12**   Frequency of a piano sound—OPL3.

FM algorithms for each of the voices. The richer-sounding four-operator instruments are not available. The end result is almost like having a card with two OPL2 chips on it. The other two modes of operation are either 6 four-operator melodic sounds plus 6 two-operator melodic sounds; or 6 four-operator melodic sounds, 3 two-operator melodic sounds, and 5 percussive sounds. The first four-operator mode is capable of producing only 12 simultaneous melodic voices, while the second can produce 9 simultaneous melodic voices and 5 percussive voices.

Although the OPL3 is able to offer more simultaneous voices than the OPL2, it still falls short of the minimum requirements for GM System–Level 1 compatibility. The only mode that approaches the required performance uses the lower-quality two-operator algorithm. In a similar manner to the OPL2, the OPL3 is unable to reproduce realistic percussion sounds and still has the limitation to the same 5 basic percussion instruments. This number of percussion sounds, as well as the specific assignment of sound to operator, greatly reduces the flexibility of the device. This structure doesn't allow for dynamic allocation of the base percussive instruments, as required for GM compatibility. To this is added the great difficulty in properly modeling unpitched timbres with the FM algorithms, resulting in the same poor-sounding percussion instruments found on the OPL2.

Although the OPL3 is able to offer much better-sounding melodic instruments than the OPL2, the limited number of four-operator voices generally results in many applications using the two-operator algorithms to generate more simultaneous sounds. Sound cards using the OPL3 may be viewed as a reasonably good choice for a multimedia device if the music-synthesis quality for melodic instruments can suffer a bit, and if there is no need for full GM System–Level 1 compatibility.

**Wave-table lookup/sample-based.**   The wave-table lookup method of synthesis is a relative newcomer to the PC sound card market. This method differs from the FM-based systems in that it uses looped samples of instruments to synthesize the musical notes. This method generally offers a higher quality of synthesis than the FM methods, due to the more complex harmonic information contained in the instrument samples. Figures 27.13, 27.14, and 27.15 show the waveform, amplitude envelope, and frequency spectrum of a piano sound generated with a wave-table/sample-based synthesizer.

When compared to the corresponding FM methods, it is readily noticeable that this method produces a more complex waveform, envelope, and frequency spectrum, resulting in a sound that is a great deal closer to that of a real piano. This complexity comes from modeling the instrument with two sampled waveforms, each having a complex, logarithmic 8-stage envelope that allows for more control of the output amplitudes as the note decays. One of the important benefits this method offers is the ability to synthesize the complex, unpitched percussion sounds from straight PCM sample tables.

This higher quality does come at an additional cost, in the form of the large amounts of ROM needed to store the library of wave-table loops and samples.

**Figure 27.13**   Synthesizer-based piano-sound waveform.

**Figure 27.14**   Synthesizer-based piano-sound amplitude.

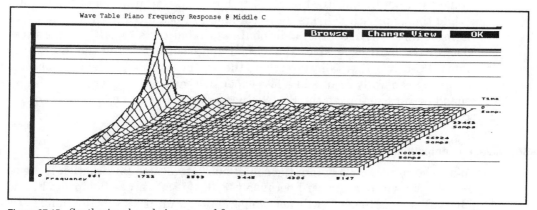

**Figure 27.15**   Synthesizer-based piano-sound frequency.

It is at this point that sound cards using a wave-table/sample-based synthesizer will begin to vary in both price and quality. The sound ROMs may be 8 or 16 bits wide, and vary in size from 0.5 to greater than 4 megs of stored samples. To approach professional quality, a system typically has to be made with 4 megs of 16-bit samples. Where professional quality isn't quite necessary, a 0.5-meg ROM is large enough to build instruments for the General MIDI map that are considerably better-sounding than either of the FM techniques. Another option found on some sound cards based on this style is the addition of RAM banks that allow the user to create custom instruments on the PC. This is especially beneficial for applications that require sound effects. The wave-table/sample-based sound cards on the market today offer GM System–Level 1 compatibility with a performance range of 24 to 32 dynamically allocated voices, depending on the synthesis chipset being used.

Although wave-table/sample-based synthesizers sound a great deal better than the FM solutions, the needs of the end user must still be the criterion used to determine which of the many sound cards using this method is best for the application. The best method of deciding is to set a purchase-price range and then audition the available cards that fall within that range.

### MIDI and the sound card

To complete the GM System–Level 1 compatibility requirements, the sound card must offer some means of interpreting the stream of MIDI commands into the data required to set up and play the various instruments. This is accomplished through the use of a MIDI interpreter, which intercepts the MIDI messages and translates them into the format expected by the synthesizer. Depending on the design of the card, this interpreter will reside as part of an audio driver on the PC or be built into the hardware on the card through the use of a microcontroller. The method of implementation essentially comes down to a cost versus functionality issue.

The complexity of the interpreter would require the addition of a microcontroller and additional ROM or RAM to handle the translation of MIDI data. While this approach delivers a system able to work directly with more existing software packages, the additional associated costs typically make these devices the most expensive. The second approach is to build the interpreter into a PC-driver that talks directly to the synthesizer. Implementation of this approach generally results in a less expensive card, at the expense of a larger sound-driver existing on the PC. Neither approach has an effect on the quality of the synthesis.

### Soundblaster compatibility

Whenever a new card enters the sound market, a catch-22 situation is created. No one will buy the card because very little software will support it, and the software developers will not support a card until it is in the hands of a large number of consumers. Although this has been alleviated somewhat through the development of the multimedia extensions under Windows 3.1, the most important support comes from the independent software vendors (ISVs), the companies that make the games. Because of this, it has become something of a necessity that new cards be backwards-compatible with a Rev. 1.5 Soundblaster card. This compatibility gives the card both instant support for existing applications as well as continued support from new titles, until the ISVs begin to support the new card in its native mode.

It should be noted that the need for this compatibility is starting to fade as newer software titles are switching to the use of audio APIs that allow software vendors to use one audio driver library that talks to secondary drivers supplied by the sound card manufacturers. The introduction of this philosophy allows these vendors to offer native-mode support of any sound card that supplies the secondary driver.

This feature is meant solely for use of the sound card with older entertainment software that was written with sound support for Yamaha's two-operator FM chip (OPL2) and the single 8-bit digital-audio channel found on the old Soundblaster cards. There are currently three methods being used for offering this compatibility; two work very well, and the other is a kluge that is prone to problems.

The first way to emulate Soundblaster is to design what is essentially a Soundblaster clone. This method will use either the Yamaha OPL2 or the backwards-compatible four-operator OPL3 chipset for the FM music synthesis, and a PCM channel that responds in the same way as on a Soundblaster card. Many sound cards on the market use this approach and are able to offer full compatibility with the older card. The net result is that all of these cards use the same tinny FM sound for both older and new applications, and are unable to offer the higher-quality wave-table and sample-based synthesis methods now appearing on the market.

The second way is to offer register (hardware) -level compatibility to make the card appear like a Soundblaster to the applications, but use a digital signal processor (DSP) to emulate the two-operator FM synthesis algorithms and handle the command interpretation. This method is then able to offer support to the older applications that were written for the Soundblaster, as well as to implement the higher-quality wave-table and sample-based synthesis methods for newer applications at no extra cost for additional hardware. The drawback to this approach is that the complexity of emulation may force the emulation to use a lower sample rate for the synthesis than what is used by the Yamaha OPLx chipsets. This causes a reduction in the reproducible bandwidth, resulting in a slightly duller sound.

The third method currently being used is the trickiest to implement and results in the least reliable form of emulation. This method uses a combination of a Terminate and Stay Resident (TSR) program on the PC, which intercepts the commands and data being written to the soundblaster, and a wave-table-based synthesizer. Many potential problems exist with this style of implementation.

Without getting into detail, the following drawbacks are found with this implementation. The lower memory used by the TSR is in some cases too large to allow the game to operate with full functionality. If there isn't enough lower memory available, the game either will not run or will run in some form of reduced functionality. Most software developers will drop or reduce the audio support first, to ensure that enough memory remains to let the rest of the game operate, rendering the TSR useless.

The second problem lies in the CPU overhead taken by the TSR. As some of the more complex games attempt to use all of the available processing power from the PC, the TSR's overhead may cause the game to slow down.

The third problem lies in converting FM parameters to a wave-table sound. The difficulty found in this conversion can result in the occasional wrong sound being played. This occurs most often when creating special effects from an FM operator.

The final potential problem is that the method of trapping the commands and data may not be supported by the hardware found in all machines. On the up side, the games that do work properly with this method will have a greatly improved soundtrack, as well as be able to offer at no increased cost the higher-quality wave-table and sample-based synthesis for newer applications.

## The Digital Signal Processor Platform

As with so many high-technology purchases today, the consumer's underlying fear is of obsolescence. This concern is justified when it comes to purchasing a sound card for multimedia applications. Just within the last year (1993), four significant advances in audio-processing technology have arrived in the multimedia sound card market. These include speech recognition, speech synthesis, audio compression routines, and Qsound™ three-dimensional audio. Each of these technologies has one thing in common: each uses computation-intensive algorithms that require powerful microprocessors with special architectures to run in real time. To get an idea of the processing power required to implement these new features, look at this table, showing the percentage of utilization some of these algorithms require when they are executed on a 10-MIPS digital signal processor:

| Algorithm | Percentage of 10-MIPS DSP |
| --- | --- |
| Speaker-independent speech recognition | 33 |
| ADPCM compression—mono, 22.05-kHz | 32 |
| ADPCM decompression—mono, 22.05-kHz | 25 |
| Qsound 3D audio—22.05-kHz | 24 |

With the majority of sound cards being designed as closed systems that offer only the basic features, the only ways to introduce this new technology would be (1) with hardware changes and daughter boards, (2) by the purchase of a newer device, or (3) by relegating the processing overhead of new technology to the PC. The first two methods come at considerable expense to the consumer and shouldn't even be considered at this time. While the third approach doesn't require additional hardware, it is limited by the type of audio application and by the performance required to execute the algorithms in real time.

Algorithms such as speech recognition, speech synthesis, and ADPCM are able to function as a PC-based application. This is because these algorithms process the audio signal either after it has been recorded or prior to its being played back. In the case of speech synthesis, the application itself generates the digital signal. The only consideration for running these algorithms on the PC is the large processing overhead needed for real-time operation. The utilization table just given shows how large this overhead is. Other algorithms such as Qsound 3-D Audio and any type of reverb or chorusing effect require a much more integrated design that allows these functions to operate on both the PCM audio and music-synthesis signals. The only way to implement this would be to build these algorithms into the hardware. This could be done only on an open-ended system.

One of the newer entrants to the sound card market makes use of the open architecture required for implementing new technology while avoiding the expense of purchasing additional hardware and without taxing the limited resources of the PC. This architecture will use a multipurpose digital signal processor (DSP) as the main controller of all audio signals in the digital domain. The key feature of this system in the DSP is a dedicated microprocessor specifically designed to implement the computation-intensive algorithms that are the backbone of the new audio technology entering the multimedia market. The open architecture allows for new DSP applications to be developed and downloaded to the sound card. This allows the vendor to upgrade consumers with new developments at a very low cost, and without placing a heavy processing burden on the host PC.

Apart from the introduction of new technology, a sound card designed using the DSP platform gives the sound card the ability to perform functions that it is either not possible or practical to do on the PC. These functions may include the application of signal-conditioning algorithms on the digital audio stream, in the form of digital filtering to remove image frequencies and to avoid aliasing and noise-shaping algorithms and thereby mask the effects of signal manipulation in the digital domain. Other applications may take the form of real-time 3D audio, reverb, and chorusing algorithms, applied to the output of the music synthesizer on a voice-by-voice or MIDI-channel basis. These applications just can't be done on the PC, and can't be added to a closed-architecture system without additional dedicated hardware.

At this time, choosing a sound card that is based upon an open architecture and uses a digital signal processor is the wisest choice for the end user concerned about obsolescence. Even if upgrades to future technologies are not a primary concern, the additional processing taken on by the sound card frees up the PC to perform other functions.

## Acknowledgment

I would like to thank Bill Arab for his patient editing and constructive criticism of this article—man, is he quick with a pen!

# 28

# Bringing the Senses to Multimedia

## Serge Timacheff

## Adapting Machines to Humans

Narcissism runs rampant in the computer industry. We wallow egocentrically through technological developments and growth stages, believing we're the only ones who have experienced the process. This is a natural tendency, because it is shrouded by the technology itself—it's hard to believe that history is repeating itself when the products and inventions are so unique and different from anything ever created. In truth, however, many other industries, including the automobile, telephone, radio, and television industries, have experienced parallel stages of development, and taking a look at them can provide us with insights into our own efforts. Multimedia, in particular, takes advantage of a number of technological innovations and developments, and consequently it is more easily understood when its precedents have been seen from the perspectives of other industries.

### Cars and computers

The IBM PC is barely more than 10 years old. It's easy to forget that, so prevalent is it in our lives. Yet that prevalence pales in comparison with the penetration of the automobile into everyday life. While millions of people do not know how to use a personal computer, an adult that does not know how to drive a car is not so much a rarity as an oddity. How did the car get to this point in our lives, and what does that have to do with the PC industry?

The beginning of any technology is characterized by the attempt to replace and better an existing process. The automobile was created as a replacement for the horse and buggy, and early cars looked very much like buggies. In fact they were capable of little more than buggies, and most people felt no compelling urge to buy one. The early computers, likewise, were simply replacements for typewriters and calculators, and held little promise of doing more than adding unnecessary complications to our lives.

Other manufacturers became interested in automobiles, which is when the design and form factors began to change. Although relatively few autos were being sold, the companies making them believed the market would grow if people could use them for tasks unsuited for horse-drawn vehicles. The only truly interested "users" were tinkerers who were willing to dedicate a great deal of effort to understanding the technology and dealing with the problems. And so it was for the early PC adopters. Essentially, the computer "nerd" and the car mechanic were of a piece—humans who had adapted to a machine.

Business became interested as auto designs and the roadways accommodated the needs of business. Cars became more reliable; roadways and car designs permitted transport of products; cars' speed and relatively low maintenance costs and issues (live animals were more difficult to maintain) made them more attractive. While autos were still not very easy to operate (they had many levers and parts, broke down frequently, required extensive maintenance and difficult-to-obtain parts, etc.), they began to service business in ways an animal-drawn vehicle could not. The official interest of business in this new technology served to legitimize it as a unique, accepted solution that bettered the previous method.

Similarly, businesses began to adopt PCs to do word processing, spreadsheets, and databases, which were essentially tasks that had been done by hand before but could be done faster and more accurately by a machine. As workable, reliable software became available, and compatible means of exchanging data, data entry and output, and other necessities became standardized, the PC quickly began to replace typewriters, calculators, manual methods, and other less sophisticated tools. As with autos, the interest of business in computers legitimized the PC as a unique tool for meeting basic needs.

When businesses began to order automobiles, and manufacturing became more automated and voluminous, prices dropped. At the same time people at home witnessed the advantage businesses and government derived from using vehicles for everything from mail and milk delivery to mass transit. With prices within reach of the family, "home users" became interested in automobiles because they allowed them to go places they couldn't reach before. Our national support and interest in large parks was largely tied to the ability of the average person to reach them recreationally. And the freedom of being able to drive to work independently without having to rely on mass transit was a new sport in itself.

While there was an early interest in "home computers," the home market didn't truly blossom until after computers had been firmly established in the workplace. The development of significant brands and choices of personal-productivity, recreational, educational, and home-office software helped to drive the interest in using computers at home. Furthermore, powerful laptop and notebook computers could be taken home from the office where family members could use them, or so that information could be transferred from one to the other.

With growth, however, come new problems. In the case of the auto, no matter how affordable, powerful, or reliable a car might be, it was of limited use if there were no roads to travel on, no standards of navigation, or no maps to guide people. Operational standards, as well, became an issue, so that a person would not have to go through a steep learning curve each time a new vehicle was purchased or driven.

Of course compatibility, network connectivity, standardization of hardware and software, and consistency of operation are issues that continue to plague the computer industry. In many cases users have found computers to be of limited use in circumstances where necessary hardware or software is unavailable, underpowered, or incompatible. For the average user, and for the new user in particular, these problems can be the greatest impediment and source of frustration in PC wrangling.

At the same time as it was tackling issues of navigation and accessibility, the auto industry was embarked on the exploration of another issue critical to technological product design, acceptance, and use: ergonomics. There are two halves of ergonomics, although only one is popularly recognized. When most people hear the word *ergonomics,* they think of what scientists call *physical ergonomics:* how a product is shaped to fit the body. This means making a seat that fits the average person but also adjusts for other sizes; developing a steering wheel that is at the right distance and with the proper (or adjustable) height, with controls accessible while driving, and so on.

Researchers commonly refer to another half of ergonomics, however, known as *cognitive ergonomics,* or in other words how a product is shaped to fit the *mind.* In the instance of an automobile, this would mean making a dashboard that includes symbols and gauges that can be easily read at a glance (before you careen into a tree), and placing controls in logical locations. When you rent a car, it is cognitive ergonomics, made consistent, accessible, and universal, that permit you to easily read the controls and immediately drive away safely.

One good example of faulty cognitive ergonomics is the common kitchen stove. While the burners are positioned in a square, the knobs operating them are arranged in a line, thus requiring labeling (e.g., left rear, right front, etc.). The product has not been designed to logically fit the user's mind, even though the physical positioning of the knobs and burners may be perfect.

Physical ergonomics have been an important consideration in the computer industry for some time, including as they relate to such issues as radiation dangers from monitor emissions, proper office furniture and its positioning for the prevention of back pain and eye strain, and repetitive stress injuries like carpal tunnel syndrome. In software, having dark text on a light background, colors that are friendly to the eye, and even the ability to randomly access any point on the screen using a mouse (instead of cursor keys) make a difference physically. All of these factors continue to play a major role in the development of computers and computer-related hardware and software products.

Cognitive ergonomics play a role in both hardware and software, as well. Opportunities to make software more intuitive and accessible continue to abound, and products such as Microsoft Windows have increased personalization and customization capabilities dramatically. This makes for products far better tuned to the mind of the user. From a hardware perspective, the addition of a capability such as being able to attach a double-click to a single button on a multibutton mouse not only increases and simplifies usability, it also decreases repetitive motions and therefore has a physical benefit as well. As with the previous example of the stove, the logical placement of buttons, controls, disk drives, and the like can play a meaningful role in increasing cognitive connection between user and product.

While the auto industry presently has much more penetration into mainstream users than PCs, nevertheless the PC is on a similar track of development. Down that track will come additional opportunities as well as challenges. Today PCs are becoming even more like cars in that the market has become one of commodities, and it has become increasingly difficult to differentiate between products. Original, unique products are becoming more rare. Where is this track taking us, and what can we learn from the automobile?

There is still a long way to go before PCs are as common as cars. However, the recent and ongoing trend of systems toward the integration of sight, sound, and touch enhances the physical and cognitive-ergonomic attributes of the PC as well. By opening up the use of multiple senses, our access to multimedia is widened proportionally.

## Adding Senses to Computers

If a person is hammering a nail into a board with a rock, the mentality of today's computer industry is to invent a complicated, overly "techie" device, hand it to the person, and expect him or her to somehow integrate the device into his/her set of tasks. Other industries that have been through the technological "gap," such as the auto industry, will observe the person with the rock, develop a tool—in this case, a hammer—give it to the person and say, "Try this; see if it does the job better."

We can no longer afford to throw technology at potential or actual computer users and expect them to integrate it with what they're doing. They just don't want to take the time. This simply will not work when it comes to the mass consumption of a technology—which is why the average person cannot program his or her own VCR. Perhaps the most fundamental and critical element of technological development is user perspective. While manufacturers realize that the general public is interested in their products, they should also realize that listening to the user is a critical part of the development process. Developers walk a fine line between leading with technological innovation and listening to what needs to be changed in existing technology.

Clearly, what users want from multimedia is integration, simplicity, and consistency. It's wonderful to be able to use sight, sound, touch, video, music, and everything else associated with multimedia, but if there is no easy way to use or learn to use these products together, once again people are frustrated. The industry seems always to stay one leap ahead of users, tantalizing and frustrating them with a glimpse of a higher, more exciting platform of technology just as they had managed to climb up to the previous one.

How can this be achieved? With the massive features sets and capabilities required of the average multimedia software package today, how can we possibly simplify product usage?

## Consistency

Our first step in laying a path toward technological viability and user acceptance of multimedia applications and hardware must be to come up with consistency of interface in both hardware and software. If consistency is unachievable, then it must be replaced by simplicity. Microsoft Windows was a conceptual leap for the industry by offering the potential for a consistent interface among applications. Suddenly users were able to try out numerous applications without first reading the manual extensively, remembering large sets of commands, or wallowing through a tutorial.

Yet there is enough complexity and flexibility in the design of Windows applications that consistency can be lost, often with negative results. Very often this occurs when applications incorporate modules designed by separate groups or even separate companies. Corel Systems has been through this process in its development of CorelDraw 4.0, a popular Windows-based software package that integrates drawing, image-editing, animation, presentation graphics, charting, and other modules. Earlier versions of the program included modules that did not feature a consistent interface with the primary drawing module, and consequently these were used less, if at all. In some cases, such as with the Corel Photo-Paint image-editing module, the company actually went back and brought modules in house to develop from scratch so that they could be made consistent. This effort is paying off for the company in usability, reviews, and general success for the product overall.

The implementation of standards such as APIs (application program interfaces) to allow consistent access and interaction between various types of hardware and software also is as important as having common types of gasoline or consistently threaded gas-tank caps. The TWAIN standard, developed by Caere, Logitech, Aldus, Kodak, and Hewlett-Packard and supported by a multitude of hardware and software vendors, provides various Windows applications with direct support for digital scanners, cameras, and other imaging devices. Users are assured of a consistent interface and system for acquiring images with their hardware, no matter what application they are using (providing it is TWAIN-compliant). These types of standards make access to complex technology that much easier for the average user to gain.

Hardware consistency is important when it comes to products that incorporate significant hands-on control. Keyboards have faced this issue for some time; little explanation is necessary, other than to say that any new keyboard designs are faced with the challenge of keeping the keys in the same place while making significant other changes, such as making the board more ergonomic or incorporating a pointing device such as a trackball on-board. Another example is the DIP switches and jumpers on boards, which can be a nightmare to figure out when installing a new one into a computer; the answer here is to eliminate them completely and allow the user to make any changes through the software during installation.

There is an ongoing need to incorporate consistency in all applications, environments, and hardware. It is difficult to retrofit, and lack of foresight can be costly. It is in the design phase that the implementation of consistency must take place.

### Touch, sound, and sight—the present and future of Senseware

By making a computer more "human," we adapt it to the user, instead of forcing the user to adapt to the machine. The way in which we give this more human character to a PC is by giving it human attributes—in particular, the basic senses of sight, sound, and touch. This general category of computing products and capabilities is broadly referred to as *Senseware,* a term coined by Logitech in 1992 as an umbrella definition of its diverse product line.

Unwittingly, the development of the graphical user interface (GUI) actually fits into the Senseware definition and largely facilitates the use of the senses in computing. Instead of remembering and typing commands, GUI users can visually navigate through programs and environments, can reach into the program using a mouse or other pointing device and "touch" things and move them around, and today can hear various things happen or can attach sounds or music to objects. Since a GUI is largely a standardized, consistent environment, users can wander and meander around relatively fearlessly and quite comfortably.

Scanners, digital cameras, and other imaging devices give computers a sense of sight; various types of pointing devices give it a sense of touch; and sound products give it hearing and speech. Various GUIs, as mentioned above, permit visual navigation using multiple senses.

The future of Senseware is not necessarily in the addition of smell and taste to the "sensorium." Rather it may be in the enhancement of the existing PC senses to make them more highly defined and sensitive.

**Touch.** The incorporation of three-dimensional, interactive touch is a necessary and important step in the development of this computer sense, and will be of great use in multimedia. Today most users associate touch with being able to move and manipulate objects in a two-dimensional environment. In the near term, three-dimensional pointing devices will become widely popular and affordable. Today they are much more common in specific markets such as gaming, animation, robotics, and CAD. The mouse and trackball as we know them today will become antiques, as a variety of 3D devices emerge to accomplish all tasks necessary. This type of product will provide the same full range of three-dimensional motion (technically known as *six degrees of motion: x, y, z* axes combined with pitch, roll, and yaw) that your hand does.

Another very important development of pointing devices will be the incorporation of advanced interactivity. Almost all pointing devices today are limited to input only; however, to truly affect the sense of touch, the ability of the user to "feel" when inside the computer is necessary. Ultimately we'll be able to feel surfaces, textures, gradations, and the like with our pointing devices. Logitech has come up with a device, recently (1993) announced, which represents a primitive beginning of this new phase; the product, CyberMan, is a combination of a trackball and a mouse that includes full three-dimensional control along with a vibrator incorporated in the device. The device is called a "three-dimensional interactive controller," and is specifically designed for interactive role-playing games such as Castle Wolfenstein from ID Software. Every time the user is "zapped," the vibrator goes off. The 3D control allows the user to navigate easily through a full environment with one hand (joysticks, mice, trackballs, and other conventional pointing devices are all limited in their control of the 3D environment).

When these 3D pointing devices become more common in business and home use, we'll see some true enhancements to the way we compute. For example, in 3D it is much easier to store information; just as you stack information on your desk or in a filing cabinet, you can do the same on your PC. If you had a 3D "filing cabinet," you could use your 3D pointing device to rifle through the file "folders," read the label of each, pick one and pull it out, and open it. Users will find this a much more natural way of learning about accessing data than having to look for and call up files in a conventional text-based system, or even in text sections of a GUI.

In multimedia, pointing devices are critical to developing and controlling presentations, and as the multimedium grows, so will the need for more sophisticated devices and their capabilities. Three-dimensional, interactive control will become the standard, as will support for remote devices that allow a presentation to be controlled from a distance.

**Sound.**   Almost more than any other medium, sound can add incredible depth, power, and variety to communication. The range and diversity of sound can be fully utilized with voice, sound effects, and music, but to do so the PC must be equipped to handle sound with a device that can acquire and output sound. Today, most PCs are limited to being able to record sounds, embed them and share them among applications using object-linking and -embedding techniques (OLE), and play them back via speakers or headphones. Unfortunately, sound on the IBM PC and compatibles is somewhat of a retrofit, since support for sound is not natively supported; this means that sound must be added as an aftermarket product.

The use of sound to control a computer will become increasingly popular, but it will not supersede pointing devices or other navigational GUI controls. Certainly, however, the use of sound to control PCs will have become commonplace well before computers are able to understand language or even to perform basic tasks such as taking dictation. This is true primarily because navigational control of software by a sound device is limited to the sound software having to recognize only a limited set of commands ("open," "close file," "search for," etc.). For a PC to take dictation is much more akin to OCR, with every word and sound in the language having to be recognized—which represents exponentially more detail and accuracy.

Sound is a critical element of multimedia, and will continue to play a leading role. Virtually every package supporting presentations or even graphics today includes support for sound, and as a result the hardware market supporting it is burgeoning, as is the software aftermarket of add-on products such as clip-sounds and music. Much like the revolution in clip-art and graphics that was ushered in by the explosion of the graphics market 5 years ago, sound is experiencing the same growth.

**Sight.**   While graphics are common in today's PCs, the ability to acquire them has not always been a simple or natural process. In the last few years, broader and more sophisticated support of scanners and other digital-imaging devices has made it easier for users to work with images; additionally, the various software applications supporting images can take advantage of the huge CD-ROM clip-art and clip-photo market. As mentioned earlier, standards such as TWAIN make it significantly easier to give a computer a sense of sight.

Multimedia images can be still- or motion-based, but in either case are indispensable elements on PCs today. Animation of graphic images (no matter what their source), and digital-graphic techniques such as morphing and warping, are now enhancing those images. The challenge is to make the integration of motion and still images an easy process for the average user, and to bring images and video up to the level of quality users have come to expect from home stereos, televisions, and cameras. The problem once again lies in the retrofit: the average IBM PC–compatible, no matter how powerful, simply was not designed to acquire, manage, and transmit the sheer volume of data required for sound and imaging today.

As we move on to future systems, the need for easy access to large information-storage areas and the ability to easily transfer that information among systems are critical issues for multimedia. Increasing the bandwidth of communication by increasing the sensory capabilities of the PC also increases the amount of information that must be processed and transmitted.

## Conclusion

We know from research that the employment of multiple senses in the use and delivery of information is more effective, leads to better retention, and has greater impact. The ability of the system to incorporate these senses is a critical precedent to the use of multimedia. Without a Senseware-compatible system, multimedia is senseless.

Yet there are problems. Lack of consistency continues to plague users, an overabundance of often unnecessary features clutters the average application, and massive amounts of data crowd hard disks, as well as modem and network lines, as badly as Grand Central Station on a Monday morning.

A growing notion among manufacturers is that working interactively with users so as to understand their needs on physical, emotional, and cognitive levels is central to the development of successful products. Furthermore, companies are learning that strategic alliances can do more than just achieve saleable bundles—they can help companies to benefit from common experiences and can serve to develop more consistent standards in both hardware and software.

Before multimedia capabilities can be delivered to the masses, a number of key milestones will have to be passed. Other technologies have passed or are passing through similar curves of societal acceptance, and these provide a great deal of insight into our own plight in the computer industry.

The incorporation of the senses into computing is but one of these milestones. However, it will help computing to seem more natural to the uninitiated user, enhance existing applications, and be a necessary component of others. The computer equipped with senses is a computer equipped to communicate more effectively and efficiently with its user. It ceases to be an office machine and becomes an intellectual partner, a unique, creative tool suited and personalized to the unique and creative needs of its user.

# Using Audio in Multimedia Applications

## Potential Applications and Design Considerations

**Mary F. Whiteside**

**J. Alan Whiteside**

## Types of Audio

Several different types of audio output—speech, music, and sound effects—can be incorporated into multimedia. To use each type effectively, multimedia developers need to learn more about how each of the types can be used to improve their programs.

### Speech

Two types of speech are available for use by multimedia developers: *digitized* and *synthesized*. Digitized speech provides high-quality, natural speech, but requires significant disk-storage capacity. Synthesized speech, on the other hand, is not as storage-intensive, but may not sound as natural as human speech (Jones, 1989). Even with improved techniques for generating speech, it is not incorporated into multimedia programs as often as it could be. This may be due to a lack of understanding of how high-quality speech is produced, as well as to an undervaluing of the impact speech can have on computer-delivered instructional or informational programs. Speech is an important element of human communication and can be used effectively to transmit information. One advantage of using natural speech is the power of the human voice to persuade (Johnson, 1987). Another advantage is that speech can potentially eliminate the need to display large amounts of text on the screen (Dean and Whitlock, 1989).

### Music

Like speech, music is an important component of human communication. Unlike speech, however, music usually does not carry the primary or instructional message of a multimedia program. Most often, music is used to set a tone or mood, provide connections or transitions, add interest or excitement, and evoke emotion. Music, especially when combined with speech and sound effects, can greatly enhance on-screen presentations of text and visuals. To make full use of its power, developers need to become more sensitive to the effective uses of music. Music should be considered as a powerful tool that can help to ensure the success of a multimedia program.

### Sound effects

Sound effects are used to enhance or augment the presentation of information and instruction. Two types of sound effects are *natural* and *synthetic*. Natural sounds are the unadorned, commonplace sounds that occur around us. Synthetic sounds are those that are produced electronically or artificially. The sound effects produced for radio shows in the past elevated artificially produced sound effects to an art form.

In addition there are two general categories of sound effects: *ambient* and *special*. Ambient sounds are the background or "atmosphere" sounds that communicate the context of the scene or place to the listener. Special sounds, on the other hand, are uniquely identifiable sounds, such as the ring of a telephone or the slam of a door, that complement narration and/or visuals. Similar to the use of music, sound effects are an effective way of telling a story and communicating information.

### Reasons to Use Audio

Audio can improve a multimedia presentation in many ways. However, *channel redundancy* and *motivation* are two reasons to use audio to ensure that the goals and objectives of the program are met. Since channel redundancy and motivation are principles that have emerged from research on human learning, they are particularly related to programs that have an instructional message. However, these principles also apply to informational presentations in which understanding and persuasion are important.

### Channel redundancy

The research of Hsia (1977) shows that redundancy is the key to better communication. He defines redundancy as *the transmission of the same or closely related information to the receiver or learner through two sensory channels (usually the aural and visual channels)*. The capacity of the human information system is limited, and therefore information loss and error do occur. Redundancy is probably the key to minimizing these factors. Thus, presenting information via more than one communication channel increases the chances that the message will be attended to, understood, and remembered.

However, two conditions influence the effectiveness of using multiple channels:

1. Information presented in each modality must be congruent (similar and not contradictory).
2. Identical presentations of words in sound and text should be avoided.*

As an additional communication channel for multimedia, audio can improve a user's ability to understand and learn the information presented.

## Increased motivation

The extent to which the instruction or information presented in a multimedia program will be received, understood, and remembered depends to a great extent on the user's motivation and interest. Motivation affects the amount of effort potential users will put into a program, and thus affects their commitment to accomplishing the goals or objectives of the program. A multimedia developer needs to be concerned about stimulating the users' motivation in all parts of a program, not just in the beginning. Audio can be an important tool for accomplishing this.

At the beginning of a program, the user's attention can be grabbed by inserting an interesting story delivered by a narrator or actor, or music can be used. In addition, using audio to vary the way different components or chunks of information are presented can stimulate curiosity and maintain the user's interest in the program.

Analogies or metaphors that are used to connect the program material to the processes, concepts, and skills familiar to the user will help to improve motivation (Keller and Burkman, 1993). Audio can be used to support these techniques. Music and sound effects can augment the use of metaphors, and narrative can be used to provide oral analogies and explanations.

Motivation also is improved by the use of anecdotes or vignettes related to the area of study or the information being presented (Keller and Burkman, 1993). Audio can be very effective in providing stories, interviews, or conversations that highlight the human or personal element. In fact, narrative speech can be used in a variety of motivating ways by relating the information to the user and making the presentation more personal. Music and sound effects also can increase motivation by adding realism and interest to visual presentations.

Audio also can provide an alternative learning mode and, therefore, attract learners who prefer to learn by listening. The use of multiple channels to present information does provide motivation for those learners who may have difficulty learning; they may find more success when learning from programs that use audio and visual modes. These users will be motivated by greater success or increased ease of learning.

---

*Hannafin and Hooper, 1993.

Motivation can be increased in a variety of ways by integrating audio. A skilled multimedia developer will capitalize on the use of audio to ensure that the goals of either an informational or instructional program are met.

## Suggestions for Developing or Selecting Audio

Since the use of audio is new to many multimedia developers, few have had opportunities to learn how to integrate audio into informational or instructional programs. Very few published sources provide information about writing narration or selecting music and sound effects. However, general suggestions can be drawn from techniques applied in other media.

### Developing speech

To produce high-quality recorded speech, a script should be written and professionally recorded. Digitized audio and small, high-quality microphones are now available, which means that recording can be accomplished without the use of sophisticated recording studios and expensive equipment. However, having a professional narrator with clear diction and the ability to correctly pronounce the technical words in the script is still a big plus.

To provide balance, both female and male narrators should be used. Nonprofessional narrators, such as subject-matter experts or corporate officers, may be used to provide credibility, and occasionally audience peers may be used to add interest to a program. However, when content needs to be explained or information needs to be delivered accurately, a professional should be used. Professional narrators usually can be relied upon to follow the specifications of the script and to deliver a professional-sounding audio track.

Overall, narration for multimedia programs should follow the general rules and conventions followed for other media, such as video, that integrate speech as part of the presentation of information or instruction. In general, to be effective, a narrator should

- Vary intonation to motivate, explain, provoke, exhort, or empathize
- Use a conversational tone
- Be amiable, candid, sincere, and straightforward
- Avoid sounding arrogant, pretentious, flippant, disrespectful, or sarcastic
- Avoid a lecturing tone
- Vary tone of voice to help viewers/listeners understand what is important

When you are recording narrative speech, be sure to eliminate background or ambient sound unless it is used to provide a realistic environment. On occasion, incorporating ambient sound can be effective, since it can be used to help establish a mood or to increase the feeling of reality.

Good writing techniques are essential to the development of successful multimedia programs. Thus, to integrate speech as an effective tool, developers must learn to write effective narration as a part of a program script. Very few of the many books and articles that explain how to develop computer-based or interactive videodisc-based programs include information about writing or using narration. However, general guidelines can be gathered from the techniques used for scriptwriting in other media. To develop narrative scripts for integrating speech, multimedia developers should

- Write the way people speak
- Use language the audience can understand
- Write as if the narrator were teaching or speaking with one person
- Write in a clear, straightforward manner
- Write in short sentences that can be spoken in a single breath
- Use second-person pronouns—*you* and *your*
- Use contractions and other simplified forms that are used in speech
- Emphasize clarity and simplicity
- Omit needless words
- Avoid slang
- Avoid the oral presentation of figures and statistics
- Use humor when appropriate
- Present information in small chunks
- Emphasize the objectives or goals of the program
- Interpret what the user or learner is seeing rather than simply describe it
- Make the visuals and narration go hand-in-hand; usually the visuals tell the story and the narration interprets, explains, or elaborates
- Adhere to time limits and length requirements
- Understand the capabilities and limitations of multimedia hardware and software, especially as related to the use of speech

Narration written for presentation in multimedia should be read aloud and then revised if it sounds awkward, stilted, or boring. Reading the narration aloud also allows the developer to check timing; timing is important, since the narrative often must be synchronized to the visuals being presented. As the narrator explains, elaborates, or focuses attention on visual images on the screen, visual effects such as changes in color, position, or size can be used to emphasize specific points.

Many writers suggest that narration is more human when it relates ideas to people. In other words, they say that we should develop topics in terms of people's problems, interests, and activities. To raise the level of user interest, quotes, conversations, and case studies could be included in audio scripts. Swain and Swain (1991, p. 60) write that "too often we let the element of life slip out" of written scripts. To improve the naturalness or personal tone of narratives, Langdon (1973) recommends that narration be produced in an audio format by recording oral explanations or discussions, then transcribing them without changing the natural style of the verbal information. The transcription can be used as the basis for a script that can be recorded using a professional narrator. Clarity and conciseness must not be sacrificed in the name of spontaneity and naturalness, however.

### Selecting music

A wide variety of prerecorded music is available in digital format on compact discs from commercial music libraries. Many of the companies that market music for multimedia applications provide demonstration disks with samples of the types of music they offer. In addition, original music can be recorded and edited through a musical instrument digital interface (MIDI), which is a way to connect synthesizers, keyboards, and other musical instruments to computers.

Few articles or books have been published that provide detailed information or guidelines about the effective use of music in interactive programs. Some authors, especially those writing about producing video, do provide brief suggestions about the usefulness of music (Arwady and Gayeski, 1989; Cartwright, 1991; Van Nostrand, 1989). Van Nostrand (1989, p. 178) states that incorporating music begins with "identifying the function of music and making it an integral element of the script." Thus, the use of music needs to be considered as the program is being visualized and the script written. Generally, music can be used to

- Establish mood
- Set pace
- Signal a turn of events
- Indicate progress and activity
- Provide transitions and continuity
- Evoke emotion
- Accompany titles or introductory information
- Emphasize important points
- Support visual information
- Add interest, realism, and surprise

Since multimedia is designed to communicate with users, music should be selected that will become an integral part of a program's message by reaching people on an emotional level.

Music can have a wide variety of effects on listeners. Consider how music is used in movies and television commercials. It is not only "background," but also works in conjunction with the visual message to provide interest, excitement, tension, and realism. Nostrand (1989, p.178) suggests that scriptwriters "may need a wide range of musical-listing experiences to draw on: classical, pop, rock, folk, hillbilly, jazz, avant-garde, show tunes, blues, film scores, etc." Certainly, to use music effectively, developers need to become familiar with various styles of music, as well as gain an understanding of the effects of tempo, rhythm, activity, and style (Mullin, 1992).

Since music plays an important storytelling role, it should fit the pace and mood of the presentation and appeal to the audience's lifestyle, taste, and workplace position (Mullin, 1992). Burger (1992, p. 75) provides the following guidelines for choosing the right music:

- Make music an integral part from the start, rather than try to find music to "go with" the imagery later.

- Choose a music style that conveys the mood you wish to create.

- Convey personality through instrumentation.

- Use recurring themes as musical signatures to help the audience feel familiar with a character, place, or segment.

- Use tempo, dynamics, and pitch to establish energy levels.

- Use different styles of music and instrumentation to suggest time periods, cultures, locations, and a sense of place.

- Use musical genres to communicate to specific audiences; e.g., big band sounds for older audiences, or rap, metal, or pop for teenagers.

- Know when to hold them, when to fold them. Music should not compete with the narration or overwhelm the message of the program.

Listening to music in a variety of categories will help developers to gain an awareness of various types or styles of music and how they can be used to enhance multimedia. One way to do this is to review the demonstration disks provided by commercial music libraries. Since these companies use descriptive labels to categorize their music, developers can listen to selections in different categories and learn more about how different types of music can be used to establish different moods and pace. Sample categories include slow-tempo, medium-tempo, up-tempo, industrial, solo, specialty, and multimedia (Network Music, Inc., San Diego, CA).

The industrial category contains music that is called "highly motivational"; solo music features one or two instruments, and the specialty group is composed of Christmas, comedy, and other specialized styles. Interestingly, the multimedia category is described as "themes with recorded vocals" as well as "melodically similar instrumental elements" (Network Music, Inc., San Diego, CA). Another music library, Killer Tracks (Hollywood, CA) uses categories such as blues, comedy/animation, drama, fantasy, hi-tech, mellow, power/industrial, retail/institutional, warm/romantic.

## Selecting sound effects

Natural, ambient sounds are an integral part of our daily lives. We use them to help us interpret and assess our surroundings. For example, "we listen to the thunk of a car door to find out if it has closed properly, to the gurgle of pouring liquid to know if a container is almost full, and to traffic noises to assess the danger of crossing a street" (Gaver, 1989, p. 70). In other words, sound provides us with valuable data that we process in a variety of ways. In multimedia applications, sound effects can be used with great benefit to inform users; affect their attitudes, emotions, and perceptions; and direct their focus of attention.

One researcher has noted that sound or nonspeech audio can provide different types of messages, including alarms or warnings and status or monitoring messages (Buxton, 1989). Alarms and warnings are signals that interrupt and alert a listener. These sounds, such as fire alarms and police sirens, normally are loud and easily identifiable. Status and monitoring messages are sounds that give us information about ongoing tasks. The click of the keys of a keyboard or the beep of the bar-code device at the supermarket are examples of these typically short sounds. Status and monitoring sounds fade rapidly from the listener's awareness and are significant only when they indicate a change; for example, when the sound does not occur.

In addition to these types of messages, Mountford and Gaver (1990) note that sound provides information about

- *Physical events.*  We can identify whether a dropped glass bounced or shattered.

- *Invisible structures.*  Tapping a wall helps us to locate where to hang a picture.

- *Dynamic change.*  As we pour liquid into a glass, we can hear when it is full.

- *Abnormal structures.*  We can tell when our car engine is malfunctioning by its sound.

- *Events in space.*  We can hear someone approaching by the sound of footsteps.

Not only can sound effects provide specific information about an environment or setting, they also can be used to accomplish the following tasks:

- Create atmosphere
- Add realism
- Emphasize important points
- Indicate progress or activity
- Increase interest
- Establish mood
- Cue or prompt users
- Increase users' motivation

Recognizing the range of functions performed by nonspeech audio can help developers to identify ways that sound effects, both ambient and special, can be used to enhance understanding and learning in multimedia programs. Such recognition can be built by studying how sound effects are used in film and television productions, as well as in radio plays and commercials. Rather than being a cute afterthought, sound effects are a legitimate and substantive form of audio, and they should be integrated into the program script so as to enhance and lend credibility to the narrative, visuals, and music.

Three significant considerations should govern the use of sound effects:

1. They must be clear and easily identifiable.

2. They should not overwhelm the primary message.

3. They should be appropriate to the intended audience.

However, special sound effects often are difficult to record and, when recorded by amateurs, lack the required distinctiveness, subtlety, and appropriateness. Therefore, sound effects libraries usually are an excellent source of specialized sounds.

As with music libraries, sound effects are categorized by the type or use of the sound. For example, Sonic Boom (Anaheim, CA) lists pneumatics, buttons, switches; signals, levers, ratchets, gears; friction, stress, servo motors; small motors and mechanisms, electrical effects; compartments, doors, tape machines; and machines, motors, and engines. Background categories are labeled: interior work and manufacturing; packing, shipping, and conveyors; exterior work, labor, and industry; and constant-tone environments. Another company, Valentino (Elmsford, NY) provides more general categories: transportation, backgrounds, military, household, machinery, animals, and environmental. Companies that market sound-effect libraries provide an enormous selection of sounds on compact discs that have been professionally recorded using state-of-the-art equipment.

On the other hand, ambient sound usually is recorded as an integral part of a video production or as part of an audiotaped interview, conversation, or explanation. The background sounds are used to provide a realistic setting for the video or audio, and therefore slight imperfections add to the realism. Occasionally, however, background or ambient sounds are recorded alone so that they may be used as part of a still-media or textual presentation. As in the case of specialized sound effects, care should be taken that the ambient background does not overwhelm the narration or conversation and/or become annoying.

## Current and Potential Applications of Audio in Multimedia Applications

Audio can be a powerful addition to many multimedia programs. Narration can be used to eliminate the need for long sections of on-screen text, increase understanding by using a second channel of communication, and provide interest through interviews and conversations with real-life people. Music can be used to establish a mood or to cue users about specific segments. Also, music adds a professional quality to a multimedia program. Sound effects can be used to add realism by integrating environmental or ambient sounds with narration or conversations, or by using special sound effects to augment visual and narrative information.

### Speech

Since speech is one of the most common forms of human communication, it is a natural form of interaction, and one that can add an important dimension to a multimedia program. In some applications, speech is a necessity. For example, natural speech is required in programs designed to teach a foreign language or the pronunciation of new terminology. Spoken glossaries often are a valuable addition to programs where learners are faced with the task of acquiring a new vocabulary. Additionally, speech must be an integral part of programs designed for audiences with low literacy levels. Even for audiences without reading problems, the addition of the spoken word adds interest and increases learning by presenting the same message as the text.

Narration can be used to guide a learner through a task or procedure such as completing a form, assembling a piece of equipment, or setting up an experiment. Rowntree (1986, p. 246) refers to this as a "talk-through" technique. Even synthesized speech can provide guidance to a user. The "Postal Buddy" multimedia kiosk being field-tested by Electronic Data Systems (EDS) interacts with a potential customer through text, graphics, and the synthesized voice of an animated character (*The Dallas Morning News,* June 13, 1993, p. 11). In addition, the spoken word is effective in providing a general familiarization with technical and nontechnical content. However, if complex ideas or calculations are being presented, speech should be accompanied by succinct textual material and appropriate visuals.

The use of speech is particularly important when an audience member or learner is required to attend to more than one chunk of information at a time. For example, if learners must read detailed information that explains a chart, graph, or table, they are not able to study both the visual and the text explanation at the same time, especially if the two are on different screens. Using an audio explanation allows the learner to focus attention on the information or data displayed. Langdon (1973) suggests that additional learning effectiveness and efficiency can be expected when speech is used for tasks that require the user to attend to more than one chunk of content concurrently.

Speech also can be used in training or instructional experiences to provide discussions or interviews with practitioners or experts. For example, a multimedia program could provide audio segments of managers explaining how they dealt successfully with specific types of personnel issues. These segments would be accessed by the learners when they wanted additional information about the use of certain techniques or the solutions to difficult problems. Personal reactions, advice, interpretations, and commentaries can provide excellent background material related to the principle or issue being addressed. Also, conversations between patient and physician or salesperson and client could be effective in programs designed to teach questioning, listening, or interpersonal skills.

Speech, especially when coupled with environmental sounds, can also enhance simulations by adding an additional measure of realism to text and visuals. For example, an interactive patient-diagnosis simulation designed for medical students could be made more realistic by incorporating a patient's complaint as a narrative audio presentation with accompanying visuals and text.

Overall, speech can be a compelling element in a multimedia production. The persuasive qualities of the human (or even synthesized) voice should not be overlooked as a technique for improving the effectiveness of programs and maintaining the audience members' attention and motivation.

## Music

The most obvious potential applications for the use of music in multimedia are those programs that deal with music as content. For example, a program such as *The Magic Flute* by Warner Audio Notes provides the complete opera by Mozart as well as on-screen commentary and annotation. Instructional programs about musicians and different types of music that include text, visuals, and music are useful applications of multimedia.

However, music can be a valuable addition to many other types of instructional and informational programs. Since music is an excellent way to "set the stage" or establish a mood, it could be used as a type of "advance organizer" to help viewers prepare for a change in the program (Arwady and Gayeski, 1989). For example, in a sales training program that provides a sample sales call, music could be used to indicate to the viewer/listener that something is going wrong with the salesperson's presentation to the customer. In addition, important points or ideas can be emphasized by the use of readily identifiable chords or a series of musical notes. In short, appropriately selected music can help to establish a feeling of expectation or excitement.

If the goal of a multimedia training program is to change attitudes, music can be an especially valuable tool. For example, in a program designed to increase the sensitivity of workers in long-term health-care facilities toward their elderly clients, appropriate music integrated with narration by patients and their families could provide a powerful new perspective for employees. In addition, Arwady and Gayeski (1989) suggest that somber music can be used to set a serious tone for training subjects such as safety instruction.

Musical signatures and custom jingles can also be used in multimedia programs. For example, a musical signature might be employed to tell the viewer when to use off-line materials such as workbooks or reference manuals (Arwady and Gayeski, 1989). This cueing function also can indicate to users when they are in a specific section of a program or when the program is accomplishing a specific function. A recognizable series of musical notes can be used to identify the practice session of each lesson or the end of an information segment. In a related cueing function, music can be used to provide a time for reflection or time to assimilate the information just presented. Custom jingles can be used by a company using multimedia to present a new product to its sales and service force (Arwady and Gayeski, 1989).

Overall, the use of music is an excellent way to add sparkle or glitz to a multimedia production. In other words, effective use of music can make a program come alive. For example, the appropriate use of music to set the pace and mood throughout various parts of a program will help the audience to relate and interact with the program, thus increasing the likelihood that the message will be understood and remembered. Additionally, music adds a professional, polished quality to a production, especially when it is used to tie program segments together in a cohesive unit.

## Sound effects

Ambient sound often is included in video productions when the surrounding environment is being used as the setting. An example of one of the most effective uses of ambient sound is an interactive videodisc (IVD) program developed by Joseph Henderson, M.D. (Henderson, Pruett, Galper, and Copes, 1986). In this program, which is designed to teach specific procedures to physicians working under combat conditions, the noise and confusion of a field hospital, including the roar of the approaching and landing helicopters, are an integral part of the audio track. This sense of realism is continued even when the physician/user of the IVD program is branched to text menus and decision screens. Thus, as the physician is faced with making a decision based on information provided by a text screen, the audio track with the sounds of helicopters and field noise continues. This provides a realistic environment so that the physician feels at least some of the tension and pressure he or she would have to deal with in a real-life situation.

Ambient sounds can be used both to provide a sense of realism and to add interest to interviews, conversations, and explanations that are a part of multimedia training and informational programs. For example, an interview with a plant foreman could be audiotaped on location in the shop, so that when the interview is selected by users the information provided seems that much more true-to-life. Such "on-location recordings" can then be presented with digitized video, still media (such as photographs and graphics), or text screens. Explanations can be significantly enhanced by the addition of appropriate ambient sounds. Floyd (1991) reports that an overview of a manufacturing process, even though technically well produced, will be "fairly pedestrian" without the use of sound. However, with the addition of ambient sounds and a fast-paced music score, the same segment can be a powerful attention-grabber.

Simulations developed using either motion or still media can be made more realistic by the use of ambient sound. For example, a program designed to teach emergency medical technicians about specific procedures will simulate on-the-job conditions more closely if it contains street sounds recorded at an accident scene. For programs that do not incorporate speech or narration, the use of ambient sound can be an effective addition. Thus, a program about wild animals could present text, photographs, and illustrations about each animal, accompanied by an audio track of the animal's sounds in its natural environment.

Special sound effects or uniquely identifiable sounds can be used to add interest as well as to improve communication. Examples of the effective use of sound effects with still media are found in HyperCard stacks such as *Beyond Cyberpunk* (The Computer Lab, Louisa, VA) or *If Monks Had Macs* (BMUG, Berkeley, CA). In the *Beyond Cyberpunk* stack, the main menu is accompanied by a variety of appropriate cyberpunk sound effects; in *If Monks Had Macs,* the menu screen, which shows a monastery courtyard with a fountain, is accompanied by the sounds of a bird chirping and water flowing. Sound effects also are effective when used in conjunction with music and narration. Ringing telephones accompanied by up-tempo music can provide a secretarial training program with the right aura of a busy office. A troubleshooting program would be enhanced by simulating the sounds of equipment with various types of problems as they are examined and explained with visuals and narration.

Sound effects can be a powerful addition to the design of a multimedia program. We are familiar with sound effects as part of the interface of a personal computer. For example, a specific beep usually tells us when we have taken an incorrect action. When you are contemplating the use of sound effects as part of a multimedia program, keep in mind that the sounds should be appropriate, both in terms of the audience and the content. Also, sound effects should not distract or confuse the users. In most cases, since sound effects can add interest and realism, they are likely to increase user motivation to use and interact with the application.

## Sound as part of the human-computer interface

Related to the use of sound in instructional and informational programs is research involving the use of audio as it relates to human-computer interface design. Specifically, Gaver (1989; Mountford and Gaver, 1990) has researched the use of auditory icons based on his work with an auditory interface called the SonicFinder, which provides auditory as well as graphical feedback. The SonicFinder extends the visual desktop of the Macintosh Finder by using information available from the existing interface to initiate the output of sounds sampled from recordings of everyday, sound-producing events (Gaver, 1989). In addition Blattner, Sumikawa, and Greenberg (1989) investigated the use of *earcons* or audio messages integrated into a human-computer interface to provide information and feedback to the user about computer objects, operation, or interaction. Simply defined, an earcon is *a brief succession of discrete pitches, usually no fewer than three and no more than six, structured to transmit specific pieces of information* (Blattner, Greenberg, Kamegai, 1992).

Based on investigations at the CommTech Lab at Michigan State University, several guidelines for the use of sound as feedback to users' actions have been suggested by Heeter and Gomes (1992):

- An auditory response should accompany every user-initiated command.
- Auditory responses should be diverse.
- Selected sounds should be meaningful, and related, if possible, to the function performed or the metaphor used.
- Within an application, sounds used for different functions should have a consistency or similarity that indicates relationship, not sameness.
- Each function should have a single, identifiable sound throughout an application.

Heeter and Gomes say that sounds may be short music clips, identifiable real-world sound effects, interesting noises, or speech, but that they must be short, unobtrusive, and distinctive. Investigations by these and other researchers will help multimedia developers to understand how sound can be more effectively incorporated into multimedia so as to meet a variety of purposes and goals.

## Design Issues Related to the Use of Audio

If audio is to be fully integrated into an interactive multimedia program, a variety of design issues must be considered. Being aware of these issues early in the analysis and design process will help multimedia developers to avoid the pitfalls that ensnare those working with unfamiliar technology.

### Clearly defined purpose

The reasons for using audio in a multimedia program need to be clearly defined from the beginning of the project. Each of the three types of sound—speech, music, and sound effects—can be a powerful addition to a multimedia program. However, developers need to analyze how each type of audio will help to impart the message or instruction to the users. Unless it is selected and integrated with care, audio can turn into a distracting or disorienting element in a program. Thus developers should use audio as a tool to explain, augment, or enrich the content or information being presented. For example, speech is effective when users are required to comprehend technical information, especially when it is presented in detailed graphs, tables, or schematics; ambient sound is effective for increasing realism in a training simulation; and music is effective for establishing a mood, setting the pace, or cueing the user. Audio that is not effectively used can interfere with the program's message.

### Audio as an option

Determine early if audio will be included as an integral part of the program or if an option will be provided for users to turn it off. Developers need to analyze the audience, the delivery environment, and the goals of a multimedia experience before determining if audio will be optional. Audio often is made optional if it is used primarily to repeat on-screen text. This technique is used most often when the target audience contains a segment of low-literacy-level users. Even though repeating on-screen text as audio can be effective for low-literacy-level audiences, speech (as well as music and sound effects) can be used more effectively to supplement, enhance, and elaborate the information being presented on the screen.

Often, audio segments are designed to carry an important part of the message or instruction. Audio then becomes crucial to the effectiveness of the program. In such a case, the option to turn off the audio track should not be provided. However, developers should carefully examine the environment in which the program will be delivered. The need for user privacy, or the need to eliminate sound that could be distracting to other workers, are both important issues. Certain settings, such as offices in which workers are in close proximity to each other, may require that sound be optional or that the users wear headphones so that coworkers are not distracted or disturbed by the audio.

Also, if headphones are being considered, remember that they must provide high-quality sound and be as lightweight and comfortable as possible, especially if users will be wearing them for long periods of time. Some audiences may dislike wearing headphones, and this attitude could sabotage an otherwise effective program. A thorough investigation of the audience and the delivery setting, as well as the goals of a program, will help a developer to make the appropriate decision as to optional or integrated audio.

### Branching

Many multimedia programs are nonlinear and designed to increase user interactivity through questions and choices the user can make. Since audio is linear, sound segments should be designed so that they can respond to the user's need to repeat the audio as well as the on-screen text and visuals. Thus, sound segments need to be designed to branch to different sections of content based on user responses. This may mean that several transitions need to be written, recorded, and integrated for each branching point.

In addition, care needs to be taken as the branches are programmed that users are provided with appropriate audio connections from each branch to the next viewing segment, as well as connections back to the previous instructional segment for review. When using audio, especially narrative, simply branching the user back to a specific segment of on-screen material may be disconcerting if the branch takes the user to the middle of an audio segment. Ensuring that audio is designed appropriately for all branching options is an important factor in the effective use of audio in nonlinear multimedia.

### Aural versus visual processing

Even though listening can be as effective as reading for many purposes, transmitting information orally can be slow (Johnston, 1987). One reason for this may be that we can read or comprehend information faster than a person can speak (Fulford, 1993). Thus an important consideration in the use of speech to present information is whether normal speech will be too slow and cause users to lose interest.

One technique that has been investigated to alleviate this problem is the use of compressed speech (Fulford, 1993; Sticht, 1969). These studies found that increasing the speech rate from a normal rate of 175 words per minute (wpm) to approximately 260–275 wpm was effective. Fulford (1993) investigated the use of systematically designed text alone, text with normal speech, and text with compressed speech (262 wpm); she reports that the text with compressed speech was (1) as effective for mastery of objectives, (2) as efficient as text alone, and (3) more efficient than text supported by normal speech. Fulford (1993) suggests that systematically designed materials (those that are comprised only of "need-to-know" information, with little or no "nice-to-know" content) may have a high density of information and thus be "over-compressed" when speech compression is used. This is an important consideration if you are contemplating speech compression as a way of increasing the efficiency of speech delivery. Thus, incorporating carefully designed compressed speech with text and visuals can increase motivation and improve the effectiveness of a multimedia program.

### Music selection

An issue related to the effective use of music concerns how the music selected for the multimedia application will affect the listener. A tune that has pleasant associations for a given developer could cause unpleasant reactions in the viewer/listener (Cartwright, 1986), in which case the music selection would interfere with the goals of the program. Cartwright suggests that indistinguishable tunes should be used whenever possible, since music should be used to call attention to the content of the program, not to elicit unrelated memories.

### New skills

To use audio effectively, team members may need to acquire new skills, or new personnel may need to be hired. The use of audio requires skills that relate to writing narration, selecting and using music, using ambient sound, and identifying and integrating sound effects. For example, music selection requires an understanding of different types of music and their impacts, as well as a knowledge of how to mix techniques in order to achieve the appropriate blend when using music with narration and/or sound effects. Since audio is a tool that has not been widely used in the development of multimedia, many team members have not had the opportunity to learn how these new tools can be used to enhance a program.

### Increased development time

Developing or selecting appropriate audio is a time-consuming task. For example, additional time will be required during the design and development processes to write the narrative script, locate a narrator, record the narration, and integrate the narration into the program. Additional time also will be required to develop appropriate transitions for all of the branches in the program. If the development team is considering the use of music, time is required both to determine when and how music should be incorporated into the presentation and to select, acquire, and then integrate the music into the appropriate parts of the program. Sound effects present similar time-intensive tasks: decision making as to how and where either ambient or special sound effects will be used, and then the selection, acquiring, and integration of the sound effects, or the recording of the required ambient sound. However, once developers have gained expertise in the use of audio and have built a library of music and sound effects, the time requirements should decrease. Most importantly, remember to weigh the increased development time (and associated costs) against the increased effectiveness of the multimedia program being developed.

## Copyright

Copyright issues are complicated, particularly if the application is going to be sold to a client rather than used internally. The development organization should only use audio to which it holds the rights. This is especially true when using music and sound effects. Obtaining permission to use popular songs can be a long, complicated, and expensive process. Commercial-music and sound-effects libraries are excellent sources for obtaining the rights to use both types of audio in multimedia productions, and most libraries offer several different license or purchase options depending on the needs of the program (Mullin, 1992). Schneier (1992) provides several guidelines for ensuring that the material used in multimedia is legal; his guidelines suggest that developers should know what rights are being purchased, be persistent in tracking down permissions, and make sure that all relevant copyrights have been obtained.

## Audio quality

The quality of the speech, music, and sound effects used is an important issue in multimedia applications. Audio needs to be clear, and free of distortion and extraneous noise. Therefore the audio must be professionally recorded and edited. Audio quality is especially important in the case of music. The internal capabilities of some computers are sufficient for speech and most sound effects, or for short music sequences. However, if music is to be a significant part of a program, an external speaker probably will be required.

An additional consideration related to quality is that the better the audio quality, the more disk or storage space it occupies. Thus the storage capacity of the delivery platform must be sufficient to contain the application at the audio quality-level chosen. A more technical discussion of the quality of audio recording may be found in Burger, 1993.

### Response time

The response time required for an audio segment to play can sometimes be slow. Therefore, be sure to test segments that have been incorporated into the program and play them back on the delivery-system platform, to ensure that all types of audio will respond in a timely manner and without breaks or distortion.

## General Guidelines

The following guidelines are presented as a way of summarizing our suggestions for using audio effectively in multimedia programs:

- To maximize the use of audio, analyze carefully the target audience, delivery environment, and content.
- Clearly define why and how audio will be used.
- Whenever possible, integrate audio into the whole program, and do it from the start of the project.
- Develop detailed scripts or storyboards.
- Allow learners to control audio, except when it carries the primary message.
- Make sound effects meaningful.
- Use the highest-quality audio possible, given the storage constraints of the delivery platform.
- Collaborate with others who have experience using different types of audio.
- Learn more about the use of sound, especially music.

## References

Arwady, J. W. and Gayeski, D. M., *Using Video: Interactive and Linear Designs,* Educational Technology Publications, Englewood Cliffs, NJ, 1989.

Blattner, M. M., Sumikawa, D. A., and Greenberg, R. M., "Earcons and icons: Their structure and common design principles," *Human-Computer Interface,* 4, 11–44, 1989.

Blattner, M. M., Greenberg, R. M., and Kamegai, M., "Listening to turbulence: an example of scientific audiolizaton," in M. M. Blattner, and R. G. Dannenberg, eds., *Multimedia Interface Design,* pp. 87–107, ACM Press, New York.

Bove, T. and Rhodes, C., *Que's Macintosh Multimedia Handbook,* QUE, Carmel, IN, 1990.

"'Buddy' system automates postal services," *The Dallas Morning News,* June 13, 1993, p. 11H.

Burger, J., "In the mood: choosing the right music for a soundtrack," *NewMedia,* 2(11), 75, 1992.

Burger, J., "Sound thinking: audio in multimedia production," *NewMedia,* 3(7), 54–63, 1993.

Buxton, W., Introduction to this special issue on nonspeech audio, *Human-Computer Interaction,* 4, 1–9, 1989.

Cartwright, S. R., *Training With Video,* Knowledge Industry Publications, White Plains, NY, 1986.

Dean, C. and Whitlock, Q., *A Handbook of Computer-Based Training,* Kogan Page, New York, 1989.

Floyd, Steve, *The IBM Multimedia Handbook,* Brady Publishing, New York, 1991.

Fulford, Catherine, "Can learning be more efficient? Using compressed speech audio tapes to enhance systematically designed text," *Educational Technology,* 33(2), 51–59, 1993.

Gaver, W. W., "The SonicFinder: An interface that uses auditory icons," *Human-Computer Interface,* 4, 67–94, 1989.

Hannafin, M. J., and Hooper, S. R., "Learning principles," pp. 192–231 in Fleming, M., and Levie, W. H., eds., *Instructional Message Design: Principles from the Behavioral and Cognitive Sciences,* Educational Technology, Englewood Cliffs, NJ, 1993.

Heeter, C., and Gomes, P., "It's time for hypermedia to move to 'talking pictures,'" *Journal of Educational Multimedia and Hypermedia,* 1(2) 255–261, 1992.

Henderson, J. V., Pruett, R. K,. Galper, A. R., and Copes, W. S., "Interactive videodisc to teach combat trauma life support," *Journal of Medical Systems,* 10, 271–76, 1986.

Hsia, H. J., "Redundancy: Is it the lost key to better communication?" *Audio-Visual Communication Review,* 25(1), 63–85, 1977.

Johnston, J., *Electronic Learning from Audiotape to Videodisc,* Lawrence Erlbaum, Hillsdale, NJ, 1987.

Jones, M. K., *Human-Computer Interaction: A Design Guide,* Educational Technology Publications, Englewood Cliffs, NJ, 1989.

Keller, J., and Burkman, E., "Motivation Principles," pp. 3–53 in Fleming, M. and Levie, W. H., *Instructional Message Design: Principles from the Behavioral and Cognitive Sciences,* Educational Technology Publications, Englewood Cliffs, NJ, 1993.

Langdon, D. G., *Interactive Instructional Designs for Individual Learning,* Educational Technology Publications, Englewood Cliffs, NJ, 1973.

Mountford, S. J., and Gaver, W. W., "Talking and listening to computer," in Laurel, B., ed., *The Art of Human-Computer Interface Design,* Addison-Wesley, Reading MA, 1990.

Mullin, B., "Music libraries: the producer's friend," *Video Systems,* 33–42, September 1992.

Rowntree, D., *Teaching Through Self-Instruction,* Kogan Page, New York, 1986.

Schneier, B., "Practice safe multimedia: wear a copyright," *NewMedia,* 2 (12), 32–33, 1992.

Sticht, T. G., *Learning by Listening in Relation to Aptitude, Reading, and Rate-controlled Speech,* Human Resources Research Organization, Technical Report 69-23, 1969.

Swain, D. V., and Swain, J. R., *Scripting for the New AV Technologies,* 2d ed., Focal Press, Boston, 1991.

Van Nostrand, W. J., *The Scriptwriter's Handbook,* Knowledge Publications, White Plains, NY, 1989.

# Digital Video a la Carte

**Josh Hendrix**

**Alton Christensen**

## Introduction

It is now possible to use high-end personal computers and workstations to create broadcast-quality video off-line, without the use of an on-line suite. This is not the only way that a PC and video software can be integrated into the video postproduction process, and at the moment it is not the prevalent way. Nevertheless, low-cost computers and workstations are rapidly taking over many of the chores of postproduction, and in the process replacing traditional equipment that costs 100 times as much. The authors believe that within 3 to 5 years' time this scenario will have become almost commonplace.

This chapter is a guide to creating a broadcast-quality digital-video studio by choosing various products in an a la carte fashion. It contains information about the various pieces of hardware and software that can be combined together to create a custom studio that can have as much or more raw capability as much more expensive traditional video solutions. It answers the question, "What is the minimum set of equipment I need to produce video that is of high enough quality to be broadcast?"

One cautionary note should be sounded from the start. Due to the current speed of computing equipment, the digital studio described herein is by necessity a completely off-line environment. This is necessary because consumer-level computers and workstations currently are not fast enough to manipulate video in real time (30 frames per second), and consumer-level storage media also are not fast enough to retrieve it at that rate. Compensating for these factors does take time, and it has been said that the old adage "Time is money" is nowhere more true than in the broadcast business. If the nature of a project is such that time is the overriding critical factor (as in, "get it done yesterday"), then at this level of development the traditional editing suite should be used.

However, the advantages of a completely nonlinear editing environment, combined with the substantial cost savings over traditional solutions, can offset this time disadvantage for less time-critical projects. Furthermore, computing power and storage and retrieval speeds have been rapidly improving for several years at the consumer level. This trend shows no sign of slowing, which means that the time disadvantage will rapidly disappear. As less expensive, more capable equipment becomes available, one conclusion becomes clear: the future of video is digital.

It would be impossible to attempt to cover every single product within the scope of this chapter. By the time the ink dried on the pages of this book, the information would be obsolete. Instead, this guide talks in general terms about some of the types of products available. The goal is to give the reader a sense of what kinds of products are out there, and a vision of the minimal set of tools necessary to broadcast quality video on the desktop.

Let it also be noted, as a point of clarification, that in this chapter we will be referring to software and hardware that runs on a PC. We mean by that the generic term *personal computer.* Most people think of PCs as being IBMs or compatibles, or those machines that run the DOS or Windows operating system. However, most of the software and hardware available as of this writing, and thus in the authors' experience, operates on an Apple Macintosh®. We expect this to change as more software becomes available for Microsoft Windows™ and particularly when the PowerPC platforms emerge. However, the facts of our experience cannot help but color our perspectives, and the reader should take that into account.

## Broadcast Quality

The term *broadcast quality,* as it is used in different contexts, generally has either a *subjective* or an *objective* connotation. It is important to distinguish between the two uses. Video technicians tend to use the term in its objective sense. Technically, whether a video image is of "broadcast quality" has nothing to do with the subjective impression of "image quality" that appears on-screen. Rather, a broadcast-quality image is one that conforms to Federal Communications Commission specification RS170-A, which all television broadcasters must comply with by law. The RS170-A specification addresses the synchronization and other physical characteristics of the video signal as it is transmitted. Broadcast quality in this sense of the term can be measured by a machine. This contrasts with the subjective use of the term, in which case its meaning is a matter of educated opinion.

In its subjective sense, *broadcast quality* refers to the subjective impression of image quality that a video clip leaves with the viewer. In other words, is the image "crisp" and "clean," devoid of artifacts? Are the colors true? Is the motion smooth? Have the "jaggies" been anti-aliased out? The answers to all of these questions will go to form the viewer's subjective impression of the quality of the image.

Among video producers, there are tacit standards of image quality that vary somewhat but are generally well agreed upon. At one time network television was widely thought of as a minimum standard for subjective broadcast quality. This has changed in the last few years, however, because the major networks and many cable stations have begun to broadcast, in the context of news shows and humorous home videos, some footage shot in the Hi-8 format. This has caused the definition of broadcast quality to become more a matter of content than of image quality. The skill with which the content is composed and shot is becoming the only clear line that can be drawn; there is no substitute for talent and experience when it comes to capturing content. In terms of image quality, however, video pros now tend to benchmark against the quality associated with different video-storage formats such as $\frac{3}{4}$-inch, Beta-SP, and D-1.

Both connotations of the term come into play when the characteristics of video software and hardware are being assessed. Various manufacturers of both claim that their products are of broadcast quality. When this claim is heard in reference to software designed for the composition of video clips it should be taken, unless specified otherwise, in the subjective sense. The software company is saying, "Our product helps you to create output that looks good enough to be broadcast on network television." This is a safe assumption, since most software is concerned with editing and creating effects, whereas special hardware usually is required to actually move video from computer to videotape.

The claims of hardware manufacturers require more thought. Hardware can affect both kinds of image quality, subjective and objective. Seen subjectively, broadcast-quality hardware must be able to store and display the digital image in a manner that does not notably degrade its visual quality. Seen objectively, broadcast-quality hardware that encodes a digital image for transfer to videotape must generate a video signal that conforms to the aforementioned FCC standards. Most hardware can pass the objective test, but one must carefully analyze and test all subjective claims.

Generating broadcast-quality video from a PC has less to do with the computer itself than it does with the output device and with the software that creates the video. It is the old computer principle of "garbage in, garbage out" in action. If the digitizing board is of poor quality, the resulting video will be no better. By the same token, if the output device for recording to tape is of poor quality, this will be reflected in the image that is recorded to tape. Thus if you want to do broadcast-quality work from a PC, it will be worth your while to spend the extra money for high-quality input and/or output devices. When it comes to other factors that affect the subjective quality of your video, tradeoffs can be made, but it is best not to compromise when it comes to input and output devices.

## The Basic Video Creation Process

The process of creation, with respect to digital video at least, is once again evolving so as to embrace the new capabilities that advancing technology brings with it. The use of PCs as the sole video-creation engine is as yet so new that there are no commonly agreed-upon methods. Then too, PCs have a variety of still graphics and animation software already available, which means they often offer more capabilities than traditional methods of producing the same kinds of graphic elements in post. With so many new variables, and with software capabilities changing so rapidly, the process of evolution may never slow down again.

The following sections will depict a fairly common sequence of events that could take place in the creation of a video on a PC. Since the computer brings the creation process into the nonlinear age, none of these steps really has to follow in exact sequence except the last two, which can occur only when the video-editing process has ended. Assuming that the storyboarding process has been completed, the following steps can occur.

### Gathering source material

This task should be familiar to video postproduction specialists, and thus requires little explanation. Production facilities and personnel may be employed to create new footage for editing and manipulation, or stock footage may be gathered. The effects of the nonlinear editing process may be felt even here, however, because it allows editors to play "what if" with the story line in an unprecedented manner. Thus additional footage may be shot at this stage, and more footage may be required later if the story line is allowed to evolve. The computer is itself capable of generating text, graphics, and even 2D and 3D animations. As such, these types of source material may not need to be *gathered* so much as they need to be *planned.*

### Digitizing

Before any editing can take place, the source video must be converted into digital form by the computer and stored on disk. This process is known as *digitizing,* and involves special hardware. This is an important bottleneck in the process, not just in terms of time but also in terms of quality. An investment in high-quality digitizing boards is essential if broadcast-quality results are to be achieved.

Video input can come from many kinds of input devices, from consumer-quality VHS machines to traditional high-end tape equipment. However, the quality of the digital image is directly dependent on the quality of the medium from which it comes. While there are several methods of digitizing, they all depend on the quality of the source device. Thus the rental or purchase of a high-quality deck should be factored into the overall cost of equipment. Still frames to be included in the production can be created in the PC or brought in through a high-quality scanner.

## The nonlinear video creation process

Once the visual raw materials have been digitized, the creation process can begin in earnest. Traditionally this process has been a linear one, due to the linear nature of the underlying technology. By facilitating a nonlinear editing process, however, the personal computer makes possible a great deal of freedom. The price of this freedom is that many more options are available, harder choices must be made, and creativity must sometimes be restrained as deadlines approach. The following steps may be engaged in almost any order within the limits of time, budget, and common sense.

**Editing nonlinearly.**   The nonlinear editing process has many advantages. Most software products handle the editing process by facilitating the creation of an off-line, or a "model" of the final video, rather than by actually composing the video themselves on-line. This model contains information about how the video is to unfold over time. Various video clips are trimmed and then sequenced together with intervening transitions, wipes, and keys, and some programs have DVE-style layering for motion effects. Rather than manipulate the video files themselves, the model contains information about the files and pointers to them, much like a traditional off-line. Since the model is in the computer's memory, it can be continuously altered and updated with little time penalty. Also, multiple versions of the same project can be created from the same source, and stored for later evaluation.

Since video files are stored on disks for random access, cueing to a particular frame is almost instantaneous. Rearranging shot sequences and substituting one shot for another can be done with ease, letting the computer worry about the time codes. If special effects are being applied, their parameters can be tweaked repeatedly until the results are exactly as desired. Nonlinear editing enhances the creative capabilities of editors and producers by providing better tools and performing more of the "gruntwork" than did the traditional systems of the past.

**Creating additional source.**   Since the computer is a general-purpose tool, it can be used for more than just the editing process. Static graphic elements can be assembled by means of professional-quality graphics programs, text can be generated, and 2D and 3D animations can be created. Changes to all of these production elements can be made right up to the last minute. It surprises some newcomers to the world of personal computers that the quality of output can be as good as or better than traditional postproduction tools.

**Multiple storyboards.**   The computer allows the editor to create and store a model of the video project without creating the actual video. Since this model can also be duplicated, and the duplicate can be altered without altering the original, it is possible to create several different models of the same project. This means that the editor has the freedom to explore several different options (time permitting) and choose the best elements of each. Last-minute changes also are much more feasible.

**Previews.**  One disadvantage of the fact that the computer is assembling a model of the production and not the actual production itself is that on some systems it may not be possible to immediately see the results of one's work in full motion. To work around this, most editing software allows the user to preview a portion of the video by assembling a low-quality version of it. This version may be smaller in dimension, at lower quality, or play at a lower frame rate than the final video. However, previews generally are good enough to give the editor an accurate notion of what to expect in the final product and to aid in decision making when choices must be made.

**The final render.**  Once the creation process has ended, the resulting video model must be used to create an actual video. Simple editing such as cuts and transitions may not need to be explicitly rendered, but most complicated effects such as layering, compositing, and computationally intensive image-manipulation such as blurring do require it. During the rendering process the computer proceeds frame-by-frame through the model and performs all operations necessary to create a complete frame at the desired resolution and quality. This process can be very time-consuming, depending on the complexity of the model and the duration of the video. A business video with one or two layers, some graphic overlays, and transitions will take much less time to render than a music video with 20 or more layers composited together, multiple special effects, morphs, etc. There is no general rule of thumb for predicting how long a particular video will take to render; the best guide is experience.

This stage constitutes one drawback to this type of editing process, due to its time requirements. However, since many compositing and special-effect computations are very processor-intensive, three sure ways to speed the rendering process are to (1) purchase a faster computer, (2) accelerate your current machine, or (3) take advantage of multiprocessor hardware and software to operate in parallel. Also, the final rendering step usually can be completed by the computer unattended. This means the machine can be left to render overnight when it would not otherwise be in use.

### Recording to tape

The frames of the final production can be recorded to tape either in conjunction with the final rendering stage or after that stage is complete. To render and record at the same time, it is necessary to be able to record frame-by-frame to tape, because the computer usually will not be able to render the frame in under $\frac{1}{30}$ of a second. In this case, the frames may or may not be written to disk at the same time. Note that in order to save time using this method, the software involved must be able to cue the tape to record the next frame at the same time as the next frame is being rendered. Otherwise (i.e., if cueing and rendering happen sequentially), this process will be no faster than completely rendering the video before recording.

If the rendering stage is completed first, several options then exist for recording. In all cases, a device controller will be necessary to help the computer cue and otherwise control the recording deck. Recording frame-by-frame is the oldest and most widespread method, and generally produces the best-quality recordings. Newer devices exist that allow brief segments of the video to be sequentially recorded in real time from memory. A few seconds at a time of the video are loaded and played out to the recording device. Then the tape is recued while the next few seconds are loaded, and the process repeats itself. This hardware is a more expensive option, but it can pay for itself in recording time saved.

These five steps give you a general overview of the digital-video creation process on a personal computer or workstation. They are the context in which a system should be planned and put together. The following section describes the basic components of a digital-video studio.

## The Basic Components

The fact that digital video has burst upon the scene may be attributed to several factors that have come together at the same time.

### Fast machines

Central processing units, the brains of the computer, are getting faster and cheaper, and this trend will accelerate. It is commonly shared wisdom in the computer industry that processor speed doubles every 2 years, although it is now being debated whether that figure is closer to every 1.5 years. As computer hardware becomes commoditized, manufacturers have no choice but to fiercely compete on speed and price. This works to the benefit of the consumer. For digital-video manipulation, it is recommended that the fastest possible machine be bought that your budget will allow. Slower machines are just as capable of producing the same-quality output as the fastest machines available, but faster machines can accomplish much more in a given amount of time.

Speed claims by computer manufacturers are notoriously misleading, however. Currently, the best benchmark to use for comparison between different brands and platforms is the *specmark*. This set of tests measures the speed with which computers perform tasks most similar to those they are actually asked to perform in the real world. While not a perfect measurement, specmarks are more reliable than most other benchmarks such as MIPS (millions of instructions per second) and MFLOPS (millions of floating point operations per second). If your local retail outlet cannot supply these figures for the brands you are comparing, contacting the manufacturer should do the trick.

### High-quality input/output devices

The quality level at which you can digitize and record video is the most important hardware consideration in a digital-video suite. If your input and/or output devices are not of broadcast quality, then the results won't be either. Broadcast quality comes at a high price, however, sometimes as high as or higher than the computer itself. But these costs will still be one to three orders of magnitude less than the cost of buying traditional video equipment.

If you do not need to record video for editing and manipulation, and you only need to create stills, cel animation, or animation in two or three dimensions, then you may only need to buy a high-quality output card. If you do need to record video, then you can buy devices that combine input and output or those that specialize in one or the other.

Add-in boards exist that can digitize long video clips directly to disk in real time (e.g., 30 fps), but generally these will not create broadcast-quality input. Different and more time-consuming methods are necessary. One method, digitizing from videotape frame-by-frame, is an older and a very common one. A newer method is to digitize to a RAM disk (a large bank of memory) in real time. There are advantages and disadvantages to each.

Digitizing frame-by-frame trades off time for quality. The highest quality is obtained at the expense of taking a longer time to digitize and store each frame. Frames usually are recorded as a series of separate numbered files that can be altered or reordered. Several components are needed to digitize in this manner.

First, a high-quality digitizing board must be installed. This type of add-in board is called a *frame grabber*. In order to automate the process of digitizing a large number of frames, an additional board must be purchased to control the storage device from which the video is taken. This "device control" board is connected to the video deck either via the computer's serial port or through a port on the board. Both of these boards come with software that allows unattended batch recording of multiple video frames to the hard disk. This recording does not take place in real time. Rather, it can take up to 30 seconds per frame to cue the tape to the appropriate frame, digitize the frame, and save it to disk.

Methods of recording in real time exist, with different tradeoffs. With one option known as recording to a "RAM disk," a sequence of frames can be digitized at broadcast quality in real time, but the frames are digitized into memory, not to disk. This is possible because the time it takes to store information in memory is a fraction of what it takes to store it on a disk.

To digitize in this manner, a digitizing board and a device controller are both needed. The memory may be in the computer or in a special device designed to hold large amounts of it. The memory is filled over and over again by subsequent groups of frames from the deck. After memory has been filled, the deck is paused and recued, and the frames can be saved to disk either uncompressed or compressed at a low compression ratio that does not affect the visual quality of the frame. In this case, the number of frames that can be digitized is limited by the amount of memory available. NTSC-size uncompressed video takes up about 1 Mbyte of space per frame, so 1 second of video takes up about 30 Mbytes of memory or disk space. Some computers can hold up to 128 Mbytes of memory, and RAM disk devices exist that can contain hundreds of megabytes. Obviously, there is an additional cost to each extra megabyte, but memory costs have dropped sharply in recent years, and for many of us the time saved will justify the expense.

The most desirable state of affairs would be to digitize directly to disk at broadcast quality, losslessly compressing the video so that the visual quality is unaffected. At the time of this writing (early 1994) there are no products on the market for PCs that can do this. Boards presently exist that can digitize directly to disk with compression, but the compression ratios necessary to achieve this must be high enough that the quality of the image is degraded below broadcast levels (the extent to which this is true is a hot topic of debate). The authors expect this to change quickly, however, so by the time you read this, products may exist in the marketplace that accomplish this feat.

Another broadcast-quality input option exists for video professionals and those who have access to postproduction facilities of some sort. It is of course possible to digitize video into an Abekas disk recorder or similar storage medium. One can then copy the video from the Abekas to a digital tape that can be read and written to by an Exabyte or similar tape drive. Some Exabyte drives, for instance, come with SCSI ports and thus can be attached to and used by a PC. Software is required to convert from the Abekas format to one that is PC-readable, and this is the time bottleneck here. However, the resulting video quality can be very high, and the costs can be lower in the short run than buying an expensive digitizing board and device controller and gaining access to a good deck.

The process of getting finished video out of the computer works almost exactly in reverse. Most digitizing boards also allow video to be recorded from the computer to tape. Batch recordings can be made one frame at a time, or recordings can be made in real time from memory, but the amount of memory limits the duration of video that can be recorded on a given pass. In either case, the device control board and software handle tape cueing and synchronization. Recording one frame at a time can take more than 30 seconds per frame. The average time per frame will be less for the RAM option, but this comes at greater hardware expense.

Note that the digital tape process also works in reverse for output. A video file is created by the computer software. This file is then converted to the Abekas or similar format (again, this step takes a significant amount of time) and recorded to some digital broadcast medium. As before, the long-term costs are those charged by the production facilities for conversion from Exabyte tape (for instance) to the Abekas or other storage medium.

When you are doing broadcast graphics on a PC platform, it is highly recommended that you purchase an NTSC monitor in addition to a standard computer monitor, attach it to your computer, and use it to view your work in progress before rendering your final output. You may be able to do this via your output board. There is a great difference between a computer monitor that is non-interlaced and flicker-free and a standard NTSC monitor that is interlaced. In general, the computer's graphics capabilities exceed those of the target output medium, videotape, since the computer monitor displays at a higher resolution and is capable of a wider range of saturations and luminances.

For example, thin lines that look fine on the computer monitor may beat or flicker on an NTSC monitor due to its lower resolution. Color saturation and luminance levels need to be watched so that they are "legal" for broadcast. Access to waveform or vector-scope monitors is a preferable but expensive option. Viewing your work before rendering it and recording to tape can help you to pinpoint and avoid these problems.

### Time-based media storage formats

In order to store and retrieve massive amounts of time-based data such as digital video, special storage formats have been devised. File formats such as Apple's QuickTime™ and Microsoft's Video For Windows™ allow users to store and randomly access video and audio as well as other time-based information. The main advantage here is standardization of the storage format.

For instance, any QuickTime file generated by a video application can be read by any other QuickTime-compatible application. The same is true for Video For Windows–compatible applications. This eliminates time-consuming conversions between custom formats from different software developers, and frees programmers to concentrate on building better tools. Note, however, that conversion must take place between QuickTime files and Video For Windows files, and also that Apple supports QuickTime both on the Macintosh and on Windows™ platforms.

Other advantages include random access within the video file, and data compression. Random access eliminates the time-consuming process of cueing up that is necessary with a linear storage format such as videotape. Rather, any frame of the video can be instantaneously accessed at any time. This is necessary to support a nonlinear editing process.

Video compression is used to decrease the size of the video file, thus increasing the amount of video that can be stored on a given disk. Compression algorithms generally work by analyzing each frame and expressing the information contained therein more compactly. This is like writing & in place of *and* on a piece of paper. The ampersand takes less time to write and takes up less space, yet expresses the same information. An analogous process occurs in the compression of digital video.

Currently, digital-video compression is a two-edged sword. On the positive side, compressing digital video is necessary because (1) the storage requirements for digital video are enormous, and (2) compression increases the effective throughput of digital-video playback devices, which facilitates increased frame sizes and higher frame rates. On the negative side, some compression algorithms sacrifice the visual quality of the video in order to achieve smaller files.

A compression ratio is simply a ratio between the size in bytes of a frame before compression and its size after compression. The higher the compression ratio (i.e., the less space each frame takes up on disk), the greater the amount of information that has been removed. If the compression ratio is low enough, the visual quality will not be notably affected by the compression process. A rule of thumb is that compression ratios higher than 2:1 (considered a low ratio) probably will not affect visual quality. For more technical information on compression, see the appendix on p. 30.17.

## High-capacity, high-sustained-throughput hard drives

Hard drives are a critical part of the digital-video studio. Time-based media in general, and video frames in particular, can have large storage requirements. Buying the right hard drive can make the difference between productivity and frustration. Depending on budget, a choice must be made between buying a hard drive and a disk array. Disk arrays store data more quickly by spreading the video data across multiple drives and writing it almost in parallel. They are correspondingly more expensive than a slower hard drive of the same capacity, but the performance increase is often worth the price.

There are four factors to consider when purchasing storage: sustained transfer rate, seek time, capacity, and price, in that order.

The *sustained transfer rate* is the average rate at which data can be written to or read from the disk, usually in megabytes per second. It has the highest priority, because all digital-video programs will spend an enormous amount of time just reading and writing frames to and from the disk. At the time of this writing, standard SCSI hard disks have transfer rates of about 1 to 2 Mbytes per second. More expensive, higher-throughput disk arrays can have transfer rates of 3 to 5 Mbytes per second. This is one piece of information that is harder to find than other attributes of a drive, so a call to the manufacturer may be necessary.

*Seek time* comes into play because, internally, a hard disk is structured somewhat like a record player. The disk is a platter than spins around at high speed, and the read-write head moves toward and away from the center of the disk and is able to reach almost any part of it. Seek time is the average time it takes for the read-write head to move from one area of the disk to another, and usually is measured in milliseconds. In general, seek times range between 7 and 15 milliseconds (0.007 and 0.015 seconds), and as technology advances these times decrease. Seek time is important because a disk drive, unlike a record on which all songs are stored sequentially in the record's groove, can break long files such as digital video into chunks that are located in physically separate areas of the disk.

For instance, a 2-minute-long video might be broken up into three separate chunks. To play this video, the disk head must move to the physical location of the first chunk and begin reading frames into the computer for display on-screen. When the head is done reading frames from the first chunk, it must move to the physical location of the next frame. This move must happen in a split-second, because a high (longer) seek time will cause a pause in the action while the drive head moves, whereas a low (fast) seek time will not cause a noticeable pause. Thus, seek time becomes important for digitization and playback of video in real time. The lower the seek time, the better.

*Disk capacity* is simply the amount of information a hard disk can hold. Due to the storage requirements of digital video, the typical digital-video studio requires at least one gigabyte of storage space. If digital archiving of original footage is desired, a tape-drive backup system can be a cost-effective solution. Prices per megabyte for 1-Gbyte-capacity-or-greater hard drives have recently fallen under $1.20 for external drives. Prices for disk arrays, which have the advantage of higher sustained transfer rates, have fallen below $2 per megabyte. The better the performance characteristics (sustained transfer rate, seek time, etc.), the higher the cost per megabyte. To put this in perspective, however, these prices are still fractions of the cost of the traditional equipment performing the same function in post houses today. See the appendix (p. 30.17) for more technical information about hard drives.

### Broadcast-quality software

Software for personal computers and workstations now exists to create stills, edit video nonlinearly, create transitions, perform composites, render special effects, animate in two and three dimensions, and so on, and all at high enough quality for broadcast or transfer to film. No one package can do it all, however, so it is important to research the capabilities of different software from different vendors. The minimum feature-set necessary to ensure broadcast-quality output is comprised of 24-bit color manipulation, subpixel positioning, anti-aliasing, Alpha channel support, text generation that supports anti-aliasing of Postscript™ and TrueType™ fonts, field-rendering, and control of the output gamut. Special effects also are useful, but not essential. All of these features are now described.

**24-bit color.**   The most common representation of color in personal computers is familiar to video professionals as "component" video. Here, colors are composed of three channels: red, green, and blue. Each channel is represented by 8 bits (1 byte), for a total of 24 bits per pixel. Programs that generate 24-bit color output are essential to broadcast-quality work, because this color scheme can represent more than 16 million separate colors, more than the human eye can distinguish. Any program with less will not allow colors to be manipulated with sufficient subtlety. For a more technical explanation of this color scheme, see the appendix .

**Subpixel positioning.**   If your software has DVE-like features, subpixel positioning is essential for achieving smooth-looking motion of video layers and important for compositing. To achieve broadcast-quality motion, it is necessary to compensate for the computer's limited screen resolution. This is accomplished by creating the illusion that the number of screen pixels per inch is much greater than it actually is. Subpixel sampling is the frame-processing method that creates this illusion. The appendix contains more technical information about this process.

**Anti-aliasing.**   Anti-aliasing becomes important when the edges of any graphic object are diagonal to any degree, when rectangular shapes are rotated, or when smooth curves are desired, as with character generation. Like subpixel positioning, it is a method of compensating for the limited resolution of the screen. It accomplishes this by removing "jaggies" (stairsteps that appear as edges that contrast sharply with the surroundings), thereby smoothing diagonal lines and curves.

Without anti-aliasing, the edges of any object that is not perfectly vertical or horizontal will become jagged. If the resolution of the broadcast medium is lower than that of the computer, this effect will be exaggerated when the video is broadcast. This feature is so important that PC programs exist that do nothing else but anti-alias stills or animation sequences. If your chosen primary editing software does not support this feature, it is still possible to eliminate aliasing problems, but with a substantial time penalty.

**Alpha channel support.**   The Alpha channel contains transparency information for each pixel. Many video professionals are surprised to find that some PC-based graphics software, such as Photoshop™, is more capable of creating and handling Alpha channel information than, for instance, a Quantel Paintbox (the de facto standard broadcast paint system). To the video professional, this transparency information is a key signal that defines which parts of the video frame are transparent, which opaque, and which semi-transparent.

The most common example of this may be seen on most newscasts. The character-generator used to overlay the type on the screen contains an Alpha channel. The layering device (a switcher) uses the Alpha channel to determine which parts of the overlay (the letters) will be opaque and which parts will be filled with the background image (a reporter standing in front of City Hall, for instance). This is similar but not the same as a chromakey, in which the key signal is generated from a chrominance value based on the incoming video.

There are a variety of standard uses for the Alpha channel. As mentioned above, overlaying text and graphics onto video is one such use. In addition to defining completely transparent and completely opaque areas, you also will want to use the Alpha channel to better blend graphic elements with the background in a subtle manner that mimics the appearance of a real object. This is done by making the edges of the object semitransparent, and it is essential for the creation of high-quality composites of any kind. Animation software, especially for three-dimensional animation, can benefit enormously from the including of an Alpha channel with each frame. This allows the compositing of 3D, computer-generated graphic animations into 2D backgrounds with ease, for example. Special effects that are aware of the Alpha channel can be used to warp images and their transparency information at the same time, allowing for greater realism in the effect.

There are, however, some drawbacks to using the Alpha channel. Storing transparency information for each frame of an animation means that storage requirements increase by 33 percent for each file containing an Alpha channel. Also, to obtain proper composites, several additional operations must be done to each pixel of the image when compositing, to take the transparency information into account. This increases rendering time by a fair amount. These drawbacks are small, however, compared to the benefits derived from using the Alpha channel.

**Text generation.** The wide variety of high-quality fonts available for most PCs makes them a natural choice for text generation. Many video programs support both Postscript and TrueType, meaning that almost any typeface imaginable is available. Most software allows not just character-generation but on-the-fly editing late in the production process. Anti-aliasing is essential to the creation of clean-looking curves and edges, and text that has not been anti-aliased is generally considered to be not of broadcast quality. Text-keying usually is accomplished by means of Alpha channel manipulation. Special text effects include texturing, coloring, and stretching and warping.

Given all of these advantages, it is surprising to find that PC character-generation software generally has not reached the same level of professionalism that other kinds of software have. While most editing software facilitates basic titling, little attention has been paid to kerning issues and scrolling credits, two fundamental components of proper video typesetting. Until such tools become available, it may be necessary to use other programs that have kerning features, or to break credits down into manageable groups and convert the text to graphic elements separately and then import the resulting graphics into the video project.

**Field rendering.** Since the final digital output must be recorded by analog-video equipment for broadcast, the analog format in which the video will be stored must be respected. NTSC video is recorded at 30 fps (frames per second), but each frame is made up of two fields of scan lines, meaning that the true recording rate is 60 fields per second. This avoids a staccato effect in the appearance of moving objects, because effectively the screen is changing 60 rather than 30 times per second.

Software must respect fields if it is to maintain broadcast quality. Since computer-generated animation files generally do not contain fields (unless the animation software specifically supports them), a way around this difficulty is to render the video at 60 fps, record to an output device, then play back at double speed. In this case the software generally will take twice as much time to produce an animation of a given duration (since it is creating twice as many frames), but the motion of objects will be much smoother when recorded to tape. Smarter software that respects fields will render at the same frame rate but store only the even or odd scan lines for a given frame, which will take about the same amount of time. It also is important to be sure that the recording software for both digitizing board and device controller are field-aware and can extract fields from a file that contains them.

**Output gamut control.**   It is important to note that many PC-video software programs will allow the use of colors that have higher saturation or luminance values than are legal for broadcast. To correct for this, prebroadcast processing may be necessary, and some programs have methods for altering "illegal colors" so as to conform to broadcast specifications. It is important to preview these alterations just in case, to compensate for any undesirable visual results. The best way is to preview on an NTSC monitor before rendering. It is possible to correct for this with traditional equipment after recording, but this increases time and expense requirements.

**Visual effects.**   The wide variety of visual effects available from microcomputer video applications amounts to a strong argument for going digital. Visual effects include standard transitions, DVE-style video motion control, layering and compositing, video image manipulation, keying, morphing, and too many more to mention. All these effects are not available in all programs, but they are all possible through various video applications on the PC. Indeed, it is possible to put together a suite of PC video tools that offers more video-manipulation capabilities than traditional video equipment costing upward of $500,000. Doing this at broadcast quality requires most of the software features mentioned in this section, however.

## Tradeoffs

### Trading old bottlenecks for new

The bottlenecks associated with traditional video-editing equipment are switcher capabilities, generation loss, and the limit to how many VTRs can be rolled at one time. All of these bottlenecks disappear when editing in a non-linear environment on a PC. Switcher capabilities become moot, because the computer effectively becomes a switcher with infinite inputs. Since all video is stored on a random-access disk, any portion of any file can be accessed at any time. This also renders the number of virtual VTRs effectively infinite, since the physical limits to the number of files that can be made available are seldom encountered. Generation loss, which occurs when working around switcher input limits, also becomes unnecessary. The number of layers that can be composited together at one time is limited only by memory.

The *new* bottlenecks are speed and disk space. The speed of the editing process depends upon the speed of the computer's CPU, the speed of the disk drives, the speed with which video can be digitized and recorded, and the efficiency with which the software being used was written. Disk-space requirements will always be large, and disk-space management tasks become routine if backing up and keeping old digitized footage is required. Fortunately, the severity of both of these problems is continually diminishing as faster machines and peripherals and higher-capacity drives continually are introduced. Since the need for speed and disk space is not restricted to the video marketplace, increased competition in these areas greatly speeds improvements in existing products and spurs development of new technologies.

### Quality versus time

Whether one is speaking of digitizing, rendering, or recording, there are explicit tradeoffs that can be made between image quality and time. It is possible to digitize video at real-time frame rates, but the quality of the quicker process and the necessity of compression for storage prevent this from resulting in broadcast-quality input. When rendering, subpixel positioning, anti-aliasing, Alpha channel manipulation, and special effects all can be performed at various quality levels or not at all. The lower the quality, the less time needed to perform the operation. Just as with digitization, it is not possible to play normal-size video at 30 fps without compressing to such a degree that loss of quality results. With all of the above operations, the speed of the computer will make a big difference, so it is best to get the fastest machine your budget will allow.

### Quality versus expense

As previously mentioned, nowhere will the tradeoff between expense and quality be more apparent than with digitizing and recording hardware. With the rare exception you get what you pay for, and the price of broadcast-quality input and output can be greater than the cost of the computer itself. One way around this is to purchase a PC-compatible tape drive, with tapes that also can be read by a local postproduction facility. A tape drive of this type costs less than digitizing and recording hardware, but the post facility will charge a fee for transferring the video to a broadcast storage medium, so this may not be cost-effective in the long run.

Software with broadcast-quality features generally will cost more than software without them, but this is not always the case. Careful and thorough research into different software packages and their capabilities can result in the discovery of inexpensive software gems. They exist. Both computer magazines and now video magazines publish reviews of different software packages that can be highly informative. Once a list of potential candidates has been narrowed down, it is helpful to visit a local systems house or VAR (value-added reseller), where you can actually try the software and ask questions of salespeople intimately familiar with the program.

## Conclusion

This has been an attempt to cover, in a generic fashion, the necessary tools for creating broadcast-quality video direct from the desktop. The capability to do this has really existed only for a short while, and the market is constantly changing as new products are introduced with more and better capabilities.

Today, however, it is indeed possible to use various combinations of software and hardware to achieve this end. The authors both share the firm opinion that the configuration described herein will bring the same revolutionary changes to video that desktop publishing brought to the publishing industry. This means that, while the need for high-end postproduction facilities will always exist, the personal computer will bring many of their technical capabilities out onto the desktop by virtue of its low price and high level of performance. Many more talented people will have the tools "all to themselves," because those tools will be affordable for individuals for the first time. Furthermore, as computers become ever cheaper, more and more developers will be lured into the arena of video production.

## Appendix

### More about compression

Many compression algorithms rely on the fact that there is much redundant information in an uncompressed frame. This can be removed in such a way that the human eye cannot perceive the difference. If enough information is removed, however, the eye *will* notice the difference as a loss of visual quality in the frame. There is thus an implicit tradeoff between visual quality and file size when compressing digital video.

Once digitized, one uncompressed frame of a standard NTSC-size video in true color (24 bits per pixel) takes up almost 1 Mbyte of disk space. At 30 frames per second, 1 second of uncompressed video takes about 30 Mbytes of storage. Although high-capacity storage devices are constantly falling in price, the costs for this much storage are still considerable.

Each compression algorithm is designed to be most effective for a certain type of video content. Ideally, different compression algorithms will be used for different types of video. Motion JPEG, for instance, is useful for "normal video" content, such as might be recorded by a news camera at the scene of a crime or a political rally. This type of video is considered "noisy," because the content is rich and varies greatly and, once digitized, the chance that any two adjacent pixels will be exactly the same color is rather low, but the chance that they will be similar is rather high. This contrasts with computer-generated animation, which is much less noisy, and in which the chances of any two adjacent pixels being exactly the same color is much greater, but the chance that any two adjacent pixels will also be very different is also greater (edges and boundaries are much sharper). The Motion JPEG algorithm will quickly begin to degrade the quality of computer-generated animations even at low compression ratios. Algorithms designed to compress animations well may actually increase the size of a "normal video" file. Thus, it is also important to match the appropriate compression method to the video content.

### Hard drives

To understand why the sustained transfer rate is crucial, recall that 1 frame of uncompressed video takes up 1 Mbyte. It will take a drive with a transfer rate of 1 Mbyte per second about 1 second to retrieve 1 frame at sustained rates, whereas it will take a disk array between $\frac{1}{5}$ to $\frac{1}{3}$ of a second. Multiply this difference ($1 - \frac{1}{5} = \frac{4}{5}$ seconds per frame) by 30 frames and it will equal 24 seconds saved for each second of video rendered to a disk array, just in transfer time alone. Of course, since most video is compressed, the actual time savings will be smaller, but it will still be significant.

Where the video file is broken up into three separate chunks, frames 0:00:00 to 0:07:27 might be stored in one chunk near the center of the disk. Frames 0:07:28 to 0:43:12 might be stored in the second chunk halfway toward the disk's edge, and frames 0:43:13 to 1:59:29 might be stored in a large chunk along the disk's outer edge. To play a video, the head must read each frame sequentially. When the head is done reading frame 0:07:27, it must move to the physical location of the next frame. If the computer has been playing the video at 30 fps, this move must happen in a split-second in order to avoid a pause in the action as viewed on screen.

More specifically, $\frac{1}{30}$ of a second equals 0.0333 seconds. At 30 fps, 0.0333 seconds is the maximum time that the computer has to perform the following tasks: (1) move the disk head to the correct location, (2) read the frame into memory, (3) decompress the frame, and (4) copy the frame to the screen. The bulk of this time will be spent on steps 2 and 3, leaving very little time for steps 1 and 4. From this perspective, even 15 milliseconds seems rather sluggish with respect to the need to play 30 fps.

### 24-bit and 32-bit color

One bit is the smallest unit of information in a computer, representing two numbers, either 1 or 0. A byte is a group of 8 bits, each of which can be switched on or off. This means that a byte can represent $2^8 = 256$ numbers. If we start counting from 0, then the maximum number that 1 byte can represent is 255. Twenty-four-bit color means that a given color is specified by 24 bits, or 3 bytes, within the computer. It is common for each of these 3 bytes to represent the amount of red, green, or blue used to make up the color of 1 pixel. One byte specifies the amount of red, the next byte the amount of green, and the last byte the amount of blue used. Since each byte can hold 256 possible values, and since the value in each byte is independent of the values in the other two, the number of possible colors that can be represented in this way is $256^3$ = more than 16 million colors, more than the human eye can distinguish, and more than enough for video.

The next most common step downward in terms of the number of possible colors a program can handle is by more than three orders of magnitude, to 16-bit color. In this representation, the amounts of red, green, and blue are specified by groups of 5 bits. Each group can represent $2^5$ = 32 numbers, and the three groups together can specify up to $32^3$ = 32,768 colors, or about 500 times fewer than 24-bit color can represent. The general consensus is that this is too few for broadcast quality.

In a 32-bit color scheme, the red, green, and blue channels for a pixel are represented by 1 byte each, and the Alpha channel is represented by an additional byte. Thus 32-bit color is really just 24-bit color with 1 byte of transparency information stored for each pixel as well. Since 1 byte can represent 256 possible values, there are 256 levels of transparency per pixel available in a 32-bit color scheme.

## Subpixel sampling

To be sure that we understand why this technique is important, let's review the way in which visual elements are represented on the computer screen. To the computer programmer, the screen is a grid of square dots or *pixels* (for *picture elements*). Consumer-level monitors generally support up to 80 or so pixels per inch (or dots per inch, abbreviated dpi). This is the computer's *screen resolution*. The programmer has control over the color of each individual pixel, and exercises this control to create the graphical user interfaces that make using computers easier, as well as to display a frame of video on-screen for the user.

Similarly, one frame of video is stored as a grid of pixels, each of which can be manipulated. To display a stored frame of video on a computer screen, the programmer must somehow map the pixels from the video frame to the appropriate pixels in the computer screen. This "mapping" process sometimes can become complicated.

In the simplest case, suppose the computer screen has a resolution of 80 dpi and is 8 inches wide. If the video also was digitized at the same resolution, then to display a nonrotated video frame the programmer can use a one-to-one mapping, which means that each pixel from the video frame corresponds to 1 pixel on the computer screen. For convenience, let's assume that column numbers begin with 1 for the leftmost column and increase by 1 to the right, with the rightmost column being number 640 (80 dpi × 8 inches). Assume that row numbers begin at 1 for the first row and increase by 1 down-screen. Proceeding from the left column to the right, the program would then color the pixel in column 1, row 1 of the screen the same color (bright red, for instance) as the pixel in column 1, row 1 of the video frame. This would then be repeated for columns 2 through 640, then start over again with column 1, row 2. The process would end when all screen pixels had been colored the same as their video-frame counterparts.

Suppose now that the programmer wants the video image to move horizontally to the right over time, creating the "reveal-right" transition. To create this motion, the programmer would again copy the pixels from the video frame, but with an offset from column 1. The value of the offset is determined by the speed of the reveal. Thus for the second frame of video, the screen pixel in column 1, row 1 would be colored black (the background color as revealed), and the screen pixel in column 2 (1 plus the desired offset), row 1 would be colored bright red, the same as the video pixel in column 1, row 1. Similarly, the color of each screen pixel would be determined by the video pixel in the same row, but in a column determined by the desired offset.

Note, however, that this means that the on-screen image can move only in increments of $\frac{1}{80}$ of an inch, due to the resolution of the screen. The video moves a certain number of pixels to the right according to the offset, but only to distances that are multiples of the width of a pixel. Problems arise when the speed of the push creates offsets that should be some fraction of an inch that is not a multiple of $\frac{1}{80}$. This might happen with a very slow push, for example. In this case, rounding the offset to the nearest $\frac{1}{80}$ will not create smooth motion. Rather the motion will appear choppy, abruptly jumping one pixel to the right. This is one example of video output that most video professionals would consider to be below the subjective threshold of broadcast quality.

Subpixel sampling involves coloring screen pixels according to a weighted average that takes into account the true value of the unrounded offset. In the example above, the screen pixel in column 1, row 1 was colored black, while the pixel in column 2, row 1 was colored bright red. With subpixel sampling, the screen pixel at column 1, row 1 would be colored neither black nor red, but some color that reflected a weighted average of black and red, with the weights being set according to the offset.

## Acknowledgment

The authors wish to state that this chapter was inspired by Thomas A. Ohanian's excellent book *Digital Nonlinear Editing* (Focal Press, 1993). This tome contains in-depth coverage of the past, present, and future of nonlinear film and video editing, as well as explanations of the underlying technology, and is highly recommended to those who wish to explore these issues more thoroughly. We just had to cover the little bit that he left out.

# Real-World Applications for MPEG Digital Video

**Ray Harris**

## What Is MPEG?

MPEG stands for Moving Picture Experts Group, a joint committee of the International Organization for Standardization (ISO) and the International Electrotechnical Commission (IEC). MPEG is broken into two different specifications, MPEG I and MPEG II. MPEG I was designed for limited-bandwidth transmission such as a CD-ROM on a PC. MPEG II is used for the high-bandwidth transmission typically used in satellite-based broadcast television.

MPEG I was finalized in December of 1991, with the goal of a compression standard that would deliver 30-fps "movies" over a limited-bandwidth channel such as a CD-ROM. MPEG II is under development, and as of this writing (early 1994), only the video had been finalized. MPEG II is aimed at the broadcast television market and will most probably not be suitable for low-cost PC use. This chapter will concentrate on the MPEG I standard.

## Reference frames and redundancy

In most movie scenes, the background remains relatively stable while action takes place. The background may move, but a great deal of the scene is redundant. MPEG starts its compression by creating a reference frame called an *I* or *Intra frame*. These I frames are placed every 10 to 15 frames. Each of the following frames is then transmitted as an annotation to the reference frame.

## Inside an MPEG stream

The three types of pictures in an MPEG stream are

1. Intra (*I*)
2. Predicted (*P*)
3. Bidirectional interpolated (*B*).

Intra pictures provide entry points for random access, but only with moderate compression. Predicted pictures are encoded with reference to a past picture (Intra or previous Predicted), and in general will be used as a reference for future Predicted pictures. Bidirectional pictures provide the highest amount of compression but require both a past and a future reference for prediction. Bidirectional pictures never are used for references.

**Finding the macro block (motion compensation).**   The reference picture is divided into a grid of 16 × 16 pixel squares called *macro blocks*. Each subsequent picture is also divided into these same macro blocks. The computer then searches for an exact, or near exact, match between the reference-picture macro block and those in succeeding pictures. When a match is found, the computer transmits only the difference through what is called a *vector movement code*.

**Tracking the changes (spatial redundancy).**   After finding the changes in location of macro blocks, the MPEG algorithm will further reduce the data by describing the difference between corresponding macro blocks. This is accomplished through a math process call *discrete cosine transform* or *DCT*. This process divides the macro block into four subblocks, seeking out changes in color and brightness. The MPEG committee found that human perception is more sensitive to brightness changes than to color changes. Armed with this research, the MPEG committee specified the MPEG process so that the MPEG algorithm would devote most of its efforts to reducing color space rather than brightness.

## Developing Markets for New Technology

The key to growing a market is to first have an industry standard that is (1) affordable and (2) easy to implement. At first release, MPEG met neither of those requirements. The algorithms required to execute the MPEG compression schemes were complex, and available only from a few firms in the first year after the standard was established. This limited the early acceptance of MPEG I and spawned numerous PC-based alternatives. These ranged from simple software products offering postage-stamp-sized video in a window, at a very low frame rate per second, all the way up to true high-quality video-compression hardware.

As the PC industry struggled to decide which alternative would replace the standard, the video industry wholeheartedly embraced MPEG I as being the true high-quality standard the committee had envisioned it would become. This schism between the PC and video industry explains why most PC-based users and analysts have failed to see the rapid growth of digital-video applications. The PC industry is now also looking to move more strongly toward the MPEG specification. This change in direction is due purely to a lowering of the price point at which MPEG may be delivered. While the first PC-based MPEG players were priced near $2000, the next generations are expected to come in well below the $1000 mark. The near future will bring us MPEG playback hardware for the PC priced under $500. These lower prices will spur the growth of MPEG and add a great deal of stability to the standardization of video compression on PC-based applications.

### Early adopters

As is true with any new technology, there were the early adopters. These users are driven by technical needs and by a strong desire to establish themselves as leaders in their respective markets. In the case of digital video, the early adopters also saw a direct increase in functionality tied to a decrease in costs. These early adopters are now integrating MPEG digital video into a surprisingly diverse assortment of applications. These applications range from cable television to video kiosks, but all have one thing in common: the need for professional-quality visualization.

Early adopters of MPEG I saw the technology as a replacement for expensive videotape recorders and video laserdiscs. These video players have been heavily used in the video-kiosk, interactive-training, ad-insertion, and preview-channel markets. The advantages of digital playback are readily apparent when it is compared to the industry-standard videotape and laserdisc players. Its main advantages are delivery of video over a network and over phone lines, lower maintenance costs, and lower system costs. These are the keys to an understanding of the early and continued growth of MPEG I.

## Applications

The applications for compressed digital video are enormous. Nearly every facet of our life will be touched by this new technology. Our videotape recorders, televisions, games, and shopping will all be enhanced by the addition of MPEG digital video. Given the global size of the digital-video market, it should come as no surprise that the silicon chip manufacturers all are looking at MPEG as the largest chip market ever to evolve. The following applications are just a sampling of actual uses of MPEG currently in development or being shipped.

### Video kiosks

The kiosk market has evolved from a posted sign on an obelisk to a true multimedia application. Today's kiosk developers have a myriad of tools available. Touchscreens, software authoring packages, CD-ROM writers, and digital video all are enabling kiosks to impart a stronger, more interactive message than ever before.

The simple self-running tape in the grocery store's meat department has now become a tailored message on how to prepare one's food of choice. The video store that runs out of this week's top hits can offer an interactive kiosk that will help the potential customer to choose an alternative, complete with a 30-second movie trailer. In every case, the addition of interactive digital video to a kiosk increases a retailer's sales through the dissemination of usable information.

In the near future, walk-up bank tellers and auto dealerships will feature video kiosks with professional-quality digital video. These future kiosks will perform at even higher levels than today's advanced systems. The future will add complete interaction, transaction processing, and demographic processing for the developer. The video kiosk is a low-cost, highly effective tool for delivering an interactive, high-quality message that will soon encompass many aspects of our daily lives.

### Cable TV advertisement insertion, and barker channels

Today's cable television is delivered from the satellite to head-end stations, and finally to the home. The head-end station is an unattended building that receives the incoming signal, mixes it with local content, and sends it out to the home. These head ends are filled with high-quality, fully automated, analog videotape recorders and laserdisc players. These analog-video devices are used to deliver local advertisements and previews of upcoming pay-per-view events.

MPEG professional-quality digital video is a perfect replacement for the high-maintenance analog devices found in the head-end station. The benefits of using digital video over analog are tremendous. Local advertisements that, with analog, previously required a physical delivery to every head end, can simply be downloaded electronically with a digital system.

This change in delivery of the ad spots represents a savings in terms of personnel and also benefits the customer via faster response times. Under the current analog-based system, the customer may have to wait 2 to 3 days for his or her advertisement to be copied and delivered to all of the pertinent head-end stations. With the new fully digital system, the customer's advertisement can be electronically transmitted to the head-end stations within hours of its creation. This increased flexibility will allow advertisers to adapt their message to timely changes in events. In addition, the digital-video system requires far less maintenance than the traditional analog players, with all of their moving parts.

### Interactive training

The training and education market has long been a volume user of laserdisc players. These players deliver high-quality video content to students, corporate executives, and others. The two drawbacks of laserdisc players are (1) that they cannot be shared over a network and (2) that their level of interactivity is very low.

Replacing a laserdisc with MPEG digital video solves both the network and the interactivity problems. The content may easily be sent over standard networks in a "store-and-forward" mode, or interactively on a properly configured network. The addition of network capability opens up the access users have to the prepared content.

Interactive video is far more enticing than traditional closed-access systems. Digital video is a natural tool for the development of interactive training content. Touchscreens, pointing devices, and keyboards become the gateways to high-quality corporate training and educational media.

## Arcade games and simulations

Arcade games and simulations are very similar in their construction and content. Both typically use computer-generated graphics or laserdisc video to create a simulation of a real-world experience. These applications require quick response from interactive media.

Digital video is the ideal solution to this application. The high-quality nature of MPEG, along with its minimal storage requirements, make it well suited both to arcade games and to simulations. Future arcade games will move from low-quality, computer-generated graphics to fully interactive graphics mixed with real video footage. The heightened sense of reality undoubtedly will create increased demand to play these new games, and subsequently increase revenue for the arcade owners.

## Video on demand

*Video on demand,* or *VOD,* is a widely used term that has no specific meaning. In reality, any application that provides video at the request of a user is demonstrating a VOD capability. In the hospitality and home arenas, video on demand has come to be synonymous with certain applications such as movies. Given the nebulous nature of the term *VOD,* the potential areas of usage will be discussed individually.

**Institutional video.**   Hotels and hospitals currently provide movies on a pay-per-view basis. These movies actually are played on a scheduled basis from videotape players located on the property of the institution. The drawbacks of such a physical solution are limited playing times and a limited selection of movies.

Switching to digital video with MPEG completely changes the scope of the service such institutions can provide. With properly networked MPEG videos, users can chose from dozens of movies and watch them at their own convenience. The benefits to the institutions are increased viewing and increased revenues from rentals.

**Video dial tone.**   The phone companies are very aggressively going after their piece of the VOD market. Their vision is that we will all order, and receive, our movies through high-speed phone lines. Unlike the CATV infrastructure, which will have to be upgraded to provide sufficient bandwidth for VOD, the entire United States currently is wired to provide sufficient capabilities for the regional phone companies to enable this technology.

In essence, every home that wishes to have access to VOD through the phone lines will be required to have an MPEG decoder sitting on top of their television set and connected to their high-speed phone line. Users will interactively select the movies they wish to view, then sit back and enjoy. In the background a massive file-server will have been put into action, finding the requested movie and serving it up to the correct home. Virtually all of the regional phone companies are active in this area.

**Cable TV.**   Interactive services and VOD are hot topics for the CATV industry. The drawback here is that given the current infrastructure, it is estimated that the cost to the CATV operators to upgrade their serviced homes to be VOD-ready will be around $11 billion. This figure is based on an estimate of there being a $200 set-top television decoder hooked to the cable system. Given the enormity of the investment, and the complexity of switching all of the head-end stations to large servers, this is expected to take several years to complete.

The first step for the CATV operators will be to use video compression on their satellite transmissions. This alone will enable the fabled 500-channel scenario. The next step will be to make the head ends capable of supplying an increased number of channels. The final step will be to install a TV decoder in every household. While many CATV operators are actively going forward with interactive CATV units, the prospect of widespread demand for VOD through the use of these interactive units appears to be at least a few years away.

### Consumer applications

A number of consumer applications will utilize MPEG digital video to enhance the user's experience. These products include the Philips CD-I player with the FMV option, the JVC Video Karaoke, and the Interactive player from 3DO. The Philips CD-I and the 3DO will use MPEG to decode feature-length movies, add excitement to games, and possibly to act as a television decoder for cable broadcast. The JVC Karaoke represents the logical next extension to what has become an extremely popular pastime in the pubs and nightclubs of the world.

### MPEG Is Transparent

In the coming few years, MPEG I and MPEG II will be used in numerous applications that affect our daily lives. The beauty of the MPEG algorithms is that most people will never know that the video they are watching has been switched from analog to digital. We, as users, will only know that we have been given a far greater number of choices in the movies we may watch, that our lives are touched by greater amounts of easily disseminated information, and that the world has become just a little bit smaller.

# 32

# Introduction to Digital Video and Audio

**Ken Morse**

## The Real World

Television was designed to reproduce natural images and sounds, and nature is basically analog. In nature, the brightness of an object can have any value, and the object can be shaded with minute graduation. Likewise, a natural object can take on any position that is consistent with the action of gravity, and it may be moved smoothly with microscopic precision. Real images and sounds thus are made up of intensity values and positions that can have any level—continuous functions in both space and time—that is analog.

The digital world of the personal computer can deal only with discrete levels, and it cannot process continuous values. Hence the video and audio signals must be converted into discrete values in time for manipulation by the computer. The following section introduces the principles of analog video as it is used in the television industry today.

## Analog video

We've already established that most things in nature are analog. Real images and sounds are based on light intensity and sound-pressure values, which are continuous functions in space and time. Conversion of images or sounds to electrical signals is accomplished through the appropriate use of sensors, called *transducers*. Sensors for converting images and sounds to electronic signals are typically analog devices, with analog outputs. The world of television and sound recording is based on these devices. Video cameras and microphones (the sensors) are familiar objects to almost everyone, and their purpose generally is well understood. This section introduces the chief concepts associated with analog video, from its origin in a video camera to the thing itself. Right now, however, we will concentrate on how video cameras work.

### Video cameras

Video cameras have become commonplace in today's society. Once found only in the domain of television studios, a modern video camera can now fit in the palm of the hand, due to advances in technology and integration.

The video camera converts an image in front of the camera into an electrical signal. Electrical signals are one-dimensional, i.e., they can have only one value at any instant in time. However, images are two-dimensional and have many values at all the different positions within the image. To convert the two-dimensional image into a one-dimensional electrical signal, the image is scanned in an orderly progressive manner called a *raster scan.* Scanning is achieved by rapidly moving a single sensing point over the image. The complete image must be scanned fast enough to capture the complete image before it changes too much. As the sensing point moves, the electrical output changes in response to the brightness or color of the image under the sensing point. This varying electrical signal from the sensor represents the image as a series of values spread out in time and is called the *video signal.*

Figure 32.1 shows a stationary monochrome image being scanned in raster fashion. The image scan begins at the upper left corner and progresses horizontally across the image, making a scanning line. At the same time, the scanning point is being moved down at a very much slower rate. When the right side of the image is reached, the scanning point returns to the left side.

Due to the slow vertical motion of the scanning point, it is now below the starting point of the first line. It then scans across again on the next line, snaps back to the left edge, and continues until the entire image has been scanned vertically by a series of lines. As each line is scanned, the electrical output from the scanning sensor represents the light intensity of the image at

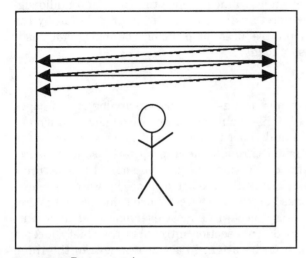

**Figure 32.1**   Raster scanning.

each position of the scanning point. During the snap-back time (known as the *horizontal blanking interval*) the sensor is turned off and a zero-output (or *blanking-level*) signal is sent out. The signal from a complete scan of the image is a sequence of line signals, separated by horizontal blanking intervals, called a *frame*.

## Aspect ratio

An important parameter of the scanning process is the *aspect ratio*. This is the ratio of the length of a scanning line horizontally on the image to the distance covered vertically on the image by all the scanning lines. It also can be thought of as the width-to-height ratio of a frame. Aspect ratio for television was standardized very early on at 4:3. Other systems, most notably movies, use different aspect ratios that can be as high as 2:1.

## Synchronization

If the video signal is used to modulate the brightness of the beam in a cathode-ray tube that is being scanned exactly the same way as the sensor, the original image will be reproduced. This is exactly what happens in a television set in the home or in a video monitor. The electrical signal(s) sent to the monitor must contain some additional information to ensure that the monitor's scanning will be synchronized with the sensor's scanning. This information is called *sync information* and consists of horizontal and vertical timing signals. It may be included with the video signal itself during the blanking intervals, or it may be sent on a separate cable (or cables) meant just for the sync information.

## Horizontal resolution

As the scanning point moves across one line, the electrical signal output from the sensor changes continuously in response to the light level of the part of the image that the sensor sees. One measure of scanning performance is the horizontal resolution of the pickup system, which depends on the size of the scanning-sensitive point. To test the horizontal resolution performance of a system, which also measures the capability to reproduce horizontal fine detail, closely spaced vertical lines are placed in front of the camera. If the sensor area is smaller than the space between the vertical lines, the lines will be reproduced, but when the sensor is too large the lines will average out under the sensor and will not be seen in the output signal.

To achieve a realistic measure, the horizontal resolution must be related to other parameters in the image for consistency. In the television industry, horizontal resolution is measured by counting the number of black and white vertical lines that can be reproduced in a distance corresponding to the raster height. Thus a system that is said to have a horizontal resolution of 300 lines can reproduce 150 black and 150 white lines alternating across a horizontal distance corresponding to the height of the image.

Scanning a pattern of black and white lines results in a high-frequency electrical signal, and it is important that the circuits used for processing and transmitting these signals have adequate bandwidth. Broadcast television systems require a bandwidth of about 1 MHz for each 80 lines of horizontal resolution. Since the North American broadcast television system uses a bandwidth of 4.5 MHz, a theoretical limit to the horizontal resolution is 360 lines.

### Vertical resolution

The second resolution parameter of interest is the vertical resolution, and this simply depends on the number of scanning lines used in one frame. The more lines there are, the higher the vertical resolution. Broadcast television systems use either 525 (North America) or 625 (Europe) lines per frame.

Not all of the vertical lines contain image information. A small number of lines in each frame are devoted to the vertical blanking interval. Both this and the horizontal blanking interval were originally intended to provide time for the scanning beam in cameras or monitors to retrace so as to start the next frame or the next line. In modern systems these intervals have many other uses, since they represent nonactive picture time during which different information can be transmitted along with the video signal. Video studios have used the vertical blanking to encode time-stamp information into the signal, and many television systems encode teletext or closed-caption information on these lines.

### Frame rates for motion

If acceptable motion video is to be produced, many frames must be scanned each second to produce the effect of smooth motion. Standard broadcast video systems use frame rates of 25 or 30 frames per second (depending on the country). Although these frame rates are high enough to provide smooth motion, they are not high enough to prevent a video display from having flicker. The human eye can perceive flicker in a bright image that is refreshed at less than 50 times per second. However, to increase the frame rate to that range while preserving horizontal resolution would require a speeding up of all the scanning, both horizontal and vertical, and would therefore increase the system bandwidth. To avoid this difficulty, all television systems use *interlace.*

Interlace means that more than one vertical scan is used to reproduce a complete frame. Broadcast television uses 2:1 interlace—2 vertical scans for a complete frame. With 2:1 interlace, one vertical scan displays all the odd lines of a frame, then a second puts in all the even lines. At 30 frames per second (North America), the vertical rate is 60 scans per second. Since the eye does not readily see flickering objects that are small, the 30-per-second repetition rate of any one line is not seen as flicker, but rather the entire picture appears to be refreshed at 60-per-second. Other specialized systems have used higher interlace ratios, but the 2:1 broadcast standard is prevalent.

## Color television systems

The color cameras just described were producing three output signals: red, green, and blue. This signal combination is called *RGB*. Most uses of video involve more than a single camera connected to a single monitor. The signal probably has to be recorded; we may wish to combine the outputs of several cameras together in different ways, and almost always we will want to have more than one viewing monitor. Therefore we usually will be concerned with a color-video system, containing much more than cameras. In RGB systems, all parts of the system are interconnected with three parallel video cables, one for each of the color channels.

However, because of the complexities involved in distributing three signals in exact synchronism and relationship, most color television systems do not handle RGB (except within cameras), but rather the camera signals are encoded into a composite format that may be distributed on a single cable. Such composite formats are used throughout television studios, for video recording, and for broadcasting. There are several different composite formats used in different countries around the world—NTSC, PAL, SECAM—and each will be discussed in the next section. Here we will concentrate on some of the conceptual aspects of composite color-video systems.

Composite color systems originally were developed for the broadcasting of color signals by a single television transmitter. However, it was soon found that the composite format is the best approach to use throughout the video system, so it is now conventional for the composite encoding to take place inside the camera box before any signals are brought out. Except for purposes such as certain video-manipulation processes, RGB signals do not exist in modern television plants.

All composite formats make use of the luminance/chrominance principle for their basic structure. This principle says that any color signal may be broken into two parts: *luminance,* which is a monochrome video signal that controls only the brightness (or luminance) of the image, and *chrominance,* which contains only the coloring information for the image. However, because a tristimulus color system requires three independent signals to achieve complete representation of all colors, the chrominance signal is actually two signals, called *color differences.*

Luminance plus chrominance is just one of the many possible combinations of three signals that could be used to transmit color information. They are obtained by a linear matrix transformation of the RGB signals created in the camera. The matrix transformation simply means that each of the luminance and chrominance signals is an additive (sometimes with negative coefficients) combination of the original RGB signals. In a linear transmission system, the number of possible matrix transformations that might be used is infinite; we just need to be sure that we use the correct inverse transformation when we recover RGB signals so as to display them on a color monitor. Psychovisual research (research into how images look to a human viewer) has shown that by carefully choosing an appropriate transformation, we can generate signals for transmission that will be affected by the limitations of transmission in ways that will not show (as much) in the reproduced picture.

In a composite system, the luminance and chrominance are combined by a scheme of *frequency-interleaving* in order to transmit them on a single channel. The luminance signal is transmitted as a normal monochrome signal on the cable or channel, and then the chrominance information is placed on a high-frequency subcarrier located near the top of the channel bandwidth. If this carrier frequency is correctly chosen, very little interference will occur between the two signals. This interleaving works because of two facts:

1. The luminance channel is not very sensitive to interfering signals that come in near the high end of the channel bandwidth. This is especially effective if the interfering signal has a frequency that is an odd multiple of twice the line-scanning rate in adjacent scanning lines, for visually the interference tends to cancel out. The selection of the right carrier frequency for the chrominance ensures this interlace condition.

2. The eye is much less sensitive to color edges than it is to luminance edges in the picture. This means that the bandwidth of the chrominance signals can be reduced without much visual loss of resolution. Bandwidth reductions of 2 to 4 are appropriate.

Thus, a composite system is able to transmit a color signal on a single channel that has the same bandwidth as each of the three RGB signals we started with. The transmission is not perfect, but it is good enough to be the basis of our worldwide television systems. This packing of the three RGB signals into the same bandwidth once used only for one (black-and-white) signal may seem like we are getting something for nothing, but that's not the case. What is really happening is that we are utilizing the spaces in the channel that are unused when transmitting only a single television signal, as we are also making compromises in the reproduction of the color information based on our knowledge of what the viewer can and cannot see in the final image.

### Color video formats—NTSC

The NTSC color television system is the standard broadcasting system for North America, Japan, and a few other countries. NTSC stands for National Television Systems Committee, a standardizing body in the 1950s that chose a color television system for the United States. The NTSC system is a composite luminance/chrominance system, as just described. An important objective for the NTSC system was to be compatible with the monochrome color system, already in place with millions of receivers long before color television began. This objective was met by making the luminance signal of NTSC just the same as the previous monochrome standard, so that existing monochrome receivers see the luminance signal only, and the color signal present at the top of the bandwidth does not show up very much on monochrome sets.

In NTSC, the luminance signal is called the Y *signal,* and the two chrominance signals are *I* and *Q.* The color carrier frequency, which must be maintained very accurately, is 3.58 MHz. As already explained, the I and Q color difference signals have reduced bandwidths. While the luminance can utilize the full 4.5-MHz bandwidth of a television channel, the I bandwidth is only 1.5-MHz, and the Q signal is chosen so that it can get away with only 0.5-MHz bandwidth.

When the I and Q signals are modulated onto the color subcarrier of the NTSC system, they result in a color subcarrier frequency component, whose amplitude represents the saturation values of the image; the phase of the color subcarrier represents the hue values of the image. NTSC receivers usually have controls to adjust these two parameters in the decoding of the NTSC signal.

Figure 32.2 shows a single line of composite video, and illustrates the modulation of chrominance information on the luminance signal.

It should be pointed out that the NTSC system was designed to deliver satisfactory performance with the kinds of signals created by looking at real scenes. Today we also can generate video signals with computers, and problems can arise if a computer-generated signal does not follow the rules when it is expected to be passed through an NTSC system.

**Color video formats—PAL**

The PAL system, which originated in Europe, is also a luminance/chrominance system. It differs from NTSC primarily in the way in which the

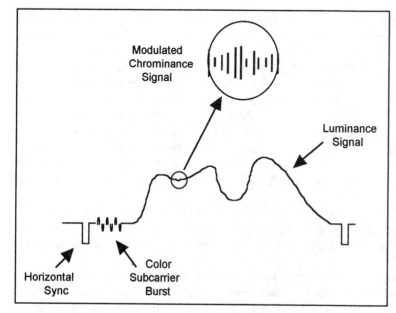

**Figure 32.2**  Baseband analog video.

chrominance signals are encoded. In PAL, the two chrominance signals have the same bandwidth (1.5 MHz) and hence a different set of chrominance components is used, called $U$ and $V$ instead of $I$ and $Q$. In addition, PAL signals are more tolerant of certain distortions that can occur in transmission paths that affect the quality of the color reproduction.

## Digital Video

A digital-video system is any system in which the information for images is represented as a series of digital bits. The most common digital-video system is the display portion of any personal computer. In a PC, the information for the video display is represented as a pattern of bits contained in the PC's memory. These bits are accessed by the display circuitry and manipulated to provide the computer displays that are so familiar. Two processes are examined in this section that form the backbone of digital-video systems. First the process for converting analog video into the digital domain is explained. This is followed by a description of the reverse process required to display the final image.

### Sampling

Analog waveforms are continuous both in time and in value (amplitude). For an analog waveform to be converted into a digital signal, both of these dimensions must be changed into noncontinuous values. The amplitude is represented as a digital integer (with a specific number of bits) and time is represented as a series of these integer amplitude values taken at equal steps in time.

The process for converting amplitude into discrete values is called *quantizing,* and the process of converting time into discrete values is called *sampling*. These two processes together are referred to as *analog-to-digital conversion (A/D),* or sometimes *digitizing*. Since the continuous analog signal is converted into discrete steps by the A/D process, an approximation of the original signal is created. If care is taken in the choice of the correct numbers, A/D conversion can be carried out with sufficient precision that the approximation errors cannot be detected when reproduced by the digital system. The approximations of the initial conversion process may be the only approximations, since digital systems reproduce digital values exactly. Further approximations or errors may be introduced, but only if the designer introduces them.

Figure 32.3 illustrates the sampling process. For every clock pulse the instantaneous value of the analog waveform is read, thus yielding a series of sampled values. The sampling-clock frequency is referred to as the *sampling rate*.

Since the input analog signal is continuous, the value changes over time. The A/D conversion process takes a finite time to complete, hence the input analog signal must be held constant during the conversion process to avoid

**Figure 32.3**  The sampling process.

conversion problems. This task is carried out by a sample-and-hold circuit. At this stage if the clock frequency is high enough, the samples will be a good representation of the analog waveform. However, it is important to note that at this stage the signal is discrete only in time, each sample is still analog, and each may have any value in a continuous range.

### Quantization

Now all analog samples must be converted into digital values. This is achieved by quantizing them. Quantization establishes a series of equally spaced levels in amplitude, as shown in Fig. 32.4. In the figure there are 16 quantization levels, and the span between each two thresholds in amplitude is given a value from 0 to 15. Each sample is matched to the appropriate threshold level and assigned the corresponding numerical value. This value can then be represented digitally and coded. This simple digital-coding stream is called *pulse code modulation (PCM)*. Digital coding is not limited to a linear series of quantized values; it can replace the sampled and quantized values with any set of consistent numbers. Such non-integer coding is called *nonlinear quantization,* or more frequently *companding.*

Returning to the example of 16 quantized levels, the numbers for each level can be coded as digital values of 4 bits. Hence the quantization is at 4 bits per sample. To achieve an adequate representation of the analog signal, there must be a sufficient number of quantization levels. This digital signal may then be reconstructed by the reverse process of digital-to-analog conversion, which will be covered in a subsequent section.

From the previous discussion it is now clear that there must be a high enough sampling rate, and enough quantizing levels, to acceptably approxi-

**Figure 32.4**  Quantization.

mate an analog signal. To better understand the effect of sampling rate, take a look at Fig. 32.5.

In this figure the analog signal to be converted is a high-frequency sine wave. In the first case the sine wave is sampled at a very high rate, so that 10 samples are generated for each cycle of the sine wave. In this first case, the samples represent the sine wave adequately. A sampling rate that is lower than the sine-wave frequency is used in the second case, with only one sample acquired for every two cycles of the sine wave. The output from this process in no way resembles the original signal. The third example illustrates a special case in which exactly two samples are taken per cycle of the sine wave.

At this rate, the frequency of the sine wave is present in the output but the waveform is square rather than sine. This special case illustrates the *Nyquist limit,* where the input sine wave is at the highest frequency that can be sampled with the sampling clock. The Nyquist theorem states that to reproduce a waveform that has a maximum frequency component *F,* the waveform must be sampled at $2 \times F$. Any attempt to digitize at a lower rate will result in an output that is incorrect for any high-frequency components in the input.

Care must be taken when sampling information above the Nyquist rate, since spurious output components are produced. This is known as *aliasing,* and most systems include an analog low-pass filter on the input before sampling, to remove any frequency components above half the sampling rate. Most modern designs will use a sampling rate higher than twice the input bandwidth, since analog filters cannot be designed to have an absolute cutoff (they cut off gradually with increasing frequency). With the introduction of competitively priced digital signal processors (DSPs), filtering can be carried out in the digital domain, where it is much easier to attain sharp cutoff characteristics.

The only limit on the quantizing process comes from the number of quantization levels used. It is very difficult to define how many levels should be

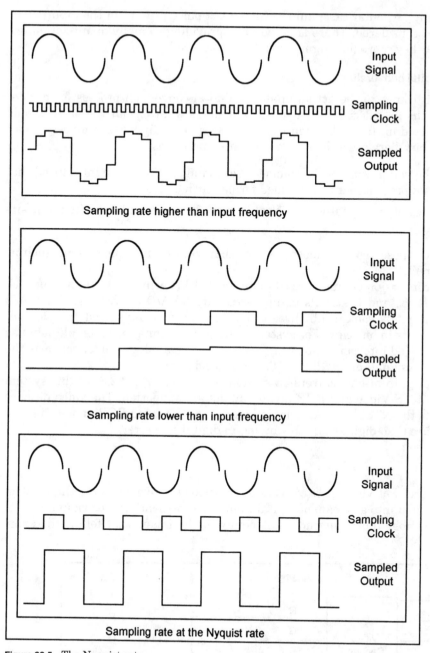

Sampling rate higher than input frequency

Sampling rate lower than input frequency

Sampling rate at the Nyquist rate

**Figure 32.5** The Nyquist rate.

used in a particular case, but the amount of noise present in the input signal must be considered. There is no point in providing so many quantization levels that they reproduce signal variations that are less than the noise.

### Video analog-to-digital conversion

When it comes to the actual analog-to-digital conversion process for a video signal, the first decision that must be made is what format the video should be digitized in. It will be seen that it is possible to digitize a composite video signal, but there are at least two associated problems:

1. By the very nature of the composite-encoding, artifacts are introduced that are not present in a non-encoded format such as RGB.

2. The resultant digital-video signal is difficult to manipulate in its composite form.

For both these reasons, most systems digitize a component scheme such as RGB or YUV.

The conversion of analog RGB to digital RGB is achieved by digitizing each of the R, G, and B signals using three parallel A/D converters. Video A/D chips normally contain all three converters and the associated sample-and-hold circuits in one chip. For systems where the original material already has been encoded into composite—e.g., videotape—an analog decoder converts the composite signal into RGB or YUV ready for digitizing.

A typical front-end conversion system is shown in Fig. 32.6. In this system composite, S-Video and RGB analog inputs are supported. The video decoder converts the NTSC- or PAL-encoded video into baseband RGB analog signals, which are then digitized by the analog-to-digital converter.

### Pixels

The process of video A/D conversion described above converts the analog-video signal into a stream of digital numbers representing the original image. Each number represents adjacent points in the image that follow the same

**Figure 32.6**   A simple video digitizer.

pattern as when the camera originally scanned the image. Each of these numbers represents a pixel, and when the image is reconstructed each pixel will be shown as a small rectangle filled with a color based upon the number. How realistic the resultant image looks is dependent on the number of pixels used and the color-encoding scheme used.

Every digital-video display can be viewed as a two-dimensional array of pixels. The sampling rate for digesting must be accurately related to the number of pixels required, and locked to the scanning frequencies of the input signal. Failure to do these two things will result in a digital image that has an incorrect aspect ratio.

## Pixelation

The number of pixels in a digital image is analogous to the horizontal and vertical resolutions of an analog system, but the appearance to the eye of pixels is very different from that conveyed by the analog system. The analog signal is continuous, and as such provides smooth transitions horizontally as the image changes. In the vertical direction there is a step from one line to the next, which can provide some artifacts. A common artifact can be seen when watching sports coverage that includes boundary lines such as the markings on a basketball court. If the viewing camera shows the court from one of the court corners, the resultant diagonal lines appear to be stepped (also known as *the staircase effect*). This is because the video signal is not continuous in the vertical direction. Most systems today provide a form of filtering that helps to remove the staircase effect and blend lines together.

In an analog system with low resolution the picture will become fuzzy, but in a digital system an effect known as *pixelation* occurs. As the resolution decreases, each pixel represents a higher proportion of the entire picture, but it can provide only a single color to represent that area. With dwindling resolution, the resultant image starts to take on a blocky appearance. The human eye is very good at picking out edges, and as the resolution decreases the edges of each pixel become more obvious due to the increased color difference from one pixel to the next. If you are viewing low-resolution digital images, notice how they often look better when viewed with slightly closed eyes. This has the effect of blurring the edges of the pixels, and some low-resolution digital systems use a low-pass filter on the display output to create the same effect and reduce the pixelation.

How visible pixelation is depends on the distance from which the image is viewed. For example, for a typical 13-inch computer screen viewed from a normal desktop distance of 18 inches, 540 pixels vertically are required. Taking a 4:3 aspect ratio into account means that the desktop display should be at least 720 × 540 to avoid pixelation.

It already has been noted that there is no active picture information during the blanking periods. Digitizing the analog-video signal as has been described will also digitize the blanking intervals. This means that when you are

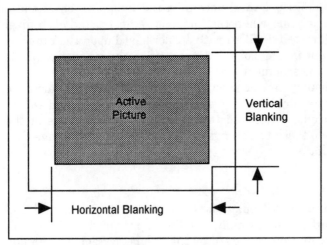

**Figure 32.7**   Removal of blanking intervals.

digesting video signals, the blanking-period data may be discarded and only the active image area is stored, as shown in Fig. 32.7.

### Bits per pixel

By this stage there is a bitmap of pixels stored in memory, ready to be displayed. The realism of the image displayed is dependent on the number of possible colors, which in turn is determined by the number of bits per pixel. Different systems use different values, ranging from 1 to 32 bits per pixel. A 1-bit display system can display only two colors, usually black and white. Such a system has a place for computer graphics but cannot display a realistic image. (It also has a low memory requirement, which can be advantageous.)

What is required for realistic image display? It will be easiest to consider monochrome images first. We suggested earlier that a good signal-to-noise ratio for a video system is 46 dB, which generates a video signal with about 3 percent peak-to-peak noise. Using the earlier criteria for quantizing, set one level equal to the peak-to-peak noise. That will require 33 levels for the 46-dB system, with 3 percent noise. This could then be reproduced by digitizing with 5 bits (32 levels). However, images quantized at 5 bits do not look acceptable, due to a digital artifact known as *contouring*.

### Contouring

The contouring effect occurs because all analog levels that fall between two thresholds of the quantizer are replaced with the same digital value, and thus will be reproduced at the output of the digital system with the same value also. Any part of the image that has a slowly changing analog level will be converted into stairsteps by the quantizing. The stairsteps will be clearly visible even when they are smaller than the random noise that was on the analog signal, because they are correlated with the image itself. (The analog noise was random and constantly changing—that is why 3 percent noise is not very visible.)

For noise patterns that are coherent, or correlated with the image, the visibility threshold is more like 0.5 percent. That is $\frac{1}{200}$ of the amplitude range, and would be achieved by quantizing with 8 bits per pixel (256 levels). For contouring to be invisible in monochrome or luminance signals, 8-bit-per-pixel quantizing is required.

## Introducing color

It is now time to leave the realm of black-and-white monochrome images and return to the real world of color images. Processes similar to those in the monochrome case must be applied in the case of each of the three color components (RGB, YUV, etc.) if color images are to be reproduced digitally.

One common approach is to generate 24-bit RGB pixel values by using three A/D converters (8 bits for each of R, G, and B) in parallel. 24-bit RGB gives excellent reproduction, since the 24 bits are capable of generating more than 16 million colors. However, there are several problems with 24-bit systems. They are very expensive in terms of memory usage, storage, and the processing power required to manipulate the images.

Earlier reference was made to the process of digitizing the composite analog-video signal and handling that digitally. Eight bits per pixel is adequate, but the signal must be sampled at a rate of at least 3 times the color subcarrier frequency, which leads to an average size of around 420K for a 640 × 480 image. After one has considered the problems associated with manipulating the image in this format, it becomes clear that it is unsuitable for use in computer video systems. However, in the broadcast television industry the D2-standard digital-video recorders use this technique to overcome the analog limitations associated with multiple-generation recording.

Many systems use 16 bits per pixel as a compromise; 5 bits red, 6 bits green, 5 bits blue is a common split, since the human eye is most receptive to the green area of the spectrum. Sixteen bits gives over 65,000 colors, which works well with highly colored images and will exhibit contouring only in images that have subtle shadings of colors over large areas.

Techniques to reproduce good images with fewer bits than the above numbers are called *video-compression techniques*. There are a wide range of techniques available, and these will be described later. The introduction of video compression brings with it at least two additional concerns other than simply the image-quality compromises that may be necessary.

First, compression and decompression operations require some processing power that must be provided by the CPU unless additional hardware is provided. Second, it is very awkward to manipulate images when they are in compressed form. They must be decompressed, manipulated, and then recompressed, with all the inherent additional time and processing problems that go with this.

### Color-mapping

The previous discussion of RGB24 and RGB16 described the mechanisms for displaying an image in which the pixel values directly represent the color values. There is another way of using a bitmap in memory to represent an image in which the pixel values do not directly represent the color sample values, but instead the pixel values are an index to a color lookup table (CLUT) that holds the actual color value.

This technique, called *color-mapping,* allows the number of colors represented by the pixel value to be a subset of a much larger set of colors (the *palette)* represented by the number of bits per pixel (bpp) in the color table. This subset of colors in the CLUT may be changed for each image displayed. For example the bitmap may be 8 bpp, but 24 bpp in the CLUT. This would be a system that can display 256 out of a palette of 16,777,216 colors, as illustrated in Fig. 32.8.

To display a realistic image with a CLUT system, the image must be processed by an algorithm that chooses the 256 colors that occur the most to create the CLUT. The pixels then are assigned the index value from the table

**Figure 32.8** Color lookup table (CLUT) operation.

for the color closest to each pixel's actual color. Both the CLUT and the pixel values are then stored to save the image. When the image is later loaded for display, the CLUT data is loaded into the CLUT hardware and the pixels into the display memory. When the display hardware reads out the pixels to refresh the display, the pixel values will be converted to the color values by looking them up in the CLUT in real time.

By tailoring the color map to the image (which can take a lot of processing time), fairly realistic images can be constructed. One important exception is an image that contains skin tones, which may require too many of the CLUT colors to obtain the satisfactory smooth shading.

Color-mapping provides the simplest approach to compression to 8 bpp while still delivering an approximation to realism. The results depend on the number of colors in the image; images with few colors may look good, whereas elaborately colored images may suffer from severe contouring.

One final problem with color-mapping occurs when more than one image is to be displayed concurrently. In that case the palette will be split between the two images, and each will suffer a loss in quality unless there is a strong correlation between the colors in both. Either way, a large amount of processing power and time must be provided to calculate the optimum palette.

**Overlay**

In many digital-video systems there will be a need to allocate some of the bits in a pixel to purposes other than color values. For example, it may be desirable to define a region of the image where another image (maybe from an outside source) will be placed (or keyed) into the first image. With appropriate hardware responding to one bit in each pixel, this technique can provide a window of any shape on the screen where the video from an external VCR or other live source could be displayed.

For this to work correctly, there must be proper synchronization of the two signals (called *genlocking*). This technique can be extended to use 8 bits from each pixel to control a video mixer, which will allow a video dissolve between the computer's image and an external source. Twenty-four-bpp systems often are extended to 32 bits for such purposes. In most cases, the application of extra bits in this way will require additional special hardware, either inside the system or externally, to respond to the extra bit values and to carry out the desired process.

**Analog-video generation**

The final step toward displaying a digital image is the conversion process back to the analog realm used by video monitors. This is accomplished by using a D/A converter, which typically consists of a single chip containing three D/As, one for each of R, G, and B. The D/A converter simply contains some digital switches, which are controlled by the signal bits to deliver analog values equal to the value represented by each bit. These values are summed at the output to create an analog signal. Most computer systems use chips called *RAMDACs* that contain this function, and the color lookup tables required for color-mapping, in a single package.

As mentioned earlier, the visibility of pixelation can be somewhat reduced by including an analog filter on the output of a D/A converter. A filter with a bandwidth equal to the Nyquist limit for the pixel rate used will not change the resolution very much, but it will smooth some of the sharp transitions between adjacent pixels—only in the horizontal direction. Not all digital-video systems use these filters, however. Of course the results will be best when there are enough pixels that the eye will not see them anyway.

## Video compression

The desirability of video compression should be clear to you from the discussion in the previous sections. Reducing the amount of data needed to reproduce images saves storage space, increases access speed, and is the only way to achieve digital motion video. Therefore, video compression is an important element in reaching a fully capable digital-video system.

A typical still image, 640 × 480 with 24 bits per pixel, consumes just under 1 Mbyte of storage. Obviously the storage of even a few images could pose a problem, and this is before the implications of digital motion video have been explored.

The example just given clearly illustrates how the digitization process results in a large number of bits for each image. However, the number of bits actually required to represent the information in an image may be substantially less because of *redundancy.* In general, three types of redundancy in digital images can be identified:

1. *Spatial redundancy,* due to the correlation between neighboring pixel values.

2. *Spectral redundancy,* due to the correlation between different color planes (e.g., in an RGB color image) or spectral bands

3. *Temporal redundancy,* due to the correlation between different frames in a sequence of images.

Compression schemes may exploit any or all of these aspects of redundancy. Another thing to keep in mind about displaying a digital-video image is that there is no need to display more than the viewer will be able to see. The human eye has poor spatial acuity for certain colors. Because of this characteristic of the viewer, you need not provide independent color values for every pixel—the color information can be transmitted at lower resolution. This principle is used successfully in NTSC and PAL color television, and it can be utilized in a digital-video compression system as well.

Image compression aims to reduce the number of bits needed to represent an image by removing these redundancies. There are many approaches to image compression, but they can be classed in two basic groups, *lossless* and *lossy.*

In lossless compression, the reconstructed image after compression is numerically identical to the original image on a pixel-by-pixel basis. Obviously, lossless compression is ideal, since no information is compromised. However, only a modest amount of compression is possible.

In lossy compression, the reconstructed image contains degradations relative to the original. As a result, much higher compression can be achieved than with lossless compression. In general, more compression is obtained at the expense of more distortion. It is important to note that these degradations may not be visually apparent.

Over the past few years, JPEG (the Joint Photographic Experts Group) has become the de facto standard for the compression of continuous-tone-color images. It is a discrete cosine transform-based algorithm that removes redundant image and color data.

JPEG can compress images at ratios of about 20:1, with no noticeable loss of quality. Compression ratios of up to 100 to 1 are possible, but the higher the ratio the greater the loss of detail and, sometimes, the more likely the appearance of artifacts.

Another advantage of JPEG is that it is a symmetrical compression algorithm. The same hardware or software can be used to compress and decompress an image. In addition, compression and decompression times are about the same. This does not hold true for most video-compression schemes, which are asymmetrical.

JPEG is also among the standards used for motion-video compression today. It can be used to compress video frames individually through a process called *intraframe coding*. This allows users to randomly access any individual frame within the compressed video, making it ideal for digital applications in which access to every frame is necessary, such as video preproduction. The downside of using intraframe encoding alone is that even at high compression ratios, a few seconds of 24-bit color video stored as motion JPEG takes up a lot of space.

The standards organizations that sponsor JPEG—the Consultative Committee in International Telegraphy and Telephony, and the International Standards Organization—have defined a compression standard called *MPEG* (Motion Pictures Experts Group) specifically to handle motion video. In addition to intraframe encoding for removing redundancies within individual frames, MPEG also employs interframe coding, which eliminates redundant information among frames. If the background of a video clip stays the same from frame to frame, for instance, MPEG will save the background once and store only the differences between those frames. MPEG supports compression ratios of up to 50 to 1, assuming the standard MPEG resolution of about 320 $\times$ 240 pixels for full-motion video. (MPEG-2 was proposed in 1992 for handling higher-resolution, broadcast-quality images.)

In addition to its interframe coding capabilities, MPEG differs from JPEG in its asymmetrical approach to compression, using more hardware and computer power to compress full-motion video and audio than to decompress it.

## From Analog to Digital Audio

In contrast to digital video, digital audio has been available as a standard feature of personal computers since the introduction of the Apple Macintosh in 1984. On such systems it originally was used to generate system sound prompts and simple sound effects for entertainment titles. In the last few years there has been an explosion in the audio marketplace when it comes to personal computers. A wide variety of add-in audio adapters are available, providing a cost-effective audio solution.

The use of audio on personal computers has matured since the early days of beeps and squawks. Today's systems use audio to implement interactive help systems and to provide the soundtrack to digital-video movies as well as musical scores.

This section will describe the processes involved in bringing audio into the digital domain, as well as provide an overview of the compression techniques available and an introduction to synthesized audio.

### Digital audio

A common initial first impression is that digital audio is much simpler compared to digital video, since the bandwidth of audio is hundreds of times less than that for video. This, unfortunately, is not the case. Although digital audio requires many of the same considerations as digital video, there is one aspect that is very different. With video it is possible to impose a structure of lines and frames. With audio this is impossible—audio is a continuous signal with no blanking intervals or other structural features that could make the signal easier to handle.

In addition, there's no equivalent to a still frame in audio. When the processor gets behind in manipulating video, it can always display a still frame while it catches up. If this is not held for too long, the viewer will not notice. With audio it is impossible to stop without causing a loss of information and of synchronization. Hence, audio has its own problems that easily compensate for its lower bandwidth.

Although audio most often is associated with accompanying video, there are many applications that involve audio only. Sound effects in modern computer games, help systems, and musical scores are but a few examples.

### Analog audio

Natural sounds are analog. Sounds cause very small pressure variations in the air, which can be picked up by various pressure-to-electrical transducers. The most common of these made specifically for sound pickup is the microphone. It is designed to model the frequency-range and the pressure-value characteristics of the human ear. The output of the microphone is an analog electrical signal that closely matches the pressure variations in the air around the microphone.

The audio industry is a mature one, and a full range of equipment is available for storing, processing, and reproducing analog-video signals. The equipment suppliers serve the three main markets: broadcast, professional, and consumer. Traditionally, audio production has taken place in the analog domain, using microphones and tape recorders. The music industry utilizes some of the most complex audio production facilities available. These can be found in most major cities around the world and they allow audio from many sources to be equalized, effects to be inserted, and the sources to be mixed into the tracks that will be used by the final application. Typically an audio production house will work with many parallel tracks on magnetic tape—24-track machines using 2-inch-wide tapes are common.

There is an emerging trend in audio production and postproduction to move to digital equipment. This trend started in the broadcast market and has moved down through the professional market into the consumer market. The driving force toward an all-digital process was the release of the compact disc medium to the consumer in 1983. Now, a decade later, the CD is king, and many record companies are discontinuing vinyl record production altogether. Studios and production houses have fully digital recording suites and mixing systems that allow recordings to be digital throughout the entire recording, production, and transmission cycle. Digital audio tape (DAT) was released several years ago and embraced by recording studios but not by the consumer market, which was skeptical of yet another potential standard. The last year has seen the release of the digital compact cassette (DCC) and the minidisc (MD), both of which attempt to address the consumer requirement for digital-audio recording. Time will tell whether either of these formats is accepted.

## Audio analog-to-digital conversion

To process audio in the personal-computer environment, the analog-audio signal must be converted to digital using an A/D converter. (Alternatively, if the audio is already on a digital medium, such as DAT, only a simple format conversion is required.)

As with video, the A/D process consists of sampling and quantizing, but at much lower frequencies than those attributed to video. In audio systems the maximum bandwidth is 20 kHz, hence sampling rates need to be between 40 and 50 kHz. These rates are slow compared to video, but they are slightly offset by the need to have lower quantization and hence more bits per sample. In the earlier discussion of video sampling, a signal-to-noise ratio of 46 dB was considered good. An audio signal of the same quality is not acceptable, and signal-to-noise ratios of greater than 70 dB must be attained if the noise is not to be heard during normal listening. When the additional requirements of production are taken into consideration, the standard for audio digitizing becomes 16 bits per sample, giving a signal-to-noise ratio of 96 dB.

## Audio compression

The standard quantizing method for 16-bit digital audio is *linear pulse code modulation (PCM)*, with each quantization step having equal size. It is this format that was adopted and used on audio compact discs. If samples have less than 16 bits per sample, several other quantizing methods may be used. A form of PCM known as *companding* (or *nonlinear PCM*) is best used when 12 or 14 bits per sample are available. In this approach the quantization steps at low signals are smaller than the steps at high signal levels.

Higher levels of compression can be achieved by the use of *differential pulse code modulation (DPCM)*. This time only the differences between adjacent samples are coded by the quantizer, rather than the samples themselves.

This approach rests on the assumption that most of the time the difference between samples will not be as large as the samples themselves, and therefore fewer bits can be used for coding. This works well if adjacent samples are of similar amplitude, but if the signal contains a lot of frequency components that are near the Nyquist limit, the adjacent samples will be very different. The DPCM system will be unable to keep up and will cause severe distortion of the high-frequency sections of the audio.

An adaptive system was introduced to solve the problems inherent in DPCM. This system, called *ADPCM,* applies a scale factor to the difference bits that can dynamically change, depending on the signal level or high-frequency content of the audio signal. Hence when the signal is small, the difference bits control small steps of amplitude, and when the signal is high they control much larger increments. Since an ADPCM playback system must know the scale factor, it is contained within the stream of difference bits that the decoder processes. There are many ADPCM implementations, the most popular of them based on a CCITT standard that uses ADPCM at 4 bits per sample and is commonly referred to as *ADPCM4.* The quality of the reproduction can be increased simply by increasing the sampling rate, but with the inevitable increase in bandwidth. Distortion may be heard when a large amount of adaptation is required by a sound that changes too fast for the system.

The MPEG specification includes a section devoted to digital-audio compression to accompany digital video. These compression schemes are highly computationally intensive and make use of the audio-masking characteristics of the human ear. Even when such techniques are used, compression ratios are limited to a factor of 6:1, which is enforced by the lack of structure in an audio signal and the resultant low possibilities for any redundancy.

### Synthesized audio

The rapid advances in electronics and computing have also enabled a new breed of musical instruments: electronic synthesizers. Synthesizers have come a long way since the early analog-sound-generator-equipped Moogs. Synthesizers have made the transition to the digital world, and modern examples can be used to recreate almost any sound imaginable. Yamaha introduced a synthesis method known as *frequency modulation (FM) synthesis* with their early DX line of synthesizers, which revolutionized the marketplace. FM synthesis works by generating a sound by modulating a series of sinewaves together. By careful selection of the frequencies, and modulation, a wide variety of sounds can be achieved. Since then many other techniques have been introduced, as equipment manufacturers have battled to produce the most natural-sounding systems.

Until recently, the controller and the sound generator had been part of the same piece of equipment. Today, however, the controller and the sound generator have been separated, and there are digital sound generators that can be controlled by any kind of player interface. For example, controllers are available that play like guitars or violins even though the sound generation is electronic.

How is this flexibility achieved? They key ingredient is MIDI, the Musical Instrument Digital Interface, a communications specification that enables the exchange of musical information among electronic musical instruments, computers, and peripheral audio equipment. When combined with music-synthesis capability, MIDI allows a personal computer to become the control center of a musical production system. Although initially used by musicians to perform music, MIDI is now an integral part of the audio-generation technology for multimedia productions.

MIDI augments the use of waveform audio in multimedia. Waveform audio normally is used to reproduce speech and many nonmusical sounds but, as stated previously, requires a large amount of memory to faithfully reproduce music. MIDI represents music using far less storage and allows greater editing flexibility, but does require a music synthesizer to generate the actual music. MIDI describes music in terms of high-level command sequences, for example "Play Middle C on the French horn loudly for one second." This is encoded into 6 bytes, 3 bytes to start the sound and 3 to terminate it. Compare this to CD-quality PCM data at 176 kbps for the same "information."

Because MIDI is a symbolic representation of music, not the audio waveform data itself, the quality of the sound is related primarily to the quality of the music synthesizer, not the MIDI data. Most synthesizers produce stereo sound, and some can very convincingly reproduce acoustic musical instruments. Speech and sound effects, recorded as specific musical sounds, are limited by the synthesizer's memory.

MIDI messages can be stored on a computer as MIDI files. Playing back MIDI files on a suitably equipped system reproduces the recorded performance exactly. In addition to allowing you to simply play the file back, the performance may be edited, instruments changed, the tempo or the musical key modified—all by simple modifications to the MIDI data.

The amount of data required to store a performance is many orders less than that required to sample the performance in the traditional methods described previously. Hence MIDI is an alternative mechanism that augments the use of waveform audio in multimedia titles. With the number of MIDI-enabled systems growing, and given the rate of development for music, it is expected that every personal computer soon will have a built-in capability for realistic audio.

## Conclusions

This chapter has introduced the principles of digital audio and video. Both are rapidly extending the capabilities of personal computers to present information in new and exciting ways. The large bandwidth requirement of digital video has accelerated the research effort with regard to video compression. Large reductions in the bandwidth requirement may be accomplished by removing redundant information in the video sequences. Such reductions are possible only because of the inherent structured nature of video (lines and frames). Audio, however, does not exhibit a structured nature, which consequently limits the amount of compression achievable. High-quality compression schemes attempt to model the acoustics of the human ear to determine which components might be redundant within the audio signal.

Broadcasting is moving into the digital realm with the introduction of digital broadcast radio and with the first field trials of interactive televisions based on standard video-compression schemes such as MPEG. Such systems enable applications such as "video-on-demand," bringing the age of consumer-driven television that much closer.

# 33

# Understanding PC Video

**Claude Leglise**

## Enhancing Business Communications

Imagine trying to explain to someone how to tie a shoe—using only written or spoken words. Even if you use pictures and diagrams, it's still awkward and time-consuming to "talk" someone through this everyday procedure. People are likely to respond with "Just show me!", because they catch on far more quickly when they can *see* how something is done rather than read or listen to instructions. Likewise, many types of business information cannot be conveyed effectively with words and images alone. This information requires a much richer mode of communication, one that not only includes visual elements to enhance the spoken word but also captures movement and visual expression as well.

The personal computer (PC) has enhanced business communications dramatically in the last decade, allowing people to communicate information with text, data, and graphics. The next logical step is the addition of motion video to PCs. PC video integrates visual elements with the spoken word and motion, bringing a rich new data-type to PC communications. It combines the impact of video with the PC's ability to manage, access, and present data.

Off-the-shelf hardware and software that support PC video are available today. New technologies are making PC video not only affordable but also easy to install and use. As a result, we are beginning to see exciting business applications that use video to enhance the effectiveness of business communications. This chapter will take a close look at PC video and its applications, and explain how easy it is to add video to your PC.

## PC Video Applications

The PC is rapidly becoming the platform for communicating and distributing information. People already are using PCs to send and receive documents, faxes, and e-mail messages over LANs and across phone lines. Video is a natural and powerful extension to PC-based communications and information distribution.

Given the ready availability of PC-video software, and the ease of incorporating and using video, you can get started right away enhancing your business communications. In fact, products such as Microsoft's Video for Windows, with Intel's Indeo video technology, allow you to play back video clips that have been incorporated into existing applications such as word processors, spreadsheets, databases, and presentation graphics. It's as easy as pasting in a graph or a drawing. And with the addition of video-capture hardware, you can record video right at your desktop. Think of the possibilities...!

## Business presentations

PC-based business presentations are rapidly increasing in popularity because they look good, are easy to create, are highly portable, and can be played on just about any PC, including portables and laptops. Over one hundred million PCs have been installed to date, so you can show your presentation in almost any business office without scheduling a conference room or setting up additional equipment. Or you can hook up a flat-panel projector to your PC and project your presentations using an overhead projector.

With PC video, you can add a whole new dimension to your business presentations. Imagine the impact of a sales presentation that includes "live" customer testimonials, or electronic product brochures that include video product demonstrations. PC video offers other benefits as well. For example, you can quickly create a marketing clip on a new product without the expense of producing a full-blown video. Sales and marketing are not the only areas in which you can use PC video. You can also add impact to staff presentations, announcements, and many other corporate communications.

## Education and training

Because of the rich and portable nature of video communication—not to mention its cost-effectiveness—videotaped training programs are heavily used in business. Video adds impact to training programs and holds an audience's attention. In addition, a 1991 study by Inteco Corp. shows that video presentations increase audience retention of information by up to 38 percent.

However, videotaped training programs have their limitations. Because videotape is sequential, sequences cannot be randomly accessed; videotape cannot be integrated with computer-based training; and people typically cannot view videotapes at their desks. PC video overcomes the limitations of videotape. It combines the benefits of computer-based training with the impact of a video presentation.

Video on the PC is convenient, and even more portable than videotape—it can be run on just about any i486-based PC. And it's easy to combine video with text, graphics, and other data types so as to optimize communication. You can use PC video for many training and education purposes: employee orientation, human-resource updates, sales training, product training, electronic employee newsletters, safety courses, and many others. For example, service and maintenance manuals can be enhanced to include video clips of certain operations, such as installing an oil filter in a car.

### Video databases

Video databases combine the power of video with the ability of computers to manage, access, and present data. Imagine going into a real estate office, entering into a PC your requirements for a new home, then viewing video clips of houses that meet your specifications and budget. Real estate is only one of many areas that can be enhanced with video databases. Physicians in remote locations can take advantage of a video database containing medical procedures; and video can be added to insurance claims databases.

### General-purpose video communications and information distribution

Just as e-mail has revolutionized communications, so too will PC video eventually revolutionize e-mail. Video e-mail is particularly effective at facilitating cooperative projects in which several coworkers need to share information. For example doctors can share patient records, engineers design approaches, and insurance adjusters claim information. Video e-mail also can be used to distribute information—such as service bulletins and product updates—quickly and effectively.

### Next-generation applications

In addition to enhancing existing applications such as presentations, PC video opens the door to new applications that simply were not possible before. One exciting example is desktop videoconferencing, in which users may not only see the other party, but also send, annotate, and share documents in real time. As a result of these applications the PC will become an even more powerful business tool, one that allows interactive business communications combining text, graphics, voice, and video.

## Minimum System Requirements

What hardware and software you'll need to run PC video will depend on whether you plan to record video at your desktop or simply play back video clips recorded by others.

### Requirements for playing video

Your PC may already be capable of video playback. All you need is an Intel 486 microprocessor-based personal computer running the Windows operating

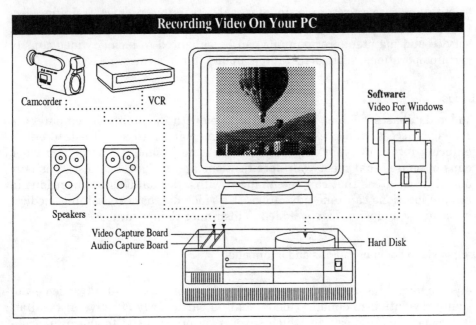

**Figure 33.1** Components needed for recording video.

system. The PC should have a i486SX/25-MHz CPU or higher, a hard-disk drive, and a 256-color VGA board or greater. You'll also need a PC audio board and speakers or headphones, which are readily available and easy to install.

With this setup you can play back video titles that have been recorded elsewhere and supplied to you on diskette, CD-ROM, or via a network. This means that tens of millions of i486 microprocessor-based PCs are potential video-playback units. As you can see, playing back video to your PC is easy, and doesn't require a lot of expensive equipment.

### Requirements for recording video on a PC

If you also wish to *record* video on your PC, you'll need a few additional components, as shown in Fig. 33.1:

- A video-digitizing (or capture) board, to convert the analog-video signals to digital information

- A hard disk with a minimum of 30 Mbytes of free hard-disk space, or more

- A source of video input such as a video camera, VCR, or laserdisc player, which you connect to the video-capture board

- Video software (such as Video for Windows) that includes video-capture, compression, playback, and basic video-editing utilities

You cannot play back video at a higher quality than was captured, so you should give particular attention to the quality of video recording.

By recording at the highest level of quality possible, you ensure that you will achieve the highest-quality playback when you need it. Video image quality depends primarily on three factors: viewing-window size, video "frame rate," and color-presentation capability. What it is important to note is that quality depends on a combination of these three factors. Therefore remember, when you are evaluating video software and hardware, that it is important to look at all three quality factors.

In addition, the level of video quality that you enjoy is directly related to your PC hardware configuration, in particular to the PC microprocessor, the graphics board, and the speed of the hard disk. We'll discuss the relationship among hardware and video capture and playback quality later. But first let's look more closely at the three factors that jointly create video quality.

### Viewing-window size

Viewing-window dimensions are expressed in pixels—for example, 320 × 240 or 160 × 120 pixels. Note by way of reference that a standard VGA screen is 640 × 480 pixels, which means that a 320 × 240 video-playback window takes up about one-fourth of a VGA screen. Standard PC video-window playback sizes, as shown in Fig. 33.2, are 160 × 120 ($\frac{1}{16}$ screen) and 320 × 240 ($\frac{1}{4}$ screen).

### Video frame rate

The *video frame rate* specifies the number of frames per second (fps) of video images displayed on the screen (see Fig. 33.3). The higher the frame rate, the more fluid the motion appears. The highest-quality, or best-quality, frame rate available is 30 fps, which appears to the human eye as completely fluid motion. Lower frame rates (below 10) still appear as motion, but are noticeably "jerky."

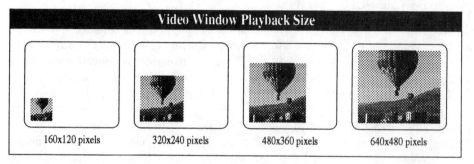

Figure 33.2   Video-window playback size, expressed in pixels.

**Figure 33.3**   Frame rates range from 0 (still) to 30 fps.

For reference, 0 fps is a still frame (no motion); 24 fps is the frame rate used in motion pictures; 30 fps is used in television; 10 to 15 fps is the rate that most people find acceptable for fluid motion.

### Color presentation capability

Color presentation capability depends on the color depth and the spatial color resolution. The term *color depth* refers to the number of different colors available. The more colors, the higher the quality and the truer the representation. Color depth on PCs ranges from a VGA palette of 4 bits (16 colors) up to 24-bit true color with 16.7 million hues. You'll need at least a 256-color VGA card, or higher, for video. The term *color resolution* refers to the spatial "graininess" or "blockiness" of the color. The highest quality results when every pixel is assigned its own color.

Blockiness results when the same color is assigned to all four pixels in a $2 \times 2$ area or larger. Many compression algorithms reduce file sizes by grouping pixels into color blocks. To help reduce the graininess during playback, interpolation or dithering techniques are employed to smooth out the color over the blocked-out areas.

### Recording Video on Your PC

Recording video on your PC is a simple process. You can capture live action using a video camera, or you can capture existing video clips from a VCR or laserdisc player. Video cameras, VCRs, and laserdiscs communicate video information to a television set using a standard analog-video format such as NTSC (North America and Japan), PAL (Western Europe), or SECAM (France and Eastern Europe).

The video-capture board in your PC converts this analog-video signal into digital information, and records it on a hard-disk file. The file format depends on the video-recording hardware and software used. Raw uncompressed digitized video files are quite large. For example, 1 minute of video can range from 35 to 50 Mbytes on your hard disk, depending on preset capture parameters. So it's necessary to compress—or shrink—raw video files to a size that is more manageable on a PC.

## Compression

Video-compression techniques take advantage of the fact that, as you move from one frame of video to the next, much of the "information" remains the same. Compression routines look at each frame and identify and save only the changes from frame to frame—for example, changes caused by motion. Additionally, compression routines "eliminate the redundancy" within each frame. If, for example, an area of the screen is made up of a group of pixels all the same color, the compression software stores color information about the area as a whole rather than storing separate color information for each pixel.

These compression techniques dramatically reduce video file sizes. For example, video software that incorporates Indeo video can compress a 50-Mbyte raw video file to about 9 Mbytes. Indeo video, Intel's advanced video compression/decompression software technology, is a key component of Microsoft's Video for Windows and Apple's QuickTime products. IBM also has endorsed Indeo technology and plans to incorporate it into its operating environments. This will allow users to interchange video files freely between Windows, Macintosh, and OS/2 platforms.

## One-step versus two-step capture and compression

There are two basic video-capture techniques: one-step capture and compression and two-step capture and compression. Older video-capture boards use a two-step process. Capture and compression are two separate steps because video input comes into the PC faster than the compression routine can process it. In the first step, you capture the video and store the raw digitized video information on a hard-disk file. In the second step, you compress this file off-line (see Fig. 33.4).

This two-step process requires disk space to hold not only the uncompressed video file but also the compressed file (for a total of 45 to 60 Mbytes for 1 minute of video). In addition, the off-line software-compression step takes a lot of extra time: as much as 15 to 30 minutes for every minute of video. During that time the PC is completely dedicated to compression, and cannot be used for other work. Fortunately, newer compression technologies use a combination of software and hardware to compress video much more quickly. For example, The Intel Smart Video Recorder digitizes, compresses, and stores the video data all in one easy step (see Fig. 33.5).

This is accomplished by incorporating Indeo technology and Intel's i750 video processor into The Intel Smart Video Recorder board. Real-time, single-step capture and compression offers important advantages. It minimizes the cost of PC video, because it uses far less hard-disk space (9 Mbytes of hard disk for 1 minute of video in a 160 × 120 window, versus 45 to 60 Mbytes). This often eliminates the need to add large and fast hard-disk capacity to

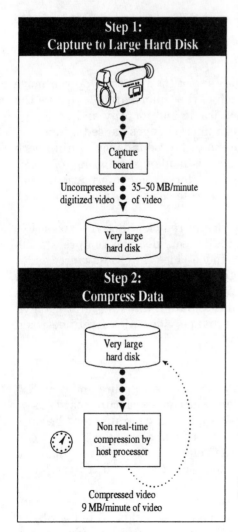

**Figure 33.4** Two-step capture and compression.

your PC. It also offers convenience and time savings, because there is no lengthy compression process involved.

### Video-capture quality

Single-step capture and compression has an important advantage, in that the video quality is not as sensitive to the hardware configuration as it is when two-step capture and compression is used.

With two-step capture and compression, video quality is directly related to your PC hardware configuration: the more powerful the microprocessor and the faster the hard disk, the higher the quality. With two-step capture and compression, all uncompressed video data must be transferred directly to the hard disk. In many configurations, the speed of the microprocessor and hard disk cannot keep pace with the large volume of incoming data. The system

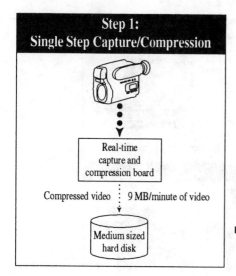

**Figure 33.5**  Single-step video.

becomes overloaded and begins to "drop" frames. So you may not be able to achieve the full frame rate (quality) that is specified for the video-capture board.

For example, a two-step video-capture board rated at 30 fps may in reality capture far fewer fps on less powerful hardware configurations.

One-step capture and compression, on the other hand, compresses video data before it is transferred to the hard disk. As a result the amount of data that the hard disk must handle is dramatically reduced—by a factor of up to 6 to 1. Thus very few frames, if any, are "dropped" during capture. A single-step video-capture board rated at 30 fps will deliver 30 fps even on less powerful system configurations.

## Distributing Your Video

You can distribute your compressed video files just as you would any other file type—either on diskette or over a network. People who have Video for Windows can play your video clip without any additional software. If you are planning to distribute your video clip to people who don't have Video for Windows, you will need to attach a copy of video-player software (also called a *runtime player*) to the compressed file. Video-player software is included with Video for Windows and with the Intel Smart Video Recorder.

### Playing video files on your PC

You can receive video files for playback on diskette or through a network. You can view these files even if you don't have any specialized video-playback hardware on your PC. If you have video-playback software such as Video for Windows, you can take advantage of its simulated push-button controls, which look much like those on a VCR or cassette player.

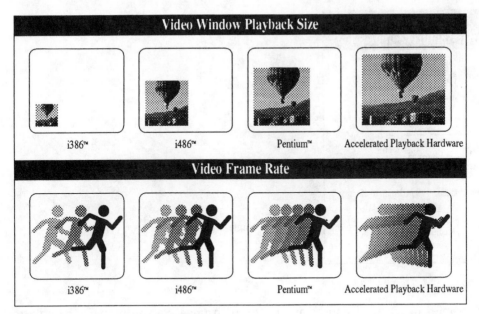

**Figure 33.6**  Increasing the quality of video.

### Playback quality depends on hardware

As you move up in processing power, such as from an i386 to an i486 to a Pentium microprocessor, you can take advantage of larger playback window sizes and faster frame rates, enhancing playback quality. The result is a larger viewing area and more fluid motion, as shown in Fig. 33.6. The table below shows how different hardware configurations affect video-window playback size and video frame rates.

Depending on the hardware configuration, you may need to make tradeoffs between window size and frame rate to optimize video quality for particular purposes. For example if the most important thing to convey is motion, then you would opt for a smaller window playback size to get a faster frame rate. If however you are more interested in visual details, you would trade off frame rate for a larger window playback size. The following table shows typical window sizes and frame-rate tradeoffs for popular hardware configurations. The numbers shown depend on the specific hardware configuration, and may vary based on such factors as disk-drive speed, available RAM, and the VGA card installed.

**Playback Performance Tradeoffs**

| System | 180 × 120 | 320 × 240 |
| --- | --- | --- |
| 486SX/25 | 15 fps | 4 fps |
| 486DX/33 | 20 fps | 5 fps |
| 486DC2/66 | 30 fps | 8 fps |

All systems based on 8 Mbytes RAM; 11.8-millisecond hard-disk speed; VGA card with 512-kbyte memory and 256 colors.

### Smart video software

Because of the variety of hardware configurations available, a wide range of playback qualities are possible. As a result, video software should be "smart" enough to determine what hardware is available and optimize playback quality for that hardware automatically—without requiring you to change the software or the video clip file.

This intelligence is sometimes referred to as *scalability*. During playback, Indeo video's scalable technology automatically determines what hardware is available and optimizes playback quality for that configuration. When recording Indeo video files, the Intel Smart Video Recorder's one-step capability ensures that frames are never lost. As a result, more powerful PCs are able to tap into this stored video data during playback, delivering progressively faster frame rates. Therefore, as computer users upgrade their systems with faster Intel microprocessors, they benefit from the security of knowing that video recorded on The Intel Smart Video Recorder will "upgrade" along with them.

Scalability protects your investment, because video recorded today will play faster on tomorrow's machines. This is not the case for video clips captured on two-step boards, which often lose frames. These lost frames never can be recovered and played back, no matter how fast your upgraded CPU. Without scalability, video quality will be the same on the faster CPU as it was on the older one.

## Video Trends

Recent advances such as Intel's Indeo video technology bring PC video to the business user. PC video is affordable and easy to install and use.

As a result, you immediately can begin to use video to enhance your business communications: presentations, educational and training programs, video communications and information distribution, and even video databases.

### PC hardware

Today's microprocessors have the horsepower necessary to handle the demands of high-quality video. The next generation of microprocessors, such as Intel's Pentium microprocessor, will be even better equipped for running video-based applications. And your investment in video is protected, because Indeo video software technology is scalable. That means the video you capture today will run on tomorrow's hardware to the full extent of the quality of the video capture. In addition, storage capacities are increasing and costs are plummeting. Disk drives of 200 to 300 Mbytes are now standard on many PCs.

### Video hardware

Intel offers a variety of video boards to simplify video capture and to enhance playback quality by using Indeo video technology and the i750 video processor. Intel recording boards offer all the advantages of one-step capture and compression, which result in significant disk-space savings, time savings, and higher recorded frame rates.

### Operating system software

Microsoft, IBM, and Apple have all committed to supporting video in their operating system software. Video for Windows and QuickTime, which incorporate Intel's Indeo video technology, are available today from Microsoft and Apple. IBM has announced its plans to incorporate Indeo video into OS/2.

### Video tools and utilities

A number of video-capture, editing, and playback tools and utilities are already available for working with video on your PC. Many of these programs have been integrated with operating environments such as Video for Windows.

### Video clip art

Clip-art suppliers are beginning to market "video clip art," offering you a wide selection of prerecorded video that you can incorporate into your business documents. Video for Windows includes one of these video-clip libraries on CD-ROM.

### Applications

Existing standards such as Object Linking and Embedding (OLE) make it easy to include video in the Windows operating environment. Over 150 existing business applications support OLE, including word processors, spreadsheets, databases, and business presentations. This paves the way for the integration of video into compound documents without the need for specialized software. OLE ensures that you can easily incorporate video into existing files, even if these were created before PC video capabilities were available.

### Distribution

Distribution infrastructures such as LANs and the telephone network are already in place and can support limited digital-video transmission, such as low-volume store-and-forward. As video-compression techniques advance and network bandwidths widen, we'll be able to increase the volume of store-and-forward video transmission so that large-scale video e-mail becomes a reality. Advancements in digital communications technology such as the Integrated Services Digital Network (ISDN) are making it possible to send video beyond the local-area network.

Ultimately we'll be able to handle the transmission of full-motion video in real time, enabling videoconferencing and other exciting new video applications. As we have seen, many PC video capabilities already are available. And they are only the beginning. New advancements are occurring every day, at all levels of information technology. The next generation of PC hardware will include more powerful microprocessors, larger disk drives, and faster graphics subsystems, resulting in even better PC-video quality. In addition, higher compression rates will enhance our ability to send and receive video via the telephone or local-area networks. As new technology becomes available, prices will continue to drop, making PC video even more affordable.

## Conclusion

PC video is here today, and it's here to stay. It's affordable, it's easy to use, and it opens the door to numerous applications that can dramatically enhance business communications. New technologies such as Indeo video make playback easy and affordable—often without any additional hardware.

In addition Indeo technology, in conjunction with The Intel Smart Video Recorder, permits single-step capture and compression, making the process fast and efficient so that you can create your own video clips right at your desktop. Through the continuing development of more powerful microprocessors such as the Pentium microprocessor, Intel is paving the way for more sophisticated video applications that will allow PC video to fulfill its true potential.

# 34

# System Support for Integrated Desktop Videoconferencing

Amy Pearl

## Introduction

In the last 15 years, the ability of computers to capture, store, and manipulate information has been augmented by an ability to transmit that information to other computers. As computers become increasingly connected by means of various networks, they increasingly are being used as communication tools. Much of that communication comes in the form of forwarded and stored data such as electronic mail and bulletin boards (*Byte*, 1985). These tools support asynchronous communication between people, allowing communication to occur even if the recipient is absent. However, such tools have not replaced the need for interactive, or synchronous, communication, even in computers. For example, for as long as computers have supported multiple users, people have found simple text-based interactive "talk" programs useful. Our research at SunSoft is focused on the new possibilities for interactive collaboration between remotely located workers who use networked workstations. One of the early prototypes we developed is a digital, integrated videoconference application called *videoconf*.

Videoconferencing is a technology that has been emerging over the past 30 years, motivated by a recognition of how much of our face-to-face communication is visual, or nonverbal. For example, there have been efforts to augment telephones to include the transmission of visual images. Recently the Computer-Supported Cooperative Work (CSCW) community has been exploring the use of computer-controlled analog audio and video transmission to support group work (Root, 1988; Olson and Bly, 1991; Vin et al., 1991). Recent advances in media-compression technology, along with shrinking component size and cost, are making digital video feasible. Unlike analog video, digital video can take advantage of the growing number of digital communication networks, including phone (e.g., ISDN) and institutional networks (e.g., LANs and WANs). It is also possible for programs to manipulate digital video, the effects of which are just now being explored (Liebhold and Hoffert, 1991). An example of this is the morphing of video images.

At Sun Microsystems Laboratories Inc. (SMLI) and SunSoft, our conferencing and collaboration project explores issues in computer-assisted collaboration for geographically distributed small groups. Videoconf is part of a set of workstation tools built for use studies. (For reports on related use studies see Tang and Isaacs, 1993, and Isaacs and Tang, 1993.)

The videoconference application was built on the Advanced Multimedia Platform (AMP) (Calnan 1991), also developed at SMLI. AMP was designed to provide system support to network multimedia applications. AMP defined multimedia as *the combination of standard data types (text, graphics, images, etc.) with data types that have timeliness constraints (or time-critical data)*. It provided applications with support for managing the resources required for multimedia, including hardware devices. AMP used a video board to capture, digitize, compress, and display video in windows on the workstation. Our goals for developing the videoconference application were to (1) determine the feasibility of integrating digital audio/video conferencing into a standard networked UNIX desktop workstation, (2) exercise the AMP multimedia platform, and (3) evaluate how much system support AMP was providing for the development of collaborative applications.

Through our early videoconferencing prototype, we learned about the requirements for integrating videoconferencing into a networked workstation. After describing the system support that applications require in order to name, protect, share, and optimize the resources needed for videoconferencing, this chapter will describe our application architecture in light of past CSCW literature. Finally, it will describe features we expect to see prototyped, and the further system capabilities required to support them. This includes an important addition to the class of time-critical data: general-user actions in multiuser applications.

## Requirements

Most of the difficulty in a videoconference application is in handling aspects of the network: finding conferees and the necessary resources (such as video cameras and video displays), providing access control and security, sharing resources, and sharing network bandwidth fairly.

### Resource naming

One of the first problems a distributed environment must address is how applications locate and reference services or resources. For videoconferencing, there are three things we need to be able to find and reference: people, devices, and conferences.

**Figure 34.1**  Identifying people prior to initiating a conference.

When users start a conference, they think in terms of the people to whom they want to talk or the name of the meeting they want to join. Applications need system support if they are to map the names of people ("Connect Amy's camera to John's and Dave's video displays") and conferences ("Add me to the SMLI staff meeting") to the resources and attributes associated with them. AMP associated multimedia resources, such as video and audio devices, with machine names, and provided references to those devices. In order to allow users to refer to people or conferences by name, an application needs to map those names to the relevant machines.

Videoconf provided a phonelike invocation model, in which users needed to know the name of each person with whom they wished to confer (Fig. 34.1). However, users found videoconf's phone-call model very limiting. Individual applications can provide their own mapping of people and conference names to the appropriate machines, but this support should be provided by a collaboration platform.

Users want the ability to join a conference in progress (in which case they usually are referred to as *late joiners*). For example, if two people are conferencing and a third contacts one of them, they may want to add the caller to the existing conference. Users of videoconf were unable to do this for two technical reasons: AMP provided no support for finding a conference, and AMP references to devices could not be shared between applications. Truly general-purpose platforms for multimedia and collaboration should provide support for these capabilities. At a lower level, this means that the underlying network protocol must support the adding and deleting of connections dynamically.

## Security

Once there are network-connected cameras and microphones on individuals' desks, with software allowing remote access of these resources, it becomes possible to eavesdrop on conferences and to monitor individuals. There are two areas of security, security *of access* and security *of transmitted data,* and two reasons for providing security mechanisms at the platform level:

1. Security is a service that many multimedia applications require, especially those that provide group support, and it shouldn't have to be replicated by each of them.

2. It is critical that these mechanisms be robust, and that users of these systems be able to trust that they are secure. This requires that security implementation be embedded at a level out of reach of the end user.

### Security: access

At a minimum, users want to know if someone wants or attempts to view or listen to them. They may also want to restrict access to their local multimedia resources in various ways. This is an issue of concern in any distributed multimedia environment that has multimedia devices located on desktops that can be accessed remotely. Because security was not a focus of our research, AMP provided minimal security. Whenever a video camera is initially accessed on a machine, AMP audibly notifies the user on that machine and prints a status message in the console window (the global workstation status window). This mechanism does nothing to restrict access, relying as it does on users' awareness to mediate security.

Videoconf provided additional security by imposing a more restrictive access policy, symmetry of functionality ("If I can see/hear you, you can see/hear me") (Borning and Travers, 1991). While this meets the requirement of having a simple model and is simple to implement, it is not a very scalable, flexible, or practical model.

In our experience with a system that provides very little security control, we saw that much of access control can be socially mediated. This may in part be true because our target users are those who work closely together. We plan to prototype communication applications with a less restrictive policy than symmetry of functionality. For example, many more of our workstations are equipped with audio than with video. We would like to be able to impose symmetry on audioconferencing only, and allow video to be used, if available. In such a case, either the access policy may be socially mediated or the application may impose a policy of symmetry of security ("I am unable to see you unless I have permission to see you and you have permission to see me"). This would require that the system include the concept of user-access permissions for each resource.

In the example of symmetry of permissions, the access control was on the basis of each resource. It can be useful for conferences to have permissions. In the example of locating and finding a conference ("Add me to the staff meeting"), the policy may be that conferences that have a privacy attribute have a more restrictive admission procedure. In such a case, users may have to contact and obtain permission from a conference leader first, or no one may be allowed to join who is not already on the membership list.

### Security: data

Users who transmit sensitive video data may want to prevent some people from monitoring it. Digital video opens up a wide array of data-protection possibilities.

For example, both analog and digital images can be altered, but it may be easier, through techniques such as *checksums,* to determine the authenticity of a digital image than to authenticate an image on paper. We can protect digital images through powerful digital encryption techniques such as DES. However, while we must be concerned with issues of individual privacy when there are new ways to invade it, we also should consider just how private many of our current communication transmission mechanisms are. Conventional paper mail can be compromised in many ways. Electronic mail is often notoriously lax in its security. Telephone communication over lines can be tapped, and wireless communications are even more vulnerable. Many of our uses of communication and media rely on socially agreed-upon security mechanisms, not technical ones.

No security system is invulnerable; therefore the most important design goal is that the security model be well understood by programmers and end users. The security requirements of collaborative applications vary widely. When applications are geared toward sharing big collections of information among large, loosely connected groups of people, the security requirements are likely to be much greater than for the sharing of targeted collections of data among a closely connected work group. Security mechanisms should be flexible and sophisticated, so as to accommodate a wide range of needs.

### Shared resources

Once applications have located their resources and the system has verified that they may access them, multiple clients may potentially share the same resources. Sharing resources is not unique to collaborative applications, but it is inherently part of them. There are many ways in which resources may be shared, and there are different requirements for each. Some resources are shared by partitioning them, so that users are protected from each other. For example, our digital-video board supports up to four independent video displays. Other resources are shared outright, and the actions of one user may affect others. For example, a user may pause in the transmission of his or her video camera for privacy during a conference; all display clients of that camera are then effectively halted.

Our videoconference application required three kinds of sharing:

1. Multiple receivers must share the data from a source.

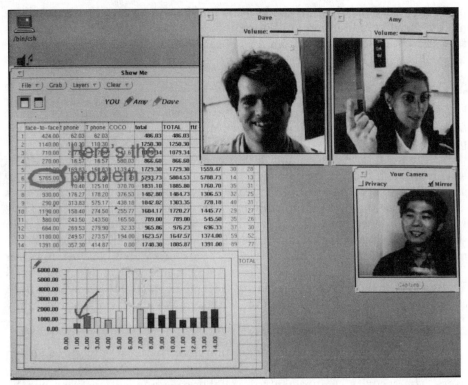

**Figure 34.2**   A three-site conference in progress.

2. A display of multiple video images shares a single frame buffer.

3. Multiple users share control of video streams.

Let's look at each of these more closely.

1. *Transmitting each video camera output to multiple users' displays.* Each conferee's camera must transmit its data to a display on each conferee's machine. The displays share the camera data stream either by getting their own copy of the stream or by monitoring a single broadcast stream (see the discussion of optimization of video data transmission). AMP handled these connections and the choice of transmission.

2. *Displaying video streams from multiple cameras on each user's workstation.* The video board on each conferee's workstation must display the multiple streams it receives (Fig. 34.2). Again, this was handled by AMP, since the need for multiple video displays on a user's workstation is not limited to collaborative applications.

3. *Allowing multiple users to share control of each video stream.* In our videoconference application, each of the users receiving the video data was able to control its behavior by pausing or resuming it. This could affect the view of others receiving that stream. AMP provided no mechanisms to negoti-

ate sharing control of resources. As a result, that capability was provided only in a very limited way by videoconf. Those resources may be shared by multiple applications that have no knowledge of each other. Any platform that manages shared resources must provide applications with the ability to negotiate control of those resources. Because the AMP platform did not do so, videoconf does not provide users with the ability to manipulate many shared video characteristics such as frame rate and image resolution.

Users of a desktop videoconferencing program really don't share data in the same sense as users of a multiuser editor do. The data that videoconference users share is really only the multiplexing of the video sources to all the relevant displays. Unlike a shared editor, a videoconference does not contain persistent data that is manipulated in different ways by the various users who receive it.

## Performance characteristics

Digital videoconferencing has very specific performance requirements. This is because of the need for interactivity, the need for multiple video displays on each workstation, and the large volume of data in a digital-video stream. People perceive audio delay when it lasts longer than 200 milliseconds. Our video board allowed conferencing between up to five people at a time. Like several existing digital-video standards, the compression scheme AMP used generated over 1 Mbit per second for each video data stream at full-motion-video rates.

Prior to the development of our prototype system, we at Sun conducted a study of dedicated videoconference rooms between the east and west coasts of the United States (Tang and Isaacs, 1993). The vendor-supplied systems enforced audio and video synchronization. Users found that the significant transmission delay (over 500 milliseconds) interfered with natural verbal communication. Users frequently switched over to using the telephone for an audio channel, because the absence of delay made conversation more natural and productive, even though the audio and video were then out of sync.

Our multimedia platform originally was designed to support media stream synchronization, achieved in part by liberal use of buffering, which introduces delay. Our videoconference-room study showed that this approach is at odds with the needs of low-latency conferencing. The platform was redesigned to take this into consideration. Because a multimedia platform hides details such as buffer size from applications, its design must carefully take into account the requirements of all multimedia applications. The importance of low audio delay may also mean that some audio data should be treated at a higher priority than other time-critical data.

The volume of data is an important consideration when it comes to both data storage and transmission. Generally, the higher the quality of compression technique used, the more computation required to achieve the results. For single-user multimedia applications, it makes sense to use whatever computational resources are available for decompression of that user's data streams. In conferencing, however, we want to display multiple streams at once. In addition, the number of streams is variable. This means that, unless the system can dynamically scale the complexity of the decode algorithm appropriately, it is desirable to use a less computationally intensive decode algorithm, even at the cost of lower quality or higher data rate. The AMP platform provided a very simple algorithm with a relatively low compression ratio (about four times). It also required relatively little computation. Our system had usable results with this algorithm, and as better compression techniques become available, either image quality will improve or the data rate will get lower, or both.

The goals for integrating video into a desktop collaboration environment must include sensitivity to the use of the shared network resources. A single desktop-video data stream often will have multiple destinations. Examples are three-way conferencing and broadcasting a lecture. In a bus-based network like Ethernet, there are three ways to have multiple destinations receive the data: through point-to-point addressing, broadcast, and multicast.

*Point-to-point addressing* requires sending each of the destinations a copy of the data. Replicating video data for each destination adds significant load to the shared network bandwidth.

A *broadcast* mechanism sends a single stream of the data out on the network, and all machines on that network receive it. Broadcast has two disadvantages; first, by convention, broadcast messages are limited to a local network in order to prevent wide-area-network overload; second, every machine on the network receives the video data, whether it is interested in it or not. This puts significant extra load on processors not even involved with the conference.

*Multicast,* or *group addressing,* sends a single stream out on the network, but only machines with users interested in the data can receive it (Deering, 1990). AMP used multicast connections when possible, minimizing applications' impact on the network. While multicast transport is not explicitly a requirement of interactive video, network performance optimization is.

## Application Architecture

There are two general approaches to designing multiuser applications: a *centralized* approach, in which a single copy of the application is run on one machine, and is explicitly or implicitly connected to user-interface code on each participant's machine; and a *distributed* approach, in which each user interacts with a separate copy of the application, and some mechanism is used to keep all copies of the application synchronized. The advantages and disadvantages of both schemes have been well documented in the case of applications employing text and graphics (Lantz, 1986). In applications that make heavy use of audio, video, or high-resolution still images, performance considerations often will dictate that at least the media-intensive parts of the application should be distributed.

In our case, one of the most useful functions provided by AMP was the management of distributed multimedia. Applications used AMP to allocate resources and to hook them up in the desired way. This took care of distributing the flow of media. We then had to decide whether to make the videoconference application itself centralized or decentralized.

Beyond having AMP and the network window system allocate and connect resources, the application's primary function is to mediate user requests to pause, resume, and exit. Because of the CSCW literature and the fact that we were building a conferencing application, we expected that it would be preferable to write videoconf as a distributed application. However, because the application was a prototype, it was expedient to write it as a centralized application. It was much simpler to write that way, because all the communication was within one process. Much to our surprise, as we sought to establish which functionalities were not provided by our centralized implementation, we found that the only one was reliability. Reliability in the face of machine failure, though a classic advantage of distributed architectures, is not a major issue when it comes to the small-group collaboration addressed by our application.

It is worth noting that, while the sophistication of distributed computer systems is increasing, the number of applications taking explicit advantage of this new sophistication is not (Rodden and Blair, 1991). Our experience with AMP has been that the environment finally is becoming rich enough to make distributed functionality easier. This is good news for those working on collaborative applications.

## Future Work

### Extending the platform for conferencing support

The application-specific data that is exchanged in a multiuser collaborative application is also time-critical, and is subject to exactly the same synchronization problems as the audio and video. Consider the example of an application that employs audioconferencing and provides a shared telepointer. A user who says "Look at the picture I'm pointing to" wants some assurance that collaborators on remote machines are receiving the utterance and the pointer update at approximately the same time. This suggests that the services required of multimedia by CSCW environments are not simply audio- and videoconferencing. Application-specific data also must be delivered in the same timely manner as the media.

Like most general-purpose computer operating systems and networks, ours do not currently recognize data as having time-critical requirements. In an effort to minimize its impact on other network traffic and other processes on the workstation, such as other current multimedia efforts, AMP made three assumptions about the time-critical characteristics of multimedia:

1. Data is sampled at regular intervals.
2. Individual data samples decay quickly (if one arrives late, it rapidly loses relevance).

**Figure 34.3**   Characterizing time-critical data.

3. Synchronizing multiple streams of data (e.g., audio and video) is a priority.

These assumptions drive the design and implementation of multimedia toolkit support. However, these assumptions are not true for all time-critical domains.

In Fig. 34.3, time-critical data samples have been characterized on two axes: how regularly it is sampled, and its need for guaranteed delivery. The top-left quadrant contains traditional real-time events. These kinds of events, for example on a factory floor, occur at predictable intervals, and the servicing of these must be guaranteed. Samples from a videocompression algorithm that captured and transmitted a complete data sample 30 times every second would be in the "predictable interval, nonguaranteed" quadrant. That data requires regular sampling and delivery within the sampling interval, and each sample is independent of the others. Data samples that don't correctly and completely arrive before the next interval may be discarded; they will be replaced by later samples with more current information. Some compression algorithms send full base frames at less frequent intervals, supplemented with frames containing just the difference information in the intervening intervals. Because the base frames require reliable delivery and the difference frames do not, such algorithms are a hybrid on the full/incremental update axis. AMP supported exactly this class of events.

Events in multiuser applications occur at unpredictable intervals. These events need to be shared in a timely manner, and some require guaranteed delivery while others do not. In general, keyboard events and mouse events (such as mouse-up, mouse-down) must be reliably delivered, even if some delay is involved (top-right quadrant). Events generated by drawing continuously using a mouse or stylus do not require guaranteed delivery. Delivering fewer events results only in a coarser representation, not an inaccurate one. These are the kinds of data generated by shared drawing. A platform for collaboration must support this class of time-critical events.

Once we have a platform that supports a wider range of collaborative applications, we can expand our concept of a conference on the workstation beyond that of a videoconference. A conference can be an object that contains a set of applications, including a videoconference application. That set can be dynamic, and actions in the different applications could now be synchronized, or be subject to shared attributes. Interesting future directions for conferencing include exploring richer models of conference naming, characterizing, and browsing; other models of security; and shared user control of parameters during a conference, such as security attributes, recording function, video frame rate, and image size and resolution.

## Summary

One of our goals was to determine if it was feasible to develop a videoconferencing prototype on a standard UNIX workstation. The software platform on which we built the application provided many of the services required for conferencing, and it was relatively easy to build a simple videoconference application for up to five conferees, running on a standard network.

While our distributed multimedia platform provided much of the system support needed to accomplish our goals, additional requirements are needed for a collaboration platform. For example both platforms need to provide applications with the ability to name network entities, such as people and devices. Additionally, a collaboration platform needs to provide the ability to reference conferences, or sessions. Both platforms need to be able to associate attributes with their entities, e.g., access permissions and whether the data need to be secure. Collaborative applications also need to have elements of a conference, such as the people and applications required, be part of its attributes. Both a multimedia and collaboration platform need to provide the resources for multiple displays on each workstation, but a collaborative platform must also provide the ability to deliver a source, such as the data from a camera, to multiple destinations. Both multimedia and collaborative applications require platform support to be "good network citizens." Both can benefit from data compression, but collaborative applications also require intelligent connection management.

A collaborative platform needs to provide some services not required by strictly multimedia applications. It must provide applications with support for negotiating the sharing of control of shared devices. Collaborative applications may have strict timeliness requirements for some data streams such as interactive audio. A collaborative platform also should be able to support the application-specific data of multiuser applications in a time-critical manner, just like video and audio.

## Acknowledgments

First and foremost, I must acknowledge the contributions of my two COCO project collaborators, David Gedye and John Tang. Their insights and contributions were and are innumerable, and always invaluable. I also am grateful for the contributions, both in thought and practice, of our colleagues on the AMP team, led by Greg McLaughlin. In addition I thank Roger Calnan, Trevor Morris, Alan Ruberg, Rab Hagy, and Brian Raymor for guidance and comments on this paper.

## References

Borning, A., and M. Travers, "Two Approaches to Casual Interaction Over Computer and Video Networks," SIGCHI 1991 Proceedings, pp. 13–19.

*Byte* magazine, December 1985 issue on Computer Conferencing, vol. 10, no. 13.

Calnan, Roger S., "The Advanced Multimedia Platforms Project," 2nd International Workshop on Network and Operating System Support for Digital Audio and Video.

Casner, S., K. Seo, W. Edmond, and C. Topolcic, "N-Way Conferencing with Packet Video," Technical Report ISI/RS-90-252, USC/Information Sciences Institute, Marina del Rey, CA, 1990.

Deering, Stephen E., and David R. Cheriton, "Multicast Routing in Datagram Internets and Extended LANs," *ACM Transactions of Computer Systems,* vol. 8, no. 2, May 1990, pp. 85–110.

Isaacs, Ellen, A., and John C. Tang, "What Video Can and Can't Do for Collaboration: A Case Study," Proceedings of the ACM Multimedia '93 Conference, August 1993, Anaheim, CA, in press.

Lantz, K. A., "An Experiment in Integrated Multimedia Conferencing," Proceedings of the ACM Conference on Computer-Supported Cooperative Work, ACM, NY, NY, 1986, pp. 267–275.

Liebhold, Michael, and Eric M. Hoffert, "Toward an Open Environment for Digital Video," *Communications of the ACM,* vol. 34, no. 4, April 1991, pp. 103–112.

Olson, Margrethe H., and Sara A. Bly, "The Portland Experience: A Report on a Distributed Research Group," *International Journal of Man-Machine Systems,* vol. 34, no. 2, February 1991, pp. 211–228. Reprinted: *Computer-Supported Cooperative Work and Groupware,* Saul Greenberg, ed., Academic Press, London, 1991, pp. 81–98.

Rodden, Tom, and Gordon Blair, "CSCW and Distributed Systems: The Problem of Control," Proceedings of the Second European Conference on Computer-Supported Cooperative Work–ECSCW '91, Kluwer Academic Publishers, Bannon Robinson and Schmidt, eds., 1991, pp. 49–64.

Root, Robert W., "Design of a Multi-Media Vehicle for Social Browsing," Proceedings of the Conference on Computer-Supported Cooperative Work, Portland, OR, September 1988, pp. 25–38.

Tang, John C., and Ellen A. Isaacs, "Why Do Users Like Video? Studies of Multimedia-Supported Collaboration," *Computer Supported Cooperative Work: An International Journal,* in press. Also available as Technical Report TR-92-5 from Sun Microsystems Laboratories, Inc.

Vin, Harrick M., Polle T. Zellweger, Daniel C. Swinehart, and P. Venkat Rangan, "Multimedia Conferencing in the Etherphone Environment," *IEEE Computer,* vol. 24, no. 10, October 1991, pp. 69–79.

# 35

# Voice-Recognition and Voice-Response Systems

**Mike McGonagle**

In the movie *Star Trek IV: The Return Home,* Chief Engineer Scott sits down in front of a twentieth-century computer and prepares to communicate with it. He addresses it: "Computer." Once more, with feeling, when it doesn't respond: "Com*pute*r!" Dr. McCoy hands him the mouse and Scotty turns it over in his hand and speaks into it: "Hello, computer!" At this point his host says, "Just use the keyboard," to which Scotty dryly replies, "The keyboard. How quaint."

While this scenario is humorous in its comparison of current versus futuristic computer usage, it is typical of almost all literary and movie references to computer interfaces in the future. Users will be able to talk normally to computers, and they will not only understand but respond verbally as well. Predicting the distant future is a difficult and often frustrating activity. Better just to ask, how close are we to this vision today? Can we build a system today that would satisfy Chief Engineer Scott?

## Introduction

This chapter will discuss the technologies that enable computers to understand spoken language and to respond in kind: voice recognition and voice response, respectively. Already there are many examples of this technology in use, mostly in "consumer" sorts of applications such as banking, telephone dialing, VCR control, etc. As the quality of these systems has improved, they also have been applied to providing handicapped people with access to computers, and to educational areas such as foreign language training. Since the focus of this chapter is on multimedia, we will touch on such applications only briefly in our discussion of technology.

Principally we will discuss voice recognition and response as general interface options in building multimedia systems, as input/output mechanisms to be used in conjunction with or instead of keyboards, mice, touchscreens, graphic displays, sound files, etc. This is a logical extension for many multimedia systems, since this technology is supported by many of the commercially available sound cards. The main focus of the technology examples and applications dealt with in this chapter will be on the PC, but this technology is equally available on MacIntosh, UNIX, and many other platforms. Although the chapter will mention and discuss several voice-recognition and -response products, it does not intend to be a comprehensive product comparison. Products are mentioned in order to illustrate various features, and the inclusion or exclusion of a specific product or company should not be construed to be either an endorsement or rejection of them. A list of the companies mentioned in this chapter, with addresses and phone numbers, is included at the end of the chapter, to assist anyone interested in investigating this technology in more detail.

The vision inherent in voice recognition and response is one of computer systems that are able to fully understand normal spoken language for command and data input, and that are able to formulate responses in the same way, speaking in a natural-sounding (i.e., nonmechanical) voice. This is a natural extension in the development of human-computer interfaces. Humans communicate principally via spoken language, with writing being used primarily when the communication is not going to be immediate and interactive. As our use of computers has evolved from batch-oriented processing to real-time, interactive computation, the interest in building voice-oriented computer interfaces has naturally increased.

Man's interest in "talking automata" dates from ancient times, when statues were made to speak via hidden voice tubes. This fascination continued down through the Middle Ages, and through the early decades of this century. For an interesting discussion of these historical efforts, I would refer readers to Chapter 2 of Gordon Pelton's book *Voice Processing* (see the References at the end of the chapter). Since the advent of computers in the middle of this century, the focus of these efforts to create speaking and hearing automata has been shifted to the computer.

There has been academic and research interest in speech generation and recognition for several decades, and there have even been commercial products in these areas for much longer than most people realize. Actually, over the last several years there has been a minor explosion of products in these areas. This explosion has been fueled in part by the availability of general sound-processing boards, such as the Sound Blaster from Creative Labs and the ProAudio Spectrum 16 from Media Vision, which have tremendously increased the number of workstations able to produce quality sound. Once quality sound was available, it was a natural step to go beyond playing music and sound snippets to processing speech input and output.

Users want speech processing, and vendors see it as a way to make their sound-board products more desirable in the business world. There are now several software-only products available that provide speech synthesis or voice recognition via any number of the most popular sound boards. While most of the high-end systems still come with their own specialized hardware, many of these vendors also offer a lower-end version of their product that works with industry-standard sound boards. This trend can be expected to continue, providing users with increasingly robust and affordable products.

A brief analysis of human-to-human spoken interaction will point out some of the serious challenges to accomplishing voice recognition and response.

In conversation, our voices rise and fall to give emphasis, pose questions, etc. This characteristic is called *prosody*. The prosodic features of what we say often convey more information than the actual words themselves. Anyone who has ever repeatedly said "Come here" to a stubborn dog has had first-hand exposure to this effect. Although the dog may recognize the wave forms that compose the phrase "Come here," it is the tone of the speaker's voice and which word receives the emphasis that tell the obstinate animal whether it is in trouble or not. Some words even change their meaning under different pronunciations. *Permit* is a noun with the emphasis placed on the first syllable, but a verb when the emphasis is shifted to the second syllable. Anyone who has ever had to read a passage aloud has probably experienced the embarrassment of misemphasizing a word or phrase, thereby completely changing the meaning of a sentence or rendering it as gibberish. Properly dealing with these prosodic features is critical to the production of human-sounding computer speech.

In listening, we often use our visual sense as well as our auditory one. This is especially important in determining who is actually being addressed. So too, the computer has difficulty detecting that you have turned your back to it and are speaking to someone in the doorway to your office, not still giving it commands. (In a scene from *Star Trek: The Next Generation,* Worf turns away from the computer console and says to Data, "You mean it's alive?", to which the computer answers: "Insufficient data to support that conclusion." Worf then turns and says acidly to the computer: "I wasn't talking to you!" Apparently this problem has not been solved even in the twenty-third century!) In listening, we also determine the meaning of words and phrases by the context in which they are used. For example, a person can easily tell whether a speaker said "I'd like *to*" or "I'd like *two*" based on the context of the conversation.

The correction of misunderstandings, whether between humans or between a human and a computer, is also an important component of any spoken interface mechanism. People normally do not understand 100 percent of what is said to them. To compensate for this, they take a guess at what was meant based on the context in which something was said. For example, the phrases "wreck a nice beach" and "recognize speech" are similar-sounding, but obviously differentiable based on the context in which they appear. In face-to-face communication, we can interrupt the speaker to ask him or her to repeat, or to clarify, what was said. This poses problems when building a human-to-computer interface, partially because of the difficulty in modeling both the interaction and the context awareness, and partially because of the loss in accuracy that may occur when comparing voice input with normal keyboard and mouse interaction. While a voice-driven system has great appeal due to its natural and intuitive feel, if it means that our work becomes more error-prone, it will not be used.

It is these interface-oriented challenges that are in many cases more difficult to overcome than the mechanics of word or phrase recognition and synthesis. Therefore, the primary focus of current systems is on those applications in which the interface can be sufficiently well defined so as to limit these problems, rather than on the free-form communications depicted in the science-fiction literature. But even working within these limitations, voice recognition and response have tremendous potential today, as interface options, to build effective and user-friendly systems.

## Technology Overview

### Voice recognition

Before beginning our discussion of applications, a brief review of the technology and the terms used is in order. This will allow us to more accurately categorize and compare products, and to look at how they fit into different application areas.

In the voice-recognition area, products typically are categorized as utilizing either *continuous* or *discrete* recognition, as being able to handle either a small or large vocabulary, and as either *speaker-dependent* or *speaker-independent*. Normal human speech is continuous, with an unlimited vocabulary, and speaker-independent, but in many applications none of these characteristics is required.

In products that utilize discrete recognition, the speaker must pause briefly between words or phrases, the delay normally in the range of a few milliseconds. This type of system usually can recognize as single entities either individual words or short phrases. In products that utilize continuous recognition, the speaker can talk normally without pausing between words/phrases, and the system is able to pick out the words that were spoken from this continuous stream. In a voice-dictation system, this would mean that all of the words were recognized and processed, whereas in a voice-command system only the *command* words would be picked out of a continuous stream of speech, all other words being ignored. Because of the difficulty inherent in continuous human speech in detecting word boundaries, discrete word systems are much easier to implement and generally more accurate. On the other hand since this is not a natural speaking style, they can be awkward to use in those situations (e.g., dictation) where a continuous mode of speech normally is used.

Vocabulary size in voice-recognition systems is generally categorized as small or large, with the former being under 1000 words/phrases and the latter above it. This delineation is important not only because of the obvious difference in the number of words recognized, but also because it requires changes in the way the system is set up. Several commercially available systems manage several vocabularies, organized in a tree-structured fashion. When a command is recognized that starts or returns to a different application, the voice-recognition software replaces the current vocabulary with one for that specific application. This mechanism allows each individual vocabulary to be limited in size, while still supporting a large number of diverse applications. Vocabulary size can be an important consideration, since processing time, as well as the resources required for recognition, can grow in a nonlinear fashion as vocabulary size increases. In addition the *confusability* level of the system, i.e., the amount of difficulty the recognition mechanism has in differentiating similar words, also goes up rapidly as vocabulary size grows.

The difference between speaker-dependent and speaker-independent systems is fairly self-explanatory. In the former case, the system needs to be trained to recognize each user's individual voice patterns, while the latter type of system contains a general voice model that is meant to allow any user to be understood. Given all of the differences in accent, pitch, inflection, etc., speaker independence is a difficult challenge, and most of the commercially available systems are speaker-dependent. While most provide a generic voice template that users can attempt to utilize, they normally provide much better recognition rates if users take the time to train them for their individual speech patterns.

The type of training these speaker-dependent systems require varies according to the specific system and vocabulary size. Most small-vocabulary systems require the user to repeat each word a number of times. This information then is used to create both a model of the word, and a *variability factor*. This last element helps the recognition engine to take into account changes in pronunciation, since each utterance of a word will differ slightly.

As an example of this, Fig. 35.1 shows the waveform generated by three repetitions of the word *multimedia,* each said in succession. As you can see, they are similar but not identical. In order for a voice-recognition system to work consistently, each of these waveforms must come to be recognized as the word *multimedia.*

Large-vocabulary systems, by their very nature, usually require a different training mechanism. Repeating several thousand words several times each would be both time-consuming and of dubious value, given the effect of overuse on the user's voice. It also would not reflect the way in which many large-vocabulary systems perform the recognition task, since they often base their recognition on elements smaller than a word such as syllables or phonemes.

*Phonemes* are the smallest distinguishable sounds in a dialect of a language. Each phoneme actually represents a family of sounds, since the actual pronunciation of a specific phoneme varies according to the surrounding phonemes, an effect called *coarticulation.* A specific instance of a phoneme as

**Figure 35.1**   Waveform of three repetitions of the word *multimedia*.

spoken is called an *allophone*. Phonemes are important, since there are far fewer of them than there are words in a given language. Only around 40 phonemes are required to speak in the English language, which is comprised of over 40,000 words. For a more thorough discussion and analysis of the mechanics of speech production, I would refer the reader to either Gordon Pelton's, *Voice Processing* or Chris Rowden's *Speech Processing* (see References section at end of chapter).

The training of systems that base their recognition on phonemes, or similar entities, typically involves the repetition of a series of words, phrases, and/or sentences that allows the recognition system to build a voice model for these subword units. Undertraining of any speaker-dependent system can lead to very unsatisfactory results, so care should be taken that training is thorough. Retraining of the system also may be required occasionally, due either to changes in the user's voice caused perhaps by a cold or hay fever, or to a change in equipment, such as a different microphone.

It also is important to use a normal voice when training the system. Many people, when they think of "voice training," think of teaching a young child to speak. In the latter case most people will speak slowly and clearly, using careful enunciation, and may even speak in a louder-than-normal tone. This is precisely the wrong approach to training a voice-recognition system, for the system needs to be able to recognize the user's normal, everyday speaking voice. Training in an artificially "careful" voice may actually reduce the accuracy of the system.

A fairly recent development is the introduction of *speaker-adaptive* systems. A speaker-adaptive system is constantly updating its word models based on the actual speaking patterns employed during use. This can allow an operator to start using the system sooner, since it can shorten the formal training time required, and it also helps to build word models that represent true speech patterns. It can be difficult to get people to relax and speak naturally during training, as just mentioned, which often means that the system is being trained to listen to a different voice than that which will be employed during actual usage. The current feeling in the industry is that a speaker-adaptive system, built on top of a basic speaker-independent model, offers better recognition accuracy than the strictly speaker-dependent system.

## Voice response

In the voice-response arena, systems are divided into *synthesized* versus *digitized* (or *recorded*) voice systems. In the latter case, words and/or phrases are spoken, recorded, indexed, and saved. These speech fragments then are pieced together by the application to form the spoken response. Chris Rowden, in his book *Speech Processing,* refers to this technology as *copy synthesis,* so as to differentiate it from the capture and playback of complete, unfragmented, digitized voice messages, as in voice-annotation systems. Although the vocabulary that can be handled is limited by the storage requirements of the recorded speech segments, the quality of the speech usually is very high, since it is actual recorded human speech. Extending the vocabulary of a digitized voice system can be a problem if the same person is not available to record the new phrases. Mixing fragments recorded by different speakers may be obvious and therefore distracting to the users.

For the most part this chapter will deal with the other option, synthesized speech, since it seems to have much more applicability to the building of multimedia interfaces. In general, synthesized-speech systems allow a much larger vocabulary, unlimited in some applications, but their quality is limited by the quality of the synthesis hardware/software. At the low end, the voice produced is very mechanical-sounding, but higher-end systems provide much more control over both the quality and the characteristics (i.e., sex, pitch, tone) of the voice.

All of these systems either have rules for pronunciation that they use to determine how a given word should sound, or are table-based, in which case each word is looked up in a pronunciation dictionary. Many current systems are hybrids, using a combination of rules in conjunction with a basic pronunciation dictionary. The quality of a speech-synthesis system is directly related to the robustness of these rules, and in order to account for English's many exceptions to the rules most speech-synthesis systems allow the user to define entries in an *exception dictionary*. The pronunciation for a given word is placed in this dictionary, usually specified phonetically, and the system will look there first when attempting to pronounce a word. The system may provide a basic set of exception words, but it will be up to the user to load any special technical words or, especially, peoples' names, since this latter group frequently require foreign rules of pronunciation.

In order for a text-to-speech synthesis system to be well accepted, it must provide the following:

- *Correct pronunciation.* Because of the importance of speech in our lives, people tend to be very critical of a speech-synthesis system that consistently mispronounces words. Mispronunciations also can prove distracting, drawing the listener's attention away from the content of the message and actually lowering the effectiveness of the system. Rowden describes the problems in this area as "related to the irregular correspondence of the written form of the language, the orthography, to the sounds of the spoken form, the phonology." While he is speaking of British, as opposed to American, English, the statement holds true for both. He cites an example of this by comparing the written representation, versus the spoken pronunciation, of the syllable *cam* in the following four words:

1. cam
2. came
3. Cambridge
4. cameo

■ *Intelligent interpretation of content.*   In a free-form text-to-speech system, it is critical that the speech-synthesis system be able to correctly handle nonword items such as abbreviations, numbers, symbols, etc. The speech engine also needs to be able to differentiate the end of an abbreviation from the end of a sentence. Rowden cites five sentences as an example of how various elements such as these should be handled. They are:

1. Kiteflying is such fun, I'd do it all day!
2. Mr. Smith lives in St. George St.
3. 121,040,011 is a large number, $65,000 is a 'city salary,' 508-229-4980 is a 'phone number.'
4. World War II broke out on 3/9/39; will NATO prevent another one?
5. I arrived at 8:00 and stayed till 3:30.

To get an idea of how one commercial system handles these, take a look at how Monologue for Windows (a description of this product will come later) read each of these sentences. Monologue is a very low-end system, but did a fairly good job on these sentences. The results were these:

1. *Kiteflying* was pronounced more like *kitfling,* but Rowden anticipated that that word would be a problem. Inserting a space, i.e., making it *kite flying,* or placing it in the exception dictionary handled the problem.
2. This sentence was pronounced almost perfectly. *Mr.* was expanded to *mister,* the first St. became *saint* and the second became *street.* But the system hesitated at each period, treating them as an end-of-sentence marker.
3. The phone number was interpreted as an arithmetic string (i.e., five hundred eight minus two hundred twenty-nine...) but the other num-

bers were handled correctly, including the inclusion of the word *dollars* in the appropriate place.

4. II was not read as a roman numeral and so was spelled (i.e., /ay/ /ay/), but the rest of the sentence was handled correctly. 3/9/39 became March ninth, nineteen hundred thirty-nine, and NATO was correctly pronounced.

5. The system didn't recognize 8:00 or 3:30 as being in time format, so it read each component of them separately (i.e., eight zero zero, and three thirty).

Of the 15 items identified in Rowden's analysis as points of interest in this test suite, Monologue handled 9 correctly without having to resort to adding items to the dictionary or respelling items.

- *Correct prosody.* Since this information is not inherent in the text but usually is supplied by the reader based on knowledge of the material or application of common knowledge rules (e.g., how to properly change inflection to convey a question), speech-synthesis systems often can sound flat and monotone. Since a flat, monotone voice is a cultural trigger to the listener that the information is boring, the listener can be tuned out simply by the presentation.

- *Nonmonotone presentation.* This is different from prosody, which has accepted rules for inflection. This category relates more to the voice control that an experienced speaker uses, varying speed and loudness not to convey information but to keep the audience listening. These characteristics generally are referred to as *delivery,* especially when applied to actors.

The above criteria are most important for a free-form text-to-speech system. In the case of a system that needs only a limited vocabulary, the application can do things, such as spell words phonetically, that will make up for shortcomings in the underlying speech engine.

## Application Overview

### Voice response

In the voice-response area, applications can be roughly divided into two areas: *computer reading,* and *interactive voice response* (*IVR*). The latter generally is associated with interactive telephone-response systems, but the same type of applications can just as easily be built around an interactive computer interface as the phone.

**Computer reading.** This area encompasses a number of different actual and potential applications, ranging from reading free-form text, as would be found in a memo or a mail message, to proofreading applications that deal with a more limited vocabulary, as might be found in a typical spreadsheet. To date,

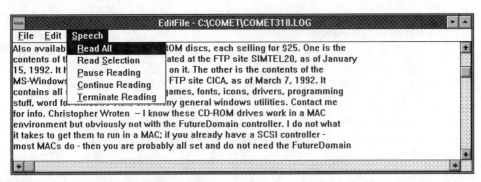

**Figure 35.2**   Sample speaking-editor interface.

free-form text-to-speech reading applications have most commonly been found in systems built for handicapped users. The main reason for this is that the current technology has difficulty producing a pleasant, non-machine-sounding voice. The technology therefore is suitable for providing access for people who could not use the system otherwise, but a visual interface is preferable when at all possible.

Reading a passage aloud does have its uses, since often it is easier to pick out grammatical problems by hearing them than by looking at them. Spelling errors also can become obvious when the speech-synthesis system pronounces the misspelled word. As an example of this type of application, let's look at a speaking text editor that I've built as a test system for working with text-to-speech technology. The basic interface is shown in Figure 35.2, illustrating the speech options that are available.

In building this application I used ProVoice for Windows from First Byte, described more fully later in the chapter. This product, which provides a pro-grammatic interface for performing text-to-speech conversion, allowed com-puter reading to be easily added on top of the normal editing functions. The total code was approximately 100 lines, on top of that already in place for the base application. The editor code uses functions provided by ProVoice to first parse the text sentence by sentence. Each sentence then is converted to a pho-netic string, which is passed to the speech engine to be said. An even simpler interface could be constructed that would just pass the entire block of text and have it spoken as a single step. However by breaking it out the way I have, I provide the ability to interrupt the computer after each sentence. Otherwise the user would have to wait until the entire block of text had been completely spoken, which clearly could become annoying if it was a large section of text. This points up an important consideration when purchasing or building a text-to-speech system: How easy is it to interrupt when it is speaking?

The same type of functionality illustrated in this simple example can be added to many other products, even without "programming," by using inter-process communications mechanisms such as DDE under Microsoft Windows, or Sun Solaris's ToolTalk on Sun Sparcstations. Some third-party applica-tions provide powerful macro-writing capabilities, which potentially could also be used to extend the applications you are using today and allow them to perform text-to-speech conversion. Some products, such as Microsoft's Window Sound System and First Byte's Monologue for Windows, provide this type of proofreading capability, for spreadsheets, as part of the product. When using this feature, the current cell or selected range is read directly from the spreadsheet. This can be a great aid in checking a row or column of numbers to ensure that they were entered correctly, since it allows the user to validate the data in an "eyes-free" mode rather than continually shift from the monitor to a sheet of numbers.

**Interactive voice response.**   The area of interactive voice response holds a great deal of potential for building interactive, multimedia-oriented interfaces. On the one hand there are an increasing number of small devices, ranging from laptops to personal digital assistants (PDAs) coming into everyday use. Screen real estate is a valuable commodity with these devices, and therefore IVR offers you the ability to convey important information without having to display it. Even on desktop systems with full-size monitors, our visual senses often are inundated. This problem becomes especially acute when dealing with graphic-intensive applications such as CAD/CAM, or drawing applications. Many of these applications require that attention be focused on the spot where you are currently drawing, even as they provide coordinate information at the bottom of the display.

Anyone who has had the experience of trying to accurately position an object while shifting his or her eyes back and forth between two areas can appreciate the benefit of having the coordinate information provided orally. Adding speech synthesis to applications in this manner can greatly increase their usability, and can be done easily by utilizing existing text-to-speech technology. Concerns about mispronunciation and monotone delivery are greatly reduced for this type of limited application.

A related but unique potential area for speech synthesis is in providing warning and alert messages. The current range of computer beeps and bells is becoming greatly overworked as a means of gaining a user's attention. As a user, I can't tell if my workstation beeped to say that my file transfer has been completed or that I received a mail message, or to alert me that a network node has failed. If I'm concentrating on some other task, I may not want to be interrupted in the first case, but may in the last two. A solution that would have the computer announce which event has occurred has been proposed by several people, even to the point of giving the voice different characteristics for different events. Today's workstations assume that they already have the user's undivided attention, but as the ways in which we use computers change, this assumption increasingly will become less valid. Our computers will need to learn to get our attention, just as that visitor standing in your office doorway does.

**Voice recognition.**   In the voice-recognition area, applications may be divided into two categories: *voice command* and *voice dictation*. Voice-command systems allow a user to run the computer via voice, either in conjunction with or as a replacement for the keyboard and/or mouse. The entire system can be operated by voice command, customized voice-driven applications can be built, or both options can be supported. Voice-dictation systems basically are voice-driven typewriters. There are systems currently in use in areas such as medical-report dictation, and by handicapped people unable to use the keyboard and/or mouse. The differentiation between these two types of systems is important not only because of the variance in usage, but more so because of the distinctions in the criteria for selecting an appropriate system. The two types of systems, at least as we are dealing with them here, can further be defined by the following characteristics:

- *Vocabulary size.*   In a voice-command system, this can run from the handful of commands needed to operate a highly specialized application to the several hundred commands needed to operate Microsoft Windows as defined in the Microsoft Sound System. This means that a small-vocabulary system can be used, and is in fact more desirable due to reduced processing time, confusability concerns, and resource requirements. A voice-dictation system, on the other hand, generally will require a large-vocabulary system if it is to be useful. This may range from moderate size, for a restricted-use voice-dictation system such as medical diagnosis, to unlimited size, for a "voice typewriter" style of application.

- *Continuous versus discrete word/phrase recognition.*   In a voice-command system, the user generally is issuing short, specific commands, with a pause at the end of each. This means that a discrete word/phrase system can be used and it will still feel natural. The restriction of having to pause between words in a voice-dictation system could lead to reduced productivity, as the users were forced to adjust their working style to the limitations of the tool. Therefore continuous recognition would seem to be far preferable in voice-dictation systems. There is a certain amount of debate on this point since, as Biermann et al (1985) hypothesize, "Users seem to be able to learn to speak machine-recognizable discrete speech more easily than they are able to speak machine-recognizable connected speech."

- *Speaker dependence/independence.*   In voice-command applications such as telephone dialing, speaker independence is mandatory, but in the types of multimedia interface developments being addressed here, most voice-command systems will have a well-defined set of users. Using a speaker-dependent system is therefore desirable because of its higher accuracy rate, since voice-command systems must operate in a near error-free mode, as opposed to voice dictation, where the minimum goal is to perform better than a human typist. In the voice-dictation area, the issue is more how a speaker-dependent system can adequately be trained, given the assumption of a large vocabulary.

Now let's look at these areas of voice command and voice dictation separately.

**Voice command.**    Accuracy is of paramount importance in building a general, voice-driven user interface. As was mentioned earlier, any significant increase in the error rate of the work produced will often lead to the new interface being scrapped in favor of the more reliable keyboard and/or mouse approach. There are several types of errors that can occur in a voice-command system:

- *Failure to recognize a spoken command.*    In this situation, the system does not believe that what was said matches any of its known commands. While this may just mean that the command must be repeated, it can quickly lead to frustration. The natural tendency is to repeat the command with increased emphasis, which may make it that much less likely that the command will be recognized. This is another example of a fundamental difference between conversing with people and talking to a computer.

- *Misrecognition of a spoken command.*    In this case the operator issues one command but the system mistakenly takes it for another (i.e., the user says, "Page down," and the system hears "Page up") This mistake, often a result of poor training, can range from the slightly annoying to the catastrophic, depending on what action the computer carries out. Since a voice interface is inherently less accurate than keyboard/mouse input, care should be taken to ensure that there are confirmation dialogues associated with "dangerous" actions such as file deletion.

- *Recognition of a spoken command when none was given.*    This error may occur because someone else said something that the computer picked up and interpreted, or may be caused by the operator answering the phone or turning to talk to someone, without remembering that the computer is desperately attempting to interpret what they are saying as valid commands. As with the previous point, this mistake can range from the slightly annoying to the disastrous. To handle circumstances such as these, most systems have a simple mechanism that turns off recognition. The challenge to you, the operator, is to remember to use them!

Training, or retraining, can go a long way toward the reducing of these errors. The equipment being used, especially the microphone, also can be an important factor in this. Quality noise-canceling and/or unidirectional microphones are those that most voice-recognition system suppliers recommend. In my own work, I have gotten the best results with a relatively inexpensive headset microphone. It picks up very little outside noise, and the fact that it is a constant distance from my mouth helps to reduce the variability in my voice. The speed of the underlying system also can be a factor, at least with some voice-recognition packages. I have experienced a difference in accuracy of more than 10 percent when moving from a 386/33 to an equivalent 486/33 machine, given the greater accuracy of the faster machine.

Many voice-command systems operate by issuing a series of keystrokes that correspond to the command that was detected. Examples of such systems are the Microsoft Sound System, Media Vision's ExecuVoice, and Command Corporation's IN3 product. This is a very direct and intuitive way of adding voice command on top of an existing interface, such as Microsoft Windows. Since this type of installation is becoming so popular, let's take a moment to ask some of the questions you will want to ask when you are evaluating products.

*How easy is it to turn off recognition if I need to converse with someone else?* Some systems have a command-bar button that allows the recognition state to be toggled on or off via a mouse click. Some also support turning recognition off and on via voice command. This does not actually turn voice recognition off, but rather limits the valid recognizable vocabulary to a single phrase, which will turn full recognition back on. This is a very convenient feature, although care must be taken not to turn it on inadvertently when speaking on the phone or to another person.

*How are commands executed?* Some current systems have "macro" commands, such as EXEC, that allow a program to be started without having to go through the "FILE, RUN..." sequence, while others require that each command be converted into a specific series of keystrokes. This latter approach can be bothersome if the system handles these keystrokes as if they actually had been typed at the keyboard, since some people may find the flickering menus distracting.

*How well is the system able to handle background noise?* This may be only a minor consideration in a typical office environment, but it can be critical to the usability of a system intended for a factory, sawmill, etc. In general, if a system is going to be deployed in one of these noisy environments, a higher-end system, such as that produced by Verbex, will be needed.

*Does the voice-recognition system interfere with the operation of other parts of the system?* Some of the lower-end products, at least in the Microsoft Windows environment, do not allow sounds to be played while the voice-recognition software is active. This is an unacceptable situation, since it forces the user to choose between having the system listen or speak.

*How responsive is the system?* This can be a function of either the basic workstation configuration or the voice recognition software, or a combination of the two. When you are deciding on a system, both of these factors will need to be taken into consideration, and tests run that use the actual target configuration. The ease of use of a voice-command interface will mean little to you if it is appreciably slower than your current keyboard-and-mouse usage.

*How easy is it to add commands, and to train the vocabulary?* Most systems seem to have a simple, easy-to-use training mechanism. However, with some, if the word model becomes "corrupt," as it may if the user mistakenly says the wrong word during training, the only remedy is to delete and reload the command. This is due to the fact that the existing word-pronunciation model, based on a different word, is so different from the correct one that the system cannot reconcile the two, thereby causing it to reject new attempts to retrain the command with the correct word.

In terms of adding new commands, most systems make it easy for an individual user to perform this function. In a corporate environment, however, vocabulary definition may be performed centrally and then distributed to the individual workstations. Most of the low-end systems do not support this concept very well, but some of the higher-end ones do allow a vocabulary to be defined and trained as independent tasks.

## Putting Together a Voice-Command System

In this section we will describe the six steps you should take to build a voice-command system. As a real-world example of the application of each of these steps, I will be citing a multimedia technology demonstration system built for the Computer Corporation of America (CCA). This system was intended to demonstrate the integration of CCA's client-server tools with state-of-the-art personal computer technology, including voice recognition. The system was set up as a travel-planning aid, displaying a series of maps and, ultimately, detailed information about specific locales. The user could issue voice commands to navigate through the maps and the detailed information windows.

The six steps are as follows:

1. *Decide whether the system will support multimode input (i.e., keyboard, mouse, touchscreen, pen, etc.), or whether it will be a voice-only system.* This will determine what options are available to correct those errors that arise from misrecognition.

In our example system, the decision was made to support keyboard, mouse, and touchscreen input, as well as voice recognition. This was done so as to have an adequate mechanism to handle voice-command errors and to allow users who had not trained the speaker-dependent system to access the application.

2. *Define the vocabulary for the application.* If possible, this should be set up in a hierarchical fashion, since many products will support this type of structure. What this means is that certain commands are valid only after other commands (see Fig. 35.3 for an example of a hierarchical vocabulary structure, taken from the Microsoft Sound System's Voice Pilot). This allows the total vocabulary to be divided into a series of subvocabularies, only one of which is valid at any point in time. Therefore the voice-recognition software can limit its search for the correct word or phrase at each point, improving accuracy and response time. The initial vocabulary for the example system was around 45 words/phrases and is shown in Fig. 35.4. Because of its small size, it originally was set up without any structure, but the need to use the same phrase to perform different actions based on the application context eventually dictated a hierarchical structure.

3. *Choose the hardware/software products that will be used to support the voice-recognition aspects of the application.* This decision will be based on factors such as vocabulary size, speaker dependence/independence, operat-

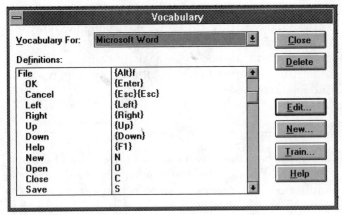

**Figure 35.3**  Hierarchical structure of a vocabulary.

| Amsterdam | Exit | New York | San Diego | Yes |
|---|---|---|---|---|
| Back | Good Bye | Next | San Francisco | |
| Baja | Help | Next Window | Size | |
| Boston | Maximize | No | Switch To | |
| Cabo | Menu Bar | OK | Tab | |
| Cabo San Luca | Mexico | Page Down | U.S. | |
| Cancel | Minimize | Page Up | UK | |
| Caribbean | Move | Paris | United States | |
| England | Nashville | Previous | utah | |
| Enter | national parks | Previous Window | Window | |
| Europe | new orleans | Restore | wyoming | |

**Figure 35.4**  Sample application vocabulary.

ing-environment characteristics, etc. A discussion of several commercial products for voice command will be presented later, in order to compare their features.

The example system had a small vocabulary and was intended to be used in a controlled, relatively quiet environment. It also was intended to have a limited number of predetermined users, so a speaker-dependent implementation was preferable. Since the system also required a general sound-support capability, the Microsoft Windows Sound System was selected. It contains a sound card as well as voice-command software, and allowed our custom vocabulary to be created and supported. It was also, at the time, one of the only inexpensive options available, although of late this has changed dramatically.

4. *Select a microphone to use with the system.*  If you are to make the right choice, you will need to take into account the operating environment of the system (i.e., hands-free operations, background noise, etc.), and also to ensure that the microphone chosen does not introduce recognition errors into the system by inconsistent operation, picking up background noise, etc.

Since the example system supported keyboard, mouse, and touchscreen input as well as voice, a hand-held microphone was deemed unreasonable. Testing showed that accuracy was better with a microphone that attached to the user (i.e., lapel or headset) than with a stationary type. Fashion concerns dictated the use of the lapel microphone.

5. *Assuming that a speaker-dependent system is being used, remember that it must be trained by the user community.*   Initially there were two users for our example system, and in order to ensure the highest possible accuracy, separate profiles were created for both the lapel and headset microphones, giving a total of four "users." Training of each profile took only 5 to 10 minutes.

6. *Put the finishing touches on the miscellaneous aspects of the system.*   In our example system, this mainly involved selecting the proper PC configuration to use. Testing yielded much better results using a 486-based system over a 386, so the former was chosen.

As we ran the example system cited here, the voice-command software performed very well. Recognition was in the 90 percent range, which was good although not perfect, and the system's responsiveness was excellent, working by voice as fast as with any of the other input modes. The one problem occurred when one of the operators was suffering nasal congestion due to a bout of hay fever. This required that we retrain the system in order to compensate for the change in voice characteristics, after which the system once again performed excellently.

This experience points up an important issue that real-world voice-recognition systems need to handle, since an individual's voice can change due to colds, allergies, etc. and also can have different tonal qualities at different times of day. The volume level of an individual's speech also changes in response to different situations. This problem is especially pronounced in voice-recognition systems when it becomes necessary to repeat commands.

It is only natural to add extra emphasis when repeating a command, but with most systems this reduces the chances of successful recognition. Retraining our small-vocabulary example system was easy, but a large-vocabulary system should help you to avoid retraining by having greater flexibility to handle changes in an individual's voice.

Thus far our discussion of voice-command systems has focused on interfaces that convert a recognized word into a series of keystrokes, and in fact this is how most of these systems operate. There may be situations in which a program calls for direct access to the commands spoken, as when there is no keyboard and/or display involved. Examples of this include mail sorting, manufacturing control systems, and financial trading, where a direct programmatic interface is desired of the kind supplied by Verbex Voice Systems, IBM, and Dragon Systems. In a custom application development effort, using a direct programmatic interface may make for a more intuitive, voice-oriented interface, as opposed to attempting to overlay voice commands on top of a morass of existing menus, buttons, and dialogue boxes.

## Voice dictation

When people think of voice-recognition systems, most commonly they think of voice dictation, in which the computer is able to transcribe everything that is said to it. Although systems of that kind (those produced by Dragon Systems, for example) have been available for a few years, they have not been widely implemented. This is partly because of cost (these systems are expensive) and partly because of the interface (they are speaker-dependent, discrete word systems). This requires an investment in training the system, and an adjustment to speaking style in order to utilize the system. To date these systems have been most popular among handicapped users, where they are necessary in order to access the computer. Many of these folks are very happy with their voice-dictation systems and report that they have adjusted their speaking style without any problem, but most computer people have been reluctant to give up their keyboards.

This reluctance may begin to erode over the next few years, as advances in continuous-speech recognition, coupled with a continuing drop in the cost of technology, make voice dictation both more affordable and more usable. IBM's recent announcement of their Interactive Speech Server Series gives a good indication of the technological side of this trend, if not the economic. This system can accept dictation at a rate of 70 words per minute, which is much faster than most users can type, although slower than a skilled typist.

There are really two types of voice-dictation systems that can be envisioned, differentiated by where the user's attention is focused. In the classic voice-activated-typewriter case, the user is focused on the computer as well as on the material being input. This means that error correction can be immediate, and that the system can prompt the user for information in the case of an unrecognized or ambiguously recognized word. In the other case the user's attention is directed elsewhere, and he or she is basically "thinking out loud" so that the computer can capture those thoughts. An example of this type of system is the radiological dictation system that IBM markets in Italy. This application allows a radiologist to dictate a report while examining an X-ray film, and clearly it is important that the system not distract the user in the middle of dictating to ask for clarification. Errors, if they occur, would more appropriately be flagged and dealt with later, when possible. In both cases the recognition system may need to handle long pauses and unintended noise that the speaker may make while formulating his/her next thought.

These problems will crop up most frequently when the user's focus is on the creation of material, not the dictation of a document.

The challenges facing a voice-recognition system increase rapidly as the vocabulary size goes up, and as the system attempts to process continuous rather than discrete speech. This explains why there are relatively few voice-dictation systems in use, especially when compared to the burgeoning voice-command area. But as the technology continues to improve, this area will receive more and more attention.

## Commercial Applications

Commercial applications are not the focus of this chapter, but it is appropriate to discuss them briefly, if for no other reason than that most people's first exposure to voice-recognition and voice-response systems will be in this arena. One of the common threads that runs through almost all of these applications is that they are telephone-oriented. This comes as no surprise, since what the telephone does well is to handle voice, both as input and output. It is not, however, a very good data-entry tool when having to use the keypad, as anyone who has ever had to type a long name into a voice-mail system can attest. As more and more services from banking to computer dating are developed around telephone access, the need to improve the overall user interface becomes increasingly important.

One of the first steps in telephone applications was the introduction of interactive voice response (IVR), which was in fact the technology that got this whole industry off the ground. Using IVR technology, systems could be built that provided the user with instructions at each step of the process, not to mention the information that was the eventual goal of the entire exercise. Most of these systems were and still are built using digitized voice technology. This is appropriate in telephone management applications, since the vocabulary generally is limited and the quality of the voice is of paramount concern. Some telephone applications, such as interactive catalogs, use synthesized speech because of the size and variability of the vocabulary that they must handle.

The next step, currently (1994) in full swing, is to add limited voice recognition to these systems. This is being done to improve the interface of some systems by limiting the amount of number-punching required, and also to provide access to these services from the 39 percent of homes and offices equipped with non-touchtone phones. Since these services are accessible by large numbers of people, speaker independence is required, but the fact that only a limited vocabulary is needed simplifies the problem greatly. Continuous-speech processing also is a requirement, since the general population will not adapt easily to a discrete-word speaking style. These systems can further be improved by the incorporation of word-spotting algorithms. Word-spotting allows the system to pick out or spot words within a continuous stream of speech, so that the system could pick out the account number if the user says, "Let's see...I think it's here. Okay. 81364."

Current product offerings of voice recognition in the commercial area already cover a wide range of applications. Customers accessing telephone-based services can now say their zip code, account number, etc. rather than punch it on the telephone's keypad. As another example, some cellular phone companies are offering a service that allows customers to place phone calls by voice command, to anywhere in the world, by saying the name of the person to be called. This is done by first dialing a central number that gives the customer access to the voice-recognition portion of the system. Field-testing of some of these systems has yielded accuracy rates of as high as 97 percent.

Another application of voice-recognition technology in the commercial area is in voice control. Examples of this include car phones that can make calls in a hands-free mode, by voice command, and the VCR voice controller. This latter device allows users to control their TVs and/or VCRs by speaking commands into a control unit, thereby simplifying the user interface greatly. As voice-recognition technology improves, expect to see more applications of this type. Providing nontechnical users with a simple, voice-driven interface to what is otherwise an intimidating and nonintuitive system will be an extremely well-received initiative.

There are many other examples of commercial or specialized uses of voice recognition and response, ranging from voice-alert systems that can dial a phone number and call for help to the voice-driven navigation system on an America's Cup yacht. We will not go into them here, but it should be noted that as computers steadily infiltrate our lives more and more, the technologies that they bring with them, such as voice recognition and response, also will play an ever-increasing role in our everyday lives.

## Product Breakout

This section briefly will describe several products in both the voice-recognition and voice-response areas. This is done to give the reader some sense of the different features and characteristics to be found in commercial product offerings, not to compare or recommend them. For further and more current information, the reader should contact these companies directly.

### Voice-response systems—digitized-speech systems

A great number of companies offer products in this area, but since most of them are focused on telephone management systems and are not targeted at general multimedia usage, I won't list them here. Still, there are some interesting developments in this market segment that are worth mentioning. The first is the joint interest shown by multimedia developers and telephone-management application-builders in editing digitized sound files. Right now the sound-file-editing companies seem to be focusing on one segment of the industry or the other, but undoubtedly this will change over time, thereby bringing more robust multimedia-editing packages to the market.

Another interesting development in digitized speech is the Smooth Talker product from Parity Software. This is a digitized voice system with a twist. It stores alternate pronunciations of words in its vocabulary, which allows different inflections to be used when using the same word in different contexts. For example, Smooth Talker would pronounce the word *two* differently in the phrases "ninety-two," and "two hundred and one."

**Microsoft Corporation.** The Microsoft Windows Sound System Proofreader is the one product that it seemed appropriate to talk about in this section. Offered as part of the Microsoft Windows Sound System product, this component can be used to read to the user sections of a Microsoft Excel and/or Lotus 1-2-3 for Windows spreadsheet. It comes with digitized speech fragments to handle the type of data normally found in a spreadsheet, i.e., numeric data in different formats. It can be extended to recognize items, such as text strings, and play back a user-recorded speech fragment when one is encountered.

As with most digitized-speech systems, the quality of the voice is very good. The inclusion of user-recorded speech fragments can be somewhat distracting, since they utilize a different voice than the surrounding items, and even the digitized voice can sound somewhat mechanical and choppy due to the small fragments that are being strung together. For example, the entry "$1,086.49" would consist of the fragments

(one)(thousand)(eighty)(six)(dollars)

(and)(forty)(nine)(cents).

Despite this, the overall effect of this system is quite good.

## Synthesized speech systems

**Digital Equipment Corporation.**   Digital Equipment Corporation produces DECTalk, a very flexible and high-quality speech-synthesis system. DECTalk is positioned more as a telephone management tool, but it also has the capability to be used as a general voice-response system. The DECTalk product gives the user control over a variety of the elements of the speech produced, such as

Male, female, or child's voice

Speaking rate (from 120 to 350 words per minute)

Baseline pitch

Pitch range

Breathiness

Smoothness

Head size

Forte

Laryngealization

Pauses

The ability to control all of these elements, along with the completeness of the rules used, allow a pleasant voice to be produced, although one readily identified as produced by a machine. The text to be spoken is passed to the DECTalk unit, which can be configured either as a separate, external box connected via a serial communications link or as a board within the PC. The external option makes DECTalk very flexible, in terms of its ability to be connected to a wide variety of systems.

**First Byte.**   First Byte produces Monologue for Windows, a very inexpensive (street price of less than $100) speech-synthesis system. There also is a version of Monologue that runs under DOS. Monologue for Windows, as well as ProVoice discussed next, works on any multimedia personal computer

(MPC)–compliant sound card. (It also can be used via the standard PC speaker, but on most PCs the quality of the voice produced in this manner is so poor that it is not a viable option.) The voice is mechanical, but clear and understandable, and the price will allow many users to get their first taste of voice response without having to spend an arm and a leg. The Windows product, Monologue for Windows, supports three different interfaces. Text can be copied to the Windows Clipboard, and Monologue can then be told to speak it. On a more automated note, a DDE interface also is supported that allows macros and/or programs to directly pass text to be spoken to the speech engine, without user intervention. Monologue also supports an Excel mode, which allows spreadsheets to be proofread, similar to the ProofReader feature of the Windows Sound System.

First Byte also produces a "sister" product to Monologue, called ProVoice for Windows. This product provides an application-programming interface (API) for performing text-to-speech conversion directly under program control. When it comes to building custom applications, this mechanism is far preferable to any of those offered in the Monologue product. The API is robust enough to cover functions for dictionary lookups, conversion of text to phonetic strings, and actually speaking a string, and even for coordinating an animated character's mouth with the actual words being spoken.

### Voice-recognition systems—voice-command systems

**Command Corp.**  Command Corp. offers the $IN^3$ (pronounced *in-cube*) voice-command system. This originally was offered on Sun Sparcstations, and is now available for Microsoft Windows as well. On the PC, IN3 can run on any MPC-compliant sound board. IN3 utilizes continuous-recognition and word-spotting technology, so it is able to pick commands out of a string of continuous speech. It comes with a standard command vocabulary for its target environment and can be extended with additional, user-supplied commands. The company has taken a somewhat unique approach to spreading the word on their product. In addition to the normal marketing channels, there is a "demo" version of IN3, available on several bulletin board services such as Compuserve, that allows potential users to try the system out, in a limited but useful fashion.

**Microsoft.**  The Windows Sound System, Microsoft's business-oriented sound board, comes with Voice Pilot, a Windows voice-command system. This system is based on technology licensed from Dragon Systems (to be discussed in a moment), and works only with the Windows Sound System board. It comes with an extensive set of vocabularies for operating Windows and many of the more popular Windows applications. It also is extendable, so that a user can create new voice commands within an existing vocabulary and/or create new vocabularies for custom applications.

**Verbex Voice Systems.**  Verbex offers a product called Listen for Windows in a number of configurations; it runs on Verbex's own Speech Commander DSP (digital signal processing) sound-processing card. Listen for Windows can handle continuous speech in a speaker-dependent mode, and is oriented toward the development of custom voice-aware applications rather than the overlaying of a voice-to-keystroke mechanism on top of existing applications. The software is priced based on the size of the vocabulary it can handle, while the Speech Commander hardware comes in several configurations, including a plug-in PC board, an external desktop unit for non-PC hardware platforms (i.e., UNIX, VAX, etc.), and a portable unit that works with laptop and notebook computers. Verbex also allows the vocabulary to be defined, in a text file, independent of the voice-processing system. This text file is passed through a conversion utility to build the preliminary binary vocabulary, which then is ready to be loaded onto the board and used.

**Covox.**  Covox has been supplying consumer-oriented voice-recognition systems for the PC longer than anyone else. Their traditional product offering uses Covox's own Sound Master family of hardware, and runs under DOS. Recently they have extended their product line with Voice Blaster, a voice-command facility that operates under either DOS or Windows on most MPC-compliant sound boards. Both of these systems are speaker-dependent, discrete-word systems, and both handle a small vocabulary. As with several other products in the Windows voice-command area, the total vocabulary can be organized into several smaller "subvocabularies," only one of which is active at any one point in time. It should be noted that, in order to operate, the Voice Blaster product requires a "dongle," a hardware security device that attaches to the printer port. This device does not interfere with normal printer output but should be tested with other printer-port-attached devices, such as tape or CD drives.

**Media Vision.**  Media Vision recently has begun to offer a voice-command package with their ProAudio Spectrum line of sound cards. This package, named ExecuVoice, is based on technology licensed from Dragon Systems and will work with any MPC-compliant sound board. It comes with a predefined vocabulary, but currently is not extendable. This means that it probably is adequate for running Microsoft Windows and most popular applications, but is not adaptable to custom applications.

## Voice-dictation systems

One note to be made before discussing Dragon Systems' and IBM's offerings is that, while their larger vocabulary systems clearly are targeted to the voice-dictation market, they both also offer configurations that are usable as voice-command systems. All of their products are discussed under this single heading for simplicity, but they also should be considered when evaluating voice-command systems.

**Dragon Systems.**  In many ways, this company is the leader in the voice-recognition area. This claim can be made based on the length of time they have been installing systems, and on the number of companies that have licensed their technology for inclusion in their own products. These include

- *IBM*.   IBM VoiceType Control for Windows and IBM VoiceType 2 are based on Dragon's similar products.

- *Microsoft*.   The Windows Sound System's Voice Pilot is based on technology licensed from Dragon.

- *Media Vision*.   ExecuVoice also is based on technology licensed from Dragon.

- *Articulate Systems*.   Voice Navigator II, a Macintosh voice-command system, is based on Dragon's speech-recognition technology.

In addition to all of this, Dragon also markets its own line of voice-recognition systems. Three examples are: DragonDictate-30K, DragonWriter-1000, and Dragon Talk-To Plus. All three use discrete word recognition and are speaker-dependent, although the DragonWriter-1000 is better described as speaker-adaptive. The DragonDictate-30K is a large-vocabulary system intended to be used in general, free-form, voice-dictation applications. DragonWriter-1000 can access a 1000-word active dictionary and is more focused on voice-command, or constrained voice-dictation applications. This product also has an API available, for use in developing customized voice-aware applications. Both of these products require that Dragon's speech-recognition board be present. The last product, Dragon Talk-To Plus, is a small-vocabulary system, supporting a 64-word active vocabulary at any point in time. It is aimed at voice-command applications and supports third-party audio boards.

**IBM.**  IBM offers a number of different products in the voice-recognition area, a couple of which were mentioned a moment ago. This section will describe two products based on IBM-developed technology. The first is the IBM Speech Server Series. This recently announced offering from IBM runs on OS/2-based personal computers; RS/6000 machines running the AIX operating system (IBM's version of UNIX); or on a combination of the above in a client-server mode. This system supports a large vocabulary (20,000 words, plus 2000 user-added words), is speaker-dependent, and operates in discrete-word mode. In addition to extending existing applications to accept dictated speech, the system also provides an API that can be used in the development of customized voice-aware applications.

The other product is the IBM Continuous Speech Series. This is a small-vocabulary system, although that calls for some explanation. The system will support a 20,000-word vocabulary, total, but this is organized into twenty 1000-word vocabularies, only one of which can be active at any point in time. The system is speaker-independent, and accepts continuous speech. Because of the small active vocabulary compared to the Speech Server Series product, this product is focused not on general dictation usage but more on voice-command or constrained-dictation applications such as medical reports. As with the previous product, it also provides an API for users who wish to develop customized voice-aware applications.

Both systems require that a special IBM audio-capture and playback card be installed.

## Summary

With any emerging technology there are champions and critics, and the situation is no different in the voice-recognition and -response area. I hope this chapter has helped you to see that this technology is here to stay, as evidenced by the large number of diverse applications available today. In the report *Voice Recognition and Response Markets,* Market Intelligence projects that the advanced-voice-processing-technology equipment market (in the United States) will triple from $700 million in 1991 to $2.5 billion in 1998, growing at a 20 percent compound annual rate. This same report predicts that voice-recognition systems will grow from 9 percent of this market in 1992 to 11 percent in 1998. During this same time frame, voice synthesizers will expand from 10 to 13 percent. In support of these projections are the number of voice-recognition and -response products on the market, many of which have been discussed, and the introduction of related products such as Wen Technology Corp.'s 486 Super-Note-Voice notebook computer, which comes complete with voice-recognition and speech-synthesis capabilities.

John Oberteuffer, president of Voice Information Systems, has predicted the obsolescence of the keyboard by the early 2000s. While he may be right, the focus of this chapter has been on the much nearer term, to illustrate how this technology can be applied *today.* As has been discussed, total voice dictation and response is not quite ready to replace the keyboard and monitor in all instances, but voice command, as another axis of control along with the keyboard and mouse, is certainly available, and in many cases both technologies can make users much more productive today.

In applying this technology, care must be taken when selecting not only the hardware and software to be used but also the target application. Today's operating systems and applications are mouse- and keyboard-oriented, and some may be more amenable to a voice-centric approach than others. This is obviously less of a problem when building custom applications, where the voice-command integration can be incorporated right from the start.

In applying speech synthesis, care must be taken to tailor the application to both the linguistic and acoustical abilities of the user, and to take account of the complexity of the material being presented. As the material's technical and/or linguistic complexity increases, the need for the speech-synthesis system to be acoustically correct in its pronunciation also increases. The interface may also need to change, since most people, when faced with a difficult passage in a book or technical journal, will go back and reread it several times, if necessary, until they understand what is being said. A computer-based reading program should be able to support this mode of operation.

The length of the text being read by a speech-synthesis system is also a concern, because while there are no empirical studies to support this, it seems intuitively obvious that comprehension on the part of the listener will decrease as the length of a monotone passage increases.

Voice recognition and response is a hot topic in the world of academic and industrial research and development. Over the next several years you can expect to see advances in many different areas, such as

- The introduction of operating systems and applications that were developed from the beginning to be voice-oriented. A shift away from the current menu-navigation-oriented systems to a more direct-command type of interface will make the integration of voice recognition much more seamless than it is today.

- The application of technology, such as wave-guide, to the problem of speech synthesis. Wave-guide technology, which produces sound based on a computer model of the physical instrument being mimicked, holds out great promise in terms of allowing more natural voices to be produced. This is only part of the challenge of producing human-sounding speech, but overcoming it will represent progress.

- The development of speech *understanding,* not just *recognition,* in computers. The difference between these is that recognition deals with the problem of having the computer determine which words were said, while understanding addresses the issue of what the speaker actually *means.* Clearly, human conversation deals with speech understanding, voice recognition simply being a necessary but insufficient condition for arriving at this understanding.

- The ability of the computer to determine when it is being spoken to. Simple methods, such as microphone arrays, may hold out short-term hope of dealing with this problem, while research in the area of visual speech analysis may bear fruit in the future.

This research eventually should lead to the development of voice-oriented systems, such as those depicted in the science fiction movies and literature. But users do not have to wait for that day. Voice-recognition and -response systems are robust enough to be used today, and early adopters of this technology can begin to reap the productivity gains right away.

## Vendor List

Articulate Systems
600 W. Cummings Park, Ste. 4500
Woburn, MA 01801
800-443-7077
Voice Navigator voice-command
  system
Apple Macintosh

Command Corporation
3675 Crestwood Parkway
Duluth, GA 30136
404-925-7950
IN³ voice-command system
Sun Sparcstations
PCs

Covox
675 Conger St.
Eugene, OR 97402
503-342-1271
Voice command systems
PCs

Digital Equipment Corporation
146 Main St.
Maynard, MA 01754-2571
508-493-5111
DECTalk speech synthesis
All platforms

Dragon Systems
320 Nevada St.
Newton, MA 02160
617-965-5200
Voice dictation/command
PCs

First Byte
3100 S. Harbor Blvd., #150
Santa Ana, CA 92704
714-432-1740
Speech-synthesis products
PCs

IBM
White Plains, NY
800-772-2227
Voice dictation/command
PS/2
RS/6000

Media Vision
3185 Laurelview Court
Fremont, CA 94538
510-770-8600
ExecuVoice voice-command
  system
PCs

Microsoft
Redmond, WA 98052-6399
800-227-4679
Windows Sound System
PCs

Parity Software
25 Stillman St., Ste. 106
San Francisco, CA 94107
415-931-8221
Smooth Talker digitized-voice
  system

Verbex Voice Systems
1090 King George's Post Road
Building #107
Edison, NJ 08837-3701
800-275-8729
Voice-command systems
All platforms

Wen Technology Corp.
11 Clearbrook Road
Elmsford, NY 1052
800-377-4936
Voice-oriented laptop computer

## Bibliography

Acero, Alejandro, *Acoustical and Environmental Robustness in Automatic Speech Recognition,* Kluwer Academic Publishers, Boston, 1993.

Bailly, G. and Benoit, C., *Talking Machines: Theories, Models, and Designs,* Elsevier Science Publishers, Amsterdam, 1992.

Biermann, A. W., Rodman, R. D., Rubin, D. C., and Heidlage, J. F. *Natural Language with Discrete Speech as a Mode for Human-to-Machine Communication,* Communications of the ACM, vol. 28, 628–636.

Blattner, Meera M. and Dannenburg, Roger B., *Multimedia Interface Design,* ACM Press, New York.

EDGE, Work-Group Computing Report, vol. 4, no. 149, March 29,1993.

Haber, Lynn, "Searching for the Speech-Recognition Holy Grail," MIDRANGE Systems, vol. 5, no. 11, June 9, 1992.

Laface, Pietro and De Mori, Renato, eds., *Speech Recognition and Understanding,* Springer-Verlag, Berlin, 1990.

Linggard, R., *Electronic Synthesis of Speech,* Cambridge University Press, Cambridge, 1985.

Markowitz, Judith, "The power of speech," *AI Expert,* January 1993.

Market Intelligence Research Corporation, voice-recognition, -response, and -synthesis markets.

Pelton, Gordon E., *Voice Processing,* McGraw-Hill, New York, 1993.

Rowden, Chris, *Speech Processing,* McGraw-Hill, UK, 1992.

Tucker, Tracey, "Voice for the masses: voice mail extends its reach," *Teleconnect,* April 1993.

# 36

# MIDI Means Music!

## Rob Wallace

### The General MIDI Specification, and How to Use a MIDI File

MIDI is an acronym for musical instrument digital interface, which enables keyboard samplers/synthesizers, sequencers, sound cards, and computers to be connected. MIDI hardware and the MIDI data format are defined in such a way that devices, cabling, and data flow all are spelled out for uniform compatibility.

A Copy of the Level 1 Specification documents for General MIDI is available at a cost of $5 from the International MIDI Association, 5316 West 57th Street, Los Angeles, CA 90056.

Recently, the uniform implementation of instrument patches has been defined. A *patch* is a program number assigned to a musical instrument within 16 families of instruments with 8 groups each (see Fig. 36.1).

General MIDI also includes a "percussion key map" (see Fig. 36.2).

### The MIDI file format (MFF)

"Opening.mid" could be the name of the file that contains all the MIDI data that will make the sound card in the system running your program play your opening music when the program is evoked.

Please understand that "opening.mid" *does not* contain *any digital sounds* whatsoever. A MFF file contains only a stream of data that instructs a MIDI device to perform functions as specified within the data stream. The .mid file tells the sound card to play patch #1, the Grand Piano, on channel 1 at a certain volume and velocity within the left/right pan position using a particular pitch bend, if any, with or without sustain, and—most important of all— which notes to play, when, and at what tempo. A richly orchestrated 1-minute .mid file will contain only 5 to 35 kbytes! The same music digitized at 22 kHz in a .wav file played through a 16-bit sound card in stereo would be more than 10 Mbytes in size!

| Program number | Instrument | Program number | Instrument |
|---|---|---|---|
| (1–8   PIANO) | | 36 | Fretless Bass |
| 1 | Acoustic Grand | 37 | Slap Bass 1 |
| 2 | Bright Acoustic | 38 | Slap Bass 2 |
| 3 | Electric Grand | 39 | Synth Bass 1 |
| 4 | Honky-Tonk | 40 | Synth Bass 2 |
| 5 | Electric Piano 1 | (41–48   STRINGS) | |
| 6 | Electric Piano 2 | 41 | Violin |
| 7 | Harpsichord | 42 | Viola |
| 8 | Clav | 43 | Cello |
| (9–16   CHROMATIC PERCUSSION) | | 44 | Contrabass |
| 9 | Celesta | 45 | Tremolo Strings |
| 10 | Glockenspiel | 46 | Pizzicato Strings |
| 11 | Music Box | 47 | Orchestral Strings |
| 12 | Vibraphone | 48 | Timpani |
| 13 | Marimba | (49–56   ENSEMBLE) | |
| 14 | Xylophone | 49 | String Ensemble 1 |
| 15 | Tubular Bells | 50 | String Ensemble 2 |
| 16 | Dulcimer | 51 | SynthStrings 1 |
| (17–24   ORGAN) | | 52 | SynthStrings 2 |
| 17 | Drawbar Organ | 53 | Choir Aahs |
| 18 | Percussive Organ | 54 | Voice Oohs |
| 19 | Rock Organ | 55 | Synth Voice |
| 20 | Church Organ | 56 | Orchestra Hit |
| 21 | Reed Organ | (57–64   BRASS) | |
| 22 | Accordion | 57 | Trumpet |
| 23 | Harmonica | 58 | Trombone |
| 24 | Tango Accordion | 59 | Tuba |
| (25–32   GUITAR) | | 60 | Muted Trumpet |
| 25 | Acoustic Guitar (nylon) | 61 | French Horn |
| 26 | Acoustic Guitar (steel) | 62 | Brass Section |
| 27 | Electric Guitar (jazz) | 63 | SynthBrass 1 |
| 28 | Electric Guitar (clean) | 64 | SynthBrass 2 |
| 29 | Electric Guitar (muted) | (65–72   REED) | |
| 30 | Overdriven Guitar | 65 | Soprano Sax |
| 31 | Distortion Guitar | 66 | Alto Sax |
| 32 | Guitar Harmonics | 67 | Tenor Sax |
| (33–40   BASS) | | 68 | Baritone Sax |
| 33 | Acoustic Bass | 69 | Oboe |
| 34 | Electric Bass (finger) | 70 | English Horn |
| 35 | Electric Bass (pick) | 71 | Bassoon |

**Figure 36.1**   Uniform implementation of instrument patches.

| Program number | Instrument | Program number | Instrument |
|---|---|---|---|
| 72 | Clarinet | 100 | FX 4 (atmosphere) |
| (73–80 PIPE) | | 101 | FX 5 (brightness) |
| 73 | Piccolo | 102 | FX 6 (goblins) |
| 74 | Flute | 103 | FX 7 (echoes) |
| 75 | Recorder | 104 | FX 8 (sci-fi) |
| 76 | Pan Flute | (105–112 ETHNIC) | |
| 77 | Blown Bottle | 105 | Sitar |
| 78 | Skakuhachi | 106 | Banjo |
| 79 | Whistle | 107 | Shamisen |
| 80 | Ocarina | 108 | Koto |
| (81–88 SYNTH LEAD) | | 109 | Kalimba |
| 81 | Lead 1 (square) | 110 | Bagpipe |
| 82 | Lead 2 (sawtooth) | 111 | Fiddle |
| 83 | Lead 3 (calliope) | 112 | Shanai |
| 84 | Lead 4 (chiff) | (113–120 PERCUSSIVE) | |
| 85 | Lead 5 (charang) | 113 | Tinkle Bell |
| 86 | Lead 6 (voice) | 114 | Agogo |
| 87 | Lead 7 (fifths) | 115 | Steel Drums |
| 88 | Lead 8 (bass + lead) | 116 | Woodblock |
| (89–96 SYNTH PAD) | | 117 | Taiko Drum |
| 89 | Pad 1 (new age) | 118 | Melodic Tom |
| 90 | Pad 2 (warm) | 119 | Synth Drum |
| 91 | Pad 3 (polysynth) | 120 | Reverse Cymbal |
| 92 | Pad 4 (choir) | (121–128 SOUND EFFECTS) | |
| 93 | Pad 5 (bowed) | 121 | Guitar Fret Noise |
| 94 | Pad 6 (metallic) | 122 | Breath Noise |
| 95 | Pad 7 (halo) | 123 | Seashore |
| 96 | Pad 8 (sweep) | 124 | Bird Tweet |
| (97–104 SYNTH EFFECTS) | | 125 | Telephone Ring |
| 97 | FX 1 (rain) | 126 | Helicopter |
| 98 | FX 2 (soundtrack) | 127 | Applause |
| 99 | FX 3 (crystal) | 128 | Gunshot |

**Figure 36.1** (*Continued*)

The MFF is assembled, usually in real time, by the computer musician playing a MIDI-able keyboard controller through a MIDI interface card sitting in a slot that sends the data to the CPU, which routes the data to the sequencer software in the system. The file data captures the performance exactly, and can be played back through another MIDI device.

When I write a .mid file I "echo" the data in real time to my General MIDI sampler, so that when I play a note I hear it in real time while it is being cap-

| Key No. | | Key No. | |
|---------|-----------------------|---------|-----------------|
| 35 | Acoustic Bass Drum | 59 | Ride Cymbal 2 |
| 36 | Bass Drum 1 | 60 | Hi Bongo |
| 37 | Side Stick | 61 | Low Bongo |
| 38 | Acoustic Snare | 62 | Mute Hi Conga |
| 39 | Hand Clap | 63 | Open Hi conga |
| 40 | Electric Snare | 64 | Low Conga |
| 41 | Low Floor Tom | 65 | High Timbale |
| 42 | Closed Hi-Hat | 66 | Low Timbale |
| 43 | High Floor Tom | 67 | High Agogo |
| 44 | Pedal Hi-Hat | 68 | Low Agogo |
| 45 | Low Tom | 69 | Cabasa |
| 46 | Open Hi-Hat | 70 | Maracas |
| 47 | Low-Mid Tom | 71 | Short Whistle |
| 48 | Hi-Mid Tom | 72 | Long Whistle |
| 49 | Crash Cymbal 1 | 73 | Short Guiro |
| 50 | High Tom | 74 | Long Guiro |
| 51 | Ride Cymbal 1 | 75 | Claves |
| 52 | Chinese Cymbal | 76 | Hi Wood Block |
| 53 | Ride Bell | 77 | Low Wood Block |
| 54 | Tambourine | 78 | Mute Cuica |
| 55 | Splash Cymbal | 79 | Open Cuica |
| 56 | Cowbell | 80 | Mute Triangle |
| 57 | Crash Cymbal 2 | 81 | Open Triangle |
| 58 | Vibraslap | | |

**Figure 36.2**   Percussion key map.

tured as data. The file is constantly edited and new tracks are added, then balanced, until the final version has been completed.

The sequencer I use is very much like a word processor, with a full battery of editing and authoring tools.

### Making the music for your project

Before your composer gets to work, you should be able to tell him or her what kind of music you need in your project, and where. Write down your ideas. Be as descriptive as possible about the mood and even the type of instruments you want to hear. Use examples of existing music to draw parallels with what you want. Write down the styles or artists that evoke the mood or feel you need. A good composer can better produce for you when you can communicate your concept clearly and specifically.

On the other hand if your trust level is high, and your experience with the composer is such that you can give him or her free creative reign over your project, then you may just end up with something better than anything your mind could have conjured up! Producers I have worked for tend to balance their direction by drawing on both of these two styles.

## Tweaking your music

Some elements of a MIDI file are relatively easy and simple to change, some are not. As the producer, you can alter these musical elements to fit your vision. If, however, the basic music isn't right, none of the following suggestions is likely to help.

Changing patches is simple. If you want to hear instruments from the list shown in Fig. 36.1 playing certain parts such as the melody, bass line, or percussion, tell the composer, "I want to hear a trumpet or some sort of brass instrument playing the melody." Or, "There isn't a punchy enough rhythm feel; bring up the percussion and add some bongos, congas, or something."

Tempo is easy to fix. Tell your composer to speed it up or slow it down a few bpm (beats per minute). Find out at what bpm your song currently is, for a reference point. A ballad usually is 60 bpm, a rock ballad 90 bpm; a typical universal tempo falls between 100 and 120 bpm, and a typical hard rocker is 150 to 200 bpm. It is amazing how shifting tempo can alter the character of a piece.

## MIDI hardware—which soundcard?

I will not endorse a particular manufacturer here, although there are many people who will be glad to tell you which one is best. First you need to ask yourself what quality and what type of sound you want for your project, and decide how dependent your project is on music.

There are two types of sound reproduction, *FM synthesis* and *wave-table synthesis*.

**FM synthesis.**   Not that long ago, all you heard from a computer was a beep or series of beeps, perhaps at different frequencies, through the PC speaker.

You heard only one at a time (monophonic). Then along came the Adlib™ sound card, and shortly thereafter Creative Labs' Sound Blaster, and polyphonic music began to flow from your computer.

The heart of the technology is the Yamaha OPL chip and its various incarnations through the OPL3. The OPL chip produces sound by FM synthesis, FM meaning frequency modulation of an operator(s) that can produce a variety of waves: sine, sawtooth etc. By changing elements of the waveform such as attack, delay, and frequency multiplier(s), different timbres are produced, from clarinets and flutes to the wacky arcade beeps, boops, and sci-fi-like sweeping sounds associated with computer games and arcade games.

FM synthesis has its limitations. In some applications, such as Windows™, you can play only 9 or 11 notes at once. By definition, you can hear only synthetic instrument tones. FM cards can't begin to sound like a real piano and many other instruments.

FM cards are severely limited when it comes to producing the percussion sounds familiar to us on other media. FM percussion sound is essentially variations on white noise, and leaves much to be desired when contrasted with traditional percussion.

As the technology progresses, we will see FM synthesis slip farther and farther into the background.

**Wave-table synthesis.**   More and more sound cards are appearing that use wave-table synthesis to produce outstanding musical sounds. When you hear a grand piano or timpani on one of these devices, it sounds very close to the real thing—mostly because it *is* the real thing captured in a "sampled" form in ROM. This sample contains digital recordings of the actual instrument, mapped in such a way as to faithfully reproduce the acoustic range of the instrument.

Leading manufacturers of wave-table synthesis devices often have proprietary techniques of reproducing instrument sounds. Among the leading MIDI sound card devices in this category are The Roland Sound Canvas family, SC-55, SCC-1, SC-7, and TAP 10; Creative Labs' Wave Blaster; Turtle Beach's Multi Sound; the Aria chipset family of cards; Gravis's Ultrasound; and The Ensoniq Soundscape. This listing is by no means complete, and new devices are coming on-line rapidly.

When you are choosing among these, base your decision on which device sounds best to your ear. If you don't trust your "ear" for music, get some recommendations from your composer and your hardware advisers.

### Supporting diverse sound cards?

If your project requires that your MIDI file or digital waveform files must play on more than one type of card, then you need to use the AIL drivers from Miles Design for your MIDI data, and the digital drivers available from The Audio Solutions' DigPak toolkit.

For AIL, you may leave a message for John Miles on the following BBS: 512-454-9990. To get information on DigPak, leave a message for John Ratcliff or the Sysop at 314-939-0200. If you e-mail me on Compuserve, I will provide you with their compuserve addresses. I can be reached at 71042,1410. AIL and DigPak have been used successfully by entertainment and educational software developers on hundreds of products.

### The MIDI interface

To deal with MIDI data, you must have a MIDI interface within your system. Some sound card manufacturers build a MIDI interface into their cards, but you may need to use a stand-alone interface card. In any case, the interface is a hardware requirement not unlike a controller card for your drives or the card for your CD-ROM.

## MIDI Music Is a Powerful Tool

Luckily for you as a producer, the hardware and software now exists that allows you to integrate MIDI files into your project that can play devices astounding in their depth and musical quality. You also can play digital voice and sound effects on top of this music, and create a true multimedia mix of sound. Even though the ability to do this is recent, the tools are stable enough that you can maintain control of this power and develop it for a reasonable cost within a reasonable time line.

You are limited only by your imagination and that of your computer musician/composer. Today the PC has even more powerful abilities to deliver sound than film, TV, and radio, because ours is an interactive environment by nature. There are ways to have the music change the mood instantly to fit what the user is doing within the program.

Interactive musical scores are here, now. And they sound fantastic!

## Glossary of Terms Found in the MIDI Domain*

**Accent**   Stress given to a musical tone.

**Accidentals**   In music these are sharps, flats, or naturals not indicated in the key signature. MIDI software programs tend to represent accidentals as sharps (e.g., F-sharp rather than G-flat).

**Access**   In computing, the verb is encountered more often than the noun. *Synonymous phrase:* "to communicate with." *Illustration:* A sequencer that lets one directly access hardware.

**Aftertouch**   The change in pressure on a key after the initial attack. Determines vibrato and other characteristics.

**Algorithm**   A step-by-step procedure for problem solving.

**Apple Macintosh**   Apple computers were among the earliest to offer MIDI-computing capacity. Others now in the field include IBM-compatible PCs, Atari, and Amiga.

**Articulation**   The percentage of a note's duration that actually plays. This could represent the difference between a staccato and a legato effect.

**Attack**   When the musical note begins. *Antonym: release.*

**Audio**   Sound, or its transmission and reproduction.

**Auto accompaniment**   Sometimes called *orchestration* or *auto chord,* all the terms refer to the rhythmic styles that sound when a fingered or one-finger mode is selected. Auto accompaniment usually comprises a drum pattern, a bass line, and other enhancing sounds such as a piano arpeggio or a strummed guitar.

**Bar**   A synonym for *measure:* musical time, a grouping of beats.

---

*Reprinted by permission of Eugene A. Confrey, Ph.D.

**Beat**   Literally, a single stroke or pulsation. Tempo is expressed in beats per minute (bpm). The beat value affects the metronome. *See also* Tempo.

**Buffer**   A temporary storage area in memory.

**Bulk dump**   Denotes a series of system-exclusive messages. Sometimes this involves transferring a mass of data, such as several choruses of a song that have been stored in memory, from the keyboard to the sequencer or vice versa. Settings at both ends must be coordinated. A keyboard "bulk-dumps" to a sequencer as a system-exclusive message (Syex). Conversely, a keyboard can receive such data as a system-exclusive message.

**Cancel**   An often-misunderstood command. It does not mean delete (e.g., the file) or "send it to the moon." Usually it means, quite simply, "turn off the display now on the screen."

**Channel**   In ordinary language, a channel is a path for passing data. In MIDI, channels are used to separate different sections of a song that are going to play together. Each channel is assigned to a single instrument in any particular instant of time. One channel usually is reserved for a percussion voice. To *channelize* means to move to another channel.

**Choking**   What happens when the sequencer receives too much continuous data. *Result:* Tempos slow down and speed up randomly.

**Chord**   Three or more tones—preferably harmonious—sounded simultaneously.

**Classical music**   A broad umbrella term, usually contrasted with jazz, folk, rock, pop. The "classical" tradition is best illustrated by examples: symphony, opera, chamber music. *See also* Jazz; Rock.

**Clef**   It's that sign at the beginning of a staff—the one that determines pitch.

**Clock**   A clock is used to synchronize two devices. In MIDI, the term *clock* is used to denote a single time source, which everything plays along with. MIDI clocks actually are special messages sent 24 times (normally) per beat, and used to synchronize two sequencers or a sequencer and a drum machine. Usually the sequencer's clock is the important one. Other clock sources rarely are used, and, typically, only when doing a final recording.

**Codes**   In MIDI, as in general computing, the term *code* refers to program instruction. One type is a *source code* (human-readable). Another is a *machine code* (executable).

**Compose-arrange**   Two activities that can be facilitated by MIDI-computing. The composer creates music, the arranger enhances it—by scoring for other voices or instruments.

**Compression**   In MIDI-computing, the phrase *compression and expansion* refers to the process of changing the range of a song. Compression makes the loud parts softer, the soft parts louder.

**Continuous data**   Controllers, pitch bend, aftertouch...

**Controller**   Most often, the term refers to the instrument: keyboard, guitar, drums, etc. (as in *master controller*). A second meaning, in sequencing, refers to a setting, a parameter, as in "Controller 7 = Volume." In this sense, a controller is a MIDI event.

**Controller change**   This event will be displayed in the Event List editor. It refers to a change in the synthesizer setting. There are 128 controllers. *Example:* the loudness of notes. *See also* Program change.

**Count in**   A command in a sequencer that plays a metronome for several measures until you are ready to record.

**Crescendo**   A gradual increase in volume. Antonym: *decrescendo*.

**Cut-and-paste**   In word processing, this function means moving text from one place in a document to another. In MIDI, one can copy a section of a musical passage and paste it elsewhere.

**Damper**   The damper pedal on an acoustical piano functions to stop the vibration of a piano string. (In contrast, the sustain pedal holds or prolongs the note.) Unfortunately, sustain pedals on electronic pianos often are called *damper* pedals, thus blurring the distinction. *See also* Sustain.

**Data bytes**   These follow the status byte in a MIDI message; e.g., what note has been struck, how hard. *See also* Status byte.

**Default setting**   In MIDI, as in general computing, this is a choice made by the program (when the user does not specify an alternative).

**Design; Program**   Two distinct functions. The *designer* of a sequencing piece of software, for example, conceives and plans the product and all its functions. The *programmer* addresses the issues of programming languages, data structures, how data is stored and manipulated, etc.

**Digital**   In MIDI, the phrase *digital recording* is contrasted with *analog recording*. Long-playing phonograph records are analog recordings. That is, they capture information in a continuously variable form, a fluctuating waveform. Telephone lines work on the same principle. Digital, in contrast, involves binary numbers, 1's and 0's. MIDI-computing represents digital encoding.

**DLL**   A file extension standing for "dynamic link libraries." A DLL is part of an application's executable files, and often it is used to link the application to the hardware.

**Downbeat**   The maestro's downward stroke, indicating the first beat of a measure. In contrast, the upbeat is unaccented.

**Dubbing**   Making a new recording of sound already recorded. Sometimes used to describe the process of mixing sounds from several sources into one recording.

**Duration**   The length of time (number of beats) of a note or chord.

**Dynamics**   Variation in the intensity of musical notes.

**Edit**   Editing, in MIDI, involves altering, deleting, revising the musical passages that have been captured in a digital recording and are now displayed on the monitor screen. This display will offer two options. In the first, the notes are listed by track and number, by event (such as "Note on"), by the specific note G4, the beat, the channel, etc. The second option for editing is to use a musical notation display. Here the notes are arrayed in clefs, (1) like a piano roll (the piano-roll display sometimes is referred to as *graphic notation*) or (2) in conventional musical notation. Editing options include changes in notes, measures, transpose, volume.

**Enable; disable** Antonyms, meaning *to turn on* or *to turn off*. Synthesizers and sequencers have many controls requiring such action (such as MIDI THRU).

**Engraver-quality** A complimentary descriptive term, referring to a professional-looking job of printing music.

**Entry-level** An adjective used to describe beginners (those trying to learn MIDI, for instance). They may be devoid of experience in computer engineering or in electronic music.

**Envelope** The changes of a tone; e.g., attack, sustain, decay, release.

**Error messages** The message says "Something's wrong!" In MIDI, you could be told that "memory is full," that you've committed a "track error," or made a "protect error" (attempted to write to a protected disk).

**Event** In ordinary language an occurrence, a happening. In MIDI, the signal that is transmitted, such as note on, note off, program change, control change. *See also* Program change, Control change.

**Event-chasing** Scans data in a sequence before the start-point of the recording. Looks for patch changes, for example.

**Event list** An alphanumeric display of all MIDI events on a single track. *Examples:* notes, time signature, tempo, program changes, control changes.

**Faders** Controls for changing effects gradually, such as decreasing loudness.

**Field** Traditional computing defines this as a location in a record. *Examples:* name, address, zip code, etc. *Illustrative fields in MIDI:* Song title, track name, instrument, channel.

**File types** A MIDI File Type 0 is a single (multiple-channel) track. A MIDI File Type 1 contains one or more simultaneous tracks.

**Filter** The noun and the verb, in MIDI, are used primarily in connection with events (note on, program change, tempo change) and with channel changes. Each event is either filtered (deleted), transformed, or passed through.

**Fingered mode** Provides automatic rhythm, bass, and orchestral accompaniment. The bass and orchestral accompaniment reflect the notes in the chord of the left hand. *See also* Auto accompaniment.

**FSK** Frequency-shift keying. Modulation involving two different frequencies.

**Ganged** When tracks are "ganged," they will move simultaneously. *Analogy:* A variable capacitor in an early radio receiver.

**Gate time** The length of a produced sound (e.g., legato, staccato).

**General MIDI mode** A convention specifying how a sequence (song) should be constructed, so that it will play on a variety of hardware.

**Glide** This effect plays the sound of a semitone below the pitch, then slides up to normal pitch.

**Global editing** Affecting an entire file or program. Transpose is illustrative. The contrasting function is *local editing,* such as changing one event.

**GUI** Graphical user interface. A display that permits a user to select commands, menu items, by pointing at an icon (with a mouse) and clicking.

**Hardware sequencer**  Sequencing can be performed by software programs or by hardware. Hardware sequencers also work with synthesizers, controllers, sound modules to create and edit songs. A hardware sequencer is—as the name implies—hardware, containing a single-purpose program, one designed to provide sequencing.

**Humanize**  A term used to refer to the introduction of random irregularities in note-timing and velocities, in order to reduce the mechanical character of a performance. *See also* Quantization.

**Implementation chart**  Look for the MIDI Implementation Chart in the manual of your master controller (e.g., the keyboard). This will tell you what is transmitted (or recognized) for the various functions such as note number, velocity (pressure on a key), aftertouch (change in pressure), pitch bender, control change, program change, system-exclusive message, etc.

**Import**  To bring data from one program into another. *Antonym: export,* meaning to transfer to another program. (Some sequencer manuals use the term *export* to mean convert and save—as a MIDI file—preparatory to transferring elsewhere.)

**Initialization**  *Initial* means first. To initialize is to set a program to a starting position, to prepare the program for use.

**Instrumentation**  The selection of instruments in a MIDI arrangement.

**Intros and fills**  The jazz man's vamp—a couple of measures repeated before a solo.

**Inverse video**  The reversal of light and dark on a screen character. *Example:* an indication of whether Automatic Rewind is on (enabled) or off (disabled).

**Jazz**  Another umbrella term, often (erroneously) defined in terms of volume and tempo. Its basic ingredient is improvisation, accomplished melodically, harmonically, or by rhythm changes. *See also* Rock.

**Keyboard**  A reminder: In MIDI-computing, one has to remember which one is involved in a documentation reference, the computer's or the controller's.

**Key signature**  Musical notation shows this in terms of sharps and flats after the clef. Software sequencers sometimes show a song key as "F major/D minor" and indicate the number of sharps or flats. B-flat major/G minor has two flats, for example. *See also* Accidentals.

**Looping**  Used to repeat a section of a recording.

**Marker**  Something used to record a position. MIDI markers identify, for example, musical cues. They work like tab stops on a word processor.

**Mapping**  The process of identifying patches and keys, so that sound files can be played properly. A *key map* will translate values for MIDI messages, so that the correct keys will be played. A *patch map* functions to identify the correct patches (sounds, instruments).

**MCI**  Media control interface. Standard used primarily by Windows, for all media interfaces.

**Measure delete**  This command removes specified measures (e.g., measures 4, 5, and 6). *See also* Measure erase.

**Measure erase**  The contents of specified measures are erased, but the length of the song is unchanged. *See also* Measure delete.

**Media Player**  Microsoft's term for the Windows application that will control the playing of sound cards, CD-ROM drives, and videodisc players. It also will play MIDI sequencer files.

**Melody**  One of the three basic elements of music (the other two being harmony and rhythm). Melody is a succession of tones—hopefully pleasing.

**Merge**  To combine or blend into one. *Example:* merging two tracks.

**Messages**  The net effect of MIDI-computing is sound: melodies, harmonies, rhythms. But the MIDI message (the MIDI event) itself is not a sound. Transmitted are digital commands—about 1000 events per second.

**Meta events**  In ordinary language, the prefix *meta* often means *above* or *beyond.* In computing, a *meta*character conveys information about other characters. In MIDI, a meta event would be illustrated by such things as track name, patch name, tempo, time signature, etc. Meta events are contrasted with *data streams.*

**Meter**  The basic pattern of note values, e.g. beats per measure. *See also* Time signature.

**Metronome**  A device that marks time by producing a repeated tick. The older type, a triangular box with a vibrating arm, was succeeded by an electrical unit. In MIDI, the ticks are computer-generated.

**MIDI**  A protocol. The musical instrument digital interface comprises a MIDI card and cables connecting the computer to an electronic instrument, such as a keyboard. The MIDI card (a printed circuit board) normally is mounted in an expandable slot inside the computer. Keyboard synthesizers also can communicate with other synthesizers by means of a MIDI connection.

**MIDIEX file**  Created by saving the current contents of the buffer. MIDIEX is a standard format containing raw MIDI data without a header (a line identifying the program).

**MIDI Mapper**  Microsoft's utility program, which can help you to remap patch, channel, etc. during playback.

**MIDI pitch wheel switch**  Determines whether continuous controller information (e.g., note on, key pressure, control change, program change) will be recorded.

**MIDI sound generator**  For authentic reproduction of acoustical instruments. It uses samples—instrument sounds stored as digitized audio. This actually is another term for *synthesizer*—converting MIDI events into real audio sound.

**MIDI Thru**  One of three ports (connections): MIDI In, MIDI Out, and MIDI Thru. MIDI In receives information from other equipment. MIDI Out sends information to other equipment. MIDI Thru duplicates the information, and sends it to other equipment. By means of the latter, a synthesizer can echo messages to other synthesizers.

**Modulation**  In music, one usually thinks of modulating as passing from one key to another, by means of intermediate chords. In MIDI, modulation usually means applying a vibrato effect to a sound.

**MPU-401–compatible**  The reference is to a standard interface. (It derives from Roland's initial design.) *Important:* MS-DOS MIDI software often supports this user base, but not always.

**Multitimbral**  In sequencing, a multitimbral sound module can play several parts on different channels simultaneously. A multitimbral device is one that is prepared to sound like more than one instrument at a time.

**Multitrack recording**   Normally, one records on a single track ("normal-mode" recording). Multitrack recording is feasible, however. *Example:* from a guitar, with each string on a different channel.

**Multivoice mode**   A setting on a multitimbral tone generator (such as a keyboard) for receiving multiple MIDI channels, each channel having a different voice (instrument).

**Musical score**   Most often, the written copy of a musical composition. Compose in MIDI, print the notation, and voilà!—there it is.

**Mute**   A sequencer command to turn off specified tracks. *Reason:* so you can listen exclusively to one track. *See also* Solo.

**Noise**   That disturbance of a signal that can occur if your MIDI cables are too long— exceeding 15 meters in length, for example.

**Normal mode**   When a (controller) keyboard has this setting (as contrasted with *split,* or *fingered* modes), the sounds, from the lowest note to the highest, are all of one voice. In this mode, the resemblance is to an acoustical instrument. *See also* Split mode, Fingered mode.

**Octave notation**   MIDI software and electronic keyboards use notations such as F4 to represent the specific note F located in the fourth octave of an acoustical piano.

**Open command**   Loads an existing disk file.

**Pads**   (Sometimes *multipads*). On keyboards, where you store percussive sounds.

**Pan**   To *pan* is to move the sound between full left and full right in a stereo sound field. It resembles the "balance" function of a stereo receiver-amplifier.

**Parameter**   A tough word to define. In mathematics, it's a variable or an arbitrary constant. In MIDI, it's a value assigned at the beginning of an operation. *Examples*: pitch bend, sustain, voice number, volume, reverb.

**Patch**   In some early keyboard synthesizers, one selected "instruments" to play (e.g., vibraphone, clarinet.) Later the term *voice* emerged, in part because some of the sounds went beyond instruments (police whistles, human voices, etc.). In contemporary MIDI-computing the word *patch* is prominent, one reason being that a single keyboard setting, such as 99, may encompass a large range of percussive sounds. In any event, to a sequencer, the patch setting will determine the nature of the sounds.

**Patch layout**   A potential source of trouble for MIDI users. Manufacturers of synthesizers have not standardized the correspondence between patches and numbers. The celesta patch number might be 24 on a Roland keyboard, 09 on a Yamaha. Microsoft's MIDI Mapper is designed to help rectify this situation. *See also* MIDI Mapper.

**Pattern recording**   Establishing a pattern, e.g. a bass drum beat, then embellishing it.

**PCM**   Pulse code modulation—a process of digital recording.

**Percussion**   A percussive instrument is sounded by striking or shaking it. *Examples:* Bass drum, snare, bongo, cymbal, high-hat. By extension the term also encompasses so-called "background sounds" such as wind chimes, thunder, voices.

**Piano-roll editor**   A common notation used for editing by many sequencers. The notes of each track are shown as horizontal bars, the vertical position representing pitch, the horizontal length representing duration of the note (or chord). *See also* Edit; Event list editor.

**Pitch**    The property of a musical tone—determined by frequency.

**Pitch bend wheel**    A wheel on the keyboard that allows notes to be bent up or down. *Example:* a sliding trombone sound. "Pitch bend" is a MIDI message.

**Platforms**    Computer hardware. Some MIDI software will run on one platform (e.g., IBM PCs) but not on another (e.g., Macintosh).

**Player**    In the realm of MIDI-computing the sequencer is still the virtuoso, but MIDI players are prominent too. They play the sound files. They compile play lists of songs and sometimes group them into albums.

**Play list**    A list of tunes to be performed in succession. The sequence is preprogrammed.

**Polyphony**    From the Greek, meaning "variety of tones." In MIDI the question is, "How many notes can be played simultaneously?" Maximum polyphony cannot be exceeded.

**Port**    A location in the hardware from which data is passed in and out. In setting up MIDI one must make port assignments, so that channels can be correctly addressed.

**Port address and interrupt settings**    *Addresses* are locations within the computer. These addresses are used by devices (such as a MIDI keyboard) to communicate with the software. An *interrupt setting* signals when the device is ready to send or receive data. Addresses and interrupts must be unique for each device.

**PPQN**    Pulses per quarter-note. A measurement of time resolution.

**Program change**    Like controller change, this event will be displayed in the event list editor. An illustrative program change would be the introduction of a new voice (instrument). *See also* Controller change.

**Pulse**    The tick of a computer clock is sometimes referred to as a *pulse. Example:* one clock pulse defined as $\frac{1}{240}$ of a quarter-note.

**Punch recording**    A feature that allows automatic on-off recording at specified points.

**Quantization**    To *quantize* is to force all notes played to fall on the nearest beat specified. It shifts events (like note-on) to an exact rhythmic position.

**Radio button**    A small circle in a menu display. When it is pressed (clicked), it activates an option.

**Real time**    In MIDI there are two types of recording procedures, *real-time* and *step-time.* The former resembles traditional recording—as with a tape recorder. Step-time recording really is sequential: note-by-note, chord-by-chord.

**Record**    In the world of sound, to register something reproducible on a disk, such as a phonograph record, or on magnetic tape. Traditional recording captures the amplitude (height) and frequency (number) of wave forms. MIDI-computing does not really "record." It encodes messages, digitally—by means of numbers. Because of established usage, however, the words *record* and *recording* often appear in MIDI-computing, along with *play, rewind, fast forward,* and so on. In MIDI-computing, these words really are metaphors. A typical sequencer will "record" all of the MIDI events received, along with the time they were received.

**Reset**    Keyboards, like computers, sometimes "lock up." To restore normal operation, the *system reset* is used. There is another meaning of *reset* in MIDI software: to return to the first measure.

**Rest**    In music, a rhythmic silence. *Examples:* a two-beat rest, a quarter-note rest.

**Ritard** As a verb, to gradually slacken tempo (sometimes used at the ending of a song). *Antonym of the noun:* accelerando.

**Rock** Like "jazz," a broad umbrella term. Rock is a form of popular music, usually played on electronically amplified instruments, with a heavily accented beat.

**Sampling** Emulating the sound of an acoustical instrument by digitizing (converting to digital sound) the waveforms produced by the instrument.

**Save as...** If no file name has yet been assigned, this is the command to use. If your MIDI file already has been christened, and you have edited it, the appropriate command is Save.

**Select** Do you want to edit (insert, delete, copy, cut)? You must first "select," i.e. highlight, block.

**Serial** Appearing in succession, one at a time. For instance, MIDI messages, as displayed in an Event List.

**Sequencer** So called because such a program arranges melodic and harmonic patterns in successive positions. Strictly speaking, one should define a sequencer as something that stores note-on and note-off events in memory, then plays them back.

**Sequencer memory** It is in RAM (random-access memory). It is measured in the number of events that can be accommodated.

**Slider** An input device to increase or decrease volume. Also refers to an on-screen image (such as a button control) that one can move with a mouse.

**Snap-to-grid** A grid consists of two sets of lines that crisscross. A snap-to-grid feature facilitates step-entry of notes.

**SMPTE** Usually indicates a standardized time code developed by the Society of Motion Picture and Television Engineers. The time code is used in the MIDI world as a way of synchronizing MIDI to external events.

**Solo** If you want to listen exclusively to one track, you can mute all other tracks. *Alternative:* Select a track to "solo" (a feature that some sequencing programs offer). *See also* Mute.

**Song clear** To erase the contents of all tracks. *See also* Track clear.

**Sound device** Any device is part of the system's hardware. (*Examples:* a printer, mouse, modem, etc.) A sound device could be, for instance, a MIDI synthesizer, a CD-ROM drive, a videodisc player.

**Sound driver** Device drivers are software that control communication between devices (a mouse, printer, modem) and the computer. A sound driver controls the sound card or the sound device, such as a MIDI-compatible synthesizer. The sound driver must be correctly configured for your computer.

**Sound module** The component in a device (such as a keyboard) that produces the sound (e.g., a violin melody, a drum rhythm). This is another term for MIDI sound generator.

**Sound recorder** A Microsoft Windows accessory that can play, record, and edit sound files in the WAVE (non-MIDI) format.

**Speed; pitch** Perhaps the most important benefit gained from using a sequencer is that tempo can be changed without affecting pitch. Thus a difficult passage can be recorded slowly, then played at a faster tempo—with no change in pitch.

**Split mode**   Divides a keyboard into two sections, each of which can play a different instrument. *Example:* From the split-point (say, C#3), the left hand can be producing the sounds of an organ, while the right hand plays a flute melody line. *See also* Normal mode.

**Split-point**   In a split mode, the location on a keyboard where one voice (instrument) is differentiated from another. G2, for example, might be set to allow one voice (say, choir) in the left hand, another voice (say, violin) in the right hand. *See also* Normal mode.

**Standard MIDI file**   Identified by its extension (.MID; sometimes .MFF or .SMF), this is a file that can store MIDI messages, such as songs. The data in a MIDI file can be played, manipulated, edited. A MIDI file comprises actions performed on an instrument (keys pressed, how hard). There is a standard MIDI file format. A principal advantage of a MIDI file: It uses comparatively little disk space, but more importantly it is standard across platforms and sequencers.

**Status byte**   In a MIDI message, this announces what kind of message is being sent, e.g. "note-on." *See also* Data bytes.

**Staves**   Plural of staff—those horizontal lines and spaces.

**Stomp boxes**   Floor pedals for enhancing tones, used principally by guitarists.

**Sustain**   To sustain is to hold a note (or a chord). The musical tones fade out gradually. *See also* Damper.

**Synchronize**   To make synchronous or simultaneous. *Example:* to synchronize a drum pattern to play with melodies and chords on a synthesizer. MIDI synchronization is a coordinating function—involving a sync signal.

**Syncopation**   Changing a regular metrical accent, e.g. by coming in early or late on a beat. It is a form of rhythmic improvisation. *See also* Jazz.

**Synthesizer**   (Often shortened to Synth.) A device driven by a microprocessor that contains a programmable chip. *Examples of instruments that can control synthesizers:* Guitar, keyboard, wind, string, drum controllers. The keyboard itself does not produce musical sound. A synthesizer circuit, built into the keyboard, accomplishes this function. Originally a synthesizer was so called because it synthesized acoustic instruments. Nowadays the term refers to the sound-generating circuitry of any MIDI gear. Another term is *sound module.*

**Sysex**   Short for a system-exclusive message. *Illustrative data:* voices, drum patterns.

**Tempo**   In music, the rate of speed (such as allegretto). Electronic keyboards provide controls to set or change tempo. A quarter-note setting may range from 40 to 240 beats per minute. Software sequencers also set and change tempo. *Examples of tempo settings:* Viennese waltz—190 bpm; disco-rock—104 bpm; swing—166 bpm. Sequencers display the exact beat (e.g., beat number 29) of the music being recorded or played. *See also* Beat.

**Time base**   The number of clock ticks per beat. *Illustrative range:* 120–768.

**Time signature**   In traditional musical notations, this is expressed as a fractional sign, such as $\frac{3}{4}$. The denominator indicates the unit for the beat; the numerator shows the number of notes per measure. *See also* Meter.

**Tone generator**    Essentially, a synthesizer without a keyboard.

**Touch response**    A feature of some electronic keyboards, enabling one to control loudness according to how hard the keys are pressed.

**Track**    In MIDI, the term *track* designates a location where one records or plays back a musical message—usually a portion of the total arrangement. To illustrate, one might record an oboe melody line on Track 2, then record a bowed bass line on Track 3. When played, the sounds can be simultaneous. Most MIDI software now accommodates 64 tracks of music, enough for a rich orchestral sound. *Important:* Tracks are purely for convenience; channels are required. *See also* Channel.

**Track clear**    To erase the contents of a specific track. *See also* Song clear.

**Track merge**    To merge the contents of two tracks and store in a third track.

**Track names**    Names such as "melody line," "bass line," "left hand," etc. are assigned to tracks to help determine the instrumentation of a sequence.

**Transcription**    The word has been used extensively in music. *Example:* arranging for some instrument or voice other than the original. In MIDI, a common usage refers to converting a MIDI file into musical notation for printing. This is accomplished by means of notation software.

**Transpose**    To perform a musical composition in a different key. Both synthesizers and sequencers can carry out this function.

**Tuning**    440 hertz is the normal tuning value. However, the pitch of a synthesizer can be altered—raised or lowered. Changes in the tune value are expressed as plus or minus signs.

**Tuplet**    A *triplet* always designated three notes over two beats. The word *tuplet* is a generic term—in fancy language, "non-integral duration values." Think of quintuplets (5) or sextuplets (6). (Notes, not offspring from a single birth.)

**Undo**    This command could be a lifesaver. It reverses your last mistake, such as inadvertently recording or inserting MIDI data. "REDO" undoes an "UNDO."

**User-friendly**    A popular "buzzword" in computing. *Synonym: intuitive.* It means "directly comprehended." For many users, a method of pointing at icons and clicking is more "user-friendly" than entering many keystrokes to select menu items, like commands. Intuitive programs are more quickly grasped by the "computer-naive" (another buzzword).

**Velocity**    Velocity is the MIDI way of determining how hard a note has been pressed on the keyboard controller.

**Waveform**    A representation of a wave's amplitude over time.

**Zoom**    To magnify the image on a monitor screen; especially useful when editing notes in Standard MIDI files.

# References

## Books

Eiche, Jon F., *What's MIDI?,* Hal Leonard Publishing Corp., 1990.
Microsoft Press, *Dictionary of Computer Terms,* 1991.
Starr, Greg R., *What's a Sequencer?,* Hal Leonard Publishing Corp., 1990.

## Articles

Petzold, Charles, "An introduction to the Musical Instrument Digital Interface," *PC* magazine, March 17, 1992.

Kendall, Robert, "MIDI goes mainstream," *PC* magazine, March 31, 1992.

Wilkinson, Scott, "Sequencing made easy," Parts 1 and 2, *Electronic Musician,* March and April 1992.

Petzold, Charles, "MCI, MIDI, and the nature of time," *PC* magazine, September 29, 1992. (A more advanced discussion.)

# 37

# Multimedia and Video Editing

Marco Pinter

## The Need for Multimedia-Based Editing

The computer age has resulted in revolutionary advances in many fields, cutting costs and labor by factors of 10 or even 100. A case in point is the publishing industry. Prior to the widespread use of computers, producing a simple newsletter with some different typefaces and a few photographs required equipment costing several hundred thousand dollars and many hours of specialized labor. Since the advent of desktop publishing in the 1980s, an amateur with a $5000 system can produce in a short amount of time the same newsletter of essentially the same quality.

The 1990s are seeing a similar revolution occurring in the video industry. In the early days of videotape, the editing process consisted of physically splicing tape segments under a microscope, using equipment costing several hundred thousand dollars. Over the years the process has been simplified somewhat, and today a low-end videotape-editing suite can be assembled for under $10,000.

These systems, however, have a number of problems. Most importantly, they are completely *linear*. A linear editing solution means that the user needs to constantly seek from one portion of a tape to another in order to view various segments, which is very time-consuming. Nonlinear solutions are available, such as systems that incorporate a number of videodisc machines, but these generally cost at least $100,000. Then too, performing even the simplest video effects, such as wipes and dissolves, calls for additional equipment starting at $30,000.

Clearly, there has to be a better way. Many industries, from training to education to public relations, use video constantly, and simply cannot afford such expensive systems. Desktop video has provided the answer. Today, for

$1000 to $5000, one can purchase hardware and software capable of nonlinear editing with special effects. True, a more expensive solution is required if one wishes to preserve the original picture quality, just as one needs more equipment than a simple desktop publishing suite to print at a high resolution. However, these advances are coming rapidly, and probably will have been incorporated into low-cost solutions by the year 2001.

The advent of the multimedia age also has affected desktop video in other ways. With the release of QuickTime on the Macintosh, and Video For Windows on the IBM, most personal computers now are capable of motion-video playback. This has created a large market for computer-based video programs in the areas of entertainment and education. The developers of these programs, as well as interested consumers, now need video-editing solutions for their multimedia video. Unlike users in the videotape realm, these people are using the computer as their medium, not just as a tool. They need to repeatedly update and reedit their video, and see it instantly in their applications. To these users, desktop video-editing programs are critical, an integral part of their authoring workstations.

Current desktop-video-editing needs can thus be classed in two major categories, which we will focus on in turn:

1. *Computer as Tool* encompasses those users whose goal is to edit videotape, and who use the computer as a tool to accomplish this task more efficiently and effectively.

2. *Computer as Medium* describes the exploding market of multimedia users who are editing digital video on the computer, with the goal of incorporating the video into their interactive programs.

## Desktop Video Editing—Computer as Tool

### Analog editing systems

Before we can discuss the revolution in desktop editing, we first must look at analog systems. This will provide us with a clearer vision of the advantages of using the computer as an editing tool.

Simple analog systems consist of the following, at a minimum:

1 playback VCR (or camcorder)

1 recording VCR

Picture/sound monitor (i.e., television)

Controller

The *controller* is a hardware device that interfaces with VCRs and controls the following functions: play, rewind, fast forward, pause, step, and seek. The seek function causes a VCR to cue up at a particular frame. Editing technology identifies individual frames by a *time-code* stamp, which gives every frame of video a distinct number. (Time-code standards are described in the subsection Formats, Time Codes, and Standards on the next page.)

One factor that separates low-end from high-end editing systems is the *frame accuracy* of the edit control. Medium- to high-end systems usually are 100 percent frame-accurate, which means they can play back and record from an exact frame with no margin of error. Low-end and consumer-grade systems typically have lower frame accuracy. Generally this is due to the quality of the playback/record decks. Fully frame-accurate VCR decks start at $3000 and can go up to $100,000. Cheaper, non-frame-accurate systems usually specify the margin of error in terms of frame offset, i.e., ± 5 frames. For normal scene-editing, a few frames of error, which amount to less than a tenth of a second, are unnoticeable. However for montage-style edits, as in many music videos, frame accuracy is critical.

The edit suite that has been listed is a bare-minimum configuration. It does not allow for any transitions between scenes. Transitions are used to change between scenes in a smooth, visually appealing way. Typical transitions include

*Wipes.*   Scene B wipes across Scene A.

*Dissolve.*   Scene B fades into Scene A.

*Iris.*   Scene B appears as a small circle on Scene A, and enlarges until it fills the screen.

Transitions use a process known as *A/B roll,* which means that two source decks are playing simultaneously and the image from deck B must be merged with that of deck A. This process requires the following setup (see Fig. 37.1):

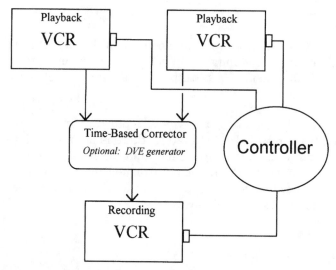

**Figure 37.1**   What's needed for an A/B roll.

2 playback VCRs

1 recording VCR

Picture/sound monitor (i.e., television)

Controller

Time-based corrector/digital video effects (DVE) generator

The time-based corrector (TBC) allows for synchronization of the signals from the two playback decks. Without a TBC, the final video image would be unstable. The digital video effects unit, typically combined with a TBC, performs the actual transitions. This DVE unit often also includes functions for color correction (i.e., tint and contrast), as well as overlay of titles and graphics.

Overlays of this kind are accomplished through a process known as *keying,* in which one image (i.e., titles or graphics) is set on a black background. The DVE unit allows video to pass through any black area, leaving colored areas on top. In the example shown in Fig. 37.1, the key color is black. Keying also can be used to mix two video signals, for instance a weatherman keyed on top of a satellite map. In these cases the weatherman is filmed in front of a blue background, and blue becomes the key color.

The functionality described in the previous paragraphs is typical of analog editing systems. These kinds of systems can cost from $40,000 to $300,000. This price point limits these systems to video production houses and large corporate clients. Others have had to settle for hybrid solutions. For instance, many people edit a "rough cut" on a low-end system, then rent time at a production house to perform their final edit. This usually runs them at least $250 per hour, and clearly is inconvenient as well. These factors have been the major reason behind the drive toward desktop editing solutions.

### Formats, time codes, and standards

If you are entering into video editing, whether analog or digital, you will need to understand different formats and standards, in order to ensure compatibility of tapes, cameras, and equipment. Here we provide a summary of these issues.

**Video signal standards.**    It is by means of the video signal that images are electronically stored and transmitted. Unfortunately, there is no international standard for this. Therefore an American VCR cannot be hooked up to a German television and a French VCR cannot be attached to an American television. Some signals also differ with regard to the number of images per second that appear. The standards are as follows:

NTSC (USA, Japan): 30 frames per second

PAL (most of Europe): 25 frames per second

SECAM (France): 25 frames per second

**Video signal formats.** Distinct from the issue of signal *standards* is that of signal *formats*. Signal formats include

Composite

Y/C (luminance/chroma)

RGB (red/green/blue)

The most common format is *composite*. The video signal that comes out of your VCR or into your television is composite. High-end video equipment also supports Y/C and RGB formats. The Y/C format splits the video signal into its brightness and color components and stores these separately. The RGB format splits the video into three signals, one each for red, green, and blue. These component formats provide higher-quality video signals.

**Tape formats.** Most people are familiar with differing videotape formats. For instance your VCR requires a VHS tape, while your camcorder may use an 8-millimeter tape. Tape formats include the following:

VHS ($\frac{1}{2}$-inch): Consumer video

8-mm: Consumer camcorders

Super-VHS: Midrange video

Hi-8: Midrange video

Betacam: High-end video

U-Matic ($\frac{3}{4}$-inch): High-end video

D1/D2: High-end video

Type B (1-inch): Broadcast video

Type C (1-inch): Broadcast video

Typically, within a certain standard (i.e., NTSC), one can connect decks using different formats. However some decks, e.g., Super-VHS, can use component signals (Y/C), while other decks, e.g., VHS, can function only with a composite signal.

**Time code.** As already discussed, time code is used to number individual frames of video. The international standard is called *SMPTE time code*. This format can be encoded on a tape in two ways: *longitudinal (LTC)*, and *vertical interval (VITC)*. Also, broadcast video often is recorded using *drop-frame* time code, which means that every few minutes a frame value is skipped. Most users, however, use standard, non-drop-frame time code.

**Edit decision lists (EDLs).** Video producers typically like to keep track of the choices they have made during an edit session, so that they can return to a project later without having to start from scratch. Most editing systems store this information in an *edit decision list (EDL)*. There are several formats for displaying and storing the EDL information. Common formats include CMX/ASCII and Grass Valley. EDLs also can be saved during a "rough cut" and brought to a production house for a fast final edit. In this scenario, the rough cut is called *off-line editing* and the production level session is called *on-line editing*.

**Linear/nonlinear.** *Linear* editing is the norm in the analog world. The user scans back and forth through the tape, and locates all desired scenes. Then the controller sends commands to the decks, which assemble the scenes in order. This method is very time-consuming for the user, who spends long periods of time rewinding and seeking through the tape.

*Nonlinear* editing is the superior solution. Essentially, this technique provides a way to store many individual sequences separately, so that any sequence may be viewed or modified immediately. In the analog world, these systems are extremely expensive, because they involve storing to laserdiscs or large numbers of tape decks. However, as we will see, digital video provides a much more efficient solution.

### Moving to the digital desktop

In the previous sections we have demonstrated the need for a cost-effective, computer-based solution to video editing. The role of the computer in editing works at many levels, and we will be examining each of these in turn.

First, we have seen that there is a need for a more efficient method of basic editing. Since production houses typically charge $150 to $500 per hour for off-line editing, the average user needs something more affordable. Many of these users have turned to computer-based controllers to perform their editing.

On another level, most people quickly become dissatisfied with the general analog editing process. It involves watching scenes many times and recording a scene with obscure time-code numbers. This is a tedious and nonintuitive process. At the next level of computer editing, the computer digitizes one or more still images from a video sequence and uses these *thumbnails* to represent each scene.

These solutions, however, still require the user to wait as decks are rewinding and seeking. The final solution, then, is purely digital. The computer digitally records all motion-video sequences and stores them on the hard drive. Some people use these solutions to perform their rough cut as efficiently as possible. Others, however, take computer-based editing to its highest level by using the computer to convert the finished digital-video sequence back to tape.

### The computer as control device

Using a computer to control video decks is not a new idea—it's been done for over 20 years now. The earliest CMX systems used computer control, but at that time these solutions cost several hundred thousand dollars.

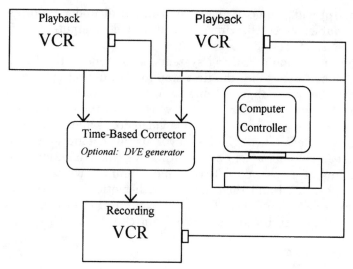

**Figure 37.2**  Computer-controlled editing suite.

The typical computer-controlled editing suite has the following components (see Fig. 37.2):

2 playback VCRs

1 recording VCR

Picture/sound monitor (i.e., television)

Computer controller

Time-based corrector/digital-video effects (DVE) generator

In all of these systems the computer acts as the control device, sending messages to playback and recording decks. In some systems with digital overlay boards, the computer also acts as the monitor, passing through video and audio on the screen.

The interface with computer control typically is done through mouse control. VCR controls appears as buttons on the screen, which can be clicked on. The computer then sends messages to the VCRs by means of a *control language*. Consumer-based control languages include Control-L/LANC and ViSCA control. The ViSCA control language works specifically with the Sony V-Deck and V-Box.

Frame accuracy is achieved through the use of time code. In addition to the professional SMPTE time code, desktop editing solutions often use rewritable consumer (RC) time code. Computer-based solutions also sometimes make use of a control network to access several decks. Popular networks include V-LAN by Videomedia Inc., and the ARTI system (Advanced Remote Technologies Inc.).

A popular computer-control program for PCs is Gold Disk's Video Director. This program uses Control-L and infrared to control standard camcorders and VCRs. It does not provide frame-accurate control, but at under $200 the program is very affordable. Video Director also will provide computer monitoring if a digitizing board is present.

Perhaps one of the most popular editing systems of all time is the Video Toaster by Newtek. This system takes the first step toward digital video and can be thought of as a "digitally enhanced" analog A/B-roll system. The Video Toaster is a hardware/software combination that works with the Commodore Amiga computer. The system can control multiple video decks and provides a wide variety of special effects through the clever use of computer video. However, the Video Toaster is *not* a nonlinear editing system. Transitions are accomplished by means of a "pseudo A/B roll" paradigm, in which a still image from deck B is captured and then merged with motion video that is passing through from deck A. A number of other systems also use the pseudo A/B roll method, such as Studio Master Pro from the AT&T Graphics Software Lab.

### Nonlinear digital editing

The step to fully digital video editing is a long one, and has many ramifications. First, digital video has very high storage needs, requiring huge amounts of disk space. Depending on the video-compression method used, digital video can require from 9 to 30 Mbytes per minute. Therefore an adequate nonlinear system will use multiple gigabytes of storage. Currently, magnetic storage costs about $2000 per gigabyte. Another solution is optical storage, which is gaining popularity and rapidly decreasing in price.

Digital editing has two main uses. The first is as a tool, for making a rough cut or work print, with EDL output used for subsequent on-line editing. The second use is the pure digital solution, and involves outputting the completed digital movie directly to tape. The advantage of the latter method is that computer software can provide almost infinite flexibility when it comes to creating transitions and special effects, which would cost a fortune if produced with a hardware DVE generator.

Unfortunately, digital video has disadvantages when printing to tape. Digital artifacts appear, such as pixelation, contouring, and aliasing. While artifacts also exist in the analog world (smearing, streaking, and color-fringing), the general public is very tolerant of these, as they have been a part of our lives through television for decades. By contrast, since digital artifacts are a recent phenomenon, most people are intolerant of them. As a result many producers are hesitant to print from digital format to tape, unless the digital video is stored with a very high resolution and color depth.

A nonlinear desktop editing system consists of the following (see Fig. 37.3):

1 playback VCR

1 recording VCR

**Figure 37.3** Nonlinear desktop
editing system.

Computer

Note that the computer has taken on the roles of controller, player, recorder, and DVE generator.

One popular nonlinear editing system on the PC is D/Vision by TouchVision, Inc. This system uses DVI technology to digitize, compress, and play back video. It provides a number of transitions and effects, as well as overlays and titling. Systems such as D/Vision typically range from $4000 to $15,000, depending on configuration and options.

## Platforms and systems

Often one's first decision when exploring desktop video is what type of computer to buy: PC, Macintosh, or something else? For the most part the host computer is relatively unimportant, as long as it is compatible with the editing system that best fits one's needs. Because of the widespread use of the PC, there is more software for that environment than its competitors. However, some very good packages exist for all platforms.

One platform that does offer some specific advantages is the Amiga. The Amiga features coprocessors for audio, graphics, and animation. Also the Amiga's video-signal-timing is compatible with NTSC, which makes it ideal for systems like the Video Toaster. However the Amiga also has some graphics limitations, and outside the video-editing world the Amiga has a fairly small market share.

A number of editing systems exist on the various platforms, other than those already mentioned in this section. Of note are Sundance 2.0 by the

Sundance Technology Group, Video F/X by Digital F/X, and the Avid Media Composer. The Avid system is quite popular but is somewhat higher-end, and ranges from $30,000 to $70,000.

The use of the computer as a tool for editing videotape has grown rapidly in the past few years. The software and hardware systems are rapidly evolving and coming down in price as competition increases. However, with the advent of low-cost multimedia hardware, another parallel market for editing is beginning to explode. This will be explored in the next section.

## Computer as Medium

The previous pages have described the evolution of desktop systems for editing videotape. These systems are used by a variety of professionals, ranging from broadcast-television producers to advertisers to small production shops, with uses ranging from movies and commercials to wedding videos. Certainly the market for videotape will be there for years to come.

However, recent technological advances have brought about the evolution of a new market for video. This market focuses not on videotape but on the digital motion video used by computers. Applications are widespread, and range from interactive training programs for industry to multimedia encyclopedias and entertainment programs for consumers. The video content of these applications also needs to be edited. This has brought on a new set of tools designed specifically for this purpose, adding new features that would be impractical in a tape-editing system.

If you are going to effectively use and edit digital video, you must first explore the issues of formats and compatibility. With the knowledge that exploration brings you, you will be able to produce and edit quality digital videos that can be ported to multiple platforms.

### Digital video as a medium

We've already explored the relative advantages and disadvantages of digital versus analog video. For various reasons, the quality of most digital video on a computer appears inferior to that of television. Compounding this problem is the fact that computer users typically are less than 2 feet from the computer screen, whereas the TV set is viewed from a much greater distance.

Digital-video quality is primarily affected by three issues:

1. *Data rate.*   How many bytes per second are used by the file
2. *Compression degree.*   How much the video frames are compressed (more compression produces lower-quality images)
3. *Use of interframes.*   How often there are "key" frames

Item number three requires additional explanation. Most video-compression methods, e.g., MPEG and DVI, use what is known as *interframe* or *delta-*

*frame* compression. This means, for instance, that only 1 in 15 frames is stored as a true image and all other frames store only the *difference* from the last frame, which is essentially any movement that has occurred. The 1-in-15 true-image frames are called *key frames.* This type of compression affects performance, because video sequences with large amounts of movement, such as pans, may appear jittery. Some compression methods, e.g., JPEG, do not use interframe compression, but this lowers the effectiveness of the total compression.

It would be easy to ignore these issues and work with uncompressed video that had no limits on data rate. As we shall soon see, this is impossible, because there is a limited amount of space to work with and many storage units, such as CD-ROM, can retrieve only a certain amount of data per second. To illustrate this, let us look at a hypothetical scenario.

We will say that an uncompressed image requires 100 units to store, and that the data rate we are using allows for 300 units per second, or an average of 10 units per individual frame. We therefore need a 10:1 compression ratio.

Let us now say that our compressor gives us 5:1 compression on still frames, and results in acceptable quality. If we also use interframe compression we can cut the data rate in half, resulting in 10:1 compression. However, this will limit motion. Yet if we do not use multiframe compression, we will need to push our compressor to 10:1 for each image, which results in lower quality. In the end there is no clear answer, and one simply must find the best solution for each situation.

This example is an oversimplification, but it does well represent the thought process involved in producing multimedia video. Other factors affecting data rate include the following three:

1. *Frame size.*   Video at 640 × 480 pixels looks excellent, but takes 16 times the data of video at 160 × 120.
2. *Frame rate.*   Producing video at 10 frames per second will result in 3 times less data, but also will make motion look stuttered.
3. *Color depth.*   Decreasing the number of colors available to video can save significant space, but may cause the video to appear "cartoonish."

The first two issues, *frame size* and *frame rate,* are straightforward. The third, *color depth,* is an important one that must be well understood. The technical term for this is *bit depth,* and refers to the number of bits per pixel used for color. The best-quality images are 24-bit, where each pixel can be any of 16 million colors. This level of quality typically is used only for photographic and broadcast-quality imagery. A popular midrange format is 16-bit, in which each pixel can be any of 65,000 colors. This still produces good-quality video, when used with a VGA monitor that can support that many simultaneous colors. However the most common format is 8-bit, where there are only 256 colors to choose from. This format is used because it requires less data, and because currently most computer monitors can support only 256 simultaneous colors. The 256 colors used must be chosen carefully, and are placed in a *palette* or *CLUT* (*color lookup table*). If one chooses 256 shades of gray, the resulting video will be high-quality black-and-white. However since using color is much more popular, most editing programs allow one to *optimize* the best palette for a video once it is complete. It is possible to optimize different palettes for different sections of a movie, but on most computers this produces an awkward and unpleasant flash on the screen called a *palette change*.

There also is another type of color depth used, called *color subsampling*. Popular subsampled formats include 9-bit, 4-1-1, and 4-2-2. Basically, these formats store more brightness information than color information, because humans are perceptually less aware of changes in color than changes in brightness. These formats result in high-quality images at a reduced data rate. Usually, however, one does not need to worry about this, because most 16- and 24-bit compression algorithms do color subsampling internally.

### Digital-video formats

A digital-video format essentially is a specification for the storage of interleaved video and audio data. There is an important distinction between *format* and *compression*. Some digital-video formats, e.g., Video For Windows, can support multiple compression algorithms within the same format.

The primary video format on Apple computers is QuickTime. On the PC, the most popular format is Video For Windows (established by Microsoft). There also is a QuickTime for Windows format, which is identical to the Apple QuickTime format. This allows those files to be played on both the PC and Macintosh. Also, around the time this was written, Microsoft announced drivers for playing Video For Windows on the Macintosh. In addition, as one might expect, there are conversion programs that allow one to go back and forth between each format.

Other formats exist for specialized uses. One popular format for training and marketing applications is the AVS format, used only with Intel-hardware-supported compression methods. This format exists on the PC, in DOS, Windows, and OS/2.

### Compression options

Compression of video data is an absolute necessity if such data is to be used in computer applications. One frame of video data, at $512 \times 480$ resolution and 24-bit color depth, requires 737,280 bytes of data. At the same time digital video often is distributed on CD-ROM, which has a maximum data throughput of 150,000 bytes per second. Since usually there are 30 frames of video per second, this makes a requirement of 147:1 compression ($737,280 \times 30 = 22$ million $= 150,000 \times 147$). This level of compression is not easy to obtain, and over the years a number of compression algorithms have appeared to perform this task.

Compression can be accomplished either in hardware, during the capture/digitization process, or later in software. Generally the choice depends on the cost of the capture hardware.

Low-end capture boards, such as Video Blaster, run from $250 to $350. They capture motion video as a series of uncompressed images, in a very large file. Later one can filter this file through an editor and compress the video in software to a more manageable size. On the PC, files typically are compressed with the Microsoft Video Compressor, the Indeo algorithm (by Intel), the RLE algorithm, or the Cinepak codec. While inefficient, boards such as Video Blaster are an excellent value for the money, and have helped to put digital video into the hands of many consumers.

It should be noted that RLE (run-length encoded) compression does not provide a high compression ratio, but it is lossless, which means the compressed image has 100 percent of the quality of the original. RLE is best used for animation, as well as with video having only small areas of motion.

Midrange boards generally include real-time compression with capture. These boards, ranging from $400 to $600, include the Video Spigot (using Supermac compression), Intel's Smart Video Recorder (using Indeo compression), and MediaVision's Pro-Movie Studio (using Microsoft Video Compression).

High-end hardware, starting at $1500, also includes hardware-assisted playback. This means that special hardware decompresses the video very fast and can play it back full-screen, giving the highest video quality. Unfortunately this limits distribution, because only users with the special decompression hardware can play the video.

One very popular high-end board is ActionMedia II, made by both Intel and IBM. The ActionMedia board supports Intel's DVI and Indeo compression algorithms. Also, VideoLogic sells the MediaSpace board, which provides motion-JPEG compression and decompression.

Other higher-quality proprietary compression algorithms exist that require you to send your video to special sites. Intel's PLV (production-level video) is one such algorithm, and costs approximately $200 per video-minute to compress, at sites such as Horizons Technology in San Diego, CA. One drawback, however, is that, once compressed, these videos cannot be manipulated, and editing is limited to very simple cut-and-paste operations.

### Digitizing issues

Anyone editing and producing computer-based video needs to be aware of capture and digitizing issues if they are to get the best-quality product. First, one should capture video with the highest-quality video deck. Using consumer-grade VCRs brings the problems of both analog and digital artifacts into the final product, and thus should be avoided.

The analog-video format generally is unimportant in the digital realm, but one needs to make sure that the output format of the deck, e.g., Y/C or RGB, is compatible with the input formats of the capture board.

Finally, if at all possible one should use a time-based corrector. TBCs synchronize and stabilize the video picture, making for a much better digital image when captured.

**Figure 37.4**  SPLICE editing software.

### Editing software—Macintosh

The most popular editing software for digital video on the Macintosh is Adobe Premiere. This program allows for a number of interesting transitions and special effects, and is very flexible. Also popular is DiVA VideoShop, which allows easy incorporation of edited clips into applications.

### Editing software: PC

Several digital-video editing programs exist in the PC environment, most under Windows. One popular program is SPLICE (see Fig. 37.4). SPLICE is compatible with the following formats: Video For Windows, QuickTime, and AVS, and can convert between any two of these formats. SPLICE has an intuitive time-line-based interface, and a number of special effects and video filters. The product also ships with a CD-ROM of sample video clips, which can be used in editing. In addition many other effects and filters are available as add-ons to the SPLICE product.

Also available is ATI's MediaMerge, which includes support for Video For Windows and QuickTime. MediaMerge incorporates an audio editor and several layers of video overlay.

Finally, there also are a number of programs for postproduction video effects. One popular consumer program is Morph by Gryphon Software. This program allows one to add morphing effects to Video For Windows sequences.

## Editing and the Authoring Process

Video production and editing is an integral part of the interactive video authoring process. Many have tried to separate them and have ended up reshooting and reediting large amounts of material later, when it was discovered that important sequences were missing from the program. The process should be carefully planned and organized. A description of the five key steps follows.

1. *Make a flowchart.*   Always make a detailed flowchart of any sections of the program that will incorporate video or audio. Be sure that *all* branches are accounted for, so there will be nothing missing as the program is being authored. Such deficiencies can cause large delays in programming.

2. *Write a script/storyboard.*   Write a detailed script for every scene. Accompany all changes in action with a storyboard, which sketches out the scene that is to be shot. Note that with interactive video, similar events often are repeated with different outcomes. Working from a careful script will help you to avoid unnecessary shooting of certain pieces and keep costs down.

3. *Review and digitize.*   All raw footage should be reviewed. If your digitizing is to be done externally (as with PLV video), you will need to make a precise chart of the time code to be used, making sure that you choose only important clips. This should be done carefully, since recompressing extra segments later will bring on big delays in development. Also, unnecessary digitization can cost over $200 per minute.

For in-house digitizing, you will simply need to digitize those general sections of the tape that are needed. Precise cutting can be done by the video-editing program.

4. *Synchronize video and audio.*   Individual clips now can be loaded into the editing program. Many interactive video productions incorporate narration that was recorded separately. Editing programs such as SPLICE allow one to visually lay out video and audio on a time line, to allow for precise synchronization. Often you also will want to add background music or external sounds, e.g., an alarm ringing. Most editing programs have a second audio track used for mixing. You will want to make sure your program has relative volume control and audio fading, to allow for the best-quality soundtrack.

5. *Match images and audio.*   Most interactive programs have long segments of audio that are interspersed with still images. Before authoring, it is very important that you lay out a chart listing audio files, image files, and appropriate frame numbers for insertions. Time-line-based editing programs

are very helpful in this process, for they allow the user to slowly step through audio files and locate exact frames corresponding to specific words on the soundtrack.

## Desktop Editing Tips

A number of "rules" exist for video editing, rules that establish meanings for various types of cuts and transitions. They were established a century ago during the production of the first black-and-white films. Though we are not conscious of them as viewers, we expect these rules to be followed and we understand the "language" that is presented through them. For instance, in a static scene, we expect the action to be *balanced* in the center two-thirds of the screen. If the action is off-center, we get a sense of motion or urgency. Ignoring these rules can confuse the viewer, whereas following them helps you to take advantage of subliminal cues that were not present in the original footage.

*Continuity* of action is critical. If at all possible, make sure the video is shot from multiple vantage points, for additional flexibility in editing. Cutting from a medium shot to a closeup is common, and can suggest emotion. Never cut between two shots of the same scene at the same distance. This is known as a *jump cut,* and is very distracting to the viewer.

Edited scenes should follow the action. If you have a training sequence of someone operating machinery, cut to a closeup of the hands, giving a sense of the importance of a particular action. At the same time, always keep in mind the *pace* of your movie. A rapid number of cuts in sequence, as in music videos, suggests excitement. Relaxed subject matter should be edited at a slower pace.

Transitions between scenes can be enhanced by means of *transparent editing*. Programs such as SPLICE allow one to manipulate video and audio tracks separately, so that audio from the first scene can lead into the second, or vice versa. For instance, in the first scene two characters may be talking about where they are going. When cutting to the second scene, continue the audio of the conversation from the first for an extra two or three seconds. This produces a smoother, more meaningful transition.

Many editing programs offer a variety of interesting special effects and transitions. One must fight the urge to overuse these. Effects sometimes can distract from the action of a scene. If possible, use them only when they complement the action. For instance, when cutting from a scene of a character thinking of his/her friend to a scene of the friend, you might use an *iris effect,* originating from the head of the character and opening to fill the screen. Used in this way, effects can enhance a movie considerably.

## Consumer Distribution

When it comes to applications that will be mass-distributed to a consumer market, several issues should be kept in mind during the editing process.

First, remember that most consumers have low-end machines that probably will play back video more slowly and less smoothly. As a result, you may want to add more flash and excitement to the video to compensate. Image-warping and video-morphing are popular techniques. Keep in mind, however, that a fast, flashy transition may be skipped over entirely by the video driver on a slow machine.

When putting together a program, you also should be careful as to the palettes used. Since digital video usually is no more than 320 × 240, often it is framed on a background screen. If the background screen is made up of more than 20 colors, and if palettes are not carefully chosen, video play will cause unsightly palette changes unacceptable to the consumer. The SPLICE program allows the user to incorporate a base palette of background colors when optimizing palettes for a new movie. This allows several movies to play on the same background without altering the visible palette.

As discussed previously, data rate for video is a key issue, as most programs are delivered on CD-ROM. Also, CD-ROMs can hold only 70 minutes of video. Some applications require more, which calls for a further limiting of frame size and frame rates. Some developers have turned to a new compression technique (developed by Iterated Systems) called *fractal compression*. This provides higher-quality video at lower data rates.

Most developers are very interested in cross-platform compatibility. We've discussed various video formats and the platforms on which they run. The most important issue, however, is the type of compression used, since you can always convert between video formats.

Finally, performance is always an important issue when delivering to consumers. Compounding this is the fact that, as of this writing, the Video For Windows drivers do not guarantee video and audio synchronization. This means that on a slow machine, video can look like a badly dubbed foreign film, with the mouth moving out of sync with the voice. Unfortunately there is no good solution for this, other than to limit the amount of closeup speech.

## Future Directions

The 1990s are witnessing a rapid evolution of editing technologies. Costs have dropped dramatically, and will continue to do so.

Increasingly faster computers also will affect editing systems. The need for hardware-accelerated video playback may dwindle, as CPUs and VGA boards grow both in power and speed. Also, as more consumers are able to play smooth-motion videos on their PCs, the market for digital-video tools and applications will burgeon dramatically.

# Adding Full-Motion Video to Multimedia Presentations

**Bruce A. Rady**

## Introduction

Software capture/edit tools provide all the functions of conventional video-editing systems but offer many additional benefits. These tools store your video and audio files digitally on computer disk, using advanced video-compression techniques.

Well-featured capture/edit tools will have the capabilities described in this chapter.

The *disk storage method* means that these tools can provide virtually instant access to any scene or frame in any random order you choose. The need to wait for videotape to cue is completely eliminated.

Given the digital storage of video and audio, and the random access to any frame or scene, the more sophisticated capture/edit tools now available provide the user with "nonlinear" editing capabilities (see Figs. 38.1, 38.2, 38.3, and 38.4). Nonlinear editing allows you to place a new scene or shot in between existing ones without having to copy any of the subsequent scenes. This saves considerable time.

Since nonlinear editing is much faster and you can see the results instantaneously, it's easier to experiment with different edits. Nonlinear editing also makes it possible to "undo" edits, even to save different versions of a program. And because the editing is done without copying tape, video (and audio) quality are maintained regardless of the number of edits.

## Overview of the Creation Process

### An introduction to software capture/edit tool capabilities

The new breed of software capture/edit tools have everything you need to help you create edited digital "movie" files that can be played in other multi-

**Figure 38.1**  Linear editing means copying.

**Figure 38.2**  Nonlinear editing means disk-skipping.

media programs. They allow you to "capture" original material from virtually any video or audio source, and provide you with easy-to-use yet powerful editing capabilities.

These tools also allow you to export video programs to Microsoft Video for Windows (AVI) files, or Apple's Quicktime (MOV). Video for Windows allows you to play motion video and audio on a PC without any compression hardware at all. This means that the audience for your multimedia program can be any PC running Windows 3.1. To hear audio, an audio card and speakers are required.

**Figure 38.3**   Linear changes are difficult.

**Figure 38.4**   Nonlinear changes are easy.

The better capture/edit tools are ideal for Video for Windows, because they allow you to capture and edit at the highest digital-video quality and then export your program to a variety of formats with differing qualities/data rates. The same video program then can be sent to a very wide audience, from Video for Windows customers at the low end to videotape users at the high end. This flexibility to maximize the audience for your multimedia products is an important consideration.

Additional software tools allow you to add "interactivity" to the edited video you create with capture/edit tools. IBM's Ultimedia Tool Series, for example, offers a variety of compatible products to give you a complete "suite" of functions to develop exciting, rich, interactive multimedia. Many of these tools have versions both for the occasional user and the frequent "professional" user.

The balance of this chapter will show you how to create full-motion, interactive multimedia programs using capture/edit tools.

### The multimedia development process

Developing a multimedia program consists of seven basic steps (see Fig. 38.5).

1. *Script and plan.*   Creating a good multimedia program should start with a good script and plan. Determine exactly what you are trying to accomplish with your program, who your target audience is, and what messages you are trying to convey to them. Then write a complete script and plan out such things as the type of video/audio segments you will need, where animation, graphics, or text would be effective, the type of music you want, a flowchart of any interactive branching, etc. A "shot list" of the camera positions you want is also an important part of the script. Even if you are using the most flexible capture/edit tools, a good script is likely to save a large amount of time and money that otherwise would be wasted.

2. *Shoot the video/audio.*   Using your shot list, shoot your video. Also, record any narration or extra audio you need. While you're shooting video, get some "on-location" sound effects such as keyboard typing, machine sounds, ambience, and other audio unique to your story. These are very easy to edit in and they will greatly add to the realism of your program.

3. *Create graphics/animation/titles.*   Using an animation, paint, or graphics package, create the graphic, animation, and textual elements you desire. Depending on which capture/edit tool you use, these elements can be stored in a Targa, PCX, or other file format and then directly imported. Or you can create them in almost any format and convert them using utilities such as HiJack. The Ultimedia Tool Series includes a number of tools that perform these functions.

4. *Capture video/audio.*   Capture the video and audio you shot during Step 2. *Capture* means digitize the audio and video onto your computer's hard-disk drive. Also you can capture "wild" audio such as music from CDs, audio tapes, sound effects, direct microphone narration (use your camcorder's mike if nothing else), audio-only portions from your videotape, etc.

5. *Edit motion video/audio.*   Using your capture/edit tool's edit function, create your edited movie or sequence. If the tool offers nonlinear editing capabilities, you easily can change your sequence at will and even capture more video/audio/graphics after you've edited a rough version of your story. Using a nonlinear editor, the process becomes "iterative" and allows you to change your script quickly if you're not happy with the results. When you're done, you can output an edited digital-video file in formats such as Microsoft's Video for Windows (AVI) or Apple's Quicktime (MOV).

**Figure 38.5**  The multimedia development process.

6. *Create the "interactive" portion.*   Using a multimedia-based presentation or authoring program, add the "interactive" aspects of your program: icons, branching, hypermedia, etc. Include digital-video windows in which you play the edited motion-video files you created using the capture/edit tool. Bring in animation, graphics, and titles from Step 3 directly, if you so desire. Again, you have a number of choices of presentation and authoring tools available to you from the IBM Tool Series. Many of these also include a run-time "player" version that you can use to distribute your interactive program to your target audience's computers.

7. *Distribute the program.*   This can be done via CD-ROM if you are publishing a title, on a network for video e-mail, or kept on a laptop for a sales or business presentation.

Of course, there are many variations on these steps. For example, if you simply wanted a motion-video file to play in a window under Windows or OS/2's Media Player, you could skip Step 6 and exclude any "interactivity" from your program. In that case, just call up into the Media Player the file you created using the capture/edit tool.

## Capturing Video and Audio

### Defining *capture*

Steps 4 and 5 described above are performed using the capture/edit tool. Step 4 actually consists of two steps, *capture,* a required step, and *logging footage,* an optional step.

Capture is the process of digitizing and compressing video and audio into your computer and storing it on hard disk. You can capture from any NTSC video source (NTSC stands for National Television Standards Committee and is the standard TV format in both the United States and Japan) such as a VCR, camcorder, etc.

You also can capture audio—either simultaneously with, or separately from, video. For example, you can capture from a CD player or audiotape recorder without any video. You then can easily synchronize this with the video any way you like, using the capture/edit tool.

Once the video or audio source has been properly connected, you simply play it into the computer and the system captures it in "real" time—that is, 1 minute of video takes 1 minute to capture.

During capture, the video will be compressed using hardware such as Intel's i750B chip on the ActionMedia II board. Compression is a method used to remove unneeded data from the incoming video and make it take up less space in the computer.

This crucial step makes high-quality motion video on a PC possible. For example if you just digitize video without using any compression, 30 seconds of video will require approximately 600 Mbytes of hard-disk storage space. However, that same amount of storage space will hold over an hour of video when it has been compressed by the ActionMedia board.

**Figure 38.6**  Capture screen.

The end result of capture is an AVS file (audio/video subsystem file) in which both the digitized video and audio are stored. This file can be converted into a variety of formats including a Microsoft Video for Windows (AVI) file, either before or after editing.

## A sample capture session

This subsection will "walk you through" 12 steps that will show you how to capture material using one capture/edit tool, D/Vision. This particular tool allows you to capture in real time at a variety of picture resolutions/data rates. It also gives you the option of "marking" a still frame image as a reference for a video segment. During editing, this reference still frame is displayed as a "thumbnail" for fast retrieval of the video segment.

1. Figure 38.6 shows the "Capture Screen" in D/Vision. The image from your video source is shown in a video window on the upper left. The "DVI Input" window is on the lower left, and the "Capture File" window is on the upper right.

2. Load a tape into your VCR. If you are going to capture to a new file, select the "Video Config" icon in the Capture File window. Figure 38.7 appears, allowing you to select from four different resolutions. Each of these has a different data rate, as indicated by the number in the parentheses:

   ▪ SupeRTV (1000 kbytes/second)
   ▪ High-res (1000 kbytes/second)

**Figure 38.7**   Video configuration screen.

- Medium-res (300 kbytes/second)
- Low-res (150 kbytes/second)

The higher the data rate, the better the picture quality, but also the more hard-disk space required per second of video running time. Data rate versus picture quality is discussed later, in the section Outputting a Digital Video File. Once a resolution setting has been chosen for an AVS file, it cannot be changed later (however, you can intercut between different resolutions during edit). In Figure 38.7, the selected resolution has a checkmark next to it.

3. If you are capturing footage to an existing file, choose the "AVS Files" icon in the Capture File window and the "Select AVS File" screen will appear (see Fig. 38.8). The new video you are about to capture will then be appended onto the end of the selected file.

4. Select the name of the file you wish to use.

5. Move your VCR to the start of the footage you want to capture, and put it in pause. Then click on the "Digitizer Control" icon in the DVI Input window. The Digitizer Control's pop-up window appears.

6. Adjust the Digitizer Control to obtain the picture you want (see Fig. 38.9). You may also want to play a segment of the tape and adjust the

**Figure 38.8**   Select AVS File screen.

**Figure 38.9**   Digitizer controls.

Digitizer Control. Then move back to the start of the section you want to capture. The upper-four "slider" icons are similar to the controls that exist on a TV set, a professional video monitor, or a time-base corrector. These controls are

*Contrast.*   How much difference there is between the light and dark areas in your picture. The contrast and brightness of your image are related, since once an overall brightness level has been fixed, the picture can be made to look darker or lighter by contrast adjustment.

*Brightness.*   How dark or light the overall picture is.

*Tint.*   The actual colors in the image. This control makes flesh tones look natural, or colors appear realistic.

*Color.*   The "saturation" of color in the picture. This does not change the actual color but only how "strong" it is.

To operate the slider controls in this example, you would use the computer's mouse to click within any control.

7. Put your VCR into "Play" and let it come up to speed. Then hit the "Begin" icon to start capturing to disk.

8. If you wish to "mark" a reference still frame, hit the "Enter" key where a new shot begins (i.e., where the scene content significantly changes). This allows the use of a "Source Catalog" of "thumbnail" still images for fast retrieval during the editing process. (*Note:* Marking is an optional step. You can capture—and even edit—your material without it.)

9. Repeat Step 8 as long as you want to continue capturing. Each time you see the content change, hit Enter, and a new still image will be stored for display in the Source Catalog.

10. When you have reached the end of the portion of the tape you want to capture, pause RTV Capture by hitting the F3 key.

11. You can easily add more to the end of any file by going back to Step 3.

12. "Logging footage" is an optional step in which you enter information such as shot descriptions or scene and take numbers, for each segment of video and audio. A well-featured capture/edit tool will let you log footage as you capture it, eliminating the need for a separate logging step. These tools also may have a cataloging function, to greatly speed up searches performed during editing.

## Editing Audio and Video

### Introduction to editing

When capture is complete, your next step is to edit the audio and video. Editing is done using the AVS files created during the capture process.

Using D/Vision as an example, Fig. 38.10 shows the unedited source files being displayed in one video window (on the left) and an edited "movie" sequence in another video window (on the right). This is the D/Vision Edit Screen.

This Edit Screen simulates two videotape recorders. The window on the left "plays" the source video and audio, the window on the right "plays back" your recorded edited program. The controls under the windows act just like the controls of a VCR. They are

1. *Play.* Lets you view the video (and hear the audio) at the normal speed of 30 frames per second.

2. *Jog.* Lets you use a computer input device, such as a trackball, to look at the video footage at variable speeds, from frame-by-frame jog to 50 times normal speed, forward or reverse.

3. *Seek.* Allows you to locate specific frames in the footage.

**Figure 38.10**   Edit screen.

4. *Rec. (record).*   Available only on the right-hand "Record" window, this
control instantly "records" material from the source into your edited program.

Figure 38.11 shows how you can access video material quickly via a "Source
Catalog," which presents a visual catalog of the digitized source material.

Each of these still images is from a different shot that has been captured,
so you can easily and quickly see all of your editing options. Just select the
shot you want, and it's instantly loaded into the source window.

Next you play or jog the video or audio segment to "record" a shot on the
record window. Select which portion of which shot you want first, then second, then third, etc., until you have assembled an entire edited "movie" or
"sequence." Figure 38.12 is an example of how an edited sequence might
appear on what is called a "Time Line" on the Edit Screen.

There is a block for each of four elements: overlay (graphics), video, audio
channel 1, and audio channel 2. Wherever the blocks are vertically connected,
the video and audio are "sync"—that is, the audio originally was recorded
with the video. In the example shown in Fig. 38.12, all the audio is sync for
each shot in the Time Line. A vertical line called the "Time Line Cursor" tells
you where your recorded program is "cued to."

The more sophisticated "nonlinear" editing tools can play back the sequence
without assembling an edited digital-video file. They display a simulation of the
edited movie that is so real it cannot be distinguished from an actual edited file.

**Figure 38.11**   Source catalog screen.

**Figure 38.12**   Time line #1.

Here is how the "nonlinear" simulation is accomplished. The address of each segment chosen is called an "event" and is stored in an edit decision list (EDL). Capture/edit tools using this method will use the EDL to direct the PC's hard disk to skip around during the simulation, picking up only the video and audio segments you want. The software is so fast that the "playback" is completely seamless, with no pauses or glitches at edit points. Not only is the video "nonlinear" but so are up to six audio tracks and a graphics overlay "track." Regardless of where the video, graphics, and audio are stored—on the same disk or on different disks—the simulation is seamless and plays at a true 30 frames per second.

Nonlinear capture/edit tools with this simulation capability provide you with tremendous flexibility when it comes to making creative choices. They allow you to add, remove, or rearrange material anywhere in the edited sequence, and instantly see the results. You can edit in "wild" sound on two or more separate audio tracks completely independent from the video. You can even make many different edited versions from the same source material, and recall them one after the other to decide which is the best.

All this is done without copying or rerecording any material. The differently edited versions are simply different EDLs, directing the disk to pick up video/audio/graphical elements in a different sequence.

Furthermore, nonlinear tools allow you to "undo" multiple previous edits, or create special video effects such as dissolves and wipes. During all of this editing and reediting the tools continuously—and transparently—update the EDL with the latest changes.

Software capture/edit tools also can provide powerful multitrack audio mixing capabilities, with CD-quality digital audio (44.1 kHz, 16-bit sampling).

## Editing video only or audio only

The editing described thus far has used both video and the original audio that goes with it. But it is also useful to be able to edit audio or video separately and independently. For example, you may wish to edit in a narrator, or the audio of interviewers, over the video of their subject. Or you may want to edit silent video over a piece of music.

To accomplish these kinds of edits, the software capture/edit tool must treat audio and video as two completely independent entities. This means that at any point in the edited sequence the video can come from any frame in the source material, regardless of where the audio comes from and vice versa.

Moreover, if two or more channels of audio are fully independent of each other, you have increased creative flexibility. You can then combine three elements that come from different parts of the same disk or from entirely different disks—still with seamless playback.

Figure 38.13 shows how a Time Line can give you an intuitive visual display of the relationship between your video and audio elements. It visually indicates when the video and audio elements are in sync by connecting them vertically.

The "Mode" icons (see Fig. 38.14) at the left of the Time Line determine which of the elements—graphics overlay, video, or one of the several audio channels—are affected in any editing operation. One or any combination of these may be selected to determine which element will be affected by editing.

To record audio only or video only and have the new material overwrite (replace) existing material, you "insert" the new material by selecting the Insert icon and one or more Mode icons. You may select any combination of these icons. The mode(s) selected will determine which elements from the source footage get recorded. The recording of any element will be made at the location of the Time Line cursor. Since this example assumes Insert editing, no change will occur in the positions of the video and audio events following the new shot you're recording.

**Figure 38.13**   Time line #2.

**Figure 38.14**   Mode icons.

**Figure 38.15**   Time line—video-only editing.

**Figure 38.16**   Time line—after-video recording.

Figure 38.15 is an example showing the recording of a video-only insert shot. The shaded region on the Time Line will be replaced by the new shot, and the total length of the video will stay the same. When the recording has been completed, the Time Line will appear as in Fig. 38.16.

You will see the "over the shoulder" (OTSH—GOOD MORNING) while still hearing the "medium shot" (MS—GOOD MORNING, WALTER). It is also possible to turn Insert off and then record new footage that "pushes" everything else down in the sequence.

### Creative audio editing and mixing

Creative audio editing is one of the most powerful dimensions to motion pictures. A well-featured software capture/edit tool will give you the same flexibility for handling audio that it gives you for video.

With this degree of capability, you can mix and edit multiple audio tracks in sync with, or completely independently from, your video. You can fade down music and fade up a narrator's voice, or cross-fade from one piece of music to another. A particular word or phrase can be made louder or quieter, edited out, or even rearranged. These capabilities easily let you fine-tune your audio and make your finished program a polished, professional presentation. Up to six overlapping audio channels can be edited and mixed while editing audio.

In addition, by creatively using the editing functions, you can add many different types of sounds into an edited program. A virtually unlimited number of audio channels can be "layered" together, six at a time, by editing the output of one sequence into another.

### The audio profile

The audio levels at any point in the sequence and on any channel can be changed dynamically. One way to represent this is to use a series of lines and points known as the *audio profile*. A typical audio profile is shown in the Aud 1 and Aud 2 elements of the Time Line in Fig. 38.17 (see the white lines and dots).

The audio profile shows you the volume setting at each point in your edited sequence. You have complete control to change the audio profile at any point, as often as you like—up to once every three frames. All the changes you make are memorized by the system and played back when you choose "Play" or "Jog" under the Record Window. This is like having an automated mixing studio right in your computer.

The black horizontal line running through the middle of each audio channel represents the "normal" volume level for each channel. This is the level at which the audio originally was captured, and represents no attenuation or boost (i.e., it is "flat" audio). This is 0-dB "line level" if your incoming audio was 0 dB. Whenever the audio profile is "flat," the Profile line covers the "flat" line. In the example shown in Fig. 38.17, Aud 1 in the event "THE YEAR WAS..." is flat audio.

When the audio volume is boosted above normal, the Profile is above the flat line; when the volume is lower than normal, the Profile is below the flat line. By setting the two channel's audio profiles, you can vary the relative levels and create mixed audio tracks.

The audio profile actually consists of a series of points connected by lines. These are called *mix points* and they represent the points in time at which you have made changes in the audio levels.

**Figure 38.17**  Audio profile.

**Figure 38.18**   Audio-mixer window.

### The "Audio Mixer" window

When you insert or adjust a mix point, the "Audio Mixer" window appears, as shown in Fig. 38.18.

This is the main control panel used for setting or changing a mix point. It contains the following functions.

1. The vertical "Faders" labeled "Aud 1" and "Aud 2" on the left are used to adjust the volume. Volume can be adjusted from approximately − 40 dB to + 30 dB, as indicated by the scale between the Faders. The lower, light area on each Fader is the actual volume setting; the higher it is, the higher the volume. Using an input device such as a trackball, you can point and click inside the Fader to the level you want.

2. The "Pan" bars underneath each Fader adjust the left and right balance for each channel.

3. The "Fade to" icon determines whether or not the audio profile into a mix point will fade (up or down) from the previous mix point. If it does not fade, it will step to a new level at the point.

4. "Fade from" determines whether or not the audio profile will fade (up or down) from the current mix point to the next one. If it doesn't fade, it will step to a new level at the mix point.

5. "Lock 1 & 2" locks the levels on both channels together, so that a change made to one channel automatically changes the other as well.

6. "Flat" automatically resets both Volume and Pan controls to normal (0-dB) levels.

It is important to turn on the Mode icons on the Time Line for the channel(s) you want to adjust before clicking on the Mix icon. This determines which channel is active in the Audio Mixer window. If a channel is not active, its fader is "ghosted" and cannot be adjusted.

### Creating special video effects

Until now we have discussed only "straight cuts" between events. Using a "Special Effects" ("Spfx") function, you can change a straight cut into a special-effect transition such as a dissolve or wipe. The following four categories of special effects are very useful:

1. *Dissolve.*   The end of one scene is superimposed over the beginning of another.

2. *Wipe.*   The picture will show a portion of the end of one scene, along with a portion the beginning of the next. Many different types of wipe patterns are available. For examples, see Fig. 38.19.

3. *Fade.*   The start of a scene fades up from black (fade in) or the end of the scene fades out to black (fade out).

4. *Freeze-frame.*   The video at any point in an event can be still-framed for as long as you want.

All of these effects can be programmed for various lengths of time. It is also possible to combine a freeze-frame with any of the other three categories of effects (e.g., wiping out of a freeze-frame into a motion event). In addition, you can convert any special effect back to a straight cut at any time.

The more powerful capture/edit tools create freeze-frames instantly, and build dissolve, wipe, and fade effects in nearly "real time"; that is, a 1-second dissolve takes only about 3 to 4 seconds to build. It is created as a separate file on the disk, and you can play it back as a part of the sequence. You can even jog slowly through the effect at that point in the sequence.

In addition to these effects, graphics and overlays can have special effects. You can fade into a title or fade out a logo. Some capture/edit tools even let you animate the overlay layer in real time for rolling credits, flying logos, etc.

**Figure 38.19**  Select wipe pattern.

Another category of special effect is sophisticated multisource digital-video effects. These include split screens, dual/quad splits, "pan-and-scan" types of effects, compositing of video layers in a montage, etc. These also include slow- and fast-motion effects, including reverse motion. Since all the video is stored digitally, the number of possible effects is virtually limitless. However, many of these types of effects must be "rendered" to the disk and then edited in as "Source" material, because they are too complex to create in real time during editing.

All special effects are accurately included in your edited digital file during exporting to Video for Windows.

## Graphics

In addition to editing video and audio, sophisticated capture/edit tools let you edit graphics simply as another element. Targa, PCX, and other graphics file formats can be imported into the edit tool and edited along with the video and audio. Graphics can either be "keyed" (i.e., overlaid on the video) or put up as still images with audio running under them. It is even possible to import a series of graphics files as an animation sequence and edit that into the video, or key it over the video.

## Outputting an Edited Digital-Video File

Once you have completed your editing and have the final version of your program, you will create a real, edited, digital-video file. This is called *outputting,* and includes the steps of *assembling* an actual file and then *exporting* it to the desired resolution and file type.

The exporting utility of your capture/edit tool should let you adjust many parameters in the digital video. For example, you may be able to convert high resolution to low resolution, or introduce "frame-differencing" to reduce the data rates.

### Assembling and exporting a digital-video file

An *Assemble* function automatically and frame-accurately recreates all video edits, audio edits, audio mixing levels, qraphics, overlays, animations, and special video effects that you have edited.

The assembled file then can be exported into a variety of formats, including

- Microsoft's Video for Windows (i.e., AVI) file format
- Apple's Quicktime (i.e., MOV) format
- Intel/IBM's DVI file format
- WAV file formats for audio-only files

These edited digital-video files can be played in any authoring or player packages that support, for example, Video for Windows. In fact, using Object

Linking and Embedding (OLE), you can play a Video for Windows file on any computer with Windows 3.1—even if it does not contain Video for Windows. (You will, however, need a sound card and speakers to hear the audio.)

This means that you can send a video clip embedded in WordPerfect, MS-Word, or Excel documents, and the recipients can play them instantly when they view the document, even if they don't have any special software or hardware installed (other than Windows 3.1 and a sound card and speakers).

A digital-video file may be stored on any hard disk, CD-ROM, rewritable optical disk, or other medium having adequate space and data-throughput capability. Also, the file can be networked, allowing motion video/audio to be sent over standard digital networks.

### Data rate versus picture quality

A fundamental issue in digital video is the data rate of the video file. Digital video requires that the user make a tradeoff between data rate and picture quality. The higher the data rate, the better the picture quality. However, higher data rates also mean that the files take up more space on the disk and require faster computer platforms to play them back. For example, a digital file that plays well on a fast hard disk may freeze periodically or not play at all on a CD-ROM. For a file to play back without interruption, the data rate of the player platform *must exceed* that of the digital-video file.

It is extremely important to determine the data rate of the target platform on which your digital-video file will play. The disk is a major factor affecting data rate. A fast SCSI hard disk can sustain 500 kbytes per second or more, while most CD-ROMs may be limited to approximately 150 kbytes per second.

Other factors affecting data rates include CPU type and speed, disk controller, operating system overhead, wait states/CMOS setup, etc. Many disk manufacturer's specifications give burst data rates or rates of the controller and not of the disk itself, so often it is very difficult to determine the ongoing, sustainable data rate of a particular platform.

It is *strongly* recommended that you prototype sample digital files on your slowest target player platform, using exactly the same configuration and operating system your audience will use for your final product!

Because of the picture-quality/data-rate tradeoff, some capture/edit tools allow you to easily adjust and experiment with different picture-quality/data-rate tradeoffs in your exported file. To see how this is done, look at Fig. 38.20.

During the outputting procedure, this "Select Export File Type" window appears. By choosing one of the following top five checkboxes, you can select a type of file and a level of picture resolution for your exported file.

1. *High-res AVS.*  This provides a standard Intel DVI file with the best-looking video quality, but it requires the most disk space and the highest data rate (approximately 600 kbytes per second). If the target player system has a fast, unfragmented SCSI disk, and your operating system has been configured for fast video playback, this is your best option.

**Figure 38.20**   Select export file type.

2. *Medium-res AVS.*   This provides a standard Intel DVI file at medium picture quality and half the data rate of "high-res" (approximately 300 kbytes per second). If the target player system has an unfragmented IDE or fast MFM disk, this is a good choice. You may also have to configure your operating system with larger buffers/files and other adjustments to allow fast video playback.

3. *Low-res AVS.*   This provides a standard Intel DVI file at low picture quality and data rate (120 kbytes per second). If your target system will use a CD-ROM or slow hard disk, or your operating system cannot be configured for fast video playback, this is your best option.

4. *Video for Windows (AVI file).*   This provides a direct output to Microsoft's Video for Windows file using Intel's Indeo algorithm video file and "WAV" audio file formats. This is not an AVS file, and its data rate is low enough to allow playback of files from slow hard disks and CD-ROMs in most systems.

5. *Quicktime (MOV File).*   This provides a direct output to Apple's Quicktime file. It is used on the Mac platform, and its data rate is low enough to allow playback of files from slow hard disks and CD-ROMs in most systems.

A sixth option, WAV, is for audio only. All six options actually are simplified presettings of many parameters that can be adjusted using the "Advanced Options" icon at the bottom of the "Select Export File Type" window. The Advanced Options allow you to "tweek" the quality of the video and audio to bring it in line with the target-player platform you are using.

Note that it is not possible to increase the resolution of the exported file beyond what was used during capture. However, you can *decrease* it. Therefore, be sure to capture the video at or above the highest resolution you will want to export.

## Conclusion

Software capture/edit tools make the production of video programs much easier and faster than it is when you are using conventional videotape-editing methods. They also tend to offer you greater creative freedom, since making edits does not require the recording or copying of material. This encourages that creative experimentation so often needed to tell a compelling, interesting story.

Because the programs created with these tools can be viewed on many platforms—including PCs without special video hardware—the potential audience for your program includes almost anyone with a PC.

# Advanced Topics

# Communications for Multimedia

**Glenn Becker**

**Vince Walisko**

## Introduction

In order to facilitate later discussions about protocols and standards, we first will briefly review the seven communications protocol layers as described by the International Standards Organization/Open Systems Interconnect (ISO/OSI), as shown in Fig. 39.1.

The *application* layer defines the task being performed from the user's perspective. Examples include e-mail, computer conferencing, and computer-based training.

The *presentation* layer handles any conversions required to prepare files for presentation to the user, including controls of the desktop PC to play an audio file or display an image file. The *session* layer includes access control and addressing of the information being delivered. Access control can be

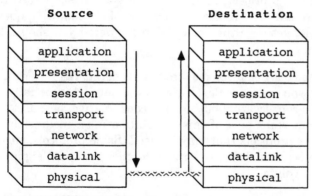

**Figure 39.1** ISO protocol layers.

implemented by password or by keys built into the application software. Addressing is an important feature when it comes to delivering information to the appropriate place and not using up excess communications capacity and storage for files.

The *transport* layer is responsible for end-to-end file delivery. This layer includes protocols for detecting and correcting errors that occur during file transfer. The *network* layer is responsible for delivering packets of information that will be assembled into files in the transport layer. Routers operate at the network level to determine which *path* can be used to access the destination computer. Routers also can offer congestion control, which should improve overall system performance. CCITT X.25 is one common example of a network layer protocol.

The *data-link* layer defines the frames of data traveling through a network, as well as correction and retransmission schemes. The frame format may include CRC checks and error-correction codes, which allow the link to appear virtually error-free to the user. LAN protocols (Ethernet and Token Ring) and passive bridges are implementations of data-link protocols.

The *physical* layer defines how unstructured binary digits (bits) travel over the physical media between machines. Physical-layer protocols define pin configurations for cables and voltage levels. Examples include EIA RS-232-C, RS-449, and CCITT V.24.

Standardized protocols have allowed many communications systems vendors to respond to the demand for network interoperability. By building a protocol convertor from RS-422 to V.35 (both physical-layer protocols), two otherwise incompatible systems can be connected. Protocol converters also can be built at the data-link and the network layers. Network interoperability has been a hot topic of late, since it allows users on one network to connect to a different one without having to replace one of the networks.

In this chapter we will concentrate on the physical media available for high-speed communication. For this reason most of the discussion will involve only the physical and the data-link layers.

### Determining requirements

When you are sizing a project, remember that some basic parameters define the goals and ultimately drive the solution. All of the following questions are insultingly simple, yet once they have been answered you should have your network solution.

**What is the required daily data volume through the network?**    Determine the volume of data that you expect to flow through the network on a daily basis. The goal here is to be conservative but not too conservative, because "bandwidth is money." An important part of this calculation must include the data-link and network layer protocols that may be used. Some protocols, such as packet-switching protocols or forward error correction, can add significant overhead to your data volume.

**How fast must the data arrive at the intended destination?**  The delay from the moment a unit of data is submitted to a network for delivery to that when it arrives at the destination is referred to as *latency*. Latency at the transport layer is how long the network takes to deliver a file. If your application requires the timely delivery of data such as news, stock market information, or an address from the company chairman, then latency must be reduced by increasing bandwidth and/or compression, or decreasing overhead. Multimedia applications that depend on real-time delivery of digital audio and video have very strict throughput requirements.

**How much of the data received by each destination actually is used by that site?**  This question does not directly relate to the network but addresses the storage-capacity requirements and the location of the data storage. For some applications it is more efficient to store the data at a central hub and then distribute it over a network on demand. Other applications require local storage of the data at each destination. In most cases data that is used regularly is stored locally for quick retrieval, whereas infrequently used data is stored centrally and transmitted only on demand.

**What percentage of the total data goes to many as opposed to only a few destinations?**  The answer to this question will determine whether the communications network should be point-to-point or point-to-multipoint (broadcast). If information needs to be sent to several hundred sites or more, and if more than half of the information is required by all sites, then a satellite broadcast solution usually is best. If the number of destinations or the amount of data common to all sites is low, then point-to-point transmission usually is best.

**Is the data transmission bursty and irregular, or is it steady throughout the day?**  Steady data transmission calls for full-time access to a data path. In some cases bursty data transmission is best served by networks that offer part-time usage fees or dial up access on an "as-needed" basis. If you are sending data more than 20 to 30 percent of the day, then full-time access generally is warranted. If you are sending data less than 20 percent of the time, then a part-time communications path may be more cost-effective. Many existing networks offer part-time access at reduced rates for overnight traffic, if your application lends itself to such a schedule.

**Are the destination sites friendly or hostile?**  One of the most important issues to address when designing a new network is the environment of the communications equipment at the remote sites. If this remote equipment is located in a friendly environment, where technical assistance is available and children with ice cream cones are not allowed, then installing equipment that requires regular maintenance is not a problem. If it is to be located in a hostile environment, however, the installed equipment must require little or no on-site maintenance and must be packaged in such a way as to discourage tampering and intrusive ice cream cones.

**Is the data flow one-way or two-way?**   This question is fundamental, since most communications paths are by nature either one-way or two-way. In many applications with two-way data flow, the data volumes are not symmetrical (far more data is flowing one way than the other). For such applications, two separate paths sometimes are the best solution. Consider as an example networks that broadcast many megabytes of data over satellite each day, then retrieve small data transactions from the remote sites via dial-up phone lines.

**Can you piggyback on an existing network that has excess capacity?**   Sometimes this question alone will determine which network your application will use. Often it's hard to beat free or very inexpensive access to an existing data path. Data transmission in the VBI (discussed later) of a video signal does not change the cost of sending the video signal. Remember, however, that additional equipment still is required to insert data into the VBI and retrieve it again.

**What level of security do we need?**   Requirements for data security may determine whether you use public data networks or private ones. If security is important, current encryption technology offers sufficient protection for the vast majority of applications.

**How geographically dispersed are the remote sites?**   Terrestrial communication links generally charge by distance, whereas satellite links are indifferent to distances within the "footprint" of a single satellite. The axiom of network implementation is "keep it simple." The fewer things there are to break, the better. Networks cost money to install, and more money to operate. The correct network solution must be a winner in both of those areas.

## Current Technology Options

Most of the current technology and standards for communications existed before the advent of desktop multimedia. Yet some of these technologies, such as the CD-ROM, are much more successful now due to multimedia.

### Point-to-point delivery

**CD-ROM.**   A great deal of the multimedia being delivered today is being delivered on CD-ROM. CD-ROMs have proven themselves to be a successful way to distribute multimedia reference materials such as encyclopedias, atlases, historical information, and computer-based training (see Fig. 39.2).

A single CD-ROM can hold up to 660 Mbytes of digitized audio, images, text, video, and program information. CD-ROMs can be copied in large quantities for less than $2 each. The cost-versus-data-capacity ratio for CD-ROMs makes them very attractive to publishers of reference materials, since they are much less expensive to produce than books.

- high data capacity at 660 Mbytes
- extremely low manufacturing costs in quantity
- long lifetime if handled properly

- slow data transfer rates compared to hard disks
- cannot be updated with new information

- access requires a CD-ROM drive
- each CD-ROM is priced based on the value of the information it contains

**Figure 39.2**   CD-ROM.

- generally available / easy to access
- interface equipment is inexpensive
- inexpensive

- slow data transfer rates
- long time required to establish connection

- charges for telephone usage are based on time of day, calling distance, calling region, and the length of the call

**Figure 39.3**   Dial-up analog telephone service.

Unlike hard disks, CD-ROMs cannot be updated with new information. For this reason they work well for archiving reference materials but not for applications that require frequent updates.

One limitation CD-ROMs have imposed on multimedia applications is a data-transfer rate of 150 Kbps (kilobytes per second). This data-transfer rate originated as the "Red Book" specification. However, applications started to use high-resolution color images and full-motion video. These new demands prompted CD-ROM manufacturers to start to build CD-ROM players that operate at two and four times the original data rate.

**Dial-up analog telephone service.**   Using modems to send and receive data over basic dial-up telephone lines is now commonplace in both the office and the home (see Fig. 39.3). Typical baud (bits per second) rates range from 1200 to 9600 and even 14,400.

While the available data rates do not offer much capacity for the delivery of large quantities of multimedia, dial-up service represents an inexpensive path for the sending of data updates and the retrieval of status information from remote sites.

· high data transfer rates available
· extremely low error rate

· may require several weeks to install
· cannot be re-routed if a service break occurs
  like a switched virtual link would

· fixed monthly access fee
· must buy/lease interface equipment

**Figure 39.4**   Leased-line telephone service.

**TABLE 39.1   Major Grades of Leased Lines**

| Service | Number of voice channels | Baud rate in Mbps |
|---|---|---|
| T-1 or DS-1 | 24 | 1.544 |
| T-2 or DS-2 | 96 | 6.312 |
| T-3 or DS-3 | 672 | 44.736 |
| T-4 or DS-4 | 4032 | 274.176 |

New technologies will help to keep dial-up telephone service in the multi-media ballpark. Two such technologies are CCITT V.fast and videophones. The CCITT standard V.fast will offer data-transfer rates of 28,800 baud (or 28.8 kbps) over voice-grade lines.

Videophone standards, such as M-VTS which synchronizes video and audio, will make it possible for multimedia presentations to be sent directly to your telephone.

**Leased-line telephone service.**   Dedicated high-capacity data lines may be leased from telephone-service providers. Table 39.1 shows the major grades of service and their associated data rates. T-# services typically are for short distances of 200 miles or less. DS-# services support longer distances by using the main communications paths built by the phone companies for interstate-call routing (see Fig. 39.4).

Fractional T-1 services are extremely popular for point-to-point communications and also to transfer data from a source to a satellite uplink facility. Fractional T-1 services generally are sold in increments of 56 kbps.

Some packet-switching network vendors have services that create permanent virtual circuits using the frame-relay protocol. These permanent virtual circuits are the main competition for fractional T-1.

| | |
|---|---|
| 👍 | • good combination of high data rate and "pay as you go" service<br>• very fast connection after dial |
| 👎 | • not available in many areas of the US<br>• not much penetration in areas where it is available |
| $ | • usage charged by length of connection, distance of call, regions of call, and bandwidth used |

**Figure 39.5**  ISDN.

**Integrated services digital network (ISDN).**   Currently, the infrastructure of our telephone system uses digital circuits for call-transmission and number-switching. ISDN is the underlying technology that supports such features as automatic caller identification. Only the "last mile" to your home or desktop is analog. As the ISDN continues to roll out, digital service will be available directly from your telephone.

ISDN offers basic-rate service (BRI) and primary-rate service (PRI). Basic-rate service includes two 64-kbps B channels and one 16-kbps D channel. The B channels are used for data transfer, either 64-kbps two-way transmission or 128-kbps one-way. The D channel is used for switching and flow-control information. Primary-rate service consists of 23 64-kbps B channels and 1 64-kbps D channel. If you combine all of these numbers you will see that prima-ry-rate service actually is a T-1 circuit. PRI commonly is used for LAN-bridging, since it offers far more throughput than analog dial-up service.

Broadcast delivery via ISDN has been discussed by some as possibly being desirable for multimedia applications, but no current implementation is available (see Fig. 39.5).

### Point-to-multipoint delivery

In cases where large volumes of information need to be delivered to many locations, the techniques employed are quite different from those used for point-to-point delivery. The differences are analogous to those between a letter and a newspaper. Just as it is more efficient to put a general advertisement in a newspaper than to do direct-mail advertising to everyone, so too it is more efficient to do a data broadcast over satellite than repeated point-to-point transfers to a large number of remote sites.

The basic law of satellite communications is that the more money you spend on the ground the less will have to be spent in space, and vice versa. Costs on the ground include the terminal equipment, which includes the antenna, a low-noise-block down converter (LNB). Costs in space are deter-mined by how much of the available spectrum your signal will consume. For

**Figure 39.6**   Satellite communications.

**Figure 39.7**   C-Band.

large numbers of users, spending less on each terminal and more on the space segment (which is divided by all the users in figuring a per-site cost) is more cost-effective. However, a large space segment is expensive, and many receivers are required to justify the expense (see Fig. 39.6).

The satellite section is broken up into the commonly used frequencies C-Band and Ku-Band, and then different modulation and control techniques for one-way and two-way communications. Any given system can work with a combination of these alternatives (for example, one-way C-Band).

### Operating frequencies

**C-Band.**   C-Band was the first frequency band used for commercial satellite communications on a large scale (see Fig. 39.7). C-Band employs uplink frequencies from 5.925 to 6.425 GHz, and downlink frequencies from 3.7 to 4.2 GHz. C-Band antennas range in size from 2 to 3 meters.

**Ku-Band.**   Ku-Band has come into widespread use just in the last 10 to 15 years (see Fig. 39.8). Ku-Band uplinks from 14.0 to 14.5 GHz, while it downlinks from 11.7 to 12.2 GHz. Ku-Band antennas range in size from 0.5 to 2 meters.

### Modulation techniques

**Spread spectrum.**   Spread spectrum simulates natural noise by pseudo-randomly jumping the carrier frequency around. This allows for very good signal

• antennas are small (2 meters or less) for easier shipping and installation

• antenna must be precisely manufactured
• Ku-Band frequencies are attenuated by rain, snow, and water vapor (rain fade)

Figure 39.8   Ku-Band.

• extremely small antennas
• impervious to interference
• coding scheme makes encryption inherent

• extremely large amount of space segment required in comparison to other techniques
• receiver does not lock into signal instantly

• $500–1,000 per receive site for installation
• monthly space segment costs

Figure 39.9   Spread spectrum.

• requires relatively little satellite power for the bandwidth
• low cost receivers

• data must be delivered to a common hub to be combined with other data for aggregate uplink
• changing data rate requires changing hardware

• $400–900 for receive site equipment
• monthly fee for space segment

Figure 39.10   FM/FM.

discrimination in low carrier-to-noise-ratio situations. When other technologies were more expensive, it was a good approach to distribution to large universes of users (tens of thousands). See Fig. 39.9.

**Frequency modulated on frequency modulated (FM/FM).**   The trade names for FM/FM are "FM on FM" or FM Squared. FM/FM is a series of frequency-division-multiplexed phase-modulated signals that are then collectively phase-modulated. This allows the rf high-frequency components of the satellite receiver to handle a large signal, and only after demodulation to lower frequencies are the smaller signals discriminated (see Fig. 39.10).

**Figure 39.11**   TDMA SCPC.

**Figure 39.12**   FM above video.

**Time division multiple-access, single channel per carrier (TDMA SCPC).**   The trade name for TDMA SCPC is FM Cubed. Like FM/FM, TDMA SCPC is a method of aggregating together a number of digital data signals. In this case the multiplexing is a matter of time division rather than frequency. The result is the same, in that the receiver can look at a big signal that is easier and less expensive to discriminate (Fig. 39.11).

**FM above video.**   Same as FM/FM, except that in this case data is frequency-division-multiplexed with video and other subcarriers. This is a popular method for companies that already have video transmission capabilities, since the data travels along with the video for free (Fig. 39.12).

**Single channel per carrier (SCPC).**   SCPC is a technique that can be used for point-to-point or point-to-multipoint transmission. A single data signal modulates a single rf carrier, which is relayed by a satellite (Fig. 39.13).

## Flow control for two-way VSAT networks

Two-way VSAT (very-small-aperture terminal) networks are based on a single hub site that controls the access of a large number of remote VSAT sites

- uplink to satellite can be from anywhere within range of the satellite
- data rate and number of channels are easy to change with hardware

- higher equipment costs than other alternatives
- sophisticated equipment at customer sites requires occasional maintenance

- $5,000-10,000 per site for equipment
- monthly fee for space segment

**Figure 39.13**  Single channel per carrier.

- smaller antenna size required
- good for central database accesses

- long response times for site-to-site messages
- network is vulnerable if central site goes down, backup hub is expensive

- $5,000-10,000 per site for equipment
- monthly access fee

**Figure 39.14**  Star network.

via channels in the space segment. The channels support data messages from a remote site to the hub, the hub to a remote site, and in some cases remote site to remote site. Various protocols are used to determine which site can "talk" at any given time and for how long.

**Star network.**   The star network is the most common type of control protocol, one in which the sites and the hub can "talk to each other." If a message is addressed from one site to another, it must go through the hub on the way (Fig. 39.14).

**Mesh network.**   A mesh network allows all sites to "talk" to all other sites directly (Fig. 39.15).

## Access to the Home Market

### Telephone

The most common channel of digital data communications into the home today is over voice-grade telephone lines. The current population of personal computer users is accustomed to using modems to access bulletin-board ser-

**Figure 39.15**    Mesh network.

**Figure 39.16**    Vertical blanking vertical.

vices and to send files between computers. The low data rates available on dial-up voice-grade lines make this communications method inefficient for most multimedia applications.

### Vertical blanking interval (VBI)

The vertical blanking interval is a period in a TV signal during which the raster beam travels from the bottom of the screen back up to the top of the screen. Inserting data in the VBI is a way of putting data in the unused space on a television signal, between the end of one frame and the beginning of the next. A decoder box can be attached to the TV antenna or cable. Current technology limits data throughput to 9600 baud per VBI line. Most commercially available VBI equipment handles only one VBI line. Some new systems support two lines and offer throughput of 19,200 baud (Fig. 39.16).

### TV Cable used for digital data delivery

This is an approach to using existing Cable TV channels to deliver data into the home. A decoder is connected to the cable just as a TV would be. Tests of this technology are beginning to appear across the United States. Services

· relatively high data rates are possible
· no new connection to the home is needed

· cable TV must be available and installed
· consumes channel capacity on cable which
  was used for program delivery

· monthly access and usage fees
· $100-500 per home for equipment

**Figure 39.17**  TV cable for digital-data delivery.

· inexpensive to purchase
· allows sharing of expensive resources
· supports high data rates directly to the desktop

· high maintenance requirements
· running new cabling in existing offices can
  be expensive

· purchase/lease a LAN server, cabling,
  LAN software, and network interface cards
  for each client computer
· large LANs require support staff

**Figure 39.18**  LANs.

that allow subscribers to connect to their cable, such as a LAN or a one-way data receiver, soon will be available (Fig. 39.17).

## Access to the Desktop Market

All of the communications options available to the home also are available to the office, with the exception of TV cable. Cable has not penetrated office buildings to the same extent as it has the home market.

### Local-area networks (LANs)

LANs have become commonplace in most office environments (Fig. 39.18). They offer data-transfer rates of from 4 to 16 Mbps. LANs allow many desktop users to share expensive resources such as large storage devices and laser printers.

The most common data-link protocol for LANs is Ethernet. Virtually all Ethernet implementations run at 10 Mbps. A new version called Fast Ethernet, which runs at 100 Mbps, soon will be available. On an Ethernet LAN, each system is responsible for controlling its dialogue with the LAN. If a computer needs to send information over the LAN, it checks the LAN for data traffic. If there is no current data flow, it will try to send its information. If two or more systems start to send at the same time, a collision occurs and each sending computer must stop sending and retry at a later time. The control protocol that manages the interface to the LAN is called Carrier Sense Multiple Access/Collision Detection (CSMA/CD).

The second most popular data-link protocol for LANs is called Token Ring. Token Ring avoids the collision problem by having one system, and one system only, act as the *active monitor* (*AM*). A token is passed around the network until it arrives at a system with something to send; this system starts to send and continues to send until the token-holding time limit is up, at which time the token is passed on. The system with the token is the active monitor.

The bandwidth requirements imposed on current LANs by multimedia applications often cause performance problems. Current protocols were not designed to deliver the sustained data throughput required for driving real-time digital-audio and -video presentations. New schemes for handling multimedia applications are in the works for both Ethernet and Token Ring.

### Fiber distributed data interface (FDDI)

FDDI, which offers transfer speeds of 100 Mbps, is used primarily to interconnect LANs in a metropolitan area network (MAN) or a wide area network (WAN). Copper distributed data interface (CDDI) uses the same standards as FDDI to deliver 100-Mbps traffic over copper wiring, but only for short distances (within an office). See Fig. 39.19.

### Switched multimegabit data service (SMDS)

SMDS is supplied by the phone companies and gives users with bursty high-bandwidth requirements access to DS-1 (1.544-Mbps) through DS-3 (45-Mbps) levels of service.

SMDS offers dynamic bandwidth allocation, which is ideal for delivering large multimedia files. SMDS, however, is not good for delivery of real-time data. Since the data is packetized and switched through routers, it may not

| · extremely high data rates available<br>· wide area network support |
| --- |

| · limited distance of 2 kilometers<br>· not available yet in most places |

| · monthly access fees<br>· purchase/lease gateway equipment for access |

**Figure 39.19**   FDDI.

- extremely high data rates available
- dynamic bandwidth allocation for bursty data
- routers switch data flow to avoid congested areas

- only available in a few areas of the US

- monthly access and usage fees
- purchase/lease gateway equipment the access service

**Figure 39.20** Switched multimegabit data service.

arrive in the same order it was sent, and there may be delays between the delivery of consecutive packets (Fig. 39.20).

## Emerging Technology

### Channel-modulated video delivered over existing LAN wiring

One innovative approach to delivering video over existing LAN wiring is to channel-modulate the video onto the LAN cable, just as the many channels of TV come into your home on a single cable. To leave room for FDDI bandwidth, most of these channel-modulation schemes use the frequency space from 300 to 450 MHz. Frequencies below 300 MHz are reserved for normal LAN and FDDI traffic, while frequencies above 450 MHz suffer severe attenuation.

Modulating video onto a LAN requires special equipment that can take a baseband video source and channel-modulate it onto the LAN, and then a demodulator to convert the video back to baseband at each desktop.

The pricing of this equipment follows the usual model for such systems, with the modulator costing several thousand dollars and the demodulator at each desktop costing only a couple of hundred dollars.

### Ka-Band frequency over satellite

Ka-Band is a higher-frequency band than Ku-Band or C-Band. Ku-Band uplinks from 27.5 to 31.0 GHz, and downlinks from 17.7 to 21.2 GHz. Today the Ka-Band spectrum is largely unused, but as applications for broadcasting more digital data arise, this space will be called into use.

Ka-Band offers the advantage of having very small receiver antennas (around half a meter in diameter), but it suffers more severely than Ku-Band from rain fade.

### High-definition television (HDTV)

Now that the standards are converging to make it possible for HDTV to be entirely digital, the possibility of inserting more data in the video and audio signal exists. Current HDTV plans call for delivery via tagged digital data packets. Each packet's tag describes the data contained in the packet. This tagging scheme allows some amount of data to travel along with the packets of digital video and audio.

### Asynchronous transfer mode (ATM)

In the communications world, ATM is the hottest thing since sliced bread. The infrastructure for ATM is only beginning to be built, but soon it will be competing with FDDI and other WAN interconnection networks. At first ATM will be a bit more expensive than networks already in place, but it does offer some useful advantages.

ATM packets will be of fixed size, which makes for fast hardware switching. These fast switches will compare favorably with X.25 and frame-relay switches. ATM also offers scalable "on-demand" bandwidth for bursty data-delivery applications.

Initial ATM usage will be through X.25 or frame-relay interfaces that emulate existing communications links and LAN interconnections for compatibility.

## Conclusions

When designing any network, it is important that you size the requirements early in the process. This information will focus your attention on those technologies that can do the job. You also must unit-test the transmission of your data over the prospective network, so as to get real statistics on things such as error rates, overhead, and net data throughput. Problems are inevitable in any integration project. The key to success is to find the problems early, before they can become "showstoppers."

But above all else: "Keep it simple"!

## Glossary of Acronyms and Abbreviations

**ATM**   Asynchronous transfer mode

**C/No**   Carrier-to-noise ratio; a measure of signal strength

**CCIR**   International Radio Consulting Committee (wireless and spectrum usage)

**CCITT**   International Telegraph and Telephone Consulting Committee

**CDDI**   Copper distributed-data interface

**CSMA/CD**   Carrier Sense Multiple Access/Collision Detection

**Ethernet**   IEEE 802.3 (uses CSMA/CD)

**FDDI**   Fiber distributed-data interface

**FM/FM**   Frequency-modulated, multiplexed, and frequency-modulated again

**GHz**   Gigahertz (billion cycles per second)

**IEC**   International Electrotechnical Committee

**ISO**   International Standards Organization

**ISDN**   Integrated Services Digital Network

**ITV**   International Telecommunications Union (a treaty organization of the United Nations consisting of the CCITT and CCIR)

**kbps**   kilobits per second (data rate)

**Mbps**   Megabits per second (data rate)

**MHz**   Megahertz (million cycles per second)

**OSI**   Open systems interconnection

**PAD**   Packet assembler/disassembler

**SCPC**   Single channel per carrier satellite modulation scheme

**SNA**   Systems Network Architecture; IBM proprietary standard for communications and network interoperability

**SNMP**   Simple Network Management Protocol, from Internet; also SNMP2, which has many new features including security

**10BaseT**   Twisted pair LAN

**10Base2**   Thin-wire LAN

**10Base5**   Thick-wire LAN

**TVRO**   Television-receive-only satellite terminal

**TCP/IP**   Transmission Control Protocol and the Internet Protocol

**Token Ring**   IEEE 802.5 LAN communications protocol

**VSAT**   Very-small-aperture terminal (satellite antenna)

**X.25**   A standard DTE PAD to DCE PAD protocol

# Distributed Multimedia Requirements

**Les Dunaway**

## Requirements

If we are to understand the requirements for implementation of multimedia applications, we must first focus on the objects that make up the application. In one sense multimedia is "just computing." That is, data objects are created, manipulated, distributed, stored, displayed, and destroyed. Additionally, these data objects have behaviors and relationships that change with use.

In another sense, multimedia is "a new computing paradigm." That is, the data objects are very complex and very large, have many complex, dynamic relationships, and require special hardware and software for creation, manipulation, distribution, storage, and display. While creation, manipulation, distribution, storage, and display are the actions seen by the end user, the system functions that enable them make up a different list—a list containing some of the same words, just to enhance confusion.

## Storage

The requirements for storage of multimedia objects differ from those of conventional data processing in two ways: size and complexity. Some primitive systems are unable to deal with BLOBs (Binary Large OBjects); that is, they exhibit sensitivity to certain sequences of bits, often interpreting them as control sequences. When this behavior is encountered, one must decide whether to eliminate the primitive system (good idea!) or forgo the value of multimedia (bad idea!).

## Size

Multimedia objects tend to be quite large. The smallest is quite manageable: an icon, about 1000 bytes. Audio and video files are at the other extreme, running to a storage-capacity-limited number of giga or terabytes. An uncompressed motion-video stream amounts to width × height × colors × frames-per-second bits per second; for example, a clip intended for display on a VGA monitor with only 256 colors is 640*480*8*30 or 73,728,000 bits per second or 9,216,000 bytes per second. Going to 16 bits for color, generally considered the minimum number acceptable, gives a storage requirement of 18.4 Mbytes for each second of video.

Audio is digitized by sampling. Sampling must be done at some multiple of the highest frequency to be reproduced. For audio the calculation is samples/second × size of sample × channels. For "CD quality" the numbers are 44,000 × 16 × 2, or 176 kbytes per second. It's easy to see why the compression algorithm is critical to space management. There's an alphabet soup of them: MPEG, JPEG, P*64, PLV, RTV, FIF. Each of these has its tradeoffs of speed, space, cost, and quality. That's a discussion that could fill a book, and it would be out of date before the ink was dry. For our purposes here, lets just say that the state of the art is such that compressed motion video with sound needs about 150 kbytes of storage for each second of the clip.

## Complexity

The second issue within that of storage is complexity. The storage subsystem must deal with a level of complexity that is both high and ever-changing. A video clip is an example. While a video clip can be treated as a BLOB, many applications require that it be treated as a time-sequenced set of pictures (frames) with two or more associated time-sequenced samples of sound. Further, depending upon the compression algorithm, there may be relationships between frames. For example, with RTV or PLV a full frame is compressed and then a series of frames contain only the changed pixels (bits) from their predecessor. So now we have two kinds of frames, *reference* (*full*) and *difference*. A sequence of difference frames has meaning only in sequence, following the associated reference frame. Also, playing of a section of a clip must begin at a reference frame, so an index to reference frames is needed.

Another contributor to complexity is the need to change or replace the soundtrack. Now we must deal with synchronization.

The other aspect of complexity is that of the relationships between objects. A multimedia production is made up of clips, stills, graphics, animations, text, etc. in a defined order, with defined paths between certain objects. The same set of objects may be part of any number of productions. The same production will change, over time and with use. The storage subsystem of a multimedia system must support complex and changing relationships.

## Distribution

The requirements for distribution of multimedia objects are those of traditional data-processing objects plus some new ones. The reasons for distribution have been *moving* and *sharing:* moving data to the point of use, and sharing of data or resources. With multimedia there's a new reason for distribution: *interaction*. A geographically dispersed group of people can interact, via a distributed multimedia system, with a multimedia object. For example, a floor plan can be displayed on several screens. Each participant can "mark" it with a "crayon"; each of the others can see the marks and the "owner" of the plan can decide which marks become permanent.

### Management

The requirements for management of multimedia objects in a multimedia application are similar to the requirements in a conventional system.

The objects are large, numerous, and complex. Therefore while the actions needed are familiar, the tools and procedures must accommodate these new characteristics.

The users of multimedia systems often are less computer-literate than those of traditional systems. Further, they are less amenable to training—they don't know computers, and they don't want to learn! That's one value of multimedia systems: users don't have to become "computer jocks." A basic law of human nature applies here: the less a person understands about a system, the more he/she expects of it ("Hey, if I can't understand it, it must be able to do anything I want!"). This leads to new requirements in the management of the system's objects. They must be available, they must be reliable, and they must behave as expected.

### Access

Access has two aspects: control of who can access the database, and helping them to find what they need. Access control must be both unobtrusive and effective. It must allow the user to gain access to the database in an easy and reasonable manner. Interestingly, these are the requirements for *navigation* as well.

### Storage

As we look at storage in more detail, it will be useful to consider the different functions in a distributed database and to consider the storage needs of each of these. The three major functional component types in a distributed application are the network server, the LAN server, and the workstation, as shown in Fig. 40.1.

Clearly, in a small enterprise, the network server and the LAN server can be one and the same. Even in a large enterprise, the topology may not include a network server, as shown in Fig. 40.2.

### Network server

The network server is a "server server"; that is, it provides services to machines that are, in turn, servers to workstations. A network server can

**Figure 40.1**  Major functional components of a distributed database.

**Figure 40.2**  Topology without a network server.

range from a 386 up to a mainframe. The storage requirements for this class of machine range from very large to huge.

There are two kinds of storage that may be provided by a network server: *raw* and *application*. Raw storage is simply disk space made available to the client—sometimes this is called "virtual disk," since applications on the client see it as just another disk. It is used and "owned" by the client application. The server has no knowledge of the content.

Application storage is access to files belonging to applications, and it is seen by the server as files. This is sometimes necessary, but it is always dangerous. It creates logical dependencies throughout a network that are unknown to the owner of the application. Any change can bring down all of the dependent applications. A much better approach is message passing or transaction access of the data.

## LAN server

The LAN server is what we think of as a server. It is on a LAN with workstations, to which it provides services: disk space, processing, communications, etc. The storage requirements for a LAN server will vary, depending on the applications it supports and on whether it has a network server "above." Storage on a LAN server must be big enough and fast enough to support the local application needs plus the workspace requirements of downloaded temporary objects. Careful analysis and management of this space is necessary; analysis, to ensure an adequate minimum, and management, to ensure that temporary objects are temporary.

## Workstation

Storage on a multimedia workstation can range from zero (a "diskless" workstation) to many gigabytes. Most multimedia applications can be supported across the LAN—given a reasonable number of workstations per server, and a reasonable-capacity LAN. However, some multimedia applications have data rates greater than those available on the LAN. These must run in a download or a store-and-forward mode; that is, the objects must be copied onto the workstation's disk and displayed from there.

## Distribution

Distribution is the movement of objects across a network. Objects are moved for purposes of transport, sharing, and interaction. Each of these will be illustrated by the light of the following multimedia application situation, a common one.

An enterprise has a corporatewide multimedia application. A group at one location is responsible for the creation of new and the maintenance of existing objects: clips, graphics, stills, etc. Groups at other locations must incorporate these objects into presentations: courses, product descriptions, reference documents, etc.

## Transport

An object is created by the services group and then is sent to the end user. Simple, right? Well, not really. The services group probably cataloged the object based on a work request. The end user will catalog it based on the family of presentations into which it will be incorporated. So, somehow, the work request must be related to the finished object and to the project that caused its generation, and that relationship must be used to relate the new object to the project. The transport functions must support the transport of these relationships, as well as the object itself.

## Sharing

Sharing is "virtual transport." The object is made available at another location but is not moved. We can also say that a copy is sent. However, proper sharing ensures that the identity of the original is always maintained. In terms of our example, sharing occurs when the services group wants to show work in progress to the end user, for comments or approval. A copy of the object is moved to the end user(s). It is reviewed, annotated, and returned. The original is the updated version, based on the reviews and annotations. The "old original" and the copy may be retained as a record, in which case they become part of the descriptors of the "new original."

## Interaction

Interaction is the new requirement brought to the table by multimedia. If we take the review example above and make it real-time, we have interaction. The services group schedules an interactive conference. A copy of the object is displayed on each participant's workstation. Each person can annotate or even edit his/her copy. These changes can be viewed by all the others. The owner of the object then can choose which changes will become part of the new object.

## Management

Management of basic multimedia objects resembles the management of a library. Management of the more complex objects resembles the management of an assembly process. In the first case, we are concerned with managing a storehouse where new objects are added and old objects are examined and copied but never (or seldom) deleted or changed. In the second case, we are concerned with managing the creation of new assemblies from the objects in the storehouse. In addition to these two types of multimedia object management, there is a third. This comes into play when multimedia objects are used in a controlled environment, one where the results of their use can be measured or inferred. In this environment there must be a feedback of results, which leads to the creation of new presentations and new objects. This has been called "training management," since it was born from the use of multimedia in training applications. The name is now a misnomer, as many applications can be monitored for effect and value.

### Content management

Every multimedia object database has two logical parts: components, and assemblies. The components are stills, clips, sounds, graphics, and text. These must be managed to allow their location and retrieval so that they can be used in the creation of assemblies. It is important to note that when a multimedia component is made part of an assembly, it does not necessarily lose its identity. The same physical component may be part of any number of assemblies at the same time. If the database system requires that an object be copied into an assembly, there is an unlimited market for new disk files. Also, if the database system has such requirements, it probably is defective in other respects as well.

The assemblies are the instances of the use of the components. These can be called *presentations* or *books* or *experiences* or *games* or *courses* or…Whatever they are called, they must be managed. They must be managed in order to be located and used and, indeed, to become components in yet greater assemblies.

### Training management

*Training* or *effect* or *value* management (the terms are synonymous) is simply a feedback loop that generates change and addition requests to the processes that create both components and assemblies. In general, the change requests are directed to the process that creates assemblies, and that process may generate requests to the process that creates components. Management of multimedia objects requires facilities for cataloging, indexing, retrieving, checkout/-in, export, and import.

### Access

Access is the point of all this. Most of the rest exists simply to support access to the objects in the library. There are three parts: cataloging/indexing, access support, and access control.

### Cataloging/indexing

Cataloging is the process whereby the incoming objects are entered into the "card catalog." Using the familiar book library as an example, each book is cataloged and indexed by subject, author, ISBN number, Dewey decimal number, etc. The details of the catalog/index will vary with the intended use of the multimedia database (library). However, the architecture must support storage of the objects with a basic index, additional standard indices, and an unlimited ability to create new (permanent and temporary) indices "on the fly." This requirement is one of the main reasons why relational databases are not suitable for such applications. The root of this requirement is in the way libraries are used. First, no one can predict how users will want to access the library. Second, the users must be able to make a list of their "finds" as they work.

### Access control

Access control is driven by the user profile: the library card. Each user of the library is identified and authorized by the library card. In a traditional library, building the user profile is an ad hoc process—the librarian decides if a given user should be allowed to see or check out a given book. In a distributed multimedia library, that function requires the user profile.

### Access support

Access support also depends upon the user profile. However, rather than preventing a user from accessing any particular object, it assists the user in accessing all those for which he/she is authorized and masks the fact that he/she is not authorized for all. This last is important, because people tend to react negatively to being denied access. If the system is able to help them achieve their objective without mentioning that certain objects are off-limits, they have a better image of the library and of themselves.

Access support can take many forms. It is, generically, a personalization of the library that lets each user work in the way that is best for him/her. An obvious example is an audio output of the catalog for a blind person looking for Braille or recorded materials. Another is the differences in the interfaces presented to a child of six, a teenager, a teacher, and a businessperson. Further, as a given user may play different roles, the user can be given the ability to select from a set of interfaces.

### Conceptual Design

This section sketches the major subsystems of a distributed multimedia application. The system described could support a wide range of applications: product design/development, product support, training, marketing, and others.

Figure 40.3 shows the major subsystems of a distributed multimedia application. This diagram makes the assumption that the remote sites are not connected with "multimedia-capable" communications links: backbone LAN, T1 point-to-point, etc. Therefore, the distribution manager maintains databases at each remote site containing the objects required for that site. In a backboned system, the central site library could support all of the remote sites. This would cut down on complexity (having a distribution manager), but it also would decrease robustness by making all users dependent upon one server.

**Creation subsystem.**   This provides the user interface and functions used in the creation of multimedia objects. This subsystem is made up of three major components: user interface, drawing/paint tool(s), and the window/control tool(s).

**Figure 40.3**  Major subsystems of a distributed multimedia application.

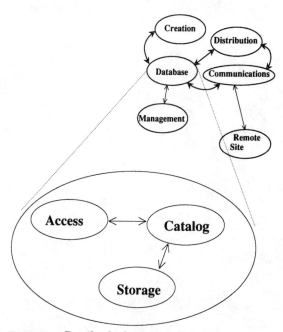

**Figure 40.4**  Details of a database system.

**Distribution subsystem.**  This provides the user interface and functions used in the distribution of multimedia objects to the remote-site servers.

**Database subsystem.**  This is detailed in Fig. 40.4.

**Communications subsystem.**  This provides the capability to connect to the remote-site servers.

**Management subsystem.**  This provides the facilities for managing the central library and, through the distribution subsystem, the remote-site libraries.
Figure 40.4 shows the details of the database system, including the access, catalog, and storage subsystems.

**Storage subsystem.**  This is the basic object database: the physical storage capabilities, recovery, transaction handling, and the object classes that make up the particular database.

**Catalog subsystem.**  This includes the librarian-user interface and the functions needed to support cataloging and indexing.

**Access subsystem.**  This includes the user interface and the functions needed to support access control, access support, and searching.

# Networks for Multimedia and Collaborative Computing

**Mike Evans**

## Why Collaborative Computing?

The multimedia applications developed in the early 1990s are only a small part of what can be achieved once a communication infrastructure supporting multimedia has been installed. As a result of the lack of such a communications infrastructure, multimedia applications thus far have not been sufficient to attract the mainstream user: the business user. Business users primarily are interested in communicating with other people, whether in the local office area, another part of the company, other companies, or in their homes.

While multimedia communication can be personal between two people, it is more likely that several people will be involved in the communication. Examples of group communication, or collaborative computing, include the sharing of work in progress such as a spreadsheet, chart, document, or photograph, so that all the members of the team can see and modify it.

Such collaborative applications can save businesses both time and money; are more effective, because the emotions of each person are visible to the entire team over both voice and video; and are more successful in team- and consensus-building and thereby in producing more effective results.

Business users prefer to have access to this type of communication directly from their own offices, and they want it to be available without the need for additional hardware on the desktop. If a desktop PC already is present, then users will be more comfortable using it rather than a combination of it and a telephone. Or, if a PC is not wanted on the desk, then the telephone can be upgraded to provide the capabilities required for collaborative computing.

## Passing Limitations

Before collaborative multimedia computing can become ubiquitous, a new multimedia-capable communications infrastructure is needed that can connect multimedia traffic from people in their local office area to people in other locations. This traffic can be real-time video and audio, and it can be data that is either synchronized or interactive with the video and audio traffic. The infrastructure must be inexpensive; it must be low-latency, to minimize irritating delays end-to-end; and it must allow full duplex traffic in both directions. A number of people in different locations should be able to access the infrastructure's services. Finally, the process of communication must appear as seamless as today's telephone call.

While desktop machines are capable of performing the functions involved in assembling multimedia communications, a number of new factors are emerging to surmount the technical and price hurdles involved in building a multimedia communications infrastructure.

### Video and audio components

Video cameras have dropped rapidly in price. Video-capture cards are available that will capture video from a camera in full color at 30 frames per second at SVGA quality. Most monitors now have SVGA screens with full color. In other words, from the video perspective, many of the components required for collaborative computing are now available at a reasonable cost.

Video compression/decompression is becoming increasingly cost-effective. Without video compression, most collaborative multimedia communications applications would not be possible.

Data rates (bandwidths) of 200 Mbits per second are required to provide uncompressed full-motion video at 30 frames per second for a single VGA screen in full color. Video compression can reduce this bandwidth requirement to about 1.5 Mbits per second, a rate that is compatible with both compact disks and with Ethernet local-area-network data rates. If the data is to be sent over the public network, the user can select smaller windows on the screen for collaborative applications, or the video-compression scheme can compress data even further.

Audio features already are being introduced on all multimedia PCs. Audio takes a small amount of bandwidth relative to video. Audio suitable for collaborative computing could use two 16-bit stereo channels, for a data rate of 256 kbits per second. This can be compressed by a factor of three if required. Voice can be compressed much more, down to data rates less than 10 kbits per second, although voice data rates are more typically compressed to 32 kbits per second. In many local area network-based multimedia applications, audio compression isn't necessary.

### LANs and Collaborative Multimedia Computing

Most business desktop PCs are now connected to a local-area network (LAN). LANs allow users to access files, e-mail, and other applications that are shared with other users in the same office. The most popular LAN today is Ethernet, with most new installations moving to 10BASE-T Ethernet. All versions of Ethernet transfer packets at a fixed data rate of 10 Mbits per second, as specified in the IEEE 802.3 standard.

With a maximum data rate of 10 Mbits per second, files the size of a megabyte take a few seconds to transfer. This transfer occurs in a number of bursts of data comprising many packets, whenever network traffic allows. Normal Ethernet, as with most standard networks including Token Ring and the first generation of FDDI (Fiber Distributed Data Interface), requires messages to wait until their is time available on the network. This type of packet transfer is unsuitable for the transfer of real-time audio and video information. Video traffic must appear smooth, and audio must be undistorted.

As multimedia applications—which require good-quality video and audio—become more widespread, the capabilities of older packet-based LANs are coming under scrutiny.

## Packet LANs and delays

Figure 41.1 shows the many applications that will need to use future LANs. Obviously, present-day applications still will need to be supported, such as accessing normal data files (probably from a file server) or new packet-based applications such as writing to printers over the LAN.

But LANs will need to support any multimedia PC for new multimedia applications. The simplest application is video playback of movies, where video files may be stored in a video server and the file transferred across the LAN to one or more PCs. Taking this example one stage further, the video

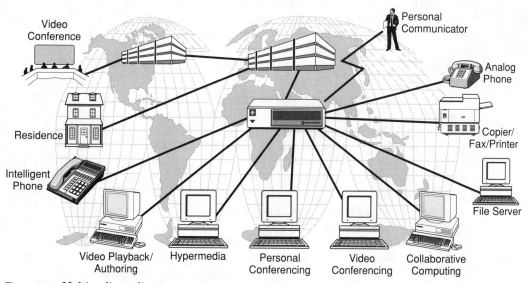

**Figure 41.1**  Multimedia applications requiring communications.

files may require interactivity, where the user can select any part of the video quickly, fast-forward or reverse, or zoom in, or freeze a frame.

Training is an example of an application that would require interactivity. An associated application is video authoring, where the user must be able to retrieve previously stored video files from the server and modify them locally, then transfer them back over the LAN to the server. These types of applications may function with existing LANs, but new applications including personal conferencing and collaborative videoconferencing have far more stringent requirements than can be supported over packet-based LANs.

Personal conferencing is two or more people talking to each other using video cameras attached to their PCs, with microphones and speakers for voice or audio. The camera can be moved to focus on any object. This kind of application is very demanding for a number of reasons: the video and audio need to be synchronized; the information being transferred is full duplex; and interactivity requires that there be minimal delays end-to-end in both directions. This kind of capability could be satisfied with an ISDN link, but the quality or window size would have to be sacrificed due to the limited bandwidth of basic-rate ISDN—128 kbits per second. The logical alternative is to use the LAN already attached to the PC, because of its higher data rate. Even so, picture quality deteriorates as more people join in the conversation, because the typical LAN was not designed for continuous traffic over long periods of time. And as more people become involved in the conference and more demands are put on the LAN, the more frustrating using the conference becomes.

### Connection path using packet LANs

Figure 41.2 shows a typical connection path for a videoconference between two multimedia PCs in different locations. The path might be through Ethernet, connected through a bridge or router to a backbone such as FDDI, and then through a router to a private or public network. There is likely to be a similar setup on the other end of the connection.

If the conference is intracompany, then there may be a T-1 link between the different company locations.

But a substantial amount of videoconferencing will take place between people in different companies. Intercompany connections will need to be made over the public network, usually using the X.25 protocol. X.25 is a protocol for conveying packet traffic between LANs at different locations. X.25 typically runs at 56 kbits per second over digital networks, or even lower over analog phone lines. Some X.25 links run over ISDN (Integrated Services Digital Network).

The problem with the protocols seen in Fig. 41.2 between the two multimedia PCs is that the delays experienced are all unpredictable—even inside each PC. Packet-based networks offer only limited control of timing. Each step has its own maximum and minimum timing parameters. Thus the first frame may experience minimal delays, the second maximal, the third minimal. For example, after the video-compression block in the right-hand PC has output the first frame into main memory, the PC then waits for the

**Figure 41.2**  Video and audio transported over a packet-based network.

Ethernet controller to add a header and then transmit the composite header and compressed video in packet format. During a two-way conference, the same Ethernet controller also is receiving incoming packets of compressed video from the other PC at random times, making the delays inside the PC even more unpredictable. The wait may be short for the first frame, if the Ethernet controller does not face delays or collisions on the Ethernet link to the hub.

At the hub, now carrying the video, there is a bridge or router to FDDI. This router may not be busy, so delays through it are minimal. Then, on the FDDI ring, the FDDI frame may instantly catch the token as it is going around the ring, so the frame can instantly be transferred to the X.25 router. Minimal delays occur in the router to the X.25 link. The packet then is sent over X.25 from the customer premises across the central offices or public exchanges of the telephone companies, and again delays may be minimal over the wide area. Likewise, the delays may be minimal back into and through the LAN at the other end. The next compressed video frame may experience maximal delays all along its route, from inside the PC through the network to the other PC. The next compressed video frame may again experience short delays all the way along. The effect of varying delays is jittery video and distorted audio, as Fig. 41.2 shows.

## Solutions for Collaborative Computing: A New Idiom

There are solutions that can help to minimize the problems of jittery video and distorted audio associated with packet-based LANs.

The first solution is to speed up the whole path. This may be possible with some of the components, by using the fastest PCs or routers, but there are no guarantees as to delays if the call goes outside the company.

The second approach is to install buffer memory into the PCs, to smooth out the variable delays. Obviously, all the PCs participating in the conference would need to have the additional memory, so again there is no guarantee that the person at the other end has installed buffer memory. Even *with* buffer memory, the maximum size of the buffer has to be larger than the worst-case delay between video frames. Such a solution will result in smooth video, but depending on the frame rate the video could arrive a full second after it was sent. While this is tolerable for one-way video such as lectures and presentations, most users find such delays intolerable for conferencing. Delays of a third of a second are considered the longest that users in a video-conference will tolerate.

A better solution that eliminates delays and jitter is a new idiom for LANs. The idiom (common in telephony, but almost unheard-of in data LANs), called *isochronous connectivity,* is to set up an end-to-end link between the two PCs at the beginning of the call, then send the video and audio down the now-established pipe in totally synchronized fashion in both directions simultaneously. Such a protocol results in minimum and maximum delays that are known, and that are much smaller than those a packet-based approach would yield. These delays are small enough that a buffer memory is not required, and the user will see smooth video, as shown in Fig. 41.3.

**Figure 41.3**  Smooth-quality video and audio over end-to-end isochronous.

## Isochronous services

There are many ways to explain isochronous services. The word *isochronous* is derived from the Greek: *iso* for *equal,* and *chronos* for *time.* But this definition hardly helps us to understand what isochronous services are.

A simple way to view the isochronous is to define it as *time-stamped data.* Isochronous services are defined by the worldwide standard 8-kHz clock used for telephone communications. In other words, an isochronous network must be able to synchronize and remain synchronized to an 8-kHz clock. The minimum number of bits per clock is 8, so isochronous data comes in multiples of 64 kbits per second.

The synchronization of isochronous services is extremely important, especially for conversations. Any delay beyond a few hundred milliseconds is sensed by the ear, and such a delay in communication is uncomfortable, at best.

## An isochronous multimedia call

Setting up an end-to-end link between two PCs at the beginning of a video or other multimedia call is known as *call setup.* The user originating the call places the call in a manner similar to today's telephone call, but through a PC. Typically the originating caller requests a certain bandwidth and the destination address. The bandwidth requirement is sent indirectly by requesting a particular screen video size and picture quality. The destination address is indirectly selected from a lookup table that links people to their phone number. This information is interpreted at each hub along the way and sent to the next hub on the path. At the far end, the receiving PC either accepts the call or does not. If the call is accepted, the message comes back to the originating PC and the two-way link is established.

This type of call setup cannot be accomplished with packet-based LANs. Call setup is part of the new isochronous LAN idiom that is a symbiosis of the best of both data and telephony solutions.

Fortunately, products supporting the new idiom became available in early 1994. Packet-based Ethernet is enhanced with isochronous Ethernet (isoENET), and FDDI with either the FDDI-II (also called isoFDDI) or the asynchronous-transfer-mode (ATM) LAN protocol. ISDN is used in the public network between customer premises. The new isochronous LANs can connect to either basic-rate ISDN (BRI), or primary-rate ISDN (PRI).

## Isochronous Ethernet

Isochronous Ethernet (isoENET™), developed by the National Semiconductor Corporation of Santa Clara, California, is a LAN standard that provides a combination of the packet-type services presently used for data LANs and the isochronous services required for collaborative multimedia computing.

Isochronous Ethernet, because it maintains packet services for normal Ethernet, is evolutionary, and allows people to build on the installed networks they already are using—it is estimated that in 1994 10BASE-T installations total 20 million. While maintaining packet-based services, it adds isochronous services for multimedia communications. National's isoENET proposal was unanimously accepted by the IEEE 802.9 standards committee in March 1993 as a working document.

An isoENET LAN offers 10-Mbit-per-second Ethernet data services, but adds an additional 96 64-kbit-per-second "B" channels for a total of 6.144 Mbits-per-second bandwidth for isochronous communications, plus a "D" channel for signaling and call setup. Each of these three paths—data, the B channels, and the D channel—is separate, both at the node (or PC) and at the hub. They are combined only on the 10BASE-T wiring, as shown in Fig. 41.4.

10BASE-T is hub-oriented and is wired, like normal office phone wiring, in a star configuration. 10BASE-T wiring uses two voice-grade unshielded twisted-pair wires of up to 100 meters in length from the desktop to the hub.

Isochronous Ethernet can use the same wiring as 10BASE-T, because it uses the same frequencies on the cable as does Ethernet. Ethernet appears as 10 Mbits per second to the user, but isoENET bandwidth is encoded with clock information that allows synchronization.

While all Ethernets use Manchester encoding, which doubles the data rate to deliver a maximum data rate of 20 Mbits per second on the wire, isoENET uses a more efficient coding scheme called *4B/5B*. This coding scheme yields a maximum data rate of 20.4 Mbits per second. This data rate is so close to the Ethernet standard that no wiring changes are required to meet FCC emission requirements. This is an important feature to MIS manager, because no rewiring is required to install isoENET if 10BASE-T is already in place.

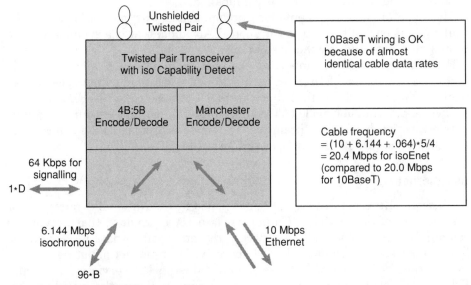

**Figure 41.4**  Isochronous Ethernet multiplexer.

Users who want to add isoENET will add an isoENET hub in the same wiring closet that already contains the LAN (and PBX) wiring. Users who do not wish to add isochronous services can still connect to the isoENET hub, and their Ethernet connections will operate normally. Any combination of isoENET and Ethernet PCs can be connected to the isoENET hub, allowing users to upgrade as they require isochronous services.

### Isochronous Ethernet data rates

The isochronous data rate used in isoENET was chosen for three reasons. First, to keep the total data speed traveling over the installed wires as close to 10BASE-T's data rate as possible. Second, because 6.144 Mbits per second is the lowest common denominator of North American and international telecommunication data rates. It is four times the T-1 data rate, 1.544 Mbits per second exclusive of the 8-kHz framing, and three times the E1 data rate of 2.048 Mbits per second. Third, because it is quite adequate for all SVGA- or VGA-based multimedia applications that incorporate video-compression technology. Most applications using video compression require less bandwidth.

### Call setup

The 6.144-Mbit-per-second data rate also is useful because it maps easily onto the standards of the public network, particularly on ISDN. ISDN uses a number of Bearer or "B" channels for information, and a "D" channel for signaling. The call setup to make the end-to-end link is done over the D channels, using the internationally accepted Q.931 call setup procedure, which includes the number of B channels required and the telephone address of the person on the receiving end. The message is passed by the PBX or some other hub to the local central office, and by each central office along the way to the person receiving the call. If the call is accepted, the signaling information is then sent back along the same path to the call originator. Basic-rate ISDN (BRI) allows the use of two B channels, while primary-rate ISDN (PRI) allows the use of from 1 to 23 B channels in North America and up to 30 B channels elsewhere.

Signaling down the D link in isoENET is very compatible with ISDN, making the translation between isoENET and ISDN quick and easy. This translation can be used when connecting either from an isoENET environment to the wide area or from an isoENET PC to an ISDN link in the same customer premises.

Once a call has been set up from one PC to another through the wide area, the video and audio are mapped into the same repeated B channels every 125 microseconds (8 kHz) for each segment along the way. This guarantees minimal delay across the wide-area network and also guarantees that the video and audio are synchronous with each other as well as with any data sent in the same manner. The data pipe is also full-duplex, ensuring that video and audio going in the opposite direction are guaranteed to have minimal delay. These features make the isoENET/ISDN connection ideal for conferencing and collaborative computing.

**Additional benefits**

Isochronous Ethernet, aside from being able to set up isochronous data pipes, offers other technical benefits that make it attractive as a multimedia communications network.

First, isochronous data is processed directly. In other words, the video and audio information can totally bypass the PC bus and memory, significantly reducing delays inside the PC.

Second, the iso paths in an isoENET hub connect separately into a circuit switch, by taking advantage of isoENET's switching protocol. This means not only that isoENET is a switching protocol, but that hubs can be designed so that the switch can be nonblocking, meaning that any PC on the link has isoENET's full 6.144-Mbit-per-second data rate dedicated to the link in both directions, independent of any other link. Thus each link can have its own 96 B channels. For example, in a 16-port hub designed with a nonblocking switch, the hub will have an aggregate bandwidth of almost 200 Mbits per second. The more ports, the higher the aggregate isochronous bandwidth, not counting the normal packet Ethernet (which also can be switched on a per-port basis).

The switching circuit in the hub allows any B channel on any link to be connected to any other B channel on any other link. These links don't even have to be within a particular LAN; the linking structure also can link from one hub to another, or to a PBX, or to an ISDN link—in other words, to any other isochronous link, including FDDI-II and isochronous ATM.

All of these features are ideal for conferencing and collaborative computing. They also significantly boost the quality and performance of other multimedia applications including one-way video playback, hypermedia, and video authoring. Therefore the applications shown in Fig. 41.1 could all utilize isoENET, as illustrated in Fig. 41.5. Any PC connected to isoENET can perform any of the different functions at different times, just as PCs do now.

Isochronous Ethernet offers smooth-quality synchronized video and audio for video playback, and it is highly interactive to any number of users on the LAN, each accessing his/her own dedicated video streams provided from a server. Video mail provided from a server can be downloaded smoothly. In video authoring, taking video shots normally requires a lot of bandwidth and local storage, but using video compression and isoENET allows the movie to be prepared at the PC, compressed, and instantly transferred directly to a server over isoENET without occupying much local storage or processor bandwidth. Similarly, for editing video, there is no need to store any video locally on the PC—it can instantly be retrieved using isoENET, then decompressed and displayed on the PC. Users can sift through video and audio hypermedia information, with optional associated data information, very interactively using B channels in both directions. The hypermedia information can be outside the user's premises and the quality and performance will still be good. For videoconferencing and collaborative computing, isoENET allows any number of users to talk to each other, including users outside the customer premises.

Isochronous Ethernet also allows any of the multimedia applications to take place at the same time on different PCs, as well as allowing normal LAN

**Figure 41.5** Isochronous Ethernet in a multimedia cluster.

traffic to take place independently. Iso. Ethernet costs only a little more than Ethernet, both in the PC and in the hub. This makes isoENET a powerful yet evolutionary protocol.

## FDDI-II

FDDI-II is an upward-compatible second generation of fiber distributed-data interface (FDDI). Both are ANSI X3T9.5 standards. FDDI-II, or isoFDDI, adds isochronous capabilities to existing FDDI in the form of a circuit-switched service. FDDI-II, similar to isoENET, can handle both packet and isochronous data. The only difference is that in isoENET the isochronous channels are added as additional bandwidth to basic Ethernet, whereas in FDDI, isochronous channels come out of FDDI's basic 100-Mbit-per-second bandwidth budget.

FDDI-II can operate either in Basic or in Hybrid mode. In Basic mode, the ring operates like an FDDI ring with packet service only. In Hybrid mode, the ring becomes a time-division-multiplexed-(TDM-) based switching matrix, which divides the bandwidth into 16 wideband channels (WBCs) of 6.144 Mbits per second each. Each WBC, as in isoENET, can be divided into 96 B channels.

### Uses for FDDI-II in collaborative computing

FDDI-II may be used as a local network where multimedia traffic is very intense.

Because its isochronous services are divided into B-channels, FDDI-II serves as an excellent backbone for isoENET's isochronous services. If FDDI-II is used in Hybrid mode, then the isochronous channels of isoENET can be directly mapped into the isochronous channels of FDDI-II, while Ethernet packet traffic can be bridged or routed to FDDI-II.

In this configuration, FDDI-II alone serves as the backbone for isoENET hubs, and links both Ethernet packet and iso traffic across all the hubs in the customer premises.

FDDI-II also can serve as a link to a file server for packet traffic using FDDI frames, and as a video server for traffic such as compressed stored movies for video playback applications using isochronous frames. FDDI-II's iso channels also can link through ISDN's primary-rate interface to either the PBX or to the central office for outside calls.

And as with isoENET, the division of isochronous capabilities into B channels or 6.144-Mbit-per-second wideband channels simplifies connection of isochronous communications to the public network.

FDDI-II also can be used purely for isochronous traffic, keeping Ethernet packet traffic separate and allowing the packet traffic to be repeated or bridged between hubs. In this configuration, a great deal more isochronous bandwidth is available for those users who require it.

### Asynchronous transfer mode (ATM)

Beginning in 1992, a number of LAN and switch developers have worked in a standards body called the ATM Forum to adapt the CCITT (Consultative Committee on International Telephone and Telegraph) broadband ISDN specification into an ATM LAN architecture.

ATM is a switch-based architecture that utilizes fixed-size cells with a payload of 48 bytes. The protocol is designed to give each connection as much bandwidth as it requires without having to contend with traffic on a shared medium.

Like isoENET and the Hybrid Mode of FDDI-II, it is a connection-oriented technology. Virtual circuits (data pipes) are established between communicating stations before data transfer begins. This enables ATM to be another viable backbone for isoENET.

The ATM Forum has defined four different physical layers for ATM. Three of these four layers specify synchronization to an 8-kHz clock to create isochronous ATM services.

Figure 41.6 shows clusters of isoENET-based PCs, each hooked to ATM by a fiber spoke with a data rate of 155 Mbits per second dedicated to each cluster. All of the spokes are connected to a central ATM switch hub, which could be a future PBX that handles telephone calls as well as isochronous data transfers. The central hub initially will connect to the wide area through an ISDN primary-rate interface, and by the year 2000 probably through an ATM-based broadband ISDN (B-ISDN). Video links can be set up from an isoENET-based PC through the ATM backbone.

Once an ATM switch has been installed, users who need more isochronous bandwidth than 6 Mbits per second can migrate to an ATM link that may be twisted-pair copper wiring if the link is less than 100 meters long. There are likely to be two bandwidth options available for these 100-meter links, 25

**Figure 41.6**  Multimedia-based LAN.

Mbits per second and 52 Mbits per second. It is unlikely that the majority of users will require more dedicated bandwidth to the desktop until the end of this century. Video-compression ratios will continue to increase, so as users demand HDTV-level video quality, there should be no volume desktop requirement for bandwidths greater than 52 Mbits per second for quite some time.

## Getting from Here to There

Isochronous services became available early in 1994 within a single office or company campus, allowing local collaborative computing. Getting a multimedia call off-campus, however, will require ISDN services.

ISDN is an ideal connection medium. Isochronous multimedia calls can be directly transferred over either primary-rate interface (designed for business users) or basic-rate interface (designed for home and small-company users). It is estimated that by the end of 1994 over 65 million users in North America may have the capability of a BRI connection. This does not mean that they will *have* the connection, only that if they then request it, it will be physically possible to deliver it. It also does not mean that if a connection is requested it will be made; that will depend on the regional Bell operating company in North America or on other countries' PTTs.

Nonetheless, as businesses begin to experience first-hand the productivity enhancement that collaborative computing makes possible within their own establishments, increasing pressure will be placed on telephone carriers to widen the installed base of ISDN.

# 42

# Networking Multimedia on Standard Data Networks

**Prem Uppaluru**

## Overview

The availability of cost-effective add-in hardware and software for integrating compressed digital video and audio into desktop computers, coupled with the introduction of video-networking products, is making networked multimedia applications possible for the first time. These trends are driving the development of new solutions for users sharing business-video information over networks, in applications that require the capturing, storing, retrieving, and playing of frequently updated video clips. Examples include

- Integrating business video into networked applications, such as on-line information services, video databases, and on-line help systems

- Delivering networked multimedia courseware to school classrooms from a central file server

- Updating point-of-information and point-of-transaction kiosks with new products or services from remote locations

- Delivering just-in-time training in shop-floor applications over the network, providing shared access to video data, and enabling rapid content updates in response to changing information

Digital video represents a new data type for computers and networks, requiring the management of real-time, high-bandwidth, continuous flows of data. The capture, storage, distribution, access, and presentation of digital video requires specialized system software capable of managing real-time continuous data streams within a network computing environment.

## Networking Video: Technical Challenges

Industry leaders, including Apple, IBM, Intel, and Microsoft, currently offer *stand-alone* digital-video products integrated into personal computers. These products consist of digital-video compression/decompression and capture/presentation hardware, as well as digital-video management-system software. All of these products depend on the interleaved storage representation of audio and video for the support of audio/video synchronization, and support networking of digital video by accessing video data through a file redirector. However, seeing as today's packet-based networks are not designed for motion video, performance over the network is limited by several fundamental technical challenges:

- *Real-time data over non-real-time networks.*   Computer data networks are designed for asynchronous transmission of data, but digital video and audio are inherently synchronous, real-time data types. Network delays that have little impact on text or graphical operations can cause audio and video data streams to lose synchronization and even to drop out critical information.

- *High data rates, limited network bandwidth.*   Full-motion compressed digital video requires relatively high data rates to transmit and display as digital information. Depending on the compression algorithm and the compression ratio used, a single video and audio data stream can range from several hundred kilobits per second to several megabits per second. In a standard 10-Mbits-per-second Ethernet or 10BaseT network, where only 6 to 7 Mbits per second is available for data transfers, the capacity to support motion-video data rates is limited—especially when typical applications require the network to support video playback from several clients at the same time.

- *Unpredictable availability of network bandwidth.*   As network usage and traffic varies, so does available bandwidth. When available bandwidth decreases below the minimum data rate required by a digital-video stream during playback, video and audio quality deteriorate sharply. Making video a practical data type in networked applications requires that video and audio be resilient to network bandwidth variations.

## Solving the Network Problem with Scalable Video

The key to solving this networking dilemma is support for scalable video—the capability to dynamically adapt video data rate to available network bandwidth, allowing motion video with synchronized audio to be sustained even under heavy load conditions.

The goal is to incorporate client-server session-management protocols and stream-transport protocols that support independent handling of audio and video over networks, and rate control techniques for digital video that prioritize audio over video and support adaptive load-balancing in standard local-area networks.

## Audio/video stream separation

A main feature of scalability is the separation of audio and video into two distinct streams early after retrieval from storage. The software retrieves a file, parses the information according to the specified file format, and dynamically separates the audio and video information into its internal representation. The separation and independent handling of audio and video streams, coupled with the human perceptual tolerance for variation in quality and frame rate in the presentation of video, allow *dynamic* scaling of video and audio over the network.

Typically, people perceive motion when video presentation rates exceed 15 frames per second. Moreover, instantaneous smooth variations in video presentation rates are practically unnoticeable. However, human aural perception is quite intolerant of variations in the presentation quality or rate. Typically, humans perceive noise when presentation rates are not adhered to, and clicks when brief periods of silence are injected into audio streams. Scalable video takes advantage of these inherent human perceptual constraints and prioritizes audio transmission and delivery over video. This prioritization of audio over video extends over the entire data flow of audio and video streams, starting from their retrieval from storage containers and ending up with their presentation.

By prioritizing the retrieval, transmission, decompression, and presentation of audio over video within a network computing environment, and by relying on their resynchronization before presentation, scalable video optimally can utilize the available computing, compression, and network resources while maintaining an acceptable presentation of audio and video.

## Adaptive load-balancing

Server software must manage the flow of video and audio data to requesting clients, and monitor the rate of delivery to the client. As the delivery rate slows under network load condition, impacting video and audio quality, the server smoothly slows the rate at which it sends data, allowing the client to "catch up" with the data stream without causing irritating breaks in video and audio quality. When the data bottleneck clears, the server responds by increasing the data rate on the video stream, resulting in improved video quality at the client's end.

The system administrator must be able to configure the maximum number of users allowable at one time, as well as the maximum data rate available to each client on the network. This allows the administrator a large degree of control over how much of the total network bandwidth will be consumed by video and audio data streams.

To avoid situations where data cannot make it to the client in time for synchronized playback, video and audio must be processed in a "read-ahead" manner, preparing the data for quick transmission across the network. It also applies adaptive rate-control algorithms that selectively drop video data when it is clear the entire data stream cannot be transmitted.

## Configuring Networks for Multimedia

The number of users who can simultaneously play video segments over the network is based on many factors, including the speed of the server's CPU, network card, and fixed disk, as well as the network topology. Multiple Ethernet or Token Ring segments may be connected to a single file server to increase the number of video users per server.

The following lists define optimal system requirements for the network, server, and clients to ensure acceptable video/audio playback quality on clients. The requirements are based on the assumption that approximately 6 multimedia clients playing stored files back at 1.2 Mbits per second (Mbps) can be supported per Ethernet network segment. Therefore, if users are playing back at rates lower than 1.2 Mbps, more clients can be supported.

Network requirements

For 5 users: One Ethernet segment on one or more repeaters, or one token ring

For 10 users: Two Ethernet segments on two or more repeaters, or one token ring

For 25 users: Four Ethernet segments on four or more repeaters, or three token rings

Server requirements

Software

NetWare Version 3.11 or 4.0.

Hardware

**For 5 users.**  You can install Fluent's FluentLinks®, a NetWare®-loadable module (NLM), on your standard network server and support five audio/video clients with no hardware changes. However, for optimal performance, the recommended configuration for a server PC supporting five users on one Ethernet segment or Token Ring is

- 386 EISA or MCA personal computer with a 33-MHz processor
- 8 Mbytes of RAM

- One 16-bit Ethernet network card
- One hard drive with 12 milliseconds (ms) or less access time and 2 Mbytes per second or greater transfer rate
- One 16-bit disk controller
- Hard-disk storage (10 Mbytes per minute of stored audio/video)

**For 10 users.**  The recommended configuration for a server PC supporting 10 users distributed evenly on two Ethernet segments or one Token Ring is

- 486 EISA or MCA personal computer with a 33-MHz processor
- 12 Mbytes of RAM
- Two 32-bit Ethernet adapters or one 32-bit Token Ring adapter
- Two hard drives with 12 milliseconds (ms) or less access time and 3 Mbytes per second or greater transfer rate
- One 32-bit disk controller
- Hard-disk storage (10 Mbytes per minute of stored audio/video)

**For 25 users.**  The recommended configuration for a server PC supporting 25 users distributed evenly on four Ethernet segments or three Token Rings is

- 486 EISA or MCA personal computer with a 50- or 66-MHz processor
- 16 Mbytes of RAM
- Four 32-bit Ethernet adapters or three 32-bit Token Ring adapters
- Four hard drives with 11-milliseconds (ms) or less access time and 4 to 5 Mbytes per second or greater transfer rate
- Two 32-bit disk controller
- Hard-disk storage (10 Mbytes per minute of stored audio/video)

## Performance considerations

The performance is affected by three basic factors.

1. *The effective bandwidth of the network segment.* For example, the effective bandwidth per Ethernet segment is 6 to 8 Mbits per second (Mbps), while the effective bandwidth per Token Ring is 14 Mbps.
2. *The presence of bridges or routers between the server and clients.* Performance on a specific client may be reduced if there are bridges or routers on the network segment between the server and the client.
3. *The rate at which clients are playing back files.* For example, if each client is playing back a file at 1.2 Mbps, then the configuration described can support 5 to 6 clients on a single Ethernet segment or 10 to 12 clients

on a Token Ring. If however each client is using software video decompression to play back the same files, 10 to 12 clients per Ethernet segment or 20 to 24 clients on a Token Ring can be supported, since the data rate is much less.

## A Sample Configuration

At NetWorld '93, Fluent demonstrated a 24-client video network consisting of a 486-based server with NetWare 3.11, FluentLinks 1.0, and four Ethernet segments of six computers each. The first part of the demonstration showed that this configuration, without FluentLinks software, supported 3 to 4 video playback sessions before video and audio quality degraded severely. In the second part of the demonstration the FluentLinks NLM was loaded, and all 24 client PCs retrieved and played video clips with imperceptible degradation in video and audio quality.

At Brainshare '93, Fluent and Novell demonstrated a 96-node network supported by a 486-based server, including 24 video clients and 72 clients running a variety of popular spreadsheet and word-processing applications. The Brainshare configuration consisted of the following:

*File-server.*    486/50 DX2 EISA server, with 2 Gbytes of storage and four 32-bit Token Ring cards

*Network Operating System.*    NetWare 4.0

*Video-networking software.*    FluentLinks 1.0 NetWare Loadable Module

*Network topology.*    4 Token Rings of 6 video-enabled personal computers each, plus 1 Token Ring of 72 nonvideo clients, all connected through a Token Ring concentrator

*Video-enabled personal computers.*    486/33 or higher models running DOS 5.0 and Windows 3.1, with 8 MBytes of RAM, VGA adapter and display, 16-bit Token Ring card, speakers, and motion JPEG cardset supporting motion-video compression and decompression.

*Video data.*    Video clips were compressed in ISO JPEG format to an average data rate of 2 Mbps, and stored in a single volume. During playback over the network, the actual data rate fluctuated in response to available network bandwidth, resulting in actual streaming data rates of 1.5 to 2 Mbps, and displayed video frames rates of from 20 to 30 fps.

The following list shows expected performance per segment for various network topologies, based on transmission of video streams recorded at a resolution of 320 × 240 pixels and a data rate of 1.5 Mbps:

*Ethernet.*    10-Mbits-per-second bandwidth available, generally 6 to 7 Mbits per second usable for data; application performance per network segment: 4 to 12 users at 12 to 30 frames per second.

*Token Ring.*    16-Mbits-per-second bandwidth available, 13 to 14 Mbits per second usable. Estimated application performance per network segment: 8 to 20 users at 12 to 30 frames per second.

*FDDI.*    100-Mbits-per-second bandwidth available, 80 to 100 Mbits per second usable. Estimated application performance per network segment: 40 to 100 users at 12 to 30 frames per second.

Now desktop computer users can integrate time-important, full-motion video into applications over businesswide networks, instead of distributing CD-ROMs or videodiscs. The key benefits of scalable video are shared storage, efficient video distribution and access, and compatibility with existing NetWare installations.

# 43

# Building a Standard for Cross-Platform Delivery

**John Colligan**

**Joseph Dunn**

**Joseph Fantuzzi**

**Donna Hefner**

## Introduction

The rapidly changing multimedia industry is challenging developers to consider many issues when they are producing interactive multimedia titles. Among these is choosing the best platform—or platforms—to deliver multimedia productions.

While no single hardware leader has captured the multimedia market, two distinct types of systems have emerged: personal computer and consumer platforms, as shown in Fig. 43.1. Today, standards do exist on the personal computer side—Macintosh and Windows. This is not true for consumer platforms, and it is likely that no leader will appear anytime soon.

Macromedia believes that standard platforms cannot be imposed on an emerging market, but rather must develop from it. Because of this, authoring software must support a variety of platforms, allowing multimedia developers to do the same. This chapter will explore the delivery options today's developers encounter, offer tips to make cross-platform delivery easier, and illustrate the kinds of cross-platform projects developers are creating now.

## Creating a Standard for Multimedia Software

Like producers in Hollywood, multimedia developers want their productions to play on screens everywhere. But the multimedia industry does not

**Figure 43.1**    Number of Macs and PCs to double by 1995 (units in millions).

have one "big-screen" standard as the movie industry does. Rather, the market is comprised of several little screens, each incompatible with the next.

Industry analysts predict that by the turn of the century, multimedia will be a multibillion-dollar industry. As hardware manufacturers scramble to get a piece of the market with their new multimedia machines (and new platforms), multimedia developers are looking for the best way to leverage their time and resources so as to produce titles for a broad audience without reworking productions for each machine. Macromedia makes this easy by providing standard multimedia software to ensure that productions are played on screens everywhere.

Designing cross-platform applications is becoming increasingly popular, because it allows developers to leverage their resources to turn a profit. Off-the-shelf software packages such as Authorware Professional and Macromedia Director are helping to simplify the conversion process to the most popular systems, thereby opening new markets to developers in a timely and affordable manner.

## Creating Cross-Platform Applications

More than 1000 multimedia titles are available today and 3000 others are under development, according to GISTICS, Inc., a market research firm based in Larkspur, California. By conservative estimates, more than 5000 multimedia titles will be on the market by 1995. Authors of these titles want them to play on multiple platforms without requiring significant additional time and resources.

Designing an application for multiple platforms, however, can be quite a challenge. Even the most highly compatible file formats cannot account for all

**Figure 43.2**   Binary-compatible files enable cross-platform development.

the differences among systems, such as individual machine performance, screen size and resolution, use of color, use of fonts, and sound support. Because of these differences, a developer sometimes needs to create similar but separate versions of a production for it to run smoothly on different machines.

Developing cross-platform applications does become easier with experience, as authors become familiar with each system and adjust their techniques to work around the differences. Some cross-platform applications, such as Macromedia's Director Player for Windows and Authorware Professional, are packaged with in-depth design guidelines so as to simplify the transition between platforms.

## Working with differences in machine performance

When creating multimedia projects, developers must assume that their customers have the appropriate hardware to play back the productions. However, even with sufficient hardware, machine performance varies widely from machine to machine.

The amount of memory available on a particular machine affects how fast a multimedia production will run. Although a machine with low memory may have the capacity to play a particular production, that application may run more slowly than desired. To optimize performance, use general memory-management techniques:

- When creating a large production, use scripting to control and optimize performance. For example, unload data from memory if it is not needed, and design load time at places where the CPU is idle and the user will not notice (while they're reading or looking at a still).

- Use memory-intensive effects, such as bitmapped images and large internal sounds, wisely. Consider cutting large bitmaps into pieces or using external sound, if necessary.

- Be sure to test the production on a range of machines, so as to check both highest- and lowest-level performance.

### Ensuring good color

Colors can be difficult to manage in cross-platform projects, because different platforms use different palette-mapping systems. A color Macintosh, for example, has millions of colors available, while PCs with VGA Graphics offer only 16 colors, and PCs with Super VGA graphics offer millions of colors. When converting a Macintosh file to Windows, all colors are mapped to their nearest equivalents. Several authoring techniques help to guarantee the truest possible colors:

- Make sure you use color palettes that can be recognized by the destination platform. For example, consider working with a standard VGA palette while authoring on the Macintosh, and creating cross-platform productions for the PC, if you will be delivering to 16-color computers.

- Optimize color quality by saving the original images in high resolution and applying an 8-bit diffusion dither to the images in Adobe's PhotoShop. For highest quality, use a product such as Equilibrium's DeBabilizer to dither the original images to a customized palette that works well with a variety of images in your production.

- When crossing from a computer-based RGB display to a consumer-based NTSC display, do not rely on the use of color to communicate information, because palettes may vary considerably. Programs such as Macromedia Director allow use of a custom NTSC palette to help keep colors true on television screens.

### Working with different monitors

Many multimedia presentations keep the same pixel resolution when converted to other platforms. Because the pixel resolution may differ from platform to platform, movies can fill the screen or window differently on each. Here are some rules for good design:

- Use the "TV-safe" area of the screen—720 × 486 pixels or less—when creating for consumer platforms. This keeps you from unintentionally cropping the picture or text in your productions on different-sized screens.

- To avoid unintentionally cropping a production when it plays on different computer screens, create it in 640 × 480 pixels, the size of a Macintosh 13-inch display and the typical PC-system display.

- Many Macintosh customers own 12-inch monitors, 512 × 384 pixels. When designing productions for these screens, place a color, texture, or PICT image in the background, for playback on larger screens.

- When designing for consumer platforms, keep text to a minimum, and at least 18 points in size. Also, consider using shadows behind the text to help it stand out. The resolution of a NTSC television screen is much lower than that of a computer monitor, making copy hard to read.

- Avoid single-pixel horizontal lines, graphics, and animations when delivering to NTSC displays. Because these displays use an interlaced signal, single-pixel images may result in flickering.

### Mapping fonts

If a project includes text in fields, or requires the user to enter text, developers may incur font problems (specifically size and shape issues) when crossing platforms. The Macintosh and Windows environments, for example, create visually different text, even when created from the same font and size information. Therefore, when working with text, keep in mind the following techniques:

- For text in boxes, center the text, leaving open space on each side so as to avoid possible word-wrap.

- For the closest possible mapping of text, use a standard font such as Times, which usually is available on different platforms. Also consider TrueType and Adobe Type Manager fonts, which provide standard fonts for Macintosh and Windows. These fonts still vary in size on each platform. (See Fig. 43.3.)

- Avoid high-level ASCII characters, as well as outline and shadow styles; these are not commonly supported on multiple platforms.

- To guarantee that text will look identical on both platforms, convert it into bitmaps before converting the file. Be aware, however, that bitmapped text uses much more memory than standard fonts, and cannot be edited.

### Using sound

Although every Macintosh provides at least 8-bit audio, only PCs that meet the MPC standard are guaranteed to have this capability. In fact, many Windows-equipped PCs have no digital audio capabilities at all, and require an additional sound card with an appropriate driver to play sounds. When creating sound files in cross-platform productions, keep in mind the following:

- Many sound cards do not support all of the commonly used sampling rates on the Macintosh. Use 11-kHz and 22-kHz 8-bit audio for best results and compatibility.

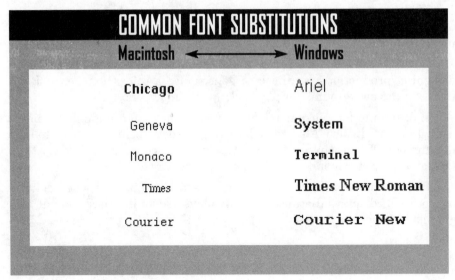

**COMMON FONT SUBSTITUTIONS**

Macintosh ◄─────► Windows

| Macintosh | Windows |
|-----------|---------|
| Chicago | Ariel |
| Geneva | System |
| Monaco | Terminal |
| Times | Times New Roman |
| Courier | Courier New |

**Figure 43.3** Font substitutions.

- Make sure that sound files and any linked external sounds are in an appropriate format for the destination platform. Common Macintosh sound file formats include AIFF, SND, and SoundEdit. Common Windows sound file formats include PCM, WAV, and MIDI.

- Consider using Red Book CD audio by including it on the multimedia CD-ROM. That way, you can play the audio directly from the CD-ROM drive as the production is running from the hard drive. This saves memory, and frees the CPU for better performance.

### Designing different user interfaces

One of the most basic (but often overlooked) rules of thumb for cross-platform delivery is to be sure a title's content is *appropriate* for a specific platform. While new software is making it easier to leverage development work across platforms, the dynamics of *how* a user interacts with these platforms are quite different. In general, you would do well to follow these guidelines:

- Be sure to design the interface consistent with the published guidelines of the destination platform.

- Use a computer-based platform if the program requires a lot of text, or use of a keyboard. Most consumer players do not have a keyboard and use a low-resolution NTSC television screen, making text difficult to read.

- When creating productions for both computer- and consumer-based platforms, make each interface element large enough to touch with a finger, enabling it to be run on platforms that use a touchscreen display.

## Multimedia's Future Direction

As the multimedia industry continues to unfold, developers will have more and more delivery options for their productions. Macromedia expects multimedia authoring and production to continue to be enhanced on the leading computer platforms: Macintosh and Windows-based PCs.

Eventually, after a hard-fought battle among contenders, multimedia delivery platforms will solidify into two or three major consumer platforms in addition to Macintosh and Windows. This means that even as the market stabilizes, a single delivery platform may not be a viable business option for multimedia-title developers.

Macromedia is committed to helping developers leverage their work across platforms by supporting the leaders as they emerge. From Macintosh and Windows to ScriptX-compatible computers, 3DO, and other leading consumer players, Macromedia's multimedia software will provide a standard that ensures that productions play back on screens everywhere.

## Developer Examples

### Crossing platforms for peanuts

When Image Smith released *Yearn 2 Learn—Peanuts,* the program captured the imagination not only of children but of the multimedia industry worldwide.

*Peanuts* targets children aged 3 to 10 years by using the well-known Charles Schulz characters of Snoopy, Woodstock, Charlie Brown, and the gang* to teach math, geography, and reading in a fun, interactive way. The program automatically adjusts the level of difficulty to the child's skill level, allowing the title to interest all the children in a family and to continue to challenge them as they grow older.

*Peanuts* has been extremely well received, and the Macintosh version exceeded sales projections by 150 percent in its first 3 months on the market. *Yearn 2 Learn—Peanuts* was released for Windows in June 1993.

While the Macintosh version was developed in 8 months by a full-time team of four, one dedicated person converted the program to Windows in just 45 days. The alternative was complete recoding, which would have taken approximately six months. The Player gave Image Smith a head start in capturing the Windows market.

Image Smith's success with *Yearn 2 Learn—Peanuts* is just the beginning of a series of Yearn 2 Learn titles that set a high standard for interactivity, playability, and educational value. (See Fig. 43.4.)

### Multimedia fosters multilingualism

The Central Intelligence Agency's (CIA) Federal Language Training Laboratory and Analysis Corporation of Washington, D.C., made headlines

---

*Peanuts* characters copyright © 1992, United Features Syndicate, Inc.

**Figure 43.4**  Sample of multimedia system.

around the world when they announced their intention to commercialize state-of-the-art multimedia language courses developed for CIA employees.

The courses, developed with Authorware Professional, combine full-motion, full-screen video with native-speakers' voices, text, graphics, animation, and audio record and playback. "Interactive multimedia is the ideal medium for language learning," explains George Conrad of Analysas Corporation. "The visual and auditory reinforcement helps motivate students, enabling instructors to be more efficient by making optimal use of class time."

The first course, called Exito, covers Spanish, and it has proven itself to be effective in teaching basic Spanish to CIA officers in just 10 days, assuming 4 to 5 hours of study a day. Courses in Russian, French, and Arabic also are under development. The programs focus on everyday situations such as arriving at the airport, meeting people, asking for directions, and ordering a meal.

"Our goal for the language courses is to bring this national treasure back to the public," Conrad explains. "And to reach the broadest audience, we decided to deliver the program to both Macintosh- and Windows-based computers." Analysas uses schools and universities to test-market and enhance the courses, which are delivered on five double-sided videodiscs and one CD-ROM. Eventually they hope to market simplified versions of the CIA language courses worldwide.

"There is an incredible groundswell of interest in language learning," Conrad says. "Perhaps this will be the start of bringing multilingualism to mainstream America."

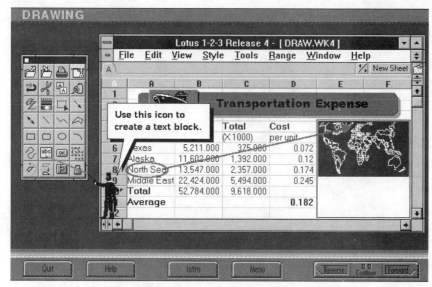

**Figure 43.5**  Multimedia training example.

## Gaining an edge with interactive introductions

Lotus Development Corporation understands multimedia's "edge" when it comes to effectively conveying new information. Recently the company developed the 1-2-3 Release 4 for Windows Guided Tour, using text, graphics, and animation to show the new features of 1-2-3 Release 4 for Windows. (See Fig. 43.5.)

The tour ships with every copy of 1-2-3 Release 4 for Windows and has received rave reviews. It opens with an animated introduction, which leads into an interactive tour of 1-2-3 Release 4 for Windows. The program includes high-impact graphics and interactivity, to keep the user engaged throughout the program.

Created exclusively for the Windows platform, the guided tour initially was designed on the Macintosh, then converted to Windows.

# 44

# Making the Move to Distributed Multimedia Computing

Peter B. Blakeney

## Introduction

Multimedia is poised to deliver fundamental improvements in how we train our work force, make our buying decisions, and communicate with one another. As a cavalcade of multimedia capabilities proliferates on the desktop, it will likely become the most popular human interface for our personal computers, extending the once-revolutionary graphical user interface (GUI). Many predict that by the year 2000 every computer will be equipped to handle multimedia applications. The resultant impact on how we do business is destined to be profound.

Multimedia combines the interactivity of a computer with a natural user interface (NUI) that includes audio, still images, animation, full-motion video, and voice recognition. Over the past decade, multimedia has proven its worth as a uniquely powerful set of technologies when used to support applications such as training, business presentations, and marketing kiosks. Most of these applications have been stand-alone, due to the limitations of the communications technologies needed to manage and transport multimedia information. While stand-alone applications may be valuable, they don't necessarily optimize the competitiveness of an organization. Therefore, for multimedia to reach its full potential, it must move beyond the limits of stand-alone technology and be integrated into the existing information-system infrastructure.

Today's organizations generate traditional information consisting of text, numbers, and graphs more productively than ever before; store and retrieve that information more efficiently through the use of databases; and share that information more effectively through the use of electronic mail, facsimile transmissions, and telephone communications. These same organizations are increasingly aware that their applications will become that much more valuable with the addition of multimedia content. They will expect just as much flexibility and transportability in their distributed multimedia networks as they now enjoy in their traditional data networks.

Most industry observers agree that even though there is a substantial and accelerating use of multimedia in industry today, it will be 1995 or 1996 before multimedia gains the widespread acceptance that it is expected to. Adoption most likely will come in stages. According to Dr. John M. McQuillan, president of McQuillan Consulting, "High-resolution graphics, photographs, drawing, and the like, will generally be the first multimedia objects that users will incorporate into an application. Audio (spoken words or music) will come second, followed by full-motion video and, finally, animation."

Note that the proliferation of multimedia also will depend on advances in related technologies. These include end-user platforms; specialized devices that capture, record, and play back video and audio; public telecommunications systems; and enabling software development tools. Corporate networks will have to adapt to multimedia applications, especially in terms of bandwidth and delay-sensitive delivery. Over time, standards will be established and interoperability achieved, and this will propel distributed multimedia into the mainstream.

This chapter will focus on the following topics:

- Distributed multimedia applications
- Enabling enterprisewide distributed multimedia computing
- Multimedia server solutions
- Multimedia standards

## Distributed Multimedia Applications

Networked multimedia information systems will inevitably improve productivity, through more effective internal and external communications. Consider the possibilities. Companies can communicate product information to customers in the format and location that those customers prefer. In advertising, creative designers can share ideas for video commercials with colleagues and customers through audio/video-enhanced electronic mail and multimedia documents. Medical professionals can collaborate by sharing diagnostic images or videotaped procedures across the world, using multimedia-enabled distributed systems. In educational settings, multimedia's power of interactive visualization is already augmenting traditional lectures and laboratories through multimedia navigational tools, and enhancing the process with self-paced instruction and distance learning. There are strategic applications across all industries in which multimedia can improve competi-

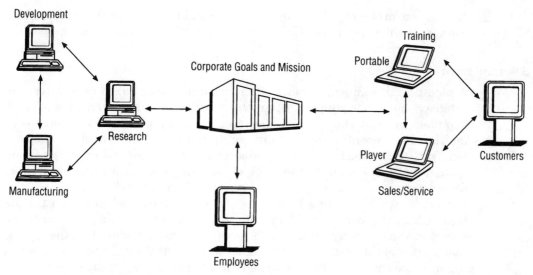

**Figure 44.1**  Business functions impacted by multimedia.

tiveness through the increased efficiency, effectiveness, and quality of communications.

To envision the magnitude of the impact and benefits of distributed multimedia on traditional business practices, consider the following scenarios (see Fig. 44.1).

### Research and development

In the development of a complex product, engineers work independently to design segments of the product and then transfer the design to development engineers for integration. They continuously change and update the design and manufacturing process throughout the life of the product. The design consists of drawings, images, text, and prototypes, and the process includes meetings and conversations, both within and across product segments. With multimedia-enabled networked systems, researchers can send voice-annotated notes with images or video clips of prototypes. Developers can videoconference across multiple manufacturing sites in order to ensure integrated product development. This multimedia collaboration solution reduces the R&D cycle and improves quality.

### Manufacturing

The R&D collaboration just described reaches into manufacturing as well. When a manufacturing problem arises, a plant-floor worker can communicate from a workstation to a development engineer to show a defective part via a videoconference. The engineer can actually see the defective part and make his or her recommendations instantly. The worker might also reference, right from the workstation, training videos, or a central video database of solutions to common problems. Training and video information on demand enables workers to solve problems quickly and to learn new techniques on the job.

### Sales and service

A high-priced, complex product often requires a specialized sales force and extensive customer support. Often the sales cycle is long and expensive. A manufacturer can shorten the sales cycle by equipping the sales force with multimedia presentation and training systems, and by providing information/transaction kiosks in stores and sales offices. A multimedia presentation system and kiosk adds to the sales effort videotaped testimonials, product demonstrations, competitive comparisons, and interactivity. Customers can request more information from a technical database and provide valuable feedback to the company. They can dial up and videoconference with an expert at the company's headquarters. Because multimedia gives the critical information to the customer at the right place and at the right time, businesses can increase service and at the same time enhance the company image.

### Training

It's not always possible, practical, or affordable to provide training the moment that it is needed, especially when training needs to be delivered to individuals at multiple remote locations. With networked multimedia technology, office workers can receive "just-in-time" training without leaving their desks. A widely dispersed class can view a lesson on PCs and interact with an instructor who is also at a PC, via fax, audio channel, or two-way video. This phenomenon, known as *distance learning,* saves on travel costs and increases productivity by allowing office workers to gain immediate access to materials rather than wait for scheduled classes. In this way multimedia protects investments in skilled personnel and helps corporations to maintain their competitive edge.

### Corporate communications

Communicating company goals and vision to employees and customers is often difficult. The CEO cannot easily make frequent visits to every manufacturing and sales site. And often the corporate message gets modified as it is disseminated through the layers of an organization. Companies now show videotaped speeches, but multimedia technology can enhance the delivery process. Rather than view a two-hour videotaped speech, an employee can access an interactive application that includes clips of the speech filed by topic, plus related information such as a response form. In such a case the one-way message becomes a two-way interactive communication.

Each of the previous applications extends multimedia from being a stand-alone application to being a networked, strategic solution for fundamental business operations.

**Figure 44.2**  Multimedia systems solutions.

## Enabling Enterprisewide Distributed Multimedia Computing

In a stand-alone environment, multimedia content, such as audio and video, is produced and captured at the viewer's desktop. In a networked multimedia environment, the audio and video may be distributed in real time from a videoserver, located in the same city or across the continent. That same videoserver may be sending the same audio and video content to multiple individuals distributed across a wide geographic area. Alternatively, many individuals may be collaborating and involved in an audio/video conference. The resulting audio and video datastreams are distributed among the workstations used by the individuals participating in the conference.

To enable enterprisewide distributed multimedia computing, existing strategic system platforms need to be enhanced to support multimedia applications. These enhancements will result in an open distributed system enabled for multimedia, as seen in Fig. 44.2.

### Distributed computing framework

Due to the large size of multimedia objects (their transmission as continuous streams of data when played or captured), and the need to control and synchronize them, key elements of distributed computing must be enhanced to support work-group collaboration and enterprise-distributed systems. In order to map the development of distributed multimedia computing solutions, we will use a "distributed computing framework" to describe those key elements of distributed computing that will be enhanced to support multimedia. This framework is targeted for heterogeneous computing, thus ensuring interoperability, data exchange, and common user access (CUA) across many dissimilar systems, with selected and emerging international de facto standards as a foundation.

An important objective of open distributed systems is to make a network of heterogeneous systems appear as a single-user system. All computing resources and services that a user is authorized to access, local and remote, appear as local resources and services. The Interactive Multimedia Association (IMA), a consortium of leading companies in the information industry, published a "Multimedia Services Request For Technology" in December 1992. The objective of this RFT is to achieve distributed multimedia services across heterogeneous systems. IBM, along with its Common Operating System Environment (COSE) partners, will be submitting to the IMA a specification for achieving distributed multimedia services, in hopes of establishing a standard.

Many facilities are required to implement location transparent, distributed computing, including application development tools, presentation management facilities, data management facilities (which use the services of interprocess communications), directory services, networking, and subnetworking. These facilities process a service request using the client-server computing model, in which one entity provides a service for another. In addition, they use relevant international and de facto standards to ensure interoperability across multivendor systems. Figure 44.3 represents a system framework that outlines the generic facilities needed to support both collaborative and client-server computing.

Two characteristics unique to multimedia will drive extensions to existing systems: object size, and datastreams. Multimedia data objects, such as digital video or high-quality digital audio, require large storage facilities. Most systems are designed to handle kilobyte data objects, not the gigabyte objects employed for a full-length movie of VHS quality. Storing many such data objects may require terabytes. Thus the automated storage management facilities that catalog, back up, migrate, relocate, and archive files must be upgraded to handle large multimedia data objects. As the number of multimedia objects increases, users have a greater need to classify, abstract, and index the objects—functions best controlled by a data management facility. Therefore, existing data management facilities must be enhanced to manipulate and deliver multimedia objects.

Multimedia data objects are unique not only in size but also in nature. Objects, such as audio and video, are time-based, continuous datastreams of information that must be delivered at a constant rate with minimal delay between source and target in order to preserve human perception. For example, digital audio from a compact disc results in two continuous datastreams, each flowing at about 706 kbps (a total of about 1.4 Mbps). Compressed VHS-quality digital video played off a CD-ROM results in a composite datastream

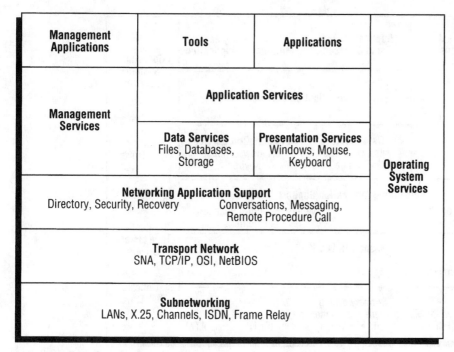

**Figure 44.3**  Distributed computing framework.

flowing at 1.2 Mbps. To manage datastreams, the lower four layers of the distributed computing framework require continuous datastream handling capabilities to provide real-time control and synchronization of the audio and video datastreams that together form the movie clip.

The objective of this chapter is to describe the requirements for integrating multimedia extensions into the existing facilities of distributed computing. The following sections examine each affected layer of the distributed computing framework, together with the extensions required for each layer to support enterprisewide multimedia.

### Multimedia enhancements to the distributed systems framework

The goals of distributed multimedia computing are two: open computing, and the integration of multimedia extensions into strategic platforms. Figure 44.4 shows all of the multimedia extensions that will be discussed in the context of a distributed computing framework.

### Application tools and services

Supporting multimedia requires new application tools, such as those provided through the Ultimedia Tools Series (UTS), an interoperable family of application development tools from IBM and independent software vendors. Most UTS tools fall into one of five categories:

**Figure 44.4** Distributed computing work enabled for multimedia.

1. *Authoring tools,* which integrate text, sound, graphics, and video into a multimedia production

2. *Graphics tools,* which enable the user to create still graphics, images, and special effects—or edit digitized photographic images

3. *Animation tools,* which add motion to graphics and text

4. *Audio tools,* which capture and edit or modify sound

5. *Video tools,* which capture and/or edit digital motion video

In addition to application tools, new application services are needed, including extensions to the following:

- Common user access services
- Object management facilities
- Data conversion services

**Common user access services.**    CUA extensions will provide standardized graphical screens for interacting with multimedia applications, including icons representing virtual volume-control buttons, virtual slide bars, and other graphical data objects. When CUA services are standardized across multimedia applications, programmers can learn consistent methods for interacting with multimedia content, such as touching a media icon with a mouse or touchscreen.

**Object management facilities.**  As multimedia applications are employed by an organization over time, an inventory of multimedia data objects will grow across various systems on the network. The interrelationships among the data objects will become more complex, and many types of data objects will proliferate. In addition, multimedia data objects will be stored as files, as entries in databases, in byte spaces, or stored on different types of storage devices such as a VCR tape. As a result, object management can become very complicated.

A distributed object management facility will be needed to simplify the access to multimedia data objects by means of application programs and multimedia tools. This facility will provide a uniform programming interface to applications.

**Data conversion services.**  Currently, there are multiple data formats for each type of digital medium. Data interchange among multimedia tools, as well as application programs, can be difficult to achieve. There is now a concerted effort in the information industry to define a unique data format for each type of digital medium. Once the standards for representing digital images, video, audio, and animation have been accepted and supported, data conversion services will be needed to convert old data formats to new data formats (and perhaps vice versa). IBM currently is making multimedia conversion services available through Multimedia Presentation Manager/2 (MMPM/2), an extension of IBM's OS/2. The Resource Interchange File Format (RIFF) implemented by MMPM/2 and Microsoft Windows is an example of the generic data structure, or *wrapper,* that will be used to standardize multimedia data formats and thereby allow data interchange among systems.

## Presentation services

In distributed multimedia computing, client systems perform the important role of presenting multimedia and datastreams to the user. The primary client platforms are the PS/2 and Value Point personal computer families. IBM has enhanced the multimedia capability of these platforms by extending the presentation-services component of OS/2 2.1 with MMPM/2. MMPM/2 provides a common programming interface to control both multimedia devices and the datastreams that flow from those devices.

## Data services

The role of data management in developing multimedia applications will grow, as more multimedia information is stored digitally and as applications evolve toward distributed client-server implementation. Data management includes three major components:

1. File systems
2. Database management systems
3. System managed storage

The ability of these three components to support multimedia data is critical to the success of distributed multimedia computing. Multimedia content (video recording, animation sequence, etc.) typically is both time-consuming and expensive to produce, and frequently represents a valuable corporate asset. Data-management technologies become key to protecting these assets and to maximizing their use, just as they have done for more traditional information assets, by sharing, saving, cataloging, archiving, and recovering multimedia content.

**File systems.**  Existing file systems provide the basic ability to "store-and-forward" blocks of media data files, and they can be used to develop a number of client-server multimedia applications, such as distributing a video training course to an employee's workstation or updating video content for use by a kiosk application. Because of the time-based, stream-oriented nature of multimedia data, file systems themselves cannot effectively deliver such data to multiple users in real time, unless the number of users on the network is severely restricted. In order to accommodate the time-based nature of multimedia data, additional client, server, and communications components must be developed.

**Database management systems.**  As the numbers of stored multimedia data objects increase, they are likely to become more important to an enterprise business. Efficient data services will be required to organize, manage, search, and deliver these objects to one or more users. These capabilities, provided by Database Management Systems (DBMSs) for more "traditional" data, are equally important to application developers and end users dealing with multimedia data.

DBMSs simplify and facilitate application development and operational procedures by providing functions that support

- Data definition, organization, storage, and navigation
- Search and retrieval
- Consistent user/application interface
- Data security, integrity, recovery
- Concurrency control for access from multiple users
- Distributed data, client-server application topologies
- Specific view of data to each application, without physical data redundancy
- Consistency of all data related to the same object

Utilizing databases will allow multimedia application developers to focus on addressing unique application requirements, rather than on solving data-management problems.

**System managed storage.**  Multimedia has a significant impact on storage requirements, due to the size of media objects. As a reference point, consider that a 500-page textbook requires 1 Mbyte of storage. Ten fax-quality images require 640 Kbytes, whereas 10 color or detailed images could require as much as 75 Mbytes. Five minutes of uncompressed voice-quality audio requires 2.4 Mbytes of storage, and 52.8 Mbytes of storage are required for premium-quality audio (compact disc, digital audio, CD-DA).

Digitized video requires the greatest storage capacity of all data forms. Without compression techniques, practical storage of digital video is impossible. For example, animation-quality video requires 147 Mbytes per minute for a one-quarter screen size video. But with today's compression techniques, this same animation-quality video can be compressed to 1.44 Mbytes (3.5-inch diskette). A two-hour, television-quality video can be compressed to about 2 Gbytes of storage.

Early multimedia applications introduced analog storage devices—such as audiotape recorders, VCRs, and laserdisc players—as workstation peripherals. These peripherals typically have been single-function, and positioned in a stand-alone environment. However, effective use of multimedia content requires shared access across the enterprise, and that shared access requires in turn networked storage systems.

Distributed multimedia applications demand storage devices and libraries that include both analog and digital devices. These applications will benefit from the flexibility of digital media storage, including not only traditional hard disks but also such optical devices as CD-ROM players, write-once, read-many (WORM) rewritable optical drives, and optical "jukebox" libraries.

As support for various types of multimedia storage devices develops, the scope of the storage hierarchy needs to be extended. High-quality digitized images, audio, and video data stored on these devices will require automated data management to store, retrieve, back up, archive, restore, relocate, protect, and control access to data. The data files will be independent of the storage device. System managed storage now offers these facilities.

### Networking application support, transport network, and subnetworking

The networking application support, transport network, and subnetworking layers of the distributed computing framework together form the "arteries" of distributed systems. The networking application support layer consists of components supporting program-to-program (or interprocess) communications, directory services, and such systems services as security, transaction management, and recovery management. The transport network includes the support for Systems Network Architecture/Advanced Peer-to-Peer

Networking (SNA/APPN), Transmission Control Protocol/Internet Protocol (TCP/IP), Network Basic I/O System (NetBIOS), and Open Systems Interconnect (OSI). The subnetworking layer includes the physical network support and network attachment.

In a multimedia-enabled network, the networking application support component expands to include both simplex (one-way) datastream communications and multiparty communications. For conferencing to become ubiquitous, standards will have to be developed that encompass a programming interface, communications protocols, and control mechanisms.

A common function of distributed multimedia computing is the delivery of audio/video datastreams from server platforms to clients in response to a media control "play" request or a request to videoconference. The videoconference datastreams have to be delivered in real time, with minimal delay, to ensure intelligible communication. The "play" request is serviced transparently; the application or user need not know whether a network was used or not.

Accomplishing this transparently can be done by means of existing transport networking facilities, coupled with careful network configuration design. However, to ensure a very robust quality of service, a new capability, network datastream handling, will be required in the transport network layer, plus extended subnetworking services that include bandwidth management and new physical network interfaces.

There exists a need for client-server video applications that efficiently utilize local-area networks (LANs) while maintaining an acceptable level of service. This can be accomplished by a digital videoserver that uses a scalable digital-video compression algorithm to adaptively control video datastream parameters such as frame rate, based on feedback about transport network performance. The client system receiving the video datastream decompresses it and presents the video at a quality commensurate to what could be handled by the network without seriously degrading every other network user.

While some applications require the real-time video transmission facilitated by scalable video, others require only conventional store-and-forward transmission of multimedia data objects. For example, multimedia objects will need to be uploaded and downloaded between clients and servers, or accessed while under the control of a distributed file management system. There is, therefore, a requirement to provide extensions to networking protocols as appropriate, so as to support the store-and-forward transmission of the large objects that accompany multimedia.

Multimedia requires changes in the subnetworking layer of the framework—the physical transmission network. There are three primary types of high-speed physical networking technologies under active development and applicable to multimedia:

1. Local area networking
2. Fiber-optic channel switching
3. Fast packet switching

**Local area networking.**   LANs and their supporting interconnect products were designed to meet the needs of high-speed data networking applications where the data-packet traffic is sent in bursts. Integrating multimedia into distributed computing requires that LAN technology be enhanced to support the transmission of unpredictable, continuous datastreams of data packets. However, any enhancement must attempt to protect the customers' existing investment in LANs, such as Ethernet and Token Ring.

Ethernet is intrinsically limited, by its access protocol and transmission speed, to supporting fewer VHS-quality digital-video datastreams than a 16-Mbps Token Ring LAN, which can support approximately 10 video datastreams.

IBM, along with its business partners, is evaluating an isochronous-transmission enhancement to Ethernet LAN products. Isochronous communication delivers a signal at a specified rate and time interval, making it desirable for delivery of continuous data such as voice and full-motion video. This enhancement requires an intelligent wiring hub that employs a time division multiplexing scheme to deliver both 10-Mbps Ethernet service and wideband circuit-switched service to a personal workstation over the same physical network interface (in this case, unshielded twisted-pair copper cable).

Token Ring LAN technology incorporates unexploited access control mechanism capability (in the form of priority scheduling for frame transmissions) that can support multimedia applications by giving isochronous traffic higher priority than asynchronous data traffic. Assigning a high priority to the frames that make up the multimedia datastream will ensure that they are among the first to pass across the LAN. The development of Token Ring adapters and the necessary network control software for managing priority assignments will allow voice, video, and data packets to flow over Token Ring LANs.

Along with evaluating how best to enhance Ethernet and Token Ring LANs to support multimedia, IBM is evaluating an alternative approach to delivering high-speed multimedia communications to the desktop. This alternative is based on the observation that limiting the number of attached systems can ensure multimedia support on the LAN. Optimizing this approach requires an intelligent wiring hub capable of a high-performance bridge that, in turn, supports many LANs, each incorporating one or only a few attached systems. This approach will provide the maximum LAN data transmission rate to each system, and confine all LAN changes to the intelligent wiring hub.

**Fiber-optic channel switching.**   Fiber-optic channel switching (FCS) originally emerged as a solution for the high-speed connection needs of high-performance computer applications. Fiber channels transmit in the 120 Mbps to 1 Gbps range over a distance of several kilometers, and typically are used to connect either engineering and scientific workstations to "supercomputers" or host computers to such high-performance storage systems as disk arrays. Electronic channel switches dynamically set up and take down fiber channel connections in microseconds. A connection usually lasts for milliseconds (enough time to transmit a burst of several megabits of data), but can stay set up indefinitely if needed. IBM sees the requirement for making FCS one of the LAN options available to client-server multimedia applications implemented on the high end of its personal workstations and ES/9000 system platform.

**Fast packet switching.** The transmission capacity demands (bits-per-second) of digital voice, data, compressed image, and compressed video are extremely varied. Controlling the performance of a multimedia network can be achieved by accepting only fixed-length packets (cells) into the network for transmission. This approach has led the telecommunications industry to explore asynchronous transfer mode (ATM), aka *cell relay,* in which a 53-byte cell, consisting of 5 bytes of header and 48 bytes of data, is presented to the network for transmission.

The design of the header assumes that the intelligence exists in the network to interpret it. The header specifies routing and network control information. It allows related multimedia connections to be set up as virtual channels that make up a multimedia conversation. These channels are grouped together into a virtual path so that they may be routed and controlled by the network and synchronized at the end points. In addition, the header allows the transmitter at the origin to indicate which cells are candidates to be discarded by the network when there is a problem.

The success of ATM will depend on the practicality of migrating existing LANs to the ATM platform. According to ATM Forum member Rob Hamilton, such a migration may proceed as follows:

> At the wiring-hub level, Ethernet and eventually Token Ring networks will be increasingly segmented into smaller networks capable of correspondingly higher performance. Backbone networks, such as fiber distributed data interface (FDDI), will continue to collapse to a centralized multiport bridge/router, improving throughput and performance.
>
> The next phase introduces local LAN hubs with ATM hub-switching capabilities, while retaining the bulk of the original LAN equipment investment. This phase retains the functional advantage of the collapsed backbone, while attaining improved throughput and performance with high-speed switching. Underlying this migration will be the transition from a FDDI ring architecture to ATM switching hubs as the core premises technology. Finally, with the ATM backbone switching and ATM on the desktop, end-to-end ATM will support voice, data, text, graphics/imaging, and video on the desktop over a point-to-point network with premises-based cell switching.

Two new developments suggest that cells and packets will be parallel technologies for the rest of the decade. One is the increase in Ethernet speed to 100 Mbps, and the other is the practice of leaving the 10-Mbps Ethernet channel alone but adding an isochronous channel above it to support multimedia applications. Ultimately, though, ATM switches will likely be the best solution for providing LANs with the stable, dedicated links that super-high-bandwidth multimedia applications will require in the future.

Broadband Integrated Services Digital Network (BISDN) is another emerging force in distributed multimedia computing, representing the telephone companies' initiative in exploiting ATM. According to Steve Crowl, Director of Broadband Service Development for Sprint,

> The term "BISDN" describes tomorrow's all-purpose, all-digital network, which will accommodate diverse user requirements by providing a wide range of service mixes, including the following:
>
> - *Synchronous services,* such as voice and video
> - *Connectionless data services,* for LAN interconnection
> - *Connection-oriented services,* for packet-switched data, such as X.25
> - Variable-bit-rate services, such as video, where only changes in scene are transmitted

### Networking cabling infrastructure

Another aspect of protecting a customer's investments in a networking infrastructure is determining how existing cabling systems may be used to deliver multimedia networking services. Today, VHS-quality digital video requires about a 1.2-Mbps transmission rate. Motion Picture Experts Group (MPEG) MPEG-II compressed broadcast digital video will require 4 to 8 Mbps; advanced digital TV will require 30 to 130 Mbps. On this basis, it will not be necessary to use fiber-optic cable to deliver video to the desktop. Copper cabling system installation is viable for most multimedia applications.

Impressive digital signal processing (DSP) advances have recently occurred that make it possible to achieve high-speed digital transmission over unshielded twisted-pair (UTP) cable. In fact, UTP cable may be used to deliver digital video to the desktop.

IBM is investigating how to achieve reliable transmission in the range of 25 to 45 Mbps over typical UTP cable lengths (e.g., 100 meters) found in the office and factory. If successful, UTP cable would be usable for most networked digital multimedia applications. Alternatively, shielded twisted-pair (STP) cabling, which provides a bandwidth of 500 MHz, offers excellent flexibility for broadband transmissions. Using frequency-multiplexing techniques, different types of transmission services may be delivered simultaneously over STP cabling, including LAN services and CATV.

### Systems management

As intelligent multimedia equipment (digital VCRs, audio/video storage libraries, digital cameras, etc.) proliferates across distributed systems, centralized management will become very important. Networked kiosk applications already have identified the need for centralized systems management to control the distribution of multimedia content to the kiosks and to perform problem determination. Multimedia-based training and education applications will become networked, allowing courses to be taken on demand or delivered "just-in-time." It is essential that system/network management products meet the system management requirements of distributed multimedia applications.

## Multimedia Server Solutions

Sharing multimedia content in a distributed computing environment poses unique challenges to the capabilities of traditional servers. New multimedia server solutions are now emerging that optimize the server's support for sharing multimedia data.

To facilitate shared access to data, multimedia servers need to control very large volumes of continuous datastreams, the media devices that store those datastreams, and the networks and communications that distribute the datastreams to and from the users in real time. Multimedia servers also have to control and manage the request-admission process, so that each data request is accepted only if the server can guarantee that the request can be satisfied without adverse impact on the execution of other requests.

Because multimedia data can be represented and stored in either analog or digital form, multimedia servers should be able to manage both data forms. Analog servers control the devices that store the data, such as laserdiscs or TV tuners. Digital servers control the data itself, retrieving it from the files or databases.

Digital servers offer a number of advantages to organizations, including the ability to incrementally add, delete, or edit stored multimedia content on an ongoing basis, often through the use of digital video editing techniques. Digital servers also allow multiple clients to have concurrent interactive access to the same media devices.

For many interactive multimedia applications, digital multimedia servers also will require digital communication of multimedia content between the server and the clients. However, for some applications, it also might be desirable to use digital servers in tandem with analog distribution, in order to exploit the 70-channel available bandwidth on existing twisted-pair Token Ring cable using F-Coupler technology. In this scenario, the data must be decompressed and converted to analog form prior to distribution. During distribution, F-Couplers merge analog TV signals and digital LAN data onto the same network cabling (see Fig. 44.5).

Synchronization and management of multiple audio and video datastreams is a challenging task even in a stand-alone environment, where a single system encompasses the datastream handlers, the data they operate on, file devices, and the playback devices. In a distributed multimedia configuration, a server owns the stored data and file devices that are remote from the clients. Client systems and their respective playback devices must connect to the server via a network, introducing the potential for delays and interruptions in the continuous delivery of datastreams for playback.

Further complicating delivery, the server and its data concurrently support more than one client on the network. Several clients can make simultaneous requests for the same or a different datastream, located on the same or a dif-

**Figure 44.5**   Multimedia server for analog and digital distribution.

ferent storage device—thus increasing the potential for server resource contention and datastream interruption.

Therefore, in addition to developing the isochronous network support capabilities, one must evaluate the development of other components that will ensure the end-to-end isochronous delivery of multimedia datastreams between server and multiple clients. These include the sync/stream management, buffer management, request admission management, file management, and communications management components.

## Multimedia Standards

Standards are one of the critical success factors in the widespread acceptance and growth of multimedia applications and products. A significant inhibitor to growth has been the "alphabet soup" of multimedia data formats, vendor-proclaimed and industry-developed multimedia standards that continue to proliferate and even to compete against each other. At the same time, widely accepted international standards to guide developers in creating applications are lacking. The result is incompatibility and complexity in data exchange among multivendor platforms. The lack of widely accepted standards also has resulted in system-specific multimedia tools, and authoring systems that produce applications that "play" only on specific platforms. This leads to obsolescence as technology evolves. Application developers and information owners need standards that can accommodate new technology as it emerges.

The growth of multimedia will be accelerated greatly through the adoption of such unifying standards. Organizations such as the IMA are driving the industry to develop a set of common standards specifying data formats, multiplatform scripting language, and distributed multimedia services. Likely results will be

- An increased willingness to invest in the production of digital multimedia content, in the knowledge that applications developed using that content will be "playable" on future systems
- A rapidly expanding set of multimedia applications
- A large number of PCs and workstations able to "play" many varieties of content
- Businesses expanding at significant growth rates

## Conclusion

Enabling open distributed systems with multimedia is a challenging goal that spans many core technologies and includes many evolving technologies from information systems, telecommunications, and consumer electronics. Over the next few years, users can look forward to a plethora of networked multimedia application solutions that incorporate international standards, and associated system integration services that span multimedia workgroup systems, enhanced desktop conferencing, and networked kiosks. As developing technologies become easier and less expensive to implement, the impact of distributed multimedia computing will be felt all over the world. What a great way to enter the twenty-first century!

# Open Distributed Multimedia Computing

**John F. Buford**

**Mark Doran**

**Jesse Bornfreund**

## Introduction

Multimedia computing will dominate the next five years of computer technology, due to the increasing need of organizations for better information and communication. Multimedia computing can deliver productivity gains to organizations because its information content is richer and more accessible, and organizational communication is integrated with the information system.

Computer-based training, multimedia authoring, group conferencing, multimedia mail, and many more applications will be available in a powerful distributed computing environment. The UNIX System is the only solution available today that can bring distributed computing and multimedia computing together on platforms ranging from laptop to supercomputer.

The UNIX System is an open model of computing developed using an open process involving users and leading computer industry vendors. The result is the most innovative technology adopted by a broad range of system vendors, application developers, and users. The corporate investment in heterogeneous computing is protected through the process of creating a truly industrywide standard. Standardization provides a technology foundation on which systems-integrators and application-developers can depend. Timely standards accelerate the growth of the market for UNIX System–based solutions.

The UNIX System holds traditional strengths in networking, client-server computing, networked file systems, and multitasking. Distributed-multimedia-computing enhancements to the UNIX System will build on these strengths to meet the real-time requirements of multimedia data and applications. As the UNIX System grows to meet these needs, it will continue to support cross-platform applications, heterogeneous computing, and emerging standards as defined by the industry and the international community. In particular, the UNIX System will evolve in compliance with the Interactive Multimedia Association's Multimedia System Services Recommended Practice, and UNIX International will participate in the technology review of this Recommended Practice.

## The Emergence of Multimedia-Based Enterprise Computing

The quest for the competitive edge, the better product, and the satisfied customer is an ongoing effort that every enterprise must make. However talented the work force and innovative the idea, the organization's investment in tools and infrastructure helps to define the starting line and map out the terrain of this pursuit. And, increasingly, the computing environment is becoming the integration point of corporate communications and information processing, the key components of this infrastructure.

The last decade has seen UNIX System–based distributed computing become pervasive. Access to services and data via local and global networks is commonplace. Powerful WYSIWYG applications for business, technical publishing, and CAD/CAM are widely used. Standardized graphical user interfaces and iconic desktops have simplified access for users. The UNIX System facilities for distributed computing have made heterogeneous computing a reality for many organizations.

The impact of UNIX System–based distributed computing will be further amplified in the next generation of computer systems due to converging developments in telecommunications, electronics, and software. These advances will bring about two significant functions that will have a direct impact on the organization's infrastructure: computer-integrated communications and distributed multimedia information systems.

### Computer-integrated communications

The networking capability provided by the UNIX System is evolving to support distributed workgroups and powerful personal communication tools. Information sharing, traditionally provided through networked file systems, electronic mail, and databases, is now advancing to permit groups of users to concurrently share applications. Such application conferencing facilitates group decision making, and can enhance and accelerate an organization's decision-making process. Workgroup technology, including computer-based conferencing and group decision-making tools, shortens the decision cycle by bringing the environment for information processing and group discussion together at the workstation desktop.

The desktop itself, which has been empowered by features such as drag-and-drop and clipboard-based interchange, will be further enhanced by new facilities for application interoperability. The incorporation of standard application interconnections will permit users to transparently utilize any application as a service, more flexibility in data interchange, and dynamic network-transparent data linkage. The interrelationships between applications and the data that these applications manage will be visible at the desktop and controlled by the user. Hypermedia information systems, envisioned many years ago by visionaries such as Vannevar Bush,* are becoming a reality.

Computer-based personal communications is an area of rapid development, driven by the proliferation of portable computers, FAX servers, wireless LANs, personal digital assistants, and other mobile computing technologies. Audio- and video-enabled workstations will extend the capabilities of computer systems to encompass telephony-like functions. Developments in public switched networks, including ISDN and digital broadband networks, are bringing traditional telephony services into integration with the private computing network. Similarly, integration of local networks and PBXs will mean the convergence of electronic and voice-mail functions.

## Distributed multimedia information systems

Simultaneously, distributed multimedia computing is appearing on the horizon. The next generation of workstations will be hardware-enabled so as to support the storage and presentation of compressed digital video and audio. In many applications, the new media forms available on the computer will provide richer, more natural, and more accessible representation. In numerous cases, materials such as pictures, video clips, and recorded speech will be easily obtained and communicate the desired information more effectively.

The support for these new media forms will impact all services and applications. Multimedia user interfaces, databases, authoring and presentation tools, interchange, and many others will become standard parts of the application framework. Today's information systems will be transformed into multimedia repositories. Information that previously had to be stored and processed outside of the computer will now be accessible in the same context as the records and reports that make up the day-to-day information flow of the organization. All information, whether text, picture, audio, or video, will be integrated, easily accessed, and shared with others over the computer network.

In the new enterprise model of computing, workgroup communication and collaboration, rich multimedia information representation, and more accessible user interfaces will be the new tools that provide the competitive edge. The UNIX System model for distributed computing is the best commercial system for enabling these developments, and is poised to deliver the functionality that will permit organizations to grow these exciting new capabilities.

---

*Vannevar Bush foresaw the era of hypermedia computing in his discussion of the memex memory extension device in the famous 1945 article, "As We May Think."

## UNIX System Strengths for Open Distributed Multimedia Computing

The benefits of multimedia information systems and group-communication tools depend upon a correspondingly solid distributed computing foundation. Without adequate interconnectivity, the organization's information base is fragmented, leading to duplication, incompatibilities, and communication delays. The value of multimedia information lies not only in the rich modes of expression but also in the web of interrelationships and the cross-references within this data. Network computing can connect an organization's islands of information and make the distributed nature of the computing environment transparent to both applications and users.

Because of inherent time-dependencies, multimedia content has transmission and presentation constraints not present in traditional data types. When multimedia data is transferred over a network for applications such as computer-based training, presentation delivery, search-and-retrieval, or conferencing, the network and operating system must be able to satisfy certain performance constraints. The UNIX System has been designed from the beginning to support multitasking, sophisticated device control, a layered network architecture, and other features necessary for meeting these demands.

One of the strengths of the UNIX System's networking is its support for client-server computing. Application software can be placed on any node on the network and accessed by any number of remote users. This simplifies software management, reduces costs, and provides higher levels of performance and reliability for users. The client-server model is being taken to new levels of capability as a direct result of the new standards for distributed object-based computing.

From laptop to supercomputer, the UNIX System covers the largest range of computing platforms. This gives organizations the greatest flexibility in building their computer environment. With the UNIX System on every platform, each system will be a full member of the distributed multimedia environment. Further, the UNIX System is an open system: it doesn't lock system designers into proprietary approaches to multimedia computing. The UNIX System evolution is determined not by a single company but by the participation of all members of the UNIX System community. This open approach protects each company's investment and offers the combined innovation of industry leaders.

The UNIX System community is committed to continued technology innovation and evolution. The UNIX System enjoys natural advantages in networking, distributed computing, and the other functions needed to build today's and the future's information systems that multimedia data will be used in. The evolution toward these future systems will be driven not by a single proprietary approach but by the combined resources of industry leaders committed to open distributed computing.

## Multimedia Applications and UNIX System Services

### Kernel support

Multimedia information has long been considered for computer applications, but the amount of data and its strict timing requirements have been an obstacle. Recent international standards for the compression of digital video and image have made it possible to have high-quality moving and still pictures with a fraction of the data storage requirements. These standards are being implemented in hardware by a large number of chip vendors, and are expected to be available on next generation workstations.

In addition to the inherent timing requirements of video, audio, and computer animations, multimedia applications often define synthetic timing relationships. These additional timing constraints are used to achieve synchronization between presentation or interaction steps. To meet the timing constraints, which can be at millisecond-resolution, the kernel must provide a facility for real-time scheduling. Otherwise the scheduler in the multitasking operating system will introduce delays and degrade the application's performance. The UNIX System has been designed for multitasking, a crucial prerequisite for real-time scheduling. Throughout the kernel, facilities accommodating the execution of many tasks have been made part of the original design.

Digital video and audio typically are transferred between secondary storage devices, or the network adapter, to or from the presentation hardware. Even though hardware compression is used, these data transfers consume significant kernel buffer space. Intelligent buffer management and interdevice data transfers are crucial kernel design issues that effect the efficiency of multimedia data delivery. Otherwise, unnecessary data transfer operations can sap the efficiency of the system.

The UNIX System accommodates these needs by providing several buffer allocation services and a common device-driver interface that supports I/O devices of all types.

### File-system support

CD-ROM will be a common vehicle for the publishing of multimedia materials because of its high density and low cost. Further, CD-ROM density is expected to double or quadruple, which will permit even larger amounts of information to be stored on a single disk. In particular, files on the order of a gigabyte or more could be stored on such disks. The current UNIX System file API and file systems, including the powerful networked file system services, are being extended to support these larger sizes.

UNIX System vendors participated in the establishment of a common CD-ROM logical file format as defined by the High Sierra Group, which led to the ISO 9660 standard. Subsequently the UNIX System community has adopted the Rock Ridge extensions for providing support for POSIX-compatible semantics for ISO 9660. This framework supports traditional UNIX System file-system features such as long file names, upper- and lowercase characters, deep directories, and symbolic links. In addition to CD-ROM and CD-ROM XA, widely used CD formats for consumer multimedia products will be supported so as to provide additional cross-platform compatibility.

Network file systems, a hallmark of UNIX System distributed computing, provide the essential service of transparent access to files on remote hosts. Files that contain multimedia information may require delivery within certain time constraints. The network file-system services will use underlying network services to meet these constraints.

### Network support

High-bandwidth network protocols such as 100-Mbps Ethernet, FDDI, and ATM are expected to make the networking of digital video and audio practical. The UNIX System network architecture, TCP/IP, is tightly integrated with the rest of the UNIX System and provides the range of services needed to support both small- and large-scale networks. TCP/IP is the basis for the Internet, a large-scale network connecting most universities and government and corporate laboratories. It provides the abstractions for supporting client-server computing, networked file systems, electronic mail, remote login, file transfer, and many other application needs of the network. As multimedia data is added to the network, TCP/IP performance when it comes to the networking of time-dependent data will be further enhanced.

TCP/IP will use characteristics of the data being transmitted, as well as performance requirements of the application, in order to optimize performance for multimedia data transmission. The application requirements for data delivery are referred to as a *quality-of-service (QOS) metric* that represents the application or user's measure of the expected quality of the delivered multimedia information. This measure indirectly effects the network resources allocated to the application or user. The network services use QOS to prioritize resource allocation, and to determine how service should be degraded as demands for network resources increase.

TCP/IP currently provides a point-to-point connection model using *the socket abstraction*. If two or more applications need to communicate, a pair-wise set of connections is made. Computer-based conferencing and telephony can use the existing connection abstraction to create multipoint connections for group-communication sessions. These sessions are logical entities that can be modified by operations such as adding a party, forwarding a call, and joining or splitting a session.

### User interface and desktop services

The user interface for the UNIX System is based on a window system, with style guidelines for application developers to follow. The window system uses the client-server model so that applications may be run from any host reachable on the network. The client-server window system is a powerful feature for the user. As digital video, digital audio, and multimedia device control are added to the UNIX System, client-server control for these media types will mean continued network transparency for UNIX System applications.

Application toolkits provide standard interface components that facilitate the construction of the user interface. Multimedia interfaces, which greatly enrich the visual dimension of current applications, will be constructed using additional application-toolkit facilities, including

- *Media API,* to provide client-server control over digital media such as video and audio
- *Device-control API,* to control external devices such as laserdisc players and VCRs
- *Temporal composition and synchronization abstractions,* to describe and control the scheduling of presentation sequences
- *Multimedia-interchange API,* to support standard multimedia formats for clipboard, file storage, and interapplication interchange, as well as selection techniques

The current crop of toolkit-based applications adhere to a common style guide, which gives the user a consistent look and feel. This consistency is an important part of the application context that the user experiences. Additional guidelines will provide recommendations regarding the use of presentation media, media controls, and multimedia-based metaphors for application interaction, so that the desktop can continue to provide the benefits of a uniform look and feel.

The desktop will have standard built-in tools such as media players, recorders, and editors, so that simple media services can always be accessed by the user through the desktop. These tools will have equivalent shell-level commands.

### Interchange services

Multimedia information has complex temporal relationships, multiple media data-types, and dynamic and interactive behaviors. The interchange and communication of such information requires specially designed multimedia data formats that are recognized by applications. These formats will be used for interchange between applications and for file storage, and by electronic mail systems.

## A Framework for Distributed Multimedia Services

The provision for multimedia information and communication in the computer affects most services provided by the operating system and network. The design of these new extensions is interrelated, as shown in Fig. 45.1. Each block in system services represents a functional area that will be extended

**Figure 45.1**  Framework for UNIX system–based multimedia services.

with additional multimedia-related facilities. These blocks are organized in a hierarchy so as to show the basic dependencies among functional areas. For example, file-system and network functions depend upon kernel functions.

There are six functional areas:

1. *Desktop.* This is the user interface component of the system services. It will include built-in tools for controlling media presentation and recording.

2. *Toolkit.* The toolkit functional area provides application developers with a standardized, high-level API, and with access to corresponding services. The services and API simplify the design of multimedia applications by providing all generic services that might be needed by such applications. The existing toolkit API provides the building blocks for the graphical user interface. Additions to the toolkit API will provide various multimedia and inter-change services, as described on pp. 45.6 and 45.7.

3. *File system.* The file system handles the logical organization and manage-ment of secondary storage devices, in both stand-alone and distributed environments. As described on pp. 45.5 and 45.6, the file system will sup-port CD-ROM, CD-ROM XA, and other widely used compact disc formats, including extensions for large files and large file systems.

4. *Application services.* The application services identified on pp. 45.6 and 45.7 that will be accessible from any point in the network are represented by this functional area. Applications typically use toolkit APIs to access these services.

5. *Network.* The network functional area provides all facilities necessary for internetworking, as discussed on p. 45.6. Extensions to the network archi-tecture will include management of multiparty connections and perfor-mance, and the use of QOS metrics as specified by the application.

6. *Kernel.* The kernel is the locus of the operating system in which the most basic system services exist, such as scheduling, memory management, and I/O control. As described on p. 45.5, real-time scheduling and intelligent buffer management will be built on the existing multitasking and generic I/O device-control architecture of the kernel.

Multimedia applications will require access to specific devices such as digi-tal-audio and -video adapters, CD-ROM drives, and adapters for network pro-tocols such as FDDI or ATM. These are shown in Fig. 45.1 as external devices. These in turn rely upon further technology standards such as ISO 9660, MPEG, or JPEG, as shown in the supporting technologies area. Further information about these supporting technologies is provided just a few pages further on.

## The UNIX System and Emerging Multimedia Standards

The nature of multimedia technology is such that a wide variety of disciplines are involved in defining it. Participants in both international standards com-mittees and industry trade groups have recognized that standardization can accelerate the development of the marketplace. As a result, "the heat is on" to create standards for monomedia formats, new network protocols, interchange formats, and APIs. The final section of this chapter summarizes some of this activity.

At the same time, vendors such as Apple and Microsoft already have defined platform-specific formats widely adopted by application developers. The benefits of multimedia information will be greatest in an environment of cross-platform interoperability and interchange. The UNIX System is open, and is compatible with heterogeneous computing environments. It will continue to be the only choice for vendor-neutral support of a wide range of computing platforms.

Standardization of multimedia system services is being undertaken by the Interactive Multimedia Association (IMA). IMA is using an RFT (request for technology) process to solicit technology that it will approve as a platform-independent Multimedia System Services Recommended Practice. UNIX International will review multimedia system service technologies submitted to IMA and provide comments to IMA regarding the adequacy of these technologies for the UNIX System. UNIX International will pursue compliance with the IMA Multimedia System Services Recommended Practice when it is available, and will use the IMA Multimedia System Services RFT as the basis for its own multimedia system-services-requirements specification.

## The Benefits of Open Distributed Multimedia Computing

The UNIX System multimedia extensions will provide the functionality needed for future distributed multimedia information and communication systems. These extensions will benefit both users and application developers by defining new facilities and APIs that will be available on every UNIX System platform. This will simplify and shorten multimedia product development and porting. Users will obtain the benefits of the integration of multimedia and distributed computing in an open system that provides cross-platform compatibility. These benefits include access to powerful tools for multimedia authoring and information processing, group conferencing and application sharing, leading to improved organizational efficiency and communication.

There are functions, such as client-server access to digital media control and device control, that are common to all multimedia applications. Without standard APIs, each developer must define and implement these facilities. This impedes the progress of applications and limits the growth of the multimedia market. By providing such functions, the UNIX System will make it possible for developers to focus on application-specific functionality.

The UNIX System has a vision of distributed multimedia computing. This vision will be based on widely adopted standards, will support the full range of platforms, and will be vendor-neutral. It is a vision shared by the leading computer industry vendors who have contributed to its definition. It is a vision of significantly improved corporate productivity through richer information processing and more integrated organizational communication.

## Glossary of Selected Multimedia Terms

**ATM (asynchronous transfer mode)**   A network-switching technique that uses short packets and that can be implemented in hardware for very high switching rates.

**DVI (digital video interactive)**   An Intel Corp. format for compressed digital video.

**FDDI (fiber distributed-data interchange)**   A standard network protocol, similar to Token Ring, that provides a raw data rate of 100 Mbps and uses fiber-optic-based transmission.

**H.261**   A CCITT recommendation, Video Codec for Audiovisual Services at p*64 kbps, developed for digital video telephony using ISDN transmission rates. Also called *p*64*.

**High Sierra Group**   An initial computer industry effort to define a common, platform-independent logical file format for CD-ROM, later subsumed by ISO 9660.

**Hyperlink**   In hypermedia or hypertext information, the structural element that connects two or more objects for the purpose of interobject navigation or traversal.

**Hypermedia**   The ability to access multimedia information by navigating interobject links.

**HyTime (Hypermedia Time-based Structuring Language)**   A standard defined by the International Standards Organization for specifying the logical structure of hypermedia and multimedia documents. HyTime is based on the ISO standard SGML (Standard Generalized Markup Language).

**Hypertext**   The ability to access text information through interaction with explicit document links.

**IMA (Interactive Multimedia Association)**   A computer industry trade group developing multimedia service and format definitions for recommended use throughout the industry.

**JPEG (Joint Photographic Experts Group)**   A committee within the International Standards Organization responsible for defining standards for digital image compression.

**MHEG (Multimedia and Hypermedia information encoding Experts Group)**   A committee within the International Standards Organization responsible for defining an interchange format for real-time multimedia information interchange.

**MPEG (Moving Pictures coding Experts Group)**   A committee within the International Standards Organization responsible for defining standards for compressed digital video (with associated audio). The current MPEG video compression standard is targeted at data rates of about 1.5 Mbps, resulting in video quality approximately that of VHS.

**Multimedia**   The use of a combination of two or more media forms such as text, graphics, image, audio, or video, possibly with time relationships, as an information representation.

**Rock Ridge Extensions**   A framework for adding POSIX support to ISO 9660, including handling long (255+) file names, upper- and lowercase characters, deep directories, and symbolic links.

**TABLE 45.1    Representative Multimedia Standards, Industry-Adopted Formats, and Recommended Practices**

| Purpose | Standard industry format or recommended practice | Organization | Description |
|---|---|---|---|
| | Recommended practice for multimedia data exchange | IMA | Multimedia interchange format |
| Multimedia Mail | MIME | IETF | Electronic mail of multimedia data |
| Document Architectures | HyTime | ISO | Hypermedia document model for SGML |
| | HyperODA | ISO | Hypermedia document model for ODA |
| Scriptware | Scripting language for interactive multimedia titles | IMA | Recommended practice for application script languages |
| | Standard multimedia scripting language | ISO | Scripting language for multimedia authoring |
| Compact Disc Formats | ISO 9660 | ISO | Platform-independent file format for CD-ROM |
| | Rock Ridge extensions | Various companies | Framework for adding POSIX support to ISO 9660 |
| | CD-ROM | Philips | Compact disc computer data format |
| | CD-ROM-XA | Philips | Extended architecture for CD-ROM |
| | CD-DA | Philips | Compact disc consumer audio format |
| | CD-I | Philips | Compact disc |
| | PhotoCD | Kodak | Photographic image CD |
| Application Architectures | Distributed object management facility | Object management group | Distributed object-oriented application architecture |
| System Services | Recommended practice for multimedia system services | IMA | Operating system extensions to support interactive distributed multimedia applications |

**Script language, or Scriptware**    A programming language intended to control interactive multimedia presentations.

## Multimedia Standards and Recommended Practices

Multimedia computing involves a broad range of technologies, many of which are being developed and standardized by collective industry participation in either trade groups or international standards bodies. A partial listing of these activities is given in Table 45.1 which categorizes these efforts into the following areas:

- Fundamental media types: compressed digital video, compressed digital image, and digital audio
- Interchange and multimedia mail formats
- Multimedia document architectures and script languages
- Compact disc formats and standards
- System services and application architectures

Each category names the standard or format, identifies the defining organization, and summarizes the principal purpose. Although specific details of many formats will be transparent to the multimedia system services, general characteristics such as data rates, synchronization requirements, and application use must be factored into the supporting system design. The UNIX System will be compatible with existing multimedia standards and recommended practices in order to fulfill the requirements of open distributed multimedia computing.

## Acknowledgments

Our thanks go out to the following individuals and their companies, for invaluable help with review and input to this chapter:

| | |
|---|---|
| David Bernstein | SCO |
| Louis Boczek | SCO |
| John Dawson | Gain/Sybase |
| David Elliott | Sony |
| Ruth Klein | USL |
| Isreal Pinkas | Intel |
| Bill Pratt | SunSoft |
| Kimihiko Iwamura | Fuji Xerox |
| Akira Kumakiri | Fuji Xerox |
| Piero Scaruffi | Olivetti |
| Murali Sundaresan | Intel |
| Rodney Wilson | Sony |

# Virtual Reality in a Nutshell

**Richard V. Kelly, Jr.**

## Forms of Virtual Reality

Most of virtual reality's essentials can be described in threes. There are three general forms of VR, for example. There are also three kinds of VR application, three levels of necessary VR software, and three general types of VR hardware peripherals.

The most common form of virtual reality, called *through-the-window VR,* is already well known to the general public through its widespread use in arcade games and motion-based seat theaters. Through-the-window VR allows a participant to look into a virtual world from a seat in the real world. The "window" the user looks through may be as small as a home-computer monitor, or as large as a two-story movie screen. Motion-based seat theaters, the most common manifestation of through-the-window VR, allow for no true interactivity. The user is simply flown through a 2D-film-based world, usually at high speed on a bumpy ride, without being given any chance to change the itinerary or to interact with objects in the world. Through-the-window arcade games, however, usually are based on computer-generated images, not film, and thus are often more effective, usually allowing both 3D effects and some interactivity.

In a through-the-window theater experience, the participant views scenes on the screen while the seat lurches and shudders in response to the images portrayed: roller-coasters, swan-dives off buildings, and cliff-edge dune-buggy rides. The images are almost always "real" images (that is, photographed with a motion-picture camera) rather than "virtual" images (created in software). And any participant who looks away from the screen during the experience "falls out of" the world and back into the reality of the theater. But the sensations of speed and rapid movement while looking at that world can be convincing.

*Immersive VR,* on the other hand, is done with a head-mounted display and emphasizes interactivity with a virtual (software-derived, not filmed) 3D environment. The head-mount allows the participant to enter and become immersed in the virtual world. The principal differences between immersive and other forms of VR include the fact that the user in an immersive system can turn around, look behind, and see something in the virtual world—swimming fish, exploding volcanoes, angry wasps, or the back door—not just the back of a theater seat. An immersive virtual world is genuinely three-dimensional and inclusive.

Usually, immersive worlds also are *interactive:* the participant decides where to travel. This freedom may even extend to traveling outside the models built by the VR world-developer, even allowing the user to fly up through the ceiling or into the walls. And immersive worlds often are manipulable; that is, the objects in the virtual world can be "collided" with and can respond with a behavior as a result of the collision. A virtual dog can, for example, after being contacted in the virtual world, back up, or disappear, or fetch a bone, or attack the user.

The head-mounted display actually has two components to it that make possible the effect of immersion. One is the display itself, typically LCDs mounted in front of collimating lenses that straighten out the light rays from the LCDs, making them appear to emanate from optical infinity rather than 4 inches from the eyes. The other element is a tracking device that records the movements of the user and sends the coordinates it collects to the computer. Those coordinates tell the software rendering the images onto the LCDs where the user is looking. Without a tracker, the user's viewpoint would not change as the head's coordinates changed, and the effect of immersion would not be cogent.

The third type of VR, *second-person VR,* uses a camera to capture the image of the participant and insert it into the virtual world. Users then watch their own images on a television or movie screen interacting with objects in the virtual world. One popular game in second-person VR features virtual hockey rinks with virtual nets and skaters, and pucks that are deflected by a real keyed-in goalie.

In most second-person systems, the insertion of the participant into the virtual world is done via chroma-keying. This sometimes creates highlights around the participant, or image-resolution differences between the participant and the background (similar to what TV viewers see when they watch the meteorologist stand in front of weather maps on the local evening news). And it often takes a minute of practice to correlate one's own body movements with what is happening on the screen. But in time the user easily gets the hang of interacting with objects and scenes in the virtual world.

A combination of second-person and immersive VR yields a hybrid type known as a *cave.* In a cave, the participant walks into a room and is surrounded by a virtual environment. The environment may be displayed on multi-TV walls or on rear-screen projections. The user can interact with the projected objects because a camera, or an optical or magnetic tracker, captures the user's coordinates and sends them to the system, notifying the computer where the user is in the world and thereby triggering responses from the virtual inhabitants, who are displayed on the walls, floor, and ceiling.

Of these three main forms of VR, the one people most often think of as "real VR" is immersive. But *virtual reality*'s definition has been stretched as widely as *multimedia*'s has, and it is likely to be stretched farther as marketers begin to call everything from 3D video games to network visualization systems "virtual reality."

## VR Application Types

There are three general types of VR application, each with its own benefits, limitations, and uses. They are *perambulation, synthetic experience,* and *realization/reification.*

*Perambulation* involves walking or flying through some form of model. This may take the form of rolling through the CAD rendering of a hospital in a virtual wheelchair, checking for architectural barriers to access. Or it may involve meandering down a human esophagus at the end of a virtual endoscope, looking for lesions or ulcers in the stomach. In a perambulation, the user is mostly interested in observing aspects of the virtual world and in discovering something about that world. Interactivity generally is limited. Interactivity may focus on moving objects around in virtual space (repositioning furniture in a virtual house), or removing objects from the scene (excising tumors from a duodenum). But for the most part, perambulation applications center on observation rather than manipulation of the virtual world.

*Synthetic experience,* on the other hand, involves the training of muscle memory. Synthetic-experience applications, such as virtual surgery or power plant-control-room operation, allow participants to safely and cheaply practice skills that are dangerous or expensive to develop in the real world. In synthetic experience, the most important aspect of the virtual world is not its appearance but its ability to allow direct interaction between a user and objects in the virtual world. A participant in such a world learns how to perform actions, usually with the hands, by practicing them (not just observing them), in the same way as a pianist learns to play a new composition.

The actions performed in a synthetic-experience world often are those that may someday mean life or death to the participant, but that occur so rarely in real life that they can't often be practiced ahead of time. Firefighters, for example, can learn to direct water onto those areas of a virtual chemical fire that will yield them the greatest fire-reduction the fastest. Police officers can learn to defuse virtual bombs. Plant workers can practice adjusting the level of flow through pipes in a virtual refinery. The goal of such VR systems is to allow participants to practice certain critical actions over and over until they become second nature, in the hope that their instinctive reactions will then serve them well when those reactions are needed in the real world.

The third type of application, *realization/reification,* allows users to see and to graphically manipulate profuse context-dependent data. *Reification* means making a thing out of an idea, and *realization,* an extension of scientific visualization and visual languages, refers to the representation of complex data in a graphical fashion. Such a representation, unlike most scientific visualizations or visual language icons, usually is both three-dimensional and interactive.

The chief uses of realization are in industries that process prodigious quantities of data in real time. These include network industries such as telecommunications, utilities, and financial services. The benefit that realization/reification offers is the presentation of directly manipulable data, i.e., something one step beyond ordinary graphical displays.

In a traditional spreadsheet, for example, what-if analysis can be done by changing a single number in the spreadsheet and watching the other columns of numbers change in response. An ordinary graphical presentation of this data allows the user to see those changes occur on a bar chart or scatter graph. VR, however, allows not only the graphical presentation of the results but graphical manipulation of the data; that is, not just graphical *output,* but graphical *input.*

A realization system allows the user to reach out into a seascape of livefeed data that the user sees as waves moving across the screen in real time. The user can view, say, Spot FX data (foreign currencies) as they emerge from a Reuters feed, and can perform what-if analysis interactively with the live data. By reaching out with a wand or glove, the user can press down on Japanese yen prices to see the system reveal the concomitant increase in wave heights for the British pound and Swiss franc, or push profits from sales of a minor currency, such as the Swedish krone, across the screen into purchases of a major one, such as the French franc, seeing the resulting predicted effect on the whole portfolio.

The engine behind such a system is the same as that behind any network predictive system: part expert system rulebase, part inductive algorithm, part neural net. What VR adds is the ability to reach out and touch data directly, and to see the results of those actions immediately displayed in the data-seascape virtual world.

## VR Software and Graphics

In order to run any of these VR applications, three pieces of software are necessary: device drivers, world model builders, and navigation tools.

*Device drivers* connect the unique devices needed to navigate in and interact with virtual worlds to the code that renders the images. They allow the user to communicate with the virtual world.

Typical devices include everything from optical coordinate sensors that track the movements and head orientations of a participant, to spaceballs that allow unlimited flight through virtual worlds, to the motion-based seats that respond to the user's movement in virtual space, to soundboards that add a sonic component to virtual worlds. All of these devices capture signals from the participants and send them to the virtual world, or take signals from objects in the virtual world and send them to the user. And it is the device drivers that process and route those signals.

*World-development kits,* the next level up in the VR software hierarchy, allow the builder to construct stationary models to later be flown through, manipulated, or animated. Most standard CAD packages can act as development environments. CAD world-development kits generally allow creation of objects in wireframe. These objects then are imported into the navigation engine, where they can be filled, animated, imbued with lifelike behavior, positioned, and lighted. World development is the construction of the stationary model to be traveled through and also the dynamic objects that act in virtual space. But another piece of software is needed to allow the user to travel in that virtual space.

The *navigation/rendering engine* (not to be confused with the hardware "rendering engine," the graphics board that provides the processing power to draw the images on the screen) is a software tool used to navigate through, manipulate, and enliven the images created by the world-development software. Navigation engines are the real workhorses of VR, the software components that make VR a possibility. Some are object-based, some C++–based, some provide their own scripting language. Some even provide easy iconic graphical environments for object construction, making them combined world-development kits and navigation engines. Others focus on navigation and rendering processing power alone.

When building a virtual world, a VR world designer has three levels of graphics with which to construct a new reality. The largest-scale level is the *geometry primitive.* Common geometries are spheres, cones, and cubes. These can be variously shaded, lighted, colored, positioned, and animated to provide a world that conveys the impression of being filled with recognizable objects.

The more detailed level below geometries is the *polygon.* Think of polygons as the faces of the cube or the sides of the pyramid. Onto these polygons can be mapped textures (scanned images such as photographs, zebra stripes, or brick patterns) that add to the photorealism of the final world.

At the lowest and most processing-intensive level are *voxels,* three-dimensional pixels. This is the level at which medical imaging is done. Because the amount of detail it can convey is huge—and, consequently, its CPU demands prodigious—voxel-level work in VR is, at least so far, not readily attainable. But as this is nothing more than a performance limitation, not requiring any fundamental breakthrough in the technology, only more horsepower, it is likely to dissolve as a limitation over the next several years.

## Peripherals

Peripheral devices also fall into three categories: audio/visual, tracking, and navigation/manipulation.

The visual side of VR encompasses everything from the movie screens at theme parks, to the standard VGA monitors that most developers use to build and test their worlds, to the head-mounted displays that occlude the peripheral vision of users and make them feel that they are inside the virtual world.

On the audio side, there are ordinary MIDI boards that release sampled sounds when buttons are pressed or virtual objects contacted. But there are also audio boards that allow for "spacialization" of sound (giving the impression that a sound is coming from a given direction and altitude). They may even allow particular sound parameters to be tied directly to objects in the virtual world, such as airplanes whose engine roars doppler-shift as they approach the listener. And because touch is still a difficult sensation to emulate in VR, many developers substitute sound cues for tactile ones. This *sonic feedback collision announcement* allows users to hear a sound cue when they have touched an object, rather than actually feel it.

*Tracking devices,* another major group of VR peripherals, are used to send the coordinates of the participant's head, hands, or body to the renderer, so that the computer will know where the user is looking. Trackers generally work within "6 degrees of freedom"; that is, they handle movement in X,Y,Z space (position) and roll, pitch, and yaw (orientation). (*Roll:* turn your chin to the left and the top of your head to the right. *Pitch:* lift your chin up, and dip the back of your head back. *Yaw:* turn your head to the right or left. In all three instances your body stays in the same X,Y,Z position, but your orientation changes.) Trackers come in optical, sonic, inertial, direct physical, and magnetic varieties.

*Navigation/manipulation devices,* the last major peripheral component of a VR system, include everything from gloves for picking up objects in the virtual world, to globes for sailing through them, to foot pedals, joysticks, wands, and gyroscopic flying mice. The more advanced work in this area is now being done in the use of biological signals as inputs to the virtual world. Biofeedback signals such as EEGs, EKGs, galvanic skin response, and myography (muscle tension) are now being used as inputs that manipulate objects, viewpoints, or actions in the virtual world. This work may eventually lead to direct linkage between human bodily processes—even thoughts—and actions in the virtual world.

## The Range of VR Applications

Not unexpectedly, the most rapid development of VR applications is now occurring in the entertainment field. Within a couple of years, VR entertainment in arcades and homes will be ubiquitous. Most arcade VR games, because they are relatively expensive and are time-fee-based, are testosterone-driven and involve little or no learning. The user simply dons a headmount or sits in a motion-based gondola and the experience begins, usually involving shooting opponents of some kind. Home-based VR tends to be far more involved and complex, because home players spend far longer inside their games and prepay a lump sum for the experience rather than a by-the-minute fee. Thus home games tend to be far richer, more learning-driven environments. However, they too tend to concentrate merely on thwarting villains.

In the field of medicine, the Holy Grail is the virtual cadaver. Attempts to develop a virtual living body are being made via four different approaches. *Film-based endoscopy* allows a user to travel down a virtual esophagus, cobbled together from several thousand photographs of real throats. *MRI-based systems* construct whole body sections, organ by organ, from scan data. *Microtome reconstructions* embed a real cadaver in wax, slice it, digitize the 2D slices, and arrange them into a 3D image in the computer. And *software-based organ development* builds models of living organs from scratch, out of polygons and voxels.

My own work in this field has centered around animating virtual organs and organ systems using the principles of Artificial Life, a technology for modeling extremely complex living processes. This method combines 3D cellular automata, neural nets, genetic algorithms, and production rules together with VR as the display mechanism, in order to portray processes such as tumor development or immune function, or to reveal approaches to gene therapy using engineered viruses as the mechanisms for site-directed mutagenesis (employing hand-changed viruses to insert their cargoes into malfunctioning cells).

In the network industries (telecom, utilities, financial services, and medical infomatics), VR work is concentrating on developing new metaphors for dealing with data: expressing relationships between vast amounts of related data; allowing users to interact directly with graphically displayed data; and representing data in three dimensions so as to elicit "intuitive understanding" of prodigious quantities of data.

The work in these fields includes the exploration of novel metaphors for the displaying of profuse data: everything from Christmas trees the color and shape of whose bulbs represent types of problems in a network, to hydraulic models that show energy-transmission lines as pipes and reveal capacity by the diameter of the pipe and usage by the height of the water in the pipe, to rolling, wavy seascapes of continuous livefeed data that can be processed and speculated against by pushing and pulling as if the data were interactive taffy.

In architecture, most VR work has focused on edifice-prototyping and -testing. Edifices range from rooms in a private residence, to hospitals, to vast chemical-plant facilities. This approach allows the user to construct the virtual building first, then test it for compliance with various regulations or for the comfort and well-being of future denizens.

Our work in this arena has concentrated on linking the construction of the virtual building to a spreadsheet, so that design considerations can be visualized and their financial outcomes viewed simultaneously. Viewers can then make changes to the building in real time, to satisfy design-versus-finance constraints. They can then view the building to see whether it looks the way they want it to look, and study the resulting spreadsheet created by the system to see if costs are in line with budget. We've also built in comments on the environmental impacts of design decisions, allowing a client to view the effects building decisions will have on the environment as well as on the purse and on the eyes.

The area of VR development currently undergoing the greatest amount of corporate and industrial exploration is the field of skill-based training. VR's unique benefit over film and ordinary 2D graphics is that it allows users to interact with its objects. This has allowed VR developers to construct worlds in which users can practice those skills they must use in the real world.

Synthetic experience investigations in my lab, for example, involve telephone-line-worker training, switching-station training, and process control diagnosis training in large plants. This has led to an interest in "living history" and "wraparound" educational applications that allow a user to become immersed in an historical environment (the Wild West, a slave auction, traveling steerage across the Atlantic to America, under the bodhi tree with the Buddha, in Thomas Edison's lab, at a summer gathering of the nations of the Iroquois confederacy, on the battlefield at Gettysburg, in Timbuktu at the height of the Kushite empire). And beyond these real-world applications lies the ability to practice viewing and working in environments that human beings have not yet experienced (a colony on the surface of the moon, en route to Mars, a journey to the center of the earth, and worlds that exist only in the imagination).

## The Real World Is Messy

In all of the commercial areas beyond entertainment, VR developers have discovered that pure VR applications seem to be relatively few. As a result, most commercial work in the field now involves either coordination with or direct integration to other technologies. Behavioral animation (the insertion of life-like behavior into creatures in the virtual world), for example, may require half a dozen technologies and techniques outside of VR. In such a working environment, VR becomes one technology among many. And it is likely that, in time, as VR entertainment develops, these same concerns will become important to game-builders as well, as they broaden their scope from just 3D graphics in a helmet to genuine artificially enlivened universes.

The future of virtual reality points in that direction, to the commingling of other technologies with VR. For example as optic fiber replaces copper, and bandwidth limitations recede, long-distance networked VR is becoming a reality. As CPU processing power increases, detailed voxel-level images are being experimented with. As GUI designers begin to work in three dimensions, desktop metaphors gradually will be replaced by "landscape" and "interactive data-taffy" interfaces. As Artificial Life begins to play its role behind the scenes in behaviorally animating virtual objects, virtual worlds will begin to take on the richness and complexity of the real world. And as all of these advancements accelerate, it will become possible for participants in virtual experiences to feel for the first time that they are *natives* in the virtual world, not just tourists.

# 47

# The Design of a Multimedia Adapter

**Ken Morse**

## Introduction

In the mid-to-late 1970s the dominant user interface was based on a keyboard, a black-and-white text display, and a complicated command line. A few machines had simple graphics capabilities, but it wouldn't be until the release of the Apple Macintosh in 1984 that bitmapped graphics became a standard feature. With this shift toward graphics, user interfaces shifted away from the command line to mouse-driven windows and icons.

Audio has taken even longer to become accepted, but in the last several years developers have incorporated it into mainstream applications such as desktop presentations, in addition to entertainment titles.

Since the introduction of the Macintosh nearly a decade ago, the basic graphical user interface (GUI) has been only modestly improved. Color graphics displays now are commonplace, but generally with a small number of colors. New graphics adapters are being introduced that accelerate graphics performance by providing an on-card graphics processor to relieve the present burden on the host CPU.

During those 10 years since the introduction of the Macintosh, there have been some staggering technological advances: VLSI densities have increased 16-fold, enabling more complex designs to be implemented; VLSI speeds have increased eight-fold, providing a leap in processing power; networks are pervasive, and high-capacity optical-storage mediums such as CD-ROM are available at low cost.

These four major advances in basic computer technology, coupled with equally major advances in digital-video compression algorithms and video-processor architecture, have transformed the monochrome graphics display subsystem of 9 years ago into today's rich and highly dynamic video subsystem. Displays can now feature full-screen, full-motion video, high-resolution video stills, video special effects, 3D real-time synthetic video, and very fast, true color graphics—all of which form the heart of a modern multimedia system.

This chapter will examine the requirements for a multimedia subsystem and use an actual adapter by way of illustration. Multimedia is not limited to personal computers and will, over time, be available in a wide variety of products, from information booths to intelligent televisions to hand-held personal assistants. However, most designs will be very similar to those now found on personal computers; the difference will be that the degree of specialization and integration will be greater in these new applications.

## Multimedia Subsystems

What is multimedia? This is a common question, but rarely does one hear the same answer. Ask one person and she will say it is the combination of graphics and text, ask another and he will add audio to the list, ask a third and he will introduce video, and so on.

My definition of a multimedia system is one that is *capable of presenting a predefined or interactive experience in a compelling and intuitive manner.* Using this somewhat simple definition, a simple graph chart could be considered a multimedia datatype. It conveys information in an intuitive manner, even if it doesn't provide compelling experience.

This section will try to provide some insights into those issues that must be addressed by a multimedia adapter designer, such as functionality, cost, and integration. The data types of still images, motion video, and audio also will be discussed, with the emphasis being on their effect on a multimedia adapter's design.

## Graphics

An obvious requirement for any multimedia system is graphics support. As mentioned earlier, the dominant interface until the late seventies was built around a monochrome text display. With the introduction of the Macintosh, bitmapped graphics started to appear as a standard feature. IBM introduced the enhanced graphics adapter (EGA) in 1985, which provided color displays at resolutions of up to 640 × 400. At this resolution, however, the number of colors on-screen was limited to 16—useful for presentations and simple line art, but not much more.

The emergence and growth of graphical user interfaces (GUIs) prompted the rush to market of new graphics adapters that provided higher resolution. The base requirement for GUIs was 640 × 480, a resolution provided by VGA graphics systems. However, users of window-based GUIs quickly found themselves in need of more room on their "desktop" displays, and new adapters, termed SVGAs, appeared, pushing the resolution up to 800 × 600.

Just as GUIs were pushing the resolution up, desktop publishing was creating a need for higher color depth. Desktop publishing applications, which ran under the GUI environment, coupled with the introduction of affordable laser printers, created an explosion in document manipulation and generation. The availability of flatbed scanners allowed real images to be read into the computer and composed with text and graphics to form professional documents. Graphics adapters of the time were able to show acceptable gray-scale images using 256 gray scales, but users were demanding higher-quality color displays.

Current graphics adapters provide resolutions of up to $1280 \times 1024$, with $1024 \times 768$ the most commonly used mode (display monitors that support $1280 \times 1024$ tend to be expensive). At these resolutions the adapters support over 65,000 colors on-screen simultaneously by using 16 bits per pixel. Each pixel specifies the color in red-green-blue (RGB) color space, with common bit allocations of RGB:565 and RGB:664. For high-end publishing applications, 24-bit RGB is used, which provides over 16 million colors for true-color representation.

One important area that has to be addressed, given the increased resolution and color depth, is performance. A GUI requires a large amount of graphical image manipulation; for example, windows may be picked up and placed in other areas of the screen. This involves moving all the pixel data in memory representing that window to a new location in memory.

Moving from an 8-bit color display to a 24-bit display increases the data bandwidth by a factor of 3, and will cause performance to degrade by a factor of 3. This problem has been addressed by the advent of graphics accelerators, which remove some of the burden from the CPU. These accelerators implement graphics primitives for such tasks as line-drawing, polygon-filling, and area moves (bit-blitting), and can speed up graphics performance to a rate 50 times that achievable by a CPU-managed display. The CPU merely requests the accelerator to carry out the required operation, which then is executed in parallel to the CPU task.

Another area in graphics that is rapidly advancing is the use of three-dimensional objects to add realism to presentations. The talk of "virtual reality" and "virtual worlds" that can be explored from the comfort of your own armchair is everywhere in the press. Much research is being carried out in this area, and technology slowly is catching up with theory. The aim is to display on a computer screen or head goggles a believable world, one realistic enough to fool the brain. This requires a great deal of processing power to produce the real-time, realistic shading and light reflections of the natural world. High-end graphics workstations, from companies such as Silicon Graphics, are able to provide this realism. Now the challenge is to bring this technology to the wider marketplace.

## Still image support

Still images form an important part of any multimedia title by introducing realism. With the explosion of desktop publishing, images were one of the first of the multimedia data types to be added to personal computers. Initially these images were simply stored as the raw pixel values. However, given the increasing resolutions and color depths involved, their sizes became too large to be efficiently manipulated and they consumed too much memory: a 1024 × 768 image, stored as RGB24, consumes over 2 Mbytes of memory. The solution was to use compression techniques to exploit the redundancy in the image and encode the image to save both memory and storage space. In theory there is no time constraint on the compression of the image, since this is carried out only once. However, the decoding of the image must be carried out as quickly as possible, so that the least amount of delay is passed on to the user. Software-only solutions tend to be based on a run-length encoding mechanism that is easily decoded to give acceptable performance but at the cost of compression. Other more exotic schemes exist that provide much better compression but at the cost of a longer decode time.

Most compression schemes are *lossy,* meaning that they lose some image data during the compression process. The amount of data lost depends on the complexity of the original image and the compression ratio selected. The higher the compression ratio, the more data lost. Which compression ratio you choose will depend primarily on four things:

1. Image type
2. The desired resolution, which in turn depends on the context in which the image will be used
3. The amount of storage space available
4. The processing capabilities of the storage and playback devices

Over the past few years, JPEG (Joint Photographic Experts Group) has gained wide acceptance as a standard for compression of continuous-tone-color images. The algorithm is based on a combination of the Discrete Cosine Transform, quantizing, and arithmetic encoding that removes redundant image and color data.

Studies of human perception have proven that when viewing color images, for instance, the eye more readily notices changes in brightness (*luminance*) than changes in color (*chrominance*); JPEG takes advantage of that fact and, during compression, eliminates more chrominance than luminance information. JPEG can compress images at ratios of about 20:1, with no noticeable loss of quality. Compression ratios of up to 100:1 are possible, but the higher the ratio the greater the loss of detail and, sometimes, the more likely the appearance of artifacts.

Another advantage of JPEG is that it is a symmetrical compression algorithm. The same hardware or software can be used to compress and decompress an image. In addition, compression and decompression times are about the same. This does not hold true for most video-compression schemes, which are asymmetrical.

Until recently, the mechanism for translating photographic images into computer-readable form was through a flat-bed scanner. Either the photograph or a negative was scanned, providing a digital image that could then be manipulated and displayed on the computer. In 1992, Kodak introduced the

Photo-CD system, which makes the translation from photographic image to digital image much smoother. Photographs may be taken using a standard camera, and the film then taken to a developing agency. The negative is developed using standard processing techniques, but then is scanned at three different resolutions into three digital images. These images then are compressed and written to a CD-ROM. Up to 100 photographs may be stored on the CD-ROM in each of the three resolutions, using a proprietary compression scheme. It is too early to judge the success of Photo CD in the consumer market—after all, it took 5 years for audio CDs to become an accepted consumer medium. However, it certainly *is* being embraced by the multimedia development community, which now has a simple way of importing high-quality photographic images into their systems.

We see then, from our discussion up to now, that the requirement for still images is to provide a large color-depth, at an acceptable resolution, so as to support photorealistic images and to provide support for image-compression and fast decompression, and thereby to save valuable storage space.

## Motion video support

If a single picture is worth a thousand words, then motion video can tell a complete story. Motion video support comes in two flavors: live, and recorded. Live motion video, or *passthrough* video, is used when the video material is stored on media such as laserdisc or VCR tape. In this case, the laserdisc player or VCR is connected to the multimedia system and its output mixed with the computer-generated text and images. This is very popular for interactive educational and training titles whose playback devices are controlled by the computer—normally by means of a serial connection. The advantage of this system is that the picture quality is excellent, since no compression is involved. Unfortunately the additional cost, and system requirements, limit its application to niche markets.

The solution is to provide a mechanism that can store previously recorded material on the computer system and replay it on demand.

Much research has been directed toward the area of digital-video compression, and with the rapid increase in VLSI capabilities, computer-based digital motion video has become a reality. The need for compression becomes obvious when the data rates are considered. For example, a $320 \times 240$ image in an RGB16 color space requires 152 kbytes of memory. To attain full-motion digital video, the clip must be played at 30 frames per second, giving rise to a data rate of over 4.5 Mbytes per second. These kinds of data rates cannot be handled by current PC designs, and therefore compression techniques must be employed.

Most video-compression schemes attempt to reduce the data rate to that provided by CD-ROMs, 150 kbytes per second. The CD-ROM has become accepted as the medium for multimedia titles, since its large storage capacity (over 600 Mbytes) is required to contain typical multimedia titles. The 150-kilobytes-per-second requirement means that each compressed frame in a 30-frames-per-second sequence must average 5 kbytes—quite a difference from the 152 kbytes occupied by the original $320 \times 240$ RGB16 image.

Several image-resolution standards are being adopted, such as $160 \times 120$ and $320 \times 240$. The algorithms in use require additional hardware if they are to provide optimal results, but with the increase in microprocessor performance it is now possible to decode digital motion video on systems such as Intel 486s and Motorola 68040s using the CPU alone. The drawback is that most of the CPU bandwidth must be allocated to the task of decompressing and displaying the video—80 percent of the CPU cycles is a typical figure.

JPEG is also among the standards used for motion video compression today. It can be used to compress each video frame independently of other frames. This is referred to as the process of *intraframe coding*. This allows users to randomly access any individual frame within the compressed video, making it ideal for digital applications (such as video preproduction) in which access to every frame is necessary. The downside of using intraframe encoding alone is that even under high compression ratios, a few seconds of 24-bit color video stored as motion JPEG takes up a lot of space.

The standards organizations that sponsor JPEG—the Consultative Committee of International Telegraph and Telephone, and the International Standards Organization—have defined a compression standard called *MPEG* (Motion Pictures Experts Group) specifically to handle motion video. In addition to intraframe encoding for removing redundancies within individual frames, MPEG also employs *interframe coding,* which eliminates redundant information among frames. If the background of a video clip stays the same from frame to frame, for instance, MPEG will save the background once and store only the differences between those frames. MPEG supports compression ratios of up to 50:1, assuming the standard MPEG resolution of about $320 \times 240$ pixels for full-motion video. (MPEG-2 was proposed in 1992 for handling higher-resolution, broadcast-quality images).

In addition to its interframe-coding capabilities, MPEG differs from JPEG in its asymmetrical approach to compression—using more hardware and computer power to compress full-motion video and audio than to decompress it.

From this discussion it is clear that a multimedia system that supports motion video must have the ability to support high, sustained, data-transfer rates as well as provide real-time decompression capabilities for playback.

## Audio

A system with digital motion video is not much use without an accompanying audio soundtrack. Digital audio has been available as an option for PCs for several years, and is now in its third generation. The first set of 8-bit audio adapters has been superseded by 16-bit stereo audio adapters that also provide MIDI capabilities and simple FM synthesis.

PCM audio is the most prevalent form of audio found on personal computers today, but it carries a high bandwidth and storage requirement due to its uncompressed nature. Digital audio has a lower bandwidth than raw digital video but is harder to compress, since the human ear is very unforgiving.

Simple compression is achieved by reducing either the sampling rate or the number of bits per sample. Unfortunately, the effect of both of these options is very noticeable, and more complicated compression schemes are available, such as ADPCM, that provide acceptable quality with a lesser number of bits per sample.

In addition, the MPEG audio group has defined several audio-encoding schemes to accompany MPEG video. These schemes employ subband encoding to achieve compression. The audio signal is split into a series of frequency bands and then analyzed. The analysis is based on the human ear's *masking* characteristic: at an instantaneous point in time, the ear may "mask out" some frequencies close to a high-amplitude frequency component. For example if there is a strong frequency component at 6 kHz, the ear may be unable to resolve a frequency component at 6.2 kHz. Hence the data that represents the 6.2 kHz signal is redundant, and may be removed to achieve better compression. Yet even when utilizing the most complex audio-encoding schemes, the compression achieved is only a factor of 6:1.

New sound systems based on *surround sound* are being introduced that contain up to six audio channels. These systems work by adjusting the balance and delay of the audio channels between the front, back, and side speakers. Since there is a known relationship between these additional surround signals, audio-compression schemes for surround sound can achieve overall higher compression than 6:1.

The other important thing to remember about audio is that it is real-time, and therefore cannot be interrupted without the listener being aware of it. Hence, although the bandwidth is lower, the audio delivery and decode tasks must have a high priority within the system if it is to guarantee that audio data will be delivered on time.

Up to now our discussion of audio has addressed only the integration of "real-world" sounds, but there is a second category of audio: *synthesized sound*. Synthesized sound first arrived in the 1960s on Moog synthesizers, which used analog techniques to generate the sounds. With the amazing technological advances of the last 30 years, synthesized sound has made the transition into the digital domain.

MIDI, the Musical Instrument Digital Interface, is a communications specification that enables the exchange of musical information among electronic musical instruments, computers, and peripheral audio equipment. When combined with music synthesis capability, MIDI allows a personal computer to become the control center of a musical production system. Although initially used by musicians to perform music, MIDI is now an integral part of the audio-generation technology for multimedia productions.

MIDI augments the use of waveform audio in multimedia. Waveform audio normally is used to reproduce speech and many nonmusical sounds, but it requires a great deal of memory if it is to faithfully reproduce music. MIDI represents music using far less storage space, and it allows greater editing flexibility, but it does require a music synthesizer to generate the actual music. MIDI describes music in terms of high-level command sequences; for example, "Play middle C on the French horn loudly for 1 second." This command is encoded into 6 bytes—3 bytes to start the sound, and 3 bytes to terminate it. Compare this to CD-quality PCM data at 176 kilobytes per second for the same "information."

Because MIDI is a symbolic representation of music, not the audio waveform data itself, the quality of the sound is related primarily to the quality of the music synthesizer, not the MIDI data. Most synthesizers produce stereo sound, and some can very convincingly reproduce acoustic musical instruments. Speech and sound effects, recorded as specific musical sounds, are limited by the synthesizer's memory.

### Programmability

The algorithms of video and audio compression are advancing rapidly, given the release of optimized performance implementations for existing algorithms and the results of research into new compression techniques. The multimedia market is very young and, as is typical with emerging markets, there are no fully adopted standards in place. (JPEG has a foothold in the still-image fraternity, and MPEG is starting to make inroads into the motion video marketplace, but already there are a wide variety of specialized algorithms in use.) Keeping this in mind, it would be foolish to tie a particular multimedia subsystem to one particular algorithm or system.

Programmability is the key to a longer lifespan, since it enables the same subsystem to support a wide variety of algorithms and implementations. However, there is an associated price to be paid that goes along with providing a programmable solution. Programmability tends to have a twofold impact on the system. First, it increases the cost of the system, since the programmable unit must provide general-purpose facilities to support the wide variety of algorithms and implementations. Second, it tends to reduce system performance. Because it caters to a wide variety of algorithms, it is often the case that no single algorithm executes to the maximum—we are in the area of "jack of all trades and master of none." In the consumer marketplace there is a different outlook regarding programmability, as will be described later.

### Data Delivery

It has been shown in previous sections that a multimedia system will utilize a high-data bandwidth. Graphics, audio, and video data, in both compressed and decompressed forms, must be supported by the adapter, while avoiding bottlenecks in data transfer and delivery since audio and video are real-time quantities. The original PC bus—known as the ISA bus—was designed over 10 years ago, and is not suitable for high-bandwidth transfers. Hence designs must attempt to minimize the amount of data transferred across this bus. This can be achieved by ensuring that only compressed data flows over this bus. However, the multimedia adapter must be able to support local transfers of high-bandwidth uncompressed data. Hence a high-performance bus usually is implemented on the adapter, to meet those data delivery requirements.

## System Integration

Given time, many of the multimedia components such as digital audio and video will be folded into the motherboard design and become standard features on all new systems. In the short term, however, multimedia adapters must take the form of an add-in card, just like any other system add-on. This raises system-integration issues that the adapter-designer must address. For example, how is the digital motion video, provided by the adapter, to be combined with the existing graphics generated by the base machine? Perhaps the multimedia adapter should provide its own graphics system, thus making the base graphics redundant.

## Software support

All the hardware features in the world are useless if the software supplied cannot access them. The effort required for software development should never be underestimated, for it is at least as much as for hardware development. A typical software model is the *layered* approach. At the bottom layer is the hardware-specific code that communicates with the adapter and provides low-level services. Above this are the support modules, which abstract away the hardware dependencies and provide an adapter-independent application programming interface (API) for the programmer. The layered approach, and the use of hardware abstraction, make it possible for easier code migration to support follow-on hardware implementations.

Until recently, multimedia had been overlooked by operating-systems designers, but in the last two years multimedia extensions have been added to operating systems such as Microsoft's Windows and IBM's OS/2. These extensions provide a high-level set of common commands that can be used across different operating systems. For example, the commands provided in the Media Control Interface (MCI) layer in Microsoft Windows are identical (apart from a few variants) to those provided in the MCI layer of OS/2's Multimedia Presentation Manager (MMPM/2). This commonality has greatly helped developers, who now can port their titles across platforms more easily. With this in mind, any software provided with an adapter should integrate with the multimedia software extensions provided by the host operating system if it is to be fully utilized by application developers.

## Networking

Another area that has seen rapid growth in the past decade is networking. Classical networks consisted of dumb terminals served by a small minicomputer or mainframe. This configuration placed large burdens on the central computer, which was responsible for executing all the programs required by the users. With the rapid growth in microprocessor power over the last few years, this network model is changing. Terminals have been replaced by personal computers, and the central computer—the server—is often just a high-performance personal computer with a large on-line storage capability. This evolution has moved more processing power onto the terminal, allowing high-performance applications such as multimedia to be run locally. For example, consider a Token Ring network that has a 16-Mbit bandwidth. Such a network, with multimedia-equipped terminals, can easily support up to 10 digital motion video sessions (each at 150 kilobytes per second) to provide an interactive training facility.

The widespread use of networks is opening the door to *group-working,* which allows all users to share documents and communicate through the network, a simple example being electronic mail. Adding the exchange of digital video and audio over the network opens up the possibility of videoconferencing. A camera mounted on one user's machine can capture his/her image, send it over the network, and display it on a remote machine. Likewise the image of the user at the remote machine can be sent and displayed on the original machine.

Systems are being introduced for videoconferencing that use existing telephone lines and new digital (ISDN) systems to transmit the video and audio signals. Of course compression plays a large part in squeezing the large amounts of video and audio data into the relatively low-bandwidth transmission lines. Systems are not limited to the exchange of video and audio data; computer data such as drawings or charts can be transmitted, enabling real-time data exchange and presentation.

The logical extension of networking in the office is to the home. Already phone lines and video cable systems have been installed in homes, and these can form the backbone of an interactive network. Work is under way by both the phone and cable companies to run trial systems, offering such services as video-on-demand and interactive television.

A multimedia adapter that supports digital motion video could be used in conjunction with a network interface to provide the basis for such systems. *Latency* is the most critical area that must be addressed in network delivery; for example, if the latency of the compress-transmit-receive-decompress loop in a videoconferencing application is high, it will cause communication difficulties between the two parties of much the same kind as the delays experienced on transatlantic telephone conversations.

### Capture and compression

Thus far our discussion has been driven by playback concerns; how images and audio are replayed on users' machines. However there is also a market for importing real-world data into personal computers, i.e., *capture.* A capture system must encompass an array of multimedia data types; for example, a still image from a camera, a motion video sequence from a VCR, an audio track from a recital.

Such features are required primarily by multimedia title developers, and hence should not be included as part of the standard adapter but rather offered as an extension, thus reducing the cost for those users who require only playback capabilities.

A capture subsystem should allow standard devices (microphones, cassette recorders, cameras, VCRs, laserdisc players) to be connected, thus allowing as wide a range of source material as possible to be imported. We have already seen how the high data-storage requirements of audio and video require the original data to be compressed. This compression can be carried out at the time of capture, or as a subsequent process. For data types with extremely high data rates, such as motion video, compression often is carried out in tandem with the video capture and is termed a symmetrical capture-and-compression process.

An example of a case in which such a symmetrical process is required is the previous one of videoconferencing. The video sequences must be kept to a low bandwidth to match the transmission lines over which they are sent, and additionally the system must exhibit a low latency—buffering of the video and audio data must be kept to a minimum.

## Cost

Finally, there's no such thing as a free lunch! A price tag is attached to the implementation of all the aforementioned functionality, and cost plays an important part in the design process. At the end of the day the product will sell only if the customer is willing to buy at the selling price. Thus the design process tends to be a balancing act between functionality and cost. Tradeoffs constantly are made until the best product for the money has been achieved in the designers' eyes. An example of such a tradeoff is the point raised earlier, regarding the programmability of the multimedia adapter. Some implementations may address fixed functions in a high-volume marketplace, in which case a programmable solution is less desirable than a cost-effective one.

## ActionMedia II—A Practical Design

Now that we have some understanding of the requirements of a multimedia adapter, the description of an actual implementation can be presented. The adapter I have chosen is called ActionMedia II and is the result of a joint development by Intel and IBM, based on digital-video interactive (DVI) technology. The DVI technology was originally conceived in 1984 and has undergone a steady evolution, culminating in the release of ActionMedia II in 1992. Both Intel and IBM wanted to provide a system that was affordable and that had the following attributes:

- Integration to existing graphics system
- Programmable audio- and video-compression algorithms
- High-quality audio with compression
- Photorealistic still images, with compression

- Playback of video (decompression and display)
- Real-time capture and compression of video
- Passthrough of live analog-video and analog-audio material (e.g., laserdisc)
- Extendible software architecture

The following sections will provide an overview of the design, and indicate how each of the objectives listed above was achieved. As you will see, ActionMedia II is by no means an ideal solution.

## Introduction

DVI is not new. The David Sarnoff Research Center in Princeton, New Jersey, started work on DVI in 1984, when the laboratory was the central research facility for RCA. The Digital Products Research Group carried the project through the years when General Electric acquired RCA to bring it to the point of demonstration in early 1987, when it was first shown publicly on March 1 at the Second Microsoft CD-ROM Conference in Seattle. In October 1988, GE sold the DVI technology to Intel, who then brought the technology to market later that year.

The first DVI product was available as a 7-adapter set that provided reasonable-quality digital motion video output, but with an attached high price tag of $10,000 to $15,000. By 1989 IBM was looking for a partner with which to enter the desktop-video marketplace, and a joint-development agreement was entered with Intel. The first fruit of this alliance was the ActionMedia 750 (named after the 82750 chipset on-board), which reduced the 7-adapter design down to 2 adapters. This increased integration brought a new lower price and better performance, since processor power had risen due to interim advances in VLSI technology.

ActionMedia II is the latest in the line of DVI technology and takes the integration a step farther by making further use of VLSI integration techniques to reduce the design to a single adapter for playback, which retails for $1000, and a daughter card for capture, priced at $500.

The following sections detail the ActionMedia II technical design, with explanations offered, when appropriate, as to why a particular design choice was taken.

## System overview

ActionMedia II consists of a single ISA or Micro Channel (IBM PS/2) adapter, based on the i750 video-processor architecture, with an optional daughter card to provide capture capability. The motivating force behind the design of the i750 video-processor architecture was the desire to integrate all the processing functions required for multimedia into a single programmable chip set. This involved the design and development of basic video and logic building blocks that would find application over a broad range of algorithms. While a hardwired implementation may at first appear to offer better performance for a particular algorithm, a programmable approach ultimately is

**Figure 47.1**  ActionMedia II subsystem.

superior, since it can be reprogrammed to track the evolution of an algorithm or standard, and at the same time support each of the diverse algorithms required in a full multimedia system.

The ActionMedia II display subsystem is shown in Fig. 47.1. Its engine is the 82750PB pixel processor (PB) and the 82750DB display processor (DB). Separate from the host processor, PB is responsible for most of the classical data-processing and control functions in the subsystem. The pixel processor compresses and decompresses image data from memory, generates fast graphics and special effects, and acts as the master arbiter for subsystem memory and interdevice transactions.

The display processor performs real-time display functions, including data-format transactions, color translation, and pixel-value interpolation. It also provides outputs that support image-capture and video-synchronization. The DB generates all the timing signals required to drive display devices, including digital and analog RGB or YUV pixel outputs. An 8-bit digital word-of-alpha channel is provided so as to obtain a fractional mix of DB outputs, with another video source to achieve video effects such as titling and graphic overlays.

DVI technology performs its operations in YUV color space. Each YUV component is represented as a series of 8-bit samples. In this color system the luminance, or brightness, information (as given by the Y information), is separated from the chrominance, or color, information (as given by the U and V components).

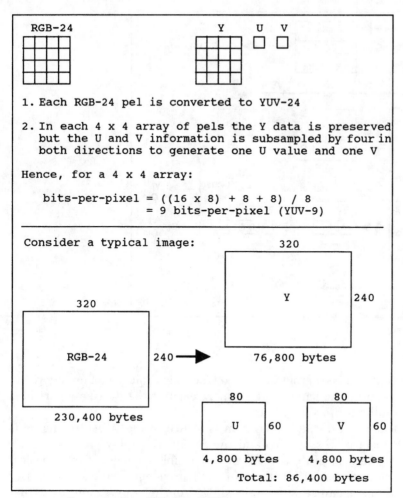

**Figure 47.2**  Conversion from RGB-24 to YUV9.

Working in this domain allows various psychovisual effects to be exploited. Most notably, color information need not be stored at the same resolution as the luminance data. For this reason, color information is stored at one-half or one-quarter the luminance density in each dimension, without significant loss of image quality. Since luminance and chrominance information are stored at different resolutions, they are placed in different bitmaps. An example of how an RGB-24 image is converted into YUV-9 is shown in Fig. 47.2.

### The 82750PB pixel processor

The 82750PB was designed as a cost-effective, real-time video-and-graphics processor for multimedia applications. Its architecture, with fully static, 25-MHz, single-cycle instruction execution, supports real-time, full-screen encoding and decoding of digital motion video at 30 frames per second. The PB can

**Figure 47.3**   82750PB pixel processor.

simultaneously perform a wide range of video effects, including scaling motion video into windows, texture-mapping video onto surfaces, and many screen-transition effects.

The PB architecture was designed to be simple, efficient, and highly parallel. Figure 47.3 is a simplified diagram of the 82750PB.

A 32-bit linear, byte-addressable, external address bus and 32-bit data bus are used to communicate with external memory and external devices. Internal data paths are either 16 or 32 bits wide and designed to allow the simultaneous processing of two or more 8-bit pixels. Functional blocks are connected to one another using one or more of these buses, and the PB can transfer data simultaneously over any one of them during any given cycle.

A 16-bit ALU, augmented by a 16-bit barrel shifter, is used to perform most arithmetic, logical, and control operations. The ALU supports 32 types of operations specific to processing video data, such as operations on dual "side-by-side" 8-bit pixel values. The ALU and barrel shifter (as well as most other functional blocks) communicate with a multiport 16-word × 16-bit register file and a 512-word × 16-bit data RAM. The RAM can be accessed from two 16-bit buses via four independent pointers. These "C-style" pointers can be auto incremented and decremented, as well as take part in general-purpose ALU operations.

The PB also contains two specialized, semi-independent structures that are optimized for image-processing tasks. First, the pixel interpolator calculates fractional spatial movement of pixels, scales groups of pixels, and is used for various filtering operations. Second, the statistical decoder decompresses video data in real time. It is a specialized input FIFO that reads variable-length serial-bit sequences from memory and decodes them into fixed-length, 16-bit values.

As mentioned earlier, multimedia operations process large amounts of data. Because of the large quantities of memory data that must continually pass through the pixel processor, four independent FIFO channels allow PB to efficiently read, process, and write data. Each FIFO packs and unpacks data words and bytes, buffers data, and initiates transfers to and from the memory array.

Two FIFO channels are dedicated to supplying continuous streams of input from memory, these containing compressed and uncompressed images as well as the microcode routines required to operate on them. The remaining two FIFOs are output channels used to store the intermediate pixel values required during the construction of complete displayable images.

Instructions are stored and executed from a pipelined 512-word × 48-bit static cache, and can be executed in a single clock cycle. A microprogrammable cache control algorithm is used to guarantee maximum cache "hit" efficiency, and can be tailored for different types of system- and device-level operations.

By coordinating the operation of the 82750 assembler with dual-word cache accesses and appropriate PB instruction control fields, zero-delay branches can be performed without conscious programmer intervention. The ability to perform any logical operation and then to effectively perform a simultaneous two-way branch based on the results of that operation yields a significant performance increase over typical microprogrammed processors.

The 48-bit PB instruction word is divided into a total of 11 different control fields, designed to allow highly parallel operations. For example, ALU operations on pixels fetched from memory can be performed simultaneously with iteration counter updates while the pixel interpolator is operating on pixels decoded by the statistical decoder—and then branch—all within a single clock cycle.

### The pixel interpolator

As long as the only objective of video data compression is the faithful reproduction of the source image, decompression itself is relatively straightforward. But if any additional transformations are required (the image is to be enlarged or reduced, scrolled, rotated, or intentionally distorted), a simple correspondence no longer exists between the original stored pixels and those destined for the display.

Simple attempts to adjust the image often produce undesirable artifacts known as *aliasing effects*. Anti-aliasing algorithms exist that eliminate those artifacts at the expense of processing cycles. Given that high cost, they are not appropriate for use in real-time systems.

An example: When the size of an image is reduced, the space between each stored pixel exceeds the space between those to be displayed. This means that each displayed pixel falls somewhere between two rows and two columns of pixels in the original image. In principle, the color and intensity of each displayed pixel can be derived by averaging the values of the four stored pixels that surround it, weighted according to how far the displayed pixel is from the rows and columns to the top, bottom, left, and right. By programming the pixel interpolator with these boundary values, the weighted average pixel values can be generated.

The pixel interpolator is designed to operate in several different modes. Most common is a *pipelined sequential* mode that allows interpolated pixels to be generated at a maximum rate of one pixel every other clock cycle. Additional modes optimized for interpolation over random pixel "quads" and different horizontal and vertical weights are included.

### The statistical decoder

The statistical decoder is a specialized input channel that reads encoded bit streams containing variable-length symbols and decodes each symbol into fixed-length values. In image compression, certain values occur more frequently than others. One means of compressing such data is to use fewer bits to encode the more frequently occurring values and more bits to encode less frequently occurring ones. This type of encoding scheme is called *statistical* (or *Huffman*) *encoding,* because it depends on the frequency of occurrence of any particular value that is to be encoded.

The statistical decoder receives long series of variable-length symbols from memory as a sequence of 32-bit data words. Each symbol encodes both its length and value, and ignores the natural boundaries between memory words or bytes. The decoder must concatenate these variable-length sequences, examine the initial bit patterns, extract the substrings, and then realign the remaining data and repeat the process for the next symbol.

Each of the above operations is performed automatically for a variety of codes (code books) and coding conventions. To use the decoder, a starting address and code book are loaded. Thereafter, programs may simply read an indefinite series of expanded symbols in parallel with other operations.

### Input and output FIFOs

The PB contains two input and two output FIFO channels that are used to read and write pixel and program data to external memory. Each FIFO has its own 32-bit address pointer that can be programmed to sequentially increment or decrement through 8- or 16-bit data types. Each FIFO double-buffers 32-bit data words so as to allow more efficient program execution and to allow hardware memory controllers to take advantage of the sequential nature of FIFO memory accesses to optimize main memory accesses.

### Microprogram performance

The 82750PB typically is 5 to 10 times faster than a conventional micro-processor at the same clock speed (even faster for operations such as image-decompression and -manipulation, which take advantage of the special hard-ware assists provided). There are two reasons for its efficiency: single-cycle instruction execution, and the inherent parallelism of the dual-bus, multifield instruction. Single-cycle execution means that instructions execute faster, and parallelism means that fewer instructions are required to complete the task.

PB does not have a hardware multiplier, but algorithms involving multipli-cation often can be implemented efficiently, using combinations of the two shifters available (single-bit parallel shifter, and multibit barrel shifter). For example, the JPEG image-compression algorithm is very multiply-intensive. However, PB can decompress a $512 \times 480$ JPEG encoded image in less than 1 second—about an order of magnitude faster than typical 25-MHz processors (including those with a hardware multiply capability). This is but one illus-tration of the power and flexibility of programming PB at the microcode level.

The PB is not limited to digital-video manipulation. For example, a PB implementation of the ADPCM audio algorithm can decode an audio stream using between 5 and 10 percent of the available PB cycles. This flexibility permits the design of low-cost multimedia systems in which a single PB pro-vides both the video and audio processing. However, in the ActionMedia II design, a dedicated audio processor was employed.

### The 82750DB display processor

The 82750DB incorporates all of the digital and analog processing elements necessary to form the basis of a low-cost display subsystem. By programming internal control registers, video timing can be modified to accommodate a wide variety of scanning frequencies and display characteristics. A large selection of bits-per-pixel, pixels-per-line, and pixel heights is available, allowing designers a wide latitude when selecting display resolution, frame rates, and memory requirements.

The display is programmable on a line-by-line basis, enabling the on-screen mixing of graphics modes. To support this feature, the CLUT also may be loaded on a line-by-line basis. A luminance interpolator is provided to assist horizontal scaling by a factor of 2:1. DB provides support for an 8-bit alpha channel, allowing the weighted mix of DB outputs and an external source enabling smooth fades and transitions. Both analog and digital RGB outputs are provided, enabling connection to a video monitor or a digital liquid crystal display (LCD).

Perhaps the two most important real-time operations carried out by DB are *chrominance interpolation* and *YUV-to-RGB conversion*.

### The chrominance interpolator

The task of the chrominance interpolator is to expand the subsampled color information up to the corresponding luminance resolution.

During programmed blanking time, subsampled chrominance data is read from bitmaps into color-information line-storage RAMs within DB. The interpolator determines when new chrominance information is needed, based on the current display position of the raster.

During active display time, when subsampled color video is being shown, DB performs a bilinear interpolation so as to expand color information to the resolution currently being displayed. To accomplish this, the chrominance interpolator expands compressed color data in both vertical and horizontal directions by a ratio of 2:1 or 4:1 in each direction.

After interpolation, DB can mix chrominance and luminance on a pixel-by-pixel basis. This ability to mix video and graphics on the same screen at any position, with any size, and with any aspect ratio, is one of the distinctive features of the i750 architecture.

### YUV to RGB conversion

The YUV-to-RGB color space conversion matrix is compatible with the CCIR 601 standard. The conversion is done fairly late in the processing cycle, after things such as color lookup table operations and chrominance interpolation have been completed.

For source data that is coded in RGB format, or for systems that draw only in RGB color space, the programmer can choose to bypass this function.

The color-space conversion is accomplished by performing a matrix manipulation on the YUV pixels. Since the coefficients all are constants, the multiplications may be done with lookup ROMs and adders. Saturation circuitry is included, to ensure that any arbitrary YUV pixel converts to an RGB value that is within the allowed ranges.

### Compositing

Since ActionMedia was designed to complement the existing graphics subsystem of the personal computer rather than replace it, a mechanism was required to mix the system graphics output with that provided by ActionMedia.

It is easiest to think of this scenario as two independent graphics subsystems that must be merged. The two systems may be displaying different resolutions and color depths, but a way must be found to combine their outputs.

Initially, since both systems are running independently, a way must be found to "lock" the two outputs together, before functions such as overlay can be considered. This is achieved by synchronizing the vertical and horizontal sync signals of ActionMedia with those provided by the system graphics—a function known as *genlocking*. Genlocking is achieved by the DB in conjunction with two phase locked loops, and this configuration can synchronize to a range of system graphics modes including 640 × 480 and 1024 × 768.

### Chroma-keying

Now that the two signals are synchronized, their outputs must be combined to form one signal to drive the display monitor. Consider the combination of

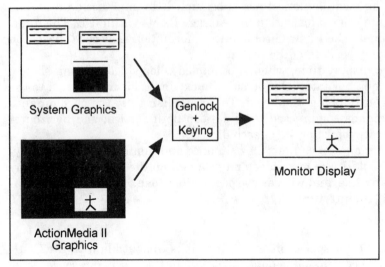

**Figure 47.4**  Combining system graphics and ActionMedia output.

images shown in Fig. 47.4. The system graphics display consists of several windows, including one that the programmer has identified as containing an image provided by ActionMedia II. Hence a mechanism is required that will identify which of the system graphics or ActionMedia graphics outputs are displayed at each point on the screen.

There are two accepted techniques for providing this mixing capability: *chroma-keying,* and *bit-mask manipulation.* The latter is achieved by providing a separate bitmap that has one bit corresponding to each pel in the display. This bit determines which of the system graphics or multimedia graphics are displayed. This technique has several disadvantages. First, the bit-mask bitmap requires valuable memory space, and second, the bit-mask can be difficult to manipulate and impose an extra overhead on the host CPU.

Chroma-keying uses a simpler approach, one that reduces the need for interaction from the host CPU and has no memory requirement.

Chroma-keying uses one of the system graphics colors to specify which of the two outputs is to be displayed for each pel position. Any area painted in this keying color is replaced by the contents of the multimedia adapter at the corresponding position. For example, black is used as the keying color in Fig. 47.4. The client area of the window that will contain the image from the multimedia adapter is painted black, and the keying circuitry then replaces any black in the system graphics by means of the multimedia adapters' output. Note that the remaining pels in the multimedia adapter display also are painted black. This ensures that any black pels in windows out of the programmer's control will still be black.

Two forms of chroma-keying exist, digital and analog, both exhibiting specific advantages and disadvantages.

**Figure 47.5**   Digital keying.

Digital keying makes use of the video feature bus (VFB) provided by the system graphics adapter in personal computers. For IBM-compatible PCs, this consists of 8-bit pel data and the associated synchronization signals. Hence the digital keying system is limited to operating in modes of 256 colors or less.

A second limitation is imposed by the bandwidth of the VFB, which limits the transmission of pel data to display resolutions up to 640 × 480. Higher resolutions cannot be digitally keyed using the existing VFB implementations. Figure 47.5 illustrates the digital keying circuitry used by ActionMedia II. The 8-bit system-graphics data is compared with the chroma-keying color, and the result used to control a multiplexor that selects which of the two graphic streams is to be sent to the display monitor. Since the incoming data is palletized, ActionMedia II must include a CLUT to convert to the actual RGB values, which are then sent to the multiplexer. For correct color-tracking, any manipulation of the system CLUT must be trapped, and the corresponding changes made to the CLUT on ActionMedia II.

To provide chroma-keying at higher resolutions, analog keying, which has no immediate bandwidth restrictions, must be used, as shown in Fig. 47.6. The operation is similar to that for digital keying but with one restriction: the keying color is fixed and is black. Since the comparator must operate in the analog domain, complete with noise, only black (which corresponds to zero-level output on each of R, G, and B) can reliably be detected. (In practice, a black threshold level is defined, and any output below the threshold is keyed.)

Most of the limitations imposed by keying will be solved in the future by using a single unifying frame buffer for both system graphics and multimedia images. This requires all the display content to have the same color depth and format, for example RGB-24. The use of a single frame buffer will reduce overall system cost, since it will remove the redundancy of providing two display systems (as found in current designs such as ActionMedia II). Many

**Figure 47.6**   Analog keying.

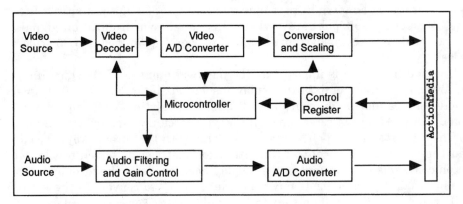

**Figure 47.7**   Capture subsystem.

companies working in the field of graphics accelerators are now starting to include multimedia as part of their requirements, and it is only a matter of time before such systems become available.

## Capture subsystem

The capture subsystem is provided as a daughter card that can be attached to ActionMedia II and provides three basic capabilities:

1. Digitization of still images
2. Digitization of motion video
3. Digitization of audio

The block diagram for the capture subsystem is shown in Fig. 47.7. The basic process for digitizing still and motion images is the same, and is as follows. A video signal with either PAL or NTSC timings may be connected to the capture subsystem using any of composite, S-VHS, or RGB connections. This signal enters the video decoder which, under the control of the microcontroller, decodes the video signal into three analog signals, R, G, and B. These signals then are digitized by the A/D converter, and provide a 24-bit RGB input to the video formatting chip.

The video formatter provides two basic tasks, *color conversion,* and *image scaling.* Incoming 24-bit RGB data may be converted to YUV or passed directly through, as in the case of high-resolution stills capture. However, for motion video, the data is converted to YUV-9 format, which greatly reduces the data bandwidth at a slight loss in quality.

Images with resolutions of up to $768 \times 576$ may be captured, but for motion video the image is scaled down to more manageable sizes such as $256 \times 240$ or $160 \times 120$.

The audio circuitry supports a single stereo input with three gain settings: *microphone, line-level,* and *CD-level.* This signal is filtered and then digitized using a stereo A/D converter and sent to the ActionMedia II as a serial digital bitstream. All operations are under the control of the capture subsystem microcontroller, which communicates with the host and the pixel processor through the control register. This local management enables more of the host CPU's and pixel processors' cycles to be used for multimedia processing.

## Audio subsystem

ActionMedia II includes an audio subsystem that provides the necessary audio functionality to complement digital video. It was not designed as a general-purpose audio subsystem, hence features such as 16-bit audio and MIDI are not present.

A digital signal processor (DSP), which forms the heart of the system, relieves the burden on the PB and the host CPU. In addition the DSP is another example of a programmable element, allowing the migration over time to different audio algorithms by simply downloading new DSP object code.

Currently, 8-bit PCM and ADPCM4 algorithms are supported in both mono and stereo at a range of sampling rates up to 44.1 kHz (the sampling rate of CD-DA). The DSP contains on-chip instruction and data memory, and reads and stores audio samples in the system VRAM.

## Software Support

The ActionMedia II software environment is provided by the *audio/video kernel (AVK),* which was jointly designed by Intel and IBM. The objectives for AVK were that it would be portable to multiple platforms and operating environments, support windowing environments, be able to expand as the power of available hardware grew, and minimize reliance on the host CPU. The architecture was able to avoid dependence on the host for processing by relying instead on the high-performance i750 multimedia processors.

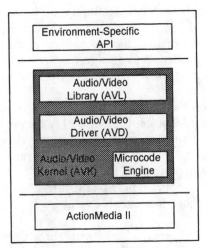

**Figure 47.8**   AVK software model.

The AVK system architecture is built in layers, as shown in Fig. 47.8. The lowest layer is called the *microcode engine,* because it includes a set of microcode tasks for the 82750PB processor; for example, a routine called DoMotion manages decompression tasks and buffers, and another routine called CopyScale copies and scales video images in real time into the display buffer.

The next layer is the *audio/video driver,* which encapsulates the details of the ActionMedia II hardware. The AVD interface provides functions for accessing the multimedia board's local video RAM, setting display formats for the 82750DB, and loading microcode functions from VRAM into the 82750PB's on-chip instruction memory. This last function is key to AVK's ability to accommodate new features and algorithms. The AVD also provides the interface for the audio subsystem and the video-capture card.

The third layer is the *audio/video library* (AVL), which supports the specialized data types needed for the manipulation of video and audio. These data types are generalized into *streams* that are then collected together into *groups.* A group is a collection of streams that need to be controlled synchronously with functions (such as play, stop, or pause) that operate on the groups. The AVL implements these functions in addition to the read and write data functions, for capture-and-display data-buffers. This layer also provides control over the attributes of these data types; for example, as functions for adjusting the volume of an audio stream or the tint of a video stream. This layer is essentially platform-independent, and so can easily be ported to other hardware and operating environments.

The AVL includes a set of functions that manage VRAM, format bitmaps, and generate and manage command lists. A *command list* is a set of microcode functions and their parameters. These lists can be built in memory and then scheduled for execution by the 82750PB as a group. Command lists can be active for a single image or for a video stream. If a list is active for a video stream, it will be executed on every frame until it has been replaced or canceled.

There's one more layer that is needed to link the architecture to an operating environment. It's an environment-specific *application programming interface (API)* that performs two critical functions for AVK. It reads and writes data into the host file system, and integrates AVK into the host windowing environment. Because these functions need to be optimized to a specific environment, they are defined as being outside the AVK architecture so as to maintain its portability.

Two examples of an API that can be implemented on top of AVK are the Media Control Interface, as defined for Windows 3.1, and Apple's QuickTime. Because AVK was designed to be independent of both the API and media formats, it will easily port to emerging standards. AVK presently is available under the Windows 3.1 and OS/2 operating systems. It is also architecturally independent of specific compression and decompression algorithms, and will easily accommodate new algorithms as they are developed.

The AVK interface was developed by identifying and abstracting a number of objects, with their associated behaviors and attributes. These objects and their relationships are shown in Fig. 47.9.

The *connector* object can be thought of as a mixer that accepts data flow, optionally manipulates the data, and sends the data to a destination. Connectors allow rectangular regions, referred to as *boxes,* to be defined for the source and destination bitmaps. Boxes can be resized and relocated in real time so as to provide good system responsiveness in windowing applications.

AVK implements a three-layered buffered data structure that provides for simultaneous execution of multiple tasks; for example, compressed data is input from a storage device by an input task, which then loads it into a compressed data buffer. A decode task then decompresses the data and loads it into a decompressed bitmap buffer. Individual bitmaps are then processed by a copy/scale task and sent to the display buffer, where a display task sends them to the screen, as shown in Fig. 47.10.

Task scheduling in AVK requires real-time response, a capability not provided by most operating systems found in desktop computers (OS/2 being an exception). The solution for AVK was to depend on the 82750PB to schedule all real-time tasks. Thus, on ActionMedia II boards, the video-processor chip also schedules audio operations. The video processor schedules tasks through the microcode engine. For example, while video streams are being processed, the DoMotion task continuously loops between the master command-list processing task and the buffer/stream processing task. For playback, the buffer/stream processing task looks for a frame of compressed data to be available, and for a free bitmap into which the data can be decompressed. When these conditions both have been met, the buffer/stream processing task calls the appropriate decompression algorithm.

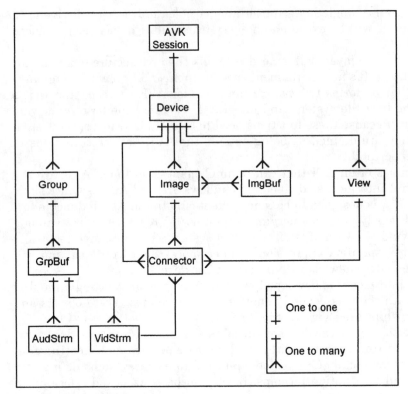

**Figure 47.9**  The AVK object model.

AVK supports two types of video algorithms that execute on the PB, *production-level video (PLV)* and *real-time video (RTV)*. PLV provides the highest achievable image quality but is very asymmetrical. PLV material is compressed off-line, without the time constraints of sending them to a display, and therefore does not need to be performed in real time. However, the PB can decompress images processed by PLV in real time.

On the other hand, RTV is a symmetrical process that PB can compress in real time. RTV supports resolutions up to $256 \times 240$ but is normally implemented at lower resolutions, resulting in data bandwidths that match that provided by a CD-ROM (150 kbytes per second). The image quality provided by RTV is lower than PLV's—a result of the real-time constraints placed on the RTV algorithm.

Both compression techniques use interframe encoding, which stores information only on pixels that change between frames. A frame for which all the pixels are defined is called an *intraframe,* and serves as an access point into the video data stream. By removing the constraints of real-time compression, PLV can employ a technique known as *motion estimation.* This time-consuming technique matches areas in the image that have moved from the previous frame, and encodes only the vector corresponding to the movement.

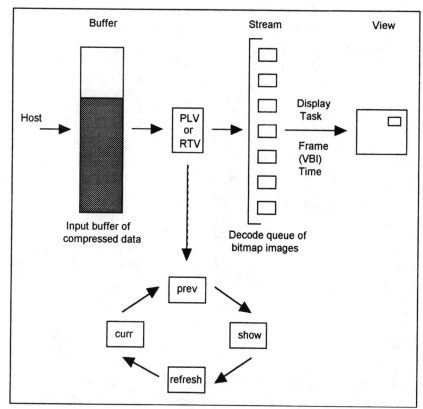

**Figure 47.10**  Video-decompression tasks.

Figure 47.11 illustrates the processes involved in RTV capture and compression. The digitized odd field from the attached video source is stored in VRAM until it is required by the display task, which then copies and scales it into the view.

The same display task takes the even field and places the bitmap in the encode queue, ready for compression. When the RTV task finds a bitmap in the encode queue, it will compress the frame—using the previous entry in the encode queue to determine whether an inter- or intraframe will be generated. Finally, the compressed frame is placed in the output buffer for collection by the host.

Still-image support is provided for images up to 512 × 480 in both YUV-9 and YUV-16 format. (This limit is based on the available memory on the ActionMedia II: 2 Mbytes.) These images may be compressed and decompressed using proprietary algorithms, in addition to an implementation of the JPEG standard for compressing and decompressing 9-bit images.

AVK's data flow and object organization have deliberately been designed to allow future enhancements. When processor power and I/O bandwidth increase in future systems, AVK's architecture will permit the number of

**Figure 47.11**  RTV compression tasks.

streams processed simultaneously to increase. By allowing the host to program its microcode engine, AVK can accommodate custom microcode for video effects and new image compression/decompression algorithms without requiring changes to the basic structure of the software.

This extendability was recently shown with the introduction of Microsoft's Video for Windows system extension. Video for Windows (VFW) provides an MCI-compliant interface for controlling digital video playback and record, and enables high-end processor-based systems (such as Intel 486's) to play back digital video without any additional hardware. This requires that the frame sizes be based on square pixel aspect ratios for optimal performance. (For example, on a 640 × 480 screen, valid square pixel frame sizes are 160 × 120 and 320 × 240.) Before the release of VFW, AVK operated on rectangular pixels with frames sizes such as 128 × 120 and 256 × 240. To support VFW, new microcode was written for RTV to support square pixel resolutions, and a new environment-specific layer was written to interface AVK to the VFW MCI layer. Figure 47.12 illustrates the basic components of the VFW system and the corresponding mapping of AVK and ActionMedia II to the new environment.

## Conclusions

The requirements for a multimedia subsystem have been presented, and an actual implementation described. Multimedia encompasses a wide range of

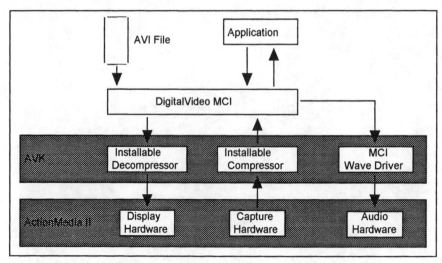

**Figure 47.12**   ActionMedia II implementation for Video for Windows.

data types, and even with the VLSI integration capabilities available today it is impossible to provide a full-function multimedia system on a single adapter. ActionMedia II addresses the areas of digital motion video and still images, and provides the audio capabilities to complement them. However, audio facilities such as 16-bit samples and MIDI are not provided.

The rapid technological increases of the last decade have made digital movies available on today's desktop systems. One can only guess what advances the coming years will bring.

# 48

# Networking Video Applications

**James Long**

**Barbara Baker**

## Introduction

Desktop video is an emerging technology that over time will come in many flavors. More and more applications in areas such as training and education are moving from the classroom to the desktop, using digital video as one of the communication tools. Today, applications using digital video have become part of familiar office-productivity software, such as spreadsheets and presentation applications. New ways of managing these desktop video applications are on the horizon. And it has become clear that many of these applications are more effective when networked and used by widely distributed work groups, not just individual users.

In this chapter we'll take a look at a few applications for networked video, their characteristics, and the requirements for and challenges of adding video to a network. We will examine the problems associated with handling video in today's networking environment, and we'll look at strategies for coping with these problems. We will provide strategies for improving servers, networks, and client computers so as to make video networking convenient, reliable, and relatively inexpensive. We'll start with a look at how applications use video today, and how they will be using it in just a few years.

## Video Applications—Today

Training applications are a natural place to integrate digital video with the desktop computer. As an innovative training method, "performance support systems" are being developed by large businesses and other institutions, and these are revolutionizing the way employees learn their jobs and perform their tasks. Instead of large amounts of up-front classroom training, performance support systems provide training on demand at the desktop. These systems call for servers that can deliver powerful audiovisual information to the desktop, so that training can truly be integrated with employees' daily workload. Training costs come down while retention increases significantly, since students learn new information in context rather than in classrooms.

Many major productivity software applications, such as those for word processors and spreadsheets, have made VHS videotape training available today. And third-party trainers are moving to desktop video courses. In addition, developers of productivity applications are taking the next step: linking digital video directly to their software's on-line help resources. For example, you can purchase a CD-ROM version of Works with multimedia on-line help and reference, and on-line tutorials for Microsoft Word, which incorporate full-motion digital video.

In the education market, most major suppliers of educational software systems are marketing or developing "integrated learning systems" that consist of student applications and teacher management systems. With an integrated learning system, teachers become better resource managers, assigning students to courseware according to their abilities and needs. Almost without exception, the developers of integrated learning systems perceive networked video as being a vital tool in the classroom, marshaling engaging and meaningful educational resources. As Marshall McLuhan said, "Anyone who sees a difference between education and entertainment doesn't know the first thing about either one."

Businesses can use networked video presentation systems to instantly send corporate resources to the desktops of all employees. Information, which for example might consist of sales videos or employee data, may be viewed on the spot (for review of important company information) or captured to create customized sales presentations. By putting the video on a server, businesses allow many people to access the resources without forcing them to travel to an audiovisual facility or to buy a VCR/television—or an editing suite!—to use the information.

## Video Applications—Tomorrow

In the very near future, networked video documentation systems will allow institutions of all kinds to maintain multiuser audiovisual databases. Advertising agencies, for example, who may have hundreds of hours of video used in a random, on-demand fashion, can use this type of system. Today these agencies use hundreds of VCR tapes that must be located, copied, and then delivered to account executives or clients. A video database would allow easier and quicker access to this information. Other potential users include health-care institutions, which have extensive audiovisual records; travel agencies, which show videos about vacation destinations; and public utilities, which need to maintain records of power-generation facilities and equipment.

For example, several state highway departments have still-video databases of every mile of their highways, allowing employees to instantly view any stretch of road.

Video teleconferencing is gradually coming to the desktop as well. In this area, businesses can own cost-effective conferencing services so as to support worldwide communication needs and thereby increase productivity. Another live-video application is distance learning, in which the teacher is not located in the same place as the students. This flavor of videoconferencing allows the teacher and students to interact almost as if they were in the same room.

## Characteristics of Video Applications

As pointed out in the previous sections, there are many good rationales for distributing video to users at their desktops. The characteristics of the video "service" required for these applications drive the type of computer system needed to support them, as follows:

- Video file services
- Video object services
- Stream management services

### Video file services

The simplest level of video application—video file services—requires store-and-play or basic file service for video. A video file service gives one the capability to store video and to retrieve it for viewing. The material generally is static, and some access delay may be tolerable. A system offering this service is much like today's data-network file servers. A good example of this level of complexity is simple playback of training or on-line help videos.

### Video object services

The next step in networked video sophistication consists of video object services, which make an application highly interactive with video information by supporting quickly changing video and audio "object" relationships. As an example, a video and audio "database" can be used to combine objects to produce a new video stream, to edit the video, or to instantly add video and audio to another document type. This requires fast access to the video objects and the ability to change their relationships to one another. Users will want to access many objects at the same time. For example, an advertising agency would require this level of video service to combine many video clips and thereby provide a quick look at a "rough cut" of a new ad concept. This is a good example of a system that needs more than just store-and-play function.

### Stream management services

The third category, stream management services, is required when many users simultaneously need access to live video. Desktop video teleconferencing and distance learning fall into this category of video applications. Video stream management service often involves live video transmission—from a variety of sources—to many simultaneous users, and management of the video streams on the network. Users may even require different data rates. Or users, for example, may need to record a teleconference for later viewing. For these applications, users may be sharing *codec pools*—expensive devices that compress and decompress the video—so that the video service can be provided to more desktops.

## Requirements for Adding Video Services

The demand for networked digital audiovisual systems will grow exponentially over the next few years, as businesses, government, and other institutions increasingly turn to digital networks. Networks will be used to distribute audiovisual information for education, presentation, and reference applications. Networked digital-video systems will allow many people to simultaneously view audiovisual information from a server, while retaining their current network functions. Applications that work on the network today should remain untouched when video is added.

From the point of view of users, therefore, video must be added to the network invisibly. Users should be able to access video files from a variety of client computers (e.g., IBM compatibles, Macintosh computers, UNIX workstations), and from a variety of applications. To avoid the need for duplication of large video files, one copy of a digital-video file should serve as many kinds of computers as possible. In addition video must be incorporated into existing applications, such as video annotation in a word-processing document or spreadsheet. Digital video used in applications comes in a variety of compression schemes, depending on the application. Networks and servers need to handle the many different compression and file formats (e.g., Indeo, Video 1, motion JPEG, PLV, MPEG, Cinepak, P*64, True Motion, and other standards as they develop).

In order to promote the widespread installation and use of digital audiovisual applications, the client network connection should be standard and low-cost. That means the use of existing network connections on the client, rather than special or additional network connections, to provide video services. By centralizing video service resources at the server, you reduce the total cost for institutions that have many video application users, particularly when you are adding additional desktop users.

## Problems and Challenges of Adding Video to Networks

Networking has become a critical technology for almost all segments of the computer market, particularly in business and education. Large and small businesses and institutions have come to depend on network servers—dedicated-purpose computers—for a variety of reasons. Today's local area network (LAN) environments were designed to handle the data and file sharing needs of typical office-productivity applications, which deal mainly with text and simple graphics files. Managing and transmitting digital video data poses two major challenges: dealing with large sizes, and handling the time-dependent demands of video datatypes. Both are particularly difficult when you are sharing the information on networks and servers.

The large file sizes associated with digital audiovisual information pose an obvious need for large disk drives or multiple-disk systems and high data transmission speeds. Even compressed video, such as Intel's Production Level Video (PLV), requires a continuous 1-to-2-Mbps transmission speed, and 0.5 to 1 Gbytes of storage for 1 hour. A less obvious problem results from the nature of audiovisual information itself, which is fundamentally different from the kind of data that typically travels across a LAN (i.e., word-processing, database, or spreadsheet data).

Digital audiovisual information takes the form of a stream of data that must arrive on time. In other words, typical LANs work with bursty requests for data. File systems and most server communication buses are designed to handle this bursty traffic. They are, however, inefficient when it comes to handling the simultaneous, continuous, large block data transfers that are needed for streaming audiovisual data. It is also extremely difficult to manage random, bursty data and streaming data applications with the same microprocessor.

Streaming audiovisual data also conflicts with the way that LANs and multitasking operating systems allocate resources via "democratic" schemes, in which applications take turns. When the network, bus, or other resource is busy, the system slows down. No data takes priority over any other data. To a typical network, bits are bits, regardless of the type of information represented. The inefficiency of democratic resource-sharing schemes is compounded by the overhead needed to allow applications to take turns and for the detection and correction of errors. These functions are important for the typical software application, but not as important for audiovisual media. The human eye can overlook one incorrect pixel in a television image, but an incorrect number in your bank balance would not be tolerated!

Audiovisual information, which is based on time, isn't useful if it slows down and speeds up according to network traffic flow. Even if the hardware and software can cope with slowdowns, the video would play back in slow motion—not acceptable! Therefore, managing data flow is key to all multimedia computing, especially in networks.

Video demands a kind of "Federal Express" attitude toward data: it "absolutely, positively" has to arrive at the client computer on time. If bandwidth isn't available for a highly reliable connection (to assure that the video information arrives on time), one of two things must happen: the server must tell the requesting application that the data temporarily isn't available, or the server must somehow reduce the amount of data (by dropping video frames, image size, resolution, etc.) to a level that the network can support reliably. Having the ability to change the video information so as to meet the bandwidth needs is known as *scalable video*.

**Figure 48.1**   Network bottlenecks.

The important network function for audiovisual media isn't fair allocation of resources or error-checking; it is making sure that data flows at the proper rate between the server and client, or between client and client, and guaranteeing that data arrives on time.

### Digital Bottlenecks for Video

Audiovisual data on a network hits a series of bottlenecks. This isn't surprising, since personal computers and networks weren't designed to handle this kind of data. Along the digital path, which connects the disk drive on a server to a client computer, these bottlenecks limit the video-stream speed or interrupt the video. The bottlenecks occur in disk drives, system buses, processors, networks, and the various interfaces and buffers that are found between the parts of the system. The problem areas are highlighted in Fig. 48.1.

Let's look at a typical setting for networked digital video: a training room with 30 PLV stations and a video server. Mission-critical training requires that users instantly view video when it is requested. In this example, high-resolution PLV requires a rate of about 1.5 Mbps per video stream. Therefore each desktop must continuously handle 1.5 Mbps, while the video server must handle an aggregate of 30 streams—45 Mbps—simultaneously.

A system such as this will run into many problems if it uses ordinary client server hardware and software. Referring to the bottlenecks diagram (Fig. 48.1), note that the storage subsystem will have to handle 30 simultaneous users—even if they were to request the same 60-second video clip 2 seconds apart. The server will have to handle the same 45 Mbps throughput internally. The network will have to handle 45 Mbps from the server and 1.5 Mbps per desktop, reliably. Finally, the client network interface will have to receive the video and still allow concurrent access to other networked applications (e.g., e-mail, text, databases, etc.). Unfortunately, a normal networked file server system could not accomplish this.

### Solution Strategies

One way to deal with the bottlenecks confronting networked multimedia data is to throw away all the software and hardware that cause the streams of data to "bump" into one another, and replace it with new software and hardware that keep each stream running at the proper rate. This works, but it means you've thrown away something of great value to almost all computer users: the network software that allows us to use our servers for many other purposes.

Four strategies offer a range of solutions for dealing with the bottlenecks:

1. Do nothing.

2. "Turbocharge" the bottleneck areas.

3. Replace the bottlenecks with higher-performance devices.

4. Install a parallel system in order to circumvent the bottlenecks.

Let's look at these four alternatives to see how well they handle both the bottlenecks and the general requirements for adding video to the network.

### Do nothing

Leave the system alone, and make sure that the data stream never exceeds the limits of the bottlenecks. This is practical for client desktop computers, which never have to deal with more data than they can decode and play. By avoiding the need for client hardware changes, you save costs, since clients far outnumber other network components. But doing nothing to standard networks and servers limits the number of users and the expected performance of the video services, since existing networks and servers have trouble handling video for multiple clients simultaneously.

### "Turbocharge" bottleneck areas

Improve the offending hardware and/or software so that it can handle more data. Like adding a turbocharger to an engine, these improvements don't replace all the existing hardware—they just make it faster. This improves the general performance of the server and network, but it may not address the different processing requirements for video and traditional data applications, such as the critical time-dependent nature of the audiovisual data.

### Replace bottleneck devices

Replace the server and network hardware altogether, with faster hardware and larger storage capacity. For example, one way to increase a network's raw capacity is to replace copper wiring with optical fiber and interfaces that can easily carry 10 times more data. Unfortunately this is expensive and doesn't necessarily solve the resource-sharing and time-dependent needs for video. By replacing the server with a higher-performance computer that has more storage, you may increase the horsepower of the server, but you still don't address the differences between video and other application datatypes.

### Install a parallel system

Install a system dedicated for video. This is all right if it means the addition of a separate server for video, but no one wants a separate physical network or a separate video computer. By establishing a parallel software world for video while sharing the same network and client hardware, you can allow the system to optimally handle both types of information. But remember, when you are using a parallel approach, to be sure that video and nonvideo information can be easily integrated within the same application.

As you can see, no single strategy gives the best solution to breaking through the bottlenecks and meeting the requirements for adding video to the network. A better approach would be to take the best of each choice and change the network so that it can cost-effectively handle data applications and video service. How can this be accomplished? Let's return to our training-room example and look at the client, the network, and the server to show how video can be added to the network.

## Handling Video Needs at the Client

Since client computers typically need only one or two streams for video, bandwidth is not a problem. The data rate for a video stream is about 1.5 Mbps—slower than the amount of data that comes from a typical hard disk. Therefore no special networking hardware is necessary at client computers. This data rate supports Intel's Indeo and PLV compression technologies, and the in-development MPEG (Moving Pictures Experts Group) standard. It's also within the capacity of a typical Ethernet network, which is about 10 Mbps—leaving plenty of capacity for other data or higher-bandwidth video technologies, such as MPEG II.

So far we've been talking about a single client. But what happens when we have *30* clients? In a typical network, all of the 1.5-Mbps streams share the same cables, quickly overwhelming a typical Ethernet network. Although upgrading to an expensive fiber-optic network (e.g., FDDI) will considerably increase the capacity, it is still a shared resource and therefore has trouble dealing with the time-dependent needs of video. A better solution can be found in a star network, such as 10BaseT Ethernet, with dedicated lines to each client computer. This network configuration already is the most popular, and as we'll see, can be turbocharged to support the video-capacity needs without expensive fiber.

## Handling Video Needs over the Network

### Star networks satisfy video requirements

The need to exchange digital data among a variety of peripherals and computers with varying operating systems (e.g., Video for Windows, QuickTime, UNIX) and applications has resulted in complex networks. Network hardware includes wires, such as the simple twisted-pair wires that also are used for telephone networks, and more exotic wiring such as coaxial cable or optical fibers. Networks can be arranged in several physical structures, or *topologies*. In the past the most common kinds of networks have used *bus* and *ring*

Figure 48.2    Bus or ring network.

Figure 48.3    Star topology (shared networks).

topologies. To create a bus or ring network, a wire snakes from one computer to the next (Fig. 48.2). Each computer on the network broadcasts data that's monitored by all computers on the network; however, only the intended recipient "pays attention" to the incoming data. To draw an analogy, a server on a bus or ring network is like a radio station that broadcasts a signal. While it is transmitting to one client, no one else can communicate with it.

Today, computer users increasingly are turning to star-topology networks based on inexpensive twisted-pair phone wire and a line for each client computer (Fig. 48.3). These networks are popular because they use inexpensive telephone-style wire and are installed in the same way as a typical phone system. Moves, adds, and changes are simplified because, as with a telephone network, each client has its own cable, unlike the "snaked" cable of a bus network, which has to be rerouted for new clients, moves, and changes. For these reasons, networking experts see star networks or "structured wiring" as the favored way to go in the 1990s and beyond. These networks also offer the best topology for serving the bandwidth needs of video.

To create a star topology, "hubs" have become increasingly common hardware features on LANs. One of the most popular hub devices is the 10BaseT type of hub for Ethernet networks. 10BaseT Ethernet already represents about 70 percent of new Ethernet installations. Another popular network, IBM's Token Ring, has used a star topology since its introduction.

Although today's 10BaseT Ethernet and Token Ring networks are wired as stars with hubs, they still operate like a bus or ring. This means that all desktops connected to the hub still share a limited amount of bandwidth (10 to 16 Mbps). This is not enough bandwidth to support typical applications, such as our example of the training room, which needs 45 Mbps. The shared nature of bus or ring networks also makes it difficult to guarantee the dedicated bandwidth required for smooth and reliable video delivery.

One solution would replace Ethernet with 100-Mbps FDDI. Not only is this very expensive, it is still a shared medium that presents problems in terms of the real-time needs of video. A better solution is to "turbocharge" the Ethernet hub so as to dedicate 10 Mbps per desktop, or several desktops, in effect giving users their own Ethernet networks (Fig. 48.4).

Although this solution increases the hub cost, it doesn't require replacement of the wire or client hardware, so the total cost is reasonable. Note also that a 10-Mbps bandwidth meets each user's video and data needs. What's more, since the "turbocharged" network gives users dedicated connections, video's real-time demands can be handled reliably. Such turbocharged or switched Ethernet hubs already are available from network vendors. This approach also works with Token Ring networks.

Star topologies with "turbocharged" 10BaseT hubs (Fig. 48.4) can handle the large amount of data required by video, giving each user enough bandwidth. However, this solution does not solve the second problem having to do with the time-dependent characteristics of video over the network, which we'll discuss in the next section.

**Figure 48.4**  "Turbocharged" switched hub network.

## Network protocols for video

Networked computers communicate via *protocols,* which are standard signals that govern the exchange of data. The computers send each other requests such as "I would like this data," "Begin sending," "Stop sending," or "Send that again, it arrived with an error." These protocols are arranged in layers, so that various parts of the computer—the hardware, the operating system, and the applications, for example—can talk to one another without needing to know special information about one another. The two main purposes of the protocols are (1) to ensure that the data arrives without errors, and (2) to ensure that the "traffic cop" functions are carried out, regulating the data flow.

In today's typical network protocols, the emphasis is on data integrity through error-control protocols. Flow control and timeliness of delivery are secondary. For the reasons we've explained, these priorities need to be reversed for audiovisual data.

One way to handle audiovisual data streams more effectively, as just noted, is to replace the existing networking protocols with special new ones. But if you throw out all the old protocols, you lose compatibility with other software. If you modify existing ones, you lose the specialty performance required for each type of data. Ideally, the network protocols for audiovisual data should peacefully coexist with the standard network software. In such an environment, applications would call for data from the server in a normal manner. The network, perceiving that audiovisual data had been requested, would use a special video protocol to make sure there was a highly reliable connection for an uninterrupted stream of data. For nonaudiovisual data, normal protocols would be used. With this "parallel-protocol" approach, audiovisual data becomes available to an application concurrently with other information on the same network.

The combination of "turbocharged" Ethernet and parallel software protocols addresses the client and network bandwidth requirements for our training-room example. The last area to address is that of the server.

## Handling Video Needs at the Server

Since video characteristics differ from other data applications, we might expect that the file server requirements would be different. Dedicated servers can eliminate the compromises that ordinary servers make between short, "bursty" data and large streams of data, optimizing performance for the latter. When dealing with audiovisual data, the server architecture should bypass "democratic" contention schemes, substituting more of a real-time system that assures reliable data flow.

Storage subsystems need to be managed in such a way that many users can access audiovisual data files at the same time. That means optimizing the storage subsystem for many simultaneous accesses to large, continuous data files. Alternatives, such as analog laserdisc jukeboxes, allow access to large quantities of video but have problems with access delays when multiple users play different segments of video. Arrays of Winchester disk drives offer a cost-effective method for storing large quantities of video data, and can be configured to support our training example of a 30-user group.

If audiovisual data is to be incorporated into existing applications, the video data should look like ordinary data to any application. To an SQL database application it should look like SQL, to a Lotus spreadsheet it should look like spreadsheet data. To the operating system, it should look like another part of the file structure. Ideally, this should be accomplished with only one copy of the data and yet support a range of computer platforms and operating systems!

Finally, a video networking solution should be able to handle any type of video application, including desktop teleconferencing. That means the server should be able to manage data streams just as a telephone switch handles audio traffic.

We've briefly described how a server optimized for video can efficiently break video network bottlenecks. To create such a server, you could either enhance an existing server or add an "application-specific" video server to the network. Enhancing an existing server will likely result in many compromises, and have a negative impact on its ability to handle nonvideo data. A video server, on the other hand, can bypass the compromises and operate in parallel with the data file server.

## Multimedia Solutions in Today's Environment

In summary, the solution for networked multimedia doesn't have to be an expensive fiber-optic network or a parallel video network. Today's star networks can do the job at reasonable cost, without special client networking hardware. A switched 10BaseT hub, or segmented Ethernet users, allow us to serve the video clients within the existing network environment. Using those parallel video-specific network protocols that coexist with today's standard networking protocols, we can maintain compatibility with current applications and deliver reliable video services on the same network. And finally, a dedicated video server can handle the processing and storage management needs of audiovisual media *and* provide superior video support, without compromising the current networked applications.

# Requirements for Pervasive Multiparty Desktop Video Collaboration

**Les Wilson**

## Defining Multimedia Communication

This author prefers to define multimedia communication as *that which enhances or transcends our current electronic communication qualities.* Without this enhanced content in the communication channel, adoption of multiparty videoconferencing may be limited, while people continue to modify a fax or e-mail image over the telephone as they do today.

Terms that accurately reflect what should happen on the desktop include *multiparty videoconferencing, teleconferencing,* and *collaboration.* Collaboration between people occurs today when two people exchange a fax and then pick up the phone to discuss the diagram on the fax. Taking the next step to enhance content in collaborative communication, the fax-like features, voice, and video of today's collaboration are integrated into a superset that we call *desktop video collaboration.*

Multiparty—more than two people collaborating—videoconferencing is generally used for consensus building, decision making, or training. The two-party conversation commonly is the execution discussion that precedes and follows a consensus meeting. This chapter will focus on multiparty videoconferencing activity. About 60 percent of the new installations of room conferencing systems support multiparty conferences, and that percentage is growing. Desktop video collaboration systems may see a similar growth.

## Market Acceptance Factors

Most workplaces can support the cost of videoconferencing and document sharing at the desktop, when the additional cost is less than one-half the cost of a personal computer or workstation. The average PC price is about $2000, meaning that for desktop video collaboration facilities to become pervasive at the desktop, they will have to cost $1000.

Just as many companies still have doubts about the value of and the productivity to be gained from computers, so too a similar doubt will slow the acceptance of desktop video collaboration.

As the desktop video collaboration application develops, users and MIS managers will decide how and when to adopt video at the desktop. The decision will be based on need, bias, cost, and corporate environmental factors. Likewise users, not the manufacturers, will decide which compression methods become standard.

There is some speculation that the "Nintendo generation," also sometimes called the "MTV crowd," will demand video simply because they are exposed to far more hours of video per day than was the previous generation of young people. The next-generation work force really understands interactive video, thanks to Nintendo's successful sales—currently estimated to be at about 90 million units.

## Defining quality

People are beginning to debate the value of seeing a person during a video conversation. Some say that *not* seeing the other person makes it easier to say what they are thinking, while others believe that seeing one's conversational partner is part of the total message.

While clear savings result when people avoid travel costs by using video-conferencing equipment, the question remains: "Was the quality of communication acceptable, and a reasonable substitute for travel or for just using a phone?" Acceptable performance is based on image quality, audio quality, and ease of data sharing. Different users will have different priorities. For some the priority may be data sharing/application sharing; for others, audio quality; and for others video quality. Good performance can mean faster results, better understanding of the message, more productive meetings, and lower costs. Travel costs are a key saving, but the most important resource we save is *time*—people really can be in two places at once.

The quality of the images used in the conversation are critical to the value of desktop video collaboration. At 7 to 10 frames per second or slower, voice and video appear to lose lip synchronization. This confuses people and usually is not acceptable. Delays in the channel greater than 300 milliseconds are noticeable.

Quality of communication also is dependent on the ability to effectively share the images that are typically part of the workgroup communication; thus data should be shared and possibly annotated by others during the conversation.

Electronic chalkboards offer several methods whereby the people in the conversation can share data. Some exchange file descriptions compatible to particular applications such as Excel. Others relay data by generating a bitmap of the application file, thereby allowing those at the other end to use a simple viewer to see a representation and to interact. Typical interactions may include reviewing a printed document and marking changes, or looking for a problem in a section of C source code. The bitmap method saves the cost of installing Excel and other applications on every remote station. In theory, a call can be "bootstrapped" by sending the chalkboard utility and file of interest through to each participant when the call is initiated.

Although video is used, it is only one part of the communication channel. Video sometimes is seen as the emotional channel, or truth channel. Body language influences the quality of the other data presented. During a sale or negotiation, body language may convey half the message. At other times video merely conveys data, such as the demonstration of a procedure, and body language does not have to be scrutinized in order to verify the quality of the data. Video can convey a procedure or technique much faster and with greater memory retention than can a written or verbal description.

As a matter of procedure, a conversation may start with a very important component called the *video handshake,* which is a visual greeting such as a nod or a hello. The video handshake is personal and helps to establish the relationship. During the conversation, data or documents may be more important, and finally at the close of the meeting video again is important, as the next meeting is arranged and good-byes are said. Perhaps negotiation meetings will continue to use video throughout, while engineering meetings will tend to proceed in the beginning-and-end manner just described.

## Market size

Let's assume that by 1995 technology can deliver quality video communication. At least some small portion of the 100 million installed personal computers and workstations now can be enhanced with the new technology. But what is really critical is reaching the last 100 meters to the desktop. Both PBX equipment vendors and LAN vendors are working on ways to reach desktops from a central hub or switch, but as of now videoconference equipment vendors are not capable of bringing their solutions that last 100 meters to the desktop, so this issue is bigger than any one company. Several forums have been established to arrive at standard methods of crossing the 100 meters and to deal with many other issues including compression and the user-interface and applications areas. The desktop is viewed as a market opportunity many times larger than the videoconference room market.

Today about 20 million desktops are estimated to have 10BASE-T Ethernet local area networks, and these can easily be upgraded to isoENET to provide desktop video collaboration.

## Factors Affecting Acceptance of Desktop Video Collaboration

Video collaboration needs have changed with end-user experience. As users are exposed to room conferencing, they find new ways to leverage the communication offered by it. This section lists yesterday's reasons justifying room conferencing and those used to justify purchases today. The last item, future plans, is significant, in that most companies with experience have a need to communicate with their customers and vendors so as to further improve corporate performance.

Yesterday's justifications for room conferencing:

- Improved communication
- Made possible distance learning
- Improved productivity
- Reduced travel costs
- Allowed more frequent worker meetings
- Facilitated company mergers
- Connected geographically dispersed offices
- Decreased time to market

Today's justifications:

- Speeds decision making
- Allows key management to conduct extensive multipoint meetings, ad hoc meetings, megameetings
- Connects to partners, leading to market wins
- Makes possible remote interviews
- Decreases cost of focus groups
- Allows traveling execs to stay in touch as they travel
- Makes possible internal research
- Aids in the development of custom applications
- Facilitates the work of product development teams

Future plans:

- Implement links to customers and suppliers
- Direct-link to government agencies to speed drug approval
- Etc.

Here are some of the key changes in companies and competitive environments that are driving the use of video collaboration:

- Business focus is becoming more global.
- Organizations are redesigning for competitiveness.
- Global workgroup teams are being empowered.
- There is an increasing focus on knowledge-worker productivity.

- Knowledge workers are becoming people-centric rather than building-centric.
- Environmental issues are emerging.
- The possible imposition of an energy tax.
- A gridlock tax encourages telecommuters.
- The desire to control pollution.
- Organizations are becoming learning organizations.
- The "video generation" is entering the work force.
- The demand for higher social content in media requires the addition of video.

## Telecommuters

An important part of the enterprise and workgroup collaboration environment is the home. Recent U.S. estimates place 34 million offices in the home. Some home offices are used by telecommuters who work at home and also in a commercial office. Desktop video collaboration will integrate home-based workers into the work force more closely, allowing them to participate in planning and ad hoc meetings. When desktop video collaboration facilities successfully connect the workplace with the employee at home, the company, the worker, and the environment all are winners.

The company can reduce the need for travel and conference rooms. Meetings can occur without waiting for a room to become available. Other employees can join a meeting as passive observers in a read-only mode, allowing them to learn from the meeting without slowing it down. Today passive observers are excluded from meetings simply because the room is too small or out of a desire to avoid overloading meeting dynamics.

Telecommuters generally spend a portion or even most of their work time at home. By reducing the number of days per week they spend in the office, workers enjoy the benefits of saved travel time as well as reduced car expenses. Just 2 days at home per week saves the average worker in California about 2 hours of travel and 60 miles of wear on the car. Due to increasing housing costs and suburban sprawl, typical commute times today are more like 40 minutes one way, or even a two-hour-and-forty-minute round trip over 120 miles of road. Everyone benefits when there are fewer drivers on the road. Potentially, road repairs and expansion of lanes are reduced. Having fewer cars on the road also helps to improve air quality. Everyone gets to work faster!

What's in it for workers? They can purchase larger houses further from work. Auto insurance companies may lower their insurance premiums, since fewer miles are driven. Workers spend less time stressed-out on the freeway and more time with family and friends.

Seeing as the public, the environment, companies, and workers all benefit from telecommuting in a multiparty framework, perhaps all of them will share the cost of purchasing equipment to make this future possible.

Here are some of these telecommuting employee benefits:

- There is easy contact with distant time zones.
- Less travel time each week means more personal time.
- People can live in their area of choice, purchase lower-cost homes with more land, greater natural beauty, and better schools.
- People will pay less for car insurance, gas, repairs.
- Sick people may recover at home, working without spreading colds and flu.

From an employer's perspective, telecommuting

- Supports dispersed work groups
- Decreases costs of office space, energy use
- Is an alternative to relocation
- Supports restructuring of the company
- Attracts employees from all over
- Reduces labor costs
- Increases productivity

Yet if telecommuting is to work, many issues must be watched closely:

- Worker must create an office at home.
- Employers must trust workers.
- Employees must be self-motivated.
- Telecommuters may work weird hours.
- Employees must be judged by their *output,* not by their mere *presence.*
- Workers still need social interaction with coworkers—*possible,* through video!
- Employers must avoid treating telecommuters as second-class citizens because they are not always "on campus."
- Telecommuting studies have measured productivity jumps of 15 to 45 percent, but could not determine if the selected individuals represented the norm.

### Specific applications

Multiparty communication serves meetings when three or more people or channels are involved. Sometimes a channel may be a feed from a database during the conversation. A typical example is training or education. Although training can be interactive with a database on a CD-ROM, the human teacher still is difficult to replace; thus, multiparty videoconferencing supports virtual classrooms. Here teachers interactively share their knowledge and skills across a group of people during the learning process. Corporate "distance learning" can train people in field offices far from corporate headquarters.

Multiparty video communication will be of tremendous benefit to medical workers. A doctor, for example, may request more than one video surgical procedure from a remote computerized database, so as to compare them and decide which procedure will be best for a particular patient. The doctor may decide to use portions of both procedures during the operation, reviewing them right in the operating room. In such a case, video quality will be very important.

Video quality is less important than interactivity in the multiperson games played by means of videoconference technology. Imagine flying your fighter jet against others you have never met. While entertainment is not a driving need in the workplace, we all do spend quite a few dollars for home entertainment. Perhaps telecommuting and entertainment will justify the consumer purchase of videoconferencing capability at home.

In any case, there are a number of issues that should be resolved to improve the application of video collaboration. The following list summarizes a few items collected in conversation, regarding how to improve what we do today, based on experience with today's videoconference rooms and existing desktop conferencing systems.

- Conference room collaboration tools are largely unused because they are not integrated with workers' desktops and PCs.

- One cannot tell the true color of garments and fabrics.

- Multipoint connections are expensive—$100,000 per multipoint control unit (MCU).

- The CCITT international H series videoconferencing standard does not yet support all areas, and leaves some issues open; therefore, minor incompatibilities result.

- All local exchange carriers (LECs) and international exchange carriers (IECs) do not yet support ISDN-1.

- Desks and offices are smaller overseas, so equipment should be smaller.

- U.S. users use white boards, whereas other cultures do not.

- Some markets have cultural barriers to accepting videoconferencing. One such barrier is a dislike of direct facial viewing, which strikes some as threatening. Video mail, however, is acceptable in these cultures.

- A limited number of circuits are available for international calls.

- The tools often are not integrated with fax.

- Some dislike the need to schedule use of the room.

- Company culture sometimes limits access or application.

- The special table shape, to meet the constraints imposed by a single camera, limits the interactions of those in the room.

- Users need training to use equipment.

- No installation proceeds without problems.

- The question arises: "Should MCU be on-premises or at-carrier?" The issue is one of encryption and security.

All of these issues must be resolved in desktop video collaboration applications.

## Relevant Standards and Proprietary Solutions

Many different standards are in development for various aspects of multimedia videoconferencing, as are a host of proprietary solutions. These approaches may be roughly divided into those standards that try to encompass the entire videoconferencing realm and those standards and approaches that relate to key portions of that realm, such as compression and local area network standards to allow videoconferencing at the desktop.

A "megastandard" that tries to encompass all of videoconferencing from the wide area network (WAN) to the desktop has been in development by the telephony industry's standards-making body, the CCITT (Consultative Committee for International Telegraph and Telephone). While elements of this standard, described in a moment, may be suited for desktop videoconferencing, much of the standard would result in equipment that is costly and that lacks the performance benefits of other solutions for desktop applications.

Resulting collaborative desktop video solutions are likely to incorporate parts of the international standard, as well as local area network standards and proprietary solutions.

### Telephony-oriented videoconferencing standards

In December 1990, CCITT completed major portions of its international videoconferencing standard. This H.320 standard series will influence, as did modem standards before it, how telecommunications companies support multiparty collaborative video. The completed portions cover two-way video between two parties. The multiparty standard was projected to have been completed by this year.

The H series of standards were defined principally by telecom-related assumptions. The bandwidth performance assumptions targeted the smallest common bandwidth, which is two 64-kbits-per-second bearer or B-channels (128 kbits per second) of ISDN (Integrated Services Digital Network, also defined by CCITT) up to the T1 connection (1.5 Mbits per second in the

| Name | Description | Status as of 1993 |
|------|-------------|-------------------|
| H.261 | Video coding (compression) | Adopted, 1990 |
| H.221 | Framing information | Adopted, 1990 |
| H.230 | Control and indication signals | Adopted, 1990 |
| H.320 | Overall requirements for ISDN systems | Adopted, 1990 |
| G.711 | 64 kilobit per second audio coding | Adopted, 1984 |
| G.722 | 48/56/64 kilobit per second audio coding | Adopted, 1986 |
| G.728 | 16 kilobit per second audio coding | Adopted, 1992 |
| H.223 | Encryption | in development |
| H.231/H.243 | Multipoint conferencing | in development |

**Figure 49.1**  CCITT standards applicable to desktop video collaboration.

United States, 2.0 Mbits per second E-1 in Europe). Although not restricting the use of local area network (LAN) connectivity, the CCITT standards do not take advantage of the higher bandwidth offered by the LAN to the desktop. The H.320/H.261 standard is also called *P*64*. The various CCITT videoconferencing standards are listed in Fig. 49.1.

Some analysts predict that by 1994 about 50 percent of telephone and other switched channels in the United States will have ISDN capacity. Pacific Bell committed to complete ISDN service capacity by 1997. In contrast, today, only a few thousand ISDN-capable connections exist in the United States.

The wide area network (WAN) capacity of Switched 56 kbits per second (SW/56, a more available digital standard in the United States) and ISDN (a worldwide standard) is important to connecting the workplace and the home with high-quality images and faster file-sharing. Today's primarily analog telephone connections (plain old telephone service, POTS) strain the idea of workgroup collaboration and productivity because their single 14.4-kbit-per-second channel greatly reduces the quality of communication. In addition, analog phones are not compatible with workplace PBX systems and are therefore not likely to become widespread in the commercial office or videoconferencing telecommuter's home. ISDN's basic-rate interface (BRI) and SW/56 are much more robust technologies for desktop video collaboration than POTS for telecommuters working at home.

### Audio/video control interface

Areas in which the videoconferencing standards are weak are multiparty conferences and user interface.

Microsoft and Apple each developed a video/audio control interface, known as AVI™ and QuickTime™ respectively. Both are targeted at reading data from mass storage devices such as CD-ROM.

Videoconferencing with multiple streams of video and audio to the LAN and WAN may be more than current versions of AVI and QuickTime can support.

### LAN standards

The CCITT's H.320, which is primarily a wide area network standard, specifies an ISDN-like connection for videoconferencing applications.

Isochronous Ethernet, a local area network technology developed by the National Semiconductor Corporation, supports this standard by delivering 96 B-channels (6.144 Mbits per second) to the desktop. Isochronous Ethernet (isoENET) equipment will be available this year. It is a superset form of switched-circuit Ethernet that brings videoconferencing the last 100 meters to the desktop with good cost/performance. The IEEE 802.9 committee, which is responsible for integrated services standards that support multimedia communication within the LAN, has adopted isoENET and is considering the adoption of its call setup procedures in the 802.9 standard. This is a step toward affordable desktop interoperability with the LAN and WAN for worldwide desktop video collaboration links.

Meanwhile, the American National Standards Institute (ANSI) X3T9.5 committee has completed work on the physical components of a second-generation fiber distributed data interface (FDDI) 100 Mbit-per-second LAN, FDDI-II, or isoFDDI, which also supports isochronous services and B-channel interfaces and will begin to be deployed this year, primarily for backbone applications.

Also working on those isochronous services that will be required if LANs are not only to connect to the WAN but also support collaborative desktop video is the ATM Forum, which is developing even higher-speed solutions than either isoENET or isoFDDI.

Another networking solution that is frequently mentioned for high-speed applications is 100-Mbit-per-second Ethernet. This is based on Ethernet's packet protocol. As a result, delays from packet collisions make this solution less than ideal for videoconferencing applications, where tolerance for delay is minimal. Additionally, users must consider the delays that accumulate over the entire Ethernet network. Bandwidth alone is not the measure of whether or not a network is suited for desktop video collaboration.

## System Design of Multiparty Communication

Digital signal processors, LAN, WAN, display, and audio and video compression/decompression (CODEC) technologies are critical to video communication systems. Software also plays an important role.

### H.320/H.261 hardware

Elements of H.320 are likely to be required as lowest-common-denominator defaults in desktop video collaboration systems. The costly hardware to implement these defaults, such as the H.261 CODEC, are likely to be placed at the LAN-to-WAN interface as a shared resource rather than burden the local area network at each desktop with their cost.

Single-channel H.261 CODEC integrated circuits are extremely complex, therefore more costly than most circuits found in a typical PC. If for example a system is designed for six locations or parties in a conversation, there are five channels of audio and video to decode and one channel, that of the sender, to encode per station. Given the $150–$400 range of cost for H.261 integrated circuits per channel, a multiparty system based on H.261 hardware CODECs may be too expensive for desktop systems. In addition there are other circuits required at the desktop; video analog-to-digital and digital-to-analog converters, an audio CODEC, video-in-a-window circuits, and LAN interface. These circuits fill multiple PC-AT boards quickly and raise system cost substantially.

## Multichannel video transmission

In the example just cited, the system supported six channels of video and audio. Six seems like a reasonable number, since meeting dynamics tend to bog down with larger groups. In addition, some people can join the group conversation from a telephone. Several channels or streams of H.261 video per desktop represent quite an investment. The H.231/H.243 section of the CCITT standards defines an MCU (multipoint control unit) that acts like a small PBX. This unit combines multiple streams of video and audio so that each user in a conference can see the other parties. Today the MCU cost is about $90,000 for a unit that can service two conversations of four parties or four conversations of two parties. The MCU cost and the additional cost of $7000 per desktop restricts multipoint videoconferencing using the H.320 specifications to special conference rooms and perhaps a few select desktops.

In contrast, an isoENET system does not need a separate MCU to create multiparty conversations, due to the high bandwidth and switch capacity of the isoENET hub. The typical isoENET hub can switch 100 to 300 Mbits per second of isochronous B-channel bandwidth, contrasted to a maximum of 2 Mbits per second per channel for H.320, thus offering much higher performance at dramatically lower cost than H.320-style systems, which also require costly MCUs. Figure 49.2 shows an example of isoENET providing multiple streams of data to each desktop, and Fig. 49.3 shows an isoENET LAN.

## Multichannel audio transmission

In the isoENET LAN, with 96 B-channels per desktop, one B-channel can support voice-grade audio without compression. In addition isoENET users may access high-bandwidth information, including hi-fidelity stereo audio, which may require from three to six B-channels. By contrast, the CCITT's G.711 standard limits users' access to one B-channel for audio. If a WAN's basic-rate interface (BRI) is installed, then communication is restricted to two B-channels, about one and a half used for video and a half for audio, and CCITT's G.728 standard defines a method of audio compression with a 4:1

**Figure 49.2**  Multiparty channel requirements.

compression ratio to fit into a 16-kbit-per-second bandwidth. Facilitating G.728 compression requires a more costly floating-point digital signal processor than does the G.711 standard.

Audio streams must be combined so that each receiver hears all senders. This combination can occur in the isoENET hub or in a node resource that conforms to the CCITT's G.114 specified delays for audio and video. Less than 150 milliseconds is considered ideal, although less than 400 milliseconds is acceptable for one-way delays.

The standard CCITT H.231/H.243 approach mixes the audio streams in the MCU. The MCU is dialed through to become part of the calling network. The typical MCU has ISDN- or SW/56-compatible ports.

The traditional MCU approach is less flexible and more expensive than using a switched isoENET hub to perform the switching, mixing, duplication, and routing of the audio and video streams. Isochronous Ethernet hubs allow each desktop to receive audio in separate streams. Separate audio streams may be used with Surroundsound-like techniques to help listeners know who is talking while they are focusing on a document.

### User interface

The user interface must be a work of simplicity if it is really to improve productivity. Workgroup video collaboration must be as easy as dialing a phone.

isoEnet: 96 B + D + E
E = 10 Mbps
D and B = 64 kbps
iso = some multiple of Bs

**Figure 49.3** isoENET Hub.

Get rid of the current LAN, which must be baby-sat and managed, and is still down twice a week. We are talking about critical real-time communications, not deferred transmission of an e-mail that gets there when the server reboots tomorrow. This system must be available for use without a call to system administration or the need for a degree in computer science.

The user display portion of the interface shows the other parties in the conversation. If voice-only members are present, an icon blinks when they talk. Users may be assigned a name or a picture during call setup. During the conversation the user should have the freedom to place the speaker windows anywhere on the screen or even behind the screen, while the screen area is shared for applications or chalkboard windows. As a person speaks, his or her image is given priority and exposed, if needed, onto the screen, while dormant speakers may be flipped to the background. With this technique six or more participants' images can share the screen with data images. Figure 49.4 illustrates a four-party conversation.

Yet to be created is the phone book that will keep all the numbers users may wish to call. Today each application has its own phone book, and users type in, once for each application, the numbers for their modem program, their fax card, and their videoconferencing equipment. One hopes that in the future a standard will create one phone-book file for all applications.

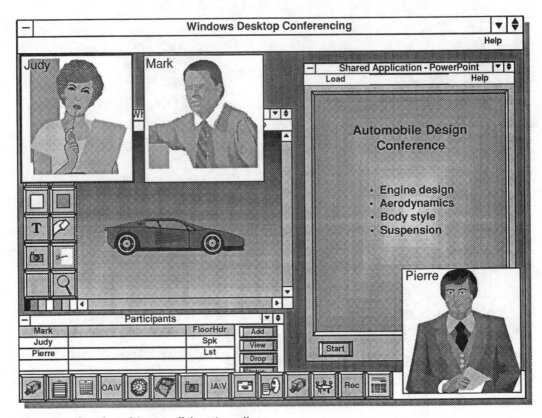

**Figure 49.4**   Sample multiparty collaboration call.

### Possible video collaboration product characteristics

The following list shows features that may be present on a desktop video collaboration product somewhere in the 1994–95 time frame. The list defines a product that could plug into a PC. The Macintosh product would be similar.

Total price (per user, plus shared MCU features): less than $2500 per station, toward the end of 1995

Multiparty conferencing over both LAN and WAN

CCITT H.320 interoperability with other WAN locations, without restricting LAN usage to H.320 limitations

Shared white board

Shared file view and annotation

Up to 6 live video windows on-screen at 15 to 30 frames per second

Up to 6 additional audio-only channels (for telephone connections)

Basic phone service

Scheduler/caller functionality

Snapshot of camera view, screen, or contents of window

Image exchange/viewer

Print images or data during conference

Clipboard—a personal note pad

Outgoing audio/video controls

Incoming audio/video controls

High-speed file exchange—up to the maximum network speed

Conference-control—speaker-management—color-coding for the floor-holder and speaker

Recorder

16-bit color VGA, SVGA, 800 × 600 or better

Six real-time windows up to 640 × 480 pixels each, overlapped—can be a combination of player, conferees, and images

Selection of visible conferees' images or icons

Hue, saturation, and brightness controls

Set frames per second (for transmission)

Monitoring user's image (self-video)

Moveable windows of variable size, variable quality

Camera and scanner inputs

Robust LAN connection—backward-compatible

Windows accelerator: BitBLT, clipping, line drawing, font acceleration

Multimedia PC (MPC)–standard compatible—Windows 3.1+:

> 16-bit stereo audio
>
> Audio mixer
>
> CD-ROM interface
>
> Synthesizer sound for presentations and games
>
> Optional midi and game ports

Full duplex speakerphone with echo cancelation

Fax—G3-, G4-compatible access through LAN–WAN bridge

Video capture, edit, play; limited authoring

Windows graphical user interface (GUI)

Unification of teleconference facilities with existing office automation facilities, i.e. voice mail, e-mail, fax, printing, collaboration tools, etc.

Voice recognition

Encryption

Video and audio quality-server-access across LAN and WAN

Video mail support

Voice mail—answering machine

E-mail X.400

Call screening

Powerful antivirus protection

Secure access to dialer so that unauthorized people are unable to use the caller's resources

Time and billing

Remote control and access

### Seamless LAN and WAN integration

The LAN and WAN connection should be transparent to the user. The LAN should simply represent the last 100 meters of connection to the office desktop. The isoENET LAN, due to its isochronous ISDN-like timing and signaling protocol, is easy to interface to the WAN. The H series protocols easily map, with some enhancements, to the isoENET LAN, thus making it easy to set up a call or tear down a call to anywhere in the world that supports digital services.

Local calls reside in the isoENET/isoFDDI/isoATM campus environment, while an out-of-campus call passes through the hub/PBX into the WAN. A typical electronic meeting could have four callers in different buildings of the campus, with a fifth caller coming in through a WAN connection. Each user in the LAN can see all others in the conversation, but the WAN-based call can be limited to two B-channels of ISDN and cannot reproduce simultaneous high-quality images of all parties in the conversation. If affordable, additional B-channels or primary-rate interface service supports multiparty viewing to WAN locations. The WAN-based user may be a telecommuter with access to either SW/56 or basic-rate interface ISDN (2B + D). To see others during the conversation, the WAN-based user can have a voice-activated switch to select who is displayed.

### Interoperability

Interoperability is a primary concern for users who purchase desktop video collaboration technologies in the expectation of fulfilling tomorrow's requirement for connection to vendors, customers, and telecommuters. Initially, new methods of compression will be introduced and used. Nonstandard methods offer lower cost or better image qualities. If H.320/H.261 standards are adopted by many users, the cost of standard systems may drop and become competitive with other methods. Still, the ideal is interoperability, and generally the use of standards delivers connectivity.

Interoperability can be achieved by means of proprietary or other de facto compression methodologies and today's standard method (H.261), working in the same environment, as long as the connection can be made to look compatible.

Theoretically, by using portions of the H series, with enhancements, and adopting a new experimental National Semiconductor software or hardware video-compression method, the cost per network is significantly reduced. Initial cost estimates for a multiparty network using National compression and isoENET are one-third the cost of a similarly equipped H.320/H.261 network. In addition, isoENET and National's multiparty compression maintains compatibility at the WAN interface and thus provides worldwide interoperability.

## Compression

Compression will be essential for desktop video collaboration. It is a way of dealing with low bandwidth and expensive storage or transport costs. Video and audio compression use different methods, due to the difference in information type and the difference in the way we perceive audio and video data.

### Video compression

Video compression typically reduces the data by discarding those things less important to our perception of the image.

The human eye is insensitive to random high-frequency visual information. It is, however, very sensitive to nonrandom high-frequency image content such as the edges of objects. Our eyes are less sensitive to color than to intensity changes, so color information may be formatted with lower resolution than intensity information, therefore affecting compression. Our vision also is more sensitive to noise in simple flat areas of an image where not much is happening. Consideration of these human factors is important when dealing with compression algorithms if we are to deliver what is perceived as high-quality video.

There are many applications for video compression, each with its different cost or performance requirements. Here's a sample list of applications:

Video conversation

Collaborative computing

White board

Multiple-person games through networks

Training

Education

Entertainment

Enhanced PC- or Mac-based games

Interactive video manuals

Video mail

Customer service

Security cameras

Many of these applications require hundreds of megabytes of low-cost storage. CD-ROM with about 650 Mbytes of storage can store images, video, and sound. Compression stores 72 minutes of movies on one platter.

Two good examples of CD-ROM storage are the following.

- *The San Diego Zoo Presents the Animals.* Features 60 minutes of video clips; more than 200 exotic mammals, birds, and reptiles; more than 1000 color photographs and descriptions; 2500 pages of habitat descriptions, articles, and scientific data
- *The Software Toolworks World Atlas.* Features motion video of the world's greatest cities; visits more than 200 countries; 1000 location photographs; currency conversion values; country and city maps; creates and combines maps, charts, and graphs

These two examples show typical uses for JPEG or still-image compression and MPEG, and other full-motion video-compression methods.

Although the general belief is that standards cut costs or widen the availability of solutions, compression used over LANs may exist with several popular de facto standards. Software compression has a niche where cost is a primary concern. Today new algorithms are developed every few months that are better than the standard H.261 or MPEG methods for some applications. The ever-increasing performance of CPUs and digital-signal-processing technologies may lead to new compression software sent to users on a floppy diskette or through the LAN with the compressed data.

In collaborative desktop videoconferencing, compression is likely to be found in two forms: software, and hardware. Software compression is ideal for one or two channels, but hardware compression accelerators will be required to support multiparty conferences.

Within the areas of data compression there are both proprietary and standards-based compression methodologies embedded in both software-compression and hardware-compression technologies.

### Standards-committee types of image compression

Four major compression standards already have been specified for image compression: JPEG, MPEG 1, MPEG 2, and those embodied in the CCITT's H.320 series for teleconferencing with video content.

JPEG is a group of methods for picture compression. The standard supports lossless compression of about 4:1 for high-quality storage, or lossy methods where compression of 15:1 is quite useful. Further compression notably degrades image quality. JPEG is used to send pictures electronically through a network, or to decrease storage requirements for a database. Some motor vehicle departments use JPEG to store drivers'-license photographs on computers.

MPEG 1 is a generic coding standard for compression of moving pictures and associated audio for storage devices (i.e., CD-ROM, DAT, disk drives, etc.) and telecommunications channels such as primary-rate ISDN in the WAN and various LANs.

MPEG removes redundancies in a manner similar to JPEG for video compression, in addition to using several prediction modes (forward, backward, bidirectional) entailing motion estimation/compensation techniques. CD-quality audio is achieved using either 64 or 128 or 192 kbits per second, and a systems transport mechanism is specified for proper synchronization and presentation. The intended MPEG application is for decode only (i.e., entertainment-quality playback), as MPEG 1 only specifies a bit-stream syntax for a decoder. MPEG 1 yields very long delays in multiparty or two-way exchanges, and therefore is not suited to real-time videoconferencing.

MPEG 2 is an extension of MPEG 1 with the intended application of distribution-quality video compression for cable television, satellite digital television broadcasting, home television theater, HDTV, etc. MPEG 2 also is a generic coding standard, since the complexity and bit rates vary between 4 Mbits per second for television programming up to 30 Mbits per second for HDTV. Technically, MPEG 2's primary differences from MPEG 1 lie in the ability of prediction modes (i.e., field/frame) to better handle odd/even fields so as to attain higher-quality video and multichannel audio modes for Surround sound, a low-frequency channel, and multilingual audio channels.

The CCITT's H.320 standard, Narrow-Band Visual Telephone Systems and Terminal Equipment, has rapidly emerged as the future standard for interoperability between videoconferencing systems. It provides for compatibility among various CODEC vendors in terms of compression, transmission, interchange, and display of audio and video. It answers the growing need for interoperability, similar to facsimile and modem technologies. Future videoconferencing systems will support the H.320 standard, at least as a default fallback, and many organizations are performing interoperability tests with H.320 standards.

Aside from interoperability testing of various implementations of H.320, a second barrier to interoperability for pervasive desktop video collaboration is the wide area network itself. Either ISDN or SW/56 is a requirement for reaching beyond the corporate campus to remote locations.

AT&T and Northern Telecom are major ISDN switch-providers in the United States. Originally they implemented ISDN differently, creating a networking barrier to interoperability. Bellcore, however, introduced National

ISDN1 (NI-1), which has been universally adopted by ISDN providers in the United States and will soon break down the WAN interoperability barrier.

Another networking barrier is the Inverse Multiplexer (I-Mux), which links a CODEC to a switched network. This function is responsible for dividing a compressed signal from the CODEC into multiple 56- or 64-kbit-per-second signals for transmission and resynchronizing at the receiver so as to provide a transparent WAN connection to multiple end stations. Since a standard was not available before the product was needed, proprietary schemes were used. Today, however, a common protocol has been adopted by a group of 32 I-Mux manufacturers calling themselves BONDING (Bandwidth-on-demand Interoperability Group), after they saw the acceptance of H.320.

Another obstacle to interoperability over the WAN has to do with providing gateways among different networks. AT&T, MCI, and Sprint already have discussed how to tackle this problem, and gateways should be available soon.

### Software compression

End users increasingly are aware of desktop video application opportunities. Video capture boards have entered the market and received an enthusiastic response from early adopters. As of now, captured video is restricted to local disk storage, and is not readily distributed. These boards use simple compression methods to compress "on the fly" at ratios of about 15:1 for storage to the disk. This restricts the application of video to enhancing presentations or video book forms.

With the increased availability of Ethernet embedded in PCs and isoENET products, users will demand the ability to channel video to other viewers in the local campus or network. Such channeling will open up new applications in education, training, and communication. These applications will be based on systems that have the following modules: a capture device (i.e., video camera or CCD lens); audio-capture analog-to-digital converter; video and audio compression/decompression (CODEC); transport and display. Today PC vendors add multimedia capabilities to their products to differentiate them and to add value. Several PCs in development carry most of the modules just mentioned.

PC processors are performing at higher levels, and some vendors include a digital-signal-processing chip on the PC mother board. This increased capacity may support compression of video and audio in software without additional board or chip resources, allowing users to use multimedia PCs for authoring, playback, and communication.

National's experimental compression method is unique in several ways that are important to the end user. The compression relies on a technique that uses 100 times less computation than the complex mathematical methods used in standards such as H.261. Since the compression scheme requires less computation power, the algorithm can run on the host PC without add-in cards.

Additionally the algorithm supports chalkboard collaboration, because it preserves the edges of text, or lines captured from the screen, or other scanned documents. The NSC method of compression supports easy scaling of size and aspect ratio, so that the end user can position the appropriate viewing resource on the screen. National's experimental compression method may be available in software versions. Additionally, it has been designed for real-time multiparty desktop videoconferencing, and therefore yields much lower delays than do other standards for high-quality desktop video collaboration. Reduced delays at the end-user desktop compensate for possible delays in other parts of the system.

### Software compression trends

Several vendors have software decoders, but few provide real-time encoding of video and audio in software. Given increasing CPU power, real-time encoding is now practical in some methods. Low-cost software can ship with the PC as part of the operating system package. In this situation there is no need to be compatible to H.261 or MPEG standards, because software CODECs can be stored on the CD-ROM or transmitted to the receiver during call setup, so no extra hardware is needed. Today all software CODECs are proprietary, and the software decoder market is still open to de facto standards.

Internet is experimenting with video over public switched and LAN networks. This is exposing thousands of users to LAN-based video mail. As a part of this experiment, Internet supplies a package called PictureWindow™ videoconferencing software, for Sun SPARC stations that connect to Internet.

The value to the desktop customer of software CODECs and compression/decompression algorithms is that some level of videoconference capability is realized at a low investment. This method of software videoconferencing can support midrange to high-end PCs and new integrated circuits that contain some standard multimedia features, thus adding additional new features almost at the same investment level. Environments that have 10BASE-T Ethernet or isoENET maintain a low-end entry point by using this software to establish simple point-to-point video capability.

Today there are few solutions for software videoconferencing. The H.320 method of video compression requires 1.5 to 3 Giga operations per second, thus requiring dedicated digital signal processing hardware.

Several vendors today offer proprietary software decoding at about 15 frames per second. For faster decoding and better image quality, a board is added. In the future new compression methods, increases in CPU performance, or very low-cost silicon may change the competitive environment.

### Sample CODEC products

Software compression will soon become a standard feature in all PCs shipped. Hardware upgrades will provide better performance and features. Analysts estimate that by mid-1993 about 1 million copies of Apple's QuickTime had shipped, and about 50,000 copies of Video For Windows. Both environments and their software CODECs continually are being improved. The following list provides a sampling of the vendors now supplying software CODECs for Macs, PCs, and workstations:

**Apple.**   Has some real-time decoders for the QuickTime environment in Operating System version seven, but the compression ratio is low, and encoding is not performed in real time.

**Digital Equipment Corporation.**   Digital's Alpha CPUs are reported to decode H.261 video (a resolution of 360 × 240 pixels) at 28 frames per second. H.261 is an asymmetrical standard, so compression is much more difficult than decompression.

**Intel.**   Has delivered a software CODEC called Indeo, packaged in the Video for Windows sold by Microsoft. Indeo cannot do real-time encoding without a special digital signal processor circuit that increases system cost. Software-only decoder performance is 15 frames per second, with 320 × 240 pixel resolution operating on an i386 33-MHz platform and 24 frames per second on an i486 33-MHz platform.

**Iterated Systems.**   Has a real-time decoder at 30 frames per second using a fractal-based method. This method yields good scaling and high quality. Fractals are very hard to code in real time, even with hardware digital-signal-processing. Microsoft's Encarda CD-ROM encyclopedia uses this method to store pictures.

**Media Vision.**   Offers 15-frames-per-second, 160 × 120 pixel software decompression. Compression is too slow for videoconferencing, but fine for CD-ROM storage. Media Vision licensed its method to Microsoft, so it is included in Video for Windows.

**Microsoft.**   Has some real-time decoders for the AVI environment in Windows, but the compression ratio is low and does not provide real-time encoding.

**National Semiconductor Corporation.**   Has developed an experimental compression algorithm that targets two-way, real-time communication, as well as storage on CD-ROM. This technology is capable of two-way communication using software alone, or supports multiple channels when using hardware acceleration. The algorithm has a low delay and preserves the quality of text in an image, thus achieving good quality and compression tradeoffs.

**Sun.**   New SunVideo™ technology includes a software compression method called CELL that can do two-way compression and decompression when running on Sun 10 workstations.

**SuperMac Technology.**   CompactVideo can display 15 frames per second in a 320 × 240 pixel window, or 30 frames per second in a 160 × 120 pixel window. The CompactVideo CODEC is licensed to Apple in version 1.5, and later versions of QuickTime. The CODEC is called Cinepak. While real-time compression in software is not practical, the decompression quality is considered quite good.

**Xing.** Has demonstrated an MPEG-like video decoder in software that uses a digital signal processor for audio decompression. The Xing product decodes in real time.

Meanwhile a host of companies, ranging from AT&T to Zoran, are offering or have announced video-compression integrated circuits that doubtless will find their way into add-in boards and perhaps into main system boards as well. Although hardware compression is more costly than software compression—adding perhaps $500 to the price of the end-user product—it is likely to be required in some multiparty desktop video collaboration applications. It is conceivable that hardware compression could reside on a local area network hub, so that hardware compression costs were spread among several users.

## Conclusions

Desktop video collaboration represents new challenges, standards, and opportunities that will serve to improve and advance the quality of remote communication worldwide. Reliability and ease of use are critical to the acceptance of a new communication paradigm. The technical challenges of multiple streams of full-duplex video and audio are clearly supported by new LAN technologies such as isoENET, isoFDDI, and isoATM, and lower-complexity, lower-cost compression methods other than H.261. Interoperability between compression methods must be established so as to spur market growth in campus environments as well as in pervasive applications. As local area network technology prepares to interface with wide area network standards, local and international exchange carriers will have to deploy ISDN in the wide area network before telecommuters, customers, and vendors are able to participate in worldwide desktop video collaboration.

# The Kodak Photo CD System

**Phil Abram**

## Introduction

The Photo CD system has fueled advancements in multimedia for a growing number of users. The core Photo CD file format is becoming established as a standard for high-quality still images in multimedia applications. In addition, the Kodak Photo CD Portfolio format makes it easy and inexpensive to produce interactive multimedia presentations with still images, audio, text, and graphics. These developments are transforming multimedia from a costly, technical specialty to one anyone can master with a minimum of experience and expenditure.

## Multimedia: A Move to the Desktop

With only minutes left before deadline, a graphic artist assembling a brochure is directed by a supervisor to change a layout. A few short years ago, when graphic artists relied on manual page makeup, making last-minute changes presented a problem. But with today's desktop-publishing software and a standard computer, the artist can make changes in seconds.

Across town, a sales representative putting last-minute touches on a presentation finds it necessary to alter the script and slide sequence. But with the presentation written, slides already in carousel, audio in place, and controlling computer program finished, the words *quick change* simply aren't in the vocabulary.

Today, advancements in technology have made speedy change as easy as changing a layout on-screen. Spurring this trend is an array of software and product developments that have transformed multimedia from a once costly, exclusive technology to one built on a broad consumer base.

No longer a technological option just for high-end specialists, multimedia is bringing a range of solid deliverables to the corporate community. Not only has the advent of these products empowered users with new capabilities, it also has significantly lowered the costs for those specialists, by amortizing the development of these tools over a much broader base of users.

## The Role of the Photo CD System in Multimedia

In the same way that CD-ROM is an outgrowth of audio CD, another CD-based technology has set the stage for today's developments in multimedia: the Photo CD system.

When Eastman Kodak Company announced it in September 1990, the Photo CD system promised to bring users a new, cost-effective, and practical way to digitize, store, and manipulate images.

Photo CD technology, which permits the scanning of high-resolution photographic images onto special compact discs, now is providing low-cost, enhanced capabilities to consumer photography and commercial applications, including multimedia.

In essence, the Photo CD system gives both consumers and commercial customers the best of two technologies. First, it provides the convenience, low cost, and image quality of traditional photography. To that it adds the benefits of digital technology: the ability to display, enhance, and transmit images electronically.

With the Photo CD system, consumers take pictures just as they always have, using standard 35-mm cameras and film. At the photofinisher, they have the film processed normally. As an additional option, users can have full-resolution images placed on a Kodak Photo CD master disc.

The Kodak Photo CD master disc is a 120-mm gold-colored CD that can hold about 100 images, or four 24-exposure rolls of film. These discs are nonerasable, so pictures cannot inadvertently be lost.

Pictures stored on Kodak Photo CD Master discs are high-resolution images. The discs offer image resolution 16 times as great as today's TV standard, and 4 times the standard currently being considered for HDTV.

The five resolutions at which each image is stored on a Photo CD Master disc are

$2048 \times 3072$ pixels (Base*16)

$1024 \times 1536$ pixels (Base*4) = HDTV

$512 \times 768$ pixels (Base) = TV

$256 \times 384$ pixels (Base/4) = thumbnail

$128 \times 192$ pixels (Base/16) = thumbnail

These are all 24-bit color (16.7 million colors) images. An additional higher-resolution image is available on new Pro Photo CD Master discs:

$4096 \times 6144$ pixels (Base*64)

The Kodak Photo CD Master disc also can function as a "digital negative," from which users may have prints made at a photofinisher.

## The Photo CD System: Commercial Applications

In addition to offering consumers a high-quality, convenient way to store and view their favorite images, the Kodak Photo CD system offers a number of specific commercial benefits. For example:

- A real estate agent can send his client a disc containing photographs of available housing.

- Photographers who are high-volume film users find that Photo CD discs make image storage less cumbersome and retrieval less time-consuming. In addition, Photo CD discs are ideal for creating disc albums made up of selected images from a photographer's personal collection.

- Photo CD–compatible CD-ROM drives can read Photo CD discs when used with Photo CD–enabled software, such as Kodak Photo CD Access software, thus giving desktop publishers a new, low-cost way to input photographs into their computers. Dozens of currently available CD-ROM drive models are Photo CD–compatible.

- The format developed for storing 35-mm photographs at full resolution can be extended to other types of images for other applications, including professional photography, catalog publishing, and medicine.

- Photo CD image files simplify the creation of "image databases," giving computer users access to images stored on-site or across local, national, or international networks.

- The technology photofinishers use to scan photographs onto Photo CD discs has changed the economies of CD publishing, making it cost-effective for many other businesses to write, distribute, and retrieve data on CDs.

Because Photo CD technology was developed for both consumer and commercial applications, each type of user receives two key benefits. *Affordability* is one: mass production of the Photo CD leads to lower prices for all Kodak-manufactured Writable CD media users. *Cross-platform accessibility* is another. Using an inexpensive CD-ROM drive in combination with Photo CD–enabled software, computers read the Photo CD discs; in addition, users may view on TV, with an inexpensive home player, the same discs used in computing applications.

The Photo CD system is doing for a range of professionals what the audio CD has done for music lovers: provide a dynamic and flexible capture medium. This, perhaps more than any other one development, has set the stage for the sweeping changes now occurring in multimedia.

## Multimedia and the Role of the Kodak Portfolio CD

The Kodak Photo CD Portfolio disc—an extension of the core Photo CD format—is a dependable, multisession CD recording medium that offers durability as well as flexibility of data input, access, and manipulation.

The Kodak Photo CD Portfolio disc lets users employ Photo CD images, or other digital image files, to create a special disc that merges those images with text, graphics, and sound. A "programmed-access" capability built into this new format enables users to create discs that are interactive.

This interactive ability is based on a sequencing that permits a user-directed "guided tour" through a collection of images and audio contained on the disc. The capacity to select and incorporate still images, text, audio, and graphics makes it possible to achieve complex and sophisticated results. In addition to programs such as training or point-of-sale presentations, the technology is being used by several major museums to document the sights and sounds of its exhibitions.

### Portfolio applications

On the consumer side, Kodak Photo CD Portfolio applications include the publishing of consumer "picture stories" such as wedding discs, or "family trees" that contain pictures and voices of family members.

The Photo CD Portfolio format also makes it possible to create educational discs. During the 1993 G-7 Economic Summit, for example, the Japanese Foreign Ministry placed 100 photographs of Japanese life, as well as accompanying narration, on Portfolio discs. Journalists attending the summit received a disc to view on television (using a Photo CD player) or on their Macintosh computers (using a Photo CD–compatible CD-ROM drive).

Books, too, are well complemented by the medium. An example is *From Alice to Ocean* (Addison-Wesley, 1992), the first book to be published with an accompanying Photo CD Portfolio–format disc. By inserting the disc into a Photo CD player or compatible CD-ROM drive with the correct software, readers can enjoy photographs from the book on a TV screen or computer monitor in vivid color, accompanied by firsthand narration and the ambient sound of the photographed scene. On-screen graphics provide a guide to the disc's contents, allowing the viewer either to watch the entire journey unfold or to select particular sections.

For the business community, a key attraction of the Photo CD Portfolio format is its ability to offer high-quality multimedia presentations at relatively low cost. It is this integration of image and audio—without the expense and aggravation of traditional animation or motion-picture editing—that constitutes a major point of value for the Photo CD Portfolio format in commercial applications. With the Photo CD Portfolio disc, users can produce a professional-quality interactive presentation with almost the same ease as they do word processing.

In effect, the Photo CD Portfolio format will do for multimedia what desktop publishing did for the graphics industry. For multimedia professionals, the Photo CD Portfolio format offers an easier way to work; it frees them from the routine details of production so that they may employ their skills on the more creative aspects of their craft. At the same time it enables a whole group of nonprofessionals to rise to a level of quality previously reachable only by specialists.

## Cross-Platform Playback

One of the great challenges facing CD title producers today is deciding on a delivery platform. The Kodak Photo CD Portfolio format offers the largest installed base of playback devices of any multimedia format.

With specialized software, a Photo CD Portfolio disc will play on most major computer platforms, using any of the many Photo CD–compatible CD-ROM drives now available. The system is especially ideal for those custom presentations that, with the aid of a portable Photo CD player about the size of a videocassette, can easily be played in home or office on TV.

Cross-platform playback goes beyond the computer platform. These same discs can be played on TV using Kodak Photo CD players, CD-I players, or other compatible playback devices. In addition to offering one of the lowest-cost playback options available, this feature makes Photo CD discs easily transportable—they can be played at the office, at home, or wherever there's a TV.

## Other benefits

Another benefit of the Kodak Photo CD Portfolio disc is its low production cost. The disc offers a still-image, static-graphics, audio, and interactive format. Because it provides no video animation or full-frame, full-motion video, it requires far lower production costs—and offers a faster turnaround.

Another benefit is that a user can develop presentations on-screen, then enlist a service bureau to produce the CD, obviating the need for the end user to purchase production software and the writer. This lowers the cost of entry into CD publishing, making it cost-effective for users in low-volume applications. When users begin to produce more discs, it quickly will become cost-effective to purchase the writer and the software.

Any 35-mm camera serves as a quality input source to this multimedia environment, and the time it takes to produce a disc is measured in hours rather than weeks. With this capability, the user can make changes on presentations and other work right up to the last moment. It can be as little as 15 minutes from the time the user makes a final decision on a presentation until the disc is produced.

Lower costs make low-volume publishing applications viable. Before the advent of the Photo CD Portfolio format, small businesses wishing to produce 10 or 20 discs found production costs almost prohibitive, due primarily to mastering costs. The Photo CD Portfolio architecture lets the user inexpensively duplicate low numbers of discs at a service bureau or on their own disc writer.

Another key benefit of the Photo CD Portfolio format is the convenience of storage, transportation, and retrieval. On a single CD the user can store up to 800 images, or 72 minutes of audio, or lesser combinations of the two (e.g., 400 images and 36 minutes of audio). This makes for a far more compact, flexible, and easy-to-handle medium than slides, audiocassettes, or other traditional presentation media. In addition, Photo CD Portfolio discs are "lights-on" media that don't require a darkened room for viewing.

The Photo CD file structure also offers random access to information. For instance, the presenter easily can jump from one image to another out of sequence, something that can't be done with traditional projectors, carousels, videotapes, or slides. This flexibility permits customization of presentations; with a Photo CD Portfolio disc, for instance, the user can place images on a single disc and then jump among them at random during a presentation, letting the presenter configure the presentation to each specific audience. In applications such as interactive sales kiosks, the audience can choose how it wants to view the information.

In sum, the Photo CD system makes it easy to store and access photographic images. The Photo CD Portfolio format lets users weave photographs with audio, text, and graphics into impressive, low-cost multimedia presentations having more flexibility than animation or video. In addition users can convert TIFF or PICT files (digital images) to Photo CD format, to be used on the same disc that contains photographs and audio.

## The Photo CD System: The Products

At the heart of the superior capability of the Photo CD system are the products that, taken together, support an impressive array of applications, many of which have directly benefited from advances in multimedia and interactive media.

### Disc formats

Kodak has applied the core technology of the Photo CD system to a variety of disc formats for specialized applications. Any disc carrying the Photo CD logo, including a mass-replicated disc made by a licensed manufacturer, can be played on a Photo CD player, a CD-I player, the Apple Power CD unit, or a compatible CD-ROM drive (with appropriate software).

In addition to the Photo CD Master disc and Photo CD Portfolio disc, discussed earlier, Kodak also offers

- *Kodak Pro Photo CD Master.*   Used by professional photographers, these discs store images from the larger film formats favored by professionals, including 120 mm, 70 mm, and 4 × 5–inch, as well as 35 mm. Depending on the film format and scan resolution, the discs can hold from 25 to 100 images.

- *Kodak Photo CD Catalog.*   This disc was designed for organizations that want to store large numbers of images on a disc and distribute those

**TABLE 50.1    Kodak Photo CD Disc Formats**

| | Kodak Photo CD Master | Kodak Pro Photo CD Master | Kodak Photo CD Portfolio | Kodak Photo CD Catalog |
|---|---|---|---|---|
| Content | 35-mm film | 35-mm, 120, 70-mm, 4 × 5 | PCD or electronic input | PCD or electronic input |
| Identifier | "Photographic quality" | "Professional photographic quality" | "Type 2 extended capacity" | "With Kodak Browser software" |
| Playback | Photo CD player Phillips CD-I player Photo CD-compatible drive | Photo CD player Phillips CD-I player Photo CD-compatible drive | Photo CD player Phillips CD-I player Photo CD-compatible drive | Photo CD player Phillips CD-I player Photo CD-compatible drive |
| Authoring system | PIW 2400 or 4200 | PIW 4200 | Portfolio authoring software | Portfolio authoring software |
| Max no. of images | 100 | 100, 25, 6, dep. on res. | 800 | 4400 (depending on resolution) |
| **Optional Features** | | | | |
| Audio | Yes | Yes | Yes | Yes |
| Programmed Access (branching) | Yes | Yes | Yes | Yes |
| Text and graphics | Yes, w/high-resolution images | Yes, w/high-resolution images | Yes, w/high-resolution images | Yes |
| Pixel edited image | No (only dustbusting) | No (only dustbusting & minor editing) | Yes | Yes |

images widely—such organizations as mail-order retailers, tourism associations, or art galleries. As many as 4400 images can be stored at TV resolution on Kodak Photo CD Catalog discs, for soft display on TV sets or computer monitors. (The images are of lower resolution than standard Kodak Photo CD Master discs or Kodak Pro Photo CD Master discs, and can't be used to make photo-quality prints.) Kodak Photo CD Disc formats are shown in Table 50.1 and Fig. 50.1.

## Players

In order to look at the images on Photo CD discs, consumers may choose among several options that bring multitiered levels of capability to an application. Using a Photo CD player, the viewer can select specific images, program them to appear in a particular order, rotate images, or zoom in on part of an image for a closeup.

Kodak and other companies now offer a number of Photo CD player models, all of which function as audio CD players in addition to letting people view Photo CD discs on TV.

For multimedia applications, one of the most useful options is the portable player. Roughly the same size and weight as a VHS videocassette, the player

**Kodak Photo CD Master**

"Digital Negative"

Written by photofinishers

Full photographic resolution images

Optional text, graphics, audio &
branching (pre-programmed access)

**Kodak Pro Photo CD Master**

Professional "Digital Negative"

Written by Professional Photo CD
Imaging Workstation

Supports larger film formats
in addition to 35 mm

Supports higher resolution film scans

Copyright notice and security features

**Kodak Photo CD Portfolio**

Created from Photo CD Master or
Pro Photo CD Master discs

Written by photofinisher or on a computer

Full or display resolution images

Optional text, graphics, audio &
branching (pre-programmed access)

Up to 800 images or 1 hour of sound,
or any proportional combination

**Kodak Photo CD Catalog**

Created from Photo CD Master or
Pro Photo CD Master discs at
photofinisher or on a computer

Contains Kodak Browser software for
computerized image access

6,000 or more low resolution images

Optional text, graphics, audio & branching
(pre-programmed access)

**Kodak Photo CD Medical**

Film based medical photographs

Digital diagnostic images: CT & MR

Compatible with many existing
medical imaging standards

All Photo CD Formats play on Photo CD Player, CD-I Player and CD ROM XA Drive

**Figure 50.1**   Photo CD formats.

provides most of the advanced viewing features found in deluxe console players, including a full-function remote control. The portable player can be connected to any standard TV in seconds, with several video-connection options.

### Photo CD authoring systems and software

Authoring systems that allow photofinishers to quickly and cost-effectively
produce discs at the desktop are another key component of the Photo CD system. A wide variety of authoring systems are now available to let photofinishers and labs automatically scan rolls of standard or large-format films.

Kodak also provides Photo CD Portfolio authoring software for photofinishers, service bureaus, or individuals who want to produce Photo CD Portfolio
discs. The software allows users to

- Develop and produce interactive multimedia presentations and titles
  directly on the desktop in the Photo CD Portfolio format, combining photos, audio, graphics, text, and programmed access

- Edit images from Photo CD Master or Pro Photo CD Master discs using off-the-shelf image-editing software, and write the edited files to Photo CD Portfolio discs for storage or distribution

- Combine photographic-quality images from Photo CD Master and Pro Photo CD Master discs with other digital images to create Photo CD Portfolio discs for presentations, storage, or distribution

- Copy Photo CD Master and Pro Photo CD Master discs to Kodak Photo CD Portfolio discs for low- to medium-volume distribution

- Merge images from an assortment of Photo CD Master and Pro Photo CD Master discs to new Photo CD Portfolio discs.

### Software for working with Photo CD images

To accommodate a wide range of desktop applications, Kodak also has developed a family of software products. This software provides easy search-and-retrieval of images stored in databases, and allows multiple users to work with individual Photo CD images in a variety of ways.

### Hardware and services for image storage and exchange

Hardware is a component of the Photo CD system that greatly extends its system capability. Special automated disc libraries, or "jukeboxes," which may hold as many as 100 Photo CD discs, allow users to store thousands of images in one place, as shown in Fig. 50.2. Also expected to be in place in the near future are imaging networks, which will use telephone lines to link image distributors worldwide (Fig. 50.3).

**Figure 50.2** Professional Photo CD image library

**Image Providers (sellers)**

Stock Photo Agencies

Publishers

Museums

**Telecommunications Network**

**Database** Directory & Service Manager

**Image Users (buyers)**

Designers & Art Directors

Publishers

Corporate Image Users

• Market Reach
• Image Asset Management
• Operating Efficiency

• Creativity
• Image Diversity
• Response Time

Figure 50.3   Picture exchange.

## Kodak Writable CD System

The Kodak Writable CD system is a complete CD-R publishing solution that includes media, disc writer, and publishing software. Kodak's Writable media offer unique features designed to protect data, including

- A carefully selected dye chemistry that resists the fading caused by light, heat, and humidity
- A protective coating that resists scratches, dirt, rough handling, or other common mishaps that may damage the disc's readability
- A unique identification number, printed in human-readable form, along with a corresponding machine-readable bar code; these provide tracking, indexing, and security advantages
- A surface design that resists fingerprints, allowing discs to maintain a "like-new" appearance even after handling

All standard hardware devices, including CD-ROM, CD-ROM-XA, CD-I, and CD audio players can read properly authored Writable CDs.

Kodak Writable CD products are designed to offer customers the most productive and convenient system available for low-volume CD publishing, with the added benefit of one-stop shopping from a single vendor. Because the sys-

**Figure 50.4**  Kodak Photo CD imaging workstation.

tem is open, however, Kodak Writable media and hardware can be used with other vendors' products.

## The Role of Interactive Media in the Business Environment

While much of the imaging industry has envisioned interactive media as a dazzling high-end phenomenon, many are now finding that the true value of interactive CD-based technology resides in its ability to deliver quality, practical multimedia presentations to the modern office. These products, in fact, are emerging as industry workhorses in multimedia applications.

The Photo CD system (Fig. 50.4) is specifically designed to offer both ease of use and advanced interactive capabilities to a broad base of users—a course of development not unlike that in desktop publishing over the past decade. Input is as easy as taking a standard photo with a 35-mm camera, production as easy as processing film onto discs at a photofinisher, assembling an interactive multimedia presentation as easy as pointing and clicking a mouse.

### Photo CD Portfolio: Multimedia (Not Just) for the Masses

What the Photo CD system has done for digital images, the Kodak Photo CD Portfolio format is doing for multimedia, by suddenly making it possible to deliver high-quality, digital color images to everyone's desktop at a reasonable cost. A significant investment with a high-end producer no longer is required to obtain quality images.

In short, Photo CD Portfolio offers a sophisticated multimedia system that the most high-end title producer can employ, but also—and most important—the ease of operation that permits use by a broader market.

More than an attractive, low-cost way of viewing and storing photographs and images, the Photo CD system and the Photo CD Portfolio format are bringing a long-needed interactive multimedia capability to a wider range of consumer and business applications.

# Annotated Resource Guide

# Keyes' Annotated Resource Guide

There's a plethora of multimedia products out there. There's also a plethora of guides that describe each of these products in painful detail. What I've done here, at the risk of incurring the wrath of literally hundreds of multimedia vendors, is to list the ones that are most interesting to *me*. Since I have the same background as most of *you*, I think you'll find these products to be interesting as well.

## Authoring

**Compel.** A simple, easy-to-use business multimedia presentations kit. You can choose from many backgrounds, and even use a menu to create buttons.

Asymetrix Corporation
110 110th Ave NE, Suite 700
Bellevue, WA 98004
(206) 462-0501

**Kodak Photo CD Access Developer Toolkit.** Available for Mac, IBM, and SUN, this kit lets developers build a flexible user interface to images stored on Photo CD discs.

Eastman Kodak Co.
343 State St.
Rochester, NY 14650
(800) 242-2424

**Authorware Professional.** Expensive (about $5000) but complete authoring package that really does give bang for the buck. Uses a visual, icon-based approach to creating multimedia systems.

Macromedia, Inc.
600 Townsend St.
San Francisco, CA 94103
(800) 288-8229

**Scala MM200.**   Limitless multimedia capabilities according to its users. MIDI, laserdisc imagery, video, still photos, backgrounds, fonts, symbols, captions, scrolling, interactive, hot keys, wipes. For the Amiga.

Scala, Inc.
  12110 Sunset Hills Road, Suite 100
  Reston, VA 22090
  (703) 709-8043

**MPower.**   Not exactly an authoring tool, but an enabler. Hewlett Packard's tool provides not only the ability to add video, audio, and graphics, but also provides the ability to do real-time collaborative multimedia. In other words, two people separated by 5000 miles can work (and even annotate) the same screen. A Unix-based product.

Hewlett-Packard
  4 Choke Cherry Road
  Rockville, MD 20850
  (301) 670-4300

**Passport Producer.**   Creates audio and visual presentations on the Macintosh. Synchronizes QuickTime movies, animation, graphics, sound, and music. Selected as "Best New Software" by Keyboard Magazine.

Passport
  100 Stone Pine Road
  Half Moon Bay, CA 94019
  (415) 726-0280

**MediaMogul 1.1.**   A CD-I authoring system. Lets you combine audio, video, sounds, images, drawings, animations. What you create runs on a CD-I authoring player with a 650-Mbyte hard disk.

Optimage Interactive Services
  1501 50th Street, Suite 100
  West Des Moines, IA 50266
  (515) 225-7000

**Quest Authoring System.**   Multimedia training courseware generating software. Has some nice features such as Flow-Chart, Search and Replace, Spell Checker, and Screen Capture.

Allen Communication, Inc.
  5225 Wiley Post Way
  Salt Lake City, UT 84116
  (801) 537-7800

**PictureLink.**   An authoring system for interactive presentations. Controls video window functions, audio, laserdisc, and NEC PC-VCR.

Multi-Media Productions, Inc.
 1855 Interrech Drive
 Fenton, MO 63026
 (314) 349-4444

**Tempra.**   Really a series of multimedia authoring software, for every level of experience and every price range. Offering full DOS multimedia, Tempra offers everything from sound to video to animation.

Mathematica
 402 South Kentucky Avenue, Suite 210
 Lakeland, FL 33801
 (813) 682-1128

**HyperWriter.**   Offers a DOS/Windows hypermedia and multimedia authoring system. It includes full hypermedia, multimedia objects, powerful navigation, royalty-free runtime. Supports: Videodisc players, Video for Windows, Intel DVI, MCI command strings, animation, DDE, object-oriented, screen-painting multiple-word-processing file formats, multiple-graphics file formats.

NTERGAID Inc.
 2490 Black Rock Turnpike, Suite 337
 Fairfield, CT 06430
 (203) 380-1280

**ProScribe.**   Offers an IBM/DOS solution for creating networked and single workstation multimedia applications. Using an object-oriented menuing system, ProScribe provides: full-motion 30-frame-per-second digital video; 16-bit photographs; dynamic text displays; crystal-clear stereo audio; animation.

Dataseek, Inc.
 7500 San Felipe, Suite 525
 Houston, TX 77063
 (713) 975-5175

**Hyperties.**   An easy-to-use DOS-based software package for creating hypertext-based materials. In a Hyperties knowledge base, text, graphics, and video are linked together. Features include unlimited articles, external interfaces, scripting language, unlimited fonts.

Cognetics Corporation
 55 Princeton-Hightstown Road
 Princeton, NJ 08550
 (609) 799-5005

**IconAuthor.**   Combines high-resolution graphics, full-motion video, text, animation, and audio, enabling you to build interactive multimedia applications for the IBM platform. IconAuthor is a visual programming tool using the concept of the structure as its building metaphor. Content, including objects, text, graphics, etc., is added to the icon structure using dialogue boxes.

AimTech Corporation
 20 Trafalgar Square
 Nashua, NH 03063
 (603) 883-0220

**HSC InterActive.**  A Windows multimedia product that incorporates graphics, images, animation, live video, music, and voice.

HSC Software
 1661 Lincoln Blvd., Suite 101
 Santa Monica, CA 90404
 (301) 392-8441

**Guide.**  An authoring system that enables users to republish existing information as interactive multimedia documents. Can combine formated text, color, graphics, sound, animation, and full-motion video.

OWL International Inc.
 2800 156th Ave. S.E.
 Bellevue, WA 98007
 (800) 344-9737

**ToolBook.**  A high-level, object-oriented software construction kit for Windows.

Asymetrix Corporation
 110 110th Avenue N.E.
 Bellevue, WA 98004
 (206) 637-1594

**Q/Media.**  An integrated tool suite that enables developers to create Windows multimedia shows with video, animation, graphics, and audio.

Q/Media Software Corporation
 312 East 5th Ave.
 Vancouver, BC V5T 1H4
 Canada
 (800) 444-9356

**Storyboard Live! 2.0.**  IBM's slick DOS-based multimedia tool offers video and audio, as well as animation.

IBM
 P.O. Box 1328
 Boca Raton, FL 33429

**StudioXA.**  A complete toolset that lets users create interactive CD-ROM-XA titles with full use of video and audio. Enables creation of interleaved multimedia files, called *streams,* for playback on CD-ROM-XA–capable platforms.

Mammoth Micro Productions
 1700 Westlake Avenue N, Suite 702
 Seattle, WA 98109
 (206) 281-7500

**Virtual BASIC.**  Although not a multimedia authoring package, it includes support for multimedia devices. It's object-oriented approach makes it popular with the professional programming crowd.

Microsoft Corporation
 One Microsoft Way
 Redmond, WA 98052
 (206) 882-8080

**Multimedia Viewer.**  Those of you familiar with Windows also will be familiar with the Windows Help feature. Viewer enables you to author multimedia titles that have the look and feel of Microsoft Windows help applications. Hypertext-oriented, you also can add sound, video, and animation.

Microsoft Corporation
 One Microsoft Way
 Redmond, WA 98052
 (206) 882-8080

**Multimedia Studio.**  A multimedia presentation system for use in creating presentations that incorporate audio, video, video-in-a-window, and graphics.

Vision Imaging
 10231 Slater Avenue, Suite 112
 Fountain Valley, CA 92708
 (714) 965-7122

**ScriptMotion.**  A DOS-based DVI authoring language.

In Motion
 Digital Interactive Media
 62 Rue des Chantiers
 78000 Versailles, France
 33 1-39-53-67-88

**Microsoft Multimedia Development Kit.**  MDK enables you to create diagrams that move, jumps to related text and objects, displays that talk, and other multisensory experiences.

Microsoft Corporation
  One Microsoft Way
  Redmond, WA 98052
  (800) 426-9400

**Multimedia Make Your Point.**   An easy-to-use end-user application for creating graphics-rich presentations that can incorporate multimedia effects.

Asymetrix Corporation
  110 110th Avenue NE, Suite 700
  Bellevue, WA 98004
  (206) 462-0501

**CD Author.**   This professional toolkit consists of a suite of menu-driven modules for conversion, indexing, and optimization of data. CD Answer, a companion product, is the retrieval software for information prepared with CD Author. This software is especially popular with those organizations that need to disseminate huge amounts of information (e.g., magazines, corporate databases).

Dataware Technologies
  222 Third Street, Suite 3300
  Cambridge, MA 02142
  (617) 621-0820

**Special Delivery.**   This is a media integration and delivery tool for the Mac that enables a user to quickly and easily build an interactive multimedia presentation. The product uses the concept of an interactive slide, and features a simple graphical technique for creating interactivity. Can combine buttons, text, pictures, movies, and sound.

Interactive Media Corporation
  P.O. Box 0089
  Los Altos, CA 94023
  (415) 948-0745

**PCPresents, MacPresents.**   For both PC and Mac platforms, this tool combines photographs, diagrams, 3D graphics, QuickTime movies, and animations. Also includes a videodisc controller.

EMC Ltd.
  7110 Ohms Lane
  Edina, MN 55439
  (612) 831-1344

**Audio Visual Connection (AVC).**   Runs under DOS and OS/2. Enables multimedia presentations to integrate images, sound, animation, video.

IBM
  Multimedia Information Center
  P.O. Box 2150

Atlanta, GA 30301
(800) IBM-9402

**LinkWay, LinkWay Live!**   These are simple, easy-to-use packages, popular in the education arena. Can integrate multimedia objects such as motion video, digital sound buttons, and digital movies.

IBM
 Multimedia Information Center
 P.O. Box 2150
 Atlanta, GA 30301
 (800) IBM-9402

**Hybrid formatter.**   Sony has come up with a way for a multimedia producer to create a single application that lets both Mac and PC users access it.

Sony Electronics
 9 W. 57th Street
 NY, NY 10019
 (212) 418-9439

## Hardware

### CD-ROMs

**PxCDS, PiCDS.**   Two multisession Photo CD, MPC and XA compatible drives, both with an average access time of 490 milliseconds. Tray-loading, 3-way eject, internal and external versions, accepts 12- or 8-centimeter-diameter CDs, plays CD audio, stereo headphones jack with volume control.

Procom Technology
 2181 Dupont Drive
 Irvine, CA 92715
 (800) 800-8600

**MultiSpin.**   NEC offers a series of high-quality CD-ROMS. What makes them unique is their multispin technology, which makes them exceptionally fast—about 280 milliseconds. Compare this to the 800 milliseconds of a typical low-cost, catalog-quality CD-ROM drive, and you'll immediately see the difference.

NEC Technologies, Inc.
 1255 Michael Drive
 Wood Dale, IL 60191
 (800) NEC-INFO

### Chinon 435
 MPC- and QuickTime-compatible
 150 kilobytes-per-second sustained-transfer rate

Data buffer—64 kilobytes

Built-in RCA jacks for stereo audio output

Headphone jack with volume control

Daisychain connection up to 7 drives

Bundles with: Multimedia Encyclopedia, The Animal MPC, World/US Atlas MPC, Sherlock Holmes MPC, Chess Master 3000 MPC, Mavis Beacon Typing MPC, Chinon Selectware

Chinon America
 615 Hawaii Avenue
 Torrance, CA 90503
 (800) 441-0222

## MacCD Station

QuickTime-compatible

SCSI interface

380-millisecond seek time

150 kilobytes-per-second sustained-transfer rate

Stereo audio output

Amplified speakers included

Lightweight headphone included

Bundled with: Mozart Dissonant CD Companion, Sherlock Holmes, Procom's Musical Sampler, Illustrated Encyclopedia, World Atlas, Shareware, Nautilus sampler

Procom Technology, Inc.
 2181 Dupont Drive
 Irvine, CA 92715
 (800) 800-8600

**CD Porta-Drive.**   A CD-ROM drive for laptop, portable, and desktop computers.

Interfaces through SCSI

200-millisecond average access time

330-kilobyte transfer rate

3.0 pounds in weight

Dual RCA phono/headphone jack

Uses a Toshiba XM-3401 drive

CD Technology, Inc.
 766 San Aleso Avenue

Sunnyvale, CA 94086
(408) 752-8500

**LapDrive.**  A portable, lightweight CD-ROM drive, with a rechargeable battery providing up to 4 hours of use.

TACSystems
 P.O. Box 650
 Meridianville, AL 35759
 (205) 828-6920

## Photo CD

**Kodak Photo CD.**  Although targeted primarily for consumers (instead of developing your trip to the beach on paper, you develop it on a CD), Photo CD offers opportunities to businesses as well.

Eastman Kodak Company
 343 State Street
 Rochester, NY 14650
 (716) 724-6404

## CD-ROM makers

**CDD 521CW Desktop CD Recorder.**  Philips Consumer Electronics' entry into the make-your-own-CD arena. Comes bundled with CD-WRITE publishing software. Can also be used to create your own audio discs.

Philips Consumer Electronics Company
 One Philips Drive
 P.O. Box 14810
 Knoxville, TN 37914
 (615) 521-4316

**CD Studio.**  For the RS/6000, CD Studio is a combination of hardware and software that enables organizations to master their own CD-ROMs. Consists of Makedisc, which is premastering software; CD Studio Controller, which is proprietary hardware, software, and dedicated hard drive; and the Philips CDD 521 CD-WO product.

Young Minds
 P.O. Box 7399
 Redlands, CA 92375
 (714) 335-1350

**Personal RomMaker, Mixed Mode RomMaker.**  JVC's personal solution for in-house CD-ROM mastering. Mixed Mode enables you to mix data (Yellow Book) with audio (Red Book).

JVC
 19900 Beach Blvd., Suite 1

Huntington Beach, CA 92648
(714) 965-2610

**RCD-202.**   An affordable (less than $4000), recordable CD-ROM drive for MAC and PC computers. Enables you to create your own HFS, ISO 9660, or audio CDs within minutes.

Pinnacle Micro
  19 Technology
  Irvine, CA 92718
  (714) 727-1913

**Personal Scribe.**   Probably the cheapest and easiest way of making your own ISO 9660-compatible CD-ROMs. All you have to do is pick the directories and files you're interested in and hit the neter key. Another advantage is that you don't need excessive hard-disk space. Prices start at less than $3000.

Meridian Data Inc.
  5615 Scotts Valley Drive
  Scotts Valley, CA 95066
  (408) 438-3100

**TOPiX.**   Supports all CD-ROM standards. Basically a desktop mastering system that is affordable and easy to use.

Optical Media International
  180 Knowles Drive
  Los Gatos, CA 95030
  (408) 376-3511

**PCD LAN Writer 200.**   This is a package that bundles Kodak's Writable CD products with Netscribe Access Client Software from Meridian Data. The net result is a turnkey system that allows any DOS or Windows user on a Novell network to produce CD-ROM discs.

Eastman Kodak
  343 State Street
  Rochester, NY 14650
  (800) 242-2424, ext. 52

### Digital cameras

**Canon Still Video Camera (RC-360, RC-570).**   Records color images on small floppy disks rather than on film. Using a separately purchased video card, you can input these images directly into your computer.

Canon USA
  One Canon Plaza
  Lake Success, NY 11042
  (615) 488-6700

**FlexCam.**  A small, flexible camera with built-in stereo microphones. Having the same quality as a SONY camcorder, the FlexCam looks somewhat like a desktop high-intensity light. It can be directly hooked up to the PC through any video board. By pointing it down at a desk, the FlexCam also can be used as a scanner.

VideoLabs
  5270 West 84 Street
  Suite 120
  Minneapolis, MN 55437
  (612) 897-1995

**DS-100 Memory Card Camera.**  Cardinal Technologies and Fuji Photo Film have joined forces to create this PC-ready digital camera. Twenty-one photos can be stored on a reusable memory card. Capabilities include auto flash/focus/exposure, 3X zoom.

Cardinal Technologies, Inc.
  1827 Freedom Road
  Lancaster, PA 17601
  (800) 722-0094

**FotoMan Plus.**  A 10-ounce, pocket-size portable camera that lets you take gray-scale digital photos. Costing about $800 retail, FotoMan is a one-button camera that holds up to 32 images and downloads those images through a serial interface. Bundled software completes the package.

Logitech Inc.
  6505 Kaiser Dr.
  Fremont, CA 94555
  (510) 795-8500

**Video**

**Adobe Premier.**  The hot ticket for Macs. Was even profiled on the Discovery channel.

Adobe Systems Inc.
  1585 Charleston Road
  P.O. Box 7900
  Mountain View, CA 94039
  (800) 833-6687

**D/Vision.**  Enables you to produce edited videotapes and multimedia video. Uses Intel's i750/Indeo digital video board. Enables instant revision and playback of editorial decisions. Good price for the power. Touts SupeRTV, which is an enhancement of Intel's RTV (real-time video); lets you "print" high-quality, full-screen video directly to videotape.

   There are actually two versions of this software. The basic system, which retails for under $500, is touted as being the lowest-cost nonlinear-editing software on the market. The Pro version, retailing for slightly under $4000, turns your PC into a professional video production studio. It even stores over 70 hours of accessible, on-line digital video.

TouchVision Systems Inc.
  1800 Winnemanc Ave.
  Chicago, IL 60640
  (312) 989-2160

**VGA Producer Pro.**   A VGA-to-NTSC genlockable encoder that enables you to transfer your multimedia work of art to videotape. Promises to be flicker-free.

Magni Systems Inc.
  9500 SW Gemini Drive
  Beaverton, OR 97005
  (503) 626-8400

**DVA-4000.**   A family of full-motion digital video adapters for IBM PC/AT, PS/2, or Mac computers.

VideoLogic, Inc.
  245 First Street
  Cambridge, MA 02142
  (617) 494-0530

**Mediator.**   High-quality computer-graphics-to-video conversion system for Mac and VGA displays.

VideoLogic, Inc.
  245 First Street
  Cambridge, MA 02142
  (617) 494-0530

**Pro Movie Spectrum.**   A playback, capture, and editing add-in board with bundled software. Enables user to bring synchronized, full-motion video sequences to the PC.

Media Vision
  3185 Laruelview Court
  Fremont, CA 94538
  (800) 845-5870

**Bandit.**   Simplifies the process of transferring images between your computer and VCR or video camera. Bandit is a peripheral device that works in the Mac and PC environments by connecting to either a SCSI or serial port.

Fast Forward Video
  18200-C West McDurmott
  Irvine, CA 92714
  (714) 852-8404

**Bravado.**  Combines full-featured, on-board VGA with live NTSC or PAL video-in-a-window and controllable pass-through audio in one board. Apparently, a single-board multimedia presentation engine.

Truevision
 7240 Shadeland Station
 Indianapolis, IN 46256
 (317) 841-0332

**Super Still-Frame Compression.**  Reduces storage requirements for captured video through JPEG (8:1 to 75:1) compression.

New Media Graphics
 780 Boston Road
 Billerica, MA 01821
 (800) 288-2207

**VideoSpigot for Windows.**  Captures digital video from cameras, VCRs, laserdiscs, etc. Includes Microsoft Video for Windows, which enables editing of motion-video sequences for embedding in any application that supports object linking and embedding (OLE). CinePak software compression lets you stores AVI files at a fraction of their original size.

Creative Labs
 1901 McCarthy Blvd
 Milpitas, CA 95035
 (800) 428-6600

**Videovue.**  Offers the ability to extract images from motion or still-frame video. Incoming video can be PAL, NTSC, composite, or S-video.

Video Associates Labs
 4926 Spicewood Springs Road
 Austin, TX 78759
 (800) 331-0547

**Intel Smart Video Recorder.**  One-step recording and Indeo compression allow a 50-Mbyte 60-second clip to be stored in a relatively small 9 Mbytes.

Intel Corp.
 2200 Mission College Blvd.
 Santa Clara, CA 95052
 (800) 538-3373

**DigiTV.**  A built-in, 122-channel, cable-ready TV tuner, with on-board, 4-watt stereo audio amplifier, lets you watch TV through your PC.

Videomail, Inc.
 568-4 Weddell Dr.

Sunnyvale, CA 94089
(408) 747-0223

**Video Machine.**  Enables broadcast-quality video editing right on the desktop.

Fast Electronics
  5 Commonwealth Road
  Natick, MA 01760
  (508) 655-FAST

**TelevEyes.**  An inexpensive tool for converting computer VGA to recordable composite video. Allows the display of computer screens on any standard composite video monitor, or the recording of VGA screens to videotape.

Digital Vision Inc.
  270 Bridge Street
  Dedham, MA 02026
  (617) 329-5400

**WatchIT.**  An add-on board that allows you to watch TV on your PC. It runs under DOS or Windows, using a pop-up remote control for TV adjustment.

New Media Graphics
  780 Boston Road
  Billerica, MA 01821
  (509) 663-0666

**PC Tele-VISION PLUS.**  A board that allows an IBM PC–compatible computer to display NTSC or composite video in a window of variable size on a VGA or Super VGA monitor.

50/50 Micro Electronics
  1249 Innsbruck Dr.
  Sunnyvale, CA 94089
  (408) 720-5050

**TapeIT.**  An inexpensive video-encoding board that converts VGA signals to NTSC or PAL.

New Media Graphics
  780 Boston Road
  Billerica, MA 01821
  (800) 288-2207

**The Indy Workstation.**  I haven't listed any multimedia PCs here, because all vendors seem to be offering them. This one, however, is unique. Silicon Graphics is now offing a workstation with a built-in color video camera for under $4995. Given the price of a multimedia-enabled PC nowadays, this workstation is certainly worth a look-see. And remember: Silicon Graphics are the guys who brought you the special effects for *Jurassic Park*!

Silicon Graphics
  2011 N. Shoreline Rd.
  P.O. Box 7311
  Mountain View, CA
  (800) 800-7441

## Media add-In boards

**ViVA.**  Truly a super board. It provides a low-cost multimedia solution by combining audio, video, and VGA—all on one board.

Omnicorp
  1734 W. Sam Houston Pkwy N.
  Houston, TX
  (713) 464-2990

**MediaTime Adapter.**  A NuBus adapter that combines CD-quality audio with 24-bit, real-time digital video and graphics display for the MAC.

RasterOps
  2500 Walsh Avenue
  Santa Clara, CA 95051
  (408) 562-4200

**Super VideoWindows.**  Enables the playing of full-motion video and stereo audio from a TV camera, VCR, still-frame camera, videodisc, or computer hard disk. Allows scalability, freeze or frame/grab, the combination of audio and video, and VGA graphics.

New Media Graphics
  780 Boston Road
  Billerica, MA 01821
  (800) 288-2207

**Super Motion Compression.**  Captures clips of high-quality video and stereo audio, compresses and stores them to hard disk, and allows instant playback.

New Media Graphics
  780 Boston Road
  Billerica, MA 01821
  (800) 288-2207

**Video Blaster.**  Integrates video and audio from a wide range of sources— cameras, VCRs, and videodiscs—then combines them with VGA graphics. Cropping, scaling, masking, and zooming capabilities. Includes a copy of Microsoft's Video for Windows.

Creative Labs
 1901 McCarthy Blvd
 Milpitas, CA 95035
 (800) 428-6600

## Sound

**AudioMan.** A portable hand-held device with a built-in microphone, speaker, and 8-bit sound digitizer. Really built to let you add verbal notes to your work, rather than handwritten notes.

Logitech Inc.
 6505 Kaiser Dr.
 Fremont, CA 94555
 (510) 795-8500

**PortAble Sound.** A parallel-port portable sound device, bundled with DOS and Windows software.

Digispeech, Inc.
 550 Main Street, Suite J
 Placerville, CA 95667
 (916) 621-1787

**SoundXchange.** A business-level audio solution, using a telephone rather than a microphone.

Interactive
 204 N. Main
 Humboldt, SD 57035
 (800) 292-2112

**Sound Blaster Deluxe, Sound Blaster Pro Deluxe, Sound Blaster 16 ASP.** A variety of cards for every need. Creative Labs creates sound cards for those interested in gaming (Sound Blaster Deluxe and Pro Deluxe) as well as those interested in 16-bit, CD-quality sound (Sound Blaster 16 ASP).

Creative Labs
 1901 McCarthy Blvd.
 Milpitas, CA 95035
 (800) 428-6600

**Wave Blaster.** A MIDI add-on daughter board to the Sound Blaster 16 card. Wave Blaster provides realistic instrument sounds rather than FM-synthesized sound.

Creative Labs
 1901 McCarthy Blvd
 Milpitas, CA 95035
 (800) 428-6600

**Audioport, Microkey.**  Two products that let you take sound on the road. With Audioport you can both record and play sound, with microkey only play sound. Both devices are tiny, fit into the parallel port of your laptop computer, and use 12-bit sampling and a 3:1 compression ratio for storage.

Video Associates Labs
  4926 Spicewood Springs Road
  Austin, TX 78759
  (800) 331-0547

**Audioport.**  An external device from Antex (not to be confused with Creative Labs' product of the same name) that offers broadcast-quality digital audio. It interfaces with PCs via the parallel port, and records or plays digital audio direct-to-disk.

Antex Electronics Corporation
  16100 South Figueroa Street
  Gardena, CA 90248
  (310) 532-3092

**Port Blaster.**  A portable solution for "on-the-road" business or multimedia presentations. Works with a parallel port.

Creative Labs
  1901 McCarthy Blvd
  Milpitas, CA 95035
  (800) 428-6600

**UltraSound.**  Can perform mixing of CD-audio, digital audio, synthesizers, a microphone, and line input.

Advanced Graphics Computer
  Technology
  3750 North Fraser Way, Suite 101
  Burnaby, BC V5J 5E9
  Canada
  (604) 431-5020

**Microsoft Sound System.**  Built primarily to add verbal notes to Windows applications such as your spreadsheet or word-processing document. Also has a facility, ProofReader, that provides an audible proofing of numbers, and another, Voice Pilot, that enables users to execute commands by voice.

Microsoft Corporation
  One Microsoft Way
  Redmond, WA 98052
  (206) 882-8080

**Roland SCC-1 Sound Card.**  This card seems to be quite popular with those interested in recording high-fidelity music.

Roland Corporation
7200 Dominion Circle
Los Angeles, CA 90040
(213) 685-5141

**Audio Solution Board.**   Basically available through OEMs, IBM's Audio Solution Board supports Windows, OS/2, and DOS. Available either in ISA (industry-standard architecture) or microchannel bus versions (for IBM's own PS/2 series), this board enables 16-bit audio.

IBM
White Plains, NY
(800) 426-3333

**Sound Galaxy.**   Offers 8- or 16-bit sounds cards, as well as multimedia upgrade kits.

Aztech Labs, Inc.
46707 Fremont Blvd.
Fremont, CA 94538
(510) 623-8988

## Upgrade kits

These enable you to upgrade your PC to be a multimedia PC.

**Sound Blaster Discovery CD 8 (and CD 16) Upgrade Kits.**   Both kits include sound card, stereo speakers, CD-ROM drive, and bundled software. The difference between the two kits is in the sound card, with the 16 being the higher-quality. In both cases, the CD-ROM exceeds MPC specifications.

Creative Labs
1901 McCarthy Blvd
Milpitas, CA 95035
(800) 428-6600

**Media Vision Upgrades.**   Media Vision has several different upgrades. The CDPC is a unit that contains everything from a Sony CD-ROM drive, Pro AudioSpectrum audio digitizer, MIDI port, and amplifier. The Pro 16 MultiMedia System includes the Pro AudiSpectrum 16 sound card, a NEC SCSI CD-ROM, Windows 3.1, Lotus 1-2-3 on CD-ROM, Compton's Encyclopedia, Nautilus Multimedia Magazine on CD-ROM, MacroMind Action! on CD-ROM. This kit also includes a joystick port and a stereo amplifier.

The PC Upgrade Kit Plus is similar to the one just described, but it has an 8- rather than a 16-bit sound card. It also has a less expensive CD-ROM drive.

Media Vision
47221 Fremont Ave.
Fremont, CA 94538
(510) 770-8600

**MediaSonic Super Professional Deluxe.**    Upgrades either Mac or PC. Includes a pair of high-quality speakers; double-speed CD-ROM drive. Also includes a collection of titles.

April One Peripherals
 4192 Fools Dr.
 San Mateo, CA 94404
 (415) 573-5170

**Turtle Beach MultiSound MPC Upgrade Kit.**    Includes a MultiSound sound board and a CD-ROM drive.

Turtle Beach Systems
 Cyber Center #33
 1600 Pennsylvania Ave.
 York, PA 17404
 (717) 843-6916

## Laserdisc players

**Teac America, Inc.**    Makers of several high-end RS-232–controllable laserdisc players for users in multimedia applications. The high end of the product line enables WORM-recordable.

Teac America, Inc.
 7733 Telegraph Road
 Montebello, CA 90640
 (213) 726-0303, ext. 659

**Pioneer.**    Manufactures a series of RS-232–controllable laserdisc players, for use in multimedia applications.

Pioneer Communications
 (800) 527-3766

**Sony.**    Manufactures a series of RS-232–controllable laserdisc players, for use in multimedia applications.

Sony Multimedia Marketing Group

Northeast (201) 833-5200

Mid-Atlantic (301) 577-4850

Southeast (404) 263-9888

Southwest (214) 550-5200

Midwest (708) 773-6110

Northwest (408) 944-4717

Western (714) 229-4267

**Networking**

The following companies make devices and/or software that can fill this tall order:

Fluent, Inc.
  One Apple Hill
  594 Worcester Rd.
  Natick, MA 01760
  (508) 651-0911

Starlight Networks
  325 E. Middlefield Road
  Mountain View, CA 94043
  (415) 967-2774

Virtual MicroSystems
  1825 S. Grant Street, Suite 700
  San Mateo, CA 94402
  (415) 573-9596

Todd Enterprises
  224-49 67th Ave.
  Bayside, NY 11364
  (800) 445-TODD

Artisoft
  691 East River Road
  Tucson, AZ 85704
  (800) TINY-RAM ext. 600

**CD-I players**

**CDI 350.** A portable CD-I player that sports a 6-inch active-matrix color LCD screen; NTSC or PAL; built-in pointing device; stereo speakers.

Philips Consumer Electronics
  1 Philips Dr.
  P.O. Box 14810
  Knoxville, TN 37914
  (800) 835-3506

**Kiosks**

These are stand-alone units. You've seen them in museums and airports, and now even in shopping centers.

**ServiceTouch Kiosk.** Fully integrated self-service kiosk. Combines the performance of a 486 computer, printer, speakers, and credit-card reader with the simplicity of a touchscreen interface.

MicroTouch Systems Inc.
  55 Jonspin Road

Wilmington, MA 01887
(508) 694-9900

**Touch Activity Center.**   The IBM Ultimedia Touch Activity Center is a suite of multimedia kiosk solutions. Each of these solutions is a stand-alone, cabinet-like enclosure (kiosk) housing varieties of IBM multimedia products.

IBM
 Multimedia Information Center
 P.O. Box 2150
 Atlanta, GA 30301
 (800) IBM-9402 X. 157

**SmartTouch.**   Touchscreen displays let you create your own kiosk solution.

Supermac
 485 Potrero Avenue
 Sunnyvale, CA 94086
 (800) 334-3005

## Software

## Sound

**Midisoft Studio for Windows.**   MIDI recording/editing software that delivers the power of a professional music studio to your multimedia PC.

Midisoft Corporation
 15513 NE 52nd St.
 Redmond, WA 98052
 (206) 881-7176

**Trax.**   Easy-to-use software for the MIDI beginner.

Passport Designs, Inc.
 100 Stone Pine Rd.
 Half Moon Bay, CA 94019
 (415) 726-0280

**Wave for Windows.**   Professional audio software for Windows.

Turtle Beach Systems
 P.O. Box 5074
 York, PA 17405
 (717) 843-6916

**Monologue.**   A software product for Windows that adds speech to your applications.

First Byte

19840 Pioneer Ave.
Torrance, CA 90503
(800) 545-7677

**IBM Speech Recognition Family.**   Brings the power of speech to AIX and OS/2
workstations. Has an active vocabulary of over 20,000 words, and a sophisticated language model.

IBM
Multimedia Information Center
P.O. Box 2150
Atlanta, GA 30301
(800) 772-2227

**20-20 Sound Editor.**   An audio-editing toolset for the IBM platform. Provides
cut, paste, copy, an 8-track audio mixer, and special effects.

MKS Compu-Group Inc.
1730 Cunard St.
Laval, Quebec H7S 2B2
Canada
(514) 332-4110

**Read My Lips.**   Not a George Bush record, but software for the Mac that
lets users record voice or sounds and attach digitized audio clips to
documents.

Praxitel
Box 452
Pleasanton, CA 94566
(510) 846-9380

**MCS Stereo.**   The complete interface to your computer's audio capability.
Controls CD-ROMs, plays, records, and edits .Wav files, and has an integrated database for all of your audio sources.

Animotion Development
3720 4th Ave. South, #205
Birmingham, AL 35222
(205) 591-5715

**FluentLinks.**   This is a NetWare Loadable Module that enables multiple users
to retrieve and play motion-video and audio segments over industry-standard
networks.

Fluent, Inc.
One Apple Hill
594 Worcester Rd.
Natick, MA 01760
(508) 651-0911

## Photographic software

**Adobe Photoshop.** Perhaps the most popular product in the photo-manipulation market. Enables user to retouch scanned photos and add significant amounts of creativity. Can make photos look like original artwork. Runs under MAC or Windows.

Adobe Systems Inc.
1585 Charleston Road
P.O. Box 7900
Mountain View, CA 94039
(800) 833-6687

**Aldus PhotoStyler.** A close second in quality to Adobe's product, but cheaper. Has all the quality and functionality you'd expect an Aldus product to have.

Aldus Corporation
411 First Avenue South
Seattle, WA 98104
(206) 622-5500

## Video

**PrimeTime.** Broadcast-quality character-generation for the PC.

InnoVision Technology
1933 Davis Street, Suite 238
San Leandro, CA 94577
(800) 238-8838

**VideoFusion.** A complete software solution for QuickTime postproduction. Create MTV-style videos that combine video, text, and graphics. Provides 2D warps, morphing, transitions, color transformations.

VideoFusion
1722 Indian Wood Circle, Suite H
Maumee, OH 43537
(800) 638-5253

**Splice.** Originally a DVI, ActionMedia II–based video editor, Splice now supports Microsoft's Video for Windows. Allows for full editing of AVS, AVI, and WAV files, as well as conversion and mixing.

Digital Media International
352 Arch Street, Suite B
Sunbury, PA 17801
(717) 286-6068

**Adobe Premier.** A Mac tool for creating high-quality QuickTime digital movies and videotapes. Premier is a powerful editing program that lets users combine video, audio, animation, still images, and graphics.

Adobe Systems Inc.
 1585 Charleston Road
 P.O. Box 7900
 Mountain View, CA 94039
 (800) 833-6687

**VideoShop.**   VideoShop enables the development of digital movies or video-tapes on the Mac platform. The system gives you the ability to combine video, graphics, PhotoCD, text, and CD-quality audio. VideoShop features include 75 digital effects and filters, graphics and titling, editing playout window, movie manager, full-screen recording, and the capacity to resize and layer movies.

Div
 222 Third Street
 Cambridge, MA 02142
 (800) FYI-DIVA

**Media Suite Pro.**   A beginner's or nonprofessional's video presentation suite that runs on the Mac. Its easy-to-use interface permits simple and rapid editing of video sequences, making you look like an expert.

Avid Technology, Inc.
 One Metropolitan Park West
 Tewksbury, MA 01876
 (800) 949-AVID

**Video Toaster 4000.**   Reportedly replaces approximately $100,000 of broadcast production equipment. Running on the Amiga platform, the Video Toaster enables users to make broadcast-quality production videos.

NewTek, Inc.
 215 SE 8th Street
 Topeka, KS 66603
 (900) 847-6111

**After Effects.**   A special effects application for QuickTime, designed to enable the Mac-based video producer to create high-quality video productions. Enables composite layering of moving video and animation; generation of moving mattes, fading them in and out over time; rotation and repositioning of images.

COSA
 14 Imperial Place, Suite 203
 Providence, RI 02903
 (401) 831-2672

**Video for Windows.**   A major extension to the Windows operating system, along with a series of utilities for creating and editing digital movies. These digital movies can be played back on any standard MPC-compliant PC. Utilities shipped with the product allow users to create, edit, and play back VRW clips in the AVI format. This product is shipped with most video add-in-boards.

Microsoft Corporation
 One Microsoft Way
 Redmond, WA 98052
 (206) 936-4423

**QuickTime for Windows.**  The Apple leader goes Windows. This is the preferred choice of experts.

Apple Computer
 20525 Mariani Avenue
 Cupertino, CA 95014
 (408) 996-1010

**FluentLinks.**  This is a NetWare Loadable Module that enables multiple users to retrieve and play motion video and audio segments over industry-standard networks.

Fluent, Inc.
 One Apple Hill
 594 Worcester Rd.
 Natick, Mass 01760
 (508) 651-0911

## Morphing

If you've seen *Terminator 2,* then you know what morphing is. Basically you choose a starting point and an ending point, then let the computer make the gradual transition between the two. You've also seen this done in one too many music videos.

Morph
 Gryphon Software Corporation
 7720 Trade Street, Suite 120
 San Diego, CA 02121
 (619) 536-8815

HSC Digital Morph
 HSC Software
 1661 Lincoln Blvd., Suite 101
 Santa Monica, CA 90404
 (310) 392-8441

## Animation

**Photorealism.**  Strata's series of packages for the Mac. There's a bunch of them. Stratavision 3D is a 3D animation program; Stratatextures are collections of realistic-looking materials that can be applied to objects.

Strata
2 W. Saint George Blvd., Suite 2100
St. George, UT 84770
(801) 628-5218

**Real3D.**  A full-featured 3D-animation, modeling, and rendering program for the Amiga. Enables objects to "rock and roll" and to react to their environment with "intelligence."

RealSoft
544 Queen St.
Chatham, Ontario N7M 2J6
Canada
(407) 539-0752

**Animator Pro.**  This one has won a bunch of awards. It's a high-resolution, 2D, paint-and-animation software program for the PC. Provides a repertoire of special effects such as tweening and color cycling.

Autodesk, Inc.
 2320 Marinship Way
 Sausalito, CA 94965
 (415) 332-2344

**3D Studio.**  The superb animation product that made Autodesk a household name. Comes with over 500 Mbytes of 3D objects, textures, and animation. Not cheap, though.

Autodesk, Inc.
 2320 Marinship Way
 Sausalito, CA 94965
 (415) 332-2344

**Cyberspace Developer Kit.**  One of Autodesk's superb animation products. It's a complete toolset for 3D visualization and simulation. In other words, lets you create virtual-reality applications.

Autodesk, Inc.
 2320 Marinship Way
 Sausalito, CA 94965
 (415) 332-2344

**Animation Works Interactive.**  A sophisticated animation system with interactivity support, multimedia extensions support, and MCI support.

Gold Disk Inc.
 5155 Spectrum Way, Unit 5
 Mississauga, Ontario,  L4W 5A1
 Canada
 (310) 320-5080

**Creative Toonz 2D CEL.** Animation software for Silicon Graphics workstations. Enables animators to experiment with up to 32 different fill colors, add 3D animations, build a picture base of images, use scanner for input.

Softimage Inc.
  660 Newton-Yardley Rd., Suite 202
  Newton, PA 18940
  (215) 860-5525

**Liberty.** A UNIX-based high-end graphics package, coupled with animation tools.

Softimage Inc.
  660 Newton-Yardley Rd.,
  Suite 202
  Newton, PA 18940
  (215) 860-5525

## Graphics

**MacroModel.** This package enables users to twist or bend 3D objects. Since there is a version for the Mac as well as for IBM-PC platforms, images created on one can easily be transferred to the other.

Macromedia, Inc.
  600 Townsend St.
  San Francisco, CA 94103
  (800) 288-8229

**223—The Stereo Paint System.** A paint system that provides the ability to create true 3D, stereoscopic images. Also permits conversion of preexisting 2D images into 3D.

Latent Image Development
  Corporation
  Digital Media Group
  111 Fourth Ave.
  New York, NY 10003
  (212) 388-0122

**Adobe Illustrator.** A powerful professional design tool. Enables designers to draw from scratch or work with existing images. Supports 16.7 million colors, text; generates separations, custom views, and page sizes; carries out object manipulations such as dividing, slicing, and combining.

Adobe Systems Inc.
  1585 Charleston Road
  P.O. Box 7900
  Mountain View, CA 94039
  (800) 833-6687

**Painterly Effects.** A UNIX-based set of filters that lets you turn boring images into classical art.

Softimage Inc.
660 Newton-Yardley Rd., Suite 202
Newton, PA 18940
(215) 860-5525

## Players

**MultiMedia Works.** A universal player that supports 40 file formats including AVI, QuickTime, DVI, FLC, FLI, CD-Audio, Wave, and Midi. Can embed into any Windows application.

Lenel Systems International Inc.
19 Tobey Village Office Park
Pittsford, NY 14534-1763
(716) 248-9720

**PACo.** An audio/visual playback system. Platform-independent. Included is PACo Producer, which creates and presents animations, digital videos, visualizations, and audio files in conjunction with Mac applications.

COSA
14 Imperial Place, Suite 203
Providence, RI 02903
(401) 831-2672

## Management

**MpcOrganizer and MediaOrganizer.** Allows users to catalog, store, and retrieve all of their multimedia objects.

Lenel Systems International Inc.
19 Tobey Village Office Park
Pittsford, NY 14534-1763
(716) 248-9720

## Virtual reality

Since this is a category unto itself, I've decided to lump hardware and software together.

**Mandala.** Almost impossible to explain. Using a video camera, this software puts you in your own virtual world. Currently used by the Nickelodeon channel.

The Vivid Group
317 Adelaide Street W, Suite 302
Toronto, Ontario M5V 1P9
Canada
(416) 340-9290

**Head-mounted displays.**  Leep optics for head-mounted displays; cyberface head-mounted displays; other stereo optical equipment (cameras, etc).

Leep Systems
 241 Crescent Street
 Waltham, MA 02154
 (617) 647-1395

**WorldToolKit.**  WorldToolKit is a virtual-reality applications development toolkit that runs on a variety of robust hardware platforms. Basically WorldToolKit is a rendering, or visualization, software package that makes the impossible possible.

SENSE8 Corporation
 4000 Bridgeway, Suite 101
 Sausalito, CA 94965
 (415) 331-6318

**ADL-1 Tracker.**  A sophisticated and inexpensive 6D tracking system that converts position and orientation information into computer-readable form. The ADL-1 calculates head/object postion with six degrees of freedom by use of a lightweight, multiple-jointed arm. Sensors mounted on the arm measure the angles of the joints. The microprocessor-based control unit uses these angles to compute position-orientation information in a user-selectable coordinate system, which is then transmitted to the host computer.

Shooting Star Technology
 1921 Holdon Avenue
 Burnaby, BC V4B 3W4
 Canada
 (604) 298-8574

**Spaceball 2003.**  A 3D control device. With six simultaneous degrees of freedom control, users are able to manipulate 3D screen models or conduct virtual scene walkthroughs or flythroughs, as easily and intuitively as if they were performing these tasks in the real world. The spaceball consists of a tennisball-sized sphere fixed on a stand. Users place their wrist on the stand and grasp the ball with their fingertips. They gently push, pull, or twist the ball to move the 3D screen object, in corresponding directions and speeds, in real time. Scene movement is smooth and dynamic. The spaceball is supported on major workstation and personal computer platforms, and in a host of applications from mechanical CAD to virtual reality.

Spaceball Technologies, Inc.
 600 Suffolk St.
 Lowell, MA 01854
 (508) 970-0330

**Flight Helmet.**  A head-mounted display.

Virtual Research
  Sunnyvale, CA 94089
  (408) 748-8712

**Grip Master.**  A force sensor.

EXOS, Inc.
  8 Blanchard Road
  Burlington, MA 01803
  (617) 229-2075

**Cyberspace Developer Kit.**  One of Autodesk's superb animation products. It's a complete toolset for 3D visualization and simulation. In other words, it lets *you* create virtual-reality applications.

Autodesk, Inc.
  2320 Marinship Way
  Sausalito, CA 94965
  (415) 332-2344

**Distant Suns; VistaPro.**  Use your PC to simulate the night sky (Distant Suns) or create electronic landscapes (VistaPro). I've heard that Arthur Clarke (author of *2001*) is using this software to get "images" for his next book.

Virtual Reality Laboratories
  2341 Ganador Court
  San Luis Obispo, CA 93401
  (805) 545-8515

**EYEGEN 3.**  A head-mounted display that uses monochrome CRTs and color wheels to improve resolution and decrease weight. EYEGEN 3 has a screen resolution of 369,750 color elements. Adjustments include inter-pupilary distance (IPD), focus, display release, double-ratchet headband.

Virtual Research
  3193 Belick St., Suite 2
  Santa Clara, CA 95054
  (408) 748-8712

**Smart 3D.**  A 3D rendering system that lets both Mac and Windows users manipulate objects in real time. The nice thing about this package is that the images wind up taking up little space: about 200 to 500 kbytes, compared to 100 Mbytes in other packages.

Macromedia Inc.
  600 Townsend St.
  San Francisco, CA 94103
  (800) 288-8229

## Catalogs

The following mail-order companies specialize in multimedia hardware/software.

Tiger Software
 800 Douglas Entrance
 Executive Tower
 7th Floor
 Coral Gables, FL 33134
 (800) 888-4437

DAK Industries Incorporated
 8200 Remmet Ave
 Canoga Park, CA 91304
 (919) 888-8220

## Databases with multimedia extensions

**Superbase4.**  Fully relational database, with extensive programming and multimedia capabilities.

Software Publishing Corporation
 3165 Kifer Road
 Santa Clara, CA 95051
 (408) 988-7518

**Oracle8.**  The latest version of this most popular multiplatform relational database adds multimedia services, including multimedia e-mail.

**Supra Relational Database.**  Features the ability to access data spread among various platforms.

Cincom
 2300 Montana Avenue
 Cincinnati, OH 45211
 (513) 662-2300

## Conversion

**Windowcraft.**  Coverts Mac HyperCard stacks into Windows execute-only files.

Windowcraft Corporation
 1000 Main Street
 Acton, MA 01720
 (508) 263-7674

## Media clips

Wallace Music and Sound, Inc., provides original music and sound effects for software developers and publishers.

Wallace Music & Sound, Inc.
6210 West Pershing Ave.
Glendale, AZ 95304
(602) 979-6201

**MusicBytes.**  Gives you access to dozens of exciting and dynamic production tunes, ranging from rock to classical and from industrial to novelty. No licensing problems.

Prosonus
1126 Weddington St.
North Hollywood, CA 91601
(800) 999-6191

**Multimedia Music Library.**  A collection of more than 100 pop and orchestral musical sequences. Royalty-free.

Midisoft Corporation
P.O. Box 1000
Bellevue, WA 98009
(206) 881-7176

**Killer Tracks.**  A series of music selections.

Killer Tracks
6534 Sunset Blvd.
Hollywood, CA 90028
(800) 877-0078

**HyperClips for Windows.**  A CD-ROM volume containing hundreds of high-quality animation and sound clips designed to accent business, sales, and technical presentations.

The HyperMedia Group
5900 Hollis Street, Suite O
Emeryville, CA 94608
(510) 601-0900

**The DigiSound Audio Library.**  Brings exciting, full-fidelity sound to multimedia, with professionally produced MIDI music, sound effects, and DigiVoice clips.

Presentation Graphics Group
270 N. Canon Dr., Suite 103
Beverly Hills, CA 90210
(310) 277-3050

Aris Entertainment offers several sets of CD-ROMs for Windows, Mac, and PCs that contain a combination of sound effects, full-color photographs, and/or video clips. Under the trade name of MediaClips the following sets illustrate the Aris offerings: Worldview: space images and sounds; Wild Places: North American photos and audio clips; Majestic Places: nature photos and audio clips; Business Background: photos, audio clips and sound effects.

Aris Entertainment, Inc.
 4444 Via Marina, Suite 811
 Marina del Rey, CA 90292
 (310) 821-0234
 (800) 228-2747

Digital Zone hires professional photographers to take stunning photos. The photos then are stored on Kodak's Photo CD and are free to be used by purchasers of one of the collections.

Digital Zone Inc.
 P.O. Box 5562
 Bellevue, WA 98006
 (800) 538-3113

**Archive Films/Archive Photos.**   Contain thousands of hours of historical and entertainment footage and stills, produced from 1894 until the present. Includes Albert Einstein, Jacob Astor, Hollywood, presidents, kings, the Depression.

Archive New Media
 530 West 25th Street
 NY, NY 10001
 (212) 620-3980

**CBS News Archives.**   Offers just that.

CBS News
 524 West 57th Street
 New York, NY 10019
 (212) 975-2875

**Buyout Music Library.**   Offers hours of royalty-free original music, on CD.

Musi-Q
 P.O. Box 451147
 Sunrise, FL
 (305) 572-9276

**Station Break.**   Contains collections of license-free music. Pick by theme, such as Crime, Haunted, etc.

Station Break Music
 40 Glen Street, Suite 1
 Glen Cove, NY 11542
 (800)-ON-AIR-99

**Video Tape Library.** Offers news clips such as L.A. Riot, gang shootings, sports.

VTL
 1509 N. Crescent Heights Blvd. Suite 2
 Los Angles, CA 90046
 (213) 656-4330

**PhotoDisc.** Contains, on each CD, 336 multipurpose images on CD-ROM from award-winning photographers: landscapes, rain forests, deserts, animals, etc. Arranged in a user-friendly slide show.

PhotoDisc
 2013 4th Ave
 Seattle, WA 98121
 (206) 441-9355

**Clipper.** A monthly clip-art subscription service. You have choice of medium: paper, floppy, or CD-ROM. Each month subscribers get a variety of themed images designed especially for Clipper from leading artists.

Dynamic Graphics Inc.
 6000 N. Forest Park Dr.
 P.O. Box 1901
 Peoria, IL 61656
 (800) 255-8800

**Masterclips.** A collection of 6000 images in 60 different categories.

Masterclips, Inc.
 5201 Ravenswood Rd., Suite 111
 Ft. Lauderdale, FL 33312
 (800) 292-2547

## Magazines/Journals/Newsletters/Books

### Magazines/journals/newsletters

**Advanced Imaging.** Monthly coverage of all facets of imaging, including video. Free.

PTN Publishing
 445 Broad Hollow Rd.
 Melville, NY 11747
 (516) 845-2700

**AmigaWorld.** Amiga gets short shrift most of the time. But it's a great multimedia platform. Monthly; $19.97/year.

AmigaWorld
 P.O. Box 595
 Mt. Morris, IL 61054
 (800) 827-0877

**AVC Presentation.**   A monthly magazine geared to those involved in visual communications. Free.

PTN Publishing
 445 Broad Hollow Rd.
 Melville, NY 11747
 (516) 845-2700

**Boardwatch.**   Actually directed to on-line users of bulletin boards, but a good source of information.

5970 South Vivian Street
 Littleton, CO 80127
 (800) 933-6038

**Business Publishing.**   Specifically for those interested in corporate publishing. Information on desktop publishing and electronic delivery. Monthly; $24/year.

Hitchcock Publishing Co.
 191 S. Gary Ave.
 Carol Stream IL 60188
 (800) 234-0733,
 (708) 665-1000

**CD-I World.**   Bimonthly CD-I magazine on paper and disc.

Parker Taylor & Company Inc.
 49 Bayview, Suite 200
 Camden, ME 04843
 (207) 236-8524

**CD-ROM Professional.**   Monthly journal ($86 per year) covering the CD-ROM and optical-publishing industries.

Pemberton Press, Inc.
 11 Tannery Lane
 Weston, CT 06883
 (203) 227-8466

**CD-ROMWORLD.**   Information on new titles and techniques in the ever-expanding world of CD-ROM. An Alan Meckler publication. Monthly; $87/year.

Meckler Corporation
 11 Ferry Lane West
 Westport, CT 06880
 (203) 226-6967

**Computer Pictures.**   Wonderful bimonthly ($40/year) graphics publication.

Montage Publishing, Inc.
 Knowledge Industries Publications, Inc.

701 Westchester Ave.
White Plains, NY 10604
(914) 328-9157

**Consumer Multimedia Report.**  Oriented toward gaming, interactive video, etc.
Monthly; $395/year.

Warren Publishing Inc.
2115 Ward Ct. NW
Washington, DC 20037
(202) 872-9200

**Desktop Video World.**  Similar to *Digital Video* magazine. Bimonthly;
$19.97/year.

Desktop Video World
P.O. Box 594
Mt. Morris, IL 61054

**Digital Media.**  A monthly Seybold publication ($395/year) providing the usual
high level of Seybold insight.

Seybold Publications
428 E. Baltimore Pike
P.O. Box 644
Media, PA 19063
(215) 565-2480

**Digital Publishing Business.**  Newsletter published for Optical Publishing
Association members. Edited by Richard Bowers.

Optical Publishing Association
P.O. Box 21268
Columbus, OH 43221
(614) 442-8805

**Digital Technology Report.**  Biweekly report ($395/year) on digital publishing
in the consumer arena.

Digital Technology Report
102-30 67th Avenue
Forest Hills, NY 11375
(718) 997-1581

**Digital Video.**  Bimonthly magazine ($24/year) published by the megatechnol-
ogy publishing group IDG. Very much oriented toward experts.

TechMedia Publishing
80 Elm Street

Peterborough, NH 03458
(603) 924-0100

**Information Today.**  Monthly magazine ($41.95/year) about information resources.

Learned Information Inc.
 143 Old Marlton Pike
 Medford, NJ 08055
 (609) 654-6266

**The Interactive Engineer.**  Publication (free) about CD-I software engineering.

Philips Interactive Media of America
 11050 Santa Monica Boulevard
 Los Angeles, CA 90025
 (310) 444-6519

**Information Standards Quarterly.**  A National Information Standards Organization (NISO) quarterly. In the United States, $40 per year.

National Information Standards
 Organization (NISO)
 P.O. Box 1056
 Bethesda, MD 20827
 (301) 975-2814

**The International CD-ROM Report.**  A bimonthly report ($72/year) on what's new and what's not in CD-ROMs.

Innotech
 110 Silver Star Blvd., Unit #107
 Scarborough, Ontario M1V 5A2
 Canada
 (416) 321-3838

**Link-UP.**  A newspaper for users of on-line services and CD-ROM. Encompasses information of interest to business people, educators, and private individuals. Published bimonthly; $26.50/year.

Learned Information Inc.
 143 Old Marlton Pike
 Medford, NJ 08055
 (609) 654-6266

**Multimedia Business Report.**  Newsletter published 24 times a year ($449/year). Covers interactive CDs, on-line services, audiotex, software interactive television, video games, integrated learning systems.

SIMBA Information, Inc.
 P.O. Box 7430
 Wilton, CT 06897
 (203) 834-0033

**Multimedia/CD Publisher.**   Newsletter with a multimedia publisher's orientation. Twelve issues, $147/year.

Meckler Publishing
 11 Ferry Lane
 Westport, CT 06880
 (203) 226-6967

**Multimedia Networking Newsletter.**  Specifically deals with the issues of networked multimedia. Published monthly, $495/year.

Publications Research Group
 P.O. Box 765
 North Adams, MA 01247
 (413) 664-6185

**Multimedia Review.**   Quarterly academic-oriented journal, $97/year.

Meckler Publishing
 11 Ferry Lane
 Westport CT 06880
 203/226-6967

**Multimedia Monitor.**   Probably the best newsletter on the market. Filled with the latest news, plus contacts and their phone numbers ($357/year).

Future Systems Inc.
 P.O. Box 26
 Falls Church, VA 22040
 (703) 241-1799; (703) 532-0529 (fax)

**Multimedia Week.**   An executive report on business opportunities in the multimedia marketplace.

Phillips Business Information, Inc.
 7811 Montrose Rd.
 Potomac, MD 20854
 (301) 424-3338

**Nautilus.**   The first magazine for multimedia published on CD-ROM. Not only does it provide the latest news, it also provides demos of latest products in the field. Well worth the money ($137.40/year).

Nautilus
 Metatec Corporation

7001 Discovery Blvd.
Dublin, OH 43017
(800) 637-3472
(614) 766-3165

**Multimedia: Nuts and Bolts.**   Quarterly CD-ROM journal that covers new products, technology, applications, "how-to," trends, and case histories.

115 Bloomingdale Lane
Woodbridge, Ontario L4L 6X8
Canada
(800) 363-3227

**New Media.**   Slick, enjoyable magazine. Great ads. A bargain ($35/year).

Hypermedia Communications Inc.
901 Mariner's Island Blvd, Suite 365
San Mateo, CA 94404
(415) 573-5170

**New Media News.**   If you're a member of the Boston Computer Society, you're in luck.

Boston Computer Society
One Kendall Sq., Bldg 100
Cambridge, MA 02139
(617) 252-0600

**Online & CDROM Review.**   An international journal of information sciences concentrating on on-line and optical information sources, systems, and services. Published every 2 months.

Learned Information Ltd.
Woodside, Hinksey Hill
Oxford OX1 5AU
United Kingdom
44 (0)865 730275

**PC Presentations/Productions Magazine.**   A new magazine focusing on the use of PC technology for better business presentations and on using products to get the job done. Easy conversational style.

PCPP Magazine
Pisces Publishing Group
417 Bridgeport Ave
Devon, CT 06460
(203) 877-1927

**Ultimedia Solutions.**   Ignore the IBM marketing pitch, and concentrate on the case histories of multimedia uses. Bimonthly. Free.

IBM Multimedia Solutions
4111 Northside Parkway
#HO4L1
Atlanta, GA 30327
(404) 238-3455

**Virtual Reality Report Magazine.**   A must-have, if you're into VR. Another of the fine Meckler publications.

Meckler Corporation
11 Ferry Lane West
Westport, CT 06880
(203) 226-6967

**Wolf World.**   Lightly written monthly newsletter covering multimedia issues relevant to PC sound card users. Available both in paper and electronic format on CompuServe via GO WESTPOINT.

Westpoint Creative
Delta House
264 Monkmoor Road
Shrewsbury SY2 5ST
United Kingdom
44(0)743 248590

## Books

*A Guide to Multimedia,* Victoria Rosenborg. New Riders Publishing, 1993.
*Apple CD-ROM Handbook,* Joel Nagy. Addison-Wesley Publishing Co., 1992.
*The Brady Guide to CD-ROM,* L. Buddine and E. Young. Brady Books, 1987.
*Building Hypermedia Applications: A Software Developer's Guide,* Gary Thomas Howell. McGraw-Hill, 1992.
*CD-I and Interactive Videodisc Technology,* S. Lambert and J. Sallis. Howard W. Sams & Co., 1987
*CD-I Design Handbook,* Philips IMS. Addison-Wesley, 1992.
*CD-I Designer's Guide,* Signe Hoffos, Graham Sharpless, Philip Smith, and Nicholas Lewis. McGraw-Hill (UK), 1992.
*The CD-I Production Handbook,* Philips IMS, Philips Electronics UK Ltd. Addison Wesley, 1992.
*CD-ROM 2: Optical Publishing,* S. Ropiquet. Microsoft Press, 1987
*CD-ROM Applications and Markets,* J. P. Roth. Meckler Publishing (11 Ferry Lane, Westport, CT 06880; 203-226-6967), 1988.
*CD-ROM: Facilitating Electronic Publishing,* Linda Helgerson. Van Nostrand Reinhold, 1992.
*CD-ROM Directory.* Biyearly from Pemberton Press Inc., 462 Danbury Road, Wilton, CT 06897; 800-248-8466.
*CD-ROM Finder,* James Shelton (ed). Learned Information (143 Old Marlton Pike, Medford, NJ 08055; 609-654-6266), 1993.
*CD-ROM Handbook,* Chris Sherman, McGraw-Hill, 1989.
*CD-ROM Marketplace 1993.* Meckler Publishing (11 Ferry Lane, Westport, CT 06880; 203-226-6967), 1993.
*CD-ROM Standards: The Book,* Julie B. Schwerin. Learned Information Ltd., (143 Old Marlton Pike, Medford, NJ 08055; 609-654-6266, 609-654-4309 (fax), 1986.
*CD-ROM: Facilitating Electronic Publishing,* Linda Helgerson. Van Nostrand Reinhold, 1992.
*CD-ROM: The New Papyrus,* S. Lambert and S. Ropiquet. Microsoft Press, 1986.
*CD-ROMs: Breakthrough in Information Storage,* Frederick Holtz. TAB Books, 1988.
*The CD-ROM Handbook,* Chris Sherman, ed. McGraw Hill, 1988.

*CD-ROMs in Print,* Norman Desmaris. Meckler Publishing (11 Ferry Lane, Westport, CT 06880; 203-226-6967), yearly.

*Compact Disc Interactive: A Designer's Overview,* Philips International, eds. McGraw-Hill, 1988.

*Digital Video in the PC Environment,* Arch C. Luther. McGraw-Hill, 1989.

*Discovering CD-I,* Eric Miller and Walden Miller. Microware Systems Corporation, 1991.

*Essential Guide to CD-ROM,* J. P. Roth. Meckler Publishing (11 Ferry Lane, Westport, CT 06880; 203-226-6967), 1986.

*Guide to CD-ROM,* Dana Parker and Bob Starrett. New Riders Publishing, 1992.

*A Guide to Optical Storage Technology,* John A. McCormick. Dow Jones-Irwin, 1990.

*IBM LinkWay: Hypermedia for the PC,* R. Harrington, B. Fancher, and P. Black. John Wiley and Sons, 1990.

*Interactive Multimedia,* Sueann Ambron and Kristina Hooper. Microsoft Press, 1988.

*Introducing CD-I,* Philips IMS, Philips Electronics UK Ltd. Addison Wesley, 1992.

*Learning with Interactive Multimedia,* Sueann Ambron and Kristina Hooper. Microsoft Press, 1990.

*Managing Interactive Video/Multimedia Projects,* R. E. Bergman and T. V. Moore. Educational Technology Publications, 1990.

*Mapping Hypertext,* Robert E. Horn. The Lexington Institute (80 Marrett Rd., Lexington, MA 02173), 1989.

*Microsoft Windows Multimedia Authoring and Tools Guide.* Microsoft Press, 1992.

*Multimedia Applications Development: Using DVI Technology,* Mark Bunzel and Sandra Morris. McGraw-Hill, 1992.

*Multimedia Interface Design,* M. Blattner and R. Dannenberg. ACM Press/Addison-Wesley, 1992.

*Multimedia Madness,* Ron Wodaski. SAMS Publishing, 1992.

*Multimedia: Making It Work,* Tay Vaughan. Osborne McGraw-Hill, 1993.

*The Multimedia Producer's Survival Guide,* Stephan Ian McIntosh. Multimedia Computing Corp. (2105 S. Bascom Ave., Suite 300, Campbell, CA 95008); 1993. Order through Avtex: 408-371-2800.

*NonLinear: A Guide to Electronic Film and Video Editing,* Michael Rubin. Triad Publishing Co., 1992.

*Publish Yourself on CD-ROM,* D. Straughan and F. Caffarelli. Random House, 1992.

*Scripting for New AV Technologies,* 2d ed., Dwight V. Swain and Joye R. Swain. Focal Press, 1991.

*Selected Resources for CD-ROM and New Media Publishers,* Richard A. Bowers. Information Arts, 1992.

*SGML Backgrounder for CD-ROM Publishers,* Richard A. Bowers. Optical Publishing Association, 1992.

*The SGML Handbook: The Annotated Full Text of ISO 8879—Standard Generalized Markup Language,* Charles F. Goldfarb. Oxford University Press, 1990.

*Text, Context, and Hypertext: Writing with and for the Computer,* Edward Barrett. MIT Press, 1988.

*Video Engineering,* Andrew Inglis. McGraw-Hill, 1993.

*The Whole Internet: User's Guide and Catalog,* Ed Krol. O'Reilly and Associates, Inc., 1992.

## Services

### On-line forums

**CompuServe.**   The multimedia forums on CompuServe, operated by Multimedia Computing Corp. under contract to Simba Information, are the leading on-line information exchanges for multimedia. Topics range from audio and video to Photo CD and CD-I. About 20 vendors offer support in the Multimedia Vendor Forum. The Forum's libraries offer a wide variety of information, programs, hardware drivers, and other useful files.

CompuServe
  5000 Arlington Centre Blvd.

Columbus, OH 43220
(800) 848-8199, operator 228

## Image scanning, slide creation

Show & Tell
39 West 38th Street
New York, NY 10018
(212) 840-2912

Digicolor
1300 Dexter Avenue North
Seattle, WA 98109
(800) 967-3714

Slide Services, Inc.
2537 25th Ave. South
Minneapolis, MN 55406
(612) 721-2434

## CD-ROM mastering

Northeastern Digital Recording, Inc.
2 Hidden Meadow Lane
Southborough, MA 01772
(508) 481-9322

MultiMedia PC Enterprises Inc.
3 Hanover Square, Suite 19A
New York, NY 10004
(212) 509-9636

Electronic Publishers International
Corporation
P.O. Box 17006
Winston-Salem, NC 27116
(800) 258-4423

International Teleproduction Society
350 Fifth Ave., Suite 2400
New York, NY 10118
(212) 629-3265

Technidisc
2250 Meijer Drive
Troy, MI 48084
(313) 435-7430

3M Prerecorded Optical Media
3M Center Blvd., 223-5N-01
St. Paul, MN 55144
(612) 733-2142

## Packaging

Ames Specialty Packaging
21 Properzi Way
P.O. Box 120
Somerville, MA 02143
(617) 776-3360

## Legal

Elman, Wilf and Fried
20 West Third Street
P.O. Box 703
Media, PA 19063
(215) 892-9580

## Conferences

MacWorld Exposition
Mitch Hall Associates
P.O. Box 4010
Dedham, MA 02026
(617) 361-0817

Winter Consumer Electronics Show
Electronic Industries Association
2001 Pennsylvania Ave. NW
Washington, DC 20006-1813
(202) 457-8700

IMEX/NOTA
ICM (Imaging Conference
Management)
Bay Colony Corporate Center
1000 Winter St., Suite 3700
Waltham, MA 02154
(617) 487-7934

Image World West
Knowledge Industry Publications, Inc.
701 Westchester Ave.
White Plains NY 10604
(914) 328-9157

Interact
Interactive Services Association
8403 Colesville Road, Suite 865
Silver Spring, MD 20910
(301) 495-4955

Annual Document and Image
Management Systems Conference

BIS Strategic Decisions
One Longwater Circle
Norwell, MA 02061
(617) 982-9500

Montage
International Festival of the Image
31 Prince Street
Rochester, NY 14607
(716) 442-6722

TechDoc
GCA
100 Dangerfield Road
Alexandria, VA 22314-2888
(703) 519-8160

Government Imaging Conference
USPDI, Inc.
1734 Elton Rd., Suite 200
Silver Spring, MD 20903-1724
301/445-4405

CONCEPPTS
Graphic Arts Show Co.
1899 Preston White Dr.
Reston, VA 22091-4367
(703) 264-7200

QuickTime and Multimedia Conference
Sumeria Inc.
329 Bryant St., Suite 3D
San Francisco, CA 94107
(415) 904-0800

Home Media Expo
American Expositions, Inc.
The Soho Bldg.
110 Greene St., #703
New York, NY 10012
(212) 226-4141.

Image World
Knowledge Industry Publications, Inc.
701 Westchester Ave.
White Plains, NY 10604
(914) 328-9157

Intermedia
Reed Exhibition Company
P.O. Box 3833 (999 Summer St.)
Stamford, CT 06905-0833
(203) 352-8254

FOSE
National Trade Productions, Inc.
313 S. Patrick Street

Alexandria, VA 22314-3567
(800) 638-8510

The Seybold Conference
  Seybold Seminars
  P.O. Box 6710
  Malibu CA 90264
  (800) 433-5200

CDISC-4
  Philips Interactive Media of America
  11050 Santa Monica Blvd.
  Los Angeles CA 90025
  (310) 444-6519

NAB Multimedia World Conference
  National Association of Broadcasters
  1771 N St., NW
  Washington, DC 20036-2891
  (202) 429-5346

Digital Video New York
  American Expositions, Inc.
  The Soho Bldg., 110 Greene St., #703
  New York, NY 10012
  (212) 226-4141

MultiMedia Expo
  American Expositions, Inc.
  The Soho Bldg., 110 Greene St., #703
  New York, NY 10012
  (212) 226-4141

TED4KOBE
  TED Conferences Inc.
  59 Wooster Street
  New York, NY 10012
  (212) 219-8993

Virtual Reality
  Meckler Publishing
  11 Ferry Lane West
  Westport, CT 06880
  (800) 635-5537

Summer Consumer Electronics Show
  (CES)
  Consumer Electronics Shows
  2001 Pennsylvania Ave., NW
  Washington, DC 20006-1813
  (202) 457-8700

REPLItech International
  Knowledge Industry Publications, Inc
  701 Westchester Ave.
  White Plains, NY 10604
  (914) 328-9157

Image World New York
 Knowledge Industry Publications, Inc.
 701 Westchester Ave.
 White Plains, NY 10604
 (914) 328-9157

CD-ROM Expo
 Mitch Hall Associates
 P.O. Box 4010
 Dedham, MA 02026
 (617) 361-0817

Online/CD-ROM
 Multimedia and CD-ROM Seminar
 462 Danbury Rd.
 Wilton, CT 06897
 (203) 761-1466

CD-ROM Expo
 Mitch Hall Associates
 260 Milton Street
 Dedham, MA 02026
 (617) 361-2001

Comdex
 Interface Group
 300 First Ave.
 Needham MA 02194-2722
 (617) 449-6600

Internet World/Document Delivery World
 Meckler Publishing
 11 Ferry Lane West
 Westport, CT 06880
 (800) 635-5537

Milia
 International Exhibition Organization
 475 Park Ave. South
 NY, NY 10016
 (212) 689-4220

Media Summit
 Strategic Forum for New Business Alliances
 ACCU-Reg
 1420 MacArthur Drive, Suite 104
 Carrollton, TX 75007
 (203) 352-8302

## Associations

**CD-I Association.**  A professional association for developers of CD-I or those interested in developing CD-I. Members receive a quarterly newsletter, *Inside CD-I,* and other publications.

CD-I Association of North America
Attn.: Laura Foti Cohen
11111 Santa Monica Blvd., Suite 700
Los Angeles, CA 90025
Phone: + 1 310-444-6619
Fax: + 1 310-479-5937

Interactive Multimedia Association
3 Church Circle, Suite 800
Annapolis, MD 21401
(410) 626-1380

International Interactive Communications
Society
IICS
P.O. Box 1862
Lake Oswego, OR 97035
(503) 649-2065

Multimedia PC Marketing Council, Inc.
1730 M Street NW, Suite 707
Washington, DC 20036
(202) 331-0494

Optical Publishing Association
P.O. Box 21268
Columbus, OH 43221
(614) 442-8805

## Consulting

**Allen Communication.**   Rex Allen runs a mean multimedia shop. Hitched to its Quest authoring tool, Allen Communication is a good consulting bet.

Allen Communication, Inc.
5225 Wiley Post Way
Salt Lake City, UT 84116
(801) 537-7800

**Corporate Media Communications.**   Specializes in multimedia applications, particularly in creative communications for large and small business meetings: multi-image slides and video and print materials for both marketing and training.

Corporate Media Applications
1530 Cooledge Road
Atlanta, Georgia 30085
(404) 491-6300

**OnTape Multimedia.**   Makes affordable and effective videotapes of PC-related products for marketing and educational purposes. Also provides consulting and purchasing advice for those interested in desktop video and PC-based multimedia.

OnTape Multimedia
 1509 S. Azalea
 Columbia, MO 65201
 (314) 874-5191

**Optibase.** A world leader in ISO implementations of MPEG, full-motion, digital video and audio products.

Optibase
 4006 Beltline Road, Suite 200
 Dallas, Texas 75244
 (214) 386-2040

**NuMedia Corporation.** Specializes in the implementation of large multimedia networks that distribute multimedia presentations nationwide. These networks use LANs, telephone lines, and satellite broadcast to facilitate the production, delivery, and presentation of multimedia. NuMedia's family of multimedia products includes options for desktop VGA presentations or for scheduled presentations playing over cable or in-house TV networks.

NuMedia Corporation
 201 North Union, Suite 400
 Alexandria, Virginia 22314
 (703) 684-9000

**Wallace Music & Sound, Inc.** Provides original music and sound effects for software developers and publishers.

Wallace Music & Sound, Inc.
 6210 West Pershing Ave.
 Glendale, Arizona 95304
 (602) 979-6201

**Multimedia Computing Corp.** A leading multimedia strategic consulting firm. The company was founded in 1988 by Nick Arnett and Tim Bajarin, two of the top computer-industry analysts. Clients have included Apple Computer, IBM, Microsoft, Hitachi, Wherehouse, and many others in the computing, telecommunication, entertainment, consumer-electronic, and publishing fields.

Multimedia Computing Corp.
 2105 S. Bascom Ave., Suite 300
 Campbell, CA 95008
 (408) 369-1233

**The Multimedia Department.** Provides corporate-communication services, including strategic video and multimedia consulting; audio, video, and interactive video production, duplication, packaging, direct mail, and order fulfillment.

The Multimedia Department
 140 West 69th Street, Suite 45A
 New York, NY 10023
 (212) 721-6117

**Performance Software Inc.**   A consultancy in starting and using multimedia.

Performance Software Inc.
 100 Shield Street
 West Hartford, CT 06110
 (800) 348-1377

**Technology Helping People, Inc.**   Does exactly what its name says, but it specializes in the implementation of multimedia.

Technology Helping People, Inc.
 1341 Canton Road
 N.E. Marietta, Georgia
 (404) 499-9800

**In Motion.**   Offers consulting (digital interactive media), training, application tools development.

In Motion
 Digital Interactive Media
 62 rue des Chantiers
 78000 Versailles, France
 33 1-39-53-67-88

**Centrimedia Company.**   Offers consulting services as well as production services for the creation of applications for the marketing, training, education, and consumer markets.

Centrimedia
 3964 26th Street
 San Francisco, CA 94131
 (415) 282-7875

**Dataware Technologies.**   Works with organizations to index and store data on CD-ROM. They use their own software tools, CD Author and CD Answer, which may be purchased separately.

Dataware Technologies
 222 Third Street, Suite 3300
 Cambridge, MA 02142
 (617) 621-0820

**R. R. Donnelley & Sons Company.**   A heavy-hitter in the traditional print world has become an even bigger one in the CD-ROM world. They will, according to their promo, "take the information you already have and target it, translate it, move it around the world, customize it, personalize it, give it more impact, make it interactive, compact, it, CD-ROM it, floppy disk it, multimedia it, on-line it."

R. R. Donnelley & Sons Company
 77 West Wacker Drive
 Chicago, IL 60601
 (800) 438-0223 (for free CD-ROM)
 (312) 326-8000

**Sasha Lewis.**  Specializes in networking and multimedia products. The author of six books, she also produces multimedia videos.

Sasha Lewis
 715 Piercy Rd.
 San Jose, CA 95138
 (408) 629-0755
 1-800-60-MEDIA.

**New Art Inc./Techinsider.**  Specializes in implementing solutions to business problems through the use of artificial intelligence and multimedia.

New Art Inc.
 200 W. 79 Street, Suite 8H
 NY, NY 10024
 (212) 362-0559

## CD-ROM Titles of Note

For the most part, CD-ROM titles are in the entertainment or consumer arenas. However, this is beginning to change. Below are some of the more interesting titles, from a business perspective, on CD-ROM.

**CD-ROMs in Print.**  Meckler, the big name in multimedia publishing, has produced a compendium of CD-ROM titles on—what else—a CD-ROM. There's also a version on paper.

Meckler
 11 Ferry Lane West
 Westport, CT 06880
 (213) 226-6967

**Business America on CD-ROM.**  Exhaustive profiles of businesses, including employment size and key contact information. Full search criteria enables users to easily pull groupings of firms.

American Business Information
 5711 South 86th Circle
 P.O. Box 27347

Omaha, NE 68127
(402) 593-4565

**Moody's Company Data.**  Moody's is a standard for information about business organizations. Now you can get that same authority on CD.

Moody's Investors Service
99 Church Street
New York, NY 10007
(800) 955-8080

**Science Citation Index.**  Enables you to view the bibliographic records of 3200 leading science journals. Also enables cross-indexing.

Institute for Scientific Information
3501 Market Street
Philadelphia, PA 19104
(215) 386-0100

**PatentView.**  A fast way for an organization to search out information on current patent data.

Rapid Patent
P.O. Box 2527, Eads Station
Arlington, Virginia 22202
(800) 336-5010

**UMI.**  Full-image retrieval from over a dozen databases, covering periodicals and newspapers.

UMI
300 North Zeeb Road
Ann Arbor, MI 48106
(800) 521-0600

**PhoneDisc.**  9.5 million businesses for about $100; 76 million families for the same price; 85 million residential and business listings for less than $200.

Digital Directory Assistance, Inc.
5161 River Rd., Bldg. 6
Bethesda, MD 20816
(301) 657-8548

**Newsweek Interactive.**  Initially bundled with the SONY Multimedia CD-ROM Player, Newsweek Interactive represents a major milestone for the multimedia industry. Available also on the DOS platform, content includes special issue topics; quarterly compilations of the full text of *Newsweek*; audio clips in support of the special issue; stories from *The Washington Post*; audio clips from the radio show "Newsweek on Air." They call it *digital journalism.*

Newsweek Interactive
444 Madison Ave.
New York, NY 10022
(212) 350-4000

**Walnut Creek CD-ROM.**  This isn't just one title. It's a catalog of 12 or so CD-ROMs, with hundreds of shareware programs. For example, the Hobbes OS/2 CD-ROM contains 2000 OS/2 programs. There's a CD-ROM for the Mac, one for DOS, etc.

Walnut Creek CD-ROM
1547 Palos Verdes, Suite 260
Walnut Creek, CA 94596
(800) 786-9907

**Wilson Business Abstracts.**  A business database providing cover-to-cover indexing and abstracting for the 350 most demanded business periodicals.

The H. W. Wilson Company
950 University Avenue
Bronx, NY 10452
(800) 367-6770

**Government Spending.**  Helps users to access the Federal Procurement Center's database of federal purchases. Contains over 145,000 records that indicate what agencies are buying, who they're buying from, and which agencies must do business with a small business.

CD Publishing
4960 Wolf Creek Trail
Flower Mound, TX 75028
(214) 724-0023

**Business Library.**  Provides the complete text of 10 popular books, all written by known experts in major business fields. Includes information on marketing, direct mail, motivation, etc.

Allegro New Media
387 Passaic Ave.
Fairfield, NJ 07004
(201) 808-1992

## New Media Invision Awards Winners (1993)

There are lots of developers doing lots of great multimedia applications. If you're stumped for an idea, just browse through the following list. Taken from the 1993 Invision Awards for outstanding multimedia implementations, the list also contains contact information.

**Business Practices Course.**  An interactive simulation designed to help personnel learn how to analyze companies and make recommendations. Students explore a hypothetical manufacturing company.

Andersen Consulting
 Professional Education Division
 (708) 377-3100

**Maintenance Continuation Training Program.**  This application consists of 210 hours of Sony View–based interactive training for Air Force maintenance technicians repairing F-15 and F-16 fighters.

Allen Communication
 (801) 537-7800

**The Interactive Courtroom.**  Eight interactive, point-of-view videodiscs were developed by the Stanford Law School Interactive Project to provide students with in-court training.

CLE Group
 (415) 324-1827

**Multimedia Smarthelp.**  An instructional application for 1-2-3 for Windows that has an animated, narrated introduction. Also offers assistance with video, and written documentation.

Lotus Development Corp.
 (617) 693-8312

**Marsbook.**  This application illustrates the industrial design proposal for the first space habitat on Mars. It was developed for NASA's Flight Crew Support Division.

Design Edge
 (512) 477-5491

**Mayo Clinic Family Health Disc.**  CD-ROM–based, this is a compendium of searchable, hyperlinked family-health-care information plus 500 color illustrations, 45 animations, and 90 minutes of audio.

Interactive Ventures, Inc.
 (612) 686-6895

**Microsoft Encarta.**  A CD-ROM–based encyclopedia for Windows. Based on Funk and Wagnall's, Encarta contains plenty of audio and animation.

Microsoft Corp.
 (206) 882-8080

**Werndl's "Feel At Home At the Office."**  A collection of 12 interactive sales presentations for the sales staff at Werndl Office Furniture Systems. Run with a videodisc, the presentation can be run either automatically or in manual mode.

Big Hand Productions
  (214) 748-2888

**Kobe Steel, Ltd. Presentation.**  Designed to represent the history, operations, and services of Kobe Steel. Includes stills, video, 2D and 3D animation.

The Whitley Group Inc.
  (704) 547-0505

**Pella Windows.**  An interactive demo disk that was bundled with the April 1992 issue of *Progressive Architecture*. It shows off Pella's line of windows and door products using interactive animation and CAD.

Grafx Group
  (714) 361-DISK

**Microbe Battler.**  An interactive, virtual reality conference exhibit game. Physicians and pharmacists are educated about the anti-infection properties of Pfizer's Unasyn® antibiotic. Players wear VR gloves and view themselves in real-time video. They interact with graphics, quelling virtual infection by hurling doses of drugs at them.

Corporate Communications Group
  (212) 268-2100

**Novato Electronic City Hall.**  A Windows-based information kiosk that provides information on public meetings, schools, services, and other activities for the city of Novato, California.

StudioGraphics
  (415) 344-3855

**Troubleshooting Techniques.**  A videodisc application for UNIX-based AT&T systems that was developed by the Federal Aviation Administration to train FAA airway facility technicians how to identify faulty components.

Applied Science Associates
  (301) 731-9200

**A.D.A.M.**  Sixty medical illustrators worked together to produce a layer-by-layer visual database of the human anatomy. It was designed as a training tool for medical students and a communication aid for doctor-patient consultations.

A.D.A.M. Software, Inc.
 (800) 755-ADAM

**State-Of-The-Art Power Plant (SOAPP).**  A multimedia database of guidelines for using advanced technology in power-plant construction. Built by the engineering firm of Sargent & Lundy and based on research by the Electric Power Research Institute, it provides graphics, photos, hypertext, and the ability to simulate the effects of new designs and technology.

Sargent & Lundy
 (312) 269-6681

**ACSC Photo Retention Project.**  Built to comply with a California law that requires auto insurers to document each insured vehicle with photos.

Auto Club of Southern California
 (714) 850-5374

# Contributors' Biographies

**Phil Abram,** Product Manager, Portfolio Authoring Products, CD Imaging, Eastman Kodak Company, has worked in the field of desktop electronic printing and publishing since joining Kodak nearly 10 years ago. He holds a Bachelor of Science degree in Electrical Engineering, and a master's degree in finance and accounting, from the University of Rochester (NY).

**Rex J. Allen** is president and cofounder of Allen Communication, Inc., a highly successful multimedia software and courseware development company. Dr. Allen has been immersed in multimedia for the past 14 years, having designed and directed dozens of multimedia training applications for clients such as IBM, Xerox, AT&T, Union Pacific Railroad, and Ford Motor. Most recently, Dr. Allen has led efforts to apply cognitive-task-analysis to multimedia training in troubleshooting skills for the U.S. Air Force. Dr. Allen received a bachelor's degree from Brigham Young University in advertising, and his MS and Ph.D. degrees at Florida State University in Instructional Design and Organizational Development, respectively.

**Barbara Baker** has been with Starlight Networks for two years as Marketing Manager. Ms. Baker has extensive experience marketing applications in emerging markets. Her background includes marketing OEM voice-processing products for Voysys Corporation, and development of vertical market voice applications through VAR channels for Octel Communications. She also has worked in the electronics practice for McKinsey and Company. Ms. Baker received her MBA from Harvard Business School, and a BA in Computer Science from the University of California, Berkeley.

**Glenn Becker** is the Vice President of Research and Development for the NuMedia Corporation of Alexandria, VA, where he has been since 1987. He has been closely involved with the design and implementation of large multimedia networks that distribute multimedia presentations nationwide. These networks use LANs, telephone lines, and satellite broadcast to facilitate the production, delivery, and presentation of multimedia. NuMedia's family of multimedia products includes options for desktop VGA presentations or scheduled presentations playing over cable or in-house TV networks. Mr. Becker also is working on his Ph.D. in Computer Science at The George Washington University in Washington, D.C. He has received an MS in Computer Science and a BS in Electrical Engineering, also from GWU.

**Bob Bennett** is a senior product manager for Autodesk's Multimedia Division. Bennett has played an active role in the computer graphics industry for most of his professional life, from developing computer-aided mapping systems to managing oil and gas lease information on Alaska's North Slope to developing state-of-the-art rendering and animation software packages. He has been with Autodesk, Inc. as a product manager for over four and a half years.

Since joining Autodesk in early 1988, Bennett has been instrumental in gaining the company's support for multimedia application development. Starting as the AutoShade product manager, Mr. Bennett then became product manager for Autodesk's award-winning software product, Autodesk Animator. Under Mr. Bennett's direction, Autodesk Animator won the PC Magazine Award for Technical Excellence in Graphics for 1989, and the Most Valuable Product Award from *PC Computing* magazine. Since receiving those honors, Mr. Bennett has had responsibility for Autodesk 3D Studio.

Educated at the University of Washington, Mr. Bennett was awarded a Bachelor of Arts degree in Urban Planning from the university's School of Architecture and Urban Planning in 1978. He is a frequent speaker at industry conferences on the topics of multimedia and animation.

**Pam Berger** is a Library Media Specialist at the Byram Hills High School located in Armonk, New York, as well as a library technology consultant for the DataSearch Group, Inc. She also is the publisher and editor of Information Searcher. Berger currently is the Conference Chair for the Databases in Schools conference. She is the coauthor of *CD-ROM in Schools: The Definitive Handbook* (Eight Bit Books, 1994) and *Guide to Information Sources in Public and Academic Media Centers* (Gale Research, 1981).

**Peter B. Blakeney,** employed by IBM since 1967, is an expert in the field of multimedia computing. As Manager of U.S. Operations, Mr. Blakeney is responsible for a wide variety of functions relative to the development, introduction, and marketing of IBM's multimedia products, as well as strategic planning for the organization.

Mr. Blakeney joined IBM's multimedia organization as a marketing support manager in 1986, after serving in a variety of field sales, headquarters staff, and management positions.

Mr. Blakeney received his graduate degree in Economics from the University of Cincinnati. Upon graduation, he joined IBM in Cincinnati, OH, in a sales capacity. Mr. Blakeney resides in Atlanta, GA.

**Jesse Bornfreund** recently joined Advantis, an IBM company. He wrote his contribution to this book while the Director of Desktop Marketing at UNIX International. Before coming to UNIX International, Mr. Bornfreund was Product Marketing Manager, UNIX, for Commodore Business Machines, Inc., and responsible for product management and marketing programs for the Commodore UNIX Amiga product line, including product launches, distribution programs, and sales and marketing programs.

Before joining Commodore, Mr. Bornfreund was Marketing Manager of UNIX Products for Rabbit Software, and Director of Operations for Telexpress, Inc. He has been involved in the UNIX industry since 1979. He is a frequent panelist/speaker at industry events, has published several articles in the trade press, and is author of UNIX International's White Paper "Desktop UNIX System V and Microsoft's Windows NT: A Functional Comparison."

**Tim Brock** is a computer graphics specialist in Instructional Technology at St. Petersburg Junior College. His work includes multimedia-based project support for faculty and staff. He received his Masters of Communication at Pratt Institute. He currently is an artist of computer-based media, and has created virtual environments and numerous computer animations. He has exhibited and presented both nonsequential and temporal works in the United States and Canada. His newest animations, Making Bread and Psalm 22, completed while in residency at the Banff Centre for the Arts, premiered early in 1993 at the Florida Film Festival.

**John F. Buford** is Director of the Interactive Media Group at the University of Massachusetts, Lowell, and a full-time faculty member in the Department of Computer Science. He serves as U.S. Head of Delegation to ISO MHEG, and has served as a consultant on multimedia standards and technology to DOD DISA, UNIX International, Siemens Nixdorf, and others. Dr. Buford is a frequent panelist on multimedia standards and has published over 20 papers. He holds a Ph.D. in Computer Science from Technische Universitaet Graz, Austria, and a BS and MS from MIT.

**Red Burns** is chair and a professor of the Tisch School of the Arts' Interactive Telecommunications Program at New York University. The focus of this graduate department is on the production of electronic multimedia and telecommunications. She is currently a coprincipal investigator of an interactive cable/telephone project. She is also the Director of the Alternate Media Center, a research and implementation center for new technologies that she co-founded in 1971.

During the 1970s and 1980s, Burns was the Director of Implementation of a series of projects such as two-way television for senior citizens, developing telecommunications uses to serve the developmentally disabled (a field trial of Teletext), media programs for drug abusers, an electronic community service on cable television, and an experimental videotex data base. Professor Burns teaches in the graduate program at NYU and has served on many committees, attended numbers of working meetings, and spoken publicly on new communications technologies.

**Alton Christensen** is a New York-and-Washington-based freelancer working on several motion graphics projects. He uses Grass Valley Group Kadenza, Quantel Harry, and, more often these days, animation software on Mac-based systems. His experience includes graphic and animation design for a variety of clients in the United States, Europe, and the United Kingdom. Alton was the senior animator in the acclaimed graphics department of the Grant Tinker/Gannett project, USA Today: The Television Show. He also was the design director for the Audio Video Design Group. He worked with NBC Sports as an animation designer for the Games of the XXV Olympiad in Barcelona, Spain, and was awarded a Sports Emmy for his work as part of the Olympics design team.

**John Colligan** is President and Chief Operating Officer of Macromedia, a company he joined in January 1989. Colligan previously worked for Apple Computer's Macintosh Division as International Product Marketing Manager for Macintosh and later as head of the higher-education marketing and sales department. He was instrumental in launching HyperCard, producing the Knowledge Navigator video, and defining Apple's initial thrust into multimedia.

Colligan graduated from Georgetown University in 1976 with a Bachelor of Science degree in International Economics, and from the Stanford Graduate School of Business in 1983 with an MBA.

**Joan Davies** is the Director of Communications for Mathematica, Inc., in Lakeland, Florida. She has coordinated marketing, press, technical documentation, training, and graphic production for the TEMPRA products since February 1991. She has an extensive desktop publishing background, and finds the transition from paper marketing to electronic marketing to be creatively exciting and potentially rewarding. She has totally "electronized" her marketing department, with all advertising and product materials developed on the computer desktop.

Davies is a Floridian who has lived in Turkey and Colorado, where she headed publicity, video production, and publication departments, before moving back to her native state. She holds a bachelor of arts degree in communication/multimedia (minor, PR) and a master's degree in interpersonal communication/theatre. She is a member of the National Association for Female Executives and the Society of Professional Journalists. She is Executive Secretary for the Deaf Service Center of Polk County, where she volunteers her desktop publishing and PR services for the deaf and hearing-impaired community.

Davies enjoys her work at Mathematica, Inc., because the company is so close to the cutting edge, it has to be careful not to fall off. She sincerely believes that no other industry can offer the technological advancements of the computer industry, and that multimedia is the "tool" that will make computers more friendly and accessible to the masses.

**Mark Doran** recently joined Intel Corporation. He wrote his contribution to this book while at UNIX International. Prior to joining UNIX International, Mark was a technical consultant with the Hoskyns Group Plc (formerly The Instruction Set), based in London, England. While at Hoskyns, Mark worked on a number of UNIX development projects as well as standards-related activities, notably with IEEE and X/Open. Mark has published a number of articles in the trade press and is the author of a book on the ANSI C programming language standard. Mark holds a Joint Honors degree in Computer Science and Electronics Engineering from University College, London.

**L. W. (Les) Dunaway** is Vice President, Multimedia, at Technology Helping People, Inc., a multimedia systems house. Les joined THP in July 1992 after 28 years with IBM. Les was part of the original team hired to set up the IBM Multimedia Division. While at IBM, Les developed the distributed multimedia architecture.

**Joseph Dunn** is Vice President of Product Development at Macromedia, which he joined in January 1991. Dunn is responsible for the development, documentation, and QA for the entire Macromedia software product line. Prior to joining Macromedia, Dunn was Director of Software Development at Frame Technology in Santa Clara, CA, where he managed the software group and succeeded in shipping two major FrameMaker versions on the SUN platform. In addition he was responsible for the development of FrameMaker as a portable application, with versions shipping on UNIX, Macintosh, and NeXT platforms.

At Acorn Computers in the UK and Palo Alto, Dunn held a variety of technical and management positions in the development of system software for personal computers. He graduated with a BS degree in Computer Science from Cambridge University in 1980.

**Mike Evans** is Director of Applications for the Corporate Technology Group at National Semiconductor. He manages several communications technology areas, including product development for the isoLan program. He is responsible for the Hong Kong design center, which recently has been incorporated into the Applications Technology Group. In 1985, Evans was instrumental in ushering National Semiconductor into the networking market through the development of Ethernet chip sets, and inventing the definition of today's industry-standard Ethernet controller.

Mike obtained his Bachelor of Science degree in Electrical Engineering from Manchester University, UK, and has designed many avionics systems. Since joining National Semiconductor Corporation in 1979, he has been responsible for developing a number of new areas for the company, including its industry-leading Ethernet chip set. Presently he is concentrating on multimedia communications.

**Joseph Fantuzzi** joined Macromedia in February 1990 as Vice President of Marketing. Before that he was Director of International Marketing at Interleaf, Inc., and project engineer at Analogic Corporation. He now holds a joint patent on 3M's laser imager. Fantuzzi received a BS in Electrical Engineering from Bucknell University in 1980, and an MS in Computing Engineering from Tufts University in 1985.

**Ken Gerlach** is Marketing Programs Manager of Hewlett-Packard's Distance Learning Systems Operation. He manages activities for the planning and introduction of integrated products and services for delivering interactive distance-learning training and education. Products include multimedia computing integrated with HP-IN (Hewlett-Packard Interactive Network), one of the most advanced interactive distance-learning television broadcast production and telecommunications services in the world. HP-IN incorporates HP's global business television network for interactive technical programming, utilizing 3 broadcast host sites and 177 remote downlink receiving sites in North America and Europe.

Ken's 12 years of experience at Hewlett-Packard have also spanned engineering project and marketing program management of computer hardware and software applications that include emerging datacom, remote conferencing, and graphic presentation technologies.

Formerly, Ken provided project leadership as a Management Consultant at SRI International on techno-economic and market feasibility studies of computer automation and telecommunications for business and institutional clients in the United States, Europe, and Asia. His early career began in project-engineering design with the world's two largest engineering consulting firms, Skidmore, Owings and Merrill in the United States and Ove Arup and Partners in London.

Ken holds an MBA in marketing from Santa Clara University, as well as an MS and BS in mechanical engineering from Pennsylvania and Portland State universities, respectively. Currently he is a part-time instructor of graduate and undergraduate business courses at the U.C. Berkeley Extension and other extended education programs. He is a member of numerous engineering and trade associations and a Chartered Engineer (Europe).

**Lewis Gruskin** joined IBM in 1968 as a systems engineer. He then became a marketing representative, with clients in the retail, apparel, and process industries. Staff and management positions followed in strategy, marketing, and channels development. In 1986, Lew joined the IBM multimedia organization, helping to develop marketing strategy, industry applications, business-partner strategy, and multimedia strategy. Currently he is Worldwide Practice Leader for Multimedia Consulting, a unit of the IBM Consulting Group.

Lew was born in New York. He and his family now reside in Atlanta, Georgia.

**Satish Gupta** is Vice President of Strategic Marketing at Media Vision. He is responsible for product strategy and for developing strategic technologies and alliances with businesses and universities. Formerly he held various technical and management positions in nearly all aspects of the IBM business, the most recent of which included managing multimedia products and DVI technology partnerships between IBM and Intel. Gupta hold a Master of Science degree in Engineering and Economic Systems from Stanford University.

**Harry Hallman** entered the U.S. Air Force at the age of 18 and was trained as a photographer with emphasis on aerial photographic recon. After four years of service, two in Vietnam, he returned to Philadelphia and continued his education while working as Head Medical Photographer at the University of Penn. Vet School.

During the year 1970 Hallman founded (with a partner) Photo Communications Corp., an audiovisual production company located in Philadelphia. The firm was an early pioneer in the creation of multi-image slide programs for use in marketing and motivational meetings. While associated with PCC, Hallman worked at a variety of jobs including writing/producing, marketing, and general management.

In 1981, Hallman sold his interest in PCC and moved to Atlanta to form a new company called Corporate Media Communications, Inc. CMC created all forms of creative communications including large and small business meetings, multi-image slides, video and print materials, for both marketing and training. Clients included AT&T, IBM, BellSouth, Texaco, and numerous other *Fortune* 500 companies.

In 1987, CMC opened a Philadelphia branch that provides similar service. As new media such as computer-based presentations, multimedia, CD-I, and CD-ROM became viable, both offices offered these services. Current CMC clients include Pep Boys, Educational Testing Services, Siemens, and many other organizations in diverse industries.

Hallman recently has formed a new venture: Hallman Electronic Publishing, a company devoted to producing and distributing video, CD-I, and other print forms of communications to the general and professional consumer.

Hallman has contributed writings to professional publications and newsletters, written for video and other media, and is coauthor of a training program currently used in industry to teach customer service. The program title is "Through The Customer's Eyes™."

**Guy Hancock** graduated from the Ohio State University College of Veterinary Medicine in 1973 and worked in small animal practices as staff member or owner until 1983, when he became Director of the Veterinary Technology Program at St. Petersburg (FL) Junior College. He serves as President-elect

(1992–93) of the Association of Veterinary Technician Educators, and as Assistant Director of the Veterinary Technology Interactive Technologies Consortium. Dr. Hancock is doing graduate study in instructional technology at the University of South Florida College of Education. Publications and presentations include the subjects of human/animal bond, pet loss and bereavement, animal-assisted therapy, dental radiology, and client relations for geriatric pets.

**Ray Harris** is a Senior Vice President of North America at Optibase. Mr. Harris has over 14 years experience in marketing and selling leading-edge technology products through OEM, system-integrator, and reseller channels. The technologies with which he has been involved include PCs, laser printers, multiuser UNIX super-micro computers, document image-processing, and multimedia full-motion digital video.

Prior to joining Optibase in 1991, Mr. Harris was Western Regional Manager for Kofax Image products, the leading developer of tools for the document image-processing markets.

Mr. Harris has delivered information presentations to numerous groups over the years. Most recently he has made presentations on MPEG and/or full-motion video to the Electronic Imaging Show, the DSP Expo, and the Digital Video/Multimedia Expo East.

Optibase is a world leader in ISO implementation of MPEG, full-motion, digital video, and audio products.

**David E. Hartman** is an Assistant Professor of English at St. Petersburg Junior College (FL), where he teaches English Composition and Greek Mythology. He received his bachelor's degree from Eckerd College and his master's from The University of South Florida. His hypertext prototype, "The Labyrinth," has been published on the Apple Community College Alliance CD-ROM.

**Donna Hefner** joined Macromedia in January 1993. As Corporate Writer, Hefner is responsible for the research and development of corporate positioning papers and other marketing materials. Hefner received a BA in Journalism from California State University, Long Beach, in 1990.

**Josh Hendrix** is a user-interface designer and quality assurance specialist. He currently works for CoSA, a Providence, RI–based software developer, where he codesigned the user interface for the company's flagship product, CoSA After Effects. He also was project manager for the company's CD-ROM–based interactive brochure, The Art of Visual Computing. He is a graduate of Brown University with a degree in Cognitive Science.

**Jeff Hooks** is an assistant professor at St. Petersburg (FL) Junior College, where he teaches literature, humanities, and creative writing. An SPJC graduate, he obtained his bachelor's degree and his MA in English and American Literature at the University of South Florida. His composition students have collaborated long-distance in real time between SPJC Macintosh labs and Jackson (MI) Community College. Students in his literature classes have studied *King Lear* with a HyperCard application he developed that keyed scenes from the play to corresponding sequences on the videodisc version of Sir Laurence Olivier's performance.

Using the Library of Congress's American Memory Project, his humanities students have created projects that displayed digitized photographs, texts, films, and recordings from the library's William McKinley–era archives. His creative writing students electronically published stories and poems by posting them to Usenet conferences on the Internet. For a year (1992–93), Mr. Hooks was on professional leave, teaching at a small college in the interior of China where his only classroom tools were books and chalkboard. Fascinated as he was by Chinese culture, and grateful for the time he had to reflect, he returned to St. Petersburg media-starved for his Macintosh and cable TV!

**Roger Karr** founded the Integrated Multimedia Solutions group at Digital Equipment Corporation. He has program-managed several multimedia-based executive information applications. He has consulted on the applicability of multimedia solutions in a number of domains, including the utilities industry, education, federal, state, and local government agencies, and the retail industry. His work focuses on application design and implementation. Roger's current work is in the area of point-of-information kiosk applications for multimedia-based, corporate communications applications, executive-profiling and succession-planning applications, and information kiosks for state and local government agencies.

**Michael Kellner,** previously of Apple Computer Inc., was responsible for the integration of QuickTime into A/UX, Apple's UNIX product. He was a contributing factor in creating an easier-to-use UNIX. Michael currently is employed by IBM's Advanced Workstation Division in Austin, TX. There, he is involved in the PowerOpen effort and in the use of multimedia on workstations.

**Richard V. Kelly, Jr.** founded and runs the Artificial Life and Virtual Reality Applications Group at Digital Equipment Corporation. He has built commercial applications in advanced technologies with and for dozens of U.S., Asian, and European corporations, and he has taught extensively in the United States and Japan. His current research and application development work is focused on the conjoining of artificial life to virtual reality in order to enliven virtual universes. Currently he is working on biomedical, telecomm, utilities, pharmaceutical, training, entertainment, and financial-services VR applications. His latest book, presently in production, will be entitled *The Future of Virtual Reality: Unexpected Consequences of a New Technology.*

**Jessica Keyes** is president of Techinsider/New Art Inc., a technology consultancy/research firm specializing in productivity and high-technology applications. She is publisher of *Techinsider Reports* as well as *Computer Market Letter.* Organizer and leader of Techinsider seminars, Keyes has given seminars for such prestigious universities as Carnegie Mellon, Boston University, University of Illinois, James Madison University, and San Francisco State University. Prior to founding Techinsider, Keyes was Managing Director of Technology for the New York Stock Exchange and has been an officer with Swiss Bank Co. and Banker's Trust, both in New York City. She has over 15 years of technical experience in such diverse areas as AI, multimedia, CASE, and reengineering. She holds an MBA from New York University.

A noted columnist and correspondent, with over 150 articles published in such journals as *Software* magazine, *Computerworld, AI Expert,* and

*Datamation,* Keyes also is the author of four books including *Infotrends: The Competitive Use of Information* (McGraw-Hill, 1992), which was chosen as one of the best business books of 1992 by the *Library Journal.* She is currently working on her sixth book, *The Productivity Paradox* (McGraw-Hill).

**Susan Kinnell** currently divides her time between being the Custom Publishing Manager at the UCSB Bookstore in Santa Barbara, California; an instructor in the Computer Division at Santa Barbara City College; and an education/computer consultant with Carty Graphics, Santa Barbara. She is the coauthor of *CD-ROM in Schools: The Definitive Handbook* (Eight Bit Books, 1994), as well as *Hypertext/Hypermedia in Schools: A Resource Book* (ABC-CLIO, 1990).

**Cliff Kondratiuk** holds a Bsc. in Electrical Engineering from the University of Alberta, and he is currently a design engineer with Sierra Semiconductor of Canada. He is responsible for the research and development of DSP operating systems and firmware for the Aria line of multimedia audio chipsets. Aria-based sound cards are designed around an open architecture utilizing a custom Texas Instruments TMS320C25 DSP. The Aria chipset is a 16-bit sound device that offers Soundblaster Rev. 1.5 compatibility, a 32-voice wavetable music synthesizer, four channels of sample playback, ADPCM compression, up to 44.1-kHz recording and playback, and firmware-based, speaker-independent speech recognition. Aria's open architecture has allowed for the recent additions of reverb and Qsound™ 3D audio algorithms as DSP tasks downloaded from the PC. His work has included the design of a DSP-based Soundblaster/Adlib emulation, audio compression and effects processing algorithms, as well as the joint development of a digital wavetable/sample-based synthesizer. He recently was awarded a patent for the development of a digital music-synthesis technique.

**Lucy Lediaev,** Manager of Developer Services at Philips Interactive Media in Los Angeles, brings to her position almost 10 years of experience in software support and CAD/CAM and in multimedia. Ms. Lediaev is a liberal arts graduate of The University of Iowa. She has been involved in the production of user-documentation, engineering-documentation, and technical-marketing support activities, and customer and engineering support services. Her current position involves the day-to-day supervision of engineering support and test personnel, who provide telephone and e-mail support to those engaged in CD-I software engineering; editing and production of *The Interactive Engineer,* a bimonthly technical newsletter for CD-I software engineers; editing and dissemination of technical notes and production notes for the CD-I community; and planning and execution of the annual Compact Disc Interactive Software Conference (CDISC). She also participates actively in CD-I support via the CompuServe Multimedia forum.

**Claude Leglise** was appointed director of Video Brand Marketing at Intel in January 1993. He joined the firm in 1982 and has held a variety of marketing and management positions. In 1985, as the i386 marketing manager, he directed the introduction of Intel's first 32-bit microprocessor. In 1987 he was appointed director of marketing of the Microprocessor Division. In 1989 he became director of the i860 Focus Group, and in 1990 was promoted to the position of General Manager of the Supercomputing Components Operation. In 1992, as Director of

Marketing for the Multimedia and Supercomputing Components Group, he managed the team that launched the Indeo Video technology.

Mr. Leglise received his MS degree in Electrical Engineering from ENSAM, Paris, France, and his MBA from Stanford University.

**James Long,** president of Starlight Networks, founded the company with Charlie Bass in early 1990 in order to develop products to enable digital-video networks and servers. In the previous 10 years, Long worked as a venture capitalist with Fred Adler and with a number of high-technology start-up companies both as a founder and in positions such as President or Vice President of Marketing. Much of his work has been in the area of real-time voice and data management, and graphics software. Affiliations include Ready Systems, Manageware, Veritas, and Unix International. Long began his career at Hewlett-Packard, where he was responsible for software development and product marketing. He holds a BS degree in Electrical Engineering and Computer Science from the University of California at Berkeley, and an MBA degree from Harvard Business School.

**Mike McGonagle** is Manager of Workstation Development at Computer Corporation of America. Mike has 19 years of experience in the software development field. He has been involved in the development of distribution and manufacturing applications, as well as systems and communications software. This work was done at companies such as Keydata, Distribution Management Systems (DMS), Cullinet, Atex, and now at Computer Corp. of America. He first got involved with voice-recognition and -response systems in the early eighties at DMS, where several prototype systems were built to demonstrate the potential of these systems in the distribution industry. This work led to the integration of voice response into Cullinet's expert system product, Application Expert.

Mike is currently in charge of Workstation Development for CCA, where his research into the commercial use of this technology continues. He has one bachelor's degree in Mathematics from Lowell Technical Institute and another in Pure Mathematics from Brown University.

**Glenn K. Morrissey** manages Asymetrix's growing multimedia business. He played a key role in developing Multimedia ToolBook, and he continues to work closely with customers in pioneering multimedia Windows applications. Morrissey is a former writer, producer, director, and musician with many years of experience in the entertainment industry.

Asymetrix Corp. is a privately held, employee-owned software company based in Bellevue, WA, committed to a mission of bringing pioneering productivity to all levels of Windows users with affordable, easy-to-use software.

**Ken Morse** received his B.Eng. in Electronic Engineering from the University of Liverpool, England, in 1986, and his Ph.D. in Electronic Engineering also at the University of Liverpool in 1992.

Since graduating, he has formed three companies. MTL was founded in 1982 to provide software security and delivery systems for cassette and floppy disk–based software in the home computer market.

Ultra Digital Systems was founded in 1986 to market digital signal-processor development systems based on the Texas Instruments TMS320 family. Multimedia Consultants was founded in 1992 as a multimedia software and hardware consultancy.

Dr. Morse has also worked as consultant at IBM Hursley, England. Currently he is working as a consultant at Kaleida Labs.

**Kurt Mueller** is founder and president of Dataware Technologies, Inc. Previously he served as general manager for the Lotus Development Corporation in Germany and Austria. He has served as a management consultant with Bain and Company in the United States and in Europe. Mr. Mueller holds a BA in Computer Science from Northwestern University and an MBA from the University of Chicago, and he has studied law at Harvard Law School.

**Amy Pearl** has been at Sun Microsystems since 1986. She runs the Enterprise Communication Initiative (ECI), a cross-functional collaboration between Sun's MIS department, Sun's training organization, Sun Laboratories, and SunSoft. The ECI is developing opportunities for multimedia communication to increase corporate productivity. While in Sun Microsystems' laboratories, she developed Videoconf, an integrated desktop videoconferencing prototype as part of a collaborative-computing research project.

Pearl received her BA in Computer Science from Mills College in Oakland in 1983. After a brief stint at Zilog, she attended Stanford University, where she received an MS in Computer Science in 1986. At Stanford she developed a protocol for automatic screen-sharing in an early network window system.

Her professional interest is in using networked computers to support people working together. At Sun she designed and developed the Link Service, an interapplication communication support service for large-scale software development. She is now involved in the design and development of network services to support distributed multimedia. She has been on the board of USACM, the ACM's Public Policy Committee, and has also been on the national executive committee of Computer Professionals for Social Responsibility.

**Tim Picraux** is Program Marketing Manager for Unisys' Imaging Systems Group. He is responsible for the definition of product requirements to incorporate imaging technologies into Unisys solutions for the commercial and manufacturing sectors.

Picraux has 10 years of experience in the automotive industry, applying computer technologies to solve engineering and manufacturing problems. He has 15 years of experience in the development and marketing of engineering systems, including CAD/CAM and document-imaging.

He holds a master's degree in Systems Engineering from Oakland University in Rochester, Michigan, as well as a management degree from the University of Michigan.

**Marco Pinter** received a bachelor's degree in Computer Science from Cornell University, and did his graduate work at the University of California. He has also served on the Computer Science faculty of Bucknell University. Pinter founded Digital Media International in the fall of 1990, and has led a number of multimedia projects, including DVI-based instructional programs for GPU Nuclear Corporation. Pinter also has led the development of several video-editing tools in the PC environment.

**Rudy Prokupets,** Vice President of R&D for Lenel Systems International, was born and educated in the former Soviet Union. He hold two master's degrees, one in Electrical Engineering from the prestigious Electrotechnical Institute of

Leningrad and the other in Applied Mathematics from the University of Leningrad. He immigrated to the United States in 1978. He worked for Bausch and Lomb and subsequently the Eastman Kodak Company, where he held positions as Senior Research Scientist and Senior Software Designer.

In 1985 Mr. Prokupets and his wife, Elena, founded Edicon, a Kodak venture company, with a focus on electronic identification and photodatabase security systems. The most successful and profitable Kodak venture company, Edicon achieved Division status in 1990.

Mr. and Ms. Prokupets left Edicon in 1990 to found Lenel Systems International, Inc. In the two years since its inception, Lenel has become a leading developer of object-oriented multimedia software and has forged development and business alliances with such companies as Microsoft, Borland, Sony, Panasonic, and Intel.

**Steven L. Raber** joined IBM in Charleston, South Carolina, in 1976 as a sales trainee. He held different marketing and staff positions until his appointment into management in 1985 in Atlanta, Georgia. Subsequently he became Southern Area Manager of Large Systems Marketing.

In 1989 Steve was named Marketing Branch Manager in Nashville, Tennessee. While in Nashville he was active in community affairs, including serving on the Board of Directors of the United Way, the Nashville Symphony, and Junior Achievement.

In January 1992, Steve was named Administrative Assistant in the office of the Chairman of the Board, and in March 1993 he was announced as Director of Multimedia Marketing.

Steve was born in Kansas and raised in southern Illinois. He attended Florida State University, where he graduated with a degree in finance.

**Bruce A. Rady** is the President and CEO of TouchVision Systems, Inc., the developer of D/Vision: The Digital Video Editor. It is a nonlinear capture/edit tool for the PC/Intel platform.

Mr. Rady has been a pioneer in the development of nonlinear video editing for over a decade. He spent 10 years as an engineering and marketing manager at Bell and Howell, where he worked in new product development. There, he headed the team that began development of the TouchVision nonlinear editing system for film production.

In 1983, Bell and Howell spun off its professional division and the TouchVision project, resulting in the creation of BHP, Inc. Rady was co-owner and head of BHP's Editing Systems Division.

Six years later, TouchVision was being used by Hollywood filmmakers for films starring the likes of Madonna and Sylvester Stallone. Development then began on the product known today as D/Vision, a digital-video version of TouchVision. Shortly thereafter, TouchVision split from BHP, and Rady began to concentrate his efforts on making D/Vision available to a wider market.

Rady holds an MBA from the University of Chicago and a BS in Electrical Engineering from the University of Kentucky. He is married and the father of three children.

**Lex van Sonderen,** Manager of Knowledge Transfer at Philips Interactive Media in Los Angeles, has as his mission the dissemination of information and training in CD-I software development. Mr. van Sonderen, who holds a master's degree in Industrial Design Engineering from the Technical University of Delft in the Netherlands, is applying his extensive experience in software engineering to the design of a CD-I training program and a CD-I developer support program under the umbrella of the worldwide Philips Interactive Media organization.

Mr. van Sonderen also is responsible for the technical component of the activities of the engineering support, text, and training personnel in the Los Angeles organization. He also is contributing editor to *The Interactive Engineer* and is a frequent contributor to the CompuServe Multimedia forum and libraries. In addition, he acts as a technical liaison between the activities in the Los Angeles organization and the Philips organization in the Netherlands.

**Serge Timacheff** is Senior Manager of Public Relations for Logitech Inc., and formerly a senior reviews editor for *InfoWorld* magazine. He is the author of two books, including *InfoWorld: Understanding Windows* (Brady Books, 1990) and *The Personalized PC* (Random House, 1993). He speaks and represents Logitech frequently on computer-related topics such as multimedia, giving senses to computers, computer personalization, business presentations, and the development of the PC industry.

Logitech manufactures and markets Senseware—products designed to give "senses" such as sight, sound, and touch to the computer, making human-to-computer communication more intuitive and natural. Retail and OEM products of the company and its affiliates include pointing devices (such as mice and trackballs), hand-held scanners, digital cameras, pen digitizers, joysticks, sound products, and related software applications for IBM, Macintosh, and other platforms. Logitech International, the financial holding company for the Logitech Group, is traded publicly in Switzerland on the Zurich and Geneva exchanges. With operational headquarters in Fremont, CA, the group maintains manufacturing facilities in Fremont; Hsinchu, Taiwan; Shanghai, China; and Cork, Ireland, and offices in major cities in the United States, Europe, and the Far East.

**Prem Uppaluru** is Vice President of Engineering and Product Marketing at Fluent in Natick, MA. Before joining Fluent, Dr. Uppaluru was Vice President of Engineering at Samsung Software America, where he participated in the development of advanced networked imaging products. Prior to that he was with Bellcore and Bell Laboratories. His areas of technical expertise include network computing, object-oriented systems, operating systems, databases, parallel processing, and computer architecture. He received his Ph.D. in Computer Science and Engineering from the University of Texas at Austin.

**Vince Walisko** has been involved in the satellite communications industry for 12 years, and in radio and television broadcasting for 20. He also spent several years working with NuMedia Corporation on the issues of communications in the multimedia computing environment. He worked extensively on the development of satellite news-gathering while at GTE Spacenet and with GEC McMichael and as a principal of Spectra Communications, Inc. Most recently Mr. Walisko has focused on the international satellite communications area while working at both PanAmSat and INTELSAT. He also is a principal in The Walisko Group, located in Washington, D.C., and Lieberman and Walisko. He has been involved in the design, implementation, and operation of satellite systems from compressed digital video and VSAT networks to shipboard television transmissions for a U.S. television network. He has tested satellite power and receive sensitivity in various parts of the world. He has taught an undergraduate course in television technology at The American University in Washington, D.C. He studied Electrical Engineering at Rensselaer Polytechnic Institute, and Television/Radio Communications at Syracuse University.

**Rob Wallace** is codeveloper and MIDI author of "Multimedia Kaleidosonics," a popular CD-ROM and DOS interactive graphic-and-music product. Wallace Music & Sound, Inc., provides original music and sound effects for software developers and publishers. Rob's credits include the musical arrangements in the Miracle Piano Teaching System for The Software Toolworks, and original music for the following: Mig 29 by Spectrum Holobyte; Snoopy's Game Club, for Accolade; Monster Bash, for Apogee; Wayne's World, for Capstone; Eagle Eye Mysteries, for Electronic Arts; Tom Landry Strategic Football, for Merit Software; and Video Poker for Windows, for Masque Publishing.

Besides dozens of other musical scores for Games and educational products, Wallace lends his character-voice acting abilities and stable of actors for complete digital voice tracks. Among them is Mario's Missing Deluxe (CD-ROM version), which contains over 2000 speeches from 57 separate roles, of which Rob voiced 15. Wallace Music & Sound, Inc., has been operating since 1989.

**Joseph Weintraub** is president of Thinking Software, a small creative software development firm in Woodside, New York; he was the first winner of the Loebner Prize Competition, held at the Boston Computer Museum in 1991. The winning software program was called PC Therapist III, and is available for the IBM/PC.

Joseph has been a Data Processing instructor at New York University and at Pace University. He is a graduate of the City College of the City University of New York, and is a member of Mensa. He has been Senior Programmer for *Time* Magazine in New York, and has authored articles for *AI Expert, AI* magazine, *PC/AI* magazine and a book for the Rosen Publishing Group (NYC) called *Exploring Careers in the Computer Field.* He is a certified member of the exclusive Developer Programs both at IBM Small Systems Division and Creative Labs.

Weintraub's current areas of research and interest include multimedia and virtual reality.

**J. Alan Whiteside,** Ph.D., is Senior Instructional Designer at Multimedia Learning, Inc., in Irving, Texas. He received his doctorate in instructional design from The Pennsylvania State University and has over 14 years of experience in designing, developing, and delivering effective instruction. Dr. Whiteside has been involved as a project manager and instructional designer of computer-based training in two large Air Force projects. In addition he has managed the development of "conventional" and multimedia projects in the financial, manufacturing, transportation, and energy sectors. Dr. Whiteside's areas of emphasis include effective integration of visuals with text and sound in multimedia, and the application of sound instructional strategies in technology-based instruction.

**Mary F. Whiteside,** Ph.D., is Director of the Media Development graduate studies program and assistant professor in the Office of Medical Education at The University of Texas Southwestern Medical Center at Dallas. Dr. Whiteside received her doctorate in instructional design from The Pennsylvania State University. She also consults with a variety of commercial firms on instructional design issues. Dr. Whiteside has managed the development of interactive videodisc and multimedia education and training programs. Currently she is project manager for an innovative performance support system designed for third-year medical students. Dr. Whiteside's interests are the integration of technology-based instruction into curricula and training programs, and the use of effective design techniques to produce multimedia.

**Frederic M. Wilf** is a member of the intellectual property law firm of Elman, Wilf & Fried in Media, Pennsylvania, a suburb of Philadelphia. The firm practices patent, trademark, copyright, and business law, with an emphasis on the computer and biotechnology industries. Many of Mr. Wilf's clients are writers, artists, photographers, software developers, and consultants, in multiple media as well as multimedia. Mr. Wilf speaks and writes extensively on topics involving computers and the law. Mr. Wilf may be reached via CompuServe at 72300,2061 and at the following address: Elman, Wilf & Fried, 20 West Third Street, Media, PA 19063, USA.

**Les Wilson** is Marketing Manager of Multimedia Communications Development for the Systems Application Technology group at National Semiconductor Corporation in Santa Clara, CA. He is responsible for providing future visions of markets and their technology requirements. Wilson currently is doing end-user market research, and for the last two years has planned the development of worldwide video networking systems that use compression, LANs, WANs, and new protocols. Wilson has over ten years' experience in developing communications architecture.

Before joining National, Wilson was involved in the development of state-of-the-art critical-care biomedical-monitoring systems that networked important physiological information, real-time, from the bedside to doctors and nurses. These graphical display instruments were designed for reliability, accuracy, and ease of use. In addition Wilson spent two years in the typesetting industry, which supplies typesetting systems to publishers.

**Andrew Young** is well known within the Unix industry for developing new directions for CD-ROM and multimedia standards. He is the principal author of two innovative Unix/CD-ROM proposals: the Rock Ridge Interchange Protocol and the Systems Use Sharing Protocol. He is currently the Chairman of the IEEE CD-ROM File System Format Working Group.

Mr. Young is president and cofounder of Young Minds, Inc., a company that provides CD-ROM and CD-recordable solutions. He holds a master's degree in Mathematics from the University of California at San Diego.

He is a frequent speaker for industry meetings and conferences such as SIG-CAT, CD-ROM Expo, Intermedia, UniForum, OnLine Multimedia, and the SCO Forum. He authored articles for *SunWorld, SunExpert, DISC,* and *CD-ROM Professional.* He also wrote the first monthly Unix column for a CD-ROM industry magazine.

# Index

## ABOUT THE EDITOR

Jessica Keyes is president of Techinsider/New Art, Inc., a technology consulting and research firm specializing in productivity and high-technology applications. She was previously managing director of technology for the New York Stock Exchange, and has been an officer with Swiss Bank Co. and Banker's Trust. She is the publisher of *Techinsider Reports* and *Computer Market Letter*, and is also the author/editor of three other McGraw-Hill titles: *The Handbook of Expert Systems in Manufacturing*, *Infotrends: The Competitive Use of Information*, and *Software Engineering Productivity Handbook*. Forthcoming from Ms. Keyes for McGraw-Hill is *The Productivity Paradox: TQM and Computer Software*.